THE TWENTIETH-CENTURY WORLD

AN INTERNATIONAL HISTORY

SECOND CANADIAN EDITION

THE TWENTIETH-CENTURY WORLD

AN INTERNATIONAL HISTORY

WILLIAM R. KEYLOR • JERRY BANNISTER • TRACEY J. KINNEY

OXFORD

UNIVERSITY PRESS

OXFORD
UNIVERSITY PRESS

8 Sampson Mews, Suite 204, Don Mills, Ontario M3C 0H5
www.oupcanada.com

Oxford University Press is a department of the University of Oxford.
It furthers the University's objective of excellence in research, scholarship,
and education by publishing worldwide in

Oxford   New York

Auckland Cape Town Dar es Salaam Hong Kong Karachi
Kuala Lumpur Madrid Melbourne Mexico City Nairobi
New Delhi Shanghai Taipei Toronto

With offices in

Argentina Austria Brazil Chile Czech Republic France Greece
Guatemala Hungary Italy Japan Poland Portugal Singapore
South Korea Switzerland Thailand Turkey Ukraine Vietnam

Oxford is a trade mark of Oxford University Press
in the UK and in certain other countries

Published in Canada
by Oxford University Press

Library and Archives Canada Cataloguing in Publication

Keylor, William R., 1944–

The twentieth-century world / William R. Keylor, Jerry Bannister,
and Tracey J. Kinney. — 2nd Cdn. ed.

Includes bibliographical references and index.

ISBN 978-0-19-542902-2

1. History, Modern—20th century—Textbooks. 2. History,
Modern—21st century—Textbooks. I. Bannister, Jerry, 1968–
II. Kinney, Tracey Jane, 1966– 3. III. Title.

D421.K49 2010   909.82   C2010-903395-7

Cover image: G-20 leaders meet during the second plenary session at the G-20 summit,
Friday, September 25, 2009, in Pittsburgh. (AP Photo/Carolyn Kaster)

This book is printed on permanent (acid-free) paper ∞.
Printed and bound in Canada

1 2 3 4 — 14 13 12 11

CONTENTS

LIST OF MAPS

LIST OF TABLES

PREFACE

In his preface to the first edition of *The Twentieth-Century World*, William Keylor noted that the book was designed to meet the need for a university textbook that reflected the remarkable advances in twentieth-century scholarship since the 1960s. In the early 1980s, when the first edition was published, there existed no such textbook. Professor Keylor's purpose, as he explained, was 'to provide a narrative account within an analytical framework of the struggle among the major nations of the world for power, prosperity, and prestige in this century'. By focusing primarily on international relations, the textbook provided an authoritative account of the crucial issues then usually glossed over as 'diplomatic history'. Professor Keylor devoted extensive coverage to economic relations, paying particular attention to trade patterns, capital flows, and competition for natural resources in the context of the global struggle for strategic advantage. What immediately distinguished Professor Keylor's textbook was its commitment to a sustained and scholarly examination of international relations. Subsequent editions built on its initial success by incorporating more recent scholarship on the extraordinary developments following the breakup of the Soviet Union.

The objective of the first Canadian edition of *The Twentieth-Century World* was to offer a monograph that would meet the needs of Canadian students while retaining as much of the original text's structure and content as possible. The ultimate goal was not a history of twentieth-century Canada but rather a study of international relations that incorporated a Canadian perspective. Given that Canada remained almost totally absent from the major English-language world history textbooks, Oxford University Press took an innovative approach to addressing this problem by creating a Canadian edition of this established world history textbook. These revisions entailed much more than simply introducing Canadian content. The author of the first Canadian edition, Professor Jerry Bannister, not only introduced Canadian standards of spelling and punctuation to the text but also adopted a Canadian perspective towards international relations. He reduced the extensive focus on the United States and Latin America and revised the discussion of ideological debates over issues such as globalization. As well, a series of new features—most notably, chapter summaries and a timeline—designed to enhance the textbook's accessibility to Canadian students were added.

This second Canadian edition retains much of Professor Bannister's invaluable material relating to Canada's role in the international history of the twentieth century, while introducing a number of new informational boxes highlighting specific elements of the general themes under discussion in the respective chapter. More than simply adding 'the rest' to 'the West', these new boxes will provide readers with a sense of the complex changes wrought by decisions made, oftentimes, half a world away. Professor Keylor's analytical framework remains intact, but, wherever possible, new material focusing on the impact of actions taken at the international level on the nations that made up the increasingly interrelated twentieth-century world has been incorporated. This edition also provides a more detailed chapter on international developments at the start of the twenty-first century, as well as new visual evidence and several new pedagogical features, including study questions and websites for further reference.

I would like to thank Jacqueline Mason, acquisitions editor at Oxford University Press, who first suggested this project to me. As well, it has been a great pleasure to work with Peter Chambers, developmental editor, on this book. This is the second time that Peter and I have worked together and he has been unfailingly helpful throughout. Finally, I must once again thank my husband, Jonathan, who continues to tolerate the demands which projects such as this one place on my time and energy.

Tracey J. Kinney
Kwantlen Polytechnic University

IMPORTANT FEATURES OF THIS EDITION

This second Canadian edition of *The Twentieth-Century World* incorporates several new features into the text. Perhaps the most significant improvement over the previous edition is the text's expanded global coverage which examines the impact of actions taken at the level of international relations on the nations that make up an increasingly interrelated world. The text also includes a wealth of enhanced pedagogy and a new chapter on the first decade of the twenty-first century, which covers recent historical events such as Canada's mission in Afghanistan and the Copenhagen Climate Summit. Highlights include:

- Expanded coverage of the non-Western world, including a new concluding chapter, Chapter Twenty-One: The Twenty-First Century, and additional text boxes such as 'The Russian Inspiration and Chinese Communism' and 'From Mandela to Mbeki'.
- New pedagogical features, including chapter outlines, questions for critical thought, and lists of further readings and websites.
- A new art program with more photos and a striking two-colour design.
- A new online suite of resources with a new instructor's manual that will make course-planning easy and features:
- Chapter Summaries

- A new study guide and companion website designed to enhance student understanding of the material including:
  - Chapter Introductions
  - Learning Objectives
  - Self-Testing Multiple Choice Questions
  - Short Answer Questions
  - Research Paper Topics
  - Suggested Audio-Visual Resources
  - Regional Timelines
  - Additional Internet Links

INTERNATIONAL RELATIONS AT THE BEGINNING OF THE TWENTIETH CENTURY

CHAPTER OUTLINE

THE EUROPEANIZATION OF THE WORLD

The most important feature of international relations in 1900 was the extent of European global domination. The expansion of European power and influence had begun in the sixteenth century, when improvements in marine technology enabled seafaring adventurers to lay claim to territory in North and South America, Africa, and Asia. European settlements were later established on the coasts of these lands to facilitate the exploitation of their economic resources, such as precious metals, sugar, and animal furs in the case of the Americas, spices in the Far East, and slave labour in Africa.

By the middle of the nineteenth century, most European settler populations in the Americas had gained political independence from their colonial masters and were busily promoting the national unification and economic development of the territories they controlled. These new states remained thoroughly European in the sense that their political institutions, economic practices, religious beliefs, and cultural traditions had all been transplanted from Europe by descendants of their ruling elites. During the same period, the Slavic peoples of European Russia were migrating eastward into Asiatic Siberia. The second half of the nineteenth century and the first decade of the twentieth, however, saw a new wave of imperial expansion as the principal states of Western Europe finally succeeded in moving into the Afro–Asian areas of the southern hemisphere that until then had remained beyond their reach. The consequence of this long process of expansion in all directions was the creation—for the first time in history—of a genuinely interlinked and interdependent world centred on Europe. Statesmen, diplomats, and military leaders began for the first time to speak of international relations in a truly global sense.

Explanations for this resurgence of imperialism have been hotly debated. Some historians have emphasized the role played by Western[1] economic interests in seeking new sources of raw materials that were in short supply at home, as well as overseas markets for industrial production and investment capital. Others have focused on the Christian missionaries who needed military intervention from their home governments when indigenous people violently resisted their efforts. Some scholars have seen the desire for strategic advantage as the principal motivating factor for this expansion abroad. Still others stress national pride and the quest for prestige. Whatever the sources of the imperialist impulse, its consequence was unmistakable: the extension of European power and influence throughout the southern half of the globe.

The first two nations to achieve world power in this way were Great Britain and France. Both had established coastal footholds on the world's non-European land masses during the first wave of imperial expansion in the seventeenth century. Over the next two centuries, Britain had disposed of the surplus population created by the Industrial Revolution by sending large numbers of emigrants to North America, Australia, New Zealand, and Southern Africa, and by the middle of the nineteenth century had also taken effective control of the Indian subcontinent. Meanwhile, France had added the North African territory of Algeria to the remnants of its seventeenth-century empire.

It was only after the opening of the Suez Canal (built by the French between 1859 and 1869 and brought under joint Anglo–French financial control in 1875) that authorities in London and Paris began seriously promoting imperial expansion. The sea route running through the Mediterranean, the Suez Canal, and the Red Sea into the Indian Ocean was much more economical—and less dangerous—than the passage around the southern tip of Africa and came to be seen as a lifeline to Britain's possessions in Asia. It was indeed a lifeline in a very real sense: since its transformation from an agricultural to an industrial economy, around the turn of the nineteenth century, Britain had customarily produced no more than 30 per cent of the food consumed by its people and an even smaller proportion of the raw materials required by its industries. Many of those vital imports came from India, Australia, and New Zealand, and Britain's survival seemed

to depend on its ability to keep open the sea lanes over which they (and the exports of manufactured products required to pay for them) travelled. Consequently, the ruling elite of Victorian England deemed it essential that Britain control the sea lanes to the Far East. This in turn required that Britain not only preserve its naval domination of the Mediterranean–Suez–Red Sea–Indian Ocean route but also establish additional strategically located bases and refuelling stations along the way.

By the end of the nineteenth century, the British obsession with protecting the passage to the East had resulted in the acquisition of a long string of islands, coastal enclaves, and their hinterlands along the southern rim of Asia and the eastern coast of Africa, as well as control of the Egyptian land bridge connecting the two continents and the canal linking the seas. These strategically situated outposts of British imperialism—Gibraltar, Malta, Cyprus, and Suez in the Mediterranean; Aden and Somaliland on opposite shores of the Red Sea; and Kenya, India, Burma, Malaya, and Singapore along the Indian Ocean basin—gave this small island nation effective control of the largest empire in the history of the world.

A third motivating factor for British imperialism was the desire for undeveloped areas in which to invest the huge profits acquired through industrial enterprise. The regions of Africa and Asia that had recently been opened to European penetration were in dire need of investment capital to build the transportation and communication systems essential for economic modernization. Soon the major financial institutions of London began to invest heavily in railway and road construction, the improvement of ports and harbours, and other ventures undertaken by British firms in preparation for colonial development. In this way, thousands of British investors were led to believe that their financial well-being depended on guaranteed markets for capital investment in the empire.

Imperialism had a moral as well as an economic dimension. All sorts of ideological justifications for the spectacular expansion of British power were proposed. For example, there was much

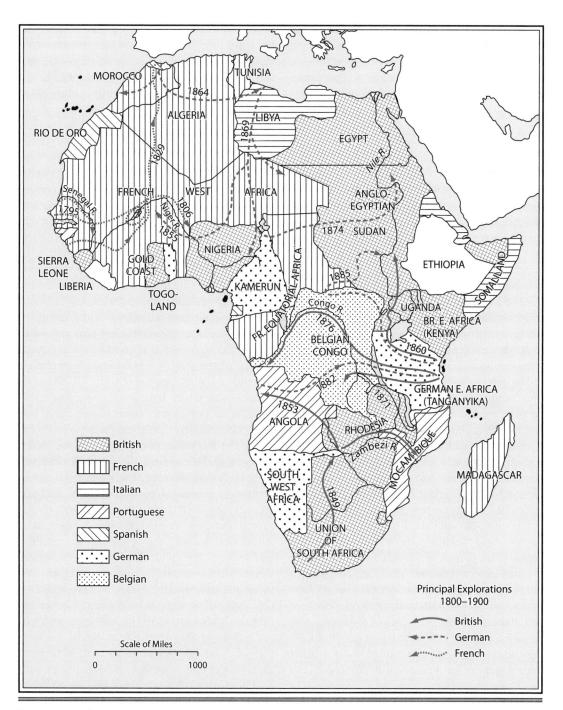

EUROPEAN PENETRATION OF AFRICA TO 1914

talk of Britain's solemn responsibility to provide the uncivilized, backward peoples of the colonial world with the fruits of its superior culture, in particular the spiritual inspiration of Christianity and the political benefits of enlightened governance. Altruistic missionaries and idealistic civil servants seem to have genuinely believed that it was their duty to rescue the indigenous populations of the non-European world from 'primitive', 'superstitious' beliefs and 'barbarous' customs. The self-justifying talk of the 'white man's burden' barely concealed the real motives for British colonial expansion, which were primarily economic. Despite the rhetoric of religious conversion and political reform, British colonial policy was designed to leave the colonies' existing social and cultural arrangements intact. All that really mattered to London was that the imperial system contribute to the efficient operation of the worldwide network of trade and investment upon which Britain depended for economic prosperity, if not national survival.

The reasons for France's acquisition of a colonial empire in the latter part of the nineteenth century are less evident. Self-sufficient in food and far behind Britain in industrial development, France was much less dependent on foreign trade for its economic well-being. It had no clear commercial incentive to seek overseas markets for manufactured goods it could not produce in sufficient quantity or sources of foodstuffs it did not require. Nor did the French financial community need colonial outlets for accumulated capital. The portion of French domestic savings invested abroad between 1871 and 1914 went not to distant regions of the southern hemisphere but rather to the state treasuries of Southern and Eastern Europe. This was so for two reasons. First, these established governments were presumed—wrongly, as it turned out—to offer greater security for investment than more speculative ventures in far-off lands in various stages of political disorganization. Second and more importantly, the flow of private capital to the developing regions of Eastern Europe was actively promoted by the French government, which was

much more inclined than its British counterpart to regard foreign investment as an instrument of diplomacy. If there was no good economic reason for France to covet a colonial empire, by the closing decades of the nineteenth century there was a persuasive diplomatic reason for it to direct financial resources eastward. France's vulnerable position in a Europe dominated by the powerful German Empire—formed at France's expense after the Franco–Prussian War (1870–1)—dictated a perpetual preoccupation with continental affairs. By encouraging private investment in the Russian, Austro–Hungarian, and Turkish empires, as well as in the fledgling states of the Balkan peninsula, the French government tried to surround Germany with a ring of states dependent on France's financial support and therefore amenable to its diplomatic influence.

Despite its preoccupation with Germany, France simultaneously embarked on a campaign of colonial expansion that was to leave it in possession of the world's second largest empire by the end of the nineteenth century. Historians of French imperialism have sought to explain this paradox by pointing to a motivating factor less easily documented than trade patterns or capital flows: the intangible phenomenon of the desire for prestige. Having been displaced by Germany in 1871 as the dominant power on the European continent, France (according to this analysis) sought the psychological compensation of territorial conquest in distant regions where local authorities lacked the political organization and military power to offer effective resistance. 'France', in this instance, refers not to the government in Paris (which appears to have endorsed this colonial policy belatedly and somewhat reluctantly) but rather to the military commanders and merchants on the spot, whose interests the policy served. One observer went so far as to describe the French empire as having been built by 'bored army officers looking for excitement'— and, he might have added, by railway builders and traders in search of quick profits.

By the end of the nineteenth century, approximately a third of the continent of Africa, a large section of Southeast Asia, and a few island chains in the South Pacific had been brought under French control. While imperial Germany was busy consolidating its dominant position on the continent of Europe, France joined Britain in a scramble for control of much of the rest of the non-European world. It is not surprising that France's imperial project had received the encouragement of German Chancellor Otto von Bismarck, the architect of his country's continental dominance. After all, it diverted French attention from European concerns, particularly the unhealed wound dealt to French national pride by the loss of the provinces of Alsace and Lorraine to Germany after the Franco–Prussian War. It also increased the likelihood of tension between France and Britain over competing imperial claims, and therefore reduced the danger that they would join forces to oppose Germany.

Towards the end of the nineteenth century, however, Britain and France were joined in their massive land grab by two other European states seeking a share of the remaining unclaimed territory of the non-Western world. The first was Germany itself. In the years following Bismarck's retirement in 1890, young German emperor Wilhelm II grew increasingly dissatisfied with the former chancellor's 'continental policy'. The strategy that had effectively preserved Germany's dominance in Europe began to look outdated in the age of imperialism. Britain and France were rapidly bringing under their control vast colonial domains containing millions of people and unknown quantities of valuable resources. In 1897, the German Kaiser caused a sensation by announcing that his nation would no longer be content with an exclusively European role. Henceforth it would conduct a *Weltpolitik* ('world policy') designed to project Germany's military, economic, and political power into the worldwide competition for empire. In response to British publicists' boasts about 'the empire on which the sun never sets', Wilhelm asserted Germany's claim to its own place in the sun. Within a few months, this bold declaration was translated into action. Plans were drawn up for the development

of a navy capable of contesting Britain's domination of the high seas. The Chinese port of Kiao-Chow on the Yellow Sea was seized as a potential refuelling station for a future German Far Eastern fleet. The German Empire abruptly put the other great powers on notice that it now intended to play an active role on the world stage.

Each assertion of Germany's international ambitions increased the sense of insecurity in London and Paris. In 1898, the Kaiser used a visit to the Ottoman Empire to declare himself 'protector' of the world's 300 million Muslims. This announcement represented a direct challenge to British and French positions in North Africa and the Middle East. A year later, a German firm acquired from the Ottoman sultan a concession to construct a railway from European Turkey to the Persian Gulf. German economic penetration of the Turkish Empire was interpreted by the British and French as a first step towards German expansion into the Mediterranean region and the portion of the non-European world that they had reserved for themselves.

The prospect of the dominant land power in Europe challenging Anglo–French imperial interests in Africa and Asia had precisely the effect that Bismarck had sought to avoid. The Kaiser's *Weltpolitik* prompted the leaders of the two imperial nations to resolve their own conflicting claims to colonial territory in order to oppose Germany's bid for a global role. France wanted above all to secure British co-operation in resisting the expansion of German power on the continent, while Britain sought French support against Germany's new naval and colonial ambitions. All that stood in the way of a mutually beneficial understanding was the Anglo–French antagonism along the southern shore of the Mediterranean that had developed during the period of imperial expansion. The fact that Britain controlled two approaches to the Mediterranean—through naval bases at Gibraltar in the west and at Alexandria in the east—conflicted with France's imperial interests in Morocco and Egypt. The two powers finally reached an amicable resolution in April 1904. In March 1906, at a conference of the great powers that had been convened to adjudicate Germany's challenge to France's claim of priority in Morocco, the British government solidly supported the French, and the Germans were forced to back down. Two months earlier the British foreign secretary had taken the extraordinary step of authorizing discussions between the British and French general staffs for the purpose of coordinating strategic plans in preparation for a possible war on the continent. Although London was careful to remind Paris that such an entente did not imply any obligation on Britain's part to defend France, the two nations co-operated closely to check the expansion of German power.

The other great power of Europe to pursue imperial expansion during the second half of the nineteenth century was Russia. While the seafaring nations of Western Europe projected their power across the world's oceans, the Russians had expanded from their home base west of the Ural Mountains into the vast spaces of Asia. This territorial aggrandizement brought under the control of European Russians a vast collection of peoples with different religions, languages, and traditions, who submitted to the Russian newcomers' rule because—like the indigenous inhabitants of the Americas whose lands were invaded by Western Europeans—they lacked the military power to prevent it.

As the Russian frontier began to approach the open seas beyond the Eurasian land mass—the Mediterranean, the Persian Gulf, the Indian Ocean, the Pacific—other expansionist states began to see a potential threat to their interests. Britain in particular was intent on protecting the sea communications to its empire in Asia and therefore worked to prevent Russia from securing a position of power along that route. As a result of this British policy, often pursued in partnership with France, Russia had to endure one of the most debilitating geographical handicaps imaginable for a state with ambitions of becoming a world power: during the winter months, when ice froze most of its major ports on the Baltic Sea, the North Pacific, and the Arctic Ocean, it lacked accessible harbours to accommodate its navy and merchant marine.

Russia did possess some year-round ice-free ports on the Black Sea. But the Dardanelles—the narrow body of water connecting these ports to the Mediterranean, known in diplomatic parlance as 'the Straits'—could easily be closed by whatever power occupied its two shores. For centuries, that power had been Ottoman Turkey. Turkish sovereignty over the Straits (and the adjacent Balkan peninsula in Southern Europe) thus deprived Russia of a secure outlet for foreign trade and naval power in the Mediterranean. In order to break out of this geographical straitjacket, Russia worked actively during the second half of the nineteenth century to extend its influence in the Balkans and to compel the Turkish government to open the Straits to its warships and close them to those of other powers.

The geographical attraction that the Balkan peninsula and the Turkish Straits held for Russia was reinforced by ideological and religious issues. The largest ethnic group in the European portion of the Ottoman Empire was Slavic and felt a sense of kinship with the politically dominant Slavic population of Russia. The cultural links between the Balkan and Russian Slavs had developed over time into a program for political unification. Dating from the first conference of Slavic peoples, held in Moscow in 1867, Russian proponents of the ideology of pan-Slavism envisioned the creation of a vast Slavic empire united under the Russian tsars. The tsars themselves cared little about either the tribulations of the Slavic peoples beyond their borders or the romantic reveries of the pan-Slavist movement at home. They promoted the movement's campaign partly to divert attention from domestic difficulties and partly to undermine Ottoman authority in the Slavic regions of Southern Europe. Thus Turkish maltreatment of the Balkan Slavs periodically elicited harshly worded protests from Russia together with fervent appeals from pan-Slavist ideologues and calls for liberation from Ottoman oppression.

Added to the Slavs' ethnic resentment was an ancient religious grievance harboured by the Russian clergy against the Turkish regime. The city of Istanbul (Constantinople) was the spiritual capital of Eastern Orthodoxy—the official faith of the Russian Empire—but for four centuries it had remained under the control of the Turks. The liberation of the holy city from Islam had long been a popular cause in Russian clerical circles, and each new report of Turkish misbehaviour added to the sense of grievance. The tsar was considerably better insulated from popular pressures than leaders of the other great powers, yet even he could not afford to ignore these ethnic and religious sentiments, particularly when they fell so closely in line with Russia's strategic and economic interests.

The result of these internal pressures and external temptations was a Russian drive toward the Mediterranean that produced what diplomats of the day called 'the eastern question'. Twice in the second half of the nineteenth century Russia attempted to expand southwards at Turkey's expense. It was prevented from doing so by the intervention of the great powers, militarily in the Crimean War (1854–6) and diplomatically at the Congress of Berlin following the Russo–Turkish War (1877–8). Over the next two decades, the Ottoman Empire lived up to its reputation as the 'sick man of Europe' by relinquishing political authority over the Slavic peoples of the Balkans. The independence of Serbia, Romania, Bulgaria, and Montenegro was confirmed, while the rest of the peninsula seethed with resentment against Turkish rule.

Into this political vacuum moved the Germanic empire of Austria–Hungary from the north. Though beset by ethnic problems similar to those that confronted the Ottomans, the Habsburg Empire enjoyed the decisive advantage of almost unconditional support from the most powerful nation on the continent. By virtue of the Dual Alliance of 1879 (which became a Triple Alliance with the addition of Italy three years later), imperial Germany had committed itself to the preservation of Habsburg power in Southern Europe. In the face of this joint Germanic opposition to Russian expansion toward the Mediterranean, the Russian government was eventually obliged to postpone fulfillment of its Balkan ambitions. In May 1897 Vienna and St Petersburg agreed (with the approval of the other great powers) to preserve the status quo in the Balkans. In other words, the 'eastern question' was put on ice for the time being.

Frustrated in its ambition to gain predominance in the Balkan peninsula and control of the Turkish Straits, the Russian regime redirected its expansionist drive farther east. Claims to disputed territory in southern Asia that had lain dormant for decades were revived at the turn of the century. The nominally independent but politically weak state of Persia blocked Russian access to the Persian Gulf just as Ottoman Turkey guarded the entrance to the Mediterranean. Russian economic penetration of Persia in the early years of the twentieth century resulted in a sharp rivalry with Britain. London viewed the prospect of Russian economic hegemony in Persia as a prelude to political predominance in that region and therefore a grave menace to the security of the sea lanes to the Far East. Even more threatening to British interests were the progressive Russian commercial encroachments in Afghanistan, the traditional buffer between Russia and British India.

As a consequence, Russian efforts at expansion in Southern Asia met British opposition at every turn, and British diplomatic pressure in Tehran counteracted Russian efforts to gain financial and commercial ascendency there. In 1901 a New Zealander named William K. D'Arcy secured a 60-year concession to explore for oil throughout Persia, a privilege that was to give the Anglo-Iranian Oil Company exclusive control of the rich oil fields discovered in 1908. The increasing British financial presence in Persia, supported by naval squadrons patrolling the Persian Gulf and military garrisons in India, effectively frustrated the ambitions of Russian policy in this area.

A far more promising prospect for Russian expansion lay in the Far East. Just as North American pioneers moved west towards the Pacific at the expense of the indigenous peoples and, to the south, the weak government of Mexico, Russian settlers drove eastward across Siberia toward the opposite shore of the same ocean, subduing the Native peoples and wresting territory from the impotent Manchu empire of China. In 1860, Russia acquired from China the Ussuri region on the Sea of Japan and founded the port city of Vladivostok. This new acquisition did not give Russia the coveted outlet to the open seas, for Vladivostok's harbour was icebound for most of the winter. Advocates of Russian expansion turned their attention south, towards China. As in Turkey and Persia, Russia found its access to a year-round harbour blocked by a politically unstable, economically backward, militarily weak state. Here, however, there was no European power capable of propping up the Chinese. Britain, which had traditionally served as the patron of China's Manchu rulers, was helpless to prevent the Russians from entering China by land. In 1891, the Russian government began constructing a trans-Siberian railway with the assistance of French loans intended to woo Russia into an alliance against Germany. Upon completion of that railway, military forces could be transported from the heart of European Russia to a frontier that no other great power (let alone the Chinese) could defend. The parts of China that appeared most attractive and most susceptible to Russian exploitation were the two peninsulas extending from the northeastern province of Manchuria into the Yellow Sea, which afforded access to the Pacific. The first of these, the Liaotung peninsula, included at its farthest extremity the coveted prize of Port Arthur, the year-round ice-free Pacific port of Russian dreams. The second, the peninsula of Korea, represented the key to Russia's control of the Yellow Sea and therefore command of the approaches to its prospective East Asian port. With control of these territories, Russia would be well positioned to take part in the Chinese trade that had begun to exert a strong attraction on the maritime states of the world.

Anticipating the arrival of the Russian military on the northern frontier of China to fill the vacuum produced by the collapse of Manchu authority, the great powers of Europe moved to partition the decaying Asian empire into spheres of interest. In 1897, the Germans seized the port of Kiao-Chow, sparking a scramble for economic concessions that quickly revealed the fictitious nature of Chinese sovereignty. Profiting from China's internal disarray, the Russian government in 1898 extracted from Beijing a long-term lease on the southern portion of the Liaotung peninsula (including Port Arthur), together with the right to build a railway linking the port to the rail network then under construction in Siberia. The territory in between, the province of Manchuria, also became the object of Russian ambition, since control of it would provide a secure land route to Port Arthur and the warm-water sea, together with privileged access to the vast mineral deposits that the province was believed to contain. In 1900, following the Russian army's participation in the multinational military force that had suppressed the anti-foreign Boxer Rebellion in Beijing, 100,000 soldiers remained on occupation duty in Manchuria to protect Russian interests there. Demands for far-reaching commercial concessions and the economic penetration of northern Korea soon followed. By the turn of the century, Russian domination of the Chinese Empire appeared imminent, pending only the completion of the Trans-Siberian Railroad, and the other great powers of Europe were incapable of projecting sufficient military force into the region in order to prevent it.

Russia was soon to discover that the world outside the control of the other European powers did not offer the boundless opportunities for exploitation that had been supposed. This was particularly true of the lands along the western shores of the Pacific, where a non-European power was using European techniques of economic, political, and military organization to take its share of the colonial spoils in its own geographical sphere. Whereas the continent of Africa and the southern rim of Asia lay within range of British, French, and German power, the western Pacific became, at the turn of the century, the object of Japan's imperial ambitions.

THE RISE OF JAPANESE POWER IN EAST ASIA

Japan consists of four main islands and several smaller ones off the coast of China. For centuries it was ruled by a decentralized feudal oligarchy consisting of territorial lords and an aristocratic caste of warriors. Hampered by a scarcity of natural resources and a mountainous terrain that left only 20 per cent of its land suitable for cultivation, Japan lacked the usual prerequisites for industrial development. Furthermore, the Japanese people were isolated from the rest of the world by a complex language with no close relatives and a strong sense of cultural uniqueness; they had remained inward-looking and resistant to foreign influences until well into the second half of the nineteenth century. For all of these reasons, Japan seemed destined to remain politically immature, economically backward, and militarily weak. Yet by the beginning of the twentieth century this isolated nation was about to become the first non-Western state to achieve the position of a modern industrial and imperial power.

Japan's rapid rise to world power began in January 1868, when a political revolution swept aside the feudal oligarchy and created the Meiji Restoration, with the emperor as the symbol of national unity and centralized authority. Real political power lay in the hands of a dynamic new ruling elite committed to transforming Japan from a primitive feudal society into a modern world power. The phenomenal success of the restoration was a result of the new leaders' willingness to abandon the isolationist prejudices of the past in favour of Western political, economic, and military methods. The Meiji political class recognized that the global power of the European nations was the result of their economic modernization, political centralization, and military organization and that Japan's best hope of resisting European domination lay in adopting the very practices that had made it possible elsewhere in the world.

The result of this willingness to innovate by imitation was the rapid Westernization of Japan during the closing decades of the nineteenth century. Members of the samurai warrior class were required to wear their hair in the Western style; European clothing was given official sanction; and in 1873, the Gregorian calendar was adopted. Japanese observers were dispatched to England to study financial, commercial, and naval affairs; to Germany to learn the principles of military organization, strategy, and tactics; and to France for training in law and government. The entire structure of Japanese society was thenceforth reorganized on the basis of these European models. The political and economic power of the aristocracy was transferred to a central government modelled on the European cabinet system, with a prime minister and a bicameral parliament. The military authority that had previously been the privilege of the samurai was assumed by the Imperial Army, and Japan adopted the Prussian institution of universal military service. The development of a nationwide system of banking and currency, transportation, and communication set the stage for spectacular economic growth during this period. Economic modernization in Japan began, as it had in England a century before, in the production of textiles. The silk industry captured a large share of the world market, and in 1910 Japan's silk exports surpassed those of China—a remarkable feat given the relative size of the two countries. In the meantime, the mechanization of cotton spinning and weaving proceeded rapidly. By 1900, Japan also had its own shipbuilding and munitions industries, and the value of Japanese foreign trade had increased from virtually nothing in 1850 to roughly US$200 million.

The prospects for Japan's continued economic growth were limited by several geographic constraints. Not only did the nation lack industrial raw materials and agricultural resources, but it was also in the midst of a demographic crisis. With a land area comparable to that of Newfoundland and Labrador and a rapidly expanding population (at the turn of the century it was nearly eight times that of Canada), the pressure on land capacity had become a serious problem. In the last decade of the nineteenth century, the Japanese ruling class concluded that the only hope for surmounting these geographical and demographic impediments to economic growth lay in colonial expansion. Once again, Europe furnished the instructive precedent. Just as Britain had relieved its population pressures and enhanced its economic productivity by acquiring overseas lands, Japan could find industrial and agricultural raw materials, markets for its manufactured products, and land for its excess population to colonize in the hitherto unclaimed territory in the adjacent regions of East Asia.

Scarcely a hundred kilometres to the west of the Japanese islands, on the mainland of Asia, the Korean peninsula and its Manchurian hinterland presented an irresistible temptation to Japan. In 1894–5, Japanese forces swept across Korea into Manchuria, defeated the Chinese military forces, and laid the groundwork for imperial expansion on the mainland by securing the independence (under Japanese economic domination) of Korea and annexing the offshore island of Taiwan (then Formosa). It was this expansion to the mainland that first brought Japan into conflict with Russia, which had begun its economic penetration of Manchuria and northern Korea in the same period. The collision came in 1904–5, in the first war between great powers since 1870. The Japanese navy bottled up the small Russian fleet based at Port Arthur, while the Japanese army defeated the Russian army stationed in Manchuria. When the 32 vessels of the Russian Baltic fleet arrived at the Tsushima Strait between Japan and Korea after a nine-month voyage from Europe, they were annihilated by the Japanese fleet. As a reward for its spectacular victory, Japan obtained the Russian lease of Port Arthur and the Liaotung peninsula, a privileged position in Manchuria, and a protectorate over Korea (which it annexed outright in 1910).

The Russo–Japanese War was a watershed in modern history for several reasons. It was the first instance in the modern era of a non-Western nation defeating a great power of Europe. As such it offered encouragement to the emerging leaders in the non-European world who wanted to liberate their own peoples from imperial domination. The Japanese had shown that such resistance was

possible, provided that it was backed by Western-type technology and military organization. Inspired to a certain extent by the Japanese example, nationalist revolutions erupted in Persia (1905), Turkey (1908), and China (1911). The leaders of these insurrections advocated economic, political, and military reforms in order to strengthen their peoples in the struggle against Western domination. In a very real sense, the Japanese victory of 1905 marked the beginning of Asia's half-century-long war of liberation against European colonial control. At the same time, the humiliation of the Russian Empire had the effect of undermining the political authority of the Romanov dynasty. The political revolution that swept Russia following the military defeat of 1905 compelled the tsar to grant a constitution, convoke a representative parliament, and guarantee fundamental civil liberties for the first time in the country's history. Although these concessions were diluted by various restrictions on popular sovereignty and democratic rights, the social unrest that had prompted them set in motion a wave of clandestine revolutionary activity that was to culminate in the overthrow of the imperial regime 12 years later.

From the perspective of the shifting balance of power in the world, the most important consequence of Russia's defeat in the Far East was the gradual rapprochement between Russia and Britain. Its expansionist ambitions in East Asia blocked by Japan, the Russian government began to contemplate reviving its long dormant claims to territory and influence at the other end of its empire, on the Balkan peninsula. First, though, Russia took the step of seeking to resolve its long-standing disputes with Britain over Persia and Afghanistan, the two states between Russian and British power in Southern Asia. The British government itself was anxious to reach a deal with Russia in order to ensure the security of India at a time when Britain felt increasingly menaced by the expansion of German military and naval power in Europe. The destruction of Russia's sea power in the Far East had removed one of the main reasons for British hostility to Russia, leaving Germany as the only potential threat to Britain's mastery of

RUSSIAN EMPIRE

Siberian RR

Trans-

Sakhalin

Manchuria

Karafuto
(Japan 1905)

OUTER
MONGOLIA

Chinese

Eastern RR

South Manchurian RR

Vladivostok

Hokkaido

*Sea of
Japan*

(Russia 1898)
(Japan 1905)

Peking

Port
Arthur

KOREA

Honshu

Tientsin

(Occupied 1905)
(Annexed 1910)

CHINA

Shantung
Peninsula

KIAO-CHOW
(Germany 1898)

*Yellow
Sea*

Tokyo

Wei-Hai-Wei
(British 1898)

Tsushima Strait

Nanking
Shanghai

Kyushu

Shikoku

N

Ningpo

	Japanese Empire
	Russian Empire
	Extent of Russian Occupancy (1900–1905)
	British Sphere of Influence
	German Sphere of Influence

0   200 Miles

0   200 km

FORMOSA
(Japan 1895)

THE RUSSO–JAPANESE WAR, 1904–1905

the seas. In short, these two historic rivals in Asia both regarded German power in Europe as the foremost obstacle to the pursuit of their respective national interests.

The reconciliation between Russia and Britain after 1905 was actively promoted by France, the one power that enjoyed cordial relations with both and had the most to gain from an Anglo–Russian rapprochement. In 1907, after more than a year of intensive negotiations, an Anglo–Russian agreement was concluded, settling all of the important disputes between these two imperial powers in Southern Asia. Russia recognized Afghanistan as a British sphere of influence, thereby according India the security on its northeastern frontier that London had long sought. Persia, which had been a flashpoint of Anglo–Russian rivalry for over

a decade, was partitioned into three zones: the northern zone, next to the Caucasus and including the capital, Tehran, was to be Russia's sphere; the southern zone, next to India and guarding the entrance to the Persian Gulf, became the British sphere; and the territory in between, including the Gulf itself, was to be a neutral buffer zone. Both nations agreed to block German efforts to obtain a foothold in Persia.

Though the Anglo–Russian agreement of 1907 applied only to the two powers' rivalries in Southern Asia, it paved the way for increasingly intimate diplomatic co-operation among Britain, Russia, and France. Observers began to speak of a 'Triple Entente' that had emerged as a diplomatic counterpart to the Triple Alliance of Germany, Austria–Hungary, and Italy. Fortified by its

GLOBAL RESPONSES TO WESTERNIZATION

Intellectuals and political leaders around the world were confronted by the challenge of Western power during the nineteenth and early twentieth centuries. Many modernizers in Asia and the Middle East looked favourably upon Western education and Western political systems as a means to achieve comprehensive reforms in their own countries. However, these same political leaders often struggled to find ways to meet the challenge of the West while retaining the distinctive cultures and traditions of their own peoples. Chinese reformers phrased this challenge in terms of preserving 'ti' (the essence of Chinese culture) while focusing on 'yong' (that which was useful from the 'barbarians'). Even those intellectuals who embraced the need to reform differed as to the best way to achieve this goal. Although political, economic, and military systems were imported wholesale from the West to Meiji Japan (1868–1912), the resulting Japanese equivalents managed to retain many uniquely Japanese elements, such as the constitutional recognition of the emperor's divinity. In China, demands for reforms similar to the ones successfully executed

in Japan often met strong resistance from those who sought to preserve the traditional imperial system, even in the face of ongoing foreign interference with Chinese sovereignty. Still other reformers sought strength through co-operation as in the case of the pan-Islamist and pan-Africanist movements. Meeting in Paris in February 1919, attendees at the First Pan-African Congress called for a collaborative effort to achieve eventual self-government and equal access to land, labour, and education. The fact that the delegates to the congress called for these rights to be extended first to 'civilized Africans'—that is, those who had already embraced the beliefs and methods of the colonizers—attests to the level of European penetration into the African consciousness. Despite general agreement and shared goals, those who advocated unity and co-operation often found that national and ethnic divisions worked against the core aims of their movements. Thus the twentieth century opened with a clear recognition of the potential threat of Western encroachment, but little in the way of consensus as to how best to address the challenge of the West.

amicable settlement with Britain in Southern Asia and emboldened by the diplomatic support and financial assistance from its ally France, Russia 'returned to Europe' after its disastrous adventure in the Far East. The revival of Russian aspirations in the Balkans—undertaken partly to divert public attention from the domestic troubles sketched above and partly in pursuit of long-standing interests in the region—was destined to bring the tsarist empire into conflict with Austria–Hungary and its powerful protector in Berlin.

THE EMERGENCE OF THE UNITED STATES

While Japan was emerging as the dominant power in East Asia, across the Pacific Ocean another non-European state that had adopted European ways began to assert its claim to imperial status. Geographically, the Japanese empire and the American republic could hardly have been less similar. Japan lacked not only arable land and natural resources but also a large internal market for its industrial output. The United States possessed all three in unparalleled abundance as a consequence of its westward territorial expansion in the nineteenth century. Whereas Japan was overpopulated, the US had the opposite problem: underpopulation required that it import millions of immigrants to operate its farms and factories.

Amid the contrasts there were striking similarities between the two nations that explain why they both joined the ranks of the imperial powers at the beginning of the twentieth century. Both were relatively free from threats of foreign invasion because of the great distances separating them from the European centres of military power. Both were located in the vicinity of politically disorganized and militarily weak states whose abundant natural resources made them tempting targets for economic exploitation and military domination. Together, freedom from interference and proximity to economically valuable, strategically vulnerable regions propelled the United States into a policy of imperial expansion during the same period as Japan's expansion into the Asian mainland.

The simultaneous emergence of these two powers on opposite shores of the Pacific raised the possibility that their aggressive ambitions would overlap. Indeed, both societies contained advocates of trans-Pacific expansion. By 1900, eastward migration had already produced a Japanese majority in the Hawaiian Islands, and increasing numbers of Japanese nationals settled on the west coast of the United States, where residents of European stock were beginning to demand exclusionary legislation. At the same time, various US constituencies were pressing for trans-Pacific expansion in the opposite direction. Commercial interests eagerly eyed the Chinese market for American agricultural surpluses and industrial products, while missionary societies dreamed of converting Chinese people to Christianity. American bankers looked to take part in the financial reorganization of the Chinese rail network in Manchuria, and American naval officials coveted the natural harbours in Samoa, Hawaii, and the Philippines as potential bases for a Pacific fleet. The subsequent American acquisition of those three island groups at the end of the nineteenth century posed a potential challenge to Japan's imperial aspirations in the western Pacific.

As it turned out, however, the Pacific ambitions of both countries were prudently postponed in favour of expansion closer to home. In spite of Washington's determined efforts to establish an 'Open Door' to China at the turn of the century, the two new Pacific powers worked out an arrangement that removed the principal sources of conflict between them. Washington tacitly tolerated Japan's economic penetration of Korea and Manchuria, while Tokyo accepted stringent restrictions on Japanese immigration to the United States. While Japanese imperial energies were thus diverted from the Pacific to the Asian mainland, American ambitions were similarly diverted from the Pacific to the Caribbean.

DEVELOPMENTS IN THE AMERICAS

One characteristic of the western hemisphere that has had a decisive influence on the economic and political relations of its constituent states is the enormous disparity in national power between the United States and the disunited nations to its south, in Latin America.[2] This imbalance of power was a direct result of the divergent historical experiences of the settler populations that inhabited the successor states of the British and Iberian empires in the 'new world' after they achieved their political independence from Europe.

By the 1860s, the English-speaking heirs to Britain's empire in North America had partitioned that vast, resource-rich continent into two sovereign political units, both of which rapidly modernized their economies following the British model of industrialization. The United States had already extended its political frontier across the continent by the mid-1850s by alternately expropriating the tribal lands of the indigenous inhabitants and annexing territory previously claimed by Spain, France, Britain, or the newly independent state of Mexico. Pushing westward with the active encouragement of their federal government and the protection of their military forces, the American pioneers welded that continental territory into a single political and economic unit by imitating European methods of economic organization and political integration. After the failure of the Southern states' bid for secession between 1861 and 1865, this politically unified, economically integrated system combined its extraordinary natural advantages—abundant natural resources; fertile, well-watered soil; and an excellent system of navigable rivers and lakes affording access to both land and markets—with the influx of skilled labour and capital investment from Europe to become the world's most prosperous nation by the end of the century.

Meanwhile, to the north, four of Britain's remaining North American colonies had united in 1867, and by 1900 the Dominion of Canada effectively stretched from the Atlantic to the Pacific. Although still tightly linked to the British Empire, by the turn of century the young country was developing close economic connections with its powerful neighbour, becoming a major supplier of raw materials and mineral resources

to the United States and the principal market for industrial exports from there.

If the general direction of developments in North America was towards integration, it was quite the opposite in Latin America. The collapse of Spanish and Portuguese authority between 1808 and 1822 resulted in the political disintegration of the Latin American mainland into what eventually became 20 independent republics.[3] Revolutionary leaders like Simon Bolívar had dreamed of creating a political federation of Latin America, but the new nations clung to their newly achieved national identities. Even economic integration—traditionally the preliminary step to political unification—proved unattainable. As a result of tariffs, import quotas, and other impediments to regional interchange established by the ruling elites, only a small portion of the foreign trade of each individual state was conducted within the region. Instead of following the North American model, which emphasized industrialization and the development of an internal market for domestic manufactured goods, the Latin republics preserved and even intensified the neocolonial character of their economic systems. They produced raw materials and foodstuffs for export and served as markets for finished manufactured products and capital investment from the already developed industrial economies of Western Europe. To make matters worse, whereas feudal practices had been abolished early in England and were not transplanted to British North America (except for the slave system in the Southern agricultural regions of the United States), the new Latin American states had inherited from Spain and Portugal feudal land tenure systems and rigidly stratified social structures that remained largely intact after these countries achieved independence.

It has long been fashionable to believe that the establishment of American hegemony in Latin America was a consequence of the policy known as the Monroe Doctrine, according to which Washington would regard any intervention by external powers in the Americas as a potential act of hostility. That belief is mistaken. As first stated

CANADA, BRITAIN, AND THE UNITED STATES

One of the catalysts for Canada's Confederation was the American Civil War (1861–5). The secession of the Confederacy had led many on the Union side to regard the British colonies to the north as possible compensation for the lost Southern states. Fear of annexation, however, was by no means the only stimulus for the colonies to unite. A sense of national identity—'a feeling of what might be termed Canadian nationality, in contradistinction to a feeling of mere colonial . . . vassalage', as the *Montreal Pilot* described it in 1850—had been developing for some time, especially in the province of Canada. Many in Britain had come to believe that it was time for the colonies to assume more responsibility for themselves—including the cost of their own defence. Meanwhile, in the 'united' province, it had become increasingly difficult to accommodate an English-speaking Protestant majority and a large French-speaking Catholic minority within a single administrative unit. In many ways the creation of Ontario and Quebec as separate provinces within a larger Canada made life easier for both. Yet strong differences of opinion could still arise, not least in the context of the Dominion's relations with Britain and its place within the British Empire.

When, in 1899, Britain declared war against the Dutch settlers (Boers) in South Africa, the Canadian government came under heavy pressure both from London and from English Canada to contribute troops in support of the Empire. But many French Canadians were adamantly opposed.

Prime Minister Wilfrid Laurier compromised, agreeing to send a first contingent of 1,000 volunteers on condition that Britain pay for their deployment. By the time the war ended in 1901, more than 8,000 Canadian volunteers had served in South Africa. Thereafter, Laurier tried to steer a middle course between independence and subordination to London. Support for Canada's imperial commitments remained high, particularly among anglophones. But when Lord Alverstone, Lord Chief Justice of England, supported the American claim in the United States' border dispute with Canada over the Alaska Panhandle in 1903, it underscored the fact that Britain still considered Canada's national interests secondary to imperial concerns.

Troops of the Royal Canadian Regiment cross Paardberg Drift during the Boer War, February 1900. Library and Archives Canada/Miscellaneous collection/C-014923.

by President James Monroe in an address to the US Congress in 1823, that 'doctrine' was simply a warning to the European powers (especially France, which was then suspected of harbouring designs on the newly independent republics of Latin America) that any attempt to re-establish European colonial power in the New World would be unacceptable to the United States. In fact, the Monroe Doctrine was a dead letter for most of the nineteenth century, since the US had not yet developed the naval power or the diplomatic influence to enforce it. It was only by the sufferance of Britain that the Latin American republics remained free of political interference and military intimidation by the great powers of the Old World. By extracting from France a promise of non-intervention and by maintaining undisputed naval supremacy in the Atlantic and

Caribbean, Britain ensured that no European nation would seek to strengthen its position in Europe by acquiring territory in the Americas.

It was not until the 1890s that the United States, having become an industrial power of the first rank, acquired the economic and military capability to project its power into the southern half of the hemisphere. The pursuit of US strategic and economic interests in Latin America, and particularly in the Caribbean region, was justified—as has so often been the case in US foreign policy—by a high-sounding moral principle. Just as the westward expansion of the nineteenth century was touted as the 'manifest destiny' of a chosen people, the subsequent extension of US hegemony over Latin America at the expense of European powers was couched in two moralistic phrases: 'hemispheric solidarity' and, especially, 'pan-Americanism'.

The ideology of pan-Americanism was rooted in two myths about the connections—both physical and political—between the two parts of the New World. The first was the widespread misconception that the two continents of the western hemisphere formed a single geographic unit. In reality, although North and South America are connected by a narrow strip of land, most travel between them was conducted first by sea and later by air. By sea, Rio de Janiero is considerably closer to the west coast of Africa than to any port in the United States; by air, Washington is closer to Moscow than to Buenos Aires. The second myth originated in the use of the term 'republic' as a label for the governmental systems of the Latin American nations as well as the United States. As 'sister republics', these countries came to be regarded as joint custodians of a common legacy of democratic government that distinguished them from the monarchical states of the Old World. The tendency of the 'republics' of Latin America to lapse into various forms of dictatorship while the nations of Western Europe moved towards democracy belied sentimental calls for a hemispheric partnership of republicanism.

Nevertheless, beginning in 1889 with the first International Conference of American States, the ideology of pan-Americanism persisted as the moral justification for what was really a neo-colonial relationship between the North American giant and the weak states to its south (Canada did not participate). The Commercial Bureau of the International Union of the American Republics, headquartered in Washington under the supervision of the US secretary of state, promoted inter-American economic and political co-operation. Subsequently renamed the Pan-American Union, this organization of free and independent states in the hemisphere became the vehicle for the exercise of US diplomatic influence over the member governments. Although American hopes of establishing a customs union were disappointed, the groundwork was laid for a hemispheric political system dominated by the United States without interference from the European powers.

The projection of Washington's power into Latin America required a direct challenge to the previously uncontested authority of Britain in the region. Such a challenge was effectively mounted in the last decade of the nineteenth century, at a time when Britain was engaged elsewhere by issues that affected its vital national interests much more directly. The episode that precipitated this shift in the balance of power in the western hemisphere was a seemingly trivial boundary dispute between Venezuela and British Guiana. Within the disputed zone lay the mouth of the Orinoco River, the key trade route in the northern portion of the South American continent. Venezuelan appeals to Washington for support, combined with American anxiety about the possible extension of Britain's economic influence along the southern shore of the Caribbean, prompted a remarkable diplomatic initiative from Washington. In July 1895, the US secretary of state, Richard Olney, demanded that Britain agree to submit the issue to arbitration or face US intervention on the basis of the Monroe Doctrine. Declaring that 'Today the United States is practically sovereign on this continent, and its fiat is law upon the subjects to which it confines its interposition,' Olney added that 'its infinite resources combined with its isolated position render it master of the situation and practically invulnerable against any or all other powers.' The boundary dispute soon receded in significance amid the broad international implications of this new policy initiative. The US had unilaterally assumed the right and responsibility to protect the interests of its neighbours to the south by virtue of its position of superiority within its hemisphere. Britain, preoccupied with more pressing concerns, chose not to become involved and thus acquiesced in this unilateral declaration of American hegemony in Latin America.

In 1898, British imperial authority in the eastern hemisphere seemed to be threatened at every turn by the actions of rival European powers. In March, the passage of Germany's first naval law and Russia's acquisition of a naval base at Port Arthur in Manchuria heralded the entry of two new contestants in the scramble for colonies and concessions in Asia. In the fall, Britain and France edged to the brink of war over conflicting territorial claims along the Nile, while tension continued to mount between Britain and the Boer republics in Southern Africa. Consequently, the United States was able to wrest Cuba and Puerto Rico from Spain after the Spanish–American War (1898) without provoking opposition from Britain. By the end of the century, the US had embarked on an ambitious naval construction program to reflect its newly acquired status as an imperial power. The naval advantages it enjoyed over Britain in the western hemisphere soon became apparent. Although the introduction of the steam-propelled warship increased the fighting strength of the world's battle fleets, it reduced their radius of action because it meant that ships needed to remain within reach of an assured source of fuel—in Britain's case, coal and, later (after 1912), oil.

In 1902, Britain began to transfer the bulk of its Caribbean naval squadron to the North Atlantic in order to offset the growth of German naval power. It effectively conceded control of the western hemisphere to the United States and recognized Latin America as an American sphere of interest. In the same year, Britain and Japan concluded an alliance that liberated more British battleships for deployment in home waters. By these two gestures Britain accorded the US and Japan the right to control the sea approaches to their own imperial domains in order to concentrate on protecting the security of the British Isles from the perceived menace of German sea power.

The United States rapidly developed extensive strategic and economic interests in the former Spanish islands in the Caribbean and the independent mainland nations on its shores. Naval strategists, concerned about the growing strength of Japan, considered the Isthmus of Panama an ideal location for a canal linking the Atlantic and the Pacific that would permit the concentration of naval forces in either ocean on short notice. American domination of the Caribbean region came to be seen as necessary for the security of the two coasts of the country as well as for the protection of the eastern approaches of the projected Panamanian canal, just as Britain's control of the North Sea and Japan's control of the China Sea were considered essential by the naval strategists of those two powers.

Powerful economic interests in the United States began to compete with European firms for control of the natural resources of Latin America in general and the Caribbean basin in particular. This penetration of Latin American economies characteristically took the form of direct acquisition by US firms of agricultural and subsoil mineral resources. Sugar-producing interests obtained a virtual monopoly on Cuban sugar cane, and the United Fruit Company of Boston established a huge 'banana empire' in Central America, purchasing enormous tracts of land and building roads, railways, and ports to convey its produce to foreign markets. The petroleum resources of Mexico and Venezuela, Chilean copper, Bolivian tin, and several other raw materials that were in comparatively short supply in the US came under the direct control of American businesses.

By 1901, the last obstacle to American mastery of the Caribbean region was removed. By means of the Hay–Pauncefort Treaty, Britain renounced an earlier agreement stipulating joint Anglo–American construction and operation of a

Central American canal. Two years later, a revolution in Colombia's northwestern province on the Isthmus of Panama received the active support of the American government, which promptly recognized Panama as an independent republic. In February 1904, the new nation signed a treaty authorizing the United States to construct an 80-kilometre-long canal across the isthmus in a zone leased and fortified by the government in Washington. In the meantime, steps had been taken to ensure the right of the US to protect its strategic and economic interests in the Caribbean. The newly created client states of Cuba and Panama were forced to include clauses in their constitutions stipulating this right to intervene to protect their independence and preserve social order, and both were induced to authorize the construction of American bases on their territory.

In 1904, President Theodore Roosevelt extended the prerogative of intervention to embrace the entire western hemisphere south of the United States. The self-proclaimed American right to manage the internal affairs of the Caribbean nations was frequently exercised in the years following the promulgation of this 'Roosevelt Corollary'. In 1905, the US assumed control of customs collection in the insolvent Dominican Republic and established a system of financial supervision that was to remain in force for 36 years. In 1909, American agents sparked a successful insurrection against the nationalistically inclined government of Nicaragua. Three years later, US marines were landed to protect the compliant successor regime, whose transfer of authority over its customs service to Washington had produced widespread internal discontent. Though nominally independent, Nicaragua would remain under US financial supervision from 1911 to 1924.

By the summer of 1914, the United States had established its undisputed mastery of the Caribbean region. American authority was dramatically symbolized by the opening of the Panama Canal in August—the very month when the First World War began. The subsequent construction of American naval bases at Roosevelt Roads in Puerto Rico and Guantánamo Bay in Cuba gave the US command of the eastern approaches to the canal and a position of strategic invulnerability in the western hemisphere. In the meantime, the economy of the Caribbean region had become tightly linked to the superior economic system of what resentful Latin Americans had begun to call 'the Colossus of the North'. Direct American investment in electric utilities, railways, sugar, oil, bananas, and extractive industries generated substantial profits, which were repatriated to fuel the United States' phenomenal economic expansion. American control of the banking system and customs administration of the Caribbean nations served the dual functions of ensuring the repayment of debts to US investors and precluding European intervention on behalf of aggrieved debtors. Although Europe's economic domination of South America persisted well into the twentieth century, that last remnant of European power in the western hemisphere was soon to disappear as well, a casualty of the Great War and its aftermath.

TECHNOLOGY AND THE GEOPOLITICAL WORLD VIEW

The projection of Western power all around the world in the closing decades of the nineteenth century was facilitated by two key technological innovations in transportation. The first was the application of steam power to ocean transport. Although the first steamship was constructed in 1802, sailing ships were not definitively displaced until the 1850s. Liberated from dependence on the unpredictable wind and capable of previously unimaginable speeds, the coal-powered steamship enabled the industrial nations of Europe to extend both their economic activity and their military power to previously inaccessible regions. The initial beneficiary of this technological revolution was Britain, which at mid-century still possessed the most highly organized machine industry and the best supplies of coal. The problem of keeping the fleets supplied with fuel was solved by the acquisition of coaling stations across the globe. The search for refuelling stations to accommodate battle fleets and merchant marines played its part in prompting the imperialist expansion of the late nineteenth century, when other aspirants to world power joined the naval race. As a result, previously formidable oceanic barriers were transformed into channels for intercontinental relations. Warships steamed from base to base displaying the flag as a warning to potential enemies, giving rise to the catchphrase 'gunboat diplomacy'. Merchant vessels arrived at far-off ports laden with manufactured products and departed with tropical foodstuffs or raw materials for the return voyage.

The second revolutionary innovation was the application of steam power to land transportation. Just as the Canadian Pacific Railway (completed in 1885) opened Canada's Prairie and Pacific regions to settlement and resource exploitation, so did massive rail construction projects in the United States and, later, Russia make it possible for them to take effective political and economic control of the vast areas to which they laid claim. Railways also permitted the nations of Western Europe, especially Britain and France, to penetrate the interior of Africa from the coastal footholds they had established in earlier centuries. The subjugation of indigenous populations, the projection of political authority into interior regions, and the exploitation and extraction of economic resources were all facilitated by the construction of rail lines inland from the coasts.

In the same period, a device was invented to permit the rapid transmission of human messages across the airwaves. With the telegraph (and, later, the radio) came the ability to convey instructions and requests for information to and from the far-flung outposts of empires. The capacity to maintain continuous communication across the globe permitted a degree of centralized direction unheard of in the days when ambassadors, military commanders, and merchants on the spot were required to make hasty decisions that often determined the outcome of diplomatic negotiations, wars, or contests for economic advantage.

The consequences of this technological 'shrinkage' of the earth became dramatically apparent in military operations conducted around the turn of the century. The railway and the steamship greatly increased the size and mobility of military forces. No longer did soldiers have to face long marches and risky sea voyages that depleted their strength long before they reached the field of battle. Between 1899 and 1902, in an unprecedented projection of military power across the ocean, Britain was able to maintain a quarter of a million soldiers in Southern Africa—more than 10,000 kilometres from home—to subdue the army of the Boer republics. In 1904, Russia conveyed an army of comparable size 6,500 kilometres across Siberia by rail to engage the Japanese forces in Manchuria. In the past, barriers of space and time had isolated the world's land masses from one another. Now, at the beginning of the twentieth century, the entire world had become a single network of strategic and economic interaction, knitted together by the railway, the steamship, and the telegraph.

The effort to understand the implications of these changes in international relations led to the establishment of a new branch of the social sciences called 'geopolitics'. To the extent that it represented a scientific intellectual enterprise, this discipline combined the principles of geography and political science for the purpose of studying the global distribution of political power. However, geopolitics (like many other social sciences) soon forfeited its claim to scientific objectivity. Many of its most reputable scholars used its teachings to create an ideological justification for their own nations' efforts to expand and to subjugate other peoples. To the geopoliticians, the entire earth represented an arena in which rival powers struggled for control of economically valuable resources, territory, and populations. No place in the world was exempt from the iron law of geopolitics: the uneven distribution of wealth, natural resources, and strategic advantage meant that the handful of nation-states capable of projecting their power beyond their own frontiers were locked in a worldwide contest for control of the unclaimed or indefensible regions of the earth.

It is no surprise that the expanding German Empire produced the most detailed and comprehensive doctrine of geopolitics at the turn of the century. In the writings of the German geopoliticians, control of Eurasia—from Spain to Siberia, and from the northern Arctic wastes to the tip of the Indian subcontinent—would determine the outcome of what they saw as the forthcoming contest for domination of the world. Given Germany's superior industrial organization and military power and Russia's advantage in terms of territory, population, and natural resources, German scholars expected this contest to take the form of an epic struggle between 'Teuton' and 'Slav' in the borderlands of Central and Eastern Europe, where Germanic and Slavic populations had intermingled over the centuries. To the underlying principle of German geopolitics—the definition of Eurasia as a geographical space to be filled by the political authority and military power of the strongest nation—was added the Malthusian doctrine of population pressure against food supply and the Social Darwinist concept of a competition for survival among different human 'races'.

This witches' brew of geopolitics, demography, and pseudo-biological determinism supplied the requisite intellectual justification for the extension of German power eastward at the expense of Russia. The theorists and their popularizers portrayed Germany as an industrialized nation with a rapidly expanding population of 'racially superior' people but an inadequate supply of foodstuffs and natural resources within its political frontiers. It therefore required additional space for internal migration as well as agricultural land and raw materials. Such space was available in the fertile plains to the east, populated by supposedly inferior peoples, mainly Slavs, who were deemed incapable of exploiting the potentially productive territory they occupied and of defending it from foreign invaders. Had these perverse theories been confined to the universities, they might have represented little more than academic curiosities. After the turn of the century, however, influential members of the German political, economic, and military elite began to study them with interest,

and so they were transformed into prescriptions for the German conquest of Eurasia.

The most formidable obstacle to this geopolitical design was Britain, with its string of colonial holdings along the southern rim of Eurasia and its domination of the adjacent seas. It was therefore not surprising that Britain produced the other great geopolitical tradition of the period. Halford Mackinder, in a seminal paper presented to the Royal Geographical Society in 1904, reflected the influence of German geopolitical thinkers such as Friedrich Rätzel while adding a few novel concepts of his own. Entitled 'The Geographical Pivot of History', this paper extended the scope of geopolitical analysis to encompass the entire globe. The earth, according to Mackinder, was divisible into two regions. The 'world island', consisting of the interlinked continents of Europe, Asia, and Africa, was the largest, most populous, and richest of all possible land combinations. Arrayed along its periphery were the large insular groups—the Americas, Australia, Japan, and the British Isles. At the centre of the world island lay what Mackinder called the 'heartland', stretching from the Volga to the Yangtze and from the Himalayas to the Arctic. Protected against seaborne invaders by ice floes to the north and rugged mountains and arid deserts to the south, this vast land was vulnerable only on its western periphery, along the stretch of lowland connecting Western Europe to Russia. Effective political domination of this space by a single power had been precluded in the past by the limitations of transportation. The periodic invasions from east to west and vice versa by horse-riding marauders, from Attila the Hun to Napoleon Bonaparte, had failed to establish permanent control of this European gateway to the heartland because they could not ensure continual supply of men and materiel.

The invulnerability of the Eurasian heartland had been abolished, Mackinder believed, by the technological revolution in transportation. Now a powerful continental nation stood an excellent chance of extending its political control first over the Eastern European gateway, then over the Eurasian land mass, and finally over the entire globe: 'Who rules east Europe commands the Heartland; who rules the Heartland commands the world-island; who rules the world-island commands the world.' Thus Mackinder identified the geopolitical nightmare that was to haunt the world's two major sea powers (Britain and, later, the United States) during the first half of the new century—the prospect that either Germany or Russia would conquer Eastern Europe and take control of the Eurasian land mass as a prelude to gaining mastery over the entire world.

At the heart of Mackinder's theory were two basic convictions. The first was that because of railways, land power had definitively replaced sea power as the key to world domination. The second was that the eastern hemisphere (the 'world island') was of pre-eminent strategic importance in calculations of global power. Both premises discounted the United States as a potential participant in the global struggle for empire, because it was just beginning to emerge as a world power at the time when Mackinder was formulating his doctrine. For the first hundred years of its history as an independent nation, the US was able to avoid active involvement in the power struggles taking place across the Atlantic. Geographical isolation from Europe—in conjunction with Britain's policy of using its naval superiority in the Atlantic to prevent the extension of great power rivalry to the western hemisphere and the relative weakness of the states on its northern and southern frontiers—made it possible for the US to direct its energies westward toward the Pacific.

It is hardly surprising that this expansionist urge did not dissipate once the West was won. As we have seen, the American hunger for land and resources that had inspired the conquest of a continent developed toward the end of the century into an aspiration for empire in the Pacific and the Caribbean. In part, this new imperialist urge was defensive. The transportation revolution had removed the geographical basis for isolation from world affairs just as the protective shield of British naval predominance began to disappear. As distant nations became capable of projecting military power across the oceans in the form of

heavily armed, coal-fired battle fleets, they were able to pose a grave threat to the United States, with its long, vulnerable coastlines. The necessity of dividing its second-rank naval forces between two oceans, and the difficulty of concentrating the two fleets in times of national emergency, created a sense of vulnerability to attack by sea that stood in glaring contrast to Americans' sense of invincible power on the continent itself.

The sense of vulnerability to seaborne invasion, together with a growing belief in the economic benefits of empire, fed the perceived need for a powerful American navy with a network of overseas bases and refuelling stations. During the great age of imperialism, the United States had seemed paralyzed as a passive observer while the great powers of Europe divided up the unclaimed spaces of the world and competed for control of its waterways.

The consequences of US inactivity during the age of imperialism were first suggested by American naval strategist Alfred Thayer Mahan, whose book *The Influence of Sea Power Upon History*, published in 1890, supplied the inspiration for his country's rise to world power. Writing when Britannia still ruled the waves, Mahan predicted that developments in the new century would revolutionize the naval balance of power. Huge armadas of ships, supported by global networks of bases and refuelling stations, would enable the industrialized nations to wage a pitiless struggle for world domination. Any nation caught without sufficient naval power and the capacity to project and sustain it across the seas would at best be consigned to second-rank status and at worst face foreign invasion. Mahan warned that his own nation was in just such a position. The American navy throughout the nineteenth century had been designed for defence of the American coasts. The American navy of the future must represent, as the Royal Navy had for Britain, an instrument of policy designed to enhance the nation's power and prestige in the world.

The influence of Mahan's writings on his own country is confirmed by the policies that signalled America's rise to the front rank of world powers: the acquisition of naval bases in the Pacific and the Caribbean, the construction of the Panama Canal, and the decision to build a battle fleet capable of operating on the high seas. As important as Mahan's teachings may have been in promoting American imperialism, they had an equally profound impact abroad. Germany in particular learned from Mahan not only the general truth that sea power was a prerequisite to national security and prosperity in the modern world but also that Britain's undisputed naval primacy was about to vanish. The rise of Japanese and American naval power in the 1890s confirmed this prediction by challenging British naval dominance in the Far East and the western hemisphere. Only by strengthening its overseas squadrons could Britain reverse this trend and regain its pre-eminent position abroad. But it was precisely at this moment that Germany embarked on a naval construction program that threatened Britain's security in its own home waters, forcing the Admiralty to deplete rather than augment its overseas naval strength in order to preserve control of the sea approaches to the British Isles.

Germany's naval expansion was intended to frighten Britain into entering into an alliance that would nullify the threat posed by the alliance concluded between France and Russia in 1894. Instead, it drove the British into the arms of the French, who, as we have seen, renounced their old claims to Egypt in return for Britain's co-operation against Germany in Europe. Thus the arms race at the turn of the century had the unintended effect of focusing Britain's attention on the balance of power in Europe, at least temporarily. The simultaneous naval challenges presented by the United States and Japan were accepted with equanimity in London and resulted in the relatively painless depletion of British naval strength overseas. But the combination of Germany's existing military power on the continent and its potential naval power in European waters reminded British policy-makers that the greatest threat to the security of their island lay across the North Sea.

The geopolitical conception of international relations to which the governing elites of all the major nations subscribed by the beginning of the twentieth century presupposed a global struggle for power that inevitably ran the risk of escalating into a general war. The great powers thus faced the challenge of designing a political mechanism for resolving the conflicts that were bound to arise in such an unstable international environment. The avoidance of a world war until the collapse of the international order in 1914 was due in large part to the universal desire to manage international conflict by diplomatic negotiation. The Berlin Conference of 1884–5 offered a pattern for channelling expansionist pressures in directions that would reduce the chances of armed confrontation. This gathering of representatives of the principal colonial powers set down ground rules for the European conquest of Africa, permitting each power to take its share so as to prevent the development of competing claims that might provoke war. Bilateral arrangements were reached between France and England regarding territorial disputes in North Africa and between England and Russia in Southern Asia.

When diplomacy failed, multilateral intervention by third parties succeeded in limiting the geopolitical consequences of armed conflict. The Russo–Turkish War of 1877–8, the Sino–Japanese War of 1894–5, and the Russo–Japanese War of 1904–5 were all terminated by the diplomatic intervention of uninvolved powers before the victors could achieve all their major objectives. This reliance on international co-operation to preserve the balance of power in Europe reflected the great powers' conviction that war must be contained in order to preserve the international order from which they derived their power. This tacit agreement to avoid recourse to violence in the pursuit of national objectives in Europe remained generally in force until the summer of 1914. It dissolved at that time, as we shall see, because two of the European powers—Austria–Hungary and Russia—had come to consider the region of Southern Europe where their ambitions collided (the Balkan peninsula) so vital to their national interests as to justify the risk of a general war, and because their two powerful allies—Germany and France, respectively—had developed powerful reasons of their own to favour a military showdown.

THE DEVELOPMENT OF AN INTERNATIONAL ECONOMY

As the great powers sought to reduce the frictions caused by unorganized imperial expansion, they also faced other challenges that demanded co-operation among the world's major trading nations. Through the first half of the nineteenth century, most economic activity had been conducted at the local level; only in those few countries, such as Britain and France, that had managed to abolish internal impediments to economic exchange was trade conducted on a nationwide scale. Where international trade existed at all, it was usually confined to distinct commercial regions defined by physical proximity—such as Western and Central Europe, Russia and the Baltic, and the North Atlantic—in which complementary economic systems permitted the direct bilateral exchange of products. Economic activity could not expand beyond this limited regional context until two conditions were met: first, labour and capital had to be free to migrate to countries with abundant natural resources; and, second, goods had to have easy access to the markets of the world.

The end of the Napoleonic Wars in 1815 had enabled Britain to concentrate its national energies on resuming the phenomenal industrial expansion that had begun in the last quarter of the eighteenth century. The restoration of peace also promoted industrialization on the European continent as the governing elites of various states recognized the advantages of economic modernization and sought to copy the British example. During the second half of the nineteenth century, the industrializing countries of Europe had begun to produce surpluses of both labour and capital. In the meantime, the continents of North and South America, the Pacific islands of Australia and New Zealand, and the temperate zone of Southern Africa combined the advantages of a rich endowment of natural resources with the

disadvantages of an insufficient supply of labour and investment capital to exploit them. European workers unable to find work on their overpopulated continent migrated to those underpopulated spaces with plentiful resources, cheap land, and high wages (reflecting the scarcity of labour). Similarly, European banks and private individuals whose accumulated savings could no longer command high interest rates at home (because of the oversupply of domestic capital) were enticed to invest abroad to obtain higher returns from the resource-rich, capital-poor areas.

However, attempts to expand commercial and financial activities in this economically rational way were frustrated by a combination of politically imposed constraints and technological deficiencies in transportation inherited from the preindustrial era. Tariffs, import quotas, subsidies for domestic industries, and restrictive shipping regulations inhibited the free exchange of products across national frontiers. The absence of a smoothly functioning international monetary system discouraged short-term financing of trade and long-term investment in productive enterprises abroad. In the same way, the lack of cheap, reliable transportation limited the international migration of labour in search of employment.

These impediments to the free movement of workers (seeking jobs), capital (seeking high returns on investment), and exports (seeking markets) gradually disappeared during the second half of the century. The advent of steamship and railway transportation in the mid-nineteenth century launched a mass intercontinental and transcontinental migration unequalled before or since. Between 1860 and 1920, more than 45 million people left the grinding poverty of overpopulated Europe for the sparsely settled spaces across the seas. The United States received over half of them, and the rest went to other underpopulated areas of abundant natural resources and temperate climate, including Canada, Argentina, Brazil, Australia, New Zealand, and South Africa. Migrating to these lands, successive generations of Europeans transplanted the economic practices, social customs, and political traditions of the Old

World to the New while reducing the indigenous inhabitants to economic insignificance and political impotence.

Along with skilled and semi-skilled European labour, the resource-rich, underpopulated areas abroad received infusions of European capital to build their economies. France joined Britain as a major source of foreign investment in the 1860s, and the newly unified state of Germany entered the ranks of international creditors in the 1880s as its rapidly expanding economy began to generate profits in excess of domestic demand. On the whole, these long-term foreign investments in productive enterprises were concentrated either in the industrializing nations of Southern and Eastern Europe or in the overseas regions of abundant resources. In the 1890s, the United States itself began to export capital to developing economies within its own region. By 1914, roughly 40 per cent of all US foreign investment was in Mexico and almost 30 per cent in Canada, with most of the rest distributed among Latin American countries along the shores of the Caribbean. Although most of these investments took the form of purchases of foreign government securities to finance the budget deficits of the recipient states, an increasing proportion supplied capital to build what economists call 'infrastructure', the public facilities—roads, railways, ports, power plants, telegraph and telephone systems, and the like—that developing economies require before their industrial and agricultural systems can function effectively. In this way, European (and, later, American) investors supplied the capital while European immigrants supplied the labour for the development of overseas regions with abundant natural resources.

As the obstacles to immigration and foreign investment began to disappear, so too did the politically inspired impediments to international trade. Here, as in all other areas of economic development in the nineteenth century, Britain led the way. The drastic reduction of protective duties on agricultural imports to Britain (the so-called Corn Laws) in 1846 was followed in 1860 by even more substantial tariff reforms that eventually opened the British market to imports without restriction. In short order France, Belgium, the Netherlands, and, later, Germany, reciprocally moderated their duties on imports. The result of this evolution toward free trade was twofold: first, it increased the total volume of international commerce to unprecedented levels; second, it stimulated product specialization, which in turn promoted the growth of world trade.

The case of Britain provides a striking example of the increasing importance of specialization and the free exchange of products. Britain recognized that a nation could benefit from specializing in the production of those goods that were best suited to its 'domestic factor endowment'. That is, it would conserve its scarce (hence expensive) factors and draw heavily on its abundant (hence cheap) ones. Instead of using its abundant supplies of labour and capital to grow high-cost wheat on its insufficient arable land, for example, Britain took advantage of those factors to produce manufactured goods, which it sold to countries with abundant farmland in exchange for the food it required. Britain's exports and imports tripled in value during the second half of the nineteenth century. After the introduction of refrigeration in the 1870s, it began to receive beef from Argentina, mutton and wool from Australia, and dairy products from New Zealand, as well as a host of other raw materials from abroad, including iron ore, tin, copper, lead, nickel, cotton, and the like. In return, Britain shipped out finished manufactured products—mainly textiles, which accounted for half of its total exports in 1880. Although the performance of other industrialized nations was less spectacular, increasing dependence on foreign trade became the central fact of economic life in the modern world.

The explosive growth of world trade and foreign investment in the second half of the nineteenth century was facilitated by the system of international financial exchange centred in London. Importers and exporters found it difficult to conduct international operations on the basis of cash on delivery. Thus they increasingly came to rely on short-term borrowing from an emerging network of commercial banks, discount houses, and dealers in bills of exchange. This system made it possible to exchange products without having to move large amounts of gold or currency around, since most transactions could simply be cleared against one another on the books of these London financial institutions. Meanwhile, as the major British banks began to accumulate huge reserves of capital, they branched out into long-term lending to foreign governments and firms. The sale of treasury bonds, railway stocks, and other foreign securities on the London money market effectively channelled the savings of the British and other European middle classes into the developing economies of the rest of the world.

Britain's greatest contribution to the international network of trade and investment, however, was its solution to the problem of foreign exchange. Since each sovereign nation of the world printed its own currency, exporters who sold products abroad accumulated reserves of foreign money that obviously were of no use in discharging debts incurred at home. What these exporters needed was a way to exchange that foreign money for equivalent amounts of their own currency. Conversely, what importers needed was a way of paying for the products they purchased in the currency of the exporting country.

Throughout history, the world's major trading nations had been frustrated in their attempts to establish orderly relations among their respective currencies in order to permit the easy exchange of goods across national borders. This problem was effectively solved in the late nineteenth century, when the British pound sterling became a type of world currency, used by all the major trading nations to settle their international accounts. Britain's pre-eminent position in world trade and finance inspired universal confidence in the value and stability of sterling, which in the eyes of importers and exporters became literally 'as good as gold'. Between 1821 and 1914, the British government faithfully kept its promise to exchange gold for its national currency at a fixed price. The convenience of dealing in a paper currency that was fully convertible into gold on demand, at a

predetermined price, persuaded exporters and importers of all nations to conduct their foreign transactions in sterling. By the early 1870s, all the major European nations, the United States, and several Latin American countries had adopted the gold standard, linking their own currencies to gold at a fixed price. In other words, the central banks of these nations were prepared both to sell all the gold demanded of them at that price and to buy up all the gold offered to them at the same price. The result was a system of fixed exchange rates that could not fluctuate because of their relationship to a metal in limited supply whose intrinsic value was universally recognized. The twin evils of exchange instability and inflation were eliminated in this era. Never before or since has the world enjoyed such an effective mechanism for the adjustment of international accounts.

Towards the end of the nineteenth century, then, the international economic system was tightly integrated through a complex network of foreign trade and investment centred in London. Universal acceptance of the gold standard made it possible to adjust temporary disturbances in the international balance of payments. British banks financed international trade and supplied investment capital to developing regions. The British merchant fleet transported more than three-quarters of the total volume of world trade. British insurance companies such as Lloyds of London removed the risk of ocean transport. The consequent expansion of world trade and investment and the effective functioning of the international monetary system was destined to continue so long as Britain was able to retain its pre-eminent commercial and financial position in world markets. Once that virtual monopoly was contested, however, this seemingly perfect system began to show cracks. Though they did not fundamentally disturb the effective functioning of the system, they foreshadowed its demise.

The first ominous development was the simultaneous emergence of Germany and the United States as economic powers of the first rank. In the mid-nineteenth century, Britain was the only industrial power of any importance. By 1914, Germany had surpassed Britain in the production of pig iron and was approaching it in output of coal. As for the US, it had counted for little before the 1880s, but since then it had experienced the most spectacular growth of all. By 1914, it was the world's leading producer of coal, and in pig iron production it surpassed Britain and Germany combined. The threat to Britain's industrial pre-eminence was not immediately apparent, for several reasons. First, America's enormous internal market absorbed most of its domestic manufactured goods. Its impressive agricultural productivity also relieved it of the necessity to export finished products to pay for imports of food. As a consequence, export trade represented a paltry 8 per cent of US gross national product in 1913 and consisted mainly of goods from the fertile farmland of the Midwest, which gained access to foreign markets as a result of railway construction. In 1910, fully 75 per cent of American exports fell under the heading of agricultural produce or semi-finished manufactures, and were therefore complementary to rather than competitive with British exports.

Germany, on the other hand, lacked both the huge internal free trade zone and the self-sufficiency in foodstuffs enjoyed by the United States. Thus it was driven to seek foreign outlets for trade that threatened to produce an acute commercial rivalry with Britain. Moreover, by concentrating on finished steel products, cotton textiles, coal, and chemicals, German manufacturers competed directly with British industrial producers. That competition was mitigated by a mutually beneficial division of world markets. Germany sent most of its exports to Eastern and Southern Europe—a region of minimal interest to British merchants, who were content to continue profiting from their lucrative commercial relationships within the Empire and with Latin America.

Even when Britain's exports of finished manufactured products failed to keep pace with its enormous imports of foodstuffs and raw materials, the resulting deficit in the balance of trade was easily covered by 'invisible exports', income derived from investments overseas and services such as banking, insurance, and shipping performed for foreign governments, corporations, or individuals. In short, Britain's virtual monopoly on the financial and service sectors of the modern world economy provided sufficient annual income to balance international accounts and even to re-export a surplus in the form of additional investment in foreign enterprises. This dependence on invisible exports to preserve the balance-of-payments surplus also concealed an ominous threat to Britain's trade pre-eminence posed by the burgeoning industrial systems of Germany and the United States. A nation whose share of the world's industrial production had dropped from 25 per cent in 1860 to less than 10 per cent in 1913 was clearly on the decline in relative terms. It was only a matter of time before the internal market of the US would become saturated with the products and profits of American industrialism, and aggressive German exporters of merchandise and capital would begin seeking overseas markets in regions previously dominated by British interests. German and American commercial expansion was already in evidence by the turn of the century in Latin America—a traditional British preserve. To make matters worse, Russia and Japan had begun their industrial take-off in the 1890s and were expected to enter the world market in the not-so-distant future.

In the same period, political obstacles to international trade began to reappear throughout the world. Germany had ended its brief experiment with free trade in 1879, when it began imposing duties on a variety of industrial and agricultural products. France followed suit in 1892. The United States raised its tariff in 1890 and again in 1897. Other European nations quickly joined the protectionist trend, so that by the turn of the century only Britain and the Netherlands remained committed to free trade. This resurgence of economic nationalism was a result of pressure exerted on governments by domestic producers anxious to protect themselves from foreign competition at a time when a global contest for markets was widely anticipated. It marked the first significant departure from the system of free exchange of productive factors on which the new international economy of the nineteenth century depended for its survival. It also foreshadowed the collapse of the interlocked network of free trade, international finance, and intercontinental immigration that would be one consequence of the First World War.

SUMMARY

While the twentieth century arguably witnessed more changes than any comparable period of time in human history, there were also long-term continuities. New technologies and political ideologies shaped the course of world history in unforeseeable ways, yet the struggle for power remained a constant factor in international relations. A growth or decline in the economic strength of one nation would often alter the balance of military power in a region, which would in turn affect international alliances. In other words, economic vitality, military might, and political influence were intertwined. Underlying the three great conflicts of the century—the First World War, the Second World War, and the Cold War—was the ceaseless international struggle to maximize wealth, power, and security.

At the turn of the twentieth century, the world was an interdependent system of nations centred on four states: Great Britain, France, Germany, and Russia. A wave of European imperialism that had begun in the mid-1800s was at its height as these great imperial powers competed for supremacy in Africa and Asia. Britain, the industrial and financial capital of the world, sought new markets and natural resources to fuel its industrial machine; Germany, a united nation since 1871, was determined to challenge Britain's dominance; France, fearing the consequences of German growth, needed to build its own strength; and Russia wanted both to expand its territory and to acquire a port that would be ice-free all year round. Imperial competition was also indirectly responsible for a series of secret alliances between several European nations, which would have disastrous consequences in the summer of 1914.

At the same time, the United States and Japan were beginning to challenge the global domination of the European powers. Fuelled by a vibrant industrial economy and massive immigration, the former began to expand its political power in the late nineteenth century, colonizing several small islands in the Caribbean. American leaders believed that their financial dominance in the western hemisphere permitted them to assert their power while preventing European nations from infiltrating the region. Japan, for its part, had embarked on a remarkable program of modernization and economic expansion, but it possessed relatively few natural resources. To meet the pressing needs of its growing population and economy, Japan acquired a number of colonial holdings in the South Pacific and on the Chinese mainland. By the eve of the Great War, Japan was poised to become the first nation outside Europe to join the ranks of the great powers.

Since the mid-nineteenth century, the established imperial powers had relied on treaties and diplomatic negotiations to manage disputes, contain regional conflicts, and limit the spread of warfare. However, the rise of the new powers (especially Germany) upset this equilibrium. Dramatic advances in transportation and communication technologies also placed new pressures on international relations, threatening Britain's commercial dominance. As Europe braced for war in the summer of 1914, no one could have foreseen how the world would be changed.

NOTES

1. In this book the term 'Western' designates that portion of the northern hemisphere inhabited primarily by Europeans or immigrants of European stock.
2. By 'Latin America' we mean the politically independent states of Central America (including Mexico), South America, and the West Indies where Spanish, Portuguese, and French are the official languages.
3. Excluding British, French, and Dutch Guiana (which remained European colonies) and British Honduras (which became a British colony in 1962).

QUESTIONS FOR CRITICAL THOUGHT

1. To what extent was the world truly an interconnected whole, centred on Europe, as the twentieth century opened?
2. What was the principal factor which facilitated Britain's acquisition of such a massive empire?
3. To what extent did imperial motives differ among the great powers?
4. What was the main source of instability during the early years of the twentieth century?
5. Why was the United States able to develop such great regional power while the nations of Latin America appeared to languish?
6. What was the key to the avoidance of large-scale war in the years before 1914?

WEBSITES FOR FURTHER REFERENCE

History in Focus: Empire
  www.history.ac.uk/ihr/Focus/Empire/web.html

Internet East Asia Sourcebook
  www.fordham.edu/halsall/eastasia/eastasiasbook.html

Internet Modern History Sourcebook: Imperialism
  www.fordham.edu/halsall/mod/modsbook34.html

Perry-Castañeda Library Map Collection
  www.lib.utexas.edu/maps

PART ONE

THE THIRTY YEARS' WAR
(1914–1945)

On 26 July 1936, a crowd of 50,000 people gathered in France to watch King Edward VIII unveil the Canadian National Vimy Memorial. Accompanied by France's president, the British monarch spoke about the great loss Canada had suffered in the Great War and the tremendous contribution Canada had made to the Entente cause. 'It is a memorial to no man,' he noted, 'but a memorial for a nation.'

Built on the site of Hill 145, which saw the fiercest fighting during the battle of Vimy Ridge in 1917, the memorial took 11 years to build and cost $1.5 million. Designed by Canadian architect Walter Allward, the massive structure features 2 towering pylons and 20 giant sculptures situated in a 91-hectare park adorned with Canadian trees and shrubs. At the base of the memorial is inscribed: 'To the valour of their countrymen in the Great War and in memory of their sixty thousand dead this monument is raised by the people of Canada.' The names of 11,285 Canadians killed in France and whose resting place remains unknown are carved on a series of long walls. The park surrounding the memorial contains hundreds of metres of tunnels, trenches, and craters, preserving parts of the wartime landscape in order to give visitors a sense of what the Canadian soldiers faced in 1917. France donated the land to the Canadian people in recognition of their enormous wartime sacrifice, and the battle of Vimy Ridge came to symbolize Canada's emerging sense of nationhood. As one Canadian officer who fought at Vimy put it, 'I witnessed the birth of a nation.'

The Vimy Memorial was intended to convey not only the horrors of war but also the principles of national sacrifice. Walter Allward designed the statues to symbolize ideals such as truth, gallantry, and sympathy. The memorial also represents the effort by empires and nations to cope with the forces unleashed by the Thirty Years' War. But while King Edward VIII was unveiling this monument to the 'war to end all wars', the world was just three years away from a second global conflict of unprecedented fury.

◇ Spectators gather in front of Canada's National Memorial at Vimy Ridge after its unveiling, 26 July 1936. Library and Archives Canada/National Film Board fonds/PA-183544.

CHAPTER 1

GERMANY'S BID FOR EUROPEAN DOMINANCE (1914–1918)

THE ROOTS OF THE 'THIRTY YEARS' WAR'

The period from 1914 to 1945 has been called the 'Thirty Years' War' of the twentieth century. No other period of comparable length has seen so many people killed, so much property destroyed, or so much national wealth squandered. Although the land combat in the two world wars of this era was confined to the eastern hemisphere (mostly on the land mass of Eurasia, but also in Africa), most of the nations of the western hemisphere were at some point drawn into the contest for mastery of the eastern half of the world. The so-called inter-war period of the 1920s and 1930s can scarcely be regarded as an era of peace. Rather it was, as the French military commander Ferdinand Foch predicted at the end of the First World War, a 'twenty-year truce' that was punctuated by explosions of national animosities, sporadic outbreaks of violence, and great-power rivalries that eventually escalated into the Second World War. The central participant in this 30-year struggle was the economically advanced, militarily powerful state of Germany. The two world wars were to a large extent the result of Germany's ambition to dominate its geographical region and the determination of other great powers to prevent it from succeeding, by diplomatic pressure in peacetime and by military force in war.

In the course of the 1920s it became fashionable in certain intellectual circles to deny that the German Empire bore any responsibility for the outbreak of what at the time was universally known as the 'Great War'. Evidence from recently published diplomatic records was marshalled by scholars and publicists (not all of them German) to show that French vindictiveness, Russian imperialism, British duplicity, or a combination of all three had been responsible for dragging Germany into war in the summer of 1914. The image of the bloodthirsty Hun in spiked helmet and jackboots rampaging across a prostrate continent, so vividly portrayed by the propaganda agencies of the Allied governments, gradually disappeared from the scene after the end of the war. In its place arose the contrary image of a peace-loving Germany that had sought nothing more than to defend its legitimate national interests in the face of predatory powers from east and west.

It was not until after the Second World War that this revisionist conception of Germany as victim was directly challenged by a school of historians that focused attention on the grandiose and expansionist war aims of the imperial German government and its domestic supporters. The leader of this school was distinguished German historian Fritz Fischer, who drew on exhaustive research and elegant argument to show that the political, military, and economic elite of the Second Reich had deliberately planned and relentlessly pursued an ambitious scheme to acquire direct or indirect control of the European continent as well as parts of the Middle East and Central Africa. That the other principal belligerents—France, Britain, Russia, and Italy—also developed imperial ambitions of their own in the course of the war Fischer did not dispute. But what emerged from his study was a massive body of evidence of an aggressive program of economic expansion and territorial acquisition meticulously planned and actively promoted by influential members of the German ruling class from the late 1890s through the final year of the First World War. Though Fischer's work has undergone extensive criticism in recent years, its overall assessment of Germany's expansionist ambitions has stood the test of time. To comprehend the sources of this aggressive foreign policy, it is necessary to review the domestic forces at play in Germany before 1914.

PRE-WAR GERMANY

The political structure of the German Reich, as defined by the federal constitution of 1871, may be best described as a facade of a parliamentary monarchy superimposed on the structure of an authoritarian state dominated by the reactionary, militarist, landowning aristocracy of Prussia. The hereditary position of German emperor was vested in the king of Prussia, who enjoyed the

exclusive power to appoint and dismiss the head of government (the chancellor), to conduct foreign relations, to command the armed forces in time of war, to convoke and adjourn the bicameral parliament, and—through the chancellor—to initiate all domestic legislation. Prussian control of the upper house of the parliament (the Bundesrat) was preserved through a complex system of indirect and weighted representation together with the Prussian veto (required by the constitution) on legislation concerning military affairs. Even the lower house of the imperial legislature (the Reichstag), though elected by direct representation on the basis of universal male suffrage, was prevented from exercising the type of legislative authority associated with genuine parliamentary systems such as those of Britain and France. Cabinet ministers were responsible only to the chancellor, who in turn was responsible to the emperor. This meant that a government could stay in office without a legislative majority so long as it retained the confidence of the hereditary ruler.

The only significant power enjoyed by the democratically elected lower house was a negative one: the power to deny the chancellor the funds required for the state to function. Periodic debates over requests for military appropriations—an issue dear to the heart of the Prussian landed elite, which monopolized the senior positions in the armed forces—gave the Reichstag its only opportunity to circumvent the elaborate constitutional limitations on free expressions of the popular will. The legislative record in the years before 1914 shows that successive German governments received the active or tacit support of all the nation's principal political parties. This was true not only of the Conservative Party—the political mouthpiece of the Prussian landowning class (the Junkers) on which the regime was based—but also of parties representing constituencies whose interests and ideologies clashed with those of the Protestant, agrarian, military caste. The Centre Party, vigilant defender of the rights of the Catholic minority (located mainly in the southern part of the country), had good reason to resist the Protestant-dominated political apparatus in Berlin. So did the National Liberal Party, which represented the industrial and commercial bourgeoisie (concentrated in the west), whose commitment to political liberalism and economic modernization seemed antithetical to the reactionary, agrarian ideology of the Junkers. The Social Democratic Party, spearhead of social revolution on behalf of the industrial working class and opponent of militarism, constituted a potential source of violent opposition to the Prussian-dominated state.

Yet none of these parties mounted a sustained campaign against the authoritarian domestic structure and aggressive foreign policy of the empire. The Centre Party became a compliant servant of the imperial system once it had been assured that the anticlerical campaign launched by Bismarck in the 1870s would not be revived and that the Catholics of the south would be free to practise their faith. The National Liberals sacrificed their democratic principles on the altar of class interest, accepting the undemocratic political institutions of the imperial state and supporting its expansionist foreign policy for economic reasons to be sketched below. The Social Democratic Party, which by 1912 had become the largest political faction in the Reichstag, represented the most numerous and best organized industrial working class in Europe. But what had transformed the German workers into loyal subjects of the empire was the progressive system of social insurance introduced by Bismarck in the 1880s. Its unprecedented provisions for medical insurance and old age pensions, followed in the 1890s by health and safety regulations in factories, ensured that the German proletariat enjoyed more economic benefits and better working conditions than any of its counterparts in other industrial nations. It is therefore no surprise that the German Social Democratic Party ceased to take seriously the rhetoric of class conflict and evolved into a party of the loyal opposition, tacitly accepting the undemocratic political system from which its working-class constituency derived such notable economic advantages.

The authoritarian political structure of imperial Germany was reinforced by two features of the German economic system that sharply distinguished it from the economic systems of other industrialized nations. The first was the remarkable degree of co-operation between the agricultural interests centred in East Prussia and the industrial, commercial, and financial interests centred in the west. Whereas industrialization had been achieved in other countries (such as England) at the expense of the landowning class, the German industrial revolution was marked by a marriage of convenience between large-scale agriculture and heavy industry that promoted the expansion of the latter without threatening the socio-economic position of the former. Both sectors campaigned for and benefited from the protectionist commercial policies that the government adopted in 1879. The agricultural estates of East Prussia were shielded against competition from Russian and American grain, while the heavy industry centred in the Rhineland–Westphalia region of the west secured the privilege of dominating the domestic market for manufactured products. This alliance of 'rye and steel' saved the Prussian Junkers from the fate of the landed gentry in England, which had earlier been forced to choose between socio-economic decline or accession to the industrial class through intermarriage or business partnership. The second striking feature of the German economy at the turn of the century was the extent of its concentration and centralization. The key sectors of heavy industry (iron, steel, coal, armaments, chemicals, and electrical products) were dominated by a handful of gigantic firms that had acquired an extraordinary degree of control over production and distribution. The cartelization of heavy industry was actively promoted by the imperial government through public subsidies and protective legislation. At the same time, the German financial system was undergoing a similar process of concentration. By 1913, the four largest banking houses controlled 65 per cent of the nation's capital reserves and were closely linked to the oligopolistic industrial firms of the Rhineland–Westphalia complex through a system of interlocking directorates.

This formidable concentration of economic power, which united heavy industry, big agriculture, and high finance in a close partnership with the government, produced a spectacular spurt of economic growth in the quarter century before the First World War. A comparison with other industrial nations, as shown in Tables 1.1 and 1.2, reveals that Germany had far outdistanced its continental rivals and had even overtaken Britain as the most productive economic power in Europe. However, the future of this economic dynamism seemed threatened by an ominous statistic: while the value of German exports increased 185.4 per cent per year between 1887 and 1912, the value of German imports rose 243.8 per cent. This dramatic surge in imports, far surpassing the gains made by any other industrial country, signified to the industrial magnates and their government patrons that German

prosperity was becoming critically dependent on foreign sources of raw materials and foodstuffs. Equally disconcerting was the shift in the direction of Germany's foreign trade away from Europe and towards distant markets and sources of supply in the southern hemisphere.

These circumstances were not in themselves cause for alarm. After all, Britain had managed to prosper despite an even more pronounced dependence on imports from far-off dominions such as Canada, by exporting manufactured surpluses in exchange. Theoretically, Germany needed only to increase its exports of finished industrial products to cover the mounting trade deficit. But therein lay what many German industrialists feared was the ultimate constraint on future growth. The markets of the world were being penetrated, dominated, and increasingly monopolized by the three other global powers: the United States in Latin America;

TABLE 1.1   PIG IRON PRODUCTION OF THE EUROPEAN POWERS, 1870–1914 (IN MILLION TONS)

	1870	1880	1890	1900	1910	1914
Germany	1.3	2.5	4.1	7.5	9.5	14.7
Austria–Hungary	0.4	0.5	0.7	1.5	2.0	2.0
France	1.2	1.7	2.0	2.7	4.0	4.6
Great Britain	6.0	7.7	8.0	9.0	10.0	11.0
Russia	0.4	0.4	0.9	2.9	3.0	3.6

TABLE 1.2   STEEL PRODUCTION OF THE EUROPEAN POWERS, 1870–1914 (IN MILLION TONS)

	1870	1880	1890	1900	1910	1914
Germany	0.3	0.7	2.3	6.7	13.8	14.0
Austria–Hungary	—	—	0.5	1.2	2.2	2.7
France	0.3	0.4	0.7	1.6	3.4	3.5
Great Britain	0.7	1.3	3.6	5.0	5.9	6.5
Russia	—	—	0.4	1.5	3.5	4.1

Source for Tables 1.1 and 1.2: A.J.P. Taylor. *The Struggle for Mastery in Europe, 1848–1918* (London: 1954), pp. xxix–xxx. Copyright 1954 Oxford University Press. Reprinted by permission.

Great Britain in East and South Africa and South Asia; and France in West Africa, the Balkans, and Russia. Soon the Russian and Japanese empires would enter the competition for economic advantage in the Far East. Where could Germany turn for new sources of raw materials and foodstuffs and for the markets for manufactured products that were essential to pay for them?

Virtually every attempt to expand Germany's economic power beyond its traditional sphere met with disappointment after 1900. Efforts to penetrate the economies of North Africa, the Balkan states, and the Ottoman Empire encountered stiff competition from British and French firms that had already established footholds there. In the two decades before 1914, France had become the main source of capital investment for the fledgling Balkan nations as well as the Russian Empire as it entered the first stage of industrialization. These financial relationships began to spark German fears of economic encirclement by Slavic states to the east and south bankrolled by the traditional Gallic enemy to the west. Even the Ottoman Empire—a prime object of German economic ambition since the turn of the century—had begun to receive massive infusions of British and French capital, in the form both of government loans and of direct investments in the oil fields of Mesopotamia. These fears were heightened by ominous indications that the rest of the world was being informally partitioned into spheres of economic interest by Britain, France, the United States, and Japan.

Concern about the limits to German economic growth coincided with mounting apprehension in military circles that the German Empire was losing its strategic superiority over the combined armed forces of France and Russia. The Franco–Russian Alliance of 1894 had imposed on German strategic planners a burden that Bismarck's diplomacy had successfully avoided: the possibility of having to wage a war on two fronts. With France and Russia committed to defending each other against a German attack, the need to divide Germany's forces between east and west seemed to preclude any rapid breakthrough. Count Alfred

von Schlieffen, chief of the imperial general staff from 1892 to 1906, had designed a war plan that was supposed to overcome the strategic disadvantage caused by the Franco–Russian Alliance. It envisioned concentrating German military power in the west in the expectation that the numerically inferior French army could be defeated within six weeks, after which the bulk of the German forces could be transferred to the Eastern Front to meet the Russian army before it could penetrate Germany's denuded eastern defences.

The Schlieffen Plan rested on two critical assumptions. The first was that Germany would retain its overwhelming numerical superiority over France. The second was that the Russian Empire, with its primitive land transportation, would be unable to deploy its numerically superior army along the German border before Germany could deliver the knockout blow in the west. To the consternation of German military strategists, however, both these assumptions were undermined by developments in the years before 1914. In 1913, France extended the period of national military service from two to three years. This meant that, even without any population increase, France would be able to field a frontline army equal in size to Germany's by 1915 or 1916. In the meantime, the Russian government had launched, with French financial assistance, an ambitious program of strategic railway construction linking central Russia with the western frontier. Even in peacetime the Russian army was larger than the German and Austro–Hungarian armies combined, and the possibility that at some future date this mass military force could be rapidly transported to the German border upset the strategic basis of the Schlieffen Plan, causing considerable anxiety among military circles in Berlin.

It was only a short step from fearing economic encirclement and military vulnerability to advocating a preventive war. The temptation of a quick, surgical strike against France in the manner of 1870 was reinforced by the conviction that a delay of two or three years might prove fatal to Germany's pre-eminence in Europe. With France and Russia removed as counterweights on the continent, Germany could rearrange the balance of power to suit its own economic and military requirements. The idea of economic expansion and pre-emptive war received strong support from numerous pressure groups in German society representing a wide range of interests. The officers' corps of the army, in conjunction with expansion-minded civilians in the Pan-German League, pressed for territorial annexations that would simultaneously remove the twin strategic threats of France and Russia. The upper echelons of the navy advocated the construction of a fleet equal to Britain's and the acquisition of bases and coaling stations abroad. The interlocked interests of heavy industry and high finance encouraged the government to obtain—by diplomatic pressure if possible, military action if necessary—privileged access to the resources and markets that the German economy needed to sustain its dynamic growth.

Amid this atmosphere of fear mingled with ambition, the long-simmering dispute between Germany's ally Austria–Hungary and the independent Balkan kingdom of Serbia boiled over in the summer of 1914. On 28 June, the heir to the Habsburg throne, Archduke Franz Ferdinand, was assassinated while attending military manoeuvres in Sarajevo, the capital of Bosnia, which with its neighbour Herzegovina had been occupied militarily by Austria–Hungary in 1878 and then annexed outright in 1908. The absorption of those two former Turkish provinces was violently opposed not only by their Slavic inhabitants but also by Slavs across the border who dreamed of a Greater Serbia that would include them. The precise details of the conspiracy that led to the death of the archduke and his wife (including the complicity of the chief of Serbian military intelligence and the foreknowledge of the prime minister in Belgrade) were not revealed until long after the event and therefore had no bearing on Austria–Hungary's response to the killings. All that was known for certain at the time was that the assassins were ethnic Serbs and that they had committed their crime in the hotbed of pan-Slavist sentiment within the Habsburg Empire.

The immediate significance of the episode was that it gave the authorities in Vienna a convenient pretext for suppressing once and for all the pan-Slavist menace by striking at the neighbouring state that had assisted it.

It was well known to the German government that an Austro–Hungarian military operation against Serbia was almost certain to provoke Russia into intervening on behalf of its Slavic protégé. Russia had already suffered a major blow to its power and prestige in the Balkans by acquiescing in the annexation of Bosnia and Herzegovina. No one expected Russia to stand back a second time and allow the Habsburg Empire to consolidate its control of the Balkans by annihilating the only pro-Russian Slavic state in the region. It was likewise probable that a war between Austria–Hungary and Russia would set in motion the competing alliance systems to which those two empires belonged, and thus bring the entire continent to the brink of armed conflict. With full appreciation of these likely consequences, Berlin deliberately encouraged Vienna to issue a humiliating ultimatum to Belgrade on 23 July concerning the investigation of the assassination—an ultimatum that the Serbian government could not accept in its entirety without sacrificing its sovereign status. Moreover, the German government assured the Austrian government of its unqualified support in the event of hostilities. The expiry of the ultimatum led to an Austrian declaration of war against Serbia on 28 July, which—as expected—provoked St Petersburg into ordering a partial Russian mobilization against Austria the following day. The tsar and his political entourage soon learned that the Russian general staff had no operational plan for a limited mobilization against Austria alone, believing as it did that a war with one of the Germanic empires would inevitably involve the other. Hence the tsar authorized a full mobilization on 30 July as a precaution, to protect Russia's frontier with Germany during the forthcoming showdown with Austria.

Here was the first instance of military planning and preparation constraining the decision-making authority of the civilian leadership during the crisis. The second instance was to come when the German high command reminded the government in Berlin that a war against Russia alone was precluded by the Schlieffen Plan, which dictated that France must be removed from the war before German forces were concentrated in the east against Russia. Therefore, Berlin served Paris with an ultimatum that, like the earlier one delivered by Vienna to Belgrade, was designed by its blatantly unacceptable provisions to serve as a pretext for war. France was required to affirm its absolute neutrality in the forthcoming Russo–German war and, as proof of good faith, to transfer to Germany's temporary custody the border fortresses of Toul and Verdun. In short, at the end of July 1914, as the Balkan dispute escalated towards war involving most of Europe, officials in Berlin did what they could to ensure that this opportunity for a preventive showdown with France and Russia would not be lost. In its present state of military superiority, Germany stood an excellent chance of defeating its two adversaries at the opposite ends of Europe, but in two or three years, that advantage might very well be lost.

Despite the creation of the Triple Entente—a diplomatic understanding among Britain, France, and Russia in 1907—the possibility of British intervention on the side of France and Russia was discounted in Berlin. Some German officials entertained the naive hope that if the tsar could be induced to mobilize his army first (as indeed he did), the British public would refuse to assist in what could be depicted as a Russian war of aggression. More realistic observers knew that the German war plan in the west, which presupposed the invasion of France through the rolling hills of Belgium, would precipitate Britain's entry in the war. This assessment was not based on Britain's commitment to the preservation of Belgian neutrality codified in a treaty of 1839. Such obligations could be conveniently renounced in the name of national interest—as Germany, also a guarantor of Belgian neutrality, promptly proved. Rather, Britain was bound to intervene because it would never permit a hostile power to obtain

control of the eastern coast of the English Channel as a potential springboard for an invasion of the British Isles. Germany was able to accept the likelihood of British intervention because of the near universal expectation that any war would be of brief duration. Britain's naval superiority would be useless to prevent the German military conquest of France in the six-week campaign projected by the Schlieffen Plan. The small British professional army of 150,000 counted for little against the 1.5 million German conscripts that were to be hurled against France. After a lightning victory against France and the removal of British forces from the continent, Germany would be free to concentrate on destroying Russia's military power in Eastern Europe. The British—with whom Germany had no serious quarrel—could then be offered a separate peace that would confirm German dominance on the continent.

THE WAR BEGINS

Over the first few days of August, all the great powers of Europe except Italy[1] entered the conflict. The first country to define the objectives it expected to achieve in the war was Germany. Chancellor Theobold von Bethmann-Hollweg strove to mobilize a broad domestic consensus in support of the war by establishing a persuasive justification for resorting to force. This was particularly necessary in the context of the German political situation in 1914, when the Social Democratic Party—led by persistent critics of military expenditures and advocates of international co-operation—was the strongest party in the Reichstag, and the Socialist trade unions constituted the largest mass political organization in the country. In order to forestall left-wing parliamentary opposition and labour agitation, the government would have to persuade the Social Democrats and union organizations to support the war. It was widely known that the German left would oppose any war of conquest. Thus the Socialist leaders were encouraged to see the war effort as a 'defensive' operation against the imperialist aggression of tsarist Russia. On 4 August, the

Social Democrats joined the other political parties in declaring a 'party truce' in the Reichstag. Unity on the home front was thus ensured at the very beginning of the war.

Once it had secured the support of all political parties, the German government began speaking less about a 'defensive war' to prevent 'encirclement' and more about the need to obtain 'guarantees' against future military aggression and economic competition on the continent. In this way, a supposedly defensive action rapidly evolved into an ambitious project for continental domination. The government's war aims were first specified in a statement by Chancellor Bethmann-Hollweg on 9 September 1914. Despite several temporary deviations and changes in the course of the war, this 'September Program' remained the basis of German military objectives until the Bolshevik Revolution and the subsequent withdrawal of Russia from the war. Thereafter it would be extended to embrace an even more grandiose scheme of military and economic expansion, devised by German economic interests at the beginning of the war.

The September Program of the German government sketched Germany's military and economic war aims during the period of great optimism, when the German army seemed on the verge of overwhelming the Anglo–French defences in the west. The military plan called for the permanent destruction of France's military power through annexation of the territory containing its principal fortresses along the German frontier, the occupation of its major ports on the English Channel, and imposition of a crushing financial indemnity that would prevent the reconstruction of France's armed forces in the foreseeable future. Belgium would be compelled to cede its strategic fortresses and permit the establishment of German bases on the Flanders coast (which, in conjunction with the French Channel ports, would constitute a formidable barrier to the reintroduction of British military power on the continent). Once these punitive terms had been imposed on France and Belgium, Russia was to be systematically driven back from Germany's eastern border and

its hold over non-Russians broken. By removing France from the ranks of the great powers, excluding Britain from continental affairs, and driving Russia back, Germany would definitively establish itself as the hegemonic power of Europe. France was then to be offered a pact of mutual co-operation, while Britain would be given the choice of withdrawing from the war or enduring air attacks launched from ports on the French and Belgian coast.

Closely linked to these military plans was a project for continental economic domination developed by a group of spokesmen for German heavy industry and high finance who feared that competition from the gigantic economic blocs of the United States (with Latin America), the British Empire, and the Russian colossus to the east meant that Germany was destined to suffer economic decline unless it gained control of the resources and markets of the entire continent of Europe. Among their recommendations for the establishment of a German-controlled continental bloc, or *Mitteleuropa*, were the implementation of a total customs union between Germany and the Austro–Hungarian Empire, the annexation of the French iron fields in the Longwy-Briey region of Lorraine, the economic absorption of Belgium and Luxemburg, and the eventual establishment of a European common market through customs treaties linking the German–Austro–Hungarian bloc to France, Italy, Belgium, the Netherlands, Denmark, and any other independent European states that might wish to join. The principal objective of these spokesmen for German heavy industry was to rectify the potentially serious problem of inadequate supplies of industrial raw materials, particularly those required for the production of steel. Though blessed with sufficient quantities of high-grade coal located in the Ruhr and Upper Silesia, Germany's pre-war steel industry had become heavily dependent on the iron ore of French Lorraine, directly across the border.[2] In 1914, Germany's iron ore reserves totalled 2.3 billion tons, compared to France's 8.2 billion tons. Thus annexation of the French ore fields would more than double Germany's iron reserves, giving it self-sufficiency while severely weakening the French iron and steel industry as a potential competitor once the war was over.

Other regions offered tempting targets as well. The representatives of German heavy industry advocated acquiring the ore fields of Belgium and gaining control of the coal, iron, manganese, oil, and grain of Poland and southern Russia. In addition to economic value, Belgium and Poland had strategic value as barriers to Anglo–French military power in the west and Russian military power in the east. Plans for the disposition of Belgium ranged from outright annexation to military occupation of strategic fortresses and ports, control of the transportation system, customs and currency union with Germany, and administrative partition into Dutch-speaking Flanders and French-speaking Wallonia. The plan to resurrect Poland as a German client state in the east was complicated, however, by the existence of a substantial Polish population in the German territories of Posen and West Prussia that might be attracted to the idea of a reconstituted Polish state. In the eyes of some planners, that problem could best be resolved by deporting the Poles (including the Polish Jews) from the German to the Russian sector and replacing them with German colonists, who would establish a 'frontier strip' to secure Germany's eastern barrier against the Slavs.

With the failure of the German war plan in the autumn of 1914 came the realization that these ambitious military and economic objectives were unlikely to be achieved by force of arms alone in the foreseeable future. The intervention of Britain and the successful defence of Paris together with the unexpectedly rapid mobilization of the Russian army in the east produced a stationary front and the prospect of a long, drawn-out war of attrition. The unprecedented firepower supplied by machine guns and heavy artillery transformed the nature of warfare. The belligerents were compelled to abandon any hope of speedy victory. The infantry forces were issued the only tool that might allow them to escape the murderous barrage of firepower: the trenching spade. By Christmas 1914, the wasteland of northern France and Belgium was honeycombed with underground trenches that formed a network stretching from the Swiss border to the English Channel. Although the war in the east was marked by greater mobility and more frequent exchanges of territory, it too was bogged down in stalemate by the onset of winter.

'TOTAL WAR' AND THE HOME FRONT

The truism that 'generals tend to fight the last war' applies equally to their civilian superiors, and in the case of the Great War it should come as no surprise. The generation of military and political leaders who supervised their respective nations' war efforts in 1914 had reached maturity during a half-century of peace in Europe. The wars of most recent memory were those fought in conjunction with the political unification of Italy and Germany between 1859 and 1871. These had been brief, mobile engagements with limited political objectives, and their outcomes had been determined by short-term technical factors such as tactical finesse and efficiency in troop mobilization and transport. They had lasted for no more than a few months and required only minimal disruption of civilian life behind the lines. In the light of this historical experience, none of the leaders involved in the Great War had thought it necessary to devise plans for a conflict of long duration. The establishment of the stationary fronts in the autumn of 1914, however, had produced an entirely new type of warfare. The clash of armies in the field was rapidly overshadowed by an epic confrontation of whole peoples. In this, the first total war in history, events at the battlefront had direct repercussions for the civilians on the 'home front'. The challenge of mobilizing the human and material resources of entire societies transformed the domestic institutions of the belligerent nations.

The most fundamental domestic effect of total war was the centralization and regimentation of economic activity. It had soon dawned on the ruling elites of Europe that success in a war of

ICELAND

NORWAY

SWEDEN

FINLAND

GREAT
BRITAIN

DENMARK

NETHER-
LANDS

IRELAND

RUSSIA

GERMANY

ATLANTIC

OCEAN

BELG.

FRANCE

SWITZ.

AUSTRIA-
HUNGARY

ROMANIA

Black Sea

PORTUGAL

SPAIN

ITALY

SERBIA

ALBANIA

BULGARIA

OTTOMAN EMPIRE

GREECE

Mediterranean Sea

Anti-German
Coalition

Germany
and Its Allies

*Italy, though a member of the German Alliance System,
remained neutral at the beginning of the war and
joined the Anti-German Coalition in 1915.*

EUROPE IN THE FIRST WORLD WAR

Women working in the assembly department of the British Munitions Supply Company in Verdun, Quebec. ca. 1916–18. Library and Archives Canada/Department of National Defence fonds/PA-024435.

indefinite duration would require the production and distribution of war-related materials on an unprecedented scale. None of the combatant nations was able to produce enough artillery shells to meet the demand, and the conscription of farmers and agricultural labourers caused serious declines in food production. The naval blockade that Britain imposed from the start of the war disrupted the Central Powers' access to foreign sources of foodstuffs and raw materials, while the German occupation of France's most productive industrial region deprived the French of vital resources and factories, and the closing of the Dardanelles by Germany's ally, Turkey, curtailed Russia's ability to import essential materials from abroad. When it became clear that the private sectors of their economies could not avert shortages, governments stepped in to manage all branches of production and distribution related to the war effort. Vital resources and transport facilities were requisitioned, laws were passed forbidding the production of luxury items, food and fuel were rationed, substitutes and synthetics were promoted, and foreign trade was controlled—all unprecedented intrusions of state power. The prospect of labour shortages and social unrest prompted governments to pass legislation severely restricting union activity and authorizing longer working hours and the employment of women and unskilled workers in the war plants.

With the mobilization of domestic production and manpower came the mobilization of capital. Stringent controls were imposed on foreign-exchange transactions, to stem the flow of domestic capital abroad. Yet even increased taxation and domestic sales of treasury securities were not enough to meet the ever-increasing capital requirements of the wartime economies. Growing dependence on foreign sources of raw materials and foodstuffs impelled the governments of France and Britain to borrow the securities of foreign governments and private corporations held by their citizens. They then resold these securities on the open market and used the proceeds to purchase essential products in neutral countries such as the United States and Switzerland, as well as in various Scandinavian and Latin American nations.

In this way, the relatively liberal economic conditions of the pre-war era abruptly disappeared. No longer did individual citizens enjoy the freedom to sell their labour and services to the highest bidder or to invest their savings where they pleased. No longer could businesses import or export products according to their commercial requirements. The wartime needs of the state replaced the marketplace as the mechanism governing the allocation of resources, labour, and capital. The prospect of a seemingly interminable war fought by mechanized forces placed a premium on economic organization. Ultimate victory would go to those nations capable of mobilizing

and deploying the most resources—human and material—in the most efficient manner.

The periodic attempts to achieve a decisive breakthrough in the land war merely confirmed the futility of hurling unarmoured human flesh against the devastating firepower of machine guns and heavy artillery. It was the horrors of the first battle at Ypres in 1915 that prompted Lieutenant-Colonel John McCrae, a Canadian doctor, to write the famous poem 'In Flanders Fields'. The casualties incurred in military offensives were staggering: in the battle of the Somme from 1 July to 18 November 1916, the Germans and British lost 400,000 each and the French 200,000—all for a maximum advance of perhaps 11 kilometres. The Royal Newfoundland Regiment lost more than 700 of its 800 soldiers fighting at Beaumont Hamel on the first day of the battle alone. In the same year, the Germans conducted a 10-month siege of the French fortress at Verdun at a cost of 336,000 men, while the French army paid for its successful defence with 350,000 lives. At Passchendaele in 1917, over 370,000 British soldiers perished in order to gain 125 hectares of mud and shell holes. And when, after numerous Allied attempts, Canadian forces succeeded in capturing Vimy Ridge, also in 1917, the casualty rate was nearly 50 per cent.

To meet the challenge to offensive warfare posed by the machine gun, both sides sought

CANADA'S CONTRIBUTION TO THE WAR IN EUROPE

When Britain declared war on 4 August it was automatically joined by the dominions within its empire. In the case of Canada, the federal government had significant latitude in determining the kind of military contribution the country would actually make. With a regular army of only 3,000, Canada embarked on a massive program of mobilization. Public opinion, at least in English Canada, generally supported the war, but opposition (particularly among French Canadians) would become increasingly more apparent as the conflict wore on and would reach a climax during the Conscription Crisis of 1917 (see box on p. 45). Civilians volunteered by the thousands, and by November 1914, more than 30,000 men had been sent to Europe. By 1918, over 600,000 Canadians would be mobilized, of whom more than 66,000 died. Canada's casualties totalled some 3 per cent of its pre-war population. This contrasts sharply with the American casualty total, which amounted to only 0.4 per cent of its pre-war population.[3]

THE FIRST WORLD WAR IN INDIA

The description of the First World War as a 'total war' is best applied when assessing the impact of the war on the European belligerents; however, the demands of the war on non-Western nations were nonetheless substantial. India was drawn into the conflict by Britain's declaration of war on Germany. Even so, the war effort received overwhelming support across the Raj. On 12 August 1914 Dadabhai Naoroji wrote that '[f]ighting as the British people are at present in a righteous cause, to the good and glory of human dignity and civilizations, and moreover, being the beneficent instrument of our own progress and civilization, our duty is clear—to do everyone our best to support the British fight with our life and property.' Almost immediately Britain's Indian Empire was called upon to contribute in a variety of ways. Over 1.4 million Indians were recruited, equipped, and trained for overseas duty—the vast majority saw service in the Middle East and North Africa, but at least 130,000 Indian forces served on the Western Front. Military expenditure rose from £20 million to £140 million during the course of the war and in 1916 the Government of India gave a donation of £100 million to the British Government. Punjab alone contributed almost 350,000 combat troops and its financial contribution was assessed in 1918 at £700,000.

As the war progressed Indian industrialists, especially in textiles and mining, saw record profits. However, the vast majority of the Indian population experienced only inflated prices of manufactured goods and stagnant per capita income. This situation was exacerbated in those areas which experienced reduced rainfall and a resulting drought in 1918. Popular discontent, generated by wartime deprivation, worked to the advantage of Indian nationalists, such as Bal Gangadhar Tilak, who intensified their calls for 'home rule' in return for India's wartime sacrifices. Ill-timed British decisions in the immediate aftermath of the war served only to transform the appeal for Indian independence into a true mass movement under the leadership of Mohandas Karamchand Gandhi. Protests against limitations on Indian civil rights led to military action in 1919 and the subsequent massacre of civilians in Amritsar. Thereafter the Indian protest movement adjusted its tactics and adopted a combination of boycotts and non-violent Satyagraha campaigns. Nonetheless, frustration mounted in India as the British, led by strident imperialists such as Winston Churchill, refused to consider full independence.

technological breakthroughs that might restore mobility to firepower. The airplane, successfully tested in the United States 10 years earlier and first used in war by the Italians against the Turks in 1911, was originally limited to observation use. Neither side interfered with the other's reconnaissance flights until it became clear that the information they provided was useful to the armies facing each other on the ground. Thereafter machine guns were mounted in the observer planes' cockpits. When Dutch aerial engineer Anthony Fokker designed—for the Germans—an interrupter gear to synchronize machine-gun fire with the propeller so that bullets could avoid the blades, airplanes became deadly gun platforms and the fighter plane was born. Aside from adding a dash of heroism and glamour to the dreary, slogging land war, the aerial duels had no effect on the outcome of the struggle. Even the German bombing of Britain, which resulted in 1,300 deaths and 3,000 injuries as well as serious material damage, paled in comparison to the damage done to men and property by the guns on land. The planes were too small and the bombs too inaccurate for aerial warfare to break the stalemate.

The technological innovation that finally restored the advantage to the offensive was masterminded by a British colonel named Ernest Swinton. To allow machine guns to move over difficult terrain while protecting their operators against enemy fire, Swinton mounted the guns on the caterpillar tractors that had been used to tow heavy artillery behind the lines, and then armoured the resulting 'tanks' for offensive action. Once adopted by the British, the tank revolutionized land warfare and gave the allies the potential to penetrate the stationary lines of the enemy. Despite great success in the British army's first major use of tanks—during the Battle of Cambrai in November 1917—lack of imagination kept the Allies from fully exploiting their new weapon. It was only during the final German offensive in August 1918 that the tanks' value was demonstrated beyond all doubt, when the British Fourth Army used 450 of them to pierce the German defences near Amiens as part of the Allied counter-offensive that brought the war to an end.

The carnage on the battlefield, together with the economic hardship endured by civilians, severely tested the morale of the belligerent nations. With the prospect of victory fading ever further into the future, the wartime governments had to find ways

CANADA'S CONSCRIPTION CRISIS

By the spring of 1917, the Conservative government of Robert Borden faced a political crisis. The prime minister had pledged in 1914 that he would not resort to conscription, but this promise became increasingly untenable as the war dragged on. With the terrible battles of 1916–17 producing tens of thousands of Canadian casualties, Borden came under heavy pressure to find enough replacements to sustain the country's commitments. The results of earlier efforts to recruit more volunteers had been disappointing, particularly in Quebec, and the lack of popular support for the war among French Canadians contributed to a growing sense of national disunity. After visiting the trenches and attending the Imperial War Conference in London, Borden returned to Canada in May 1917 convinced that conscription was unavoidable. To bolster support for conscription, Borden tried to form a coalition government with the opposition Liberals; however, their leader, Wilfrid Laurier, was firmly opposed to conscription and refused the offer.

Even without Laurier's support, Borden's conscription bill was passed in July 1917, after a heated debate in the House of Commons. Although francophones were not the only Canadians who opposed conscription—so did many English-speaking workers, farmers (especially those in the western provinces), and pacifists—the reaction in Quebec was especially strong, and riots broke out in the streets of Montreal throughout the summer of 1917.

Meanwhile, Borden continued to seek support for his conscription policy among individual members of the opposition. After finding 10—nine Liberals and Independents, plus one Labour MP—who were willing to join his Conservatives in a 'Union government', he called an election for December 1917. The election campaign further embittered political relations between French and English Canada. The Toronto *Mail and Empire* claimed that behind Quebec's refusal 'to reinforce the troops overseas' was 'the hidden hand of the Kaiser', and one Union poster suggested that a vote for Laurier was a vote for Germany. In Quebec, the Liberals portrayed conscription as a greater threat to Canada than the Germans themselves. When the votes were counted, the Union Party had won the election but lost every predominantly French-speaking riding.

The implementation of conscription, in the spring of 1918, sparked further demonstrations, some of them violent. In Quebec City, for example, protestors attacked the military service registry as well as English-owned businesses, and when Ottawa responded by sending in troops from Toronto, four people were killed and many more injured. Ultimately, few conscripts were to see action before the Armistice of November 1918; nevertheless, the issue left deep political wounds that were to reopen during the Second World War.

of persuading their own citizens that their sacrifices were worthwhile and those in the enemy camp that theirs were not. To maintain morale at home it was necessary to suppress political criticism of the war effort. Accordingly, in September 1915, the Russian tsar suspended the Duma (parliament) for the duration of the war. In Germany, the Political Bureau of the General Staff established a virtual military dictatorship. By 1917, Prime Minister David Lloyd George in Britain and Premier Georges Clemenceau in France had acquired emergency powers unprecedented in parliamentary regimes, governing through war cabinets in utmost secrecy. And in Canada, the Conservative government of Robert Borden took the opportunity to consolidate its executive powers through the War Measures Act, passed in 1914, which gave the federal government the authority to do whatever it deemed necessary to ensure the country's security. Borden's government used this authority to pass strict censorship laws, which prevented the publication of anti-war sentiments and accurate casualty figures in newspapers and periodicals. Among other measures taken to forestall opposition to Canada's participation in the war was a law allowing the government to jail or restrict the civil liberties of people refusing military conscription on conscientious grounds, as well as those suspected of being enemy sympathizers.

POLITICAL AND ECONOMIC WARFARE

The German government began conducting political warfare behind enemy lines early in the war. The British, French, and Russian empires all contained discontented ethnic, religious, and social groups that might be susceptible to German propaganda, but the main targets for this strategy were the Islamic populations of North Africa, Egypt, India, and southern Russia. The German emperor's Damascus speech in 1898 had established his credentials as 'protector' of the world's 300 million Muslims. The military alliance between Germany and Turkey, signed on 2 August 1914, led the Ottoman sultan in his capacity as caliph

(the chief civil and religious leader in Muslim societies) to proclaim a jihad, or holy war, against the European imperialists. German money flowed to Islamic nationalist movements opposed to the rule of London, Paris, and St Petersburg, and similar campaigns were mounted to incite insurrection among the non-Russian Christian peoples of the tsarist empire. Emigrés from Russian Poland, Finland, Ukraine, Georgia, and Armenia received subsidies and encouragement from Germany for their movements of 'national liberation' against Russian oppression. At the same time, the German government established contact with and supplied funds to various revolutionary Russian emigré groups in Switzerland and Scandinavia. Foremost among these was the Russian Social Democratic Party, which alone among the major working-class parties of Europe had actively opposed the war from the start and continued to press for social revolution at home.

The German government's propaganda campaign had two purposes: to pin down British, French, and Russian military forces in counter-insurgency operations behind the lines and to establish a reputation (both in neutral countries such as the United States and among progressive forces in the enemy camp) as the protector of 'oppressed peoples' and the champion of the right to national and political self-determination. The abortive 'Easter Rebellion' of 1916 in Ireland, for example, received active support from Berlin in the form of rifles, machine guns, ammunition, and explosives. But in the first three years of the war, Germany's efforts to incite domestic insurrection in the empires of its enemies were uniformly unsuccessful.

Germany's dual strategy of forming a continental economic–military bloc controlled from Berlin while promoting the disintegration of the British, French, and Russian empires provoked a series of similar countermeasures from the governments of the Triple Entente. Indeed, it is important to note that the member states of the anti-German coalition promptly developed war aims of their own that were no less grandiose and aggressive than Germany's. In the realm of foreign economic policy, the Entente governments planned to continue their economic co-operation after the war, in order to prevent the Central Powers from rebuilding on their pre-war economic foundations. Just as this strategy represented a competitive response to the German *Mitteleuropa* project, the political strategy of the Entente constituted the reverse of the German campaign on behalf of revolution behind enemy lines. Britain concentrated on inciting an Arab–Muslim revolution within the Turkish Empire; France targeted the national groups under Austro–Hungarian rule (mainly the Czechs, the Poles, and the southern Slavs of the Balkan peninsula); and even Russia paid lip service to the cause of national self-determination, offering independence to Poland under Russian protection in an effort to win the sympathy of the Polish populations of Austrian Galicia and German Posen and West Prussia.

The Entente project for economic warfare against the Central Powers was broached at the Paris Economic Conference in June 1916, when representatives of Britain, France, Italy, Russia, Belgium, Portugal, and Japan met to discuss giving permanent form to their wartime economic co-operation. The French and British delegations pressed for the creation of an inter-Allied economic bloc linked through preferential tariffs, pooling of raw materials and shipping, and joint management of financial and currency affairs. The resolutions adopted at the conference fell short of those hopes owing to the hesitations of Italy and Russia, but they nevertheless elicited sharp reactions in enemy and neutral countries. The Paris Accords seemed to signal the definitive end of the free trade era and the beginning of an effort by the anti-German coalition to subdivide most of the world into politically organized regional markets and zones of raw materials. If an economic bloc linking the British, French, Russian, Italian, Belgian, Portuguese, and Japanese empires was ever achieved, it would seal off virtually all of Africa and Asia as well as most of Europe from economic competition from the Central Powers and neutral countries such as the United States. Germany would thereupon face a

form of economic strangulation far worse than the encirclement it had feared before 1914.

Linked to the Entente's strategy for economic warfare against the Central Powers and their allies was a political strategy of inciting nationalist revolution within the German coalition. The first victim of this policy was the Ottoman Empire, whose contribution to the German war effort had been much more valuable than anticipated. The closing of the Dardanelles had sealed Russia off from its European allies, and the Anglo–French effort to force Turkey out of the war in the Dardanelles expedition of 1915–16 (a campaign that came to be known as the Gallipoli) was a costly failure. Turkish pressure on Egypt diverted British forces that might have been deployed elsewhere. However, the sultan's appeal for an Islamic holy war against the European nations had failed to rouse his Arab subjects, whose hatred of Turkish overlordship was more intense than their historic grievance against the Christian West. This gave the British an opportunity to solicit Arab support for the Allied cause, and negotiations were opened with Hussein, the grand sharif of Mecca, the most obvious candidate to contest the Ottoman sultan's authority.

Following correspondence between Sharif Hussein and the British High Commissioner in Egypt, Sir Henry McMahon, the British government pledged its support for the independence of most of the Ottoman Empire's Arab provinces in exchange for the declaration of an Arab revolt against Turkish rule. On 10 June 1916, Hussein raised the Arabs in rebellion and was soon joined by various chieftains on the Arabian peninsula. The Arab insurrection pinned down some 30,000 Turkish troops and helped to keep the Red Sea open to Allied shipping. The British military advance from Egypt to Palestine and Syria in 1917–18 was greatly assisted by guerrilla operations against the Turks mounted by Arab contingents in contact with British officers, including the legendary T.E. Lawrence. As we will see, Britain's support for Arab nationalism was compromised by agreements made with rival claimants to Turkish territory. For the rest of the war the strategy was effective in curtailing the Ottoman Empire's capacity to fulfill its obligations to its Germanic allies.

In the meantime the Western powers were also using their weapons of political warfare to promote nationalist rebellion within the Austro–Hungarian Empire. This policy was initially developed in response to American President Woodrow Wilson's invitation to the belligerents, in December 1916, to specify their war aims. The Germans refused, but the Entente replied in January 1917 with the first public statement of the goals that its members were supposedly fighting for. In addition to the obvious demand that Germany pull its troops out of Belgium, France, Russia, Serbia, and Romania, the Allied governments explicitly formulated for the first time their commitment to the 'principle of national self-determination'. Referring specifically to the liberation of the Italian, Romanian, southern Slav, Czechoslovak, and Polish subject nationalities of the Habsburg Empire, this principle called for the disintegration of that multinational state into its constituent ethnic regions. The pronouncement had the dual advantage of arousing American sympathy for the Entente's war effort while appealing to the subject nationalities of Germany's principal ally to cast off the yoke of their German-speaking rulers in Vienna. Instances of mutiny and desertion in the Austro–Hungarian army had already occurred before the Entente's call to arms. They increased thereafter, particularly as exile groups representing the various ethnic factions established headquarters in Paris and fanned the flames of nationalist rebellion behind enemy lines.

In fact, the Allied support for national liberation within the enemy camp was no less fraudulent than Germany's hypocritical pose as the champion of the Muslims and other subject nationalities under the rule of Britain, France, and Russia. The British government's promise of support for the independence of Turkey's Arab provinces was flatly contradicted by agreements made in the course of the war, which provided for the partition of the non-Turkish portion of the Ottoman Empire among England, France, Italy, and Russia. To complicate further the post-war situation in the Ottoman

domains, an official declaration by Britain's foreign secretary, Arthur Balfour, in November 1917 endorsed the proposal advanced by the European proponents of Zionism[4] for the establishment of a Jewish homeland in Palestine—a Turkish-controlled territory on the eastern Mediterranean, which at the time contained roughly 60,000 Jewish inhabitants out of a total population of 750,000 who were mainly Arab.

Similarly, the commitment to the subject peoples of the Austro–Hungarian Empire was critically compromised in February–March 1917, when France authorized Russia to set its western border as it wished, a move that had the effect of sacrificing the independence of Poland. This concession was tendered in return for Russia's support of France's acquisition not only of Alsace–Lorraine but also of the coal mines in the Saar basin and the establishment of an independent state in the Rhineland under French military protection. Similarly, Italy had been promised territory along the Adriatic coast in direct violation of the right to self-determination of the southern Slavs who inhabited the region. These arrangements caused no embarrassment to the Allies because they were made in the utmost secrecy. By contrast, the presence of tsarist autocracy within the anti-German coalition was embarrassing because it so clearly contradicted the democratic principles that the Allies were ostensibly fighting to defend. By 1917, however, Russia was on the brink of revolution.

THE RUSSIAN REVOLUTION

The immediate causes of the revolution that gripped Russia in 1917 were the conditions created by the First World War, but their roots ran deep into the country's past. The nineteenth century had witnessed periodic outbreaks of instability, culminating in the assassination of Tsar Alexander II in 1881. In theory, Russia's royal family, the Romanovs, were an all-powerful dynasty that ruled the nation with an iron fist, but in practice the tsars' ability to enforce their rule was limited by weak institutional support and bureaucratic corruption. While the aristocrats enjoyed lives of privilege and leisure, the majority of Russians continued to labour in poverty, and even though serfdom had been formally abolished in 1861, peasants still had few civil rights; public flogging, for instance, remained legal until 1904. A number of revolutionary groups continued to plot against the tsarist regime. At this time, the Bolsheviks were only one of several rival factions within the socialist movement in Russia.

In the wake of the unpopular and unsuccessful war with Japan in 1904–5, Russia slid into a major political crisis that came to be known as the 'Revolution of 1905'. It began in January of that year, when demonstrations against the government turned bloody and 96 people were killed as they marched on the Winter Palace in Petrograd (St Petersburg). Faced with public outrage and widespread strikes, Tsar Nicolas II made some political concessions in the 'October Manifesto', which for the first time guaranteed Russians a number of civil liberties, including legalized political parties, a national parliament (the Duma), and universal adult male suffrage. But these measures did not amount to an effective democracy. The elected officials could merely advise the tsar—they did not actually run the government—and they had little real political power. Moscow also cracked down on dissidents, including Vladimir Lenin, who was driven into exile. Although the initial crisis subsided, tensions continued to seethe beneath the surface, and the country's pressing social problems went unresolved.

In the summer of 1914, the Tsar's reign appeared to be secure. There were mass demonstrations in support of the war, as Russians also became caught up in the euphoria that initially swept most European countries. By 1917, however, more than four million peasants had moved from the countryside to the cities, and this demographic shift created new social pressures. As the Russian army suffered a string of defeats, support for the war faded, and by 1917 Nicolas II again faced a political crisis. In February, a group of women in Petrograd organized a protest against the high cost of bread, demanding political reforms and an end to the war. This protest led to a series of larger demonstrations involving tens of thousands of people. Military units were dispatched to disperse the protestors, and soldiers fired into the crowd, killing about 60 people. Nicolas II, who was away at the front, had lost touch with events in Petrograd, and his government soon collapsed. Power shifted to the Duma and 'soviets'—new revolutionary councils made up of workers and peasants. Working with some of the socialists, members of the Duma appointed a provisional government. Nicolas II realized that he could not crush the revolution using military force, but he hoped to keep his family in power. To that end, in March 1917 he abdicated the throne in favour of his brother Mikhail. But Mikhail abdicated a few hours later, and Nicholas and his family were arrested.

The provisional government proved unable to address the country's economic problems (particularly inflation) or to deliver on promises of land reform. Worse, it attempted to continue Russia's military operations, despite what was now widespread opposition to the war. At this critical juncture, in April 1917, Lenin returned from exile. Since his release from a Siberian prison in 1895, he had emerged as the most powerful member of the Bolshevik faction. Lenin was uncompromising in his conviction that violent revolution was necessary; in his view, co-operation with democrats was merely a temporary strategy that would allow his party to gain total control. German officials had facilitated Lenin's return in the belief that his presence would so destabilize Russia as to knock it out of the war. As the German army advanced into Russia in September 1917, support for the provisional government dissolved. The government moved against the Bolsheviks, sending Lenin into hiding, but he returned to Petrograd in October determined to overthrow the provisional government. Working with Leon Trotsky, Lenin organized the Red Guards and conspired with soldiers to take over Petrograd. Their attack, now known as the October Revolution, toppled the provisional government, and Lenin moved to impose a regime based on the belief that all traces of capitalism had to be destroyed so that a just society could be built. In March 1918, the Bolsheviks renamed themselves the Communist Party, and thereafter Lenin worked ruthlessly to consolidate power. Using the secret police, known as the Cheka (a forerunner of the NKVD and KGB) as well as the Red Army, Lenin did not hesitate to use violence to achieve his political goals. In July 1918, Nicolas II and his family were executed, and Russia slid into civil war.

THE SIGNIFICANCE OF THE RUSSIAN WITHDRAWAL

The replacement of the tsarist autocracy with a provisional government of the moderate left, in February 1917, together with the intervention of the United States in the war against Germany a few weeks later, gave the Entente coalition an ideological consistency that it had previously lacked. The new progressive government in Petrograd was promptly recognized by the Entente powers and announced its intention to honour the military and diplomatic engagements of the old regime. In the meantime, the United States made its official declaration of war on 6 April, and even though it would not be able to contribute significant numbers of troops until the summer of 1918, the idea that it had joined the fight for the extinction of tyranny and the liberation of oppressed peoples lent weight to the moral argument for the slaughter at the front. Now slogans about making the world 'safe for democracy' and the struggle for 'national self-determination' sounded less hollow.

The euphoria induced by the American intervention was tempered, however, when the provisional government in Russia was overthrown by

Soldiers of the Bolshevik Army march through Red Square, ca. 1917. © Bettmann/CORBIS.

the Bolsheviks in October 1917. This event was widely viewed in Entente countries as Germany's first success in instigating insurrection behind the lines of the Entente. The evidence for a German–Bolshevik conspiracy might have been entirely circumstantial, but it was persuasive. German government funds had subsidized Russian revolutionary groups in exile, and Lenin's publicly announced program included an immediate end to the war, if necessary by a separate peace with the Central Powers. Entente suspicions seemed to receive further confirmation after the Bolshevik victory. Not only did the new Russian government reject the tsarist regime's debts to foreign lenders—thereby wiping out roughly a quarter of France's foreign investment portfolio—but it published the secret agreements made by the Entente powers concerning the post-war redistribution of enemy territory, causing considerable embarrassment to Britain, France, and Italy. Most serious of all, after inviting all belligerents to make peace on the basis of no annexations and no indemnities but receiving no reply from the Allies, the Bolshevik government opened separate peace negotiations with the Central Powers in the city of Brest-Litovsk on 3 December 1917.

The consequences of the Russian Revolution were felt throughout wartime Europe. After three months of wrangling (from December 1917 to March 1918), the Russian and German emissaries at Brest-Litovsk signed a peace treaty that removed Russia from the war. In line with the new German government policy, adopted after the intervention of the United States, the Treaty of Brest-Litovsk did not result in the direct annexation of Russian territory. Instead, it represented the new policy of 'association', according to which the Bolshevik regime was to cede virtually all of its non-Russian territories in Europe: Poland, Lithuania, Latvia, Estonia, and Finland in the north and Ukraine and the provinces of Transcaucasia (Georgia, Armenia, and Azerbaijan) in the south. In all these regions independence movements had sprouted after the collapse of the tsarist regime, and many of them appealed to Germany for economic and military support. The German government was

happy to oblige. By supplying 'military protection' to the fledgling nations carved out of the former Russian Empire, the German Reich hoped to achieve two of its original war aims: the removal of Russian power from Europe and the extension of German economic domination to the non-Russian border zone.

As German troops advanced into the power vacuum created by Russia's withdrawal from the war, the balance of power in Eastern Europe was transformed. Russia was virtually cut off from the Baltic by the establishment of the independent states of Finland, Latvia, Lithuania, and Estonia under German military protection. The creation of German client states in Ukraine, Crimea, Georgia, and Armenia, coupled with Turkish control of the Muslim state of Azerbaijan, blocked Russian access to the Black Sea and the mineral-rich region of the Caucasus. In the centre of Europe, a Polish state was resurrected to give Germany a transit zone through which to extend its hegemony into the former Russian territory along the Black and Baltic seas. Russia's retreat from Eastern Europe was further confirmed by the peace treaty signed by Romania and the Central Powers in May, whereby Germany and Austria recognized Romania's annexation of the former imperial Russian province of Bessarabia.

Russia's withdrawal from its European borderlands might have had long-term strategic implications, but its immediate consequences were less than spectacular. The great German offensive planned for the spring of 1918 did not take place on the scale anticipated. In fact, Germany kept large numbers of troops in the eastern theatre to preserve its hold on the enormous territory ceded by Russia. The immediate goal was economic in nature: to gain control of the foodstuffs and vital minerals in Eastern Europe and the Russian borderlands. The overall objective was the acquisition of self-sufficiency in food and industrial raw materials, not only on a short-term basis to replace resources denied to the Central Powers by the British naval blockade but also for the post-war period, when overseas sources of supplies were expected to fall within the control of the United

States and the British Empire regardless of who eventually won the war. By the spring of 1918, Germany controlled virtually all the resources it needed to become independent of foreign suppliers and establish the autarkic economic system first envisioned in the September Program. The oil fields of Romania, the Caucasus, and Turkish-controlled Mesopotamia (Iraq) would ensure self-sufficiency in that vital source of energy. The coal fields of the Don basin in Russia would supplement the rich deposits of the Ruhr, the Saar, Silesia, and occupied Belgium in the west. The iron resources of Ukraine would be added to those of French Lorraine. The manganese of the Caucasus and Ukraine (which accounted for half of the world's production in 1914 and supplied Germany with three-quarters of its pre-war requirements) would now be open to direct German exploitation. The cotton and wool of the Caucasus region offered essential raw materials to the German textile industry. And, most importantly, the fertile grain-producing plains of Ukraine, combined with those of the German vassal states in the Balkans, would give the Reich a way around the British 'hunger blockade' and ensure that in the future it would not need to rely on the US and Latin America for food, as it had before the war.

Thus by the spring of 1918, the original objectives of Germany's war plan had been attained in the east. The establishment of German strategic predominance in the Russian borderlands had tipped the continental balance in favour of the Central Powers. Groundwork had been laid for German economic domination of the region that had been evacuated by the Russian armies. The Austro–Hungarian and Turkish empires—junior partners in the coalition ruled from Berlin—opened the path for German expansion overland towards the Arabian peninsula and the Persian Gulf. This land route to the Middle East and Southern Asia, which was to be improved by the construction of a German-financed railway system, potentially represented a much more secure connection to this economically valuable region than did Britain's vulnerable lifeline on the sea.

Thus one dream of the German industrial and financial oligarchy appeared to be coming true: a vast *Mitteleuropa* bounded by compliant satellites and subservient allies chained to Germany by military and economic agreements. To complete the grandiose scheme for German control of *Mitteleuropa* and the Middle East, the expansionists in Berlin added the project of Mittelafrika: a central African empire, enlarged by the addition of former Belgian, French, and British colonies to Germany's existing possessions in Africa and protected by German naval bases on the eastern and western coasts.

All that stood in the way of Germany's realization of these plans was the Entente military force on the Western Front. As American troops began to arrive in large numbers in the spring of 1918, the German high command faced a critical decision. Negotiating a settlement of the war in France might enable Germany to preserve and even increase the spectacular military and economic gains it had made in the east. Peace feelers had been extended sporadically from London, Paris, Washington, and Berlin during 1917 and early 1918, and the German quartermaster general, Erich Ludendorff, toyed with the idea of exploiting the Allies' ideological fear of Bolshevism by posing as the defender of Western civilization. A separate peace in the west, however, would require that Germany renounce its expansionist ambitions in Belgium and eastern France, and that was something it was not prepared to do. A militarily powerful and economically viable France, together with an independent Belgium serving as a vehicle for British interference in continental affairs, would hamper fulfillment of the *Mitteleuropa* project. Hence preparations were resumed for a final offensive on the Western Front. On 21 March 1918, Germany launched 62 divisions in the long-awaited attack intended to drive France out of the war and Anglo–American forces off of the continent.

It is worth noting that all of the major political organizations in Germany had supported the program of German military and economic expansion up to the period of this last great offensive.

The Reichstag ratified the Treaty of Brest-Litovsk by a large majority, and even the Social Democrats chose to abstain rather than to oppose what the Russian government, signing under protest, denounced as a 'dictated peace'. The Centre and Progressive parties defended the treaty as consistent with the principle of 'no annexations, no indemnities' (the formula adopted by the German Reichstag in July 1917) because it did not involve the formal annexation of Russian territory. The Conservative and National Liberal parties criticized the treaty as too weak. On 13 July 1918, just before the offensive in France failed, the Reichstag once again registered its approval of the plan by passing the twelfth military appropriation law of the war.

The German offensive ground to a halt on 15 July, and three days later the Entente armies mounted a counter-offensive that by 8 August was beginning to look like a rout. With their armies retreating along a broad front during the rest of August and September, Germany's military leaders recognized for the first time that victory in the west was impossible. Ludendorff and his associates thereupon dusted off the alternative strategy that had been under consideration ever since the Treaty of Brest-Litovsk: to exploit the Bolshevik threat as a means of securing a moderate settlement with the Entente. Ironically, the new policy of retrenchment in the west was enthusiastically endorsed by the very spokesmen for German heavy industry who had earlier pressed for extensive annexations in Belgium and eastern France. In September 1918, industrialists such as Hugo Stinnes, Albert Ballin, and Gustav Krupp, in league with National Liberal leader Gustav Stresemann (also a former annexationist), urged the government to preserve Germany's economic and military gains in the east by renouncing its ambitious aims in the west. They also called for domestic political reforms that would appeal to public opinion in the Entente camp by removing the stigma of autocracy from the German political system. The internal democratization of Germany would satisfy both Wilsonian opinion abroad and progressive critics at home. A Germany serving as the bulwark of Western civilization against the menace of Bolshevism could expect to receive considerable sympathy both in France, with its enormous Russian investments threatened by the communist revolution, and in Britain, with its millions of colonial subjects susceptible to infection with the revolutionary ideas circulating in Moscow and Petrograd.

The continuing deterioration of Germany's military position in France in the fall of 1918 caused the high command to adopt parts of this strategy in one final effort to salvage the gains made in the east. On 4 October—less than a week after Ludendorff had informed the emperor of the need for an armistice as soon as possible—a 'parliamentary government' headed by the liberal Prince Max of Baden was formed with the support of the parties of the centre and left. On the same day, the German government appealed to US President Wilson for an armistice of moderation on the basis of the principles enunciated in his famous 'Fourteen Points'. When Wilson replied that he would negotiate with only a genuinely democratic government, the military and political elite in Berlin realized that the cause was lost. Ludendorff resigned on 27 October, the Kaiser abdicated on 9 November, and on the same day Social Democratic leader Phillip Scheidemann proclaimed a German democratic republic. On 11 November, the German delegates who had been negotiating with Allied military representatives in a forest north of Paris signed an armistice. It provided for the immediate evacuation of all French and Belgian territory as well as all German territory west of the Rhine River. It also required—as a final blow to the hopes of the anti-Bolshevik faction in Berlin—that Germany renounce the treaties of Brest-Litovsk and Bucharest and withdraw all of its military forces from Russia, Romania, Austria–Hungary, and Turkey.

Like the 'revolution' that had created a united German Empire in 1871, the 'revolution' that established the German republic in November 1918 was carried out from above, without the participation of the mass of citizens. The parts played by the German kings and princes in the coronation of Wilhelm I were played at Versailles by former supporters of the empire such as Stresemann and moderate leaders of the Social Democrats such as Scheidemann. The military leadership did not lift a finger in defence of the Kaiser, who slipped ignominiously across the Dutch border into exile on 10 November. The German Republic was not forged by a revolutionary movement fired by democratic enthusiasm and hatred for the authoritarian regime that had brought the nation to defeat. It was created by political leaders who had either supported or acquiesced in the expansionist policies of the empire to the very end. It was tolerated by a military class that was glad to see the civilian representatives of the democratic parties take responsibility for accepting the humiliating terms dictated by the French generalissimo in the railroad car at Compiègne following Germany's defeat in the war of conquest that its high command had planned, waged, and lost.

THE SIGNIFICANCE OF THE AMERICAN INTERVENTION

At the outset of the war in Europe, the US government had declared that it intended to remain strictly neutral. No American interests were directly threatened by the fighting across the Atlantic, and no American commitments had been made, even informally, to any of the belligerents. In the early stages of the war, sympathy for both sides was expressed by various groups within the United States. There was widespread sentimental support for Britain for reasons of linguistic and cultural identification, and French publicists effectively reminded Americans of the debt they owed France for its assistance in the War of Independence. On the other hand, pro-Entente attitudes were balanced by pro-German or anti-British sentiments among the two largest ethnic groups in the US: German and Irish Americans.

As the war became a stalemate, however, the naval and economic policies of the belligerents caused a gradual shift in the United States away from absolute neutrality and towards more active

support for the Entente. By the spring of 1915, the British navy, profiting from the overwhelming numerical superiority of its surface fleet, succeeded in driving German warships and merchant ships from the high seas. Except for one inconclusive engagement in May 1916 off the Jutland peninsula of Denmark, the German fleet was to cling to its home bases rather than face total destruction at the hands of the British. Without the protection of armed warships, the German merchant marine was confined to port for the rest of the war, forcing Germany to rely on neutral shipping for its foreign trade. But Britain imposed a blockade on Germany that effectively severed its access to neutral sources of supply and prevented it from using neutral means of transport.

According to the generally accepted custom of blockade in wartime, the blockading ships were to be stationed near the ports of the enemy country—just outside the 4.8-kilometre territorial limit. The blockading power was entitled to intercept and inspect the cargoes of merchant vessels seeking admission to the enemy port. Those ships found to be carrying contraband—narrowly defined as weapons, ammunition, and other articles of war—could be denied entry to the port until they disposed of the objectionable cargo. But the British navy violated these regulations in three important respects. First, its blockade flotillas operated far from shore, on the high seas, supposedly to avoid the risk posed by long-range harbour artillery. This 'loose blockade' enabled them to intercept neutral ships headed for neutral countries contiguous to Germany (such as Denmark and the Netherlands) and to confiscate contraband on the pretext that it might find its way into enemy hands. Second, in November 1914, the British government declared the entire North Sea a 'military area' and proceeded to mine it so thoroughly that neutral merchant ships were compelled to stop at British ports for navigational directions. Such instructions were systematically withheld if the ship's cargo included articles of contraband. Third, claiming that in total war practically every important product, including foodstuffs and textiles for clothing, was of potential value to the enemy, the British extended the definition of contraband to include virtually every item that Germany was required to import.

As a consequence of this deliberate policy of economic strangulation, Germany's trade with neutral countries such as the United States slowed to a trickle, and the nations in the anti-German coalition took up the slack, importing huge quantities of munitions, food, and other necessities from Germany's traditional foreign suppliers. Germany was driven to rely on submarines to harass British merchant shipping in retaliation against the blockade. The international rules of naval warfare required submarines to surface and issue warnings to vessels flying the enemy flag, in order to give passengers and crew the chance to abandon ship before the torpedo was released. But many of the British merchant ships were armed, and their captains were under instructions to ram or open fire on German submarines that complied with this custom. Accordingly, in February 1915, the German government defined a 'war zone' around the British Isles, within which all enemy ships would be liable to destruction without warning. Neutral merchant ships were advised to stay out of the zone to avoid the risk of mistaken identity (a distinct possibility, since British merchant ships often hoisted neutral flags to confound enemy submarine commanders). Between February and May, 90 ships went to the bottom of the sea in this newly defined zone. On 7 May, the British passenger liner *Lusitania*, laden with ammunition and other contraband material purchased in the US, was sunk by a German submarine off the coast of Ireland. The death of 128 American citizens in this incident prompted such vigorous protests from Washington that German submarine commanders were instructed to issue warnings to enemy passenger liners before mounting an attack, and in May 1916 this modification was extended to merchant ships as well, on the tacit understanding that the US government would persuade Britain to relax its 'starvation blockade' of Germany.

The United States, which possessed the third largest navy in the world in 1914, could easily have convoyed its own merchant ships across the Atlantic and compelled Britain to halt its flagrant violations of established naval practices. That it chose not to do so while continuing to protest German transgressions of the rules of submarine warfare reflected two considerations that predisposed the Wilson administration to favour the Entente over the Central Powers. The first was the strong sense of kinship with British traditions and institutions felt by key members of the American government, including the president, all of whom privately championed the Entente cause and opposed efforts to treat British and German violations of international law on an equal basis. The second and more important consideration was that since the British blockade had diverted the American export trade from Germany and adjacent neutral countries to Britain and France and their allies, American economic prosperity and corporate profits had become increasingly dependent on orders from Germany's enemies for everything from munitions to textiles, grain, oil, copper, and steel (see Tables 1.3 and 1.4).

Once the nations of the anti-German coalition had exhausted their dollar credits in the United States by liquidating their holdings of American securities, the only way they could finance future imports was by obtaining loans from American bankers. Since trade with the Allies had become a critical element in the United States' recovery from the cyclical recession of 1913–14, the Wilson administration authorized the opening of the Wall Street capital market to the Allied governments. The investment banking firm of J.P. Morgan & Company became the official commercial agent in the US for the British and French treasuries, coordinating Allied purchasing from American suppliers and organizing banking consortia to furnish the credits required to finance these operations. By the time the US entered the war, private American financial institutions had advanced approximately US$2.3 billion in loans and credits to the Allied states, compared to only $27 million to the Central Powers. The House of Morgan had placed more than $3 billion worth of contracts with American export

TABLE 1.3 AMERICAN EXPORTS TO BELLIGERENT AND NEUTRAL COUNTRIES DURING THE PERIOD OF AMERICAN NEUTRALITY IN THE FIRST WORLD WAR (IN PERCENTAGES)

	Year (First Trimester)			
	1890	1900	1910	1914
Allied nations or nations that severed diplomatic relations with Germany	64.62	74.17	87.34	88.67
Neutral countries	16.15	23.55	12.26	10.38
Germany, its allies, and occupied countries	19.23	2.28	0.40	0.95

Source: Yves-Henri Nouailhat, *La France et les Etats-Unis, août 1914–avril 1917* copyright, 1977, p. 627. Reprinted by permission.

firms on behalf of the British and French governments. In this way, the trading partnership between American exporters and Anglo–French importers, reinforced by the financial relationship between Wall Street bankers and the state treasuries of Paris and London, gave American economic interests an important stake in the success of the Allied war effort.

It was this inequality of economic treatment, together with Washington's failure to persuade London to relax its illegal 'loose blockade', that prompted the German government to announce the resumption of unrestricted submarine warfare on 31 January 1917. Concluding that the United States could hardly be more helpful to the Anglo–French cause as a cobelligerent than it already was as a neutral supplier of munitions and food paid for with American credits, German political and naval authorities chose to risk provoking American intervention. They confidently

TABLE 1.4 PRICES OF SELECTED AMERICAN INDUSTRIAL SECURITIES DURING THE PERIOD OF AMERICAN NEUTRALITY IN THE FIRST WORLD WAR

Company	Stock Price on 24 July 1914	Stock Price on 21 Jan. 1916	Gain (%)
American Beet & Sugar	22¾	66¾	193
American Hide & Leather	4	10⅞	171
American Linseed	8¾	22½	157
American Locomotive	28	64½	130
American Woollen	15½	48½	212
Anaconda Copper	30¼	87	187
Bethlehem Steel	39¼	477	1,115
Corning Products Refining	8¼	22½	175
International Mercantile Marine	2	20½	820
Republic Iron & Steel	20	51	155

Source: Nouailhat, p. 507. Copyright 1977, Yves-Henri Nouailhat, reprinted by permission.

assumed that the disruption of transatlantic supply lines would force Britain out of the war within
six months—before American troops could be
mobilized, trained, and transported through
submarine-infested waters to Europe. The US
responded to the resumption of unrestricted submarine warfare by severing diplomatic relations
with Germany and arming American merchant
vessels. Hesitant to resume their perilous trade
with the Entente, most American shipping firms
kept their vessels in port, causing widespread fear
of economic depression as products intended for
export began to pile up on the wharves of East
Coast harbours. Many of those that did risk the
Atlantic crossing were sent to the bottom by
German U-boats as they entered the war zone.
This disruption of the American export trade gave
Wilson a pretext for requesting a congressional
declaration of war against Germany, which was
granted on 6 April 1917.

At that time, the United States' regular army
of 130,000 officers and men was smaller than
Belgium's, poorly trained, and incapable of playing a role in the Allied war effort. It was not until
the early summer of 1918, after the introduction
of conscription and the creation of a military
training program, that the American military and
naval forces (which by the end of the war would
grow to 4.8 million persons) began to make a
critical contribution to the Anglo–French effort

on the Western Front. In the meantime, however,
financial assistance from Washington enabled the
Allied governments to increase their purchases of
American supplies. Once the US had declared war,
the financing operations of the New York banks
were taken over by the Treasury Department. A
large proportion of the proceeds from the war
bonds that were sold to patriotic American investors were advanced to the Allied governments to
finance their purchases in the American market.
The German navy's hope of halting the transport
of American supplies to France was dashed by
Britain's success in convoying merchant ships
across the Atlantic.

The years 1914–18 witnessed a massive international transfer of wealth from the eastern to
the western shore of the Atlantic. The liquidation
of British and French investments in the United
States in the first year of the war erased the debt
owed by Americans to European lenders. The
subsequent borrowing by Allied governments in
the American money market transformed the US
from a debtor to a creditor of the European powers that had depleted their financial resources to
pay for the war (see Table 1.5).

Accompanying this shift of financial power
from Europe to the United States was a revolution
in the system of world trade. While Germany was
prevented from pursuing its commercial interests
abroad by the British blockade, Britain and France

TABLE 1.5 THE INTERNATIONAL INVESTMENT POSITION OF THE UNITED STATES
BEFORE AND AFTER THE FIRST WORLD WAR (IN BILLIONS OF DOLLARS)

	US Private Investments Abroad				Foreign Investments in US			
		Long-Term				Long-Term		
	Total	Direct	Portfolio	Short-Term	Total	Direct	Portfolio	Short-Term
1914 (June)	3.5	2.7	0.08	n.a.	7.2	1.3	5.4	0.5
1919	7.0	3.9	2.6	0.05	3.3	0.9	1.6	0.8

Note: n.a. = not available.
Source: US Department of Commerce, Bureau of the Census, *Historical Statistics of the United States* (Washington, 1960), p. 565.

were forced to divert their industrial production and merchant shipping to wartime purposes. In the meantime, the US expanded its export trade, capturing many markets previously dominated by European firms. The American economic penetration of Latin America, which had begun at the turn of the century, accelerated during the war. Similarly, the Japanese Empire grabbed Germany's possessions in the Far East and expanded economically in that region at the expense of all three of the principal European belligerents. From an economic point of view, the First World War was won by the United States and Japan, both of which avoided territorial destruction and large-scale loss of life while gaining economic predominance within their respective regions.

The long-term implications of this fundamental shift in global economic power away from Europe passed largely unnoticed in the months following the armistice. Trade patterns and capital flows meant nothing to a European population preoccupied with post-war security and recovery. The choice of the capital city of France as the site of the peace conference that would formally terminate the war reinforced the illusion that Europe, despite its commercial and financial decline during the war years, remained the centre of the world.

THE LEGACY OF THE RUSSIAN REVOLUTION

The repercussions of the 1917 revolution extended far beyond the borders of Russia. The Russian communists saw themselves as the vanguard of an international movement destined to spread across the globe, uniting the working classes of the world in a utopian society, and even in the short term, their ascent to power had effects in other European countries. Germany, for example, experienced socialist uprisings and political instability in the aftermath of the war, and the disintegration of the Russian Empire triggered nationalist movements in Poland, the Baltic states, and other territories where tsarist rule had long been resented.

Over the longer term, the Russian Revolution shaped the course of the twentieth century in three ways. First, the rise of a communist state transformed the nature of geopolitical relations. Before 1917 there had been no substantive ideological differences among the great powers. Alliances shifted according to national and imperial interests, and the leaders of European countries (most of which were monarchies of one sort or another) shared a basic set of beliefs about how international relations should be governed. The Russian Revolution transformed this international system because it gave rise to a nation (eventually a bloc of nations) that defined itself as irrevocably opposed to capitalism.

Second, the Russian Revolution had profound consequences for the global economy. The Russian efforts to build a socialist economy created an alternative to capitalism in the minds of many people. For those who were sympathetic to Marxist ideology, communism represented progress, the future, a solution to the awful inequalities and injustices produced by industrial capitalism. Even for those who opposed communism, the Russian Revolution meant that alternative viewpoints could no longer be dismissed as inconsequential. Now that one of the world's great powers was being run by socialists, capitalism was no longer the only model for organizing a modern economy. Today, with the benefit of hindsight, we may be tempted to dismiss communism as a doomed ideology, but many people in the West regarded it as a viable economic alternative, particularly after the Great Depression had exposed the failings of capitalism.

Finally, the events of 1917 inspired generations of communist revolutionaries in countries around the world. From China to Cuba, insurrections supported by the Soviet Union toppled capitalist governments and transformed their societies. The success of the Russian Revolution meant that prospective revolutionaries everywhere had a powerful sponsor and protector. Moscow provided not only the inspiration but also the arms, the training, and the funding required by the revolutionary movements that became a defining feature of the twentieth century.

SUMMARY

The First World War destroyed the geopolitical system inherited from the nineteenth century. Between 1914 and 1918, at least 10 million people were killed, great empires were toppled, and much of Europe was devastated. The war represented the culmination of the military rivalries that had been intensifying since the turn of the century. In 1914 the great powers failed to contain a regional dispute, and the situation escalated into a full-scale war. This failure was due in part to the system of alliances and war plans developed by the great powers. Yet the First World War was largely the result of Germany's political ambitions.

The first 'total war' in history had profound social and economic repercussions. Wartime demands for industrial production, foodstuffs, munitions, and military recruits led to new levels of state intervention and government regulation. National governments became heavily involved in economic production and social policy, which brought political consequences. In addition to enlisting in auxiliary military units, women entered the domestic workforce in unprecedented numbers; their presence increasingly pressured governments to support the suffrage movement in countries such as Canada, where women were finally given the right to vote in federal elections in 1918.

Internationally, the First World War had especially dramatic impacts on the United States and Russia. Although it remained officially neutral until 1917, the US provided financial loans to Britain and France to assist in their war efforts, and this massive transfer of wealth transformed the US from a debtor nation into a major creditor. Although it would take another generation for the US to become a dominant world power, its intervention in the war contributed to a larger shift in political influence away from Europe. For Russia, the First World War created the conditions that led to the overthrow of the Romanov dynasty. The failures of the Russian Army, coupled with poor leadership and economic difficulties, undermined confidence in the tsarist regime. In 1917, Russia was plunged into a crisis that saw the abdication of Nicholas II; the establishment of a provisional government in February; and, in October, a revolution in which the Bolsheviks, led by Lenin, overthrew Kerensky's provisional government and took power themselves. These events had profound implications not only for Russia, which was forced into civil war, but also for countries around the world.

NOTES

1. Italy renounced its treaty obligations to Germany and Austria–Hungary under the Triple Alliance on the grounds that the two Germanic empires had become engaged in an offensive rather than a defensive war. With Italy's withdrawal, the Triple Alliance was no more; its remaining members came to be known instead as the 'Central Powers', an alliance later joined by Turkey and Bulgaria.

2. Had the German armies failed to seize and operate the Lorraine iron fields during the war, the German war machine would likely have ground to a halt for lack of armaments and munitions.

3. The estimated population of Canada in 1918 was 8,148,000, according to Statistics Canada (www.statcan.ca/english/freepub/98-187-XIE/pop.htm); the estimated population of the United States in the same year was 103,208,000, according to the US Census Bureau (www.census.gov/popest/archives/1990s/popclockest.txt).

4. Zionism was a political movement, founded in the 1890s by Austian journalist Theodor Herzl, that advocated the establishment of a Jewish national state as a haven for the Jewish peoples of Europe and Russia who faced a resurgence of anti-Semitism toward the end of the century.

QUESTIONS FOR CRITICAL THOUGHT

1.   What factors, if any, support the argument that Germany's quest for empire was reasonable?
2.   Why have German actions in the years before 1914 come to be viewed as more threatening than those of the other great powers?
3.   Discuss whether Germany could have denied the Austrian request for support following the assassination of Franz Ferdinand.
4.   What is 'total war'? Does the Great War qualify as a 'total war'?
5.   What were the main causes of the Russian Revolution in 1917?
6.   What was the most important turning point during the Great War?

WEBSITES FOR FURTHER REFERENCE

Canada and the First World War
    www.collectionscanada.gc.ca/firstworldwar/index-e.html

Spartacus Educational: First World War Index
    www.spartacus.schoolnet.co.uk/FWW.htm

The War to End All Wars
    www.firstworldwar.com

World War I: Trenches on the Web
    www.worldwar1.com

CHAPTER 2

THE PEACE OF PARIS AND THE NEW INTERNATIONAL ORDER

THE PARIS PEACE CONFERENCE

The peace conference that began in Paris in January 1919 was the largest and most important diplomatic gathering since the Congress of Vienna of 1814–15. Twenty-seven victorious nations were represented at the conference, including—after strenuous efforts on the part of Prime Minister Borden—Canada. (The other three of Britain's self-governing dominions—Australia, New Zealand, and South Africa—were also granted separate representation, but with those exceptions the British and French colonial empires were treated as single political units.) The enormity of the devastation wreaked by the war hung like a cloud over the deliberations. Ten million lives had been lost during the previous four years, and another twenty million people had sustained war-related injuries. The total direct cost of the war was estimated at US$180 billion and the indirect cost at more than $150 billion. Three of the four great empires that had exercised authority over hundreds of millions of people in the old world—Hohenzollern Germany, Habsburg Austria–Hungary, and Romanov Russia—had already disappeared, and the fourth—Ottoman Turkey—was soon to expire. From their ashes arose politically unstable, economically weak states whose viability remained problematic. The agenda of the conference was twofold: to repair the political and economic fabric of half the world and to ensure against any recurrence of the organized violence that had torn it apart.

The president of the United States, Woodrow Wilson, astonished his compatriots by deciding to attend the peace conference in person. The first American president ever to visit a foreign country while in office, he also shocked his critics at home by staying in Europe (except for a brief trip home) for six months, leaving his subordinates in Washington to deal with domestic problems of post-war adjustment. Wilson arrived in Europe in mid-December 1918 armed with extraordinary moral authority. His exhortations on behalf of a new world order that would forever banish the scourge of war represented a new approach to the conduct of international relations, or so it seemed to the millions of war-weary Europeans who greeted him with unrestrained enthusiasm. In those intoxicating weeks before the opening of the conference, it seemed as if a saviour had

Representatives meet around the conference table during the Paris Peace Conference, 1919. Canadian Prime Minister Robert Borden is seated near the right-hand corner of the table. Library and Archives Canada/Department of External Affairs fonds/C-000242.

come from across the sea, untarnished by the discredited traditional statecraft that had brought Europe to its present plight.

To judge by his public pronouncements on the subject, Wilson believed that war in general, and the recent war in particular, had three principal causes. The first was the practice of secret diplomacy, whereby political leaders surreptitiously negotiated military alliances and diplomatic engagements to further their own nations' ambitions. The second was the tendency of politically dominant nationality groups to oppress the ethnic minorities under their control. The third was the ability of privileged elites to monopolize political power at the expense of the population at large.

Removing these impediments to the unfettered expression of the public will, Wilson seemed to say, would abolish forever the causes of war. Free and open discussion of international issues would bring an end to secret diplomacy among imperialistically inclined national leaders. The map of Europe was to be redrawn according to the principle of national self-determination, liberating the long-suppressed ethnic groups whose struggles for independence had caused most of the wars of recent memory. And, finally, European political institutions would be democratized by removing the constraints on the expression of public opinion that had permitted the ruling elites of the Central Powers to wage war in their own interests.

The crowning achievement in this process of internal and international democratization would be the creation of a world organization empowered to resolve international disputes through negotiation and compromise, modelled on the parliaments that in democratic societies adjudicated the conflicting claims of their citizens.

It is easy to understand the appeal that Wilson's program held for Europeans. The two slogans most often associated with Wilson's name—'the war to end all wars' and 'the war to make the world safe for democracy'—symbolized the widespread need to believe that the sacrifices of the preceding four years had not been in vain. The disappointment of those hopes represented one of the greatest tragedies in modern world history. So bitter was the disillusionment that the genuine accomplishments of the Paris Peace Conference have receded far into the background of historical memory. What is recalled instead is the enormous gap between intention and achievement. Because the American leader chose to express his foreign policy in the language of humanitarian idealism, he raised expectations that could never realistically be met by the fallible human beings who assembled in Paris to redraw the political map of Europe and organize the economic recovery of the world.

The contrast between Wilsonian theory and practice became clear in the opening sessions of the conference, when the heads of government tried to establish effective procedures. The principle of equality among sovereign nations, born of the pervasive distrust of great-power diplomacy, had no place in the decision-making process at the organizational meetings. The two ranking delegates of each of the five great powers—France, Britain, Italy, Japan, and the United States—reserved for themselves the right to adjudicate important issues. The leaders of the 22 other states in attendance were reduced to pleading their cases, either in writing or in person, before the 'Council of Ten'. Later, when even this truncated decision-making apparatus proved too unwieldy, the leaders of great powers (with the exception of Japan) began to meet in Wilson's quarters as the 'Council of Four' to decide among themselves the fate of the world.

The pre-eminent position given to the great powers at the peace conference was later extended to the Covenant of the League of Nations, Wilson's cherished scheme for a world organization, which was unveiled before the delegates on 28 April. While each member state was to be represented by one vote in the General Assembly of the new organization, the principal decision-making body, called the Council, was to include permanent seats for delegates of the five great powers. A requirement of unanimity ensured that each permanent member could veto any proposal that threatened its national interests.

Other features of the League Covenant effectively preserved the inequality of power among the member nations. At the behest of the American delegation, the Monroe Doctrine was specifically excluded from the purview of the League Covenant, preserving Washington's exclusive prerogative to maintain the peace in the western hemisphere. Although the right to national self-determination was extended to the successor states of the German, Austro–Hungarian, and Russian empires in Europe, it went unrecognized insofar as the non-European populations of the colonial world were concerned. Thus efforts by spokespersons for the oppressed nationalities of the British and French empires in Asia to obtain recognition of their right to self-government were ignored, as were the efforts of Latin American delegates to invoke the League's protection against US interference in their internal affairs. The application of Wilsonian principles was evidently a privilege reserved for the white nations of the Western world, and among those favoured states the four great powers of the victorious coalition ensured their own pre-eminence.

THE POLITICAL REALITIES OF DIPLOMACY

The much-heralded Wilsonian principle of open diplomacy was another early casualty of the peacemaking process. It soon became evident that the lofty promise of 'open covenants of peace, openly arrived at' meant only that the final texts of diplomatic agreements should be made public (unlike the 'secret treaties' negotiated by the great powers before and during the war). What it definitely did *not* mean—as Wilson's own behaviour in Paris revealed—was that diplomacy would be open to the influence of public opinion as expressed by press or parliament. The Council of Four conducted its deliberations in the utmost secrecy, at first even without taking minutes. When the British delegation finally insisted on a written record of the proceedings, a secretary was admitted on the condition that his notes be withheld from public scrutiny. The press, denied direct access to the decision-makers, was forced to rely on sanitized summaries of what went on behind closed doors. Most of what we know about the deliberations comes from the notes taken by the British secretary and the French interpreter, which were published long after the conference ended.

If the press had minimal access to the decision-making process in Paris, the elected legislative representatives of the four great powers had even less. Wilson in particular ignored public opinion in his own country as it was reflected in the mid-term elections of November 1918, which returned Republican majorities in both houses of Congress. Instead of selecting a peace delegation that reflected this shift away from his own party, he chose men who either shared his own views on world affairs or lacked the authority to speak for the new Republican majority in the Senate (whose votes would be required for legislative consent to the agreements reached at the conference). In his relations with the other Allied representatives Wilson relied heavily on his hand-picked associate, Colonel Edward House, a behind-the-scenes political operator who reported directly to his old friend in the White House. Public expressions of legislative opposition to Wilson's policies in Paris had no apparent effect on the president.

The other Allied leaders were similarly oblivious to domestic public opinion. The French premier, Georges Clemenceau, imposed rigid censorship on the Paris press and denied the Chamber of Deputies any role in the peacemaking process. Like Wilson, he ignored the advice of his foreign minister (and all other senior members of his government), preferring to consult his personal assistant. British Prime Minister David Lloyd George, though more sensitive to political pressures at home, often took positions in the privacy of the conference room that directly contradicted his public utterances. Far from being 'openly arrived at', the covenants were fashioned in a secrecy strongly reminiscent of the pre-war era.

Procedural efficiency was not the only reason for these deviations from the lofty standards of Wilsonianism. The complexity and sensitivity of the questions at issue might well have required that decision-making authority be centralized in a four-member group meeting in private—but in that case the members might have been chosen by lot from among the 27 delegations. That it was those four men in particular who arrogated to themselves the authority to draft the peace treaties reflected the political realities of the post-war world. No amount of lip service to the principle of equality could conceal the glaring inequality of power relationships among the sovereign states whose leaders deliberated in Paris. The United States, Britain, France, and, to a lesser extent, Italy and Japan dominated the peace conference because they dominated the world after the defeat of Germany and the collapse of Russia. (Japan's representatives participated only when issues relating to East Asia were on the agenda.)

These were the nations that had raised the armies of millions, mobilized the economic resources, and imposed military defeat on the Central Powers. These were the nations that collectively exercised economic and political dominion over most of the earth's land surface and naval control over its waters. It was inconceivable that they would relinquish their prerogative to preside over the realignment of international power relationships. It was equally unrealistic to assume that their policies at the peace conference would reflect anything other than their own governments' ideas of what their respective national interests required.

The intrusion of national interest into the decision-making became particularly apparent during the deliberations over the redistribution of the territory, resources, and populations of the regions previously controlled by the defeated powers. For reasons to be examined below, the victorious Allies disagreed sharply on the best means of accomplishing their shared objective: the re-establishment of peace and security in Europe and economic prosperity in the world. This conflict over means eventually shattered the spirit of unity that had cemented the victorious wartime coalition. The Paris Peace Conference, which had opened with such high hopes, ended in an atmosphere of acrimony that was to hamstring future efforts to enforce the treaties it produced.

The French delegation at the peace conference had two essential goals: to remove forever the menace of German military aggression in Europe and to obtain financial assistance for the restoration of the territory in northeastern France that had been devastated by the German army during the war. All the other French objectives at the conference were negotiable. These two were not.

France's determination to prevent any revival of German military power derived from its vulnerable geographical and demographic situation at the end of the war. The long frontier with Germany, unprotected in the north by natural impediments to military aggression such as wide rivers or high mountains, remained a source of grave concern to French military strategists. This sense of vulnerability was heightened by the loss of Russia as an eastern counterweight to German power. Equally alarming were the demographic differences between the two countries. There were 39 million Frenchmen facing 63 million Germans, even with the addition of the nearly 2 million citizens of Alsace–Lorraine. The decline in the French birth rate that had begun long before the war was accelerated by the death of 1.4 million potential fathers on the battlefield. Soon the Germans would be multiplying at twice the rate of the French. By the mid-1930s, the pool of French manpower available for military service would be drastically reduced.

The focus of France's security plan was the region of western Germany between the French frontier and the Rhine River, popularly known as the Rhineland. Geographers and military strategists on all sides agreed that control of this buffer zone would determine the future power relationship between the two ancient adversaries. A German military force stationed in the Rhineland would find no geographical obstacles between itself and France's major industrial sector in the northeast (including the iron-producing region of Lorraine, which had been a prime object of German expansionist ambition during the war) and the centre of French administrative authority in Paris. On the other hand, French soldiers stationed in the Rhineland and on the bridgeheads on the opposite side of the river would be within striking distance of Germany's industrial heartland, the Ruhr Valley. So decisive was this strategic position that military occupation of the Rhineland by one of these two powers would almost certainly deter the other from pursuing an aggressive foreign policy on the continent.

In recognition of this geopolitical imperative, the French delegates proposed that the Rhineland be severed from Germany and reconstituted as an independent sovereign state under French military protection. Fortunately for the French, the separatist group that had sprouted in this region after the armistice was the most ambitious and vocal of the 'anti-Prussian' liberation movements in the predominantly Catholic portions of Germany. Unfortunately, it had failed to secure the support of the vast majority of the Rhenish population, which remained loyal to the national state whose language it shared. Forcible separation of the Rhineland from Germany would not only violate the principle of national self-determination (since a plebiscite in the region would certainly have resulted in rejection of independence); it would also—particularly in the view of Lloyd George—create another Alsace–Lorraine: a perpetual source of friction between Germany and those responsible for its loss.

In the face of intense Anglo–American pressure, including a veiled threat by Wilson to abandon the peace conference in mid-session, the French premier agreed to a compromise. In return for France's acceptance of German political sovereignty over the Rhineland, the US and British leaders would consent to a set of protective guarantees: the prohibition in perpetuity against German deployment of military forces or construction of fortifications both on the territory west of the Rhine and on a 50-kilometre-wide strip to its east; inter-Allied military occupation of the Rhineland for 15 years (at the end of which, it was presumed, the militaristic spirit of the old Germany would have been snuffed out by the forces of German democracy that had recently come to power); and, just in case, the permanent limitation of the German army to a token force of 100,000, a ban on the manufacture of military aircraft, tanks, and other offensive weapons by Germany, and an unprecedented commitment by the United States and Great Britain to defend France by force of arms in the event of unprovoked German aggression. These measures satisfied Clemenceau as minimally acceptable guarantees against a future German military threat.

No less important than the desire for security was France's economic objective of post-war reconstruction. It was a cruel irony that the defeated Germany emerged from the Great War with its national territory virtually untouched, while the most productive region of victorious France lay in ruins. The northeastern region of France that had served as the battleground on the Western Front had been devastated during the four years of combat. To add insult to injury, the retreating German army had deliberately laid waste to the territory they were forced to evacuate; there is some evidence to suggest that this was done not only to deny its resources to the advancing Allied armies but also to give German economic interests a competitive advantage after the war by crippling France's capacity for economic recovery. Coal mines flooded, railways and telegraph lines destroyed, farmland pockmarked with shell holes and honeycombed with trenches, livestock slaughtered, homes put to the torch—this was the sombre scene that greeted the Allied armies as

they liberated the war zone in the autumn of 1918. The destruction of industrial plant, agricultural acreage, and communication and transportation facilities in the northeastern region, together with the severe labour shortages caused by the wartime casualties, had gravely undermined France's productive capacity. Meanwhile, in order to finance its war effort, France had had to liquidate most of its foreign investment portfolio and take on a massive load of foreign debt. The financial demands now facing the country—to reconstruct the devastated regions; to assist the millions of refugees, widows, orphans, and disabled veterans; and to service the foreign debt—were far beyond its depleted capacity. A huge infusion of capital from abroad was needed to pay for France's post-war economic rehabilitation.

Most historians of the Paris Peace Conference have portrayed French authorities as united in the expectation that Germany should bear the costs of France's economic recovery. Recent research has revealed that key officials in the Clemenceau government hoped the money for national reconstruction would come not from the defeated enemy, but rather from France's two English-speaking associates, which had been spared the trauma of military occupation and material destruction. What led France's economic planners to anticipate such assistance from the United States and Britain was the remarkable economic co-operation that had developed among the Allied nations during the last year of the war. A number of inter-Allied organizations had been established in London to pool and allocate available cargo space on ships, as well as the raw materials and munitions essential for the prosecution of the war. In this way the US and the British Empire had provided the French with coal, oil, wheat, and dozens of other commodities that they were unable to produce domestically in sufficient quantities. The French minister of commerce, Etienne Clémentel, assisted by his enterprising young representative in London, Jean Monnet, mounted a vigorous campaign during the winter of 1918–19 to persuade American and British officials to extend the wartime system of economic co-operation to the post-war period and to treat France's economic reconstruction as a responsibility to be shared by the governments of the victorious coalition on the basis of their financial capacity.

To a certain degree this scheme embodied the spirit of the proposals tentatively adopted by the European Allies at the Paris Economic Conference of 1916. By 1918 it was obvious that the United States alone was wealthy enough to underwrite such an ambitious undertaking. At the time of the armistice, therefore, the Clémentel plan revived the Paris program of 1916, with the critical difference that now it was to include the US. Furthermore, once the economic revitalization of France and Belgium was completed, Germany would be severed from the Central European economic bloc that had begun to take shape after the signing of the Treaty of Brest-Litovsk. In this respect the French plan represented a modified version of Germany's wartime *Mitteleuropa* scheme, with the roles reversed. There was originally little serious talk in French government circles about compelling Germany to foot the bill for France's economic recovery: Germany would be expected to contribute its share to the rebuilding of the territory that its armies had devastated, but only as part of a global effort of post-war recovery to be financed in large part by the United States.

THE AMERICAN POSITION

The expectation that the American government would commit substantial public funds to the reconstruction of Europe was ill-founded. Throughout the period of US participation in the war, Wilson had insisted on his nation's separate and distinct status as an 'associate' of the European Allies. The US government had only reluctantly and belatedly associated itself with the inter-Allied economic machinery in the last year of the war, and then mainly for the purpose of limiting and coordinating the European Allies' requests for American aid. Once the victory over Germany had been assured, the United States considered the area of economic interest that it shared with its European partners to have narrowed considerably.

The first overt indication of this transatlantic parting of ways appeared on the eve of the armistice, when Washington formally rejected the French proposals that the Allies pool their economic resources on the basis of need during the period of post-war reconstruction. Even the shrewd attempt by French officials to identify this scheme of international economic co-operation with Wilson's pet project for international political co-operation, the League of Nations, failed to sway American policy-makers. The Wilson administration made it clear that it expected the European nations to finance their economic recovery by themselves; if additional funds were required, they would have to be sought through private investment channels in the US money market. In December 1918, Wilson dismantled the War Industries Board, thereby removing government controls on raw materials and industrial production in the United States, and within a month he had begun to reduce his country's participation in the inter-Allied economic committees. In the spring of 1919, the US secretary of the treasury announced that all American government loans to the wartime partners would be terminated.

Thus the French scheme for inter-Allied sharing of economic and financial resources was torpedoed by Washington's insistence on returning to the peacetime conditions of the free market. It was to be American investors and exporters, not taxpayers, who would supply Europe with the investment capital, raw materials, and products it required, and at the going price. In the face of this abrupt return to economic nationalism by the United States, France was forced to seek relief in the form of 'reparation' payments from Germany. As outlined to the Reparations Commission at the peace conference, France's claims on German resources were essentially of two types. First, France sought payment in kind in the form of vital raw materials that Germany possessed in abundance but France lacked, most notably high-grade coal. Second, it wanted relatively moderate cash payments that could be readily 'mobilized' (that is, converted into negotiable securities available for purchase by foreign investors) so as to turn the long-term German debt to France into immediately usable American credits. A high reparation bill was a mixed blessing for France, since it could be paid only from the surplus of German exports over German imports, which would require expansion of Germany's foreign trade at the expense of French exporters, who were eager to recapture foreign markets lost during the war. Moreover, France was willing to accept as payment in kind only those German goods (such as coal and timber) that did not compete with the products of French industry; to take manufactured articles from Germany would be to grant German industrialists an inroad in the French market to the detriment of their French competitors.

The French government was originally ready to abide by the relatively moderate prescriptions of Wilson's Fourteen Points, which confined Germany's obligation to the reparation of civilian damages. Such a formula would have resulted in a total German payment of only 19 billion gold marks, of which France would have received 70 per cent, based on the extent of the damage to its national territory. The fixing of a specific, moderate sum would have greatly increased the chances that Germany would accept the obligation to defray the costs of French reconstruction, which could have been discharged without a drastic reduction in the German standard of living.

That possibility was foreclosed by the intransigence of the British delegation at the Paris Peace Conference. Since Britain had sustained minimal damage to civilian property (caused by bombs dropped by Zeppelin airships and Gotha bombers in cross-Channel raids), Lloyd George persuaded Wilson to include the cost of veterans' pensions and separation allowances in the total bill to be submitted to Germany, in order to maximize Britain's share of reparation payments. This modification affected only the distribution of funds among the various recipient countries and did not increase Germany's total liability, but it still left a lasting impression of Allied greed and unfairness. To make matters worse, the peacemakers decided to postpone the establishment of a total figure for the German liability until May

1921, with the provision that Germany make a down payment of US$5 billion in the interim. The ostensible reason for this delay was the need to verify the extent of civilian damages by on-site inspection. The real reason was that political leaders had led the Allied nations to expect fabulous sums from Germany and now feared that public opinion would reject the final figure as insufficient—and take political revenge on any government foolish enough to accept it.

The failure to fix a precise sum for reparations produced widespread economic uncertainty and political resentment in Germany. Investors, both foreign and domestic, were understandably reluctant to commit their savings to an economic system facing a potentially enormous claim on its productive resources. Public opinion within Germany fulminated against the 'blank cheque' that the Allies had issued on that country's capacity to regain its pre-war prosperity. But the greatest source of German resentment against the reparations settlement was purely symbolic. The symbol in question was Article 231 of the peace treaty, which established Germany's liability for the damage to civilian property—a responsibility the German government had freely and explicitly acknowledged during the pre-armistice negotiations. Inserted at the behest of a US representative on the Reparations Commission, John Foster Dulles, this article was designed to protect Germany against any Allied claims for reimbursement of the total costs of the war: Germany was to be held morally responsible for the war and its consequences, but legally liable only for the narrowly defined damages specified in the treaty.

Somehow, though, Article 231 was interpreted as implying unilateral 'war guilt' on Germany's part, an interpretation that was entirely baseless. The word 'guilt' does not appear in the article, nor was there any evidence of a 'unilateral' indictment of Germany. Almost identical language was incorporated in the treaties subsequently signed with Germany's allies, Austria, Hungary, Bulgaria, and Turkey. Yet the myth of the 'war-guilt clause', repeated by successive German governments in the 1920s and later used to good effect by Adolf Hitler, was to become as great a source of resentment in Germany as the reparations payments themselves.

THE BRITISH POSITION

It may seem ironic, given Britain's role in preventing a moderate and definitive settlement of the reparations issue at the peace conference, that Lloyd George returned from Paris with a reputation as the most vigorous advocate of moderation. In fact, this reputation was based largely on Britain's opposition to the harsh territorial (as opposed to economic) penalties for Germany that France had sought. We have already noted Lloyd George's role in blocking French efforts to establish an independent client state in the Rhineland on the grounds that such a loss of territory would fuel renewed plans for German expansion. For the same reason, Britain clashed with France over the territorial settlement along Germany's eastern frontier. In the unsettled borderland of Eastern Europe, where a hundred million people were precariously lodged between Germany and Russia, France's policy was to promote a degree of regional security and stability that would enable the newly created or enlarged successor states of the Habsburg and Romanov empires to preserve their independence from their two temporarily weakened but potentially powerful neighbours. French officials thought the small and medium-sized states between the Baltic and the Balkans held the key to the future balance of power on the continent. The geographical barrier that they collectively formed between Germany and Russia seemed to represent the most effective means of preventing any rapprochement between those two dissatisfied powers at the expense of the victorious Allies. The new nations of Poland, Czechoslovakia, and Yugoslavia, together with the newly enlarged state of Romania, proudly asserted their right to national identity.

Declaring national independence proved much easier than delimiting national frontiers in a region where centuries of intermingling among multinational populations precluded the formation of ethnically homogeneous states. To complicate

matters even further, economic and strategic considerations led to several egregious violations of the principle of national self-determination. Thus a million German-speaking citizens of Posen and West Prussia were incorporated into the new state of Poland in order to give the latter a seaport on the Baltic. Similarly, in order to provide Czechoslovakia with defensible frontiers, 3.25 million German inhabitants of the borderlands of Bohemia were included in that new state. And the German-speaking citizens of the rump state of Austria were expressly forbidden to join Germany proper, because it was feared that a unified Germanic state would threaten the security of the newly formed nations of Eastern Europe. As in the case of the Rhineland—but this time without success—Britain opposed many of these violations of German nationality claims on the grounds that they were likely to incite perpetual German dissatisfaction with the peace settlement.

The principal motivation for this conciliatory policy may be traced directly to Britain's conception of its national interests. Lloyd George's overriding objective at the peace conference was to ensure that Germany would never again threaten the sea lanes on which Britain depended for access to supplies in the western hemisphere. Such assurance was obtained by reducing the German navy to a token force of six warships and a corresponding number of auxiliary craft, prohibiting submarines, and redistributing the German colonial empire in Africa and the Pacific among the victorious Allies as mandates under the auspices of the League of Nations. Thus restored to the continental position that it had occupied in the latter part of the nineteenth century under Bismarck, Germany no longer posed a threat to British imperial and maritime interests. Accordingly, the British reverted to their traditional policy of promoting an equilibrium on the continent that would free them to play a global role. What Britain specifically wanted was a moderate territorial settlement in Europe that would preserve Germany as a counterweight to French power on the continent. Such a balance became all the more necessary in British eyes as France began to court the new successor states in Eastern Europe, for the prospect of a French-dominated coalition in Europe was hardly less distasteful to British officials than the prospect of a German-dominated continent had been.

Because of the divergent national interests of the British and the French, the wartime coalition did not survive the peace. Soon after the treaty with Germany was signed—at the royal palace in the Paris suburb of Versailles on 28 June 1919—the fissures in the Anglo–French entente became a matter of public record. As successive French governments struggled to enforce strict adherence to the peace treaty, successive British governments chose to interpret its provisions in the broadest and most lenient ways. The most notable cause of Anglo–French friction over the application of the Versailles Treaty concerned the reparations section. Although at the peace conference Lloyd George had argued forcefully that Germany should pay punitive reparations, British financial officials feared that imposing too heavy a burden on Germany would harm Britain's own economic interests. Inspired by the writings of John Maynard Keynes—then a treasury official attached to the British delegation in Paris—British public opinion came to believe that a prosperous Germany was essential to the restoration of pre-war trading patterns between Britain and Europe.

One argument advanced in London to justify drastic reductions in the reparations bill centred on Germany's pre-war position as a major market for British manufactured products. Paying large reparations to France would inevitably reduce Germany's capacity to import and thereby deprive British industry of a potentially valuable customer on the continent. A related argument revolved around the fact that in order to transfer real wealth to France, Germany would have to generate a foreign trade surplus at the expense of British and other Allied commerce. The export trade on which Britain depended would be severely damaged if Germany were permitted to capture foreign markets for the purpose of discharging its debt to France. Such considerations were especially important during the first half of

the 1920s, when the British economy suffered a prolonged crisis of industrial stagnation and high unemployment, and as a result London's reparations policy ran directly counter to the interests of France. The reparations dispute, aggravated by Anglo–French policy differences concerning Eastern Europe, the Rhineland occupation, and the Middle East,[1] effectively dissipated the wartime spirit of co-operation.

Meanwhile, the United States—the only power with the economic resources and political influence to ease the world's transition to peacetime conditions—had withdrawn from world affairs after the close of the Paris conference. The reasons for that withdrawal are beyond the scope of this book. Suffice it to say that one group of historians blames the Republican majority in the Senate, which enfeebled President Wilson's peace program in order to avoid the global commitments that it entailed; others blame the president's own refusal to recognize domestic political realities. Whatever the cause, the US Senate withheld its consent to the three pacts signed by President Wilson at Paris—the peace treaty with Germany, the bilateral security treaty with France, and the Covenant of the League of Nations—and as a result, American participation in the peacekeeping machinery was terminated. The American return to diplomatic isolation left its wartime associates with the entire responsibility for supervising the peace settlement that Wilson had done so much to fashion. With the reduction of Britain's commitments on the continent and the temporary disappearance of Russia from the European scene, that responsibility fell to France, in association with whatever small states in Eastern Europe it could enlist in a coalition committed to preserving the political status quo.

Abstention from European peacekeeping operations did not signify the disappearance of US power and influence in the world; it merely marked a change in the way they were exercised. The United States had entered the Great War with no war aims and went to the peace conference with no demands. It wanted neither territory nor financial reparations, and it received none. All it had hoped to achieve, beyond the vague philosophical goals propounded by Wilson, was restoration of the stable peacetime conditions under which the US had become the world's strongest economic power by the beginning of the twentieth century. It was widely assumed in US government and business circles that the resumption of normal patterns of international trade and investment would stimulate a resurgence of economic growth in the post-war era. The removal of American support for the new political order in Europe coincided with a spectacular expansion of American economic power in the world, which will be treated in subsequent chapters. What policy-makers in Washington failed to realize during the 1920s was the extent to which the international economic stability from which the

US hoped to profit depended on finding an effective solution to the simmering national antagonisms on the continent of Europe.

THE IMPACT OF THE RUSSIAN REVOLUTION

By the time the United States withdrew from the new international order, Russia had already disappeared as an active participant in world affairs. The fledgling Bolshevik regime that had seized power in November 1917 had paid a high price for the separate peace it concluded with Germany four months later, surrendering a quarter of Russia's territory and over a third of its population, as well as its most fertile food-producing region and most productive industrial areas. The

THE RUSSIAN INSPIRATION AND CHINESE COMMUNISM

The October Revolution in Russia occurred almost exactly six years after the overthrow of China's moribund Qing Dynasty in 1911. The intervening years had seen little progress towards the establishment of a stable, centralized government, with control growing steadily more fragmented and local warlords moving into the power vacuum in a number of areas. Under such circumstances the nascent Chinese communist movement began to gain strength. Li Dazhao, a student of political economy and head of the Beijing National University library, became convinced that communism represented the way forward for China. In November 1918, as allied troops celebrated the end of the First World War in the streets of Beijing, he wrote at length of the global implications of the Bolshevik victory. Li argued that the war represented the victory of revolutionary socialism over the forces of militarism and capitalism. According to him, a great tide of revolution 'à la Russe' would soon sweep across the world, motivated by the wartime awakening of the European proletariat. In the face of such a movement, 'all those dregs of history which can impede the progress of the

new movement—such as emperors, nobles, warlords, bureaucrats, militarism, capitalism— will certainly be destroyed as though struck by a thunderbolt.'

Between 1918 and 1921 Li attracted a number of Beijing students to the study of Marxism. In 1921, with assistance from agents of Moscow's COMINTERN, Li and Chen Duxiu, an outspoken writer and political leader, co-founded the Chinese Communist Party (CCP). Thereafter Li worked to secure the growth of Chinese communism through an alliance with like-minded members of the Chinese Nationalist Party (GMD) under Sun Yat-sen. Sun had also evidenced a good deal of sympathy for the Bolshevik movement; his wife, Soong Ching-ling, argued even more vociferously that the new Chinese government must draw its inspiration from and maintain strong connections to the Soviet Union. According to Soong, '[j]ust as he [Sun] regarded the Chinese Communist Party as the most active revolutionary force in China, so he envisaged the Soviet Union as the most powerful revolutionary force in the world. . . . Sun was not afraid or ashamed to avow this revolutionary thesis.'

Bolsheviks defended this extraordinary sacrifice on the grounds that it would give the new regime a breathing spell while it consolidated its power. They were also supremely confident that the revolutionary forces unleashed in Russia would spread westward like wildfire, inciting the oppressed populations of all countries to overthrow their capitalist masters and establish their own 'soviet' republics. The free, independent, socialist states that would emerge from the ashes of the old empires would thereupon establish fraternal relations with the Russian regime from which they had drawn inspiration.

In the meantime, however, Lenin's authority over the shrunken remains of the tsarist empire was forcefully contested by armed counter-revolutionary groups that had spontaneously sprouted all along the periphery of Bolshevik-controlled territory. Tsarist officers raised southern Russia in revolt against the Bolsheviks while simultaneously trying to drive the Germans out of Ukraine. In Siberia, several anti-Bolshevik 'governments' sprang up under the protection of a 50,000-man legion of Czechoslovak prisoners of war and defectors who had served in the tsarist army against Austria before Russia's withdrawal from the war. In September 1918, the various anti-Bolshevik factions in Siberia united to form a provisional all-Russian government that eventually came under the control of Admiral Alexander Kolchak, former commander of the tsar's Black Sea Fleet. Kolchak assumed the title of 'Supreme Ruler' of Russia and obtained the allegiance of most of the leaders of the other anti-Bolshevik groups operating in the region, which together became known as the White Army. In the north, an anti-Bolshevik regime was established in the Arctic port of Murmansk. The tsarist General N.N. Yudenich assembled a counter-revolutionary army in Estonia to mount an assault on nearby Petrograd (from which Lenin had prudently withdrawn in March 1918 to set up his capital in Moscow).

The outbreak of the Russian Civil War gave the Allied governments the opportunity to attempt to exploit the situation to their advantage. The Americans and British feared that the military supplies they had sent to the previous Russian regime, which were stacked up on the wharves of Russian seaports on the Arctic and the Pacific, might find their way into German hands. To prevent this from happening, a small British force was landed at Murmansk in March 1918; British, American, and French troops occupied Archangel in August for the same purpose; and Japanese troops that had been landed at Vladivostok in April were eventually joined by a much smaller American contingent. These Allied military forces, which included a detachment from Canada, co-operated closely with the anti-Bolshevik governments in the hinterlands of the port cities that they now occupied. The Americans and the British confined their activities to protecting the army stores and were reluctant to become embroiled in the civil war between Red and White Russians. But the French government had much more ambitious plans. It hoped that the various groups that had taken up arms against Lenin's regime could unite to form a strong, stable government willing and able to overthrow the Bolsheviks and resume the war against Germany. In the end, however, the anti-Bolshevik factions were never able to unite on a common program because they spanned the entire political spectrum, from tsarist reactionaries on the right to Mensheviks and Social Revolutionaries on the left. Hobbled by internecine ideological conflicts and clashes of personalities, the Whites gradually surrendered all the territory they had gained. By the end of 1920 the Red Army had defeated its counter-revolutionary enemies on all fronts, and the Russian Civil War had come to an end.

The purely military rationale for Allied intervention in the Russian Civil War disappeared when Germany capitulated in November 1918. But Allied troops remained in the northern Arctic ports until the autumn of 1919, and the Japanese did not leave Siberia until the end of 1922. By the latter year the Bolsheviks had liberated Russia of all foreign troops and recovered the frontiers of the former tsarist empire everywhere except in the west. There they faced the unrelenting hostility not only of the great powers that had defeated

Germany but also of the small independent states carved out of the former Russian territory lost at Brest-Litovsk: Finland, Latvia, Lithuania, and Estonia retained their independence under the protection of British warships operating in the Baltic. The greatly enlarged kingdom of Romania

THE LABOUR MOVEMENT IN CANADA AND THE WINNIPEG GENERAL STRIKE

The immediate threat of communist revolutions may have receded in the West, but social unrest remained a significant problem for many nations. The impact of the Russian Revolution was felt even in countries far removed from the upheaval in Europe.

In Canada, high rates of inflation and unemployment, combined with low wages and the lack of a collective-bargaining process, contributed to widespread post-war labour unrest. The situation was compounded by the return of war veterans looking for scarce jobs. At a meeting of labour leaders in Calgary in March 1919, delegates to the Western Labour Conference proposed the creation of a single industrial union (called the 'One Big Union') to battle for better working conditions and social justice.

Matters came to a head in May 1919, when a walkout by workers in Winnipeg's metal trades and building industries sparked a general strike in the city and a national crisis. As thousands of workers joined the strike—which soon spread to other cities, such as Toronto and Vancouver—some political leaders feared that Canada could be facing a communist revolution of its own. Opponents of the labour groups, including representatives of the city's business and professional elite, organized the Citizens' Committee of One Thousand to put an end to the strike, and with political tensions rising, the federal government sent a detachment of the Royal North-West Mounted Police to Winnipeg. On 21 June 1919, the Mounties confronted a group of war veterans demonstrating in support of the strike, and when the protestors refused to disperse, the police fired into the crowd. By the end of the day, which became known as 'bloody Saturday', two people had been killed, many more injured, and large numbers of strikers arrested.

In the aftermath of the strike, the federal government outlawed all organizations that supported the use of force to achieve political or economic reform in Canada; membership in any such organization was made a criminal offence punishable by 20 years in prison.

Striking workers tip a streetcar in Winnipeg, 21 June 1919. Provincial Archives of Manitoba, N2762.

retained control of the former Russian province of Bessarabia that it had seized during the revolution. And, most ominous of all, the proud, assertive, strongly anti-communist state of Poland had been reconstituted at Russia's gateway to Europe, with an eastern frontier extending far into former Russian territory.

Lenin's original plans for a Europe-wide communist revolution that would free the masses from their oppressors and remove the threat of aggression from the West went up in smoke during the first few months after the armistice. The few attempts that had been made by indigenous revolutionary movements in Central Europe to establish communist regimes on the Russian model were ruthlessly crushed by counter-revolutionaries with the approval of the victorious allies. In January 1919, an insurrection in Berlin sponsored by the Spartacus League, a group of left-wing socialists inspired by the Bolsheviks' success in Russia, was quelled by the German government with the assistance of the army. A Soviet republic established in Bavaria in April was forcibly overthrown. The Hungarian communist regime set up in Budapest by Béla Kun (a veteran of the Russian Revolution) succumbed to a bloody counter-revolution supported by the invading army of Romania. In short, far from launching a worldwide socialist revolution, the Bolsheviks' triumph in Russia proved to be an isolated event. The ideological hostility of the victorious Allies, coupled with the energetic opposition of the anti-communist elites that took control of the new states in Central and Eastern Europe, succeeded in halting the spread of communism. The Allied statesmen meeting in Paris to make peace could take heart from the fact that, though the triumph of Lenin's movement seemed imminent within Russia, the 'bacillus' of Bolshevism was being quarantined at the western border of the new Soviet state.

JUDGING THE PEACE OF PARIS

With the wisdom of hindsight, it is tempting to judge the Paris Peace Conference a failure. The last great diplomatic gathering of comparable importance, the Congress of Vienna in 1815, had established a framework for international order that had prevented Europe-wide war for a century. The Peace of Paris collapsed within a generation, ushering in a terrible period of totalitarianism, genocide, and war on a scale previously unimagined. Nonetheless, it must in fairness be recorded that the Treaty of Versailles failed less because of inherent defects than because it was never put into effect. Had Germany been compelled to fulfill its treaty obligations in their entirety, it would not have been capable of endangering the peace of Europe. Reduced to a token force and excluded forever from the Rhineland, the German army would have posed no military threat either to France or to the newly independent successor states to the east. Payment in full and on schedule of the relatively modest reparation sum fixed in May 1921 would have defused France's anxiety about its precarious economic condition and probably done much to reduce Franco–German tensions. Recently uncovered evidence of a genuine French desire to cooperate economically with Germany, particularly in the critical metallurgical sector (where French iron ore complemented German coking coal), suggests an opportunity for Franco–German reconciliation that was tragically lost.

The territorial losses suffered by Germany after the Great War do not appear to have been unduly harsh. The cession of Alsace–Lorraine to France merely restored the status quo ante of 1870 and was never seriously disputed by German officials. The loss of the Baltic port of Danzig and the 'corridor' connecting it to Poland was more objectionable because it isolated the German province of East Prussia and made overland transportation to the severed province inconvenient. Such inconvenience was nothing in comparison to the economic disadvantages that a landlocked Poland would have suffered. Furthermore, the creation of the corridor was not a serious violation of German nationality claims, since a majority of its inhabitants were Polish. Nor did it entail the loss of valuable natural resources that could not easily be obtained elsewhere. The same may be said for the cession to Poland of Upper Silesia, a coal-mining region of mixed Polish–German nationality. The coal output of the Ruhr and Saar covered all Germany's domestic needs as well as the reparations it owed to France. But without the coal mines of Silesia, Poland would have had to import enormous quantities of this expensive fuel at a time when, as a fragile new state, it was struggling to put its financial house in order. Together with minor border rectifications to the benefit of Denmark and Belgium, these constituted the total amount of German territorial losses after the war.

Germany lost less territory at the peace conference than did any of its allies except Bulgaria. Among the defeated nations, Austria, Hungary, and Turkey did have grounds to complain of immoderate territorial losses. These complaints were of no consequence because they had lost all chance of regaining their former status as great powers. The terms imposed on Germany in 1919 were considerably less severe than the terms it had imposed on Russia in the Treaty of Brest-Litovsk. Despite its military defeat, Germany emerged from the Great War with the potential to become the most powerful nation on the continent. Its industrial heartland, unlike that of victorious France, survived undamaged and intact because the war had been fought beyond its frontiers. Germany's territorial losses did not decisively curtail its capacity for recovery, as the losses suffered by its allies did.

German publicists portrayed the final reparations bill as a matter of barbaric exploitation. But in fact the London Schedule adopted in May 1921 reduced the total amount owed so drastically that Germany could have managed the payments with only a moderate reduction of domestic consumption. That the German government and people refused to accept the reparations schedule and the economic sacrifices it entailed had little to do with the country's 'capacity to pay'. Rather, it reflected the German belief that *any* reparations, like *any* diminution of national territory, was unjust because in Germany's view it had *not* lost the war. In the east, it had defeated the Russian colossus and thrust it back out of Europe, according to plan. And in the west, its armies had marched home in orderly formation after their leaders had

negotiated an armistice they believed to have been based on the principle of 'no annexations, no indemnities'. There had been no destruction or military occupation of German land during the four years of the war. Under such conditions, it is not surprising that the German people would believe the charges, repeated over and over by national leaders after the war, that their fatherland had been deceived and betrayed by the victorious Allies. When all was said and done, the Versailles Treaty was not inherently unjust and unworkable: the problem was that the Germans thought it so and were able to win widespread support for that view at home and abroad.

Once Anglo–American support for the peace settlement of 1919 evaporated, the burden on France and the other continental beneficiaries of the treaty gradually became unbearable, and the new political order in Europe began to look increasingly unstable. By preserving the political and economic structure of the old German Reich while surrounding it with a variety of politically immature, militarily vulnerable, economically unstable states, the peacemakers had mandated a potentially explosive imbalance of power on the continent. The presence of substantial German-speaking minorities in the eastern successor states and the German majority in the new Austrian Republic represented constant temptation for the advocates of German expansionism. Their demands for the liberation of their compatriots and the recovery of this 'lost' territory challenged the legitimacy of the post-war political settlement long before Hitler set out to revise it. With Russia temporarily absent from Europe, the only effective deterrent to German expansion would have been a peacetime equivalent of the wartime coalition of Britain, France, and the United States, fortified by an inter-Allied military force in the Rhineland. As we shall see, the disintegration of the diplomatic coalition at the beginning of the 1920s and the premature disappearance of the deterrent force in the Rhineland at the end of that decade removed the only practical means of enforcing the treaty that was supposed to keep the peace in Europe for all time.

BOUNDARY CHANGES IN EUROPE AFTER THE FIRST WORLD WAR

SUMMARY

With the armistice of November 1918, a long and difficult peace process began. The dismantling of the Russian, German, Austro–Hungarian, and Ottoman empires during and after the war left a power vacuum that stretched from Asia to Western Europe. International boundaries had to be redrawn and new nations carved out of the old imperial territories. In addition, decisions needed to be made about how to reward the victors and penalize those held responsible for the war.

The process of establishing a formal peace settlement began in Paris in January 1919. Although representatives of 27 victorious nations attended the peace conference, it was dominated by the United States, Britain, and France. The Peace of Paris, or Versailles Peace Settlement, as it came to be known, consisted of a series of treaties negotiated between 1919 and 1923.

Competing agendas among the victors made it hard to reach consensus from the outset. In particular, Britain and France disagreed on the proper penalties for Germany and its allies. Fearing another arms buildup and an attack across its eastern border, France sought extensive economic reparations from and military restrictions against Germany, but Britain argued that such harsh measures would have disastrous effects on the post-war economy and European political stability. Russian officials sought to reclaim the large territories awarded to Germany under the Treaty of Brest-Litovsk. For its part, the United States proposed an idealistic program designed to forge a new framework for managing international relations, encapsulated in President Wilson's Fourteen Points.

The final settlement left Italy and Japan, as secondary powers among the victorious Allies, unsatisfied with the final settlement because they felt entitled to a greater portion of the territorial spoils. As for Germany—singled out as the sole instigator of the war—it was penalized with economic reparations, stripped of its colonial possessions, and prohibited from military rearmament. Although these terms were not unusually severe in world history, many people in Germany and elsewhere considered them too harsh, and support for the Peace of Paris soon waned in the United States and Britain. The opportunities for true international co-operation were squandered in the early 1920s, and the problem of European security was left to fester for another generation.

NOTES

1. France and Britain pursued divergent policies during the Greco–Turkish conflict of 1920–2, with Paris supporting the Turks and London backing the Greeks. In addition, France suspected Britain of undermining French authority in Syria, which it acquired in 1920 as a mandate under the League of Nations.

QUESTIONS FOR CRITICAL THOUGHT

1. How could the Paris Peace Conference delegates have achieved their goals of repairing the political and economic damage done by the war and of ensuring that there would be no recurrence of war?
2. Which nations would have benefited from Woodrow Wilson's Fourteen Points (as he originally conceived of them)?
3. Consider the promises made during the war and discuss whether a more equitable settlement could have been reached.
4. Were the demands of the British and French unreasonable, given the circumstances? Why or why not?
5. Why was Woodrow Wilson unable to secure American support for the peace settlement and the League of Nations?
6. Did 'inherent defects' or lack of full enforcement doom the Treaty of Versailles?

WEBSITES FOR FURTHER REFERENCE

The Avalon Project: Covenant of the League of Nations
   http://avalon.law.yale.edu/20th_century/leagcov.asp

The Avalon Project: Treaty of Versailles, 28 June 1919
   http://avalon.law.yale.edu/subject_menus/versailles_menu.asp

Canada and the First World War
   www.collectionscanada.gc.ca/firstworldwar/index-e.html

World War I Document Archive: Conventions and Treaties
   wwi.lib.byu.edu/index.php/Conventions_and_Treaties

CHAPTER 3

THE 1920s: ERA OF ILLUSIONS

THE ILLUSION OF ECONOMIC RESTORATION

The massive dislocations caused by the Great War and the pain of adjustment to peacetime conditions prompted widespread nostalgia for the economic system that had operated with relative effectiveness before 1914. As governments sought to resurrect the tried-and-true practices of the pre-war era, a handful of observers warned that the war had so transformed political and economic structures that there was no possibility of a return to the 'good old days'. But their warnings went unheeded. A superficial economic recovery during the second half of the 1920s concealed the cracks in the international economic relations that had been reconstructed on the shaky foundations of the post-war world. The return of prosperity enabled national leaders to ignore the systemic weaknesses in the world economy and avoid introducing the bold new policies needed to fit the new realities. It would take the total unravelling of the international trade and investment network in the 1930s to convince political leaders that the pre-war era was gone forever and a new mechanism for the allocation of the world's productive resources was required.

The first five years of peace were marked by severe economic depression in some countries and a general slowdown in international economic activity. The problem was not that production had declined. The world's physical capacity to produce goods and services had not been seriously reduced—except in those unfortunate regions of northeastern France, Belgium, and the European portion of the USSR that had served as the principal theatres of combat during the war. The problem lay in the channels for the distribution of productive factors—that is, the international network of trade, investment, and migration. The relatively efficient system for the international exchange that had eased the West's transition to an international industrial order in the second half of the nineteenth century no longer existed.

The sluggish recovery of world trade in the early post-war years was directly related to developments in the political and economic relations among the nations of continental Europe. Among the most important of these developments was the spread of economic nationalism. This phenomenon was a natural outgrowth of the war, which had revealed the advantages of economic self-sufficiency and the dangers of dependence on foreign markets and sources of supply. Most economic experts, and many political leaders, had recognized the folly of pursuing total self-sufficiency in Europe. None of the European nations involved in the Great War had possessed sufficient food-producing land, raw materials, or markets within its own borders to sustain itself. During the war, recognition of the need for continental economic partnerships had prompted schemes for multilateral co-operation, but by the end of the war they had been thoroughly discredited. Instead, Central Europe was reorganized following the principle of national self-determination. The number of independent economic units in Europe—within which productive factors could circulate without restriction—increased from 20 to 27 as the integrated economic systems of Austria and Hungary were shattered and parcelled out among seven states (including three newly created ones), while five new nations were carved out of the western borderlands of Russia.

A negative economic consequence of this territorial distribution was the disruption of regional economic patterns. Urban centres such as Vienna were cut off from the agricultural hinterlands that had supplied them with food; industrial sectors such as the Bohemian region of Czechoslovakia were separated from their traditional sources of raw materials in those parts of the Habsburg Empire that had been allocated to other states. New frontiers often cut across the most efficient transportation routes. The national unification process that Western Europe underwent in the nineteenth century had enlarged economic units and increased productivity and efficiency through economies of scale. By contrast, the nation-building process in Eastern Europe after the First World War reduced the size of existing economic units, decreasing productivity and efficiency. Whereas products, resources, capital, and labour had circulated relatively freely within the Austro–Hungarian Empire before the war, now they ran up against all kinds of political restrictions imposed by successor states anxious to nurture their infant industries: new tariffs, import quotas, and government subsidies inhibited the revival of

intra-European commerce after the war. To make matters worse, ideological hostility to the Soviet regime severely restricted European access to the extensive natural resources and potentially lucrative markets of the USSR.

The clogging of the traditional channels of trade within Europe was a microcosm of the commercial crisis that gripped the entire world during the first half of the 1920s. The spirit of economic nationalism was not limited to the new or newly enlarged nations of Europe. During the war, nations in the western hemisphere and the Far East had established or expanded their domestic industries in order to produce substitutes for manufactured products that could no longer be obtained from Europe. As a result, by 1918 Canada, Japan, India, Australia, and several countries in Latin America were all producing goods in direct competition with Europe's principal exports. Investors, managers, and labour groups with stakes in the profitability of those fledgling enterprises naturally clamoured for government protection against the anticipated influx of products from an economically revitalized Europe. Even the victorious powers of Western Europe—which had the most to gain from a revival of world trade because of their superior productive capacity—retained a number of wartime restrictions on imports of 'luxury items' (defined in the broadest possible sense) to preserve the domestic markets for national enterprises struggling to regain the productivity lost during the war.

The United States, for its part, adopted a strongly protectionist policy after the war. The Emergency Tariff Act of May 1921 and the Fordney–McCumber Tariff of the following year raised duties to their highest levels in modern American history. These restrictive commercial measures were the result of intense pressure exerted by domestic agricultural and manufacturing interests that feared future competition from the replanted farmlands and re-equipped industries of Europe. In conjunction with this new protectionist policy, successive administrations waged a vigorous campaign to promote the country's export trade and supported the efforts of American firms to gain access to markets and resources previously controlled by European concerns. A prime example of this business–government partnership to expand American economic power overseas was the successful campaign by American petroleum companies, strongly backed by the State Department, to break the British monopoly on the oil reserves of Iraq, Saudi Arabia, and the sheikdoms along the Persian Gulf. In the meantime, Washington mounted a spirited challenge to Britain's domination of the international carrying trade. The Merchant Marine Act of 1920 authorized the sale of government-owned vessels to private shipping companies at bargain prices, while subsequent legislation granted public subsidies for the construction of new merchant ships. Even though economists warned that it was counterproductive for the US to try to compete with European merchant fleets, since higher labour costs made shipbuilding in the US more expensive than elsewhere, national pride prevailed: American goods should be carried by American ships, regardless of cost.

The revival of protectionism and economic nationalism was accompanied by an important change in the structure and direction of world trade. We have already noted that the European powers' wartime diversion of productive capacity to the manufacturing of munitions and military supplies caused a drastic decline in their export trade—a decline aggravated by Britain's blockade policy and Germany's submarine warfare. We have also noted that this cutoff of European supplies compelled many neutral nations to compensate by developing their own industries. Other nations, however, lacked the productive factors that would have enabled them to replace European imports with their own domestic output, and these countries increasingly turned to the United States or Japan as alternative sources of industrial products. Consequently, the US replaced Britain as the principal trading partner of Latin America and surged far ahead of Germany and France, while Japan (whose output of manufactured goods doubled between 1913 and 1921) made substantial inroads into

British markets in Asia for textile products made of cotton and wool.

Similarly, the opening of new coal mines in the United States, India, and South Africa, together with the emergence of Middle Eastern petroleum as an alternative source of energy, caused a serious decline in the coal exports that, together with textiles, had accounted for the bulk of Britain's pre-war export trade. These new commercial relationships persisted after the war. When the European powers sought to recapture their traditional markets abroad, they found themselves excluded on the one hand by political restrictions and on the other by economic competition from upstart economic powers. During the same period, Europe's share of the previously lucrative American market declined precipitously. Before the war, Europe accounted for more than 50 per cent of the total value of goods imported by the US; in the 1920s that figure dropped to about 30 per cent.

One reason for the decline in Europe's share of the American market was the increase in trade between the United States and Canada. After 1918, Canada's own economic focus began to shift away from Britain and toward the US. By 1924 there was more American than British capital invested in Canada. At the same time, Canada's own share of the export market in commodities expanded significantly. The Prairie provinces produced approximately 400 million bushels of wheat annually, supplying 40 per cent of the world market, and by 1930 Canada had also become the world's largest supplier of newsprint, producing over 2 million tons each year. Nor was the Canadian economic growth of the 1920s limited to commodities. The manufacturing sector, which was concentrated in Ontario, continued to expand, so that by 1923, Canada had become the world's second-largest producer of automobiles, exporting over 30 per cent of its total output.

The extent of the shift in the direction of international trade away from Europe and toward North America and Japan is indicated by a number of statistics. For example, between 1913 and 1929, the total value of all of the world's exports increased by two-thirds. During the same period, the total value of British, German, and French exports grew by 15, 33, and 50 per cent, respectively. But the total value of US exports doubled, while that of Japanese exports trebled. What these figures show is that Europe was gradually losing its position as the undisputed master of world trade. The acceleration of the two principal pre-war trends in international economic development—the United States' economic penetration of Latin America and Japan's commercial expansion in East Asia—required drastic adjustments in the structure of international economic relationships. Such spectacular shifts need not have produced international economic instability, but they were bound to cause serious disruption unless the world's emerging economic giants grasped the extent of their international responsibilities and worked to promote harmony in international economic exchange.

Unfortunately, the United States proved reluctant to bear its new obligations as the world's leading exporter and international investor. The first sign of this reluctance was the retreat into political isolation after the US Senate rejected the peace settlement of 1919. With a few minor exceptions, the US government declined to join the numerous international organizations established to enforce the peace treaties and preserve collective security. The absence of an American voice at the various international conferences held through the 1920s to address economic and security problems diminished their effectiveness and at the same time reduced Washington's ability to coordinate its foreign economic policies with those of the other industrial powers.

A second sign of the United States' reluctance to accept its international responsibilities was the contradictory nature of its financial and commercial practices, which served to undermine the country's dominant position in the world economic order. It is wholly inaccurate to apply the term 'isolationism' to US foreign economic policy in the 1920s. While the military and diplomatic presence of the US abroad was drastically reduced, its banking and trading interests were engaged in strenuous economic expansion that definitively

established it as a world financial and commercial power of the first rank. The way this expansion was managed created problems that were to damage and eventually unravel the fragile fabric of post-war international economic exchange.

Before the war, the principal movement of capital had been from Western Europe to primary producing regions for the purposes of developing underutilized resources. During the war that pattern changed, and capital went mainly from the United States to Europe to finance human and material destruction. In 1914, the US was a net debtor on international account by US$3.7 billion; by 1929, it was a net creditor by more than US$10 billion. Though American capital was put to different uses after the restoration of peacetime conditions, its direction remained largely the same: to the European continent. That meant that the US was lending to and investing in countries whose exports directly competed with its own products. Consequently, the protectionist commercial policies adopted by post-war US governments, together with the vigorous campaign to expand American exports and to wrest control of foreign raw materials and the shipping trade from the European nations, made it increasingly difficult for European debtors to earn sufficient foreign exchange to repay their creditors across the Atlantic. Throughout the 1920s, the US maintained a balance-of-trade surplus with Europe that averaged a billion dollars annually, as well as consistent balance-of-payments surpluses.

Unlike Great Britain in its heyday as the world's premier trading nation, the United States was reluctant to accept large quantities of raw materials, foodstuffs, and semi-finished industrial products from abroad in exchange for its continually expanding exports of finished manufactured goods. The source of this 'closed door' policy can be traced to the unique advantages enjoyed by the American economy: privileged access to a vast internal market and virtual self-sufficiency in manufactured goods, basic foodstuffs, and most industrial raw materials. Foreign trade therefore accounted for only a small proportion of the United States' gross national product—less than

10 per cent in 1929. Since American productivity was not significantly affected by the surpluses and deficits in international accounts, there was little incentive for Washington to devise foreign economic policies that would promote the kind of commercial and financial stability that had been one of the principal goals of British foreign economic policy in the nineteenth century. Instead, Washington responded to domestic pressures to insulate the domestic market even further from foreign competition while at the same time encouraging the expansion of American exports. This combination of import protectionism and export expansionism violated an elementary principle of international economics. Trade is a two-way street: customers cannot afford to buy your products unless they can sell you the fruits of their own labour. Nor can your debtors repay you unless they can acquire a sufficient amount of your currency by selling you their products or services.

An equally debilitating influence on international economic stability was price inflation in the industrial countries of the world. During the Great War, most of the belligerent and many of the neutral nations had abandoned the gold standard in order to conserve scarce reserves of gold and foreign exchange. The suppression of the free international movement of gold during and immediately after the war disrupted the customary connection between national price systems and permitted prices to fluctuate independently in each nation. Some countries, including Germany, Austria, and the Soviet Union, suffered such drastic hyperinflation in the early post-war years that their currencies collapsed altogether. The scourge of inflation also hit France, where wholesale prices after the war increased by eight times their 1913 level, and Italy, where they rose about sevenfold. On the international level, exchange instability increased the risks of both short-term lending to finance trade and long-term lending to promote economic development. Thus investors were understandably hesitant to transfer their assets into a foreign currency whose value fluctuated wildly against their own, while exporters were reluctant to exchange valuable goods

for paper money that continued to lose value as domestic prices rose.

In addition to these obstacles to the free international exchange of surplus capital and production, the international movement of labour was severely curtailed by politically motivated restrictions. Just as American producers strove to exclude foreign products from their domestic market, American labour organizations pressed their government to stem the influx of foreign immigrants in order to limit competition for employment. In 1924, the US Congress established immigration quotas that discriminated against the very regions of the world (Eastern and Southern Europe and Asia) that suffered from overpopulation. Before the Great War, people inhabiting densely populated areas with poor economic prospects (such as Italy and the Austro–Hungarian Empire) migrated to underpopulated regions with plentiful resources, land, and employment opportunities (such as the United States). During the 1920s, average annual immigration to the US dropped by over 50 per cent from its pre-war level. Although the US was not the only potential destination for immigrants, this reduction meant that overpopulated areas faced ever greater internal pressures on land, food, and natural resources. As in the analogous case of tariff protection, it also meant that wages in the US remained at a higher level than would have been the case had immigrants been permitted to enter the country and compete for jobs.

Free trade and free immigration—the unrestricted international exchange of resources and labour—remained unfulfilled dreams for those who wished to restore the pre-war system of international economic relations in the 1920s. Nevertheless, a considerable degree of financial stability was restored in the world. The only obvious solution to the scourge of inflation and exchange instability in the early 1920s was a return to the international financial arrangements of the pre-war era, when a single nation blessed with substantial capital reserves—Great Britain—supplied the necessary liquidity to balance international accounts, and the gold standard ensured that national currencies were convertible on the basis of a fixed relationship to gold.

The temptation to return to the gold standard eventually proved so powerful as to overcome all objections to linking the economic fortunes of the world to what the British economist John Maynard Keynes once contemptuously referred to as 'that barbarous relic'. The return to gold was not easy for many nations, particularly those whose currencies had drastically depreciated during the war: restoring the gold standard at pre-war parities re-established exchange rates that considerably overvalued their currencies, thereby rendering their exports prohibitively expensive in foreign markets. This was precisely the position of Britain, which made the mistake of returning to the gold standard at the pre-war parity of US$4.86. Other nations, such as France and Italy, took the precaution of devaluing their currencies in terms of their pre-war parity, so as to bring their external value down to the level of their depreciated value and retain the competitive price advantage of their exports. Between 1925 and 1929 more than 40 nations, including all of those with a significant stake in international trade, returned to the gold standard. By the end of the decade, the familiar method of adjusting international accounts had been universally re-established. But, as always, it depended on the solidity of the principal reserve currencies (in this case, the British pound and the American dollar) and the willingness of the two governments that issued them to buy and sell gold at a specified price to preserve the convertibility of the world's currencies.

Equally important for international monetary stability was the revival of long-term foreign investment. By the middle of the 1920s the total amount of foreign lending had surpassed its pre-war level, with the United States replacing Britain as the principal source of this international capital flow. Between 1920 and 1929, American private lenders furnished US$7.6 billion in loans abroad, of which $7.3 billion were outstanding at the end of 1929. Though on a much more modest scale, Britain and France resumed their roles as net exporters of capital in the early 1920s. This revival of foreign lending supplied the foreign exchange required to conduct international trade, repay existing debts, and stimulate economic development.

However, the new international financial system forged in the 1920s differed from its pre-war predecessor in several important respects. The law of supply and demand should have dictated the resumption of large-scale capital flows from those nations with a surplus of savings over domestic investment opportunities as well as high labour costs to regions with abundant but under-utilized resources and cheap labour. That would have meant the export of capital from the United States and, to a lesser extent, Britain and France, to the primary producing regions of the earth (particularly Latin America and East Asia, which had already begun to receive substantial infusions of investment capital before the war). But as Wall Street replaced the City of London as the 'banker of the world', the volume, character, and direction of foreign investment were transformed.

First of all, the proportion of its gross capital formation that the United States lent abroad was much smaller than the proportion lent by Britain before 1914. The resulting accumulation of gold and foreign exchange in the US was in large part due to the speculative boom on Wall Street, which drove stock prices to heights entirely unrelated to the real assets that those securities represented. The prospect of selling these stocks at higher prices in a short period of time attracted large quantities of domestic and foreign capital that otherwise would have been available for short-term lending to balance international accounts and long-term credits to increase the productive capacity of America's trading partners and debtors. In short, the lure of spectacular capital gains on the US stock market prevented the New York banking community from assuming its rightful role as the supplier of liquidity in international economic transactions. To make matters worse, the periodic attempts by the Federal Reserve Board to dampen the speculative boom by increasing interest rates attracted a flood of foreign capital into the American money market in search of higher returns.

Second, the foreign lending that the United States

did undertake in the 1920s differed from previous British lending in both character and direction. In the pre-war years, most European foreign investments were channelled into the development of productive enterprises and transportation systems (such as railways, roads, and ports) in developing countries in order to help them produce, transport, and export products that were desired in Europe. By contrast, most American foreign loans in the 1920s went to European governments and municipalities to finance public works projects such as bathhouses, parks, and urban housing. Such consumption-oriented amenities may have been necessary, but they did not increase productive capacity of the recipient countries or improve their ability to earn the foreign exchange required to finance their imports and service their foreign debts. The proportion of American lending that did go to productive enterprises tended to take the form of short-term loans financing long-term projects. This anomalous arrangement left the debtor countries vulnerable to default in hard times and dependent on the perpetual renewal of American credit.

A great deal has been written about inter-Allied debts and German reparations as disruptive factors in the international economy of the 1920s. It has often been suggested that these intergovernmental obligations inhibited post-war economic recovery by generating international capital movements that were entirely unrelated to commercial transactions or investment opportunities.

Before the war, capital exports reflected the free choice of individual investors, or of the banks in which they deposited their savings, as they sought the highest return (consistent with safety) for their funds. After the war, however, many of the world's governments owed considerable sums to other governments for debts (either contractual or moral) incurred in the course of the war. To discharge these obligations, the debtor governments would have had to raise the funds domestically and then convert them into the currencies of the creditor nations. Thus these politically defined debts represented distortions in the normal flow of international payments.

The first category of these intergovernmental debts consisted of the roughly US$10 billion lent by the United States to the governments of 20 nations during or immediately after the Great War. More than 90 per cent of that sum was owed to the US by its three principal associates in the war: Britain, France, and Italy (see Table 3.1). These funds had been raised by the sale of war bonds to American citizens after the US entered the war in April 1917. The proceeds of these bond sales were used to finance Allied purchases of American supplies required to fight the war and, after the armistice, to begin post-war reconstruction. Although these debts appeared on the books and therefore were theoretically payable on demand, in the spirit of wartime co-operation the American government did not raise the issue of repayment until 1922, when the Harding and

---

TABLE 3.1   MAJOR WARTIME AND POST-WAR FOREIGN LOANS BY THE UNITED STATES GOVERNMENT (IN MILLIONS OF DOLLARS)

Recipient Nation	Pre-Armistice	Post-Armistice	Total
Britain	3,696.0	581.0	4,277.0
France	1,970.0	1,434.8	3,404.8
Italy	1,031.0	617.0	1,648.0
Russia	187.7	4.9	192.6
Belgium	171.8	207.3	379.1

Source: Harold Moulton and Leo Pasvolsky, *War Debts and World Prosperity* (New York, 1932). p. 426. Reprinted by permission.

Coolidge administrations prodded the European debtors to begin negotiating repayment schedules.

The Europeans resisted this prodding. They argued that these loans represented America's contribution to the joint war effort and therefore should be drastically reduced or written off altogether. The United States had basked in isolation during the first three years of combat and then taken more than a year to field a fully trained and equipped army on the Western Front, while the European Allies had borne the brunt of German military power at great cost to themselves. The French, British, and Italians could not recover their dead soldiers. Why should the US be entitled to recover the funds that it had originally sent in place of men?

To this moral argument were added numerous economic ones. American claims that the loans represented an economic sacrifice were dismissed on the grounds that the money had been spent almost entirely in the United States to purchase American products, increasing American profits and employment and even indirectly benefiting the American treasury through the taxes generated by those sales. Moreover, it was universally predicted in Europe that the cancellation of inter-Allied debts would benefit US commerce. European treasury officials repeatedly reminded their American counterparts that Britain had forgiven the debts on the loans it advanced to its continental allies during the war against Napoleon and had thereafter been repaid many times over by a prosperous Europe that imported British manufactured goods. From a financial point of view, it seemed pure folly for a major creditor nation, which had lent billions of dollars abroad through private channels, to expect repayment of these government obligations. The rules of international finance suggested that the surplus funds that had accumulated in the US during and after the war ought to be recycled into those war-ravaged countries that required working capital for reconstruction; instead, Europe was being asked to increase the American capital surplus even further through debt payments that would be exceedingly difficult to manage.

The most cogent argument for cancellation centred on the inherent contradiction between Washington's post-war commercial policy and its insistence on debt repayment. On many counts it resembled the case against reparations presented by Germany and other interested parties. The European debtors did not possess sufficient reserves to pay in gold, and in any case such massive gold outflows would destroy the value of their currencies. Even if they could raise the principal amount of their debt in domestic paper currency, however, the Europeans lacked the balance-of-payment surplus to purchase the foreign currencies required to service the debt. Their dollar receipts from 'invisible exports'—shipping and insurance services, tourist expenditures, remittances from European immigrants abroad—were far below the level required to make up the difference. Therefore, the Europeans argued, the only way that they could accumulate the dollars required to discharge their obligation was by maintaining a continuously favourable balance of trade, especially with the creditor country. But the combination of protectionism and aggressive export promotion pursued by the Republican administrations of the 1920s made it difficult for European firms to gain access to the US market, while throwing open European markets to American products. Economists on both sides of the Atlantic scratched their heads trying to figure out how the European nations, in the midst of this chronic 'dollar shortage', could possibly satisfy American demands for debt repayment.

All the economic arguments in favour of debt cancellation made good sense. What they failed to take into consideration was the extent of America's insulation from the operations of the international economic system in the 1920s. As noted in regard to the post-war commercial policy of the United States, in the absence of a sense of international responsibility domestic pressure groups exercised a decisive influence on their government's foreign economic policy. The same was true with regard to the dispute over inter-Allied debts. American taxpayers refused to bear the burden of higher taxation that would be required to redeem the war bonds at maturity if the European governments failed to pay. Sensational news reports from Europe of lavish spending for armaments and luxury items reinforced this parsimonious state of mind. American war veterans clamoured for a 'bonus' as a belated reward for services rendered to the Allied cause. They bitterly recalled how their government had chosen to forego the generous separation allowances and veterans' pensions that had been written into the reparations section of the treaty for the benefit of their British and French counterparts. Agricultural and manufacturing interests in the US were deaf to technical arguments about the necessity of permitting European access to the American market in order to make debt repayment possible. Most important, American officials saw no distinction between public and private debts. These loans were regarded as normal business transactions. 'They hired the money, didn't they?' asked President Calvin Coolidge. To forgive intergovernmental obligations would undermine the sanctity of contracts and set a dangerous precedent that European recipients of American private loans might be tempted to invoke at some future date.

Responding to these domestic pressures, the US Congress established the World War Foreign Debt Commission in February 1922 and instructed it to reach agreement with the European debtors at a minimum interest rate of 4.25 per cent and a maximum maturity of 25 years. Bilateral negotiations on the debt settlement dragged on for several years, while the State Department pressured recalcitrant governments to come to terms by encouraging an informal embargo on private loans to the guilty parties. As a result, all of the major debtors had signed funding agreements by 1926. The total interest charges more than doubled the original debt, though the rates were much lower and the maturities much longer than had been stipulated in the act creating the commission. The annual debt payments came to approximately a third of a billion dollars a year, which represented a significant portion of Europe's current dollar income from merchandise exports to the United States.

France, the major holdout, finally signed a funding agreement in April 1926, but the French parliament delayed ratification until the summer of 1929, when Germany's acceptance of the Young Plan—an American-inspired proposal for definitive resolution of the reparations problem—promised sufficient reparation payments to France to cover France's debt payments to the United States. It was the issue of German reparations, more than any other, that poisoned the atmosphere of international relations during the 1920s. Though recent research has shown that the economic consequences of the reparations settlement were less dramatic than had been feared, the political passions sparked by this issue on all sides played a major role in undermining the structure of European security that had been fashioned at the Paris Peace Conference.

Most of the issues that emerged in the course of France's effort to collect reparations from Germany in the early 1920s had already been aired at the peace conference. The first of these was the familiar question of Germany's 'capacity to pay'. How much of the German people's income could be taxed by their government and applied to the reparation debt without destroying the nation's productive capacity? No one doubted that a bankrupt, unproductive Germany (however attractive that prospect might have appeared to neighbouring nations fearful of the military consequences of German economic recovery) would be incapable of paying anyone anything. It was also universally understood that in order for Germany to discharge its obligation, its people would have to reduce their consumption and bear the burden of higher taxes. These austerity measures would release domestically produced goods for export and reduce domestic demand for imports, generating a trade surplus that would enable Germany to accumulate sufficient foreign exchange to pay the annual instalment on its reparation debt.

The German people, and the German government, refused to make such a sacrifice. Far from submitting to the deflationary fiscal and monetary policy that such belt-tightening required, the Weimar Republic[1] experienced one of the most extraordinary bouts of hyperinflation that the world has seen. Whether, as some unfriendly critics have suggested, that inflation was deliberately engineered by the German government to sabotage the reparations plan or whether it was caused by economic forces beyond anyone's control, remains a matter for debate. The result was unmistakable: the nation that was supposed to consume less and produce more in order to compensate the French for their wartime losses began falling behind on its payments as its currency depreciated and its domestic prices soared.

It may have been unrealistic to suppose that any nation would freely consent to a reduction in its standard of living in order to compensate former enemies for damage claims it regarded as inflated and unjust. But the only alternative to a mutually acceptable contractual obligation is one based on coercion. When Germany repeatedly defaulted on reparation payments throughout the year 1922, the government of French Prime Minister Raymond Poincaré chose to use military force to compel payment. On 9 January 1923, the French-controlled Reparation Commission officially declared Germany in default on coal deliveries. Two days later, French, Belgian, and Italian technicians, on the express instructions of the commission and protected by a small military force, entered the industrial heartland of Germany in the Ruhr Valley to procure the coal owed as reparations. When the Berlin government ordered the miners and railway workers to withhold their co-operation, many more French and Belgian troops were sent in to seal off the Ruhr from the rest of Germany and preserve domestic order while the technical personnel mined the coal and operated the railways that transported it to the frontier.

All nations concerned profited handsomely from the Ruhr occupation. France obtained the coal it required as the German campaign of passive resistance petered out and finally ended in September 1923. British exports of coal and pig iron soared as continental customers who were cut off from their traditional suppliers in the Ruhr turned to British substitutes. Even the German government profited (along with private heavy industry), discharging much of its domestic debt in currency debased by its profligate printing of paper money to pay unemployment benefits to the striking workers of the Ruhr. The only major losers amid the hyperinflation that engulfed the country in 1923–4 were middle-class Germans living on fixed incomes, who lost their life savings along with their confidence in the future.

The short-term benefits of French coercion in the Ruhr did not alleviate the structural weaknesses of the European economic system. Although there was little evidence that the slow pace of post-war economic recovery was caused by the reparations dispute, official opinion in Britain and the United States increasingly came to accept this explanation. In addition to the problem of Germany's capacity to pay, the transfer problem that had bedevilled the Paris Peace Conference loomed large in the thinking of Anglo–American officials as they observed the unilateral French intervention in western Germany. The problem was that the transfer of such massive quantities of real wealth across national boundaries would inevitably disrupt the economies of debtor and creditor alike, discourage foreign investment, and endanger world trade. Domestic producers in Britain feared an influx of cheap articles 'made in Germany', while British exporters feared German competition in foreign markets that they were striving to recapture. American trading interests, eagerly eyeing the German market, worried about the decline in Germany's capacity to import that such large reparations payments would entail. Wall Street investment houses hesitated to commit funds to Germany so long as its government was saddled with a huge reparations burden.

By the end of 1923, a consensus had formed in English-speaking financial circles in favour of a comprehensive reparations settlement. The onset of a severe financial crisis in France at the beginning of 1924—caused mainly by the French government's refusal to increase domestic taxation once it became evident that German reparations were not going to finance reconstruction of the devastated northeast—gave British and American bankers the leverage they needed to impose a new reparations regime on the authorities in

Paris. A committee of economic experts, headed by American banker Charles Dawes, had been appointed by the Reparation Commission to study the problem and propose a solution. The Dawes Committee Report, submitted in April 1924, proposed a complex system of annual payments that could be adjusted to Germany's capacity to pay, provided for a large private international (but mainly American) loan to Germany in order to facilitate the payment, and effectively destroyed France's controlling position on the Reparation Commission. In national elections that spring, the Poincaré government, which had carried out the occupation of the Ruhr and consistently refused all compromise with Germany, was defeated and replaced by a government headed by the more conciliatory Édouard Herriot. Alarmed by the collapse of the franc and tempted by the prospect of Anglo–American financial assistance, the new French government officially accepted the Dawes Plan at the London Conference of July 1924.

The Dawes Plan fundamentally changed the reparation section of the Treaty of Versailles by abolishing France's legal authority to compel German payment by unilateral fiat. The emasculation of the Reparation Commission and the evacuation of French military forces from the Ruhr in August 1925 removed forever the threat of military force as an option in French reparation policy. Through an elaborate financial sleight of hand, voluntary American capital investment replaced the coerced diversion of German production as the engine of European economic reconstruction. In a sense, this represented a modified version of the original French plan for European recovery, unveiled at the peace conference and subsequently rejected by the United States. The only major difference was in the source and direction of the capital movements involved. The funds would be supplied by private investment firms in New York instead of the Treasury Department in Washington. They would be recycled through the German economic system instead of flowing directly to the Allied nations in need of working capital for reconstruction and debt service. Between 1924 and 1931, private American investors lent

US$2.25 billion to Germany; Germany resumed its reparation payments to the Allied states; and the latter in turn forwarded about $2 billion to the US in repayment for the wartime loans.

These changes to the reparation system had two important long-term consequences. First, the economic recovery of Europe became directly dependent on the willingness or ability of American investment banks to maintain a continuous flow of private funds to the national and municipal governments of Germany. Second, the fact that the major portion of those funds went to Germany meant that the defeated nation was able to discharge its reparation debt and re-equip its industries with capital supplied almost entirely by its former enemy.

The apparent settlement of the reparations dispute, coinciding as it did with the influx of American capital, greatly assisted Europe's recovery. By the end of 1925, industrial production and real wages in most continental nations had returned to their pre-war levels, and they continued to rise for the rest of the decade. The only countries that did not participate in the explosion of economic activity were those in the food-producing regions of the southern hemisphere and Eastern Europe, where persistent overproduction so exceeded world demand for foodstuffs that it caused a catastrophic drop in the prices of commodities such as wheat, corn, sugar, coffee, and cocoa.

The causes of this agricultural overproduction can be traced directly to the First World War. The sharp decline in European food production during the war drove up commodity prices on the world market, which in turn prompted farmers on other continents to increase their acreage. In Canada, the result was a boom in wheat production, but prices fell as market conditions deteriorated after the war. In the 1920s, the fertile farmlands of France and Eastern Europe quickly returned to their pre-war production levels, in part because the introduction of better fertilizers and mechanization sharply increased the yield per acre. The resulting agricultural surpluses accumulated unsold because of income inelasticity in the industrial world; in other words, although incomes rose in the developed countries of Western Europe, North America, and Japan, people did not spend their additional money on more food. At the same time, regions of the southern hemisphere with large undernourished and even starving populations could not afford to purchase that agricultural output even at depressed prices. It was a tragic paradox of the inter-war period that the food-producing regions of the earth, such as the newly independent countries of Eastern Europe, brought to the world market more of their cash crops than the industrial nations could consume, and at prices higher than the hungry nations could pay. The resulting agricultural depression in turn applied a brake to the economic expansion of the industrialized nations of Western Europe, which found it increasingly difficult to sell their surplus manufacturing output to the hard-pressed primary producing areas of the world. Thus the remarkable economic growth experienced by the industrial nations of the North Atlantic region in the second half of the 1920s concealed the ominous global implications of the chronic agricultural crisis that gripped the southern hemisphere and Eastern Europe during the same period. The illusion of Western prosperity survived so long as the engine of American financial power and industrial productivity continued to operate at peak efficiency.

THE CONFIRMATION OF US SUPREMACY IN LATIN AMERICA

From 1914 to 1932, American governments intervened directly in the domestic affairs of Latin American countries. In addition to acquiring the Virgin Islands, the United States exerted military domination and financial control over Cuba, Panama, Haiti, the Dominican Republic, and Nicaragua. The US replaced Britain as the major commercial and financial power in Latin America. The establishment of undisputed strategic mastery of the Caribbean and economic preponderance in South America was facilitated by the weakening of European economic power in the western hemisphere during the war and then confirmed by the inability of the exhausted European states to recapture their pre-war positions in the 1920s.

Between the end of the Spanish–American War in 1898 and the beginning of the First World War in 1914, the Caribbean Sea had been transformed into the equivalent of an American lake. Through a variety of means—financial supervision, commercial penetration, diplomatic agreements, and military force—the United States had acquired effective control of the political and economic systems of some of the islands in the Caribbean and the mainland republics of Central America that had achieved independence. The European powers, particularly Britain, acquiesced in this extension of American power because they were absorbed by their own colonial rivalries in Africa and Asia in addition to the power struggles in Europe that would result in the First World War.

It is ironic that Woodrow Wilson, the champion of national self-determination and critic of 'dollar diplomacy'[2] in Latin America, conducted more military and diplomatic interventions south of the border than any American president before or since. Wilson had genuinely persuaded himself of the essential morality of his interventionist policies in the Caribbean. A passionate proponent of good government, he cringed at the corruption, inefficiency, autocracy, and social unrest that plagued many of the United States' southern neighbours. The progressive idealist thus set out to impose order, honesty, and efficiency on the Caribbean republics for their own good.

However, beneath Wilson's disinterested idealism lay the same preoccupation that had prompted earlier interventionist policies by his Republican predecessors: the fear that political revolution, social instability, and financial collapse in the Caribbean region would tempt the great powers of Europe to intervene to protect the lives and investments of their citizens. The prospect of European powers involved militarily, or even financially, in a region critical to the security of the Panama Canal was more than any American president could tolerate.

Behind a smokescreen of progressive rhetoric about America's obligation to foster good government in its own hemisphere, Wilson resumed William Howard Taft's policy of military intervention and dollar diplomacy in Latin America. The first beneficiary of this new form of American heavy-handedness couched in the language of Wilsonian benevolence was Nicaragua. The Bryan–Chamorro Treaty (signed in 1914 and ratified two years later) transferred supervisory authority over Nicaragua's finances from American private bankers to a commission controlled directly from Washington. The US government advanced funds to the financially strapped Nicaraguan regime to reduce its public debt in return for an exclusive concession to construct a trans-Isthmian canal and establish naval bases.

This agreement had three purposes: to protect the northern land approach to the Panama Canal, to prevent any future European-constructed canal along the alternative Nicaraguan route, and, by rehabilitating Nicaragua's finances, to remove any possible pretext for European intervention. The American marine contingent that had been landed in 1912 was retained and augmented to provide the necessary armed support for the policy of financial reorganization.

It was the right of intervention that became the focal point of attacks on US hegemony that enlivened pan-American conferences in the 1920s. This prerogative, which was generally recognized in international law and specifically codified in the so-called Roosevelt Corollary of the Monroe Doctrine, was periodically reasserted

JAPANESE POWER IN THE INTERWAR ERA

Like the United States, Japan had largely escaped any physical damage during the First World War and had seized the opportunities created by wartime economic demand to increase its own industrial production and market penetration. In 1913 Japan accounted for just 2.7 per cent of world manufacturing production. By 1928 this had increased to 5.3 per cent, equal to the output of the Soviet Union and only marginally behind that of France. Despite these achievements, Japan faced a number of challenges in the 1920s. Global demand for manufactured goods decreased in the years immediately following the war. Depressed agricultural prices and low demand for silk combined to reduce Japan's economic growth; at the same time, continuing anti-Japanese sentiment, especially in the United States (most often expressed in the form of immigration quotas), prevented the large-scale emigration of surplus population. Labour unrest which had begun during the First World War in response to rising land and food prices (the price of rice rose 174 per cent during the war) continued throughout the 1920s. In 1923 the 'Great Kanto Earthquake' devastated Tokyo, destroying almost 75 per cent of the city's buildings and killing between 100,000 and 200,000 people.

On the international front, the gains made at the Paris Peace Conference were far less than the Japanese had expected and the Japanese proposal to include a statement of racial equality (or, at least, a statement denouncing racial discrimination) in the Covenant of the League of Nations had been rejected outright by the leaders of the other great powers. Subsequent attempts to work co-operatively with Britain and the United States during the era of Shidehara diplomacy led to similar frustrations. For example, the naval tonnage allotted to Japan at the Washington Naval Conference (1921–2) was less than Japanese diplomats had originally sought and seemed to confirm the view of Japan as an inferior nation. When combined with a number of poor political decisions and a major banking crisis in the late 1920s, the net result was an increase in sympathy for radical nationalist organizations that proposed stronger government, a halt to unchecked westernization, and increased colonial acquisitions as a solution to the problems besetting Japan in the 1920s.

by Washington. The right of foreign intervention was deeply resented in Latin America as a humiliating limitation to national sovereignty. In vain the southern republics tried to secure US acceptance of the Calvo Doctrine (after the Argentinian jurist Carlos Calvo), which asserted the absolute immunity of sovereign states from external intervention and recognized the judicial system of the host nation as the final authority in disputes involving foreign citizens or corporations. Though most Latin American nations customarily inserted a 'Calvo clause' in contracts signed with foreign investors (to preclude appeals to home governments for diplomatic support in disputes with the host government), the United States would not relinquish its right to intervene on behalf of its citizens if the host country refused to arbitrate. The Latin American states refused to recognize any obligation to submit such disputes to international arbitration, denouncing it as an intolerable infringement on national sovereignty. They pressed instead for the codification of an inter-American system of international law that would enshrine the principle of absolute equality and sovereignty of the nations of the western hemisphere. The US, for its part, opposed the concept of a regional international law that would deprive it of the traditional right of intervention sanctioned by international legal precedent.

THE ILLUSION OF CONTINENTAL SECURITY

Three themes characterize political relations among the nations of Europe in the 1920s, each reflecting the interests of one of the great powers:

1. the efforts of Germany to dismantle the peace treaty that restricted its economic, diplomatic, and military power;
2. the efforts of France and its continental allies to enforce those treaty limitations; and
3. the efforts of Britain, with the tacit encouragement of the United States, to remove the features of the peace treaty that were thought to be responsible for Germany's refusal to accept the new European order created at Versailles.

Throughout the first half of the 1920s, French governments devoted their diplomatic skills to the pursuit of one overriding objective: resurrection of the alliance with Britain that had lapsed in 1920 after the US Senate refused its consent to the French security treaty signed by President Wilson in Paris. The ostensible reason for Britain's rejection of its commitment to defend France against unprovoked German aggression was purely legalistic: the Anglo–French security pact was to become operational only as an integral component of the ill-fated Franco–American agreement. The real reason—which also accounts for London's subsequent refusal to replace that moribund treaty with a strictly bilateral guarantee of France's frontier with Germany—reflected Britain's conception of its national interest.

As always, British foreign policy was dictated by the interrelated objectives of protecting the British Isles, preserving the Empire, and controlling the sea communications between them. When German policy after the turn of the century had appeared to endanger those vital interests, Britain settled its differences with France and the USSR in North Africa and South Asia, respectively, in order to form a common front against any further accretion of German power. As a result of the Great War and the peace conference that terminated it, the principal threats to the security of Britain and its empire had been removed. Together, the abolition of the German air force, the reduction of the German navy to insignificance, and the dissolution of the German colonial empire now prevented Germany from projecting its power beyond the European continent. The internal disarray of the USSR removed the other potential threats to British imperial interests: aggression by land against India, disruption of the British lifeline to Asia, and pressure against British-controlled petroleum resources along the Persian Gulf. In fact, as long as Germany was disarmed and deprived of naval power and colonial bases, the USSR was blocked in Southeastern Europe and South Asia, and Japan remained content to confine its expansionist aspirations to the region north of the Yangtze River, the only conceivable peril to Britain's imperial communications came from France. France's ambitions in its newly acquired mandates in Syria and Lebanon, along with its intrigues in Turkey, caused considerable friction with Britain, which insisted on preserving its undisputed position of dominance in the eastern Mediterranean.

In conjunction with its 'Empire first' strategy, London reverted to its traditional policy of promoting a balance of power in Europe while striving to prevent any one of the great continental nations from amassing sufficient military might (especially air and naval power) to pose any threat of invasion across the English Channel. This policy inevitably inspired British opposition to France's quest for an overwhelming margin of military superiority over Germany. France in the 1920s possessed the most formidable land army and air force in the world. With military disarmament achieved in Germany by diplomatic fiat and in Britain and the United States by choice, France was the only former belligerent to retain land and air forces of wartime dimensions. Though unmistakably intended for defence of the eastern frontier, French air power alarmed British strategists, who realized that the English Channel no longer provided the security from attack that it had before the advent of the air age, particularly since Britain had begun to dismantle its own air forces shortly after the armistice.

It is no surprise, therefore, that Britain rejected French efforts to secure a British commitment to military defence of the territorial settlement in Western Europe. Refusal to promise France military assistance did not signify any willingness on Britain's part to tolerate German aggression against France. On the contrary, officials in London repeatedly affirmed that the security of France's eastern frontier was an extension of Britain's own security interests. 'Britain's frontier is on the Rhine' was the slogan of the new era. The problem lay in the conflicting views in Paris and London of how French and therefore British security could best be preserved. The French believed that the only effective way to prevent Germany from endangering the peace of Europe was to compel its strict adherence to the Versailles Treaty, since any modification

would encourage further efforts at revision. And a Germany freed from the restrictions imposed at the peace conference would inevitably threaten the political status quo on the continent because of its position as the most populous and potentially the most economically powerful nation in Europe. By contrast, British policy-makers contended that European security could best be assured by removing the irritants embedded in the Versailles Treaty that prevented Germany from accepting its reduced status in the world. Hence Britain's refusal to promise military aid to France against Germany, its campaign to reduce Germany's reparations burden, and its opposition to French efforts to compel German adherence to the Versailles Treaty by the threat or actual application of military sanctions. Underlying the British approach to European affairs was the conviction that a productive, stable, secure Germany could be enticed to rejoin the community of great powers as a peaceful, co-operative member. A Germany torn by economic chaos, political instability, and military insecurity could be expected to harbour resentment and to dream of revenge.

The disappearance of the Anglo–American guarantee of France's border with Germany in 1920 prompted France to begin a compensatory quest for allies among the states on the European continent with their own interest in preserving the post-war political settlement. In September 1920, France concluded a military alliance with Belgium, whose acquisition of the frontier districts of Eupen and Malmédy from Germany and whose strategic location astride the historic invasion route through Northern Europe made it a likely object of German aggression in any future war on the continent. This terminated Belgium's long-standing neutrality and formed the basis of close Franco–Belgian co-operation to enforce the provisions of the Versailles Treaty.

On the opposite flank of Germany lay those states of Eastern Europe that been formed or enlarged at the expense of the Central Powers after the war and therefore were prime candidates for inclusion in the emerging continental coalition. Foremost among them was Poland, which had been carved out of German, Austrian, and Soviet territory to form an independent republic in November 1918. Poland had obtained Allied recognition of its western frontiers with Germany in the Treaty of Versailles, acquiring thereby large parts of West Prussia and Posen (the corridor along the Vistula to the Baltic Sea) as well as special economic privileges in the port city of Danzig. German resentment of Poland's acquisition of this territory and a portion of Upper Silesia (an important industrial region of mixed German–Polish population that contained Germany's largest coal reserves), predisposed the government in Warsaw to seek the military protection of France. Paris responded favourably to these overtures from a fellow opponent of German revisionism, and in February 1921 the two states concluded a military alliance that was followed by extensive French economic assistance to Poland for armaments and national reconstruction.

In the meantime, the three nations in the Danube region that had acquired territory from Hungary after the war—Czechoslovakia, Romania, and Yugoslavia—concluded bilateral alliances with one another to deter Hungarian attempts to regain this lost land. Although this diplomatic association (which came to be known as the Little Entente) was directed against Hungary rather than Germany, French officials actively promoted it in the expectation that its three member states, in combination with Poland, could replace the USSR as a counterweight to German power in Eastern Europe. French hopes for such an eastern bloc were pinned on Czechoslovakia, the only signatory of the Little Entente that shared a common frontier with Germany and possessed the industrial and military capacity to pose a credible deterrent to German aggression in the region. The presence of more than three million German-speaking inhabitants in western Czechoslovakia and the efforts by nationalist elements in Germany to exploit their grievances against the Czechoslovakian state guaranteed a sympathetic response in Prague to the French efforts at alliance-making. In January 1924, the two countries concluded a bilateral pact that

provided for mutual assistance in the event of unprovoked aggression. Subsequent treaties of friendship with Romania in 1926 and Yugoslavia in 1927 completed France's ambitious campaign to compensate for the loss of the Soviet alliance by surrounding Germany with small states committed to maintaining the political status quo.

Though formidable on paper, this informal bloc of Eastern European countries linked to France had defects that severely undermined its potential value as a peacekeeping coalition. All of France's partners in the east were multinational states whose discontented ethnic minorities represented an omnipresent threat to their political unity and social stability (see Table 3.2). Worse still, all of them were locked in bitter conflict over disputed territory either among themselves or with foreign powers other than Germany. Poland had wrested land from the USSR after invading Ukraine in 1920. Romania had seized the Soviet province of Bessarabia during the latter stages of the World War. Yugoslavia clashed with Italy over competing territorial claims along the Adriatic coast. Czechoslovakia had obtained the coal-mining district of Teschen despite the presence of a Polish majority there, touching off a bitter altercation between Prague and Warsaw that poisoned relations between Paris's two premier allies in Eastern Europe. These internal difficulties and external tensions—legacies of the Paris Peace Conference's hopeless task of reconciling conflicting nationalist aspirations in a region of heterogeneous populations—guaranteed perpetual instability in Eastern Europe, which could only work to the advantage of Germany once it succeeded in freeing itself from the demands of Versailles.

To compensate for the fragility of the French alliance system in Eastern Europe, some French officials favoured a supplementary security arrangement with Italy. But France's former wartime ally and 'Latin sister' to the south had paradoxically become an opponent rather than a defender of the territorial status quo in the early post-war years. Despite its substantial territorial gains in the Alps and along the northeastern shore of the Adriatic, Italy left the Paris Peace Conference

TABLE 3.2 ETHNIC MINORITIES IN SELECTED EASTERN EUROPEAN COUNTRIES

Ethnic Group	Number		% Total Population
Poland (Census of 30 September 1921)			
Poles	17,814,239		69.2
Ukrainians (Ruthenes)	3,898,431		14.3
Jews	2,110,448		7.8
White Russians	1,060,237		3.9
Germans	1,059,194		3.9
Lithuanians	68,667		0.3
Russians	56,239		0.2
Czechs	30,628		0.1
Others	78,634		0.3
Czechoslovakia (Census of 15 February 1921)			
Czechoslovaks	8,760,927		65.5
Germans	3,123,568		23.4
Magyars	745,431		5.6
Ukrainians (Ruthenes)	461,849		3.5
Jews	180,855		1.3
Poles	75,853		0.5
Romanians	13,794		0.1
Yugoslavia (Census of 31 January 1921)			
Serbs	5,953,000	Census of	50.0
Croats	3,221,000	March 1931	27.0
Slovenes	1,019,907		8.5
Germans	505,790		3.9
Magyars	467,652		3.8
Albanians	439,657		3.6
Romanians	231,068		1.9
Italians	12,533		0.1
Others	220,220		

Source: Hugh Seton-Watson, *Eastern Europe Between the Wars, 1918–1941* (New York, 1967), pp. 412 ff. Originally printed in 1945 by Cambridge University Press. Reprinted by permission.

dissatisfied with the new international order. This discontent was not tempered even by the resolution of Italy's principal grievance against the peace settlement in January 1924, when the Adriatic port of Fiume, which the peacemakers had wanted to assign to the new state of Yugoslavia, was finally transferred to Italy by a bilateral agreement between the rival claimants. Many Italians nonetheless continued to complain that their country had been denied the fruits of victory while Britain and France had enriched themselves with commercial advantages and colonial spoils. The deepening economic crises, social tensions, and political instability that afflicted post-war Italy fanned this smouldering nationalist resentment against the Versailles system.

The ease with which demagogue Benito Mussolini took power in 1922 and established a

Fascist dictatorship within three years reflected both domestic and international conditions in post-war Italy. The Duce's promises to spur economic growth, abolish class conflict, and restore political unity under a one-party state appealed to Italians disillusioned by the deficiencies of their parliamentary system. He also capitalized on a widespread patriotic fervour that craved diplomatic dynamism and military bravado. Italy consequently became a power on the make during the 1920s, nurturing ambitions of naval predominance in the Mediterranean and colonial expansion in Africa as part of Mussolini's preposterous dream of recreating the Roman Empire. The result was an escalating rivalry with France that posed obstacles to Franco–Italian co-operation against Germany in Europe.

Why did France not look farther east to seek an understanding with the Soviet Union, the historic counterweight to German power on that half of the continent? First, Western antipathy for Bolshevism had not abated even after the failure of the Bolshevik-inspired insurrections in Central Europe during the early post-war years. The establishment in March 1919 of the Communist International (the international organization of communist parties loyal to the Soviet Union, abbreviated to COMINTERN), together with the subsequent emergence in all European countries of communist parties that affirmed their allegiance to the Soviet Union and its Marxist–Leninist doctrines of social revolution, struck fear in the hearts of governing elites everywhere. In France this ideological hostility to the Soviet Union, which was particularly acute during the tenure of right-wing governing coalitions in the early 1920s, was reinforced by lingering resentment at the Bolshevik government's premature withdrawal from the war against Germany and its repudiation of the enormous debt owed to foreign (mainly French) investors by the tsarist regime. Thus France had been the most vociferous advocate of the Allied intervention in the Russian Civil War of 1918–20, lending its support to a succession of counter-revolutionary groups that tried in vain to strangle the infant Bolshevik regime and

encouraging the Poles during their thrust into Ukraine in the spring of 1920.

Even more significant than this ideological element in the Soviet Union's tense relations with foreign powers was the geopolitical condition that not only made it unsuitable as a prospective member of the anti-German bloc but in fact guaranteed Soviet opposition on purely nationalistic grounds to the post-war political order that France was striving to uphold. The USSR had lost much more territory and population as a result of the Great War than had Germany. Finland, Estonia, Latvia, and Lithuania had been formed out of Soviet territory along the Baltic. Romania had been enlarged by the forcible acquisition of the Soviet province of Bessarabia. The eastern frontier of the reconstituted state of Poland, which was fixed by the Treaty of Riga between Poland and the Soviet Union in 1921, included within it large numbers of White Russians and Ukrainians who had previously been subjects of the tsar. The Bolshevik government was obliged to accept these territorial losses because it was preoccupied with the immediate tasks of internal recovery and reconstruction in the wake of civil war and economic collapse. But it remained unreconciled to them and therefore shared with Germany a determination to destroy the territorial settlement of 1919 when conditions permitted. The revisionist grievances of Germany and the USSR converged over Poland, which had been reconstituted at their joint expense and therefore served as a potential basis for co-operation between them. Indeed, the permanent nightmare of Western statesmen throughout the 1920s was an alliance between these two dispossessed powers against the beneficiaries of the peace settlement. Thus the chain of successor states from the Baltic to the Balkans served in the eyes of French officials not only to shield Western Europe from the infection of Bolshevism but also to keep the two dissatisfied states apart.

The rapprochement between the Weimar Republic and the Soviet Union had begun in the winter of 1920–1 in the realm of military co-operation, but these contacts were unknown to

Allied leaders at the time. The first overt indication that the two pariahs had joined forces hit the world like a bombshell in the spring of 1922 during an international economic conference in Genoa to which Soviet representatives had been invited in order to discuss means of promoting the economic recovery of Europe in general and the Soviet Union in particular. After French officials made it clear that the USSR could expect no foreign economic assistance until it had acknowledged its pre-war debt and provided compensation for nationalized foreign property, the German foreign minister, Walter Rathenau, and the Soviet foreign commissar, Georgi Chicherin, retired to the nearby town of Rapallo to sign an agreement providing for the establishment of diplomatic relations and economic co-operation between the two states. The specific terms of the Treaty of Rapallo—the mutual repudiation of claims for war costs and damages, the USSR's renunciation of reparations from Germany, and Germany's renunciation of claims arising out of the nationalization of German property in the Soviet Union— were less important than the fact of the signing itself. It put the Western world on notice that the two most populous (and potentially most powerful) countries in Europe, though temporarily hobbled by internal economic problems, territorial losses, and the animosity of their neighbours, were committed to the pursuit of friendly diplomatic and economic relations with each other, which could only strengthen their respective positions on the continent.

The normalization of relations between the Weimar Republic and the Soviet Union and the subsequent strengthening of their mutually beneficial economic links reinforced other developments that were undermining France's effort to isolate Germany and compel it to fulfill its obligations under the Versailles Treaty. We have already noted how Washington and London had prodded Paris into granting substantial concessions to Berlin in the matter of reparations. The Dawes Plan, by effectively reducing the German debt and abolishing the coercive power of the French-dominated Reparations Commission,

represented the first major revision of the peace treaty to Germany's advantage. The lightening of the reparation burden did not produce the sudden improvement in German behaviour that the British and Americans had confidently expected and the French cautiously hoped for. On the contrary, it soon gave way to a barrage of German invective against the two other major restrictions on German sovereignty imposed by the treaty: the clauses on disarmament and the inter-Allied occupation of the Rhineland. These two issues were closely linked, at least in the minds of French policy-makers. In anticipation of American and British repudiation of the security treaties that had been offered to France instead of a permanent occupation of the Rhineland, Clemenceau had insisted on the insertion of Article 429 in the Versailles Treaty. This clause stipulated that in the absence of adequate guarantees against unprovoked German aggression, the evacuation of the Rhineland could be delayed until such guarantees were forthcoming. The logic of this precautionary article was odd, since it seemed to penalize Berlin for decisions taken in London and Washington over which it had no control. Nevertheless, French leaders used the threat of an indefinitely prolonged Rhineland occupation to persuade Germany to fulfill its disarmament obligation. In the absence of the Anglo–American guarantee, only disarmament would make perpetual occupation of the Rhineland unnecessary.

The process of disarming Germany presented difficulties that Allied statesmen at the peace conference had not anticipated. First, the rapid demobilization of hundreds of thousands of young men without marketable skills placed an intolerable burden on the economic system of the Weimar Republic in its formative years. Even more disturbing was the threat to internal security posed by the existence of organized bands of unemployed veterans who detested the republican regime and periodically conspired to topple it, often with the tacit encouragement of their former superiors in the officer corps. At the same time, these paramilitary vigilante groups performed a useful function for the German state, waging a pitiless campaign of intimidation and violence against the revolutionary left, which itself was plotting to overthrow the parliamentary republic and replace it with a communist regime on the Soviet model. The Western powers were not prepared to tolerate a right-wing military putsch that would rekindle the flame of German expansionism or a communist revolution that might inspire proletarian uprisings across the continent. The political leadership of the Weimar Republic skilfully exploited both of these Allied fears to extract concessions regarding disarmament. In June 1920, after an abortive military coup in Berlin followed by a communist insurrection in the mining districts of the Ruhr Valley, the German government persuaded the Allies to authorize an increase in the size of the German police forces from 60,000 to 150,000 in order to protect the fledgling republic from its enemies at both extremes of the political spectrum. This beefed-up internal security apparatus, equipped with artillery and armoured vehicles and soon quartered in barracks, was to supplement the regular army of 100,000 whose existence had been justified by the need to preserve internal order. Together they represented a potential force of a quarter of a million armed men. At the same time, the formation of numerous private paramilitary organizations, rifle clubs, veterans' organizations, and the like effectively allowed Germany to evade the prohibition against universal military training.

The task of verifying German compliance with the disarmament provisions of the Treaty of Versailles fell to the Inter-Allied Military Control Commission (IMCC). This unarmed inspection team met with continual efforts at concealment by German military authorities and instances of intimidation by the general population. Even without deliberate German harassment, the process of disarmament inspection was hampered by the increasingly blurred distinction between the military and civilian spheres. The potential strength of modern armies could no longer be measured simply by the number of men in uniform. Modern warfare depended to a high degree on technology that was equally beneficial to

industry—just as nuclear energy can be used both to generate electricity and to fabricate weapons of mass destruction. The post-war German chemical industry manufactured substances that could be used for either fertilizers or explosives. German aeronautics firms built commercial aircraft that could easily be converted to bombers. The Allies were unable to find a justification for prohibiting Germany from producing fertilizers for its farms or developing its civilian aviation industry, especially at a time when the country needed to recover economically in order to pay reparations. As a consequence, the IMCC was compelled to grant numerous exemptions to those sections of German heavy industry that were capable of developing products that could be readily converted to military use.

The preservation of Germany's technological capacity to wage war was enhanced by secret military arrangements between the Weimar Republic and the Soviet Union. Collaboration between German and Soviet military authorities had begun in the winter of 1920–1 and was expanded after the signing of the Rapallo Treaty in 1922. Deep in the Soviet interior, the German army was able to surreptitiously produce, test, and train military personnel to use military aircraft, tanks, poison gases, and other weapons outlawed by the Versailles Treaty. Although this program of clandestine rearmament was organized and financed entirely by the German military out of secret funds, its existence was known to and tacitly approved by German governments throughout the 1920s.

In spite of the geographical, political, and economic obstacles, the IMCC persisted in its thankless task of verifying German disarmament. It had been forced to suspend activities during the Ruhr occupation when Berlin refused to guarantee the personal security of its members; it resumed its inspection only after Britain and France informed Germany that the impending evacuation of the Cologne zone in the Rhineland, which was scheduled for January 1925 according to the timetable of the Versailles Treaty, would not begin until the control commission was permitted to verify German compliance with the disarmament sections of the treaty. In December 1924, the commission issued an interim report detailing flagrant German violations of most of the disarmament clauses. As a consequence, the Allies notified Berlin that the evacuation of Cologne would be delayed.

At the beginning of 1925, therefore, the German government faced a major foreign policy dilemma: how to liberate the Rhineland without interrupting the clandestine rearmament deemed essential to Germany's return to the ranks of the great powers. Foreign Minister Gustav Stresemann devoted the last years of his career to solving this quandary. Soon after he became chancellor of the German Republic in the summer of 1923 and terminated the passive resistance in the Ruhr, Stresemann acquired a reputation in Western capitals as a trustworthy advocate of 'fulfillment' of the Versailles Treaty. In November 1923, he was replaced as chancellor and assumed the office of foreign minister. For the next six years, until his death in October 1929, this astute diplomat became the symbol of the democratic forces in the Weimar Republic that ostensibly sought peaceful relations with the victorious Allies and the reintegration of Germany into a stable, prosperous Europe.

In reality, Stresemann was an unreconstructed German nationalist who had never accepted his country's defeat in war or its reduced status in peace. His pre-eminent objective in foreign policy was to free Germany of the detested treaty requirements of 1919. Unlike the nationalist firebrands on the extreme right, Stresemann wisely recognized that Germany's temporary military inferiority in Europe meant that the first efforts to revise the Versailles Treaty had to be conducted with diplomatic finesse rather than militaristic bluster. He identified two soft spots in the armour of the Anglo–French entente that, if properly probed, might permit the weakening of the French stranglehold on Germany. To begin with, he accurately guessed that Britain would welcome a peaceful resolution of the Franco–German dispute in Western Europe, even if it were to erase France's margin of military superiority over Germany. He also understood that France, because of its chronically unstable finances and

fear of diplomatic isolation, would be incapable of resisting British pressure to reach an accommodation with Germany over the most egregious sources of friction.

Accordingly, Stresemann mounted a bold diplomatic initiative designed to attain Germany's major foreign policy goals while satisfying the minimum security requirements of its chief antagonist. France craved assurances of security in the form of German acceptance of the territorial status quo in Western Europe, as well as the demilitarized status of the Rhineland, and a British guarantee of these two arrangements. Germany sought the evacuation of Allied troops from the Rhineland, but without having to submit to the stringent treaty requirements for disarmament. In the winter and spring of 1925, Stresemann approached London about the possibility of breaking the long deadlock between Germany and France. He hinted broadly that Germany was prepared to acknowledge its loss of Alsace–Lorraine to France and affirm the inviolability of the Rhineland demilitarized zone in return for Allied concessions on a number of points. These conciliatory overtures, coming after six years of German intransigence, were received with great enthusiasm in London and were promptly communicated to Paris with the British seal of approval. After a flurry of diplomatic activity, the foreign ministers of France, Britain, Germany, Italy, and Belgium finally met at the Swiss resort city of Locarno in October 1925. The pact negotiated at this gathering committed France, Belgium, and Germany to the formal acknowledgement of their shared frontiers. It also included Germany's endorsement of the permanent demilitarization of the Rhineland. In return for acknowledging its territorial losses in the west (Alsace–Lorraine to France and the small frontier districts of Eupen and Malmédy to Belgium), Germany received from France the quid pro quo it had so earnestly sought: the promise of a prompt evacuation of the Cologne zone of the Rhineland, the scaling down of the occupation forces in the two remaining zones, and a reduction in the size and authority of the Allied inspection team, all to begin once

Germany displayed some measure of good faith regarding disarmament.

The agreements reached at Locarno were universally hailed as an almost miraculous resolution of the Rhine conflict that had unsettled Western Europe since the end of the war. France had finally obtained what it wanted most: from Germany, assurances that the Franco–German frontier and the demilitarized Rhineland were inviolate; and from Britain (as well as Italy), the guarantee that had eluded French statesmen ever since the end of the Paris Peace Conference. Germany's prize was the promise that the Rhineland would eventually be liberated, plus the assurance that French troops would never return to German soil. Almost as important as the actual text of the treaty was the atmosphere of cordiality in which it was produced. German, French, and British officials dined together, exchanged pleasantries during festive boat cruises on Lake Maggiore, and gave every indication that the acrimony of the past had been buried in a universal enthusiasm for détente. The British foreign secretary, Austen Chamberlain (foreshadowing the misplaced optimism of his younger half-brother, Neville, 13 years later at Munich), confidently boasted that his conciliatory influence at Locarno had produced peace for his time. He shared the 1926 Nobel Peace Prize with Stresemann and the French foreign minister, Aristide Briand, for this collective achievement of reconciliation.

The euphoria engendered by this Locarno Pact concealed serious deficiencies—not in what the treaty contained, but in what it omitted. Above all, the German foreign minister had adamantly refused to affirm the inviolability of Germany's borders with Poland and Czechoslovakia. By acknowledging its territorial losses to France and Belgium while refusing to recognize the political settlement in Eastern Europe, Germany had in effect reserved the right to seek redress of its grievances in that region at some future date. By freezing Germany's frontiers in the west without extracting equivalent pledges to respect the territorial status quo in the east, Briand and Chamberlain seemed to tacitly acquiesce in Germany's eventual search for territorial compensation in that direction. The fact that neither Poland, Czechoslovakia, nor the Soviet Union had taken part in the drafting of the treaty aroused fears in those countries that the Western powers had settled with Germany at their expense.

Equally ominous was the absence of a specific German commitment to fulfill the disarmament provisions of the Versailles Treaty. Berlin had consistently objected to unilateral disarmament on the grounds that it would leave the German people perpetually exposed to armed invasion from a vindictive France. By agreeing to reduce the military control commission to a token force, the Allies had effectively entrusted to Germany the responsibility of self-supervision without requiring even an innocuous verbal commitment to disarmament. The clandestine rearmament that had begun in the early 1920s proceeded thereafter without even the threat of detection by Allied military observers. Meanwhile, the Allies scrupulously adhered to their part of the bargain. The evacuation of the Cologne zone began on 1 December 1925, the day of the official signing of the Locarno treaties in London, and was completed by the end of January 1926. In their eagerness to appease Germany, the French and British were moved in the 1930s to increase the concessions made at Locarno.

The most important diplomatic prize that Briand took home from Locarno—the British guarantee of the Franco–German frontier—was rendered worthless by the multilateral nature of the commitment: for British military power to be effective in assisting France against unprovoked German aggression, extensive Anglo–French military preparations would have been required. But such privileged contacts would have prejudiced Britain's position as an impartial guarantor of the territorial status quo in Western Europe. Hence London systematically declined to authorize prior military arrangements with any of the beneficiaries of the Locarno guarantee. The most bizarre aspect of the situation lay in the fact that the British guarantee could be invoked by Germany against France in the event of a future

French military operation in the Ruhr Valley. This meant that Germany was theoretically free to default on reparation deliveries, violate the disarmament restrictions, and exert pressure against France's allies in Eastern Europe, as long as it refrained from sending troops into France, Belgium, or the Rhineland. Any French military response to these provocations would give rise, according to the language of Locarno, to British (and Italian) intervention against France on Germany's behalf.

The Locarno treaties were to go into force when Germany was admitted to the League of Nations. This remarkable event occurred in September 1926, after several months of haggling over how to accommodate Stresemann's demand for a permanent seat on the League Council without antagonizing other aspirants for this prestigious position among the second-rank powers. To French critics of Briand's conciliatory policy toward Germany, Stresemann at Geneva seemed equivalent to the fox in the chicken coop. How could an organization dedicated to maintaining the political status quo in Europe function with the most notorious proponents of territorial revision occupying a powerful place in its midst? In fact, the question was moot since the League had ceased to operate as the forum for discussion of matters relating to European security. On the model of the Locarno consultations, the important issues of the day were thereafter settled by the representatives of the four great European powers meeting privately in Geneva hotel suites. No longer a pariah, Germany would participate on an equal footing with the victorious Allies in deliberations on the future of Europe. That the recently elected German head of state, Field Marshal von Hindenburg, was a troublesome reminder of the imperial past, or that Stresemann never concealed his disdain for the territorial settlement in Eastern Europe were matters of little import for a Europe basking in prosperity and peace. Armies were no longer on the march, intergovernmental debts were being repaid on schedule, production and employment had reached and surpassed the prewar levels. 'Away with the rifles, the machine guns,

the cannon!' Briand had exclaimed in his speech on Germany's admission to the League. 'Make way for conciliation, arbitration, and peace.' The almost hysterical enthusiasm that greeted those words suggested that they expressed the hopes of an entire generation weary of war and intent on enjoying the fruits of European détente.

Yet Briand—unjustly reviled by nationalist detractors at home as a gullible dupe of Stresemann—was fully aware of the shortcomings of the Locarno settlement. Indeed, his concessions had been given reluctantly, only after persistent prodding from Chamberlain. Though historians may never discover Briand's true motivations, since most of his private papers were destroyed, his foreign policy initiatives after Locarno reveal a profound skepticism about the good intentions of the German leadership with which he had recently made peace. To strengthen France's diplomatic and military position vis-à-vis Germany, as insurance in the event that one day Stresemann's conciliatory policy might be repudiated, Briand took a number of precautionary steps.

The first provision was put in place toward the end of the Locarno Conference itself. After failing to obtain Stresemann's formal affirmation of Germany's borders in Eastern Europe, Briand hastened to reassure France's nervous allies in that region. He concluded mutual assistance pacts with Poland and Czechoslovakia that reaffirmed and strengthened the bilateral military commitments previously undertaken in 1921 and 1924, respectively. In June 1926 he added a treaty of friendship with Romania and in November 1927 a similar pact with Yugoslavia. By the end of the decade, Briand's passion for bilateral instruments to deter German aggression had provided France with military alliances or political understandings with Poland and the three countries of the Little Entente. Considered in conjunction with the Franco–Belgian alliance of 1920, this eastern alliance system seemed to represent for France a formidable supplement to the Locarno accords. Despite the disputes among themselves, all members of the French-led diplomatic system shared a common interest in preserving the territorial settlement from which they all benefited. Moreover, these military and political links between France and the nations to Germany's east and south were reinforced by economic connections as well. French capital investment was directed to these countries both to enhance their value as allies and to secure their economic independence from Germany.

On two other occasions after Locarno, Briand attempted to reinforce the Franco–German détente by enlisting outside assistance on behalf of European peace and security. The first of these initiatives was launched in April 1927, when Briand, in a message of gratitude to the American people on the tenth anniversary of the US intervention in the Great War, inserted a suggestion that the two nations sign a bilateral treaty forswearing war between them. Since the likelihood of armed conflict between France and the United States was nil at the time, the State Department correctly suspected an ulterior motive: apparently Briand hoped to draw the US into a privileged relationship that might eventually evolve into some kind of commitment to bolster French security in Europe. US Secretary of State Frank Kellogg had no intention of agreeing to a disguised version of the ill-fated Franco–American security treaty negotiated by Wilson at Paris. But an effective publicity campaign orchestrated by prominent American pacifists, who saw in the French proposal an opportunity to establish peace through international agreement, forced the State Department to respond. The shrewd Kellogg thereupon seized the initiative, dispatching to Paris a draft treaty that transformed Briand's project for a bilateral pact into a universal declaration against war that all nations would be invited to sign. When the startled French authorities complained that such a treaty would nullify regional agreements (such as the Locarno treaties) that obliged certain powers to intervene militarily against aggressors, the draft treaty was further weakened by provisions for self-defence and regional security. In place of a bilateral agreement between Washington and Paris, what Briand got was a multilateral renunciation of war

rendered entirely innocuous by the absence of precise commitments and enforcement machinery. With great fanfare the representatives of 15 nations signed the Pact of Paris on 27 July 1928, solemnly agreeing to 'condemn recourse to war for the solution of international controversies and renounce it as an instrument of national policy'. Eventually 62 nations adhered to what became known as the Kellogg–Briand Pact, including all those whose aggression was soon to produce a second world war.

Foiled in his surreptitious effort to obtain American support for French security, Briand unveiled an even bolder scheme for the maintenance of European peace. In a historic oration to the League Assembly on 5 September 1929, Briand issued a vaguely worded but dramatic appeal for the creation of some kind of supranational confederation linking the sovereign states of Europe. This urgent plan for European union sprang from the same motivation behind the earlier proposal to the United States: Briand hoped to prevent Germany from relapsing into its former aggressiveness, in this instance by submerging it in a supranational Europe made up of economically integrated and politically interdependent states. He was thereupon invited by the League's surprised European members to draft a detailed memorandum specifying the organizational structure and function of the 'federation' alluded to in his speech. On 17 May 1930, he unveiled a formal proposal for the establishment of inter-European political institutions, a general system of arbitration and security, and a common market in which 'the circulation of goods, capital, and persons would be facilitated'.

What had appeared to be an imaginative prescription for European union proved instead to be one of the last gasps of the old order established at Versailles. As the delegates at Geneva debated the Briand plan with ever-decreasing enthusiasm, the German legislative elections of September 1930 increased the Nazi Party's representation in the Reichstag from 12 to 107, making Adolf Hitler's wrecking crew the nation's second largest political party. Within a few months the Briand proposal had been permanently pigeonholed in a committee of the League Assembly. The juxtaposition of these two events at the beginning of the 1930s was an ominous portent for the future: within a decade the continent of Europe was to be unified not by the free consent of democratic nations but by the military might of a rejuvenated Germany. Briand's project for European union, like his abortive effort to secure an American commitment to European security, was a generation ahead of its time. It would take a second world war before the United States would come to regard Europe's security as an extension of its own and the nations of Western Europe would recognize the advantages of economic integration and political co-operation.

The phased withdrawal of Allied troops from the Rhineland deprived France of its last line of defence against a resurgent Germany. Now that the Ruhr Valley was no longer threatened by heavy artillery and mechanized infantry nearby in the Rhineland, the security of Germany's industrial heartland could no longer be counted on to guarantee Berlin's good behaviour. The French strategy of offensive military action in western Germany to compel adherence to the Versailles Treaty, developed by Marshal Foch after the armistice and employed by Poincaré in 1923, was radically transformed during the second half of the 1920s. By the end of the decade, the decision was taken to replace the disappearing natural defensive barrier

Canadian Prime Minister W.L. Mackenzie King signs the Kellogg–Briand Pact in Paris, 17 July 1928.

of the Rhine with an artificial substitute: a continuous stationary fortification stretching the entire length of the Franco–German frontier, which came to be known (after the war minister who authorized its construction) as the Maginot Line.

The inadequacies of the Maginot Line strategy were demonstrated in May–June 1940. Nevertheless, it is worth reviewing the motivations behind its adoption. Above all, there was the striking disparity in human and material resources between the two antagonists along the Rhine. With 40 million Frenchmen facing 70 million Germans endowed with superior industrial (and therefore military) potential, French strategists concluded that in the event of a future conflict France's only hope for survival as a nation lay in a defensive posture designed to spare as many French lives and as much French industrial capacity as possible. This conclusion was reinforced by France's experience in the Great War: the suicidal offensives of 1914–17 were universally blamed for having squandered precious French manpower and resources. The superiority of firepower afforded by modern weapons was taken to mean that the war of movement was a relic of a bygone era.

In future conflicts the advantage would surely rest with the defensive, as it had during the war. Instead of improvising underground shelters to protect against the devastating firepower of the advancing enemy, which it had been forced to do in 1914, France would construct in advance a permanent network of subterranean fortifications equipped with all the supplies and amenities that had been lacking in the cramped, disease-ridden trenches of the Western Front: barracks, mess halls, ammunition dumps, even movie theatres and canteens, all connected by an underground railway. In these comfortable surroundings the French infantry, protected by concrete and fortified with artillery, would lie in wait for any German military force rash enough to risk repeating the bloody offensives of the Great War. The valuable time purchased by this defensive strategy would enable Britain to rearm, gather its military forces

from their faraway imperial outposts, mobilize its extensive economic resources, and enter the fray alongside France. It was even contemplated, though without good reason, that the establishment of a stationary front along France's eastern frontier would result in another influx of industrial resources from the United States.

From a purely military point of view, the Maginot Line was brilliant in conception and effective in practice. It functioned precisely according to plan when the German offensive finally came in May 1940. Nowhere along the Franco–German border was the line penetrated by Hitler's armies; it was circumvented and taken from behind. France's defensive strategy failed to prevent the German breakthrough not because it was defective but because it was not carried to its logical conclusion. In fact, the system of interconnected fortifications contained two gaps. The first was of secondary importance: a portion of the Lorraine frontier was left uncovered because it was wrongly assumed that the adjoining German district of the Saar, which had been administered by the League of Nations since the Versailles Treaty came into force, would vote (in the plebiscite scheduled for 1935) either to remain under League auspices or to be annexed by France. The second flaw—the fatal one—was the decision to terminate construction of the continuous fortified line at Longwy, leaving the entire Franco–Belgian border unprotected. This omission was striking, given historical precedent and geographical reality, both of which suggested that the Belgian lowland would be the most likely path of any German assault against France.

The decision not to extend the Maginot Line the entire length of the Franco–Belgian frontier to the English Channel was dictated by considerations of both foreign policy and domestic politics. First, the military alliance that France had concluded with Belgium in 1920 made it inappropriate even to discuss the possibility of leaving a trusted ally outside the French defence perimeter. The French war plan presumed that Belgium would request French military assistance at the slightest hint of an impending German invasion. Then a Franco–Belgian line of defence could easily be improvised behind the only natural barrier to military aggression on the Belgian plain: the confluence of the Meuse River and the Albert Canal. What made this theoretically astute strategy fatally vulnerable was that it depended entirely on the willingness of a weak little neighbouring state to maintain its commitment to joint defence with France in the face of German intimidation. Even in the unlikely event that Belgium would have tolerated a fortified line separating it from its ally and protector, northward extension of the Maginot Line would have presented serious complications in the northeastern corner of France. This highly industrialized, densely populated region was entirely unsuitable for the permanent emplacement of heavy artillery, which requires long stretches of uninhabited territory to operate without obstruction. It was unthinkable, and politically impossible, to locate these weapons of destruction behind or within a major industrial, urbanized region. These reasons for halting the Maginot Line at the intersection of the French, Belgian, and Luxembourgian borders were reinforced by the fact that French military authorities judged the densely wooded hills of the Ardennes that roll across the Franco–Belgian frontier impassable to mechanized vehicles such as tanks and armoured personnel carriers.

The construction of the costly Maginot Line had to await the definitive stabilization of France's financial situation in 1928. Begun in the following year as French troops prepared to evacuate the Rhineland, it was completed in the mid-1930s; the elaborate fortifications gave the French a feeling of relative safety in an increasingly dangerous international environment. It also helped to erase the image of post-war France, by then widespread in the English-speaking world, as a vengeful nation bent on perpetual intimidation of a disarmed Germany. What more conclusive demonstration of France's defensive intentions than a military strategy of passively awaiting events behind an impregnable fortified line? But the sentiments of

security (in Paris) and relief (in London) were not shared in Prague and Warsaw. France's adoption of a defensive strategy so soon after the Franco–German reconciliation at Locarno reinforced the skepticism of the Czechs and the Poles about the value of their bilateral alliances with their French protector. The presence of French military forces in the Rhineland during the 1920s had served as an effective deterrent to German meddling in the affairs of France's eastern allies. The evacuation of the Rhineland and the establishment of a stationary position behind the Maginot Line seemed to undermine the basic assumptions of France's ambitious diplomacy in Eastern Europe. Germany's recently acquired immunity from the threat of offensive military action by France seemed an open invitation to maintain a defensive posture on the Rhine while pursuing an aggressive policy on the Danube and the Vistula.

The reduced likelihood of effective military assistance from France compelled the Eastern European states to reassess their protective strategies. Czechoslovakia, the most highly industrialized and financially secure nation in the region, could afford to construct its own miniature version of the Maginot Line. Unfortunately, geographical considerations dictated that the line be established in the mountains along the Bohemian frontier region called the 'Sudetenland': an enclave of ethnic German settlement that was a potential object of irredentist ambition across the border. Poland, which possessed neither the money to finance elaborate defensive fortifications nor the natural geographic barriers on which to base them, responded to the devaluation of its French alliance by desperately seeking an accommodation with its two menacing neighbours. As we shall see, non-aggression pacts concluded with the Soviet Union in July 1932 and Germany in January 1934 were desperate efforts by Warsaw to preserve a precarious balance between the two powers with designs on Polish territory.

The first two years of the 1930s were dominated by the spreading economic crisis and efforts by various governments to develop policies to address it. Inevitably, those economic policies, both foreign and domestic, had consequences in the political and military realms. This was particularly so in Europe, where political stability and military security both depended on the efficient operation of the international network of trade, investment, and intergovernmental debt service. The breakdown of this system was a devastating blow to the European security system that had been fashioned in the middle of the previous decade. The death of Gustav Stresemann in the same month (October 1929) that the American stock market began its downward slide was a symbolic coincidence. The era of European détente associated with his name came to a close as the international economic order on which it depended began to disintegrate. The man whose deceptively conciliatory diplomacy from 1924 to 1929 had relieved Germany of the burden of military occupation and inspection, drastically reduced its reparation debt, and restored it to the ranks of the great powers had bequeathed to his successors a golden legacy. They had only to bide their time while the deterioration of the international economic order allowed them to complete the project that he had begun: the liberation of Germany from the remaining fetters of Versailles.

It would be a grave mistake to conclude, as many historians have been tempted to do, that the disappearance of the 'spirit of Locarno', the revival of German revisionism, and the advent of the Nazi dictatorship were direct results of the international economic collapse. The assumption of a causal relationship between economic prosperity on the one hand and political democracy and international stability on the other—widely held by government officials, business people, and financiers in the English-speaking world since 1918—may well explain the peaceful, prosperous, democratic years of Europe in the second half of the 1920s. But the converse of that causal proposition fails to account for subsequent events.

Germany began to terminate its brief experiment with international conciliation and political democracy in 1930, before the Great Depression had taken its toll. The legislative election campaign of that year, which resulted in the spectacular success of the Nazi Party,[3] was fought largely on issues of foreign rather than domestic policy. All the major parties competed for votes with nationalistic denunciations of the Versailles system and strident demands for an end to reparations, restoration of the Saar and the former colonial empire, recovery of territories lost to Poland, and an unrestricted right to rearm. The proposal for a customs union with Austria in March 1931 was less a measure for economic reform than a political assault on the Versailles system and a threat to the security of Czechoslovakia. This move toward an economic *Anschluss*[4] (torpedoed by France), together with the launching of a heavy cruiser construction program in the same year, was justified to the apprehensive British and French as ploys to outbid the Nazis in chauvinism in order to win over their supporters in the German electorate. So too were Chancellor Heinrich Brüning's insistent demands for a revision of Germany's eastern borders and his successor Franz von Papen's decision to default on reparation payments in September 1932. In December of that year, in response to German pressure, nervous members of the League formally recognized Germany's right to achieve equality of armaments. In short, the main features of the Nazis' foreign policy program were adopted by the very statesmen, such as Brüning, Papen, and Hindenburg, who advertised themselves as the only alternatives to Hitler.

The stage for Germany's internal evolution from democracy to dictatorship was likewise set during the three years prior to Hitler's accession. In July 1930, after the Reichstag had rejected the government's budget bill, Hindenburg authorized it by presidential decree, dissolved the Reichstag, and called the new elections that produced the stunning Nazi gains. Within a year, Brüning was circumventing the elected legislators altogether, invoking emergency powers to enact unpopular economic austerity measures. The fierce political infighting of 1932, during which Brüning, von Papen, and General Kurt von Schleicher succeeded one another in the chancellor's office, represented abortive attempts to patch together a governing coalition that would prevent Hitler from taking power. But the legislative elections of July 1932, in which the Nazis won 37 per cent of the vote to become the largest party in the Reichstag with 230 seats, demonstrated the extent of Hitler's popularity among most segments of German society.

Though a subsequent election in November of the same year somewhat reduced the Nazis' legislative representation, the writing on the wall was unmistakable. The guardians of the old order read it and acted accordingly. Their reluctance to embrace the upstart leader of the Nazis did not stem from any distaste for his foreign policy goals, still less from concern about his antipathy for democratic political institutions. It was the radical social program of National Socialism that alarmed these conservative politicians and the social elites they represented. Once assured that the 'socialist' element in the Nazi creed was purely rhetorical and that Hitler would leave the existing socio-economic hierarchies intact, landowners, industrialists, and upper-echelon military officers hastened to make their peace with him. The Junkers craved assurances that their vast estates would not be expropriated and redistributed to indigent veterans, as some had suggested, in order to offset the effects of the Depression; the Krupps, the Thyssens, and their fellow magnates of heavy industry coveted assured markets and sources of supply in Europe; the military leaders longed for a trained and equipped mass army; and all three sought protection against what they feared to be the rising tide of communism in Germany, as reflected in the improved performance of the Communist Party in recent elections. These things Hitler promised, either directly or through intermediaries, as part of his program of foreign expansion, rearmament, and domestic dictatorship. In return he received the support, both political and financial, of these powerful interest groups in his bid for power. Hitler's appointment as chancellor on 30 January 1933 was engineered by men who believed that they could manipulate him and his extremist movement to obtain what they wanted and prevent what they feared. Instead, the Nazi leader turned the tables on his allies among the industrial, agricultural, and military elites, using them and the resources under their control to realize his ideological plans both for Germany and for Europe.

SUMMARY

International relations in the 1920s reflected the influence of three key sets of factors. First were the economic repercussions both of the Great War itself and of the peace settlement. Persistent political insecurities contributed to a resurgence of economic nationalism among the major trading nations, resulting in higher tariffs and production costs; the European Allies were reluctant to repay the loans they had received from the United States during the war; and Germany continued to balk at paying the reparations required by the treaty. Although the US was initially unwilling to play a major role in the reconstruction of Europe, American financial experts soon realized the importance of overseas markets to the US economy. In order to boost markets for American companies, the US in 1924 introduced the Dawes Plan, which radically altered the reparations provisions made by the Treaty of Versailles.

The second key influence was the effort to stabilize international relations. The establishment of the League of Nations bolstered hopes that another world war could be avoided, but European security remained a major issue. France—preoccupied with securing its borders with Germany—formed alliances with several smaller Central European states. Meanwhile, Britain sought to ease the restrictions imposed on Germany by the peace settlement, on the grounds that a stable, secure, and productive Germany would present less of a risk than a resentful Germany bent on revenge.

The Locarno Treaties (1925), hailed by many observers as a diplomatic landmark, provided a framework for guaranteeing the security of international borders.

The third influence was the spread of authoritarian regimes based on new ideologies. Dictatorships emerged at opposite ends of the ideological spectrum in the Soviet Union and Italy, while Germany became increasingly unstable. Mussolini's Fascists took power in Italy in 1922, while Lenin's consolidation of authority in the USSR inspired communist revolutionaries around the world. By 1932, when Hitler's Nazis became the largest party in the Reichstag, the prospects for a lasting peace were already beginning to slip away.

NOTES

1. The German republic of 1919–33, named for the city in which its constitution was drawn up.

2. A foreign policy followed by Wilson's predecessor, William Howard Taft (US president 1909–13), designed to promote financial stability in a region in order to protect American commercial interests there.

3. The Nazi Party received 6.4 million votes and 107 seats, finishing behind only the Social Democrats, who claimed 143 seats.

4. German for 'union', used in the 1930s to designate the German annexation of Austria.

QUESTIONS FOR CRITICAL THOUGHT

1. What were the leading causes of the post-war economic crises?
2. Discuss whether the United States was an 'isolationist' nation in the 1920s.
3. Why was the question of war debts so difficult to resolve in the years following the war?
4. How was Germany so successful in obtaining revisions to the most egregious elements of the Treaty of Versailles?
5. The Maginot Line has been judged an ill-advised and naive strategy. Why did the French place so much faith in it in the 1930s?
6. What were the major sources of European instability in the years between 1925 and 1928?

WEBSITES FOR FURTHER REFERENCE

The Avalon Project: Locarno Pact
http://avalon.law.yale.edu/20th_century/locarno_001.asp

Internet Modern History Sourcebook: Fascism
www.fordham.edu/halsall/mod/modsbook42.html

Musée McCord Museum: Keys to History – The Roaring Twenties
www.mccord-museum.qc.ca/en/keys/games/18

Project Gutenberg (numerous Marxist writings in electronic form)
www.gutenberg.org/wiki/Main_Page

CHAPTER 4

THE 1930s: ILLUSIONS DISPELLED

THE COLLAPSE OF THE WORLD ECONOMIC ORDER

The wave of economic prosperity that swept Europe in the second half of the 1920s was largely a function of the industrial and financial strength of the United States. Hence it was inevitable that the crash of the American stock market in the autumn of 1929 would have repercussions on the other side of the Atlantic. The new role assumed by the United States in the post-war decade as the largest producer, lender, and investor in the world had made the international economic order acutely sensitive to the operation of the American economy. When that economy flourished, as it did with a few minor corrections and adjustments from 1922 through 1929, it served as an engine of prosperity for the rest of the industrial world. During the second half of the 1920s, the US had only about 3 per cent of the world's population but accounted for 46 per cent of its total industrial output. During the same period it produced 70 per cent of the world's oil and 40 per cent of its coal. Moreover, the flow of American surplus capital to Europe provided a relatively painless solution to the problems surrounding German reparations and inter-Allied debts and supplied the liquidity that the world's trading nations needed in order to balance their international accounts.

Yet symptoms of weakness in the international economy were already apparent in the boom years of the second half of the 1920s. Among them was the speculative fever on Wall Street that diverted capital investment away from those parts of the world that needed it most to the one nation that needed it least, as well as the tendency of those American investments that did go to post-war Europe to be short- rather than long-term and speculative rather than productive. Other signs of trouble included declining prices for some commodities, exchange instability, commercial protectionism, and immigration restrictions, which hindered the free exchange of capital, resources, and labour across national borders. Once the American engine of world prosperity faltered, the symptoms of economic instability that had been discounted or ignored during the boom years developed into a full-blown crisis.

The causes of the precipitous decline in the prices of securities on the New York Stock Exchange need not detain us here. What is important for our purposes is the effect of the 'Great Crash' on the economic health first of the United States and then of the entire industrial world. American economic statistics for the three years after 1929 tell the story: industrial production and national income declined by half; the real gross national product dropped by one-third; the unemployment rate approached one-quarter of the workforce; one-third of the nation's banks closed their doors; and wholesale prices fell by 32 per cent. Workers without work, banks without deposits, investors wiped out, home mortgages foreclosed, farmers and small-business people unable to sell their wares and therefore unable to pay their commercial debts—such was the domestic economic condition of the nation on whose prosperity the entire world had come to depend.

The international effect of the American downturn was devastating. The first and most obvious consequence was the abrupt termination of long-term foreign lending and the repatriation of existing foreign loans as they came due. Long-term foreign lending by private American investors declined 68 per cent between 1929 and 1933, then ceased altogether for the rest of the decade. From 1934 to 1939, there was actually a selling off of foreign assets held by Americans. This massive withdrawal of American funds had an immediate impact on the economies of those nations, particularly in Central Europe, that depended on an uninterrupted inflow of American capital to balance their budgets, expand their industrial production, finance their trade, and pay their foreign debts. The repatriation of American foreign loans and investments was soon followed by a massive transfer of foreign gold holdings to the United States in response to the political instability in Europe. Between 1931 and 1938, American banks received a net inflow of gold amounting to roughly US$6.6 billion. Together, the liquidation of American assets abroad, the acquisition of

American assets by foreigners, and the accumulation of foreign-owned gold in American banks resulted in a total capital inflow into the United States far beyond the total required to settle the world's current account deficit with the US—at a time when gold and dollars were desperately needed in Europe.

To make matters worse, the decline of purchasing power in the United States sharply curtailed the ability of Americans to pay for imports from abroad. American merchandise imports dropped from US$4.463 billion in 1929 to $1.343 billion in 1932—a 40 per cent decline by volume. Furthermore, to compensate for the collapse of domestic prices, agricultural and manufacturing interests in the US successfully lobbied for the steepest protective tariff in the twentieth century, the Hawley–Smoot Tariff of 1930, which raised the average duty on protected goods to 59 per cent. The combination of reduced demand and tariff protection in the US precipitated a drastic decline in incomes and widespread unemployment among its trading partners.

The contraction of world trade during the early 1930s also caused an abrupt decline in British foreign investment. France, the other great international lender, had already begun to divert a substantial portion of its surplus capital to gold purchases in order to bolster its recently stabilized currency. The simultaneous curtailment of foreign lending by the few nations with any surplus savings forced the recipients to acknowledge a fundamental weakness in themeslves that had been conveniently overlooked during the years of prosperity: their inability to service their enormous foreign debts (both private and governmental) without additional foreign loans.

At first, the major European nations and the United States sought to ride out the storm by submitting to the traditional cure: deflation. Thus instead of repudiating the gold standard and permitting the exchange rate of their currencies to fall in order to keep their exports competitive, they clung to the system of fixed exchange rates and prepared to endure the deflation that was certain to result. But in the spring of 1931, before this medicine had a chance to take effect, Europe was plunged into a full-fledged financial panic. The largest commercial bank in Austria was found to be on the brink of insolvency because of the withdrawal of foreign short-term funds. In response, the Austrian government froze the bank's remaining assets, setting off a precautionary stampede on financial institutions throughout Central Europe as foreign lenders scrambled to recover their deposits before other governments followed the Austrian example. After failing to stem the outflow of foreign funds by the traditional means—raising interest rates to attract foreign investors—the German government imposed exchange controls to halt the capital flight and prevent further bank closings.

By the end of the year, 11 other European nations had acted to restrict the transfer of capital abroad. In the meantime, political and financial authorities had taken steps to relieve the deteriorating economic condition of the Central European nations in general and the German Republic in particular. In June 1931, American President Herbert Hoover proposed a one-year moratorium on the payment of reparations and inter-Allied debts in order to give Germany breathing space to get its financial house in order. The central banks of the United States, Britain, and France extended short-term loans to Germany, while international bankers studied the feasibility of arranging new long-term private loans to shore up the faltering economies of Central Europe.

The financial storm brewing on the continent soon crossed the English Channel and engulfed Europe's bulwark of monetary stability. Public awareness that British banks were heavily invested in the Central European nations that had frozen foreign-owned assets or imposed exchange controls caused a widespread loss of faith in sterling. So, too, did the abrupt termination of German reparation payments after the announcement of the Hoover moratorium, which came during a period of chronic budget deficits in Britain. At the same time, the need to make large international payments forced foreign creditors to withdraw the money and gold they had on deposit in London. Together, these factors sparked a run on

the pound sterling that depleted Britain's reserves of both foreign currencies and gold. When a large loan to the Bank of England from the Federal Reserve Bank of New York and the Bank of France failed to stem the tide, the British Parliament, on 21 September, took the extraordinary step of suspending the Bank's obligation to sell gold in exchange for the national currency.

Britain's repudiation of the gold standard exposed the fundamental economic weakness of the nation that had presided for so long over the international monetary system: London was not capable of keeping sufficient reserves of gold and foreign currencies to function as one of the two financial centres of the world. The reasons behind this ignominious descent from financial pre-eminence can be found in the shifting patterns of world trade during and after the First World War. Having failed to recapture the overseas markets lost during the war, Britain's export trade was unable to resume the spectacular growth that had attracted the financial reserves of the world to London in the nineteenth century. The consequence of Britain's abandonment of gold in September 1931 was the crumbling of the international monetary system that had been re-established after the First World War.

In April 1925, Britain had returned to the gold standard at the pre-war parity of US$4.86, but by the beginning of the 1930s this decision was generally believed to have aggravated the country's chronic trade deficit by making British exports too expensive for nations that had returned to the gold standard at a devalued level. Accordingly, British treasury officials hoped that once the pound was free to fluctuate it would drop to a level that would restore the competitive position of British exports. On being cut loose from gold, the pound did fall rapidly from par to about US$3.50. But this meant new trouble, for the nations for which Britain was a major customer—and British banks the principal centre for their surplus reserves—could not afford to allow sterling to continue depreciating against their currencies for fear that their own exports would be priced out of the British market and their sterling deposits in London would lose value. By the spring of 1932, 24 such countries had left the gold standard and allowed their own currencies to float freely. Thereafter, the world's trading nations were left to devise their own temporary means of financing international transactions. The system of fixed exchange rates linked to gold, one of the pillars of post-war economic recovery, was in a shambles.

The international monetary system soon disintegrated into three distinct groups, each of which cautiously embraced its own preferred expedient. One set of countries blessed with relatively healthy financial conditions—the United States, France, Belgium, the Netherlands, and Switzerland—remained on the gold standard while striving to reduce imports by erecting protectionist tariff barriers and imposing restrictive import quotas. A second group, headed by Britain and composed of its major trading partners (including all the member states of the Commonwealth except Canada, together with 12 other nations) abandoned gold and tied the value of their currencies to the pound sterling. Exchange stability within this 'sterling bloc' was maintained through the buying and selling of the British currency by the member governments, while Britain drew on a stabilization fund to moderate exchange fluctuations between this sterling bloc and the 'gold bloc'. The third group, dominated by Germany and including many of the impoverished non-industrialized nations of Central Europe and Latin America, imposed rigid exchange controls that made their currencies inconvertible. Since the protectionist policies of the gold-bloc countries and the depreciation of the currencies of the sterling-bloc countries had the identical effect of reducing imports, the only alternative open to these 'exchange-control states' was to seek new markets and sources of imports in other nations that had adopted exchange controls.

This bilateral trade approach was increasingly adopted by Germany after the advent of the Nazi regime in 1933. The drying up of foreign loans, the closure of markets abroad, and the inconvertibility of the German mark meant that Germany was unable to accumulate foreign exchange to finance the imports of raw materials and foodstuffs that it required. It therefore increasingly strove to obtain its imports from those countries (mostly in Central Europe) that were indebted to it on current account or were willing to receive payment in marks that could not leave Germany because of the exchange restrictions. As a consequence, suppliers of raw materials and foodstuffs were required to import as much from Germany as they exported to it if they were to avoid letting the marks they earned from their sales accumulate unused in German banks. The German government also tried making old-fashioned barter arrangements with various countries to circumvent the problem of currency inconvertibility. Thus German coal was shipped to Brazil for an equivalent value of coffee, while German fertilizer was exchanged for Egyptian cotton. Even the United States flirted with the idea of a barter deal with Hitler's Germany, involving an exchange of American cotton for various German products.

The gold-bloc and sterling-bloc countries themselves abandoned the traditional system of multilateral payments through the London money market and instead made bilateral arrangements to balance their international accounts. Britain, France, and the Netherlands stepped up their imports from those parts of the world (in particular, their colonial empires) where their extensive capital investments provided the foreign exchange required to pay for those goods. As a consequence, trade between the three large financial–commercial blocs continued to dwindle.

A related cause of decline in world trade was the universal trend towards restrictions on international commerce that made the protectionist measures of the 1920s pale in comparison. In response to the Hawley–Smoot Tariff in the United States, the major trading nations of Europe enacted protectionist legislation to halt the decline of prices and the loss of jobs in their domestic industries. France and Germany erected high tariff walls and imposed strict quantitative restrictions on imports. Even Britain, the perennial champion of free trade, succumbed to the protectionist pressures of the time. The Import Duties Act of 1932 terminated three-quarters of a century of free trade by raising duties on a variety of items.

In the summer of the same year, at an Imperial Economic Conference held in Ottawa, protectionist measures were extended to the self-governing dominions of the Commonwealth. Britain raised duties on foreign agricultural commodities that competed with dominion exports to the metropole, such as Canadian wheat, Australian wool, and New Zealand dairy products; in return, British manufactured goods received preferential treatment in Commonwealth markets. Meanwhile, France and the Netherlands had devised similar preferential arrangements with their colonial possessions. As a result of imperial preference, protectionist legislation in the United States, and the bilateral trading arrangements of the exchange-control countries, the network of international trade broke down into a half dozen virtually self-enclosed commercial blocs. By 1931, tariff rates in some 15 European nations had increased 64 per cent above the 1927 level.

Throughout the 1930s, trade in manufactured products between Germany, France, and Britain declined to half the level of 1913.

International efforts to revive world trade and the international monetary system on which it depended were uniformly unsuccessful, largely because domestic pressures in the major nations prevented them from adopting policies that, though painful in the short run, might have promoted long-term recovery. The most graphic instance of this shortsightedness was the initial monetary policy adopted by the new administration of Franklin Delano Roosevelt in the United States. In early 1933, the League of Nations called an international economic conference to address the instability of the world's currencies. The US had declined to participate in previous international economic conferences at Brussels (1920), Genoa (1922), and Lausanne (1932). Moreover, although private American financial experts had played an important role in drawing up economic recovery programs such as the Dawes and Young

THE STATUTE OF WESTMINSTER

The Statute of Westminster was a milestone in Canada's evolution towards sovereign nationhood. Passed by the British Parliament in December 1931, it clarified the constitutional status of all the 'Dominions'—Canada, Newfoundland, South Africa, New Zealand, Australia, and the Irish Free State. The Statute was the legal expression of the principles set out in the Balfour Report declaration agreed to at the Imperial Conference of 1926, which declared that Great Britain and the Dominions were 'autonomous Communities within the British Empire, equal in status, in no way subordinate one to another in any aspect of their domestic or external affairs, though united by a common allegiance to the Crown, and freely associated as members of the British Commonwealth of Nations'.

Under the Statute of Westminster, laws passed in Britain could no longer be extended to Canada without the explicit consent of the Canadian Parliament. Although Prime Minister Mackenzie King had already begun to pursue an independent foreign policy, the Statute was important because it meant that Canada's autonomy was officially recognized in law. Now Ottawa had the right to negotiate its own bilateral treaties and open its own embassies in foreign countries. Despite its importance, the Statute of Westminster did not give Canada full constitutional independence. Not until 1949 did the Supreme Court of Canada replace London's Judicial Committee of the Privy Council as the final court of appeal for Canadians, and the British Parliament retained the right to amend the Canadian constitution until 1982, when it passed the Canada Act.

plans, the US government had expressly declined any official involvement. It was with considerable relief that European officials learned of the new administration's decision to send high-level representatives to the London Conference scheduled for the summer of 1933.

Nevertheless, Washington cast a pall over the talks, first by refusing to permit any discussion of intergovernmental debts and then, on 19 April, by abandoning the gold standard. Alarmed by the collapse of domestic commodity prices and subject to intense pressure from the farm bloc, the new president and his advisers mistakenly hoped to stimulate demand for American commodities abroad by deliberately reducing the foreign exchange value of the dollar. Roosevelt feared that any agreement on exchange stability would limit his ability to use monetary measures at home to raise domestic prices, and on 3 July he jolted the London Conference with the announcement that the United States would not consider even a temporary linkage of the dollar exchange rate to any international standard until prices at home could be raised.

Once the world's major currency was cut loose from gold and permitted to depreciate on world markets, the London Conference initiative for international currency stabilization was nipped in the bud. The United States soon recognized its error and renewed its commitment to exchange stability by adopting a gold exchange standard[1] in January 1934, but at a fixed price of US$35 per ounce compared to the pre-depreciation price of $20.67. It was only a matter of time before the other gold-bloc nations were forced first to devalue their own currencies in order to keep their exports competitive and finally to abandon gold altogether. In 1936 the US signed the so-called Tripartite Agreement with Britain and France (later joined by Belgium, the Netherlands, and Switzerland), by which the member nations agreed to sell each other gold in exchange for the seller's own currency at an agreed upon price. This temporary expedient kept the exchange rates of the world's strongest currencies within the narrow range of the announced gold support price of each

country and would provide an important precedent for the revival of international monetary cooperation after the Second World War. It did not offer a satisfactory alternative to the gold standard, however, because of its limited application.

In response to these financial machinations, the exchange-control countries of Central Europe and Latin America tightened their restrictions on capital transfers to protect their domestic reserves. The lack of a universally recognized mechanism to make national currencies convertible, together with the drying up of international lending to facilitate the adjustment of international payments, prevented the recovery of world trade (which at the end of 1936 stood at 10 per cent below its 1929 level) and the repayment of existing debts (most of which remained in default for the rest of the decade).

Just as the Tripartite Agreement represented the only significant American initiative to restore exchange stability in the 1930s, the earlier Reciprocal Trade Agreement Amendment to the Hawley–Smoot Tariff Act was the only American effort to unclog the channels of world trade. This legislation, which went into effect in June 1934, authorized the president to reduce existing duties by up to 50 per cent in exchange for reciprocal tariff concessions by America's trading partners. It was based on the unconditional most-favoured-nation principle, which meant that any concessions made to one country were automatically extended to imports of the same commodity from all other countries. By 1940, bilateral reciprocal agreements to reduce duties had been signed with 21 countries representing 60 per cent of the volume of American foreign trade.

In principle, the results should have been a general reduction in commercial restrictions and a corresponding expansion of world trade. In practice, US tariff negotiators attempted to limit concessions to items that did not compete with American products. Moreover, even the maximum concession of 50 per cent preserved a high degree of protection, since the rates established by the 1930 tariff act had been so steep in the first place. Finally, a number of quantitative restrictions (such as an import quota on sugar) were introduced by the Roosevelt administration. A federal law of March 1933 required US government agencies to purchase American-made products in preference to foreign imports. In sum, it may be said that the reciprocal reduction of tariff barriers during the era of Roosevelt's 'New Deal' economic measures was motivated less by recognition of the critical relationship between the US balance of payments and world economic recovery than by the expectation that reciprocity would stimulate US exports and therefore hasten domestic recovery. The fact that these agreements were all bilateral rather than multilateral reflected the American government's reluctance to participate in a genuinely international effort to revive world trade.

The narrowly nationalistic character of American foreign economic policy in the 1930s became evident when the US government insisted that the European Allies resume repayment of their wartime debts to the United States after the one-year Hoover moratorium expired. The economically battered nations of Europe could hardly be expected to resume making such large capital transfers once the lubricant of American foreign investment in Central Europe had dried up. Consequently, as the moratorium approached its expiration in the summer of 1932, the European powers held an economic conference at Lausanne, Switzerland, to discuss ways of removing those impediments to recovery. In the absence of a US delegation, the European debtors proposed what amounted to a mutual cancellation of German reparations and inter-Allied debts. The Hoover administration—which, like its predecessors, had consistently denied any connection between German reparations payments and European war debts to the US—rejected the idea. Since Germany had failed to resume the reparations payments that had been interrupted (temporarily it was thought but permanently as it turned out) by the Hoover moratorium, the other European debtors were forced to the wall. When the next instalment came due in December 1932, six nations (including France and Belgium) defaulted for the first time. In June 1933, Britain and Italy

made drastically reduced payments, and within a year all the European debtors except Finland had ceased payment altogether.

Instead of writing off the debts left over from the First World War, the Roosevelt administration retaliated with the Johnson Act of 1934, which prohibited American citizens from purchasing the securities of governments in default on their war debts. As a consequence, US financial markets were closed to Britain and France in the period when they were undertaking programs of industrial expansion and rearmament to meet the Nazi menace. Similarly, the Neutrality Act of 1935, which banned the sale of munitions to belligerents and required cash payment for all exports to nations engaged in hostilities, made it impossible for the Western democracies to obtain American supplies on credit once they went to war with Germany in September 1939. Thus to conserve their dwindling gold and dollar reserves, Britain and France were forced to reduce their imports from the United States. As American public support for the Anglo–French cause increased, Congress lifted the arms embargo in November 1939, but this belated reversal of Washington's isolationist policy came too late to be of much assistance to France, which collapsed before the Nazi blitzkrieg in June 1940. The cash-on-delivery requirement was finally removed in March 1941, when the lend–lease program authorized American exports to Britain and its allies, with payment to be postponed until after the end of the war.

In sum, to the extent that Roosevelt's New Deal rescued the United States from economic collapse—and historians have increasingly challenged that conventional judgment—it did so not by co-operating with Western Europe to develop a coordinated program of international recovery but by pursuing remedies which focused on the domestic situation first and foremost. The resumption of industrial expansion in Europe was precipitated by international strategic factors, not remedial economic measures. The rearmament campaign that began in the late 1930s did far more to stimulate demand for manufactured products, raw materials, and labour than did the modest public works projects and domestic spending programs undertaken earlier in the decade by the Western democracies. It is perhaps the most tragic irony of modern history that organized violence on a large scale, or the process of preparing for it, has proved to be the most effective remedy for the economic problems of underconsumption and unemployment.

The causal connection between military preparedness and economic recovery was most evident in Adolf Hitler's Germany, where strict state control of political and economic activity permitted the most efficient mobilization of capital, labour, and resources for military purposes and consequently generated phenomenal economic growth throughout the second half of the 1930s. The Four-Year Plan of economic development instituted by the Nazis in 1936 was designed to make Germany entirely independent of markets and resources outside its political and economic orbit. As we shall later see in greater detail, this goal of economic self-sufficiency depended on two strategies. First, the German chemical industry developed synthetic products to substitute for raw materials, such as rubber, cotton, and wool, that could not be produced domestically in sufficient quantity. Second, Germany tightened its economic grip on its weaker neighbours in Eastern Europe that possessed valuable mineral and agricultural resources. By expanding its bilateral trade relations with such countries as Poland, Hungary, and Romania, Germany obtained access to enormous supplies of wheat, lumber, oil, and other raw materials it required, as well as markets in which to dispose of its surplus industrial production.

THE UNITED STATES AND LATIN AMERICA

In 1933, US policy regarding Latin America shifted away from direct intervention towards a more indirect approach. As the unrivalled power in the region, the United States no longer needed military force to deter threats from European countries. Widely criticized for its reliance on military domination in Latin America, the US government sought to create a new image in the region. Instead of using its own soldiers, it enlisted the assistance of local leaders to pursue its imperial interests. American banks used their tremendous economic influence, and the US military trained and equipped indigenous security forces throughout the region. These indirect methods did not appear overtly instrusive but were extremely effective in maintaining control over client states.

By the early 1930s the presence of US military forces in the Caribbean region had become a source of acute embarrassment to Washington as it endeavoured to mobilize world opinion against Japan's expansionist policies in the Far East. The official justification for Japan's incursion in Manchuria—that it was necessary to protect Japanese citizens and property endangered by Chinese lawlessness—was uncomfortably reminiscent of the rationale invoked by the United States in defence of its military interventions south of the Rio Grande. Sensitive to mounting allegations of hypocrisy from the world community, the new administration of Franklin Roosevelt introduced a dramatic modification of US policy in Latin America when it took office in 1933. The groundwork had been laid by the Hoover administration in 1930, when the State Department issued a memorandum that repudiated the Roosevelt Corollary to the Monroe Doctrine as a justification for US intervention in Latin America. Although the memorandum included many qualifications and did not receive much serious attention from American officials, it heralded a new attitude toward inter-American relations. Before leaving office, the Hoover administration undertook a systemic re-evaluation of the interventionist policy that had been pursued by every American president since Theodore Roosevelt.

In his inaugural address, Franklin Roosevelt suggested that the United States should behave as 'the good neighbour who resolutely respects himself, and, because he does so, respects the rights of others'. There was no reason for his listeners to think that this innocuous phrase applied specifically to Latin America. But in a speech at the office of the Pan-American Union, Roosevelt mentioned the need for hemispheric co-operation in such conciliatory tones that commentators were soon hailing the new 'Good Neighbor Policy' of the US toward Latin America. Later in 1933, at the seventh conference of the American states in Montevideo, Uruguay, this presidential rhetoric was translated into government policy. The new secretary of state, Cordell Hull, abruptly reversed a long-standing American policy by supporting a resolution prohibiting any nation in the western hemisphere from intervening 'in the internal or external affairs of another'. Soon thereafter, the US proceeded to relinquish, one by one, its treaty rights to intervene in the Caribbean basin.

During the first two years of the Roosevelt administration, the United States withdrew its military forces from Nicaragua and Haiti, abrogated the notorious Platt Amendment of 1901 (which had restricted Cuba's treaty-making power and given the US the right to intervene militarily to protect Cuba's independence and preserve domestic order), and in 1935 enabled the government of Haiti to regain control of its finances by purchasing the Haitian national bank from the National City Bank of New York. A year later, a treaty with Panama terminated the American right of military intervention outside the Canal Zone.

Thus the Roosevelt administration accelerated the radical transformation of traditional US policy in Latin America initiated by Herbert Hoover. By 1934, no American troops were stationed in the region (except at the military and naval bases retained at Cuba's Guantanamo Bay and in the Panama Canal Zone). Washington had specifically relinquished its claim to the right of intervention to protect persons and property. Financial supervision of Haiti, the Dominican Republic, and Nicaragua was phased out between 1936 and 1940. Mexico had successfully nationalized US-owned petroleum properties in 1938 without suffering US retaliation. It truly seemed that the previous relationship of dominance and subservience between North and Latin America had been replaced by one of equality and mutual respect.

However, the changes were more apparent than real. While the Good Neighbor Policy put an end to military intervention and financial supervision, it replaced them with a less direct form of control, using non-coercive means to obtain the assistance of indigenous political, military, and business elites in preserving Washington's grip on the economic resources of Latin America. The use of American Export–Import Bank loans to tie local economies even more closely to the American economy, the training and equipping of national constabularies to suppress insurrection against pro-American regimes, and the provision of financial assistance to autocratic governments to balance budgets and stabilize currencies—these were the alternative means through which American hegemony was perpetuated after direct military force and financial control had been abandoned.

It was following Hitler's announcement of German rearmament and the Italian invasion of Ethiopia in 1935 that the US government launched its first effort to establish a system of hemispheric solidarity. In January 1936, President Roosevelt proposed a special inter-American conference to discuss how the western hemisphere might be protected from the new threat to world peace brewing in Europe. At this conference, held in Buenos Aires the following December, the American and Argentinian delegations clashed when Argentinian Foreign Minister Carlos Saavedra Lamas—the leading proponent of Latin American resistance to US domination—proposed co-operating with the League of Nations to implement sanctions against aggressor states anywhere in the world. Linking the security of the western hemisphere to the European-centred international organization that the United States had repudiated, the Argentinian plan struck at the very heart of the pan-American ideology propounded by the US. The American plan, by contrast, centred on pan-Americanism, seeking to organize the republics of the Americas in a common defence of hemispheric security. It proposed the creation of an inter-American consultative committee made up of the foreign ministers of the

21 republics, which would be authorized to hold consultations during international emergencies. In the event of war involving any of the member states, the neutral nations of the Americas would be obliged to enforce an embargo of credits and arms supplies on all belligerents.

Franklin Roosevelt abandoned the 'big stick' wielded in the years before 1914 for two major economic and strategic reasons. First, the economic recovery of the United States depended on access to the raw materials and markets of Latin America. This became all the more important as the revival of economic nationalism and the increased likelihood of war in Europe and Asia threatened to disrupt US trade with those continents. Second, the rearmament of Germany, and the increasing belligerence of Italy and Japan, revived the long-dormant issue of foreign interference in the Americas. To counter the threat posed by Nazi Germany, Fascist Italy, and imperial Japan, the US sought to strengthen its peace-keeping machinery. But the traditional methods of military coercion and diplomatic intimidation were no longer practicable in the face of sustained resistance from the Latin American republics and accusations of hypocrisy from the world community. By substituting indirect for direct methods of hemispheric domination, the Roosevelt administration relieved itself of the albatross of old-fashioned imperialism. Thereafter it would be free both to act as the defender of peace and national sovereignty in the world at large and to mobilize its clients in Latin America in a hemispheric security system based on the voluntary co-operation of juridically equal nations.

THE COLLAPSE OF THE EUROPEAN SECURITY SYSTEM

Germany's rearmament program was already well advanced by the time Adolf Hitler took power as chancellor in January 1933, and by the time he announced it publicly, in March 1935, a German army and air force had already been in the making for 15 years. The patient, subtle effort to evade the disarmament prescriptions of the peace

treaty without provoking Allied retaliation had forged an institutional structure of military power that Hitler inherited intact: a general staff, effectively concealed within a labyrinth of government agencies and military bureaus; the nucleus of a well-trained army of several hundred thousand men dispersed among various police forces, paramilitary organizations, veterans' associations, and rifle clubs; the kernel of an air force in the form of hundreds of commercial airline pilots with thousands of hours of flying time; and an elaborate infrastructure of munitions plants (located in the USSR during the period of Allied inspection and later reassembled in the Ruhr) capable of turning out huge quantities of the materiel proscribed by the peace treaty, including aircraft, tanks, artillery pieces, shells, and poison gas.

The full extent of the German military buildup was not known to the Allies, but enough evidence had been uncovered to cause grave apprehension in European capitals. The removal of the Allied inspection team in 1927 and the evacuation of the Rhineland three years later left the victors of 1918 with little leverage against a Germany that was determined to rearm. As the feasibility of enforcing the unilateral disarmament of Germany began to diminish at the end of the 1920s, the alternative of general disarmament became more and more attractive to those who wanted to see Germany's military capacity limited. This was particularly true of public opinion in Britain and the United States, two countries that had unilaterally demobilized their large land armies, dismantled their munitions industries, and voluntarily accepted limitations to their naval strength in the early post-war years. The concept of 'universal disarmament'[2] had been endorsed by the Versailles Treaty in accordance with the popular presumption that the very existence of stockpiles of munitions and large standing armies increased the likelihood of war. But no progress towards that end had been possible during the first half of the 1920s because France refused to relinquish its military superiority over Germany without an iron-clad guarantee that its eastern border was secure.

The insertion of just such a guarantee from Britain and Italy in the Locarno treaties paved the way for a preparatory commission on disarmament that first met in Geneva in May 1926 to study ways of reducing the level of armaments in the world. The tangible results were minimal because of French suspicions of Germany's good intentions, and less than five years later the commission closed up shop with little to show for its efforts. Public interest in disarmament was revived soon thereafter, when the effects of the economic crisis in the United States began to be felt in Europe. As governments hastened to reduce spending and shore up their finances, the enormous costs of maintaining defence establishments came under attack. It seemed senseless to divert an ever-increasing proportion of a nation's ever-decreasing resources to the unproductive purposes of military preparedness while businesses failed, banks closed their doors, and unemployment lines lengthened. Hence in February 1932, the great powers met in Geneva in the hope of reaching some definitive agreement on the size of national armies.

At this conference the German delegation reiterated the position that it had taken in informal exchanges with the Allied governments throughout the 1920s: either universal disarmament as envisaged by the Versailles Treaty or equality of arms between Germany and the other great powers of Europe. Frustrated by France's insistence on security prior to disarmament, the German delegates abruptly left the conference in mid-September. In December, Britain and France—desperate to get Germany back to the bargaining table—promised it 'equality in a system which would provide security for all other nations'. Although this formula simply restated the dilemma that had prevented agreement in the past, the language was sufficiently conciliatory to lure Germany back to the conference in February 1933.

But the delegation that returned to Geneva was under orders from Hitler, who had been named chancellor the previous month. The new German leader had already decided on a massive program of unilateral rearmament, which he communicated to the Reich's highest-ranking military and naval officers on 3 February, the day after his delegates reappeared in Geneva. Germany would go through the motions of negotiating an agreement for equality of arms with the other great powers while secretly building a military force superior to that of all potential enemies. The ostensible purpose of this ambitious rearmament program was mainly economic. In the short run, government spending for military purposes would stimulate employment and industrial production and thereby rescue the German economy from the depression into which it had recently plunged. The huge cost of this program would be paid through deficit financing—a drastic departure from the deflationary fiscal policies of Hitler's predecessors. More than one historian has noted the similarities between the measures to combat the Depression adopted by the National Socialist government in Germany and those of the new Roosevelt administration in the United States, whose New Deal recovery program of deficit financing and stimulative government spending was getting under way at the same time. The key difference, of course, lay in the objectives: in the German case, the primary goal was not domestic recovery but rather military superiority in Europe.

The long-term objective of this military buildup, as expounded by Hitler in his major writings and speeches, was also superficially economic in character. Briefly, Germany was suffering from the Malthusian curse of insufficient arable land with which to feed its expanding population. If its borders remained unchanged, Germany would have just two alternatives: either to cultivate the available land more intensively (a possibility that Hitler never took seriously) or to reduce the population that the land had to support. Population control through measures such as contraception or abortion was repellent to Hitler because it amounted to deliberate 'racial suicide'. Given Hitler's assumption of German racial superiority, the obvious solution was emigration. The type of emigration that he envisioned differed, both in its object and in its methods, from that employed by Britain to ease its population pressures in the nineteenth century. Instead of directing German settlers overseas, where they were likely to forget their origins and therefore represent a net loss to the mother country, they were to be relocated in the adjacent lands to Germany's east, currently populated by 'inferior races' that could be subdued and then expelled or annihilated to make way for the German pioneers.

These ideas were not new to Germany. In somewhat less brutal form they had been aired since the turn of the century by social Darwinists, geopoliticians, and racist thinkers. In the guise of the *Mitteleuropa* concept, they had played a part in the more extravagant schemes of military conquest and continental domination entertained by expansionist thinkers during the First World War. Hitler's single contribution was to give these nationalistic doctrines a specific geographical focus. The Nazi leader never deviated from his insistence that the living space, or *Lebensraum*, that Germany required was to be found in Eastern Europe and the western USSR, where fertile agricultural land and valuable mineral resources could supply the food and raw materials that Germany needed and at the same time provide an outlet for its surplus population. Moreover, that territory was inhabited by two 'racial' groups that, for personal reasons, Hitler was determined to subjugate. In his view, the Slavic majority was incapable of organizing this valuable territory politically, exploiting it economically, or defending it militarily, while the Jewish minority, together with their co-religionists in Germany itself, constituted a 'cancer' on the body of Europe that had to be removed.

Hitler's policy toward the other great powers of Europe in the early months of his rule reflected this single-minded goal of extending Germany's living space eastward at the expense of the Slavs and Jews in Eastern Europe and the USSR. Since France was the self-appointed guarantor of the existing territorial distribution in Europe and protector of the states in the east that stood in Germany's way, Hitler saw the destruction of France as a necessary prelude to his eastern conquests. With England he had no quarrel so long as it stayed out of continental affairs. Indeed, his project of eastward expansion on land was entirely compatible with the maintenance of friendly

relations with the British. Recalling the disastrous consequences for Germany of Kaiser Wilhelm II's bid to challenge Britain's position outside Europe, Hitler hoped that so long as Germany did not adopt an aggressive colonial and naval policy, there would be no reason for Anglo–German friction and therefore no reason for Britain to support France. As for Italy, Hitler's ideological affinity for his fellow Fascist dictator, Benito Mussolini—who had seized power in 1922 as an opponent of the Versailles system—was reinforced by realistic reasons for Italian–German friendship: Italy was in perpetual conflict with France over naval and colonial matters in the Mediterranean, while Germany's ambitions in Eastern Europe and the USSR posed no direct threat to Italy's vital interests.

The German chancellor took only a passing interest in the affairs of the other continents. His overriding goal was the conquest of living space in Eastern Europe and the USSR, and his plan to achieve it required the prior destruction of France, with the co-operation of Italy and the abstention of Britain. Eventually a German-controlled Eurasia could enter into global competition with the imperial blocs of Great Britain and the United States, perhaps with the co-operation of Japan, whose political system and national dynamism Hitler vaguely admired. In the meantime, the two English-speaking powers were expected to remain aloof from the continent of Europe while the Germans proceeded to subdue, organize, and exploit it for its own needs.

It is worth pausing at this point to note just how far the Nazi program for continental domination diverged from the foreign policy objectives of the Weimar Republic. The superficial similarity between the immediate goals of Stresemann and Hitler has led some historians to emphasize the continuity of German foreign policy throughout the inter-war period. Some have been tempted to view Hitler as a traditional German nationalist pursuing the policy that his republican predecessors had adopted in the 1920s: recovery of the territory lost by Germany at the Paris Peace Conference, annexation of adjacent regions with substantial German populations (in accordance with the principle of national self-determination), and restoration of military parity between Germany and the other powers of Europe. It is true that all of Hitler's official diplomatic initiatives from the date of his accession to March 1939 were aimed at securing these traditional objectives of German foreign policy. During the same period, however, Hitler also made numerous unofficial references to the expansionist program outlined above. Reversing the 'unjust' verdict of the Paris Peace Conference by recovering or annexing all German-speaking regions of Central Europe was only the first step in Hitler's grand design.

In truth Hitler cared little for the German-speaking citizens who had been incorporated within half a dozen neighbouring states in the peace settlement. Their grievances were merely a pretext for destroying the territorial settlement, and therefore the balance of power in Europe, as a prelude to conquering and exploiting the vast territories to the east where few Germans currently lived but many would be sent as colonists in some distant future. Though his grandiose ambitions beyond the regions of German settlement were not openly pursued until March 1939, with the absorption of the non-German sector of Czechoslovakia, they were frequently and forcefully expressed in speeches and writings that were well-known to the world's political leaders.

In the light of this program of eastward expansion, the disarmament talks in Geneva to which the German representatives returned in February 1933 were exercises in futility. Even the compromise plan drafted by British Prime Minister Ramsay MacDonald—parity of national armies in Europe at 200,000 men each, to be achieved by gradual reduction of French forces over five years—failed to secure the approval of Hitler's hand-picked delegation, which had been instructed to reject any multilateral restrictions on the rearmament program already underway. When Germany's demand for the immediate right to construct proscribed weapons and increase the size of its standing army encountered the anticipated opposition from France, Hitler summarily withdrew his representatives not only from the conference but also from the League of Nations (in October), dissolved the Reichstag, and staged a referendum (in November), which produced a 90 per cent vote of confidence in his recent actions in Geneva. The Führer was then free to pursue a foreign policy independent of both domestic opinion (represented by an impotent Reichstag) and world opinion (represented by an irrelevant League of Nations).

Germany's simultaneous withdrawal from the disarmament conference and the League of Nations dealt a devastating blow to the principle of collective security, which had already been severely undermined in the Manchurian affair. An incident in far-off Asia could perhaps be overlooked. But the aggressive German foreign policy adopted in the autumn of 1933 forced French officials to abandon all hope that the pressure of world opinion expressed through the world body in Geneva might function as an effective restraint.

The non-aggression pact signed between Germany and Poland in January 1934 was another dramatic reversal of German foreign policy that dealt a severe blow to France's defensive alliance system in Europe. The thawing of traditionally frosty relations between Berlin and Warsaw was prompted by Hitler's realization that a relaxation of tension with its traditional adversary in Eastern Europe would facilitate Germany's internal consolidation and military preparation. The two outstanding sources of friction were a tariff war that had raged for over eight years and the political conflict between the German-speaking majority of the free city of Danzig and the Polish government, which maintained a customs union with the city as well as authority over its relations with foreign states. Hitler promoted a temporary resolution of the Danzig issue by imposing tactical restraints on the National Socialist municipal government that had been elected in 1933 by the German-speaking majority. Warsaw, for its part, hoped that better relations with Berlin would facilitate Poland's balancing act between its two powerful neighbours—Germany and Russia—and provide access to the German market for its coal and agricultural surpluses.

The pact committed the signatories to bilateral resolution of their mutual problems and avoidance of the use of force against each other for a period of 10 years. A commercial agreement concluded in March 1934 ended the tariff war and opened up the possibility of improved trade relations between the two countries. Although the Polish government was careful to insert a reservation in the non-aggression pact acknowledging its treaty obligations to France, the German–Polish rapprochement inaugurated a diplomatic revolution in Europe. In his first foray into bilateral diplomacy since throwing off the constraints imposed by the League of Nations, Hitler had punched a hole in the French alliance system and obtained what appeared to be a considerable measure of security on Germany's eastern flank.

In response to the German–Polish pact, France decided that it needed to forge new alliances with its neighbours. The first country it approached was Italy. Even before the advent of the Fascist regime in 1922, Italy had nurtured grievances against France related to the frustration of Italian aspirations to become an imperial power in the Mediterranean basin. When, at the Paris Peace Conference, Italian Prime Minister Vittorio Orlando had failed to obtain Allied support for Italy's territorial ambitions along the Dalmatian coast, it was largely because of US President Wilson's endorsement of Yugoslavia's competing claims, but Franco–Italian relations were damaged nevertheless by Clemenceau's reluctance to take Italy's side. Another source of long-simmering Italian resentment was France's acquisition of Tunisia—a North African territory across the Mediterranean from Sicily—which came to a boiling point after the war, when France repudiated its earlier pledge to respect the special privileges of the large Italian population there.

Reinforcing these territorial and colonial disputes was an intense Franco–Italian naval rivalry. Although the two countries had been compelled to accept parity in large ships at the Washington Naval Conference of 1921–2, France offended Italy by insisting that the necessity to divide the French fleet between the Mediterranean and the oceanic routes to the French empire in Africa and Asia entitled it to more auxiliary vessels such as cruisers and submarines. Added to these Mediterranean tensions was an incipient Franco–Italian conflict in Central Europe. While Paris tried to form a diplomatic coalition with Poland and the nations of the Little Entente (Czechoslovakia, Romania, and Yugoslavia), Italy sought to gain influence in the Danube basin by extending political protection and economic assistance to Austria and Hungary and undermining Yugoslavia (by supporting Croatian separatist agitation against the Serb-dominated government in Belgrade).

In spite of these numerous obstacles to cooperation, France and Italy did share one common objective: the preservation of Austria's political independence. Since the end of the war, periodic pan-German calls for the political unification of Austria and Germany, or *Anschluss*, had caused considerable alarm in Rome. That sense of alarm increased when Hitler—a pan-German zealot of Austrian birth—came to power in Berlin. The source of Italy's anxiety was the potential effect on the German-speaking inhabitants of the south Tyrol region of the Alps, which Austria had ceded to Italy at the Paris Peace Conference. The French opposed *Anschluss* both because of the threat it would pose to their ally Czechoslovakia (which would be caught in the vise of an enlarged Germanic state) and because of the increase in Germany's population and industrial potential that such a union would entail.

Officials at the French foreign ministry hoped that this shared interest in preserving Austria's independence could serve to unite the two antagonistic blocs into some sort of economic federation and political association under the joint tutelage of Paris and Rome. The prospects for Franco–Italian co-operation in defence of the territorial status quo in Central Europe were enhanced by Italy's reaction to the 'Austrian crisis' of July 1934, when local Nazis in Vienna assassinated Chancellor Engelbert Dollfuss (a determined foe of *Anschluss*) and appealed to Hitler for assistance in their prospective coup d'état. Italian troops that had coincidentally been on manoeuvres near the Austrian border staged a show of force at the Brenner Pass, prompting Hitler to repudiate the plot that his own embassy in Vienna had played a role in hatching. The ignominious collapse of the venture enabled Mussolini to take credit for having deterred Germany from interfering in Austria's internal affairs. Impressed, French authorities hastened to seek formal arrangements with Italy to deter any similar initiatives in the future. In January 1935, French Foreign Minister Pierre Laval journeyed to Rome to sign an agreement with Mussolini, which settled most of the outstanding Franco–Italian differences in Africa, in return for an Italian pledge to consult France in the event of German violations of the Versailles clauses on disarmament and the independence of Austria.

The emerging Franco–Italian entente faced its first test in March 1935, when Hitler formally repudiated the disarmament provisions of the Versailles Treaty. It had long been apparent that the rearmament project could no longer be kept secret: the construction of a navy, an air force, and a mechanized army could not escape detection. After a plebiscite in the Saar resulted in the return of that territory to the German Reich on 1 March, Hitler was free to remove the remaining legal restrictions on Germany's military recovery. On 9 March, he revealed the existence of a German air force as well as plans to expand its size and strength. A week later, he reintroduced universal military conscription with the announced goal of creating a 36-division army (the Versailles Treaty permitted it to have 7, and the existing French army had 30). The French, British, and Italian prime ministers met at the Italian resort city of Stresa to fashion a coordinated response and issued a joint communiqué that condemned the German action and threatened joint opposition to any further treaty violations. In addition, France and Italy secretly exchanged pledges of military assistance in the event that Germany should violate either the Rhineland demilitarized zone or the independence of Austria. Italy's commitment to co-operate with France reached its apex in

June 1935, when Franco–Italian military conversations were resumed for the first time since the end of the First World War.

France's overtures to Fascist Italy in this period were paralleled by simultaneous overtures to the Soviet Union. It may be surprising that a parliamentary democracy such as France would base its system of continental security on diplomatic links with Fascist and communist dictatorships. The realities of international power at the time, however, seemed to dictate just such an ideologically contradictory policy. France needed to forge an effective anti-German coalition, and it was ready to make allies wherever it could find them, regardless of their domestic politics. The national interest seemed to require that Germany be encircled by hostile powers associated with France, and that interest prevailed over the ideological concerns of all but the most vociferously anti-Fascist and anti-communist Frenchmen. Moreover, Rome and Moscow themselves had a surprising record of compatibility: Mussolini had been one of the first Western leaders to recognize the Soviet regime in the early 1920s, and Italy and Russia had maintained remarkably cordial relations ever since.

The possibility of a Franco–Soviet alliance had the obvious advantage of confronting Germany with the prospect of a war on two fronts, after the fashion of 1914. But the obstacles were even more formidable than they had been in the case of Franco–Italian rapprochement: on the French side there was lingering resentment at the Soviet government's conclusion of a separate peace with Germany in 1917 and its repudiation of the enormous debt to French investors that had been contracted by the tsarist regime; on the Russian side there was bitterness at France's anti-Bolshevik position during the Russian Civil War and its support of Poland's military offensive against Soviet Russia in 1920. Added to these historical animosities was a basic incompatibility of foreign policy between the two states throughout the 1920s. As the major beneficiary of the peace settlement of 1919, France vigorously defended the post-war status quo in Europe, extending its financial support and political protection to the Eastern European states that had also profited from the defeat of the Central Powers. Russia, however, had lost much of its territory in Europe to those new or enlarged states; therefore, it wanted to see the post-war system destroyed, and in the 1920s it had not hesitated to co-operate with the other great revisionist power, Germany, to that end.

The rise of Hitler and the stalling of the disarmament talks precipitated a simultaneous reversal in official French and Soviet attitudes toward each other. Hitler's oft-stated intention of seeking living space in Eastern Europe at Russia's expense, together with his frequent denunciations of communism as a political philosophy, were well-known in the Kremlin. In February 1933, the Soviet foreign minister, Maxim Litvinov, officially reversed his government's long-standing support for revision of the peace treaties by openly endorsing the French position on collective security at the disarmament conference. In subsequent remarks he clearly enunciated his government's new official line: treaty revision meant war and therefore was to be avoided at all costs. The French government quickly responded to this stunning about-face, sending a military attaché to Moscow for the first time since Russia's withdrawal from the world war. By the summer of 1933, the secret collaboration between the German and Soviet armies came to a halt, all German military facilities in Russia were closed, and visits of Soviet officers to Germany were cancelled. In the autumn of 1934, with an eagerness he could scarcely conceal, French Foreign Minister Joseph Paul-Boncour took the occasion of Germany's withdrawal from the disarmament conference to approach Litvinov in Geneva about the possibility of formal Franco–Soviet co-operation to preserve collective security in Europe. The idea of a commercial agreement, intended to pave the way for friendlier political relations, was unworkable because of the incongruity of the two economic systems: the USSR required massive infusions of industrial technology for which all it had to exchange were agricultural products, while France was agriculturally self-sufficient and

had already begun to restrict imports of foodstuffs to protect its politically powerful farmers. Nevertheless, increasing diplomatic, military, and economic contacts between the two governments helped to clear the air of mutual suspicion that had kept them apart—to Germany's benefit—since the end of the war.

The appointment of Louis Barthou as French foreign minister in February 1934 marked the real beginning of France's quest for a Soviet connection. A conservative lawyer with impeccable nationalist credentials, Barthou was ideally suited to the task of allaying right-wing suspicions of the Soviet regime. Barthou proposed a dual alliance system in Eastern Europe, designed to strengthen the existing French security arrangements, which had been weakened by Poland's accommodation with Germany in the month before he took office. The first part of this proposed association was a pact of regional assistance in Eastern Europe, modelled on the Locarno treaties for Western Europe, in which Germany, the USSR, Poland, Czechoslovakia, Finland, and the Baltic states would mutually guarantee their frontiers. The second part of the proposal was a bilateral agreement in which the USSR would make a commitment to France as though it were a signatory of the Locarno treaties, while France would offer it a guarantee as though it were a member of the proposed eastern pact. Later, at Britain's insistence, Barthou invited Germany to join this bilateral agreement in order to preserve the multilateral principle of European security. As expected, Hitler contemptuously refused to become a party to France's bold campaign to freeze the territorial status quo in a region earmarked for absorption by Germany.

Barthou's effort to forge an 'Eastern Locarno' failed not because of Germany's refusal to join, which had been anticipated (Hitler's aversion to multilateral agreements that would restrict German freedom of action was well known) but rather by Poland's announcement in September 1934 that it would not permit Soviet troops to cross Polish territory to fulfill Soviet commitments under the proposed eastern security pact.

Warsaw's motives were not difficult to discern. To permit a Soviet military advance across Polish territory to engage the forces of a nation with which it had just signed a non-aggression pact would have contradicted Warsaw's policy of balancing Germany against the Soviet Union. Moreover, no one—least of all France, at the other end of the continent—could guarantee that a Red Army on Polish soil would not take the opportunity to enforce Russia's own extensive territorial claims against the Polish state. The French project for an 'Eastern Locarno' was consequently torpedoed by Poland's refusal to endanger its recent rapprochement with Germany and compromise the security of its frontier with Russia. The accidental assassination of Barthou in October ended the matter for good.[3]

Regardless of the fate of the multilateral scheme, Barthou had always intended to pursue the bilateral pact with the Soviet Union. The continuing recalcitrance of the Poles, together with the announcement of German rearmament, brought the issue to a head in the spring of 1935. Barthou's successor at the Quai d'Orsay, Pierre Laval, seriously doubted the value of an alliance with the Soviet Union. Instead, he favoured cementing relations among France, Britain, and Italy as a prelude to luring Germany into a four-power pact to manage the affairs of Europe (first proposed by Mussolini in March 1933 but never acted upon). However, on hearing of Germany's rearmament in March 1935, the French government forced Laval to complete the arrangements with Moscow that Barthou had begun. Thus on 2 May 1935, France and the Soviet Union concluded a pact of mutual assistance that was followed two weeks later by a similar agreement between the Soviet Union and France's principal ally in Eastern Europe, Czechoslovakia. For a brief moment, Germany seemed isolated by a powerful coalition of states determined to resist further violations of the peace treaty. This impression was enhanced by a dramatic policy shift at the Seventh Congress of the COMINTERN in August 1935. Whereas the communist parties outside the Soviet Union had previously been instructed to refuse all political

co-operation with 'bourgeois parties' (including the Socialists), Hitler's liquidation of the German Communist Party had revealed the dangers of this sectarian strategy. The new COMINTERN line called for communists to participate in a 'Popular Front' with all political groups opposed to fascism at home and German expansion in Europe.

This Franco–Soviet pact to restrain Germany was nevertheless a pale shadow of the military alliance that had compelled the Kaiser's armies to fight a war on two fronts in 1914–17. Laval had taken the precaution of ensuring that the bilateral agreement was strictly compatible with the multilateral provisions of the League Covenant and the Locarno treaties. What this meant in practice was that military assistance could be rendered by one signatory to the other only after an allegation of unprovoked aggression had been submitted to the League and the other signatories of the Locarno Pact (Britain, Italy, and Belgium) had given their approval. The effectiveness of the pact was further undermined by the French government's refusal to accept a military convention stipulating how the two armies would coordinate their activities in the event of war with Germany. These qualifications and omissions reduced the Franco–Soviet Pact to little more than a bilateral extension of the Stresa declaration of the previous month. The effectiveness of the Czech–Soviet Pact was similarly weakened by a provision subordinating it to the prior application of the Franco–Soviet Pact.

There were several reasons for France's hesitation to enter into an authentic military alliance with the Soviet Union to deter Nazi Germany. Not to be discounted was the surge of ideological hostility to the Soviet regime and its international organization, the COMINTERN, sparked by the formation of the Popular Front coalition in France. The French Communist Party's electoral alliance with the parties of the non-communist left in a united front against fascism had been intended to strengthen the basis for Franco–Russian co-operation in the face of the German threat to both countries, but in France it had precisely the opposite effect. Conservative critics denounced the Popular Front as a Trojan horse for Soviet interference in domestic French politics that, in conjunction with the Franco–Soviet Pact, threatened to drag France into a suicidal war with Germany for the USSR's benefit. This domestic opposition was reinforced by the intense hostility of France's Locarno partners, England and Belgium, to the idea of becoming embroiled with Germany on behalf of the Soviet regime. Considerations of geography and military strategy also recommended caution. The military value of the Red Army to French security remained questionable as long as Poland refused to grant transit rights to Soviet troops in the event of war with Germany. Moreover, the defensive military strategy of France adopted at the end of the 1920s precluded the type of offensive thrust into western Germany that a mutual defence treaty with the Soviets would imply.

Why, then, in view of all of these complications, did the governments of Paris and Moscow conclude the pact of May 1935? Apparently the most that France expected from the agreement was that it would discourage further German misbehaviour merely by raising the prospect of a two-front war. It also seems probable that Laval planned to use the threat of a Franco–Soviet rapprochement as a means of enticing Germany into a Western European diplomatic grouping, and then to leave the Soviets out in the cold. For his part, Soviet leader Joseph Stalin probably welcomed the international publicity attracted by the pact, if only as a diversion from domestic turmoil. It is also likely that he hoped to show Hitler the value of an understanding with the Soviet Union. Ever since Hitler's rise to power, the Kremlin had sought an accommodation with Berlin, not only because of anxieties about Hitler's intentions but also because the threat from a militaristic Japan on Russia's eastern flank made security in Europe all the more important. Although Hitler was willing to allow the mutually profitable trade relations between Germany and the Soviet Union to continue, he rebuffed these Soviet overtures because he was unwilling to sacrifice the propagandistic value of his anti-communist posture in

Europe or to antagonize the Poles, whose acquiescence in German rearmament he valued.

In any event, the issuing of the Stresa declaration in April 1935, the signing of the Franco–Soviet Pact in May, and the beginning of Franco–Italian military talks in June collectively gave the impression that France was well on the way towards achieving the security system it had been seeking ever since the end of the First World War. Now, having concluded alliances with Belgium, Poland, and Czechoslovakia and treaties of friendship with Romania and Yugoslavia, France finally seemed about to resurrect the old wartime coalition of Britain, the Soviet Union, and Italy in an effort to prevent further German transgressions of the peace treaty.

Yet within less than a year that coalition was in shambles as a result of the defection of Britain, Italy, and Belgium—France's three Western friends. The first crack in the anti-German coalition appeared on 18 June 1935 (the 120th anniversary of the Battle of Waterloo), when the British government tactlessly chose to unveil a bilateral naval agreement that it had negotiated in secret, permitting Germany to exceed the naval limitations of the Versailles Treaty in exchange for a promise not to increase its total tonnage beyond 35 per cent of that of the combined fleets of the Commonwealth. The British government had sought this agreement after Germany informed it of plans to construct a number of destroyers, cruisers, and submarines; faced with this evidence of intent to violate the treaty restrictions, the British wanted some assurance that its own supremacy in the Mediterranean and the North Atlantic would not be threatened. The Anglo–German agreement provided for precisely what the Stresa agreement had forbidden, a further violation by Germany of its treaty obligations. London's reasoning was obvious: it knew from intelligence sources that while Hitler planned to build a navy that would eventually enable Germany to play a global role, for the immediate future the German naval construction program was geared to assuring control of the Baltic against the Soviet Union and interrupting

France's oceanic communications with its colonies and foreign sources of supply.

The second defector from the anti-German front was Italy. This defection was caused by Mussolini's invasion of the East African empire of Ethiopia—one of only two African states (the other being the Republic of Liberia) that had successfully resisted absorption by European powers during the imperial expansion of the pre-war years. Italy's interest in Ethiopia dated from the last two decades of the nineteenth century. After a humiliating defeat at the hands of Ethiopian warriors in 1896, Italian colonial forces had retreated to the coastal enclaves of Eritrea on the Red Sea and Somaliland on the Indian Ocean. In 1906, Italy and the two other colonial powers in the region, Britain and France, agreed to guarantee the territorial integrity of Ethiopia and demarcated their respective spheres of influence there.

By the mid-1930s, Mussolini's grandiose design for a new Roman Empire around the Mediterranean revived the dormant territorial claims against the independent East African state. Britain and France, which had minimal interests in the area and were intent on securing Italy's support against Germany, did nothing to discourage its belated colonial aspirations. Meeting with Mussolini in Rome in January 1935, Foreign Minister Laval of France formally renounced his country's minor economic interests in Ethiopia and gave the Italian leader verbal assurances of a free hand there. And at the Stresa Conference in April, neither France nor Britain objected when Mussolini hinted at his ambitions in East Africa. In August London and Paris went so far as to offer Rome a privileged economic position in Ethiopia, together with the right to appoint Italian advisers to the country's civil service, army, and police—the traditional prelude to the establishment of a protectorate.

These extensive Anglo–French concessions clearly indicate that Mussolini could have gained effective control of Ethiopia through patient diplomacy. But the prospective leader of the new Roman Empire was more interested in military glory than in the impoverished territory itself. Thus on 3 October he launched a full-scale armed attack, expecting little military resistance from the ill-equipped forces of the Ethiopian emperor, Haile Selassie, and no diplomatic opposition from the European powers. On the first count he was correct. Although the rugged mountains in the interior slowed the Italian advance, with the help of air power and poison gas the Ethiopian forces were routed in the spring of 1936. In Europe, however, the Duce was first disappointed and then outraged by the unsympathetic response of his friends in London and Paris. Since Ethiopia was a member of the League of Nations, public opinion in Britain lashed out at Italy's overt violation of national sovereignty and pressured the government into invoking the principle of collective security. To Mussolini's astonishment Britain and France prodded the League to condemn the Italian offensive as an act of aggression and to vote for the imposition of economic sanctions on 18 October.

The hypocrisy of the two powers, which had divided up most of Africa between them before 1914 and had recently given Italy the green light to obtain a belated share of the spoils, left a lasting impression on the Italian leader. His feelings of betrayal were not assuaged by subsequent efforts by London and Paris to undermine the very policy that they had promoted at Geneva. A secret Anglo–French agreement in December provided for the cession of most of Ethiopia to Italy and the reduction of the rest to the status of an Italian client state, but it had to be disavowed when its embarrassing contents were leaked to the press by unsympathetic personnel at the Quai d'Orsay. Yet this abortive Hoare–Laval Pact (named for the British and French foreign ministers) did apparently reflect the true policies of the two governments, for they refused to extend the economic sanctions to oil, which Italy required to fuel its mechanized army and air force in Ethiopia and had to import from foreign sources. An effective oil embargo would have required a British naval blockade in the Mediterranean, since Italy was receiving most of its petroleum from the United States (whose oil exports to Italy more than doubled during the Ethiopian conflict). But a naval blockade would surely have meant war with Italy and complications with the US—risks much too serious to undertake on behalf of an African country of no interest to Britain or France.

The most important international consequence of the Ethiopian affair, apart from the military defeat of Haile Selassie and Italy's annexation of his empire in May 1936, was the deterioration of relations between Italy and its erstwhile partners in the Stresa front against Germany. By supporting economic sanctions against Italy and verbally condemning its actions in the League, Britain and France had antagonized Mussolini without denying him the objectives he sought in East Africa. The Hoare–Laval scheme and the half-hearted application of sanctions also undermined the principle of collective security. If such an unmistakable act of aggression against a member of the League could go unpunished,

what was to prevent Germany from practising subtler forms of aggression in Europe?

Hitler, for his part, remained neutral on the Ethiopia issue while expressing his willingness to supply Italy with iron, coal, steel, and other scarce materials. Berlin's benevolent neutrality was greatly appreciated in Rome. Thus with the two guarantors of the Locarno treaties (Britain and Italy) at loggerheads over East Africa, and Mussolini grateful for Germany's acquiescence regarding Ethiopia, the Führer judged that the time was right for a daring probe of the anti-German diplomatic coalition. The submission of the Franco–Soviet Pact to the French Chamber of Deputies for ratification in February 1936 supplied the perfect pretext for Hitler's first provocative move since his announcement of Germany's rearmament a year earlier. Before making that bilateral pact, France had prudently obtained assurances from Britain

CANADIAN FOREIGN POLICY DURING THE 1930S

When Italy invaded Ethiopia in 1935, Canada's acting representative at the League of Nations, Walter Riddell, was told by the newly elected government of Mackenzie King to take no action, but he disregarded his instructions and called for the League to impose stiff economic sanctions. Whereas the outgoing prime minister, R.B. Bennett, had believed that Italy should be punished for its aggression, King was determined to avoid involving Canada in any conflict that did not bear on its immediate national interests. He announced that Riddell's call for sanctions did not represent the position of the Canadian government, and the League effectively abandoned its effort to stop Mussolini.

Nor would King's Canada make any official protests in 1938, when Hitler annexed Austria and proceeded with his plan to dismember Czechoslovakia. At a meeting with Hitler in 1937, King had described the Nazi leader as 'a man of deep sincerity and a genuine patriot'. King also refused to support the more than 1,400 Canadian volunteers of the Mackenzie–Papineau Battalion,

which fought with the 15th International Brigade of the Spanish Republican Army against the Nationalist forces led by General Franco and aided by Hitler and Mussolini in the Spanish Civil War of 1936–9. Not only were Canadians prohibited by law from taking part in the conflict, but many of the volunteers who survived the fighting (nearly 750 died) were also investigated by the RCMP upon their return to Canada.

King's policy of appeasement was generally popular with the Canadian public, as evinced by his re-election in 1940. But his indifferent response to the European crises of the 1930s contributed to one of the darker episodes in the country's history, when, responding to high unemployment and racial intolerance at home, he imposed severe restrictions on immigration, shutting out many refugees—particularly Jews—fleeing religious persecution in Europe, and leaving Canada with one of the worst records among Western nations for admitting Jewish refugees leading up to the Second World War.

and Italy that it would not be deemed incompatible with the multilateral agreement signed at Locarno. However, Hitler warned that he would regard it as a violation of Locarno and a grave threat to his own country's security—so much so that he would feel free to renounce Germany's end of the Locarno bargain by reintroducing German military forces and fortifications into the demilitarized zone of the Rhineland.

Useless to France as a military deterrent (because of its geographical contradictions), the Franco–Soviet Pact was in fact immensely valuable to Germany as a propaganda tool. Its unpopularity in anti-communist circles in all European countries, especially Britain, allowed Hitler to raise the bogey of the 'red menace' while using the innocuous pact as justification for tearing up the Locarno agreement. France, as expected, ratified the treaty on 27 February, and on the morning of 7 March three battalions of German infantry, accompanied by anti-aircraft guns and air force squadrons, moved into the Rhineland.

The Rhineland's status as a demilitarized zone was widely regarded as the most important guarantee of good behaviour on Berlin's part, precluding any German advance against France and Belgium and, by exposing Germany to invasion from the west, deterring it from making any aggressive moves to the east. The military occupation of the Rhineland in March 1936 ought to have drawn a strong response from France, but it did not. The reasons are clear. By constructing the Maginot Line, France had in effect already written off the Rhineland as indefensible. It would make little difference which bank of the Rhine the Germans chose to place their defences on, so long as France was protected by its concrete bastion. Accordingly, the French army possessed no mobile force that could be dispatched to the Rhineland to expel the Germans, nor did it have an advance plan for such an operation, despite extensive intelligence reports indicating that remilitarization was imminent. The creation of such a force and the development of such a plan, suggested a year earlier by politician Paul Reynaud on the advice of Colonel Charles de Gaulle, was

rejected as incompatible with the defensive strategy pursued by the French general staff. So long as the German forces in the Rhineland did not appear to be preparing to attack France (in fact, Hitler had shrewdly instructed them to be discreet), the French high command believed that a military response to the remilitarization would be both unnecessary (for the strategic reasons noted above) and foolhardy (because French estimates of the Germans' military strength at the time were exaggeratedly high).

Curiously, the civilian government in Paris—a caretaker ministry in power pending elections scheduled for the following month—showed more interest in an offensive operation to expel the Germans from the Rhineland than the military authorities did. When Foreign Minister Pierre-Etienne Flandin flew to London to discuss the possibility of a joint Anglo–French countermove, he was told that the British government did not view the remilitarization of the Rhineland as a 'flagrant' violation of the treaty of Locarno because it was not accompanied by threatening moves toward the French frontier. Consequently Britain would neither participate in any military response nor approve of any unilateral French action. This narrow, legalistic interpretation of the language of Locarno was merely a pretext: the real reason for Britain's hesitation was its desire to avoid at all costs the European war that it believed would inevitably result from any attempt to drive the Germans out of the Rhineland. In this perception the British were correct. Although the German commanders in the Rhineland were under orders to withdraw their troops in the event of military opposition, such a move was to be only a tactical retreat in preparation for a renewed offensive.

It has often been suggested that Germany would have backed off if France had resisted. This is a myth. Hitler was actually prepared to risk war over the issue in March 1936, largely because he (correctly) anticipated that demonstrating his willingness to go to the brink of war would paralyze the Western powers and so make actual war unnecessary. Thus London and Paris merely issued stern protests, sponsored a pro forma condemnation of the action by the League of Nations, and authorized joint Anglo–French military conversations. The latter satisfied a long-standing objective of French foreign policy, but they were confined to meaningless generalities because of Britain's reluctance to discuss detailed plans of operations. Even Britain's rearmament in the aftermath of the Rhineland crisis gave little comfort to France, since it concentrated on upgrading naval and air forces for home and imperial defence rather than on building a land army that could be sent to the continent. In subsequent public statements the British government forcefully expressed its desire that France and Germany make arrangements to freeze the territorial status quo in Europe. Thus the remilitarization of the Rhineland was rapidly to become a *fait accompli*.

As noted above, the remilitarization of the Rhineland did not greatly alter the strategic balance between France and Germany, since the Maginot Line had already made the buffer zone irrelevant to French military calculations. Nor did it suddenly invalidate France's security commitments to Poland and Czechoslovakia, which had already been rendered incapable of realization when construction of the Maginot Line began. Still, the failure to react firmly to Hitler's unilateral repudiation of the Locarno Pact had a devastating psychological impact on all the smaller countries that had expected France to take the lead in restraining Germany. The result was a radical reorientation of the foreign policies of all of those minor powers. The chiefs of staff of the Little Entente, meeting in June 1936 to reassess the strategic situation in Central Europe in the light of recent events, concluded that their countries' future security might well require a choice between subservience to Germany and subservience to Russia. The Polish government, which faced that difficult choice even more directly, resumed with greater enthusiasm the policy of détente with Germany that had been inaugurated at the beginning of 1934. At the same time, the countries of Central and Eastern Europe retained their diplomatic arrangements with France in the illusory hope that they might receive some help.

It was Belgium, France's neighbour in Western Europe and its earliest and staunchest ally against Germany, that drew the appropriate conclusions from France's inaction during the Rhineland crisis and acted accordingly. In October 1936, after a lengthy reappraisal of its security situation, the Belgian government formally renounced its military alliance with France and reverted to its pre-war status of neutrality. This dramatic reversal stemmed in part from political tension between Belgium's two linguistic groups, the French-speaking Walloons and the Flemish-speakers, who had long resented their country's diplomatic subservience to France. It also reflected the reluctance of anti-communist elements to see their nation dragged into a war with Germany on behalf of France's new Soviet ally. But the principal reason was the belief that neither France nor Britain could or would give Belgium the kind of protection it needed. The military consequences of Belgium's defection were critical: Anglo–French forces were no longer guaranteed transit rights across Belgian territory in the event of war with Germany, and Franco–Belgian military coordination—a key element in France's defence strategy for its unfortified northeastern frontier—was abruptly terminated.

By the autumn of 1936, Germany had thus obtained protective screens on its western and eastern borders that effectively insulated it against military intervention from an alliance of great powers. In the west, a neutralized Belgium and a remilitarized Rhineland (where elaborate fortifications were now being constructed along the French frontier) shielded Germany's industrial heartland in the Ruhr valley from French military power. To the east, an increasingly co-operative Poland served as a formidable barrier against the Soviet Union. And to the south the nations of the Little Entente, geographically separated from their undependable French patron, were driven to seek improved relations with Germany. Hitler wasted no time in profiting from these advantages to expand Germany's economic and diplomatic influence in those nations of Central and Southeastern Europe whose co-operation or acquiescence would further his short-term object-ives: the annexation of Austria and the destruc-tion of Czechoslovakia. At the same time he took steps to accelerate the pace of Germany's rearma-ment and to reorient its economy in preparation for the major war that he planned to launch in the more distant future.

THE SPANISH CIVIL WAR

That the Western powers failed to recognize the implications of this process of consolidation, both within Germany and between Germany and its neighbours to the south and east, was due in large part to the fact that that their attention was fixed on the civil war that had erupted in Spain in the summer of 1936. In July, military officers in command of the garrisons in Spanish Morocco had rebelled against the left-leaning government in Madrid (elected the previous February) and organized an uprising on the Spanish mainland. When the navy and air force remained loyal to the Republican government, the leader of the coup, General Francisco Franco, was compelled to look abroad for assistance in transporting his forces in Morocco across the Straits of Gibraltar to the Iberian peninsula. This appeal from the Spanish rebels, or Nationalists as they called themselves, received sympathetic responses in Berlin and Rome. By the end of July, German and Italian planes were ferrying Franco's troops to the mainland, where they quickly established contact with the rebel-held sector in the northeast. By the fall of 1936, the quantity of German and Italian aid had markedly increased. Hitler dispatched a special air force unit, the Condor Legion, to pro-vide air cover for the rebel forces, while Mussolini contributed large contingents of Italian infantry in the guise of 'volunteers'.

Hitler's decision to assist the military rebellion in Spain was determined by a number of fac-tors. The most important military advantage to be gained (apart from the opportunity to test the bombing of civilian population centres as a ter-ror tactic) lay in the promise of access to Spain's abundant supplies of strategic raw materials.

With Germany engaged in a massive rearmament program, Hitler hoped to obtain Spanish iron and copper ores without having to pay for them in scarce foreign currency. An arrangement to this effect was reached in the summer of 1937, once the major iron- and copper-producing regions of Spain had fallen under Franco's control. Large quantities of these strategic materials, which had previously been exported to Britain, were diverted to the German rearmament program in payment for the military supplies that Hitler was furnishing Franco.

In addition, two diplomatic considerations led Germany to support the Nationalist insurrec-tion in Spain. The first was the likelihood that co-operation with Italy on Franco's behalf would cement the friendly relations between Berlin and Rome that had been established during the Ethiopian affair. This became all the more appar-ent when France and Britain organized a non-intervention committee in September 1936 to curb all foreign involvement in the Spanish con-flict. Once Mussolini had committed his personal prestige to a rebel victory in Spain, the Western democracies were bound to protest—dashing all hopes of reconstituting the Stresa coalition and driving Mussolini even closer to Hitler. Still, the most obvious benefit that Germany derived from the Spanish Civil War was the diversion of French and British attention from its projects of rearma-ment and continental economic consolidation. For this reason it was more advantageous for Hitler to prolong the Spanish conflict than to help the rebels achieve a quick victory. This he accom-plished by turning down Franco's urgent request for infantry units (after the rebel offensive against Madrid in late 1936 failed) and refusing to enlarge the Condor Legion for the duration of the conflict.

The ideological overtones of the Spanish Civil War were apparent from the outset and contrib-uted to its popular image as an epic confrontation between fascism and democracy. Franco's tactical alliance with the small Spanish Fascist movement, the Falange, and his dependence on Mussolini and Hitler for military support, seemed to herald the spread of fascism—the ideology hatched in

Bombed buildings in Guernica, destroyed during the Spanish Civil War. © Bettmann/CORBIS.

Italy and perfected in Germany—to the western tip of Europe. Conversely, the arrival in Spain of the 'International Brigades'—groups of left-wing volunteers from various countries determined to fight on behalf of the beleaguered Republic— seemed to symbolize the democratic world's commitment to oppose fascism in all its forms. The conspicuous presence of the small Spanish Communist Party in the Popular Front coalition in Madrid and the flow of military aid from the Soviet Union reflected the Kremlin's new policy of defending parliamentary institutions against the Fascist menace.

In fact this ideological dichotomy was deceptive. Franco and the military, clerical, and land-owning groups that formed his base of support were reactionaries who shared little in common with the Falangist firebrands; when the marriage

of convenience between them had outlived its usefulness, the Falange was reduced to insignificance. Once military victory in the spring of 1939 had relieved Franco of the need to rely on German and Italian assistance, he showed little interest in joining Hitler and Mussolini to mount a 'Fascist crusade'. Fears of a menace to France from a Nationalist regime across the Pyrenees proved ill-founded. The Spanish dictator was to remain neutral for the duration of the Second World War despite strenuous German efforts to secure his active co-operation with the Axis war effort.

In the opposing camp, internal tensions and contradictions undermined the political unity and ideological consistency of the anti-Fascist cause. Within Republican Spain itself, communists, anarchists, Trotskyists, socialists, and liberals clashed over political ideology and military strategy, and differences were often settled by a burst of machine-gun fire. Outside Spain, the nations supposedly committed to democratic government did nothing to prove that commitment. The Conservative government in London could scarcely conceal its distaste for the leftist regime in Madrid and refused to lift a finger in its defence. In Canada there was significant support for the Republican cause, but public opinion was divided and the federal government sought to avoid the issue, refusing to make any commitment on either side. Even the recently elected Popular Front government in France, dominated by socialists with communist support, refused Spanish Republican appeals for military supplies, for fear of antagonizing Britain and further inflaming opinion at home, where many Roman Catholics were already distressed by reports of monasteries looted and nuns murdered by defenders of the leftist regime in Madrid.

Even the Soviet Union—the only European power to furnish supplies to Republican Spain—kept the flow of aid to a minimum and demanded immediate payment in gold or raw materials. Some historians have speculated that Stalin's reasoning was similar to Hitler's, and that he restricted his assistance to Franco in order to keep the Spanish pot boiling as a diversion from domestic turmoil—in the Soviet Union's case, the purge trials that began a month after Franco's insurrection.

HITLER'S PLAN

While the Spanish Civil War occupied the attention of the world, Germany worked to put its economy on a wartime footing and mounted a diplomatic offensive in several directions in aid of Hitler's two immediate objectives: the annexation of Austria and the annihilation of Czechoslovakia. Economically, Germany in 1936 was marked by superficial signs of prosperity that concealed a structural weakness of alarming proportions. The rearmament boom, fuelled by deficit financing, had eliminated unemployment, but at the beginning of 1936 Germany had begun to suffer from a severe shortage of foreign exchange due to the import of enormous quantities of raw materials required for rearmament. Previous efforts to solve this problem by requisitioning domestic savings, restricting imports, and diverting exports to countries whose raw materials were in demand proved only partially successful. If current trends continued, the remilitarization project and the economic recovery it had stimulated could be halted in their tracks unless Germany was able to pay for the strategic raw materials that could not be produced domestically.

The import crisis of early 1936 reminded the Nazi leaders of the Great War, when Germany's dependence on foreign supplies had made the British blockade of those imports extremely effective. Thus Hitler proposed a short-term program of economic development designed to render Germany self-sufficient in the strategic materials required to prepare for the European war that was expected to begin no later than the summer of 1940. The Four-Year Plan, launched in October 1936 under the supervision of Hermann Göring, was to make Germany absolutely independent by fostering the production of synthetic materials as substitutes for the natural resources unobtainable domestically. In time the German chemical industry developed artificial rubber, textiles, and plastics, while expanding its synthetic fuels program to extract oil from Germany's abundant coal supplies. The use of Germany's low-grade iron ore for the production of steel was intensified in order to reduce the nation's dependence on the high-grade ores of Sweden and Spain.

The unfolding of Hitler's military strategy in the mid-1930s reflected the precarious position of the German economy at that time. Synthetic substitutes made up for some of the shortage of raw materials, but Germany still could not hope to win a long war of attrition against the Soviet Union and the British Empire, especially if the United States lent its assistance. Such was the lesson of the First World War. Hence Germany's adoption of the 'blitzkrieg' strategy: short, swift engagements against isolated opponents. Although the principal weapons were to be tanks and airplanes, both of which required large quantities of oil, rubber, and other products, the brief duration of these 'lightning wars' meant that they could be won with only a modest mobilization of economic resources. Eventually, the territory conquered in Europe would provide access to the raw materials that Germany needed to become self-sufficient at last.

The diplomatic counterpart of this economic–strategic program was the campaign to weaken the French alliance system in Eastern Europe and discourage the other great powers—Italy, Britain, and the Soviet Union—from joining France and its remaining Eastern European clients in resisting Germany's bid for hegemony in that region. Since the annexation of Austria was the first item on Hitler's agenda for continental expansion, it is no surprise that he endeavoured to strengthen the friendly ties with Italy—the traditional guarantor of Austrian independence—that Germany had established during the Ethiopian invasion and the early stages of the Spanish Civil War. In October 1936, following cordial discussions between the Italian and German foreign ministers, the two governments announced their agreement to co-operate, and the 'Rome–Berlin Axis' was born.

In conjunction with a secret understanding between Germany and Austria, reached the previous July with Mussolini's blessing, this agreement signalled the Italian leader's tacit acceptance of Germany's freedom of action in Austria in particular and Southeastern Europe in general. The reorientation of Italian foreign policy reflected Mussolini's conversion to Hitler's conception of the geopolitical basis of Italo–German co-operation: the complementary expansion of Italian power southward into the Mediterranean basin and of German power eastward into the heartland of Central Europe and beyond. The formation of the Rome–Berlin Axis gave Hitler two crucial advantages: it prevented Italy from objecting to Germany's designs on Austria, and it increased the likelihood of tension in the Mediterranean and North Africa between Italy and the two dominant powers in that region, Britain and France.

Throughout 1937, Hitler steadily increased the pressure on Austria to align its foreign and domestic policies more closely with those of the Third Reich. In the meantime, he encouraged the Austrian Nazis to step up their subversive activities in preparation for a peaceful takeover in Vienna that would lead to voluntary unification with Germany. In January 1938, however, the Austrian chancellor, Kurt von Schuschnigg, authorized police raids on the headquarters of the Austrian Nazis that uncovered embarrassing evidence of collusion with their counterparts in Germany. Hitler abandoned his plan for a gradual movement towards *Anschluss* and prepared to hasten the process through direct intimidation of the government in Vienna. In a meeting at his private retreat at Berchtesgaden, Austria, in February 1938, Hitler berated Schuschnigg for failing to pursue pro-German policies in conformity with the agreement of July 1936 and threatened immediate military intervention unless he allowed the Austrian Nazis to play a major role in his government. Although the Austrian leader acceded to this demand (on Mussolini's advice), he boldly decided to pre-empt Hitler's plans for a peaceful takeover by scheduling a plebiscite for 13 March, in which the Austrian people would be asked to vote on their nation's independence.

Had this plebiscite been conducted before the Nazis' rise to power in Germany, it would probably have resulted in an overwhelming vote for unification, but anti-Nazi sentiment in Austria was now strong, and Hitler was unwilling to risk the embarrassment of a negative vote. Thus, after securing the tacit consent of Mussolini, the Führer sent German troops into Austria on 12 March. They met no resistance from Austrian military forces. Having asked for advice from the British and French governments, Schuschnigg had learned that London and Paris were no more willing than Mussolini to intervene on Austria's behalf. Neither was bound by treaty obligation to defend Austria, and neither was prepared to risk war by enforcing the provision of the Versailles Treaty that forbade *Anschluss*. On 10 April, a rigged plebiscite produced an overwhelming vote for the unification of Hitler's adopted nation and the land of his birth.

GERMANY AND JAPAN

Meanwhile, Germany had also been developing a cordial relationship with the rising imperial power in the Far East. The German–Japanese rapprochement between 1936 and 1938 was actively promoted by Hitler for reasons similar to those that had prompted his fruitful overtures to Italy: it was in Germany's interest to encourage Japanese imperialism in East Asia, since Japan's expansion would put pressure on the Asian possessions of Germany's principal antagonists in Europe. Britain, for example, would be less likely to interfere with Germany's plans for Europe if it faced simultaneous threats to its imperial interests in the western Pacific and to its Mediterranean lifeline from Japan and Italy, respectively. In the same way, the Soviet Union would be deterred from fulfilling its treaty obligations to France and Czechoslovakia if it faced a Japanese threat from Manchuria.

Coordinating German policy in Europe and Japanese policy in Asia was not easy. Just as the related issues of Austrian independence and the status of the German-speaking inhabitants of the South Tyrol had delayed the establishment of the Rome–Berlin Axis, the close relationship between Germany and the Chinese Nationalist regime of Chiang Kai-shek was a serious impediment to the formation of a Berlin–Tokyo Axis. Since the mid-1930s, Germany had participated in a mutually beneficial relationship with China. In exchange for military advisers who helped Chiang modernize his armed forces and military equipment, Germany was able to obtain strategic raw materials for rearmament without having to spend foreign exchange. The presence of German military advisers in Nanking and the flow of German arms to Chiang's army understandably annoyed Japan and impeded the development of German–Japanese co-operation. But the ratification of the Franco–Soviet Pact by the French parliament in February 1936 highlighted the obvious congruity of interest between Tokyo and Berlin. Working together, Germany and Japan could restrain the Soviet Union on its European and Asian flanks to the benefit of both.

Accordingly, on 25 November 1936, the two governments unveiled an agreement called the Anti-Comintern Pact. Its ostensible purpose was to promote co-operation against the subversive activities of the Communist International and its political apparatus in each country. But since both Germany and Japan had long since suppressed their domestic communist parties, the agreement was widely—and correctly—suspected of containing secret provisions directed against the Soviet Union. A year later, in November 1937, Italy joined the same pact and the world faced the nightmare of an impending alignment of three expansionist powers.

The transformation of the Anti-Comintern Pact into a full-fledged military alliance was delayed by two considerations. The first was Germany's reluctance to sacrifice its lucrative economic relationship with China. This obstacle was finally removed in the winter and spring of 1938, when Hitler recognized the Japanese puppet state of Manchukuo, terminated all military assistance to China, and recalled Chiang Kai-shek's German military advisers as a prelude to proposing a military alliance to Japan the following summer. The second obstacle was Berlin's insistence that the proposed alliance be directed at Great Britain as well as the Soviet Union. Japan wanted to transform the Anti-Comintern Pact into a German–Japanese alliance against the USSR, its major rival in East Asia, but was reluctant to risk a war with Britain for fear of drawing the United States into the conflict. Berlin, on the other hand, was less concerned about the Soviet threat than about Anglo–French opposition to Germany's policy of continental expansion. This conflict of priorities delayed the finalization of the alliance with Japan until after the beginning of the Second World War.

GERMAN POLICY IN EASTERN EUROPE

While Fascist Italy and imperial Japan gradually gravitated toward the German orbit in the years 1936–8, Hitler worked to undermine the French alliance system in Eastern Europe and establish

German predominance in that region in preparation for the long-awaited war of annihilation against Czechoslovakia. His principal aim in this policy was to accelerate Germany's tactical rapprochement with Poland and Hungary and to establish ties with Czechoslovakia's two partners in the Little Entente, Yugoslavia and Romania. The courtship of Poland and Romania was intended to secure their services in blocking the Soviet Union's access to its Czechoslovak ally. The simultaneous approaches to Hungary and Yugoslavia were designed to encourage those two countries to settle their long-standing dispute over the status of the large Magyar minority in Yugoslavia so that Hungary could concentrate its revisionist ambitions against the easternmost provinces of the Czechoslovak state, Slovakia and the Carpatho-Ukraine (Ruthenia), with their 750,000 Hungarians.

To secure Poland's acquiescence in this plan to destroy Czechoslovakia, Hitler had only to remove the major source of friction between Berlin and Warsaw while emphasizing the one positive issue that was likely to foster Polish–German co-operation against his intended victim. The principal source of friction was the city of Danzig, where the Nazi municipal government caused trouble for Polish authorities. Directives from Berlin had effectively restrained the anti-Polish agitation of the Danzig Nazis during the period when Hitler was soliciting Warsaw's friendship. The positive basis for German–Polish co-operation at Czechoslovakia's expense was the Teschen district of Silesia, a rich industrial area awarded to Czechoslovakia in 1920 despite the presence of almost 80,000 Poles. At Hitler's urging the Polish government added its own demand for Teschen to Hitler's insistence that Czechoslovakia cede the German-speaking Sudetenland to Germany. It may have seemed hypocritical (if not dangerous) for the Poles, who presided over a variety of discontented minorities in their own multinational country, to make territorial demands on the basis of the principle of nationality. But this inconsistency caused little concern at a time when the prospects seemed excellent for Poland, as a silent partner of Germany, to acquire economically valuable territory at Czechoslovakia's expense.

Obtaining the consent of Romania and Yugoslavia for the destruction of Czechoslovakia was more difficult. Neither had territorial claims on the prospective victim, and therefore they could not be rewarded as Poland was to be. As members of the Little Entente, both were associated with Czechoslovakia and closely identified with the latter's protector, France. On the other hand, neither nation shared a common border with Germany nor had much reason to quarrel with or fear the Germans. Their common adversary was Hungary, which had lost much of its territory to them at the Paris Peace Conference and had never stopped agitating for restitution. Indeed, fear of Hungarian revisionism was the only basis for diplomatic co-operation among Yugoslavia, Romania, and Czechoslovakia. This fear was particularly profound in Yugoslavia because of its strategic position blocking Hungary's only outlet to the sea. But since Hitler was actively seeking Hungary's participation in the partition of Czechoslovakia by dangling Slovakia and Carpatho-Ukraine before the authorities in Budapest, this diversion of Hungarian attention served to allay fears in Belgrade. Accordingly, Yugoslavia and Hungary, with Berlin's encouragement, reached agreement in August 1938 on the major issues of dispute between them, in the process dealing a serious blow to the anti-Hungarian basis of the Little Entente. Simultaneous German efforts to detach Romania from Czechoslovakia were facilitated by the bitter territorial struggle between Romania and Czechoslovakia's ally, Russia, in regard to Bessarabia, a former province of the tsarist empire annexed by Romania during the Russian Revolution. Just as it was in the interest of Poland, with its large holdings of former Russian territory, to block Soviet access to Czechoslovakia, so it was in Romania's interest to prevent the Red Army from circumventing the Polish barrier to Central Europe.

Hitler's diplomatic campaign to isolate Czechoslovakia from its neighbours was bolstered by a series of commercial policies designed to subordinate the shaky economic systems of

Central Europe to the expanding economy of Germany. This economic advance into Central and Southern Europe had begun in the early 1930s when the mainly agricultural economies of those regions had begun to suffer from the catastrophic collapse in world commodity prices. Germany, with its chronic deficit in food production, became the major customer for the agricultural surpluses that were piling up in those nations. With the advent of the Nazi regime, the introduction of exchange controls and bilateral barter arrangements compelled the agricultural nations to import ever-increasing quantities of German industrial products in exchange for their foodstuffs. Subsequent political developments increased this dependence on Germany as both a market for their primary products and a supplier of their industrial needs. Yugoslavia's participation in the League-sponsored economic sanctions against Italy during the Ethiopian campaign deprived it of a major market for its grain exports, caused severe economic damage, and forced a reorientation of its trade towards Germany.

The German annexation of Austria—a major trading partner of Yugoslavia and Hungary—increased Germany's domination of those nations' foreign trade. German economic penetration of Romania was prompted by its abundant supplies of oil, required for the mechanized army and air force that Germany was constructing. In December 1937, a German–Romanian agreement provided for the exchange of German military equipment for Romanian oil to supplement the synthetic petroleum production quota of the Four-Year Plan. These commercial connections between Germany and the nations of Central and Southern Europe, though developed for rational economic reasons that promised benefits to both partners, helped to smooth the path towards more cordial political relations at a time when German diplomacy was loosening the bonds of the Little Entente to isolate Czechoslovakia.

Germany's diplomatic and commercial offensive in Central Europe severely undermined the security of Czechoslovakia. The enlistment of Poland and Hungary in the German campaign of territorial revision and the de facto collapse of the Little Entente left the Czechoslovak state bereft of defenders and surrounded by predators. Its bilateral alliances with France and the Soviet Union had been gravely weakened by the diplomatic revolution that Hitler had wrought in the two-and-a-half years since the remilitarization of the Rhineland. Profiting from the Belgian–Rhenish screen in the west, the Polish–Romanian screen in the east, and the deterrent effect that the new alignment with Italy and Japan could be expected to have on Britain, Hitler proceeded to lay the political groundwork for his blitzkrieg against Czechoslovakia.

In the summer of 1938, the Nazi leader directed a furious propaganda campaign against the Prague regime's alleged persecution of the three million German-speaking inhabitants of the Bohemian borderlands. Though better treated than any of the other Germanic minorities in Europe, the Sudeten Germans harboured genuine grievances against the government in Prague. A prime instance was the preference shown to Czech-speaking citizens in government hiring, a discriminatory practice that Berlin skilfully exploited. However, Hitler cared little about the plight of the Sudetenlanders. The last thing he wanted was an amicable resolution of their dispute with Prague that would remove the pretext he needed to destroy the Czechoslovak state by force. Accordingly, he instructed the leader of the Sudeten German Party, Konrad Henlein, to demand from the Czechoslovak government what he knew it could not grant: concessions that would lead to the political autonomy of the German-speaking region as a prelude to secession and eventual annexation by Germany.

This solution was predictably unacceptable to Czechoslovakia for two reasons. First, the loss of the Sudetenland would deprive it of its defensible frontiers and the elaborate border fortifications constructed behind them, leaving the truncated nation exposed to invasion by a German military force unimpeded by either natural or artificial barriers. Second, granting autonomy to the Germans of Bohemia would establish a precedent for similar demands by the other national minorities in the polyglot republic—the Poles of Teschen, the Hungarians in southern Slovakia and Carpatho-Ukraine, even the increasingly dissatisfied Slovaks. The result was bound to be the dissolution of the multinational state created in 1918.

As German intimidation of Czechoslovakia intensified, and as it became increasingly clear that Hitler was prepared to use force in pursuit of his annexationist aims, the French and British governments were compelled to clarify their policies toward the impending crisis. In July the Czech minister stationed in Paris was privately informed that France was unwilling to go to war over the Sudetenland, though it would remain publicly committed to the Franco–Czechoslovak alliance for the sake of appearances. The deplorable condition of the French air force, Belgium's refusal to allow the transit of French troops to Germany's most vulnerable industrial targets, and exaggerated estimates of the size of the German army and the strength of the Rhineland fortifications all contributed to France's failure of nerve. The British government, unaware that Paris had repudiated its obligation to Prague, was alarmed at the prospect of being dragged into a war between France and Germany over an issue of no importance to British national interests. Remembering the Luftwaffe's bombardment of the Spanish Basque towns, British leaders made every diplomatic effort to avert a war that might bring similar attacks on British cities still inadequately protected by the anti-aircraft artillery system and radar installations then under construction. Anglo–French pressure compelled Czech President Eduard Beneš to reach a settlement on 5 September, in which he granted all of the Sudeten German Party's main demands. Since Hitler's goal was war, not a political settlement, he instructed the Sudeten Party to fabricate a new list of grievances that could be exploited when preparations for the invasion were complete.

The German dictator was thwarted, faced with what he later said was his first diplomatic setback, because of British Prime Minister Neville Chamberlain's eagerness to take him at his word. Like many British statesmen of his generation in both major parties, Chamberlain was profoundly influenced by memories of the Great War and the Paris Peace Conference. He shared the widespread conviction that the terrible war of 1914 might have been averted by more skilful, active diplomacy. He also believed that the victorious Allies had treated Germany unfairly by refusing to apply the principle of national self-determination to the delimitation of its eastern frontiers. The convergence of these two issues in the Czechoslovakian crisis of September 1938 prompted Chamberlain to undertake face-to-face negotiations with Hitler in hope of resolving what he believed to be Germany's just grievance against Czechoslovakia, and in the hope of preventing a second world war. On 15 September, two days after Hitler approved the Sudeten German leader's withdrawal from the negotiations with the Czechoslovak government in preparation for war, Chamberlain boarded an airplane for the first time in his life and flew to Berchtesgaden in a frantic quest for a settlement.

In Berchtesgaden Chamberlain received Hitler's demand that the Sudetenland be transferred to Germany on the grounds of national self-determination. He then returned to London to try to persuade the representatives of France and Czechoslovakia to accept this peaceful solution. At first the French premier, Edouard Daladier, rejected the pursuit of self-determination through plebiscites in German-speaking areas as a dangerous precedent that would expose the rest of Central Europe to German revisionism. But his awareness of France's military weakness led him to withdraw his objection after Chamberlain—reversing a century of British foreign policy—promised to guarantee Czechoslovakia's redrawn frontiers. The government in Prague angrily rejected the Anglo–French proposal but was forced into line by the threat of an end to British peacemaking efforts and a bluntly repeated refusal of French assistance if war broke out. When Chamberlain returned to the German city of Godesberg on 22 September to tell Hitler that his demands had been accepted by all interested parties, the Führer reneged on the agreement that he himself had earlier proposed and announced that the deteriorating political situation in the Sudetenland required immediate German intervention. The grievances of Poland and Hungary on behalf of their own oppressed minorities in Czechoslovakia—now being raised with great fervour by Warsaw and Budapest, in line with their prior arrangement with Berlin—would have to be addressed as well.

Both the tone and the substance of the new German demands made it clear that Hitler was intent on war with Czechoslovakia and would not be deprived of it by diplomatic concessions. As a result, the British and French governments withdrew their earlier opposition to Czechoslovakia's right to prepare for its own defence, and Prague mobilized its armed forces on 24 September as the Godesberg talks ended in deadlock. Public opinion in Britain and France had come to support the agreement proposed by Hitler at Berchtesgaden and accepted by Beneš at the insistence of Britain and France. The German retraction at Godesberg turned many British and French appeasers into hardliners and momentarily stiffened the resolve of Chamberlain and Daladier to stand firm even at the risk of war. France began to mobilize its army and Britain announced the mobilization of its fleet on 27 September. In London and Paris trenches were dug in parks, gas masks were distributed, and children were evacuated to the countryside. Hitler ordered the attack on Czechoslovakia to begin on the morning of 30 September.

Few doubted that war would eventually lead to the defeat of Czechoslovakia. The French war plan envisioned a token advance into the Rhineland to be followed by a tactical withdrawal behind the Maginot Line for the winter. The British government could only hold out the possibility of sending two underequipped divisions to the continent. The Soviet Union, whose treaty with Czechoslovakia was scheduled to take effect once France had gone to the latter's assistance, had no way of helping its ally except by air (because of the Polish–Romanian barrier) and therefore did not even take the precaution of a general mobilization. As the hopelessness of Czechoslovakia's position—regardless

of British, French, and Soviet support—became apparent, the tragic absurdity of the situation began to dawn on officials in Paris and London: Czechoslovakia was about to be crushed and Europe to be embroiled in a war over the trivial details of how and when a previously agreed-upon territorial transfer was to take place.

THE MUNICH PACT

While resuming their preparations for war, therefore, Chamberlain and Daladier desperately searched for ways to negotiate a settlement. The British prime minister persuaded Mussolini to intervene with Hitler to arrange for a final meeting to avert war. For reasons known only to himself, the Führer agreed to postpone his mobilization plans and to host a conference of the leaders of Britain, France, and Italy at Munich on 29 September 1938. His decision to stop at the brink of war may have been influenced by the hesitations of Mussolini, the reluctance of his generals, or the refusal of Chamberlain and Daladier to stand idly by if Germany attempted to settle the Sudeten crisis by military means. In any event, he had every reason to assume that his Godesberg demands would be accepted, and he knew that their implementation would spell the early demise of the Czechoslovak state.

The Munich Conference—from which both Czechoslovakia and its ally the Soviet Union were excluded, at Germany's insistence—produced an agreement that provided for the removal of Czechoslovak military forces from the Sudetenland over the first 10 days of October, after which German troops would occupy the region in four stages. An international commission would administer plebiscites in disputed areas and fix the new frontier. Britain and France undertook to guarantee the redrawn borders of Czechoslovakia against unprovoked aggression, while Germany and Italy promised similar guarantees once Polish and Hungarian territorial claims had been satisfactorily adjudicated. On 30 September, the Czechoslovak government received this agreement in the form of an ultimatum and was denied

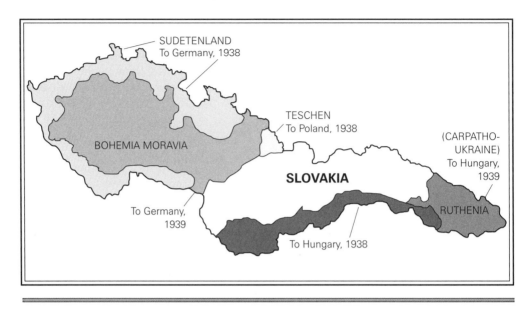

SUDETENLAND
To Germany, 1938

TESCHEN
To Poland, 1938

(CARPATHO-
UKRAINE)
To Hungary,
1939

BOHEMIA MORAVIA

SLOVAKIA

RUTHENIA

To Germany,
1939

To Hungary, 1938

The Partition of Czechoslovakia, 1938–1939

even the right to submit written objections—a right Germany had enjoyed at the Paris Peace Conference in 1919. Abandoned by its Western allies and threatened with a war it could not hope to win, the Prague government dutifully signed what its leaders knew to be its death warrant.

Upon their return to their respective capitals, Chamberlain and Daladier were hailed for preventing the arcane dispute in far-off Czechoslovakia from plunging Britain and France into a war that neither nation was prepared to fight. For those who believed Hitler's assurances that his objective in Eastern Europe was the absorption of territory populated by citizens of German descent, the Munich Pact promised an end to Germany's claims against what remained of Czechoslovakia and seemed to herald the advent of stability in the region. They ignored those passages in the Führer's speeches and writings that clearly enunciated his ultimate goal, which was not to liberate oppressed Germans from foreign rule, but rather to subject the non-German peoples of all of Eastern Europe and western Russia to direct or indirect domination from Berlin.

There were some in Britain and France who were willing to tolerate and even encourage the diversion of Germany's expansionist energies eastward at the expense of states they cared little for. But the leaders who struck the bargain with Hitler at Munich did not belong to that group of appeasers. They appear genuinely to have believed— even the more skeptical Daladier—that the annexation of the Sudetenland would remove the last obstacle to Germany's peaceful reintegration into the Versailles system. They both recognized that German domination of all of Eastern Europe would pose a grave threat to the security of their own countries, and at no time were they prepared to tolerate such a radical imbalance of power on the continent.

Far from securing the status quo, however, the Munich settlement accelerated the process of disintegration that would tip the balance of power in Eastern Europe toward Germany. What remained of Czechoslovakia was now in such a precarious state that it could not function as an independent political unit. Germany's annexation of the Sudetenland, together with the subsequent acquisition of the Teschen district by Poland and parts of Slovakia by Hungary, shattered the political authority of the government in Prague. The Slovaks, who inhabited the eastern region of the state and resented the politically dominant Czechs, seethed with separatist agitation that was actively encouraged by Berlin. The loss of the formidable string of fortifications along its western frontier—the 'eastern Maginot Line', as it was sometimes called—left the truncated Czechoslovak state wide open to invasion from Germany.

The devastating consequences of the Munich Pact for Czechoslovakia were also felt in the other countries of Eastern and Southern Europe. France's willingness to sacrifice its strongest and most trusted ally in the region encouraged Czechoslovakia's partners in the Little Entente to reorient their own foreign policies towards greater co-operation with the emerging German colossus. Shocked by France's abandonment of Prague and uneasy about threats to its own territorial integrity from Hungary and the Soviet Union, Romania resumed the rapprochement with Germany that it had begun in response to earlier indications that French power in Eastern Europe was receding. An economic agreement signed in December 1938 gave Germany access to Romanian oil and surplus wheat. Yugoslavia, also subject to Hungarian revisionism and perpetually threatened by Italian territorial ambitions along the Adriatic, strengthened its economic ties with Germany and solicited Hitler's restraining influence on its two revisionist neighbours. Hungary, which had hesitated to support Germany during the Munich crisis (and

Luftwaffe Commander-in-Chief Hermann Göring, British Prime Minister Neville Chamberlain, Italian Prime Minister Benito Mussolini, German Chancellor Adolf Hitler, and French Prime Minister Edouard Daladier at the Führerbau in Munich, 1938. Library of Congress, LC-USZ62-12187.

consequently received from Hitler a much smaller share of the Slovakian spoils than it had wanted), quickly adjusted to the new political realities. Budapest demonstrated its alignment with Berlin's foreign policy by joining the Anti-Comintern Pact and withdrawing from the League of Nations. As a reward it received Germany's approval to annex Czechoslovakia's easternmost province, Carpatho-Ukraine (Ruthenia), which contained numerous Hungarians.

THE INVASION OF CZECHOSLOVAKIA

Germany's progress towards economic and political domination of the smaller states of Eastern and Southern Europe was completed on 15 March 1939, when Hitler seized on the grievances of the Slovak minority as a pretext for the German army to occupy Prague. The western half of the country, inhabited by the Czechs, was made a German protectorate while the eastern half became the satellite state of Slovakia. In response to this spectacular extension of German military power into the Danube basin, all the states of Eastern and Southern Europe—with one important exception—were either seduced or intimidated into accepting German hegemony on the eastern half of the continent. Romania and Yugoslavia, the former allies of Czechoslovakia and clients of France, relapsed into a policy of diplomatic and economic subservience to Germany. Lithuania was reduced to the status of a de facto satellite when Hitler annexed its (mostly German-speaking) port of Memel a few days after the dismemberment of Czechoslovakia. Hungary and Bulgaria, already firmly in the German orbit, resumed their active support for Hitler's aggressive moves.

It is ironic that the single exception to the pattern of pro-German reorientation after Munich came from the principal beneficiary of Germany's eastern revisionism: Poland. Berlin's tactical flirtation with Warsaw, inaugurated by the non-aggression pact of 1934 and confirmed by the two governments' collaboration in the territorial amputation of Czechoslovakia in the autumn of 1938, reflected Hitler's intention of using Poland first as an accomplice in removing the Czech menace and later as a geographical barrier to possible Soviet interference with his planned military offensive in the west. But the government in Warsaw consistently rebuffed Hitler's demands that Poland publicly confirm its subservience to Germany by signing the Anti-Comintern Pact. Though staunchly anti-communist and hostile to the Soviet Union, the Polish ruling elite withheld this symbolic gesture because it would signal the end of the precarious balancing act between Germany and Russia that Poland had performed ever since its rebirth as a nation after the Great War. The Warsaw regime became even more intransigent after March 1939, when it saw its own western defences outflanked with the establishment of a German military presence in Slovakia—just as Czechoslovakia's defensive fortifications had been circumvented with Germany's annexation of Austria two years earlier. For reasons of national pride, the Poles were unwilling to accept the same fate as the Czechs or to tolerate the establishment of German hegemony in Eastern Europe.

Poland's refusal to submit to German foreign policy after Munich, and especially after the German march on Prague, led Hitler to change his attitude towards Poland and therefore to reverse his timetable for European domination. With an unreliable Poland to the east, he could not afford to resume preparations for the war against France and Britain that he had planned to launch after removing Czechoslovakia as a military threat and taking control of its munitions plants and raw materials. The Führer accordingly decided that the war in the west would have to wait until Poland—the only recalcitrant power on Germany's eastern flank—had been defeated as well. Since Warsaw could be neither enticed nor intimidated into acquiescence, as all of its neighbours in Eastern Europe had been, Poland would have to be eliminated before rather than after the inevitable showdown with the Western democracies. Once the decision was made (in the spring of 1939) to attack Poland ahead of schedule, the old grievances that had been downplayed during the period of German–Polish détente were suddenly revived. The alleged maltreatment of the Germans in Danzig and the economic difficulties caused by the separation of East Prussia from the rest of the Reich once again gave rise to heated protests from Berlin. When Germany demanded the restoration of Danzig to German sovereignty, as well as an extraterritorial road and railroad across the corridor to East Prussia (ostensibly to conserve the foreign exchange needed for transit payments to Poland), it met with the same polite but firm refusals in Warsaw that had greeted Hitler's earlier efforts to persuade Poland to join in the Anti-Comintern Pact. Alone among the nations of Eastern and Southern Europe, Poland seemed prepared to defend its territorial integrity and national independence, by force if necessary.

The stiffening of Polish resolve after the collapse of the Munich settlement was assisted by the abrupt change of British and French foreign policy from appeasement to resistance. Shortly after returning from Munich, Chamberlain and Daladier had taken precautions in case the agreement should come unglued. In the early months of 1939, Britain greatly accelerated the pace of its rearmament program and began to make precise plans to create a large expeditionary force for deployment on the continent, while France placed orders for warplanes in the United States (with the tacit consent of the Roosevelt government).

But it was the German occupation of Prague that caused the fundamental reversal of Anglo–French policy regarding Hitler's Germany. Unlike all previous instances of German territorial expansion during the 1930s—the Rhineland, Austria, the Sudetenland—this one involved non-Germans and therefore could not be justified by the principle of national self-determination. Public opinion in Britain and France had rallied behind the Munich agreement because it was supposed to represent the definitive resolution of Germany's nationality grievances in Eastern Europe. Its unilateral repudiation by Hitler less than half a year later left London and Paris feeling betrayed—and determined not to repeat the same mistake in the future. As the principal architect of

the Munich settlement, Chamberlain was transformed into a firm opponent of further German territorial claims. He recalled the British ambassador to Berlin, issued a stern note of protest, and suspended the Anglo–German trade talks that had dragged on inconclusively for months. On 18 March, only three days after the fall of Prague, the British Foreign Office, in concert with the Quai d'Orsay, approached the governments of Russia, Poland, Romania, Yugoslavia, Greece, and Turkey about the possibility of forming a coalition to oppose further German aggression.

Initially it was feared that Germany's next move would be against Romania, to secure control of its oil wells and grain as a way around the threat of a British blockade in the event of war. However, it soon became evident that the most likely victim of Hitler's next aggressive move was Poland, the only nation that had denied Hitler the chance to concentrate the bulk of his military forces in the west. Accordingly, the British government took two unprecedented steps that expressed its new determination to halt German aggression in its tracks. On 31 March, it publicly pledged to guarantee the territorial integrity of Poland, and on 26 April, it announced that it would request parliamentary authorization to introduce universal military conscription. Never before had Britain been willing either to promise military assistance to a nation in Eastern Europe or to institute conscription during peacetime. Such measures were unnecessary for France, since it already had a treaty commitment to Poland, as well as a large conscript army. Thus it had only to support the British campaign to organize an anti-German coalition among Poland's neighbours that could deter Hitler from taking the plunge.

THE KREMLIN CHOOSES SIDES

When Britain tried, in the spring of 1939, to persuade the minor powers of Southeastern Europe to form an anti-German bloc, it was too late. Romania and Yugoslavia had drawn too close to Germany, both economically and politically, while Greece and Turkey were geographically too remote to play a role in Poland's defence. Only the Soviet Union was willing and geographically able to join Britain and France in a common front against Germany. But the Anglo–French overture of 18 March was doomed by the refusal of Poland and Romania to be associated with the Soviet Union, and London and Paris were reluctant to press them on this point. A month later, on 17 April, Stalin offered the alternative of a military alliance of France, Britain, and Russia—the old Triple Entente of 1914—to defend all the independent nations of Central and Eastern Europe against German aggression. On the same day, however, he authorized the Soviet ambassador to Berlin to broach the subject of a Soviet–German rapprochement to officials in the German Foreign Office. In short, a month after the German absorption of Czechoslovakia, the Soviet leader simultaneously floated two trial balloons to assess the intentions of the two contending blocs that were forming in anticipation of a show-down over Poland. The two conflicting traditions of post-war Soviet foreign policy—the Popular Front–collective-security strategy of co-operation with the Western powers to restrain Germany, and the Rapallo strategy of collaboration with Germany against the West—hung in the balance.

There is no need to review the many rea-sons for Moscow to fear German hegemony in Europe. Hitler's brutal suppression of the German Communist Party, together with his well-known plans (sketched in his book *Mein Kampf* and reiter-ated frequently thereafter) to seize Soviet land for German agricultural development and resettle-ment, had made a profound impression on Stalin, converting him to the cause of collective security and the Popular Front between 1935 and 1938. But France's refusal to transform the Franco–Soviet Pact into a military alliance, Britain's hesi-tation to guarantee the territorial status quo in Eastern Europe, and above all the Soviet Union's exclusion from the Munich Conference, left Stalin with the impression (accurate or not) that the Western powers favoured the idea of Germany's eastward expansion. No doubt some influential publicists and statesmen in France and Britain did believe that their nations stood to profit from

struggle to the death between Teutons and Slavs in Eastern Europe.

Nor can it be denied that anti-communist sentiment in the West made the London and Paris governments reluctant to respond to over-tures from the Kremlin seeking their co-operation against Germany. The private comments of policy-makers in Britain and France suggest that ideo-logical hostility may actually have been less important than their lack of faith in the efficacy of the Red Army (with its decapitated command structure[4] and inadequate transportation facili-ties), together with the refusal of Poland and Romania to tolerate the presence of Russian troops on their soil. Whatever the reasons, by the time the British and French governments had overcome their reluctance to make common cause with the Kremlin in the spring of 1939, Stalin had decided that the Soviet Union's best hope for security on its western frontier lay in rapproche-ment with Germany rather than resistance to it.

One reason for this decision was the Kremlin's discovery of evidence that Hitler's plan was to make war not against Russia but rather against the Western powers. This conclusion was based on intelligence reports from a well-placed Soviet spy in Tokyo, which detailed the dispute between Germany and Japan during secret negotiations to transform the Anti-Comintern Pact into a tri-partite military alliance of the Axis powers. The Japanese insisted that any such association be directed specifically at the Soviet Union (their primary antagonist on the mainland of Asia), while Berlin had tried and failed to lure Tokyo into a military alliance aimed solely at France and Britain. Had the impending assault on Poland been merely the first stage in a plan to invade the USSR, a German–Japanese alliance against the latter would have been the most effective means of diluting Moscow's military strength by for-cing it to fight a war on two fronts. Yet this was precisely the alignment that Hitler, despite clear signs of Japanese interest, was not prepared to contemplate. The announcement of the 'Pact of Steel' between Germany and Italy on 22 May con-firmed the breakdown of the German–Japanese negotiations and signalled Hitler's intention to move against France and Britain (the only powers against which Italy's assistance would count).

Thus the Kremlin could hope to escape the threat of an immediate German invasion, which did not fit into Hitler's plan for a westward advance after the destruction of Poland. It followed that the Soviets had much to gain from assuming a defensive posture on their western frontier and much to lose from joining a military alliance with Britain and France that might provoke Hitler into revising his timetable for European conquest and dispatching his forces eastward sooner than he had planned. An accommodation with Hitler in Eastern Europe would deflect German aggression westward, and the Soviet Union could profit by standing back from a war between the capitalist powers that was likely to result in their mutual exhaustion. In the meantime, Stalin would gain a precious breathing space in which to reorganize the command structure of the Red Army (decimated by his own paranoic purges); such an interval would also permit the Soviet economy to gear up for the war with Germany that was bound to come once Hitler had secured his western flank.

These were the considerations that determined the Kremlin's double game in the spring and summer of 1939, when Britain and France belatedly solicited its help to contain Germany. Soviet criticism of the German occupation of Prague, followed by suggestions of Soviet interest in the formation of a new Triple Entente, kept the door to London and Paris open. At the same time other exploratory gestures kept the door to Berlin ajar. The most spectacular of these signals came on 3 May, when the Soviet foreign minister, Maxim Litvinov—whose Jewish ancestry and pro-Western stance would have made it difficult for him to negotiate with Nazi Germany—was abruptly replaced by Stalin's loyal henchman Vyacheslav Molotov.

This move was an unmistakable indication to Hitler that Stalin was prepared to do business, and the contacts between Moscow and Berlin initiated on 17 April soon intensified. On 20 May, Molotov himself informed the German ambassador of Stalin's interest in exploring a 'political basis' for greater Soviet–German co-operation. For the next three months, as Hitler's propaganda war against Poland reached a fever pitch, the low-level discussions between the Germans and the Soviets resumed their leisurely pace. It is likely that Stalin's mind was not yet made up when, on 25 July, Britain and France finally agreed to dispatch military missions to Moscow to explore the possibility of an alliance with the Soviet Union against Germany. The German ambassador to Moscow was convinced that the Kremlin was at that time determined to sign with England and France, if they were prepared to meet all Soviet demands.

The manner in which the two Western governments conducted their negotiations with the Kremlin conveyed neither a sense of urgency nor a determination to treat the Kremlin as an equal partner. The departure of the Anglo–French negotiating team was delayed for 11 days, and, instead of flying, the mission travelled by sea on a 9,000-tonne passenger-cargo vessel that took six days to reach Moscow. The team consisted of low-ranking officers uncertain of their negotiating powers, and they evaded the Soviets' questions about troop strength, military plans, and means of persuading Poland and Romania to permit the passage of Russian military forces across their territory. The Soviets could hardly help noting how much more eager the British and French governments had seemed in their dealings with Hitler, when Chamberlain and Daladier themselves had flown to Munich. The desultory behaviour of Britain and France also contrasted dramatically with the strong expressions of interest in a Soviet–German rapprochement that were beginning to come from Berlin. During the first three weeks of August the German foreign minister, Joachim von Ribbentrop, worked hard to secure an audience with Stalin, spurred by Hitler's belief that the Polish campaign had to be completed before winter conditions could interfere with mechanized transport and aerial operations.

Stalin's decision to receive Ribbentrop on 23 August marked the end of the double game that the USSR had played since the spring. In two meetings the German and Soviet representatives reached a series of understandings that were codified in two documents—one for public consumption, the other for the confidential reassurance of the two signatories. The public document committed Germany and the USSR to strict neutrality towards one another, should either become involved in war. Hitler thereby secured the Kremlin's acquiescence in his forthcoming campaign against Poland, as well as relief from the threat of a two-front war once he turned his forces westward against France and Britain. Stalin, like Chamberlain and Daldier had in Munich, was able to postpone a war with Germany that the Soviet Union was unprepared to fight and hence secure additional time to upgrade his strategic

capabilities as best he could. The 'secret additional protocol' confirmed the geopolitical reality that, ever since the end of the Great War, had been a potential basis of collaboration between Germany and the Soviet Union and an obstacle to Soviet rapprochement with the West. While the national interests of France and (belatedly) Britain led them to support the independence of the successor states in Eastern Europe, the national interests of Germany and the USSR pointed in the opposite direction: for them, the destruction of those successor states held out the promise of territorial aggrandizement.

Thus the two signatories secretly agreed to the partition of Poland. Finland, Latvia, and Estonia—all, like the eastern sector of Poland, former provinces of the tsarist empire—were

THE GLOBAL SITUATION ON THE EVE OF WAR

As war broke out in Europe in September 1939, authoritarian governments outnumbered democracies around the world. The combined effects of the economic crises of the 1930s and the precarious situation created by the post-war treaties had led much of the world to seek refuge in dictatorial governments which promised rapid, if not always effective, answers to their nation's problems. In the immediate aftermath of the First World War, Italian Fascism found a receptive audience and soon the country's ineffective coalition governments collapsed in the face of Benito Mussolini's manipulation of the party system. In 1933 Adolf Hitler assumed the Chancellorship of Germany as head of the largest party in the Reichstag. In Eastern Europe, the weak democracies created out of the ruins of the Austro–Hungarian and Russian empires slowly gravitated towards authoritarian leaders. By 1937 Yugoslavia, Poland, Hungary, Lithuania, Latvia, and Estonia had all seen democratic regimes replaced with more dictatorial ones. Elsewhere, the Portuguese abandoned democracy in 1926, and Spain would fall after its bloody civil war. Beyond the borders

of Europe, much of Central and South America also experienced periods of dictatorial rule in the 1920s and 1930s, including El Salvador, Guatemala, Honduras, Nicaragua, Venezuela, Peru, Brazil, Chile, and Uruguay. In Asia, Chiang Kai-shek ruthlessly suppressed his opponents and, by 1931, the Japanese parliament had lost most of its authority to a small group of military leaders. Even in Britain, whose democratic foundations stretched back for centuries, authoritarian groups such as Oswald Mosley's British Union of Fascists attracted a number of followers during the chaotic years of the Great Depression. Under such circumstances, observers could hardly be blamed for seeing some truth in Mussolini's assertion that '[i]t is to be expected that this century may be that of authority.... If the nineteenth was the century of the individual (Liberalism means individualism) it may be expected that this one may be the century of "collectivism" and therefore the century of the State.' Clearly, the difficulties of the interwar period as well as the lack of strong democratic tradition in a number of countries had led many peoples to seek alternative forms of government.

allotted to the Russian sphere of influence.[5] Germany recognized Russia's right to recover the province of Bessarabia, whose seizure by Romania during the Russian Revolution had never been recognized by the Soviet regime. Bessarabia aside, the Soviets' goal may be summarized in a single word: security. Soviet domination of Finland and the two northernmost Baltic states would provide Russia's second capital, Leningrad, with a defensive buffer in the path of the traditional northern invasion route. The recovery of the territory lost to Poland in the war of 1920 would restore the historic buffer between the Germanic and Russian populations in Eastern Europe.

The Nazi–Soviet Pact of 23 August 1939 sealed Poland's fate and enabled Hitler to launch the European war he had been planning since coming to power. Last-minute British efforts to promote a peaceful resolution of the German–Polish crisis had no chance of success: Hitler's military timetable required that the war against Poland begin no later than 1 September. He would not again be cheated out of a victory, as he had been at Munich. His evasive reply to Britain was therefore designed to split the Western powers from Poland—since he preferred to engage his enemies one by one if that could be arranged.

On the eve of 31 August, a fabricated border incident involving members of the Nazi special police force (the 'SS') in Polish uniforms was used as the justification for mounting a massive armour and air assault against Poland the following morning. The British and French governments, which had previously warned Berlin that its rapprochement with the USSR would not prevent them from honouring their commitment to Poland, dutifully declared war on Germany on 3 September, following the expiry of their ultimatum demanding that the German forces leave Polish soil. With the temporary abstention of the USSR and Italy, only four European powers were involved in the military drama that unfolded on the Polish plains in September 1939. But the limited number of participants and the geographically localized theatre of combat did not prevent journalists from referring to the conflict as a second world war.

SUMMARY

The optimism of the 1920s vanished with the onset of the Great Depression. Because of the large volume of American capital invested in other nations, the collapse of American banks in the fall of 1929 had global repercussions. In response to the economic crisis, the United States and many other countries, including Canada, raised their tariffs on imports in the early 1930s. This rise in protectionism had disastrous effects on the international economic system and obstructed the flow of capital. Economic conferences at Ottawa in 1932 and London in 1933 discussed strategies to counteract the Depression, but national interests and political rivalries made it difficult to reach agreement. American insistence that European countries continue repaying their wartime loans placed additional strains on many of the nations.

The other major concern in the 1930s was the rise of Nazism. After Hitler assumed power in 1933, European countries sought alliances to protect themselves against the renewed threat of German aggression. France worked hard to forge agreements with Italy and the Soviet Union, while Britain negotiated with Germany in an effort to meet Hitler's demands. Rejecting the Peace of Paris, Hitler withdrew Germany from the League of Nations and broke several provisions in the Treaty of Versailles. With the outbreak of the Spanish Civil War in 1936, differences of opinion regarding the Fascist rebels and the elected leftist government in Madrid further destabilized Europe and distracted attention from the growing Nazi threat.

The policy of appeasement adopted by Britain and France, and supported by Canada, culminated in the Munich Pact of 1938, which sacrificed the sovereignty of Czechoslovakia in order to avoid war. Hitler then surprised the West by signing a treaty with the Soviet Union in late August 1939; Germany invaded Poland barely a week later. That invasion shattered any remaining illusions that Hitler could be placated, and France and Britain declared war on Germany, setting the stage for what was to become the most destructive conflict in human history.

NOTES

1. The gold exchange standard differed from the traditional gold standard in one fundamental respect: under the old gold standard, each nation's currency was freely convertible to gold on demand; under the gold exchange standard, American citizens were legally prohibited from owning gold.
2. A misnomer for 'arms control'. No one advocated the abolition of all military forces and armaments.
3. He was killed while travelling in Marseilles with the king of Yugoslavia, who was assassinated by a Macedonian terrorist operating in league with Croatian separatists.
4. Four hundred officers from the rank of colonel and up had been executed during the purges of 1937–8.
5. Lithuania, assigned to Germany's sphere in the Nazi–Soviet Pact, was transferred to the Soviet sphere in a subsequent agreement on 26 September.

QUESTIONS FOR CRITICAL THOUGHT

1. What were the most important factors leading to a global economic crisis in the early 1930s?
2. Why is 'the preparation for violence on a large scale' often the most effective remedy to a major economic crisis?
3. What benefits accrued to the United States from Roosevelt's 'Good Neighbour' policy?
4. How would a stronger Franco–Soviet military alliance have affected Germany's freedom of action in the 1930s?
5. Why was appeasement such a popular policy in the latter part of the 1930s?
6. Given the political and economic circumstances of the 1930s, could the major powers have taken a stronger stance against German expansion?

WEBSITES FOR FURTHER REFERENCE

German Propaganda Archive
www.calvin.edu/academic/cas/gpa/

A Guide to the Twentieth Century – The Great Depression
www.channel4.com/history/microsites/H/history/guide20/part06b.html

Musée McCord Museum: Keys to History – The Dirty Thirties
www.mccord-museum.qc.ca/en/keys/webtours/tourID/GE_P4_1_EN

New Deal Network
http://newdeal.feri.org/index.htm

CHAPTER 5

GERMANY'S SECOND BID FOR EUROPEAN DOMINANCE (1939–1945)

CHAPTER OUTLINE

THE OUTBREAK OF THE SECOND WORLD WAR

The collapse of Poland after less than a month of fighting was foreordained by the Nazi–Soviet Pact, which ensured that Poland would not receive any military assistance from the USSR and partitioned the country between the two powerful states to its east and west. Although this agreement of August 1939 did not require Soviet participation in the military assault on Poland, Stalin prudently dispatched troops westward to lay claim to the territory allotted to the Soviet Union. Following the surrender of Warsaw on 27 September, Poland once again disappeared from the map as Germany and the USSR absorbed their respective shares of the spoils.

Both Britain and France were obliged by their treaty commitments to mount a military offensive against Germany if it attacked Poland. But no such offensive materialized. The French general staff had no operational plans in place for a drive into western Germany, believing that such a strike against Germany's heavily fortified French frontier was inconceivable and knowing that an offensive against Germany's most vulnerable point, in the Rhineland bordering Belgium, was precluded because Belgium would never compromise its neutrality by granting transit rights to French troops. As for the British, they had begun to rearm in earnest and to organize a land army based on compulsory military service less than six months before the outbreak of the war in Poland. They therefore possessed neither the weaponry nor the manpower to mount a credible deterrent on Germany's western flank, even if they could have solved the geographical riddle of how to project such military force into enemy territory.

The efficacy of the blitzkrieg—the rapid thrust of massed tank formations supported by aerial assaults from dive bombers—was so brilliantly confirmed in the Polish campaign that Hitler planned a similar offensive through the Low Countries against France for November. However, it had to be postponed twice on account of bad weather and in the end was scheduled for the second week of May 1940. As the winter set in, German forces massed along the Dutch and Belgian frontiers while British and French forces dug in along France's eastern border. The absence of actual fighting led journalists to dub this phase the 'phony war'. As one commentator put it, blitz-krieg had given way to 'sitzkrieg' ('sitting war').

Amid this eerie lack of activity in the west, world attention was suddenly turned to events in the frozen terrain of Northern Europe. In September and October, the Soviet Union began to reassert its authority over the parts of the old tsarist empire that had been lost after the revolution, a prerogative accorded by its pact with Germany. The governments of the Baltic states of Latvia, Estonia, and Lithuania were compelled to permit the garrisoning of Soviet troops on their territory and to sign treaties of mutual assistance with the USSR. When Finland, refusing to regard itself as part of the Soviet 'sphere of interest', denied Stalin the strategic bases he sought to protect Leningrad (St Petersberg), Stalin attacked it at the end of November in the expectation that it would collapse in short order, just as Poland had. But sub-zero temperatures and rugged terrain—advantages unavailable to the Poles—enabled the Finns to hold out for more than three months against an army three times larger than their own.

With public opinion in Britain and France clamouring for military intervention on behalf of valiant little Finland, authorities in London and Paris came up with a scheme ostensibly designed to relieve the Finns but in reality aimed at a soft spot in Germany's strategic arsenal. German armaments production depended heavily on imports of high-grade iron ore from Sweden, and during the winter, when much of the Baltic Sea was frozen, the ore had to be transported by rail to the ice-free port of Narvik in Norway for trans-shipment through Norwegian waters to ports in northern Germany. Plans were drawn up for an

CANADA AND THE SECOND WORLD WAR

Although Britain and France declared war on 3 September, Canada waited a week before issuing its own declaration. This brief delay was a symbolic gesture intended to show that Canada had become a sovereign nation and was no longer automatically committed to go to war with Britain, as it had been in 1914. Despite the independence granted by the Statute of Westminster in 1931, Canada was still a member of the British Commonwealth. It still had strong cultural and political ties with Britain, support for the Allied cause was high, and neutrality was never a practical option.

Canada entered the war with limited military capabilities: it had fewer than a dozen warships, only about 50 military aircraft, and a professional army of fewer than 5,000 soldiers. Over the course of the war, it would be transformed into one of the world's major military powers. Though the issue of conscription remained controversial, particularly among Quebec francophones, as it had during the First World War, the war effort received widespread public support. French Canadians supplied almost a fifth of the country's total number of volunteers for overseas service. In total, about a million Canadians out of a population of 11.5 million saw military service in the Second World War.

Volunteers in Montreal line up to enlist in August 1939. Library and Archives Canada/The Gazette (Montreal) fonds/PA-137215.

Anglo–French force to land at Narvik and move across Norway and Sweden to Finland while seizing the Swedish ore fields along the way. When Finland's capitulation, on 12 March, put an end to this plan, it was replaced by an earlier British scheme to cut off Germany's access to iron ore by mining Norway's territorial waters. Although both these schemes were complicated by the refusal of Norway and Sweden to compromise their neutrality, the British proceeded anyway.

In April 1940, the day after the British mining operation began, German forces seized the capital and major ports of Norway and occupied Denmark. British and French troops that were hastily landed on the Norwegian coast failed to secure defensible beachheads and eventually had to withdraw. Germany had instantaneously obtained a string of strategically located bases in Scandinavia that would later be used for submarine warfare against Britain. By refusing to coordinate their defence plans with Britain and France and by denying the Anglo–French armies transit rights across their territory the Nordic countries facilitated the abrupt expansion of German power into Northern Europe. Norway and Denmark paid for their neutrality by suffering German military occupation and all the privations it entailed. Sweden, however, was spared occupation because it was willing to co-operate economically with Germany. From its posture of absolute neutrality it continued to supply the German war machine with high-grade iron ore, at a handsome profit.

After Germany had secured its northern flank, the long-awaited western offensive finally unfolded on 10 May 1940. The buffer states of the Netherlands and Belgium, which like their Scandinavian counterparts had consistently rebuffed Anglo–French overtures for joint military planning, were rewarded for their scrupulous adherence to neutrality with a brutal combination of aerial bombardment and mechanized invasion.

THE FALL OF FRANCE

On paper the two sides had equal manpower (134 German divisions versus 94 French, 10 British, 22 Belgian, and 8 Dutch divisions), and Germany's three-to-one advantage in air power was partly offset by the Western Allies' advantage in tanks: 3,200 Anglo–French versus 2,500 German. But sheer numbers do not tell the whole story. In training and equipment, Germany's motorized infantry units were vastly superior to those of the Allies. Moreover, the Allies squandered their numerical superiority in armour by dispersing their tank formations among the regular infantry divisions as support groups instead of concentrating them in separate divisions to serve as spearheads for motorized infantry units. It is ironic that this tactic for the most efficient use of armour in offensive warfare had been conceived by a British military theorist (B.H. Liddell Hart) and popularized by a young French tactician (Colonel Charles de Gaulle), only to be put into practice by the Germans. Dutch resistance collapsed in five days, and Belgian forces retreated in disarray as the German juggernaut rolled toward the French frontier.

Panzer spearheads with dive-bomber support cleared the way for motorized infantry units to slash through the Ardennes upland region in southern Belgium (which had been considered 'impassable' to armour by those French military planners who vetoed the extension of the Maginot Line to the North Sea). The German forces breached the French defences at Sedan on 16 May, then veered north toward the Channel coast to sever the supply lines and communications of the main Anglo–French armies in northeastern France and Belgium. After reaching the sea on 20 May, this advance German tank contingent swung eastward toward the isolated Allied forces that had reassembled at the French port of Dunkirk, near the Belgian frontier. When the French prime minister, Paul Reynaud, requested that the rest of the Royal Air Force (RAF) be sent to the continent to defend France, Britain refused. Instead, on 28 May, it ordered the evacuation of the Anglo–French troops trapped in the vicinity of Dunkirk. Over the next eight days, 200,000 British and 130,000 French soldiers were ferried across the Channel by a hastily improvised flotilla that included civilian vessels from trawlers and fishing boats to cabin cruisers and yachts. Meanwhile the German armies turned south to deliver the knockout blow to the remnants of the French army. By 16 June, the French cabinet, which had left Paris for the south five days earlier, reluctantly concluded that further resistance was pointless. Prime Minister Reynaud resigned in favour of the octogenarian hero of the Great War, Marshal Henri-Philippe Pétain, who assembled a ministry willing to negotiate a prompt end to the fighting. On 22 June, after less than six weeks of resistance, the French government capitulated, signing an armistice that provided for the disarmament of its forces and the delivery of the northern three-fifths of the country to German military occupation.

Before the war, as an undersecretary of defence in the Reynaud government, Charles de Gaulle had been critical of the French high command's defensive approach to military strategy. Opposing his government's decision to lay down arms, he had left for London. Four days before the capitulation, the recently promoted brigadier general broadcast a message over British radio urging the French people to resist the German occupation and inviting French military and political authorities to join him in England to resume the struggle. When no one in high office responded to this appeal, he formed the French National Committee in London, which operated alongside the other governments in exile that had fled the overrun countries of the continent. The British government subsidized and encouraged this 'Free French' movement and severed relations with the collaborationist regime of Marshal Pétain, established on 2 July at the resort city of Vichy, in the unoccupied southern portion of France. Unlike the other European governments in exile that had reassembled in London after the defeat of their armies on the battlefield, de Gaulle's organization had no claim to political legitimacy, since the legally elected French parliament had voted to confer emergency powers on the Pétain regime. Nonetheless, de Gaulle assembled an army of French soldiers, sailors, and airmen who had escaped from the continent, a ragtag military force that took part in many important campaigns throughout the rest of the war.

The fall of France completed the reversal in the European balance of power that had begun with the remilitarization of the Rhineland. In just four years, Germany had come from nowhere to dominate the continent, controlling roughly the same geographical area that Napoleon had at the height of his power. Nine formerly independent states had submitted to German control in various degrees, from outright annexation in the case of Austria to a fictitious independence in the case of Vichy France. The remaining nations of the continent had become either military allies or economic vassals of Germany, except for a handful of states—Spain, Portugal, Switzerland, and Sweden—that managed to cling to a precarious neutrality. The sympathetic collaboration of the Soviet Union in Germany's drive toward the west, originally confined to Poland but soon expanded to include the exchange of Soviet grain and oil for German manufactured products, seemed to give Germany the advantage it had gained too late in the last war: protection against economic strangulation by the British blockade through access to the USSR's inexhaustible supplies of food and fuel.

THE BATTLE OF BRITAIN

The end of the Battle of France on 22 June was followed by hasty preparations for the Battle of Britain. Plans for a Channel crossing were drawn up on 2 July and Germany assembled troop transport ships along the Channel coast and organized 13 divisions in preparation for what Hitler called 'Operation Sealion'—the first attempt to invade the British Isles since the Norman Conquest of 1066. However, Churchill's decision to hold in reserve the bulk of the RAF during the French campaign forced the Germans to postpone their amphibious attack until the Luftwaffe (the German air force) could remove the threat of aerial interference. Emboldened by the astonishingly effective performance against Poland and France, Air Marshal Hermann Göring assured Hitler that the numerically superior German fighter force, after several days of precision bombing of the British bases, could remove the RAF from the skies within a month.

Apart from the courage and skill of the pilots, three technological factors enabled the RAF to foil Germany's plans for an amphibious invasion. The first was the qualitative superiority that helped to compensate for the numerical inferiority of the British air force. In this respect, Britain's belated entry in the aerial arms race had proved to be an advantage; the new Spitfire and Hurricane fighters fresh off the assembly line were faster and more manoeuvrable and possessed greater firepower than the older German Messerschmidts. The second factor was radar: the technology whereby the reflected echo of radio waves is used to detect distant objects in the atmosphere. Perfected in 1935 by the British scientist Robert Watson-Watt, this technological breakthrough resulted in the construction of 20 early warning stations along Britain's Channel coast by the spring of 1939, from which observers were able to locate approaching aircraft soon after their departure from continental bases and measure their range with uncanny accuracy. This radar network enabled the RAF fighters to conserve precious fuel by remaining on the ground until an attack was underway and then heading straight for the incoming German planes, whose limited fuel supply often forced them to return prematurely to their bases in France or Belgium. The third factor in the British air victory was the development by British intelligence of an electrically operated cipher machine capable of decoding German radio messages. This device, based on a code machine that had been stolen in Germany by the Polish Secret Service and transported to England in utmost secrecy before the war, enabled British cryptographers to crack the German code. In this way the RAF was sometimes able to obtain useful information about the German air force's plans.

Nevertheless, the major responsibility for the Luftwaffe's failure to gain control of British air space in the fall of 1940 must be placed on the shoulders of Hitler himself. When the RAF raided Berlin in retaliation for the accidental bombing of London by German planes, the Führer ordered round-the-clock bombardment of the major British metropolitan areas as punishment. He apparently persuaded himself that such brutal tactics would serve a good military purpose by sapping British morale and inciting civilian opposition to Churchill's policy of resistance. Hitler's faith in the efficacy of massive bombardment of civilian population centres (rather than military installations) was shared by an entire generation of strategists inspired by the writings of Giulio Douhet, an Italian general who had predicted that mass uprisings by the terrorized civilian victims of such air power would ensure their government's capitulation. Even though German bombs killed 43,685 British civilians and damaged or destroyed one in five British homes, they did not produce the predicted demoralization and civil unrest. On the contrary, 'the Blitz' galvanized the people behind their leaders and stiffened their resolve to carry on. In fact, the German strategy proved counterproductive because it diverted German air power from the military targets that really counted. The fighter bases of the RAF, which had been severely damaged by the initial onslaught, might very well have been wiped out if the precision bombing of the late summer had continued.

THE INVASION OF THE SOVIET UNION

The bombardment of British cities continued through the spring of 1941, but thereafter the air war in the British skies took second place to the annihilation of the Soviet Union, the project that had remained the touchstone of Hitler's foreign policy. On 31 July, two weeks before the start of the Blitz, Hitler informed his generals of 'Operation Barbarossa': his plan to invade the USSR the following May. In the early autumn, the redeployment of German forces from occupied France to the east began. The invasion was unexpectedly delayed when Mussolini, who had entered the war against France and Britain in June, imprudently embroiled Italy in conflicts in the Balkans and North Africa, which required the diversion of German forces southward in rescue operations. Italian troops based in the recently acquired protectorate of Albania had attacked Greece in October 1940 in search of a quick, cheap victory. Instead they encountered fierce resistance from the Greek army, and by March 1941 they faced the prospect of a humiliating defeat when British troops landed in Greece at the invitation of the Athens government. The sudden reappearance of a British army on the continent brought a swift response from Berlin. When the new government of Yugoslavia bravely repudiated its predecessor's pledge to grant transit facilities to the German army, Hitler launched an invasion from bases in Hungary and Bulgaria that crushed Yugoslav and Greek resistance in three weeks and forced a hasty evacuation of the British force from the Greek peninsula.

In the meantime, an offensive mounted in mid-September by Italian forces in Libya against the lightly defended British garrison in Egypt (which protected the Suez Canal and the Middle Eastern oil fields) was transformed into a rout when British forces counterattacked deep into Libyan territory. In February 1941, Hitler was compelled to dispatch an armoured 'Afrika Korps' under General Erwin Rommel to relieve the battered Italian forces in North Africa. Within two months, Rommel's panzers had hurled the British back to the Egyptian frontier. Though successful in the short run, these diversions caused a six-week delay in Hitler's timetable for the invasion of the Soviet Union. The loss of precious time during a season of favourable weather caused little concern in Berlin because of expectations (based on the French precedent) that Soviet resistance would crumble within three months, before the onset of winter. So confident was the German military command that it ordered winter clothing only for the small contingent that was to remain for occupation duty after the withdrawal of the victorious invasion force.

The German invasion of the Soviet Union began on 22 June 1941—the 129th anniversary of the launch of Napoleon's ill-fated expedition to Moscow. Four million men, 3,300 tanks, and

5,000 aircraft were sent eastward to wage what was to become the greatest land war in history. Ignoring warnings from British, American, and even Soviet intelligence sources about the impending attack, Stalin and his military advisers were totally unprepared. As the Soviet armies reeled in confusion before the offensive of that summer and fall, the consequences of Stalin's purge of the officers' corps four years earlier were clear in the tactical incompetence of the inexperienced junior officers who had replaced the executed members of the high command. In the first three months of battle, more than half the Soviet army was killed, wounded, or captured, and its tank force was reduced from 15,000 to 700. At the farthest extent of the German army's three-pronged advance—towards Leningrad in the north, Moscow in the centre, and the Ukrainian grain fields and Caucasian oil wells in the south—almost half of the Soviet Union's industrial resources and cultivated land were under enemy control.

It has often been suggested that by making a separate peace with Hitler in August 1939, Stalin bought the Soviet Union both space and time to prepare for its defence. But the space gained in the Baltic states and eastern Poland was overrun by the invading German armies in the first few days of the eastern offensive, and the time gained by Stalin for the reorganization of the Red Army and the construction of munitions factories (far to the east of the exposed western frontier) was also time gained by Hitler, who put it to good use. Once the pact with Stalin had freed Hitler from the threat of a two-front war, Germany forcibly acquired the economic and strategic resources of a dozen countries for use against the Soviet Union. With the fall of Kiev and the siege of Moscow and Leningrad in the autumn of 1941, the benefits of the USSR staying out of the war in Europe were difficult to identify. Space and time counted for little in the type of war that Germany was waging against the Soviet Union—a blitzkrieg aimed at routing the Red Army and toppling the Stalinist regime before the start of winter.

Germany's failure to deliver the decisive blow before December 1941, when the snow ground its mechanized offensive to a halt, has been traced by some military historians to the six-week delay caused by the Balkan and Mediterranean diversions of the previous spring. Others have blamed Hitler's decision to detach armoured divisions from the Centre Army Group advancing along Napoleon's road to Moscow in order to bolster the drives against Leningrad in the north and Ukraine in the south. Whatever its tactical cause, the strategic effect not only upset Hitler's expectation of a swift victory, but it also enabled Stalin's Machiavellian diplomacy during the period of Russian abstention from the war to yield its anticipated dividends. Shielded from the effects of the European war by the non-aggression pact with Hitler, the newly constructed factories east of the Urals began to compensate during the winter of 1941–2 for the lost production in the western regions that had been overrun by the invading German armies. The non-aggression pact that Stalin had signed with Japan in April 1941 freed the Soviet Union from the threat of a war on two fronts and permitted the redeployment of many troops from the Far East to replenish the depleted ranks of the troops defending Moscow. Once the promise of a quick German victory was buried in the December snows, the scales gradually began to tip in favour of the Soviet Union, whose seemingly inexhaustible reserves of military manpower and strategic raw materials were a formidable advantage in a long, drawn-out struggle.

THE UNITED STATES AND THE WAR IN EUROPE

The potential vulnerability of Germany in a conflict of long duration became evident during the six months that it waged war against two powers, Britain and the Soviet Union, that together commanded almost a quarter of the world's resources. The imbalance became all the more pronounced when the European conflict was transformed into a world war with the entry of the United States a few days after the counter-offensive from Moscow began. Though the brunt of the United States' military power could not be hurled against the

Third Reich for another two-and-a-half years, its vast economic resources were placed at the disposal first of Britain and then of the Soviet Union, just as they had been in the period before the US actively entered the First World War.

For 12 months after the fall of France, Britain, its colonies, and the larger members of the Commonwealth—Canada, Australia, and New Zealand—stood alone against Germany. During that time, the United States under Franklin Delano Roosevelt gradually moved from isolationism to a pro-British strategy as Washington came to recognize the damage that a German victory would do to American national interests. In September 1940, as the Luftwaffe began its furious air assault on the British Isles, the US transferred 50 over-aged destroyers to Britain in exchange for a 99-year lease of naval and air bases on eight British possessions in the western hemisphere, including several large bases in Newfoundland (a British colony at the time). This arrangement supplied the Royal Navy with ships it desperately needed to wage the Battle of the Atlantic against German submarines, while the acquisition of surplus American munitions enabled the British army to replace the materiel it had had to abandon on the beaches of Dunkirk. In December, Roosevelt established a defence board to plan and coordinate American assistance to Britain—a move denounced by the German government as an unwarranted intervention that compromised the neutral status of the US.

The 'cash-and-carry' provisions of American neutrality legislation—which prohibited US merchant vessels from entering the war zone in Europe and required advance payment for purchases by belligerents in the US market—had brought Britain to the brink of bankruptcy. The decline of its foreign trade, caused by the shift from production for export to production for warmaking, and aggravated by German submarine attacks on its merchant shipping, left Britain without a sufficient reserve of dollars to finance its mounting purchases. Even the sale of its remaining foreign assets and the depletion of its gold stocks would not bridge the gap for very long. In March 1941, the United States responded to the exhaustion of British dollar reserves with the so-called Lend–Lease Act. This legislation repealed the 'cash' part of the cash-and-carry requirement, authorizing the sale of American products on credit to 'any country whose defense the President deems vital to the defense of the United States'. Under its authority, a million tonnes of US agricultural surpluses were shipped to Britain between April and December 1941 to alleviate the food shortage caused by the German submarine campaign.

Terms of the Lend–Lease Act were not immediately extended to Britain's allies. Canada, for example, had in August 1940 signed the Ogdensburg Agreement with the United States, creating a Permanent Board of Defence to provide a bilateral forum for coordinating military planning. But the Act excluded Canada, which was already accumulating large trade deficits with the US as it purchased massive amounts of American equipment to supply the British war effort. Once the Lend–Lease Act exempted Britain from making cash payments for its war materials, Britain tried to extract better trading terms from Canada by threatening to place all its orders directly with the US. Worried that it would lose British business and incur heavier trade deficits, the Canadian government sought to negotiate its own agreement with Washington. In April 1941, Prime Minister McKenzie King and President Roosevelt signed the Hyde Park Declaration, in which the US agreed to increase its defence purchases of Canadian supplies, thereby easing the bilateral trade deficit. Canada was also allowed to participate in the Lend–Lease arrangement. Britain could continue to buy Canadian goods, while Canada was allowed to apply through the agreement for a portion of its purchases of US war supplies to be credited to the British account. In November 1941, the Roosevelt administration extended a US$1 billion lend–lease credit to the Soviet Union, which was struggling to defend its major cities against the German attack that had been launched the previous summer. In this way a considerable proportion of the strategic arsenal and economic resources of the US was made available to the two major powers in the anti-Axis coalition during the remaining months of American neutrality.

What finally led the United States to enter the war was not any quarrel with Nazi Germany but Japan's surprise attack on the American Pacific fleet based at Pearl Harbor in Hawaii, on 7 December 1941.[1] By the spring of 1942, all of East Asia had come under the domination of Japan. US forces had been expelled from the Philippines, Britain's major East Asian base at Singapore had surrendered, and Japanese military and naval forces had begun to fan out in three directions—towards Australia, India, and the Aleutian Islands off Alaska.

Despite the growing power of Japan and the absence of any immediate German threat to US interests, Roosevelt resolved to pursue a 'Europe-first' strategy in the war. By the summer of 1942, the United States had replaced Britain as the major foreign supplier of the Soviet Union, shipping food, clothing, and mechanized vehicles across the Atlantic to the northern ports of Murmansk and Archangel as well as to the Persian Gulf for transshipment by rail across Iran to the embattled cities of the western USSR. The menace of German submarines, which had sunk a third of Britain's merchant fleet tonnage by the time of the Pearl Harbor attack, was removed by the spring of 1943 with the help of American convoys and reconnaissance planes equipped with microwave radar to detect U-boats. In April, German naval authorities conceded defeat in the Battle of the Atlantic by recalling the submarines to their bases along the Norwegian and French coasts. Anglo-American control of the sea lanes to Europe enabled Allied strategists to envision for the first time an invasion of the continent.

BRITAIN AND THE SECOND FRONT

An Allied invasion of the continent was not soon in coming. For three full years—from June 1941 to June 1944—the Soviet army had to battle the German army virtually unaided. Although the British government concluded a mutual assistance pact with Moscow on 13 July 1941, the only help it offered its new ally was economic, not military. Although Stalin urgently requested some kind of diversionary action in Western Europe to relieve the pressure on his armies, Churchill steadfastly refused to risk such a direct assault. Instead, the British preferred to engage the vulnerable Italians in their ersatz empire in the Mediterranean basin while staging long-range bombing raids on cities (including Hamburg and Dresden) that had no discernible effect on Germany's capacity to wage its land war in the east. The US intervention did not change the situation, despite Roosevelt's professed enthusiasm for an Anglo–American landing in northern France, because the British prime minister was able to persuade the American president that such an operation was inopportune. Instead, Canadian forces were chosen to lead a large Allied raid on the French coast at Dieppe in August 1942. The attack was a disaster. In just a few hours, more than half of the 5,000 Canadian troops were either killed or captured by German units.

Extensive inter-Allied discussions about opening a 'second front' in France appear to have been intended mostly to placate the increasingly insistent Stalin. Why it took the Western powers so long to organize such an operation has remained a point of intense controversy. Defenders of the Soviet Union have detected a cynical motive on the part of the British and the Americans: a desire to see the Soviet Union bled white while its Western allies conserved their military and economic resources in order to step in at the last moment, once Germany had been defeated, and replace the exhausted USSR as the dominant power on the continent. To judge from the statements of the principals themselves, what led Churchill to oppose an early landing in Western Europe, and what persuaded Roosevelt to acquiesce, were two considerations. The first had to do with the practical concerns of an insufficient number of landing craft, the risks of transporting large numbers of American troops to Britain while German submarines still roamed the North Atlantic, and the entrenched position of the German forces along the French Channel coast. Churchill feared that a premature landing

of ill-equipped, undermanned Allied forces in northern France would suffer the same fate as the suicidal amphibious operation at Gallipoli during the First World War, for which he, as first lord of the Admiralty, had been blamed. The second consideration was the existence of a much more attractive alternative: an Allied landing in the lightly defended North African colonies of Vichy France, which could then serve as a springboard for the invasion of Fortress Europe through its back door in the Mediterranean.

The revival of the German offensive in the USSR in the summer of 1942 placed a considerable strain on the Grand Alliance—the popular name for the British–American–Soviet coalition—as Stalin continued to press for a second front in the west. The invasion of French North Africa, which took place in November 1942, was a spectacular success from the Western Allies' point of view. It led to the surrender, the following May, of the Axis armies in Libya, which were caught in the vise between the Allied forces landed in Morocco and Algeria and the British army in Egypt that had pierced the German–Italian front at El Alemein. It also brought southern Italy within range of Allied bombers stationed in Tunisia, just across the Mediterranean narrows. But the liberation of North Africa was accomplished at the expense of the long-delayed cross-Channel invasion of France. To the suspicious Stalin it seemed a disappointing diversion of his allies' military power from where it was needed in Western Europe. The trans-Mediterranean landing on Sicily in July, which paved the way for the Allied invasion of the Italian mainland in September, did little to calm Soviet anxieties about the Anglo–American strategy.

The professed objective of the strategy was to force an Italian surrender and to pin down as many German troops as possible in Italy in preparation for the invasion of France. In this the British, American, and Canadian forces were signally successful. The landing of Allied troops in Sicily, coming as it did amid desperate shortages of food, fuel, and munitions and mounting evidence of social unrest in Italy, compelled Mussolini to call a meeting of the Fascist Grand

Council—a rubber-stamp 'parliament' that had not met for years—on 24 July to shore up the deteriorating prestige of his regime. Instead, the Council voted to confer emergency powers on King Victor Emmanuel, who the following day appointed Marshal Pietro Badoglio to replace Mussolini and had the latter arrested. The new Italian leader promptly dissolved the Fascist Party, approached the enemy for an armistice (finally concluded on 8 September), and announced that his country was joining the Allied cause. The German military forces in Italy, which had been increased to 25 divisions in anticipation of just such a turnabout, proceeded to disarm the Italian army, occupy the northern two-thirds of the peninsula, and install Mussolini—following a spectacular rescue from prison by German paratroopers—as head of a new 'Italian Social Republic'. Allied forces subsequently made a long and arduous advance up the Italian peninsula, which took almost two years after the landing in Sicily. Canadian forces played a leading role in this difficult offensive, which cost thousands of lives and was one of the greatest strategic blunders of the Allied campaign in Europe.

As the Anglo–American forces cleared North Africa of Axis troops, gained effective control of the Mediterranean, and began their Italian campaign, the Soviet armies in the east finally turned the tide of battle against the German invaders. The German army had been advancing toward the strategically situated city of Stalingrad on the Volga throughout the summer of 1942, threatening to sever the railway and river connections linking the Soviet armies to their fuel sources in the Caucasus. By mid-September, the German Sixth Army had reached the outskirts of the city, the industrial and communications hub of the region, and proceeded to place it under siege. The gradual buildup of a numerically superior Soviet defence force in the autumn prompted the German commander, General Friedrich von Paulus, to request authorization to fall back to a more defensible position. Refusing to consider what would have been regarded as a humiliating

retreat, Hitler ordered a fight to the finish. After three months of senseless slaughter, von Paulus disobeyed orders and surrendered the tattered remnant of his army in February 1943. The loss of half a million Axis soldiers—dead, wounded, or captured—and the opening of a massive Soviet counter-offensive in the spring signalled the beginning of the end of Hitler's drive for *Lebensraum* in the European part of the Soviet Union. By the end of the year, two-thirds of the Soviet territory under German occupation had been liberated by the Red Army.

As the Soviet counter-offensive from the east gathered momentum, Roosevelt, Churchill, and Stalin met for the first time at Tehran, Iran, in November 1943 to plan the timing and strategy of the projected invasion of Western Europe. Churchill unveiled an elaborate proposal for an Anglo–American landing at selected points in the Balkans that would have once again deferred the long-delayed invasion of France. Stalin had little difficulty persuading Roosevelt and his military chiefs that such an indirect assault on Hitler's Europe was a poor substitute for a cross-Channel operation on France's Normandy coast, which would place the Anglo–American armies on the shortest and most direct route to the centre of Germany's industrial and war-making power in the Ruhr. Thus the American and Soviet heads of state rejected Churchill's scheme in favour of a landing in northern France, to be followed by a crossing from North Africa to the French Mediterranean coast. On 6 June 1944, five sea-borne and three airborne divisions of American, British, and Canadian troops were put ashore along the Normandy coast, quickly securing four beachheads. The Allies were supplied in part by a massive floating dock that had been prefabricated in England and towed across the Channel to compensate for the absence of good harbours in the invasion zone. On the first day of the invasion, the Canadian forces penetrated farther inland than any other Allied unit, and within a week and a half the invasion force had swollen to 640,000 well-equipped soldiers.

The greatest amphibious operation in history was facilitated by the absence of effective resistance from the two arms of Hitler's war machine that had enabled it to subdue the entire continent of Europe four years earlier: the air force and the armoured divisions. The Luftwaffe had been grounded for lack of gasoline after the US Army Air Corps's precision bombing of Germany's oil supply in the spring of 1944, while the German tank units in northern France had been held in reserve until too late, on the mistaken assumption that the Normandy invasion was an elaborate feint intended to lure them into a trap. At the end of July, the Allied forces smashed out of their coastal enclave and began a relentless offensive, which—in conjunction with the northeastward advance of Anglo–American and Free French forces landed in southern France on 15 August—cleared France of the German occupation army by the end of the year.

Washington had flirted with the idea of treating liberated France as a defeated enemy and subjecting it to an Allied military occupation. By 11 July, however, it had reluctantly recognized de Gaulle's French Committee of National Liberation as the de facto civil government. Roosevelt had long been contemptuous of the leader of the 'Free French', suspecting that he harboured authoritarian plans for post-war France scarcely less objectionable than the current policies of Pétain. For his part, de Gaulle deeply resented Roosevelt's decision to maintain diplomatic relations with the Vichy regime after the fall of France, his refusal to inform de Gaulle in advance of the Normandy invasion or to assign Free French forces a prominent role in it, and his ill-disguised efforts to promote the candidacies of potential rivals to de Gaulle within the French army. De Gaulle succeeded in taking supreme political authority in liberated France during the summer of 1944 and

Members of the 9th Canadian Infantry Brigade land at Bernières-sur-Mer, France, on D-Day, 6 June 1944. Library and Archives Canada/Department of National Defence fonds/PA-137013.

forced the United States to acknowledge his role. But his wartime dispute with Roosevelt left a legacy of bitterness and ill will that was to trouble Franco–American relations in later years.

As the American, British, and Free French armies approached Germany's western frontier in the fall of 1944, Soviet forces overran Bulgaria and Romania and advanced deep into Polish territory. In the winter of 1944–5, the inevitable collapse of Hitler's empire was temporarily postponed by desperate German counteroffensives against the Western Allies in Belgium and against Soviet forces approaching Hungary. But in February 1945 the offensives on Germany's two flanks resumed. In early March the Anglo–American armies became the first military force to cross the Rhine in combat since Napoleon's day. The Soviet army in Southern Europe took Budapest on its way to Vienna, while Soviet forces in the north decimated retreating German contingents along the Baltic coast in preparation for the march on Berlin.

The disintegration of the exhausted German armies before the advancing forces of the Western Allies from one side and the Soviet Union from the other produced a vast military vacuum in the centre of the European continent. Which of the two invading armies would fill it? This question was fraught with political as well as strategic overtones. In light of the radically different political, social, and economic systems of the Western Allies and the Soviet Union, it was inevitable that ideological hostility would resurface once the Germans' military collapse removed the only important reason for them to co-operate. On the Soviet side, Stalin's distrust of his Western allies had originated in their hesitation to open a second front in France while the Red Army engaged nine-tenths of the German army in the east. This suspicion grew in the spring of 1945, when Nazi military leaders approached American agents in neutral Switzerland with proposals for a separate peace in the west that would preserve a part of Germany's empire in the east. Neither the success of the US army in crushing German resistance nor Washington's repeated promises to observe the policy of unconditional surrender, adopted

by Roosevelt and Churchill at the Casablanca Conference in January 1943, appeared to allay Stalin's fear that the Western capitalist powers planned to allow the doomed German army to engage Soviet forces in the east while Anglo–American troops prepared to thrust deep into the continent and dictate a political settlement in Eastern Europe at the USSR's expense.

Had the decisive voice in Allied military planning belonged to Churchill, Stalin's assessment would not have been wide of the mark. Fervently anti-communist and alarmed at Soviet designs on Eastern Europe, Churchill wanted the Allied forces that had penetrated western Germany to march as far east as Berlin and as far south as Prague, where they would be in a strong position to bargain with the Soviets over the future of the former Nazi satellites. Washington rejected his plan, as it had earlier turned down Churchill's project for a Balkan landing, on the grounds that it was unwise from a military point of view. Roosevelt was counting on Soviet assistance in the war against Japan in the Far East, which his generals told him could not be won before November 1946. He also assumed that the American public would not want American troops to stay in Europe for very long after the war, and therefore saw the Red Army as a useful deterrent to any resurgence of German military power.

Consequently, the forces under US General Eisenhower in Germany were instructed to halt their eastward march at the Elbe River, while the Soviet army proceeded to liberate Berlin and Prague. On 25 April, US and Soviet soldiers shook hands at Torgau, on the Elbe just northeast of Leipzig, and on 1 May Eisenhower and the Soviet commanders agreed on a temporary occupation line that left Soviet forces in control of all of Eastern Europe, including the eastern halves of Germany and Austria. Hitler's suicide in his Berlin bunker on 30 April brought his 'thousand-year Reich' to an end 12 years after its birth. German military authorities surrendered unconditionally at Eisenhower's headquarters in Rheims, France, on 7 May and again to the Soviets in a separate ceremony in Berlin, two days later.

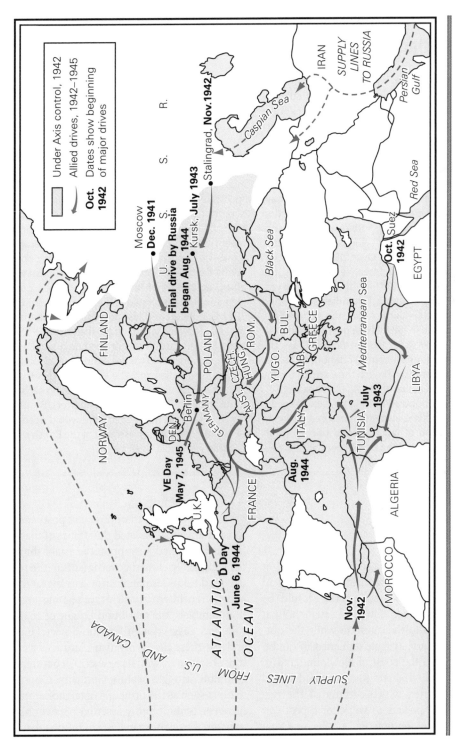

THE SECOND WORLD WAR IN EUROPE, 1941–1945

INDIAN FORCES AND THE SECOND WORLD WAR

As in the Great War, imperial forces would play a crucial role during the next great conflagration of the first half of the twentieth century. Britain, in particular, was vitally dependent on its dominions and on forces from the remainder of its empire, especially during the crucial period between the fall of France in June 1940 and the formal entry of the United States in December 1941. However, Britain continued to draw heavily on imperial troops throughout the duration of the war. Once again, India's economic and manpower contribution would be important to the British war effort. Over 2.5 million Indian volunteers, men and women, served during the Second World War; 87,031 lost their lives. The vast majority served in Burma, but Indian servicemen also saw action in North Africa, the Middle East, the Far East, and in Italy, where over 5,700 Indians died and six were awarded the Victoria Cross, the British Army's highest commendation for valour. In the brutal battles to breach the German Gustav Line at Monte Cassino alone, 431 Indians died.

The civilian population in India experienced a number of wartime austerity measures including the introduction of rationing and price controls in 1943, even as famine ravaged Bengal. Still, new economic opportunities were clearly created by the demands of war. As in the First World War, industrialists and manufacturers saw record profits. The Tata Iron & Steel Company in Jamshedpur produced 1.5 million tons a year throughout the war, making it the largest producer in the Empire. New industries, including automotive and locomotive industries, were created and traditional sectors, such as textiles and paper, saw enormous increases in output. India's geographic position—as the last bulwark against westward Japanese expansion—meant that much of northeastern India became a massive supply base for regional military operations. Despite general support for the British war effort, advocates of Indian independence grew increasingly disillusioned as the war progressed. In 1942 Gandhi drafted his most forceful statement to date regarding the need for the British to 'Quit India'. Noting that his country had no quarrel with Japan, Gandhi called for the removal of all foreign troops from Indian soil. The British, for their part, responded by arresting and imprisoning tens of thousands of Congress Party supporters. By 1945 it was evident to many that there would need to be a fundamental reassessment of the British relationship with India.

PLANNING FOR POST-WAR EUROPE

The last year of the war against Hitler brought to the fore the question of how Germany and the vast territory it had subjugated should be politically reorganized. Little serious thought had been devoted to the question while the outcome of the military struggle remained in doubt. Meeting at sea off the coast of Newfoundland in August 1941, Churchill and Roosevelt had signed the Atlantic Charter, which committed the two English-speaking powers to work for a post-war international order reminiscent of the one that Wilson had vainly attempted to forge a generation earlier. They agreed to oppose any post-war territorial change that violated the wishes of the populations concerned, to support the establishment of democratically elected governments in the regions liberated from German rule, and to favour the creation of an international peacekeeping organization to replace the moribund League of Nations.

It was easy enough for the Soviet Union to endorse these neo-Wilsonian platitudes as a gesture of solidarity with its new British partner in the common struggle against Germany. On specific matters such as the principle of territorial transfer, however, Stalin bluntly asserted his nation's right to retain the territory in Eastern Europe that it had forcibly acquired under the terms of its pact with the Nazis. Churchill reluctantly went along with this concession to the Soviets' concern with the security of their western frontiers, even though it violated the Atlantic Charter's prohibition of territorial changes imposed by force. After Pearl Harbor, the American government shrank from official endorsement of Soviet claims on the Baltic states, eastern Poland, Romania, and Finland, but tacitly accepted them in recognition of the USSR's critical role in the Grand Alliance against Hitler.

The events of the summer of 1943 forced the Allies to confront seriously for the first time the long-deferred question of Europe's post-war political future. At the first joint meeting of Allied foreign ministers in Moscow in October 1943, plans were drawn up for the inter-Allied occupation of Italy after the war. Despite Soviet efforts to obtain equal participation, effective power was placed in the hands of the Anglo–American administrative authorities who accompanied the Allied armies on their march up the Italian peninsula. At the Tehran Conference a month later, Stalin reiterated his intention to retain his country's territorial acquisitions of 1939–41 in Eastern Europe. The two Western leaders agreed, on the condition that Poland be allowed to annex German territory in the west as compensation for its territorial losses in the east to the USSR. No one thought to propose a plebiscite consulting the Poles that were to be incorporated into the Soviet Union or the Germans that were to be incorporated into the reconstituted Polish state as it 'moved west'. So the high-minded idealism of the Atlantic Charter gave way before the practical requirements of Realpolitik in the context of total war.

Once Roosevelt had definitively rejected Churchill's proposal for a landing in the Balkans as a prelude to an offensive into the Danube valley, Soviet domination of Southeastern Europe was assured, just as Western primacy in Italy, France, the Low Countries, and Scandinavia had been assured by the liberation of those countries by American and British forces. By September 1944, Romania and Bulgaria had capitulated to the Red Army, which was poised for an advance into Yugoslavia, Hungary, and Greece. Accordingly,

Churchill flew to Moscow in October to confirm and extend an informal agreement regarding the Balkans that he had proposed the previous June. The architect of the Atlantic Charter and its principled commitment to national self-determination obtained Stalin's consent to a gentlemen's agreement allotting Romania, Bulgaria, and Hungary to the Soviet sphere of influence and Greece to the Anglo–American sphere, with Yugoslavia to be split between them. Roosevelt did not attend the Moscow Conference because he was in the midst of an election campaign, but the US ambassador in Moscow kept him fully informed of the proceedings. His subsequent failure to raise objections to the cynical bargain between Churchill and Stalin may be taken as a signal of tacit acceptance of both the sphere-of-influence approach to the region's political future and the specific geographical divisions the agreement entailed.

The spirit of co-operation that had enabled the Allies to agree on the partition of the Balkans and to recognize the USSR's right to retain its acquisitions in Eastern Europe began to evaporate when the question arose concerning the fates of Germany and Poland. When the question of Germany's future status had been informally addressed at Tehran, the Big Three had seemed to agree that the only effective solution to the 'German problem' was political disintegration of the country that had plunged Europe into two great wars in less than 30 years. Reviving proposals aired by French hardliners at the Paris Peace Conference in 1919, Churchill suggested separating from Germany its industrial heartland in the Rhineland–Westphalia region and establishing a central European federation linking the south German states, Austria, and Hungary. Stalin forcefully pressed for the dismemberment of the nation whose expansionist policy had brought such ruin to the Soviet Union. The original American proposal was equally harsh, but (characteristically) focused on the economic sources of German power. At the Anglo–American Conference in Quebec in September 1944, Roosevelt obtained Churchill's tentative agreement to a scheme that would see Germany's industrial base destroyed and its status reduced to that of a simple agricultural nation.

By the time of the summit meeting at Yalta, a resort city on the USSR's Crimean Peninsula, in February 1945, the Anglo–American position on Germany's future had undergone a fundamental shift from the vindictive schemes considered at Tehran and Quebec. With Allied military forces deep in German territory and the Third Reich on the brink of collapse, Britain and the United States began to have second thoughts about the consequences of Germany's political and economic disintegration. Some of the same considerations that had prompted Wilson and Lloyd George to oppose Clemenceau's harsh plans for Germany at Paris a quarter of a century earlier led Roosevelt and Churchill to resist Stalin's demands for reparations and political dismemberment. The total disappearance of German power in Central Europe would leave a vacuum that the nearby Soviet colossus was bound to fill, and the crippling of the German economic system through excessive reparation demands would have deleterious effects on the rest of the industrial world as it struggled to recover from the war.

While no definitive decision was reached on the twin issues of reparations and Germany's political future, the Yalta Conference did produce an agreement on the temporary partition of the country into military occupation zones. The Soviet army would occupy the territory east of the Elbe that it was in the process of liberating from Hitler's retreating forces. The rest of the country would be occupied by the armies of the United States, Britain, and France (whose participation Churchill demanded for fear that the US would withdraw its forces from Europe as it had in 1919, leaving Britain to face the Soviet Union alone). As in 1919, the volatile issue of reparations was postponed, though the figure of US$20 million (with half going to the USSR) was mentioned as a basis of discussion.

A bone of greater contention between the Western and Eastern members of the Grand Alliance at Yalta was the long-simmering dispute over the political future of Poland. In April 1943,

Stalin had abruptly withdrawn diplomatic recognition of the pro-Western Polish government-in-exile headquartered in London, when it appeared to give credence to Nazi accusations that Soviet military forces had massacred 10,000 Polish officers during the period of Soviet co-operation with Germany. Shortly thereafter Stalin gave his official blessing to a rival group of Polish exiles in the USSR that disputed the London group's claim to political legitimacy. On 23 July 1944, a pro-Soviet Committee of National Liberation was established in the Polish city of Lublin after its capture by the Red Army. Then on 1 August, in response to an appeal from the London Poles, the 46,000 members of the Warsaw underground rose against the German army of occupation and were joined by most of the city's civilian population. At the time of the Warsaw uprising, the Red Army had smashed through the German defences to within 10 kilometres of the city, and Radio Moscow was broadcasting messages of support for the Poles. But the Soviet forces abruptly halted their advance and stood by while the German occupiers brutally crushed the insurrection. When Churchill appealed to Stalin to allow Anglo–American planes to land on Soviet airfields after lending support to the Warsaw uprising, he was refused. The consequent death of thousands of Polish partisans wiped out the impressive political and military organization that the London Poles had managed to establish in the occupied country, thereby paving the way for the pro-Soviet rival group that accompanied the advancing Red Army. In January 1945, with Soviet military forces occupying the entire prewar territory of Poland, the Kremlin installed the pro-Soviet Polish faction in Warsaw and accorded it formal diplomatic recognition.

At Yalta the following month, Roosevelt and Churchill obtained Stalin's agreement to add noncommunist resistance leaders to the recently established provisional government. They also wrested from him the pledge that free elections, Western-style, would be conducted in Poland after the end of the war, so that Poles could determine their own future form of government. This promise was later extended to the entire continent through the Big Three's adoption of the US-sponsored Declaration on Liberated Europe. Roosevelt returned home and on 12 April died of a cerebral hemorrhage. He went to his grave apparently convinced that the 'spheres of influence' formula adopted by Stalin and Churchill at Moscow four months earlier had been superseded by a neo-Wilsonian principle of national self-determination that revived the spirit of the Atlantic Charter. His successor, Harry Truman, believed even more resolutely in this version of the wartime agreements concerning Europe's political future.

Stalin, by contrast, left the Crimean Conference apparently believing that the informal understanding on the spheres of influence reached earlier with Churchill remained in effect, and that the Yalta declaration was nothing more than rhetorical window dressing, perhaps intended to placate American voters of Eastern European descent. Western journalists and politicians had often spoken of the need to establish a post-war consortium of the three great powers in the anti-German coalition, each of which would ensure peace and stability by exercising paramount influence in its own sphere. At Tehran, Roosevelt had broached to Stalin his proposal that 'Four Policemen'—the United States, Britain, the Soviet Union, and China—maintain order in the world after the defeat of the Axis. Together, the decision at Tehran to permit the Soviet army to liberate the Balkans and the bargain in Moscow setting out the victors' spheres of influence in that region (the so-called percentages agreement) seem to have led Stalin to believe that the old concept of the great-power consortium would continue to operate in peacetime as it had during the war.

On the basis of this assumption, Stalin proceeded to execute the provisions of the Moscow percentages agreement, which had formed the basis of the armistice accords concluded with the former Nazi satellites in Eastern Europe. Soviet members of the control commissions in Romania, Bulgaria, and Hungary bypassed their Anglo–American colleagues to ensure Soviet predominance, just as the British and Americans

ignored Moscow's representatives on the control commission in Italy, which clearly lay within the Western sphere of influence. When a civil war spontaneously erupted in Greece during the winter of 1944–5 between communist and anti-communist factions within the resistance movement, Stalin withheld support from the Greek communist insurgents, thereby enabling the pro-Western government in Athens to retain its power with British military assistance. Similarly, the Kremlin instructed the communist parties in France and Italy—whose ideology had previously prevented them from participating in 'bourgeois' political administrations—to accept subordinate positions in non-communist coalitions and to behave with moderation despite their temporary status as the most popular political parties in their respective countries. The reason was that Stalin recognized those two countries, which had been liberated by Anglo–American military forces, as belonging within the Western zone of influence. The impending triumph of the Grand Alliance necessitated a resolution of these contradictory versions of the wartime decisions regarding the political reorganization of liberated Europe.

THE HOLOCAUST

As the European war drew to a close in the early months of 1945, the brutality of Nazi occupation policy was revealed. The Red Army's capture of the Nazi extermination centre at Auschwitz in Poland in January, followed by the Anglo–American liberation of the death camps at Dachau, Buchenwald, and Bergen-Belsen in Germany in April, exposed the full extent of the Third Reich's horrendous campaign to exterminate the Jewish inhabitants of German-occupied Europe. The deliberate slaughter of more than 6 million of Europe's 12 million Jews, now widely known as the Holocaust, was carried out largely by the Nazi special police force, the SS. Hitler's strategy for eliminating the Jewish population of Europe developed in three stages. The first stage, which lasted from his accession in 1933 until the summer of 1941, concentrated on efforts to organize the mass expulsion of Jews

Survivors of Buchenwald concentration camp talk to American soldiers after the camp's liberation on 18 April 1945. © The Art Archive/Alamy.

from Germany and its territories. By the beginning of the war, more than half of the Jews of Germany and Austria had emigrated to those foreign havens that would accept them. With the conquest of Poland, an additional 1.8 million Jews were brought under German control and assembled in camps in preparation for deportation to some distant dumping ground after Germany's anticipated military triumph. (With the defeat of France, the possibility was discussed of sending Europe's Jews to the French-owned island of Madagascar off the east coast of Africa.)

The second phase of Hitler's Jewish policy began in the summer of 1941, as German military forces invaded the Soviet Union. Following on the heels of the army were small, mobile SS units known as *Einsatzgruppen* ('special task groups'). It became the task of these bloodthirsty marauders to enforce the Führer's 'Commissar Order' of May 1941,

which stipulated that all communist government officials captured during Operation Barbarossa be executed on the spot in order to destroy the political infrastructure of the Soviet state. Amid this war of annihilation the *Einsatzgruppen* massacred approximately 1.2 million of the Soviet Union's 5 million Jews. This was done on the pretext of eliminating suspected communist partisans from the rear of the German armies that were driving toward Leningrad, Moscow, and Stalingrad. While the SS contingents were rounding up and murdering every Jew they could lay their hands on, Air Marshal Hermann Göring ordered SS official Reinhard Heydrich to devise a more efficient and systematic method of dealing with the millions of Jewish survivors who were concentrated in urban areas across occupied Europe. By the time Heydrich had drafted his diabolical scheme, the German offensive against the Soviet Union had ground to a halt. The winter of 1941–2 made it clear that the war in the USSR would drag on much longer than had been anticipated.

The failure of Operation Barbarossa prompted the Nazi leadership to revise both the method and the timetable for what Hitler and his henchmen thought of as 'the final solution of the Jewish problem'. At the end of 1941, the Nazis abruptly reversed their policy of promoting mass Jewish emigration and forbade Jews to leave German-occupied Europe. A top-secret meeting of senior Nazi officials in January 1942, in the Berlin suburb of Wannsee, ushered in the third and most barbaric phase of the war against the Jews. Heydrich secured approval of a proposal to replace the haphazard assassination techniques that were being employed by the roving bands of SS thugs behind the German lines in the USSR with a systematic campaign of extermination that would apply modern methods and scientific technology. Those who did not gradually succumb to disease and starvation would be dispatched en masse in gas chambers and crematoria. The death camps were established at various sites throughout occupied Poland, to which Jews and other groups considered subhuman by the Nazis—including gypsies, homosexuals, and Poles—would be transported during the years 1942–4.

After irrefutable evidence of the extermination campaign reached foreign countries in November 1942, the Allied leaders were cautious in their response. Insisting on according absolute priority to the war effort against the Axis, the US War Department refused to divert planes conducting raids near Auschwitz to bomb the gas chambers and the railway lines leading to the death camp. Only after the liberating armies uncovered the remains of the victims and saw the emaciated survivors did the victorious governments demand that the Nazi leadership be held accountable for genocide. Between November 1945 and September 1946, 22 top Nazi leaders were prosecuted in the Bavarian city of Nuremberg. The trials resulted in three acquittals and 19 sentences ranging from 10 years' imprisonment to death. They also contributed a new term to the vocabulary of international law: 'crimes against humanity'.

SUMMARY

The six-year war that began in the fall of 1939 can be divided into three chronological periods. The first stage started with the invasion of Poland and ended with the establishment of a deceptively stable front along Germany's western frontier during the winter of 1939–40. No major battles took place on the Western Front in this initial phase, which some commentators dubbed the 'phony war'. The second phase opened in May 1940 with a German offensive in the west. Attacking through the Low Countries into France, the German army quickly defeated the French, forcing the British from the continent and leaving Britain, with Canada and the other Commonwealth Allies, to face Germany on their own. In the summer of 1940, the Germans tried unsuccessfully to knock Britain out of the war through aerial bombardment of its civilian population centres. The defeat of the German air force in the Battle of Britain denied Hitler complete victory in Western Europe.

In the third stage, the European war was transformed into a global conflict. This final period began in June 1941 with the German invasion of the Soviet Union, which became the single greatest armed struggle in human history. In December of that year, Japan's surprise attack on Pearl Harbor brought the United States into the war. As the battle for Eastern Europe raged, the Third Reich intensified its campaign to exterminate Jews, communists, and other targeted groups. By the end of the war the Nazis had systematically murdered an estimated 12 million people whom they had identified as racial and political enemies. After the enormity of the Holocaust was revealed at the end of the war, the Nuremberg trials represented the first organized effort in history to prosecute crimes against humanity.

NOTES

1.   Germany and Italy did not declare war on the United States until 11 December 1941.

QUESTIONS FOR CRITICAL THOUGHT

1. What was the primary factor facilitating German military dominance in 1939 and 1940?
2. What was the most important turning point during the Second World War?
3. Why was the opening of a second front such a source of contention?
4. Discuss whether Stalin was correct in his view that the Moscow Percentages Agreement should form the basis of the post-war world order.
5. How could the wartime coalition have maintained favourable relations in the post-war era?
6. Why did allied leaders insist that the war effort retain absolute priority over any effort to halt the events of the Holocaust? Were they correct in their assessment?

WEBSITES FOR FURTHER REFERENCE

Avalon Project: WWII Documents
    http://avalon.law.yale.edu/subject_menus/wwii.asp

Historical Text Archive: World War II
    http://historicaltextarchive.com/sections.php?action=list&secid=18&total=37

US Holocaust Memorial Museum
    www.ushmm.org

World War II Archives Foundation
    http://wwiiarchives.net

Yad Vashem
    www.yadvashem.org

CHAPTER 6

THE CONFIRMATION OF JAPAN'S SUPREMACY IN EAST ASIA

PEACEFUL PENETRATION (1914–1930)

The First World War gave the Japanese empire a golden opportunity to consolidate and expand its economic penetration and political domination of East Asia without the diplomatic risks that such an aggressive policy would have previously incurred. As an ally of Britain, Japan had declared war on Germany in August 1914 and proceeded to seize all of Germany's possessions in the Far East, including the Shantung peninsula (with its port of Tsingtao) on the Chinese mainland and three island chains in the northern Pacific (the Marianas, Marshalls, and Carolines).

Having added these former German colonies to the territories and privileges already obtained as spoils of war from China and Russia, Tokyo was ready to concentrate its expansionist energies on acquiring China in its entirety. The Chinese Revolution of 1911–12, which overthrew the increasingly ineffective Qing dynasty, had sparked Japanese fears of losing the economic toehold on the mainland that it had acquired as a result of those earlier military triumphs. The Qing rulers had relied heavily on Japan for financial assistance and political advice, but the new government in Beijing looked to Europe for support, apparently hoping to loosen China's ties of dependency on its powerful island neighbour. Anxious to preserve its privileged position in southern Manchuria and Inner Mongolia, Japan took advantage of the distraction provided by the war in Europe to present the Chinese government with an infamous set of 'Twenty-One Demands' in January 1915. In its original form, this harsh ultimatum demanded not only Japanese control of China's principal natural resources but also the establishment of a protectorate in the form of Japanese advisers attached to the Chinese government. Although Tokyo rescinded its demand for a protectorate (in response to energetic protests from the United States and Britain), it did succeed in extracting from the helpless Chinese government a number of economic concessions that significantly improved Japan's economic position on the mainland.

In 1916 Japan's major European allies—Britain, France, and Russia—formally recognized Tokyo's wartime gains in East Asia, conferring the stamp of legitimacy on Japan's unilateral extension of its power. The sole obstacle to Japanese expansionism was the United States, which had expressed profound displeasure at the imposition of the Twenty-One Demands on China. Washington's mounting concern about developments across the Pacific had nothing to do with fear for the security of the American homeland: the opening of the Panama Canal in the summer of 1914, which permitted the rapid concentration of American naval power in the eastern Pacific, had virtually eliminated any naval threat that Japan might pose to the west coast of North America. Nevertheless, Washington's longtime commitment to preserving the territorial integrity of China and the 'Open Door' for trade and investment there, coupled with its concern for the security of the Philippines, led to the passage, in 1916, of an ambitious naval construction program designed to ensure the United States' naval supremacy in the western as well as the eastern Pacific. Japan's equally intense preoccupation with securing its privileged position in Manchuria and northern China seemed to preclude an amicable resolution of this impending transpacific rivalry.

Finally, in November 1917, a mutually satisfactory compromise was reached by the US secretary of state and the Japanese ambassador to Washington. The Lansing–Ishii Agreement affirmed the territorial integrity of China and the principle of the Open Door while recognizing that geographic proximity did give Japan some 'special interest' in China. This ambiguous accommodation—an executive agreement that was not submitted for legislative ratification—made it possible for the two countries to co-operate in the common struggle against Germany while postponing the inevitable showdown over China until after the end of the war.

In Japanese eyes, this 'special interest' in China represented something like an Asian counterpart of the Monroe Doctrine, with Japan as the hegemonic power. This interpretation gained even wider acceptance in Tokyo after the military collapse and political disintegration of Russia, Japan's traditional rival for the Chinese spoils. Following the Russian Revolution and the signing of the Treaty of Brest-Litovsk, the French government persuaded US President Woodrow Wilson to approve a Japanese military intervention in eastern Siberia, ostensibly intended to restore order and assist in the reconstitution of a political and military authority in Russia capable of renewing the attack on Germany's eastern front in order to relieve the embattled Allies in the west.

Japanese expansionists welcomed the opportunity to strengthen Tokyo's economic and political position in eastern Siberia and to create a buffer zone between Russia and Japanese-dominated Manchuria. Wilson reluctantly bowed to French pressure for a Japanese intervention on the condition that the expeditionary force be limited to 7,000—approximately the size of the American contingent earmarked for the Siberian campaign. But the Japanese army in eastern Siberia mushroomed to 72,000 by the end of the war. There it was to remain until 1922, long after Germany had been defeated and the small American contingent sent to Vladivostok in 1918 had returned home. Thus the political authority of Russia, the traditional counterweight to Japan, was virtually non-existent in the region just as Japanese power there reached its height.

Japan's presence at the Paris Peace Conference as one of the five dominant powers was a fitting tribute to its remarkable rise from backwardness and obscurity in less than half a century. Although it had no interest in the redistribution of European territory and resources, Japan pressed for and obtained substantial advantages within its own geographical sphere, including official control of the formerly German Pacific islands (in the form of a League of Nations mandate) and the formal right to the economic privileges formerly enjoyed by Germany on the Shantung peninsula, which expansionist business elites in Tokyo saw as a stepping stone towards further economic penetration of China. This confirmation of its wartime gains firmly established Japan as a major economic force on the Asian mainland and the principal naval power in the western Pacific at a time when Russia was still reeling from its civil war and Britain was struggling to recover financially and commercially from the First World War.

The United States posed the most formidable challenge to Japanese imperial ambitions in the Far East. Washington was apprehensive not only about Japan's territorial and economic gains at the peace conference but also about the growth of its naval power. Tokyo's spending on naval construction tripled between 1917 and 1921, by which point it had come to represent over a third of the imperial budget. Although its fleet ranked a distant third behind the armadas of Britain and the US, Japan's distance from North America meant that it was virtually immune to the deterrent effects of American naval power (which in any case had to be divided between two oceans), while its alliance with Britain (concluded in 1902, renewed in 1905 and 1911) neutralized the Royal Navy as a potential constraint on its imperial ambitions. In response to the increase of Japanese naval strength, the US transferred the bulk of its fleet from the Atlantic to the Pacific (achieving virtual parity with Japan in that ocean) after the end of the war in Europe and proceeded to open the dry dock at Pearl Harbor in Hawaii. Relieved of the German naval menace in the Atlantic by the disarmament provisions of the Versailles Treaty, American naval strategists began for the first time to make plans for the projection of American naval power across the Pacific to the vicinity of Japan.

The prospect of a costly naval race so soon after the end of the world war was unappealing to all the powers concerned. Britain still ruled the seas but was in danger of being surpassed by the United States and equalled by Japan in the near future; at the same time, chronic unemployment and industrial stagnation demanded budgetary restraint, not massive spending. In the US, the administration of President Warren Harding faced a serious post-war recession and was dominated by conservative isolationists committed to drastic cuts in taxes and government spending, as well as retrenchment from President Wilson's ambitious global commitments. Japanese leaders continued to believe that national prosperity depended on privileged access to markets and raw materials abroad but seemed to prefer peaceful economic expansion and co-operation with

the two English-speaking powers to the domestic costs and foreign policy risks of a naval arms race. It was in the context of this widespread apprehension about the economic and strategic consequences of unrestrained naval rivalry that President Harding invited the foreign ministers of eight maritime nations to the world's first international conference on naval arms control, to be held in Washington during the winter of 1921–2.

The Washington Naval Conference produced a number of agreements to limit the naval arms race in general and to reduce Pacific tensions in particular, but its principal achievement was the so-called Five Power Treaty, which established a tonnage ratio for existing capital ships (defined as warships over 10,000 tons carrying guns larger than eight-inch) of 5:5:3:1.75:1.75 for Britain, the United States, Japan, France, and Italy, respectively, and decreed a 10-year moratorium on the construction of new ships in the same category. The three great naval powers agreed to refrain from building new fortifications on their Pacific possessions (excluding Singapore and Pearl Harbor, the principal forward bases of Britain and the United States, respectively). Japan consented to leave eastern Siberia, to restore China's sovereignty over the Shantung peninsula, and to permit the replacement of its bilateral alliance with Britain—which was strongly opposed by the United States—with a multilateral agreement to respect the political status quo in Asia.

The Washington Naval Conference was widely acclaimed as the beginning of a new era in international relations. Never before had the great powers freely consented to limit the size of any of their armed forces and to refrain from building new fortifications. Advocates of universal disarmament regretted the exclusion of land armaments from the agenda—a concession to the nervous French, who insisted on the right to maintain undisputed military superiority over Germany in the absence of effective security guarantees. This omission did not dampen the joy that greeted the publication of the Washington treaty provisions. The vague commitment to universal disarmament that had been inserted in the Paris peace treaties finally appeared to be on the brink of realization, at least in the limited sphere of naval power.

The agreements relating specifically to East Asia also raised hopes for peace and stability in that unsettled region, in Washington as well as in Tokyo. American Secretary of State Charles Evans Hughes, the host and guiding spirit of the conference, had achieved his three main objectives: the termination of the Anglo–Japanese alliance, the recognition of US naval parity with Great Britain and superiority over Japan, and the evacuation of Japanese military forces from eastern Siberia. Tokyo had accepted the inferior position in the 5:5:3 ratio for capital ship tonnage because the non-fortification agreement seemed to represent an adequate guarantee of both Japan's security in its home waters and its control of the sea approaches to the Asian mainland. These compromises in strategic matters were supplemented by a series of informal pledges by Japan to abandon its unilateral quest for preferential rights in China in favour of a multilateral approach to China's economic development, in co-operation with the Western powers.

Domestic developments within Japan after the Washington Conference appeared to confirm the new orientation of Japanese foreign policy and facilitated the rapprochement between Tokyo and the Western powers with colonial holdings in East Asia. The passage of progressive social legislation and the adoption of universal male suffrage in 1924 helped to dispel the Western democracies' lingering image of Japan as an authoritarian, militaristic society. This apparent evolution toward enlightened administration and representative government caused many American bankers and business executives to change their attitudes towards the Far East. China—the traditional object of American economic interest in the region—now seemed so mired in political chaos and social unrest as to represent a poor risk for trade and investment.

By contrast, Japan acquired a well-deserved reputation as an island of stability that offered a much more hospitable environment for US economic interests. A close Japanese–American commercial relationship had developed during the First World War, when US exports to Japan increased fivefold and Japanese exports to the United States almost tripled. These economic contacts continued to expand throughout the 1920s, the US continuing as both Japan's biggest customer (absorbing 40 per cent of all its exports, including 90 per cent of its raw silk products) and its biggest supplier (providing most of the island empire's automobiles, machinery, building-construction materials, and oil). During the same period American banks supplied Japan with 40 per cent of its foreign investment. These commercial and financial connections, reinforced by the mutually advantageous naval arms agreements of 1922, contributed to an atmosphere of cordiality and co-operation between Tokyo and Washington, which in turn promoted stability in the western Pacific for the rest of the 1920s.

In the final analysis, the security of East Asia depended on Japan's willingness to continue pursuing its national aspirations by peaceful means—through economic rather than military rivalry with the Western powers. The limitations written into the Five Power Treaty confirmed Japan's naval superiority in its geographical sphere. By agreeing not to build additional fortifications between Pearl Harbor and Singapore, the United States and Britain had significantly reduced their ability to deter future Japanese aggression on the Chinese mainland or in Southeast Asia. Meanwhile, the advent of air power as a decisive factor in naval warfare increased the vulnerability of British and American possessions in the Far East. Four months before the opening of the Washington Naval Conference, the United States Army Air Corps had sunk a captured German battleship in an experimental test off the Virginia coast with foreign (including Japanese) military observers in attendance, proving that gravity-propelled bombs could send a heavily armoured vessel to the bottom.

In strategic terms, this meant that capital ships were no longer safe in waters within range of land-based enemy aircraft or aircraft carriers. Gone were the days when great battle fleets could roam the oceans with impunity, intervening anywhere at will. Thus the Anglo–American superiority in battleships that Japan had conceded at Washington was a deceptive advantage. The comforting vision of the great fleet advancing westward from Pearl Harbor to liberate the Philippines and blockade the Japanese home islands—the basis of American naval strategy since the early 1920s—was an illusion. Japan now possessed, in the form of the German mandate islands, a string of potential air bases that stretched across the western Pacific between the Philippines and Hawaii. From these safe bases Japanese bombers could conceivably block American naval access to the western Pacific, thereby isolating the vulnerable Philippine Islands from the principal American Pacific base at Hawaii.

American naval authorities decried this potential imbalance of power in the western Pacific. But policy-makers in Washington were preoccupied with European and Latin American affairs. Thus American trade with and investment in Japan continued to increase, while Tokyo gave no sign of exploiting geographical advantages or technological innovations to upset the balance of power of the region. However, the demographic, geographical, and economic realities that had spurred Japanese adventurism in the past had not disappeared. A rapidly expanding population, a limited supply of arable and habitable land, and a lack of mineral resources and fossil fuels did not bode well for Japan's future economic growth. Unless a remedy was found, Japan would have to face a drastic reduction in its standard of living, with all the social tensions and political instability that typically accompany economic stagnation and decline.

The steps taken by the Japanese government in the 1920s were reminiscent of the path followed in the previous century by Britain—another island nation plagued during its developing phase by overpopulation and inadequate natural resources: (1) encouraging emigration, to relieve domestic pressures on land, food, and natural resources; (2) promoting exports of manufactured products to finance imports of essential raw materials

and foodstuffs; and (3) pursuing political accommodation with other great powers in order to facilitate peaceful economic expansion. During this period, a progressive governing coalition of bankers, industrialists, and civil servants successfully combined a domestic program of social and political reform with a conciliatory foreign policy and drastic reductions in military spending. Such moderation did not satisfy the powerful military, naval, and bureaucratic elites who continued to dream of an East Asia free of Western influence and dominated by an authoritarian Japan. Like their counterparts in Weimar Germany, these stalwarts of the old order rejected their government's domestic reform program and its foreign policy of accommodation. Their cause was strengthened by a series of international developments in the 1920s that gradually undermined the government's co-operative relationship with the West and allowed its military critics to mobilize popular opposition to that policy. The first of those developments was the imposition of legal restrictions on Japanese immigration in the English-speaking world. Opposition to Asian immigration in the United States, Canada, and Australia, which had surfaced at the turn of the century, sharply curtailed the opportunities for Japanese nationals to migrate to less densely populated countries bordering the Pacific. Canada, which had imposed a limit of 400 Japanese immigrants per year in 1908 (when it signed the Lemieux–Hayashi Gentlemen's Agreement with Japan), revised its policy in 1923 and again in 1928, lowering the cap to 150 Japanese immigrants per year. In 1924 the US Congress went so far as to enact legislation that singled out Japanese immigrants as ineligible for American citizenship.

Though the practical effect of the US legislation was minimal, given that the previous quota system had allowed only a few hundred Japanese immigrants into the country each year, its emotional impact in Japan was considerable. Not only did it indicate that Japanese immigrants were considered undesirable, but, given that Canada and Australia had adopted similar exclusionary legislation, it also suggested a Caucasian conspiracy to deny Japan the opportunity to relieve its population pressures through emigration. Earlier Japanese hopes for the large-scale colonization of Korea, Formosa (Taiwan), and Manchuria before the war had failed to materialize. Fewer than half a million Japanese had migrated to Korea in the decade following its annexation, and fewer than 200,000 had settled in Formosa. Twenty years after Japan had gained special privileges in Manchuria, fewer than a quarter of a million Japanese had settled there. The reluctance of Japanese citizens to relocate to these neighbouring areas, despite lavish inducements from their government, has generally been attributed to the living conditions there. Whatever the explanation, expansionist-minded zealots in Japan began to raise the alarm: their country was being boxed in by the racist policies of the white English-speaking nations.

Barriers to emigration were soon followed by barriers to the expansion of Japanese trade with the English-speaking world. Commercial relations with the United States declined sharply at the beginning of the 1930s with the advent of the Depression. By 1930, Japan's raw silk prices had fallen to one-quarter of the previous year's level, and silk exports to the US fell by more than 40 per cent, ruining many peasant families who depended on this cash crop. The abrupt decline in Japanese exports caused by the contraction of US demand was aggravated by increasing American protectionism. US producers and labour organizations sponsored boycotts of Japanese goods and mounted a 'buy American' campaign, while the Hawley–Smoot Tariff of 1930 raised duties on Japanese products by an average of 23 per cent.

The government in Tokyo made matters worse in January 1930 by returning to the gold standard at the existing exchange rate. Intended to integrate the Japanese economy more closely into an international monetary system dominated by nations that had long since returned to gold, this belated decision caused a dramatic overvaluation of the yen and therefore increased the price of Japanese exports at the very moment when declining purchasing power and rising protectionism were closing foreign markets. All these developments contributed to a rise in unemployment, a sharp decrease in the real income of agricultural and industrial workers, and the beginnings of social unrest in Japan.

As opportunities for increased trade and emigration across the Pacific vanished, some Japanese revived the old dream of establishing a neo-colonial relationship with their gigantic neighbour on the Asian mainland. At the end of the Great War, Japan had seemed ideally positioned to exploit the political divisions and economic distress of China to establish its predominance there. Although the Western powers had persuaded Tokyo to join them in reaffirming the Open Door principle regarding commercial opportunity in China, the agreement lacked an enforcement mechanism. As a result, Japanese economic domination of China was unlikely to attract more than verbal protests from other countries, even if it violated the protections agreed upon at the Washington Conference.

The internal political situation in China created opportunities for Japanese intervention. The revolution of 1911–12 had failed to establish a government capable of unifying the country and liberating it from foreign interference. From 1912 to the mid-1920s, administrative authority in China was divided among regional military commanders or political leaders, most of whom passively tolerated the humiliating system of economic and legal privileges enjoyed by Japanese, European, and American trading companies. Manchuria was dominated by a local figure beholden to the Japanese, and the regime in Beijing, recognized by the Western powers as the nominal 'government' of China, was powerless either to control local warlords or to prevent foreign restrictions on Chinese sovereignty. Only Sun Yat-sen, the leader of the 1911 revolution, who had established a rival 'government' in Canton in 1917, represented a potential inspiration for Chinese national unity and sovereignty. But his regime lacked the military strength to enforce its will on the regional warlords and command the respect of foreign powers.

Weakened by these centrifugal forces, China submitted to ever-increasing Japanese economic domination. In the course of the 1920s, 90 per cent of all new foreign investment in China came from Japan and 25 per cent of Japan's total exports went to China. Japan was rapidly developing a neo-colonial relationship with the mainland analogous to that of the United States with Latin America, exchanging manufactured goods and investment capital for coal, iron, rice, soybeans, and other mineral and agricultural resources. Japan's economic penetration of China was facilitated by the system of commercial privileges established in the previous century during the age of imperial expansion. Restrictions on China's ability to impose tariffs prevented it from increasing duties on imports without the approval of the great powers, while the principle of extraterritoriality exempted foreign residents from the jurisdiction of Chinese legal authorities and permitted foreign powers to maintain their own infrastructure (such as postal, communications, and transportation services) within their concessions. Foreign powers justified such measures on the grounds that China's chronic political instability prevented it from exercising the legal authority normally associated with sovereign states. Although the US and Europe also benefited from these privileges, Japan drew the greatest economic advantage from them and accordingly became the main object of Chinese resentment.

In the West, China's demands for the restoration of tariff autonomy and abolition of extraterritoriality fell on deaf ears even among the nations that had endorsed the idea of its administrative and territorial integrity at the Washington Conference. When none of the great powers proved willing to accord China full political sovereignty, Sun Yat-sen turned to the Soviet Union, which had not been invited to Washington and which had renounced all the special privileges in China that it had inherited from the tsarist regime. The Canton government's overture to Moscow came at a propitious moment in the evolution of Soviet foreign policy, when Lenin and his successors—disappointed by the failure of the

communist revolution to spread to industrialized Europe—were turning their attention to the non-industrialized regions of Asia. In 1924, Soviet representatives of the COMINTERN were dispatched to Canton to reorganize Sun's political movement, the Kuomintang, into a disciplined revolutionary organization capable of leading a mass movement in alliance with the small Chinese Communist Party, founded three years earlier.

Following the death of Sun Yat-sen in 1925, a young military officer named Chiang Kai-shek, who had visited the Soviet Union and remained in close contact with the COMINTERN in China, set out to unify the country and to liberate it from the detested system of foreign economic privileges. He proclaimed the Kuomintang the national government of China and in July 1926 formally launched a northern military expedition to destroy the power of the regional military authorities, promote administrative unification, and expel foreign interests. In the same year popular attacks on foreign citizens and property revealed widespread support for Chiang's dynamic policy of national unification and liberation.

The communists in the Nationalist coalition did not distinguish among the various foreign powers encroaching on Chinese sovereignty, but Chiang was eager to negotiate bilaterally with any one of them that would consider phasing out the despised treaty privileges. As it happened, public and official attitudes toward China in the United States had been gradually evolving towards greater sympathy for China's predicament. This shift was confirmed in January 1927, when the US secretary of state, Frank Kellogg, announced that Washington would consider granting tariff autonomy to a central government in China that could command the allegiance of the Chinese people and protect American lives and property. Chiang soon began to pursue policies and behave in ways that endeared him to public opinion in the US. In April 1927, he turned against his former communist allies, expelling COMINTERN advisers, ruthlessly suppressing the Chinese Communist Party, and denouncing the Soviet Union as a 'red imperialist', and by the end of the year he had married the US-educated daughter of a wealthy Shanghai businessman, after promising to convert to her Christian faith. In July 1928, Kuomintang forces occupied Beijing, bringing most of China under their control. In the meantime, the Nationalist government had caused a furor in Tokyo by announcing plans to construct a railway in Manchuria to compete with the existing Japanese line, encouraging thousands of Chinese to immigrate there, and harassing Japanese economic interests in the region. Soon thereafter boycotts were organized against Japanese goods, and in December 1928 Manchuria was formally reunified with China.

This nationalist revival hastened the process whereby the United States changed its paternalistic attitude towards China. The military successes, administrative reforms, and anti-communist political orientation of the Nationalist regime appealed to those Americans anxious to see a stable, pro-Western, Christianized China open to US trade and investment. Thus the US unilaterally accorded tariff autonomy to China in July 1928, in exchange for a reciprocal most-favoured-nation agreement. American business executives and bankers began once again to consider the potential value represented by the vast mainland of China, politically unified and stabilized by a vigorous national government.

In Tokyo, however, the revival of Sino–American friendship, together with the impending collapse of foreign privileges in China and the challenge to Japanese interests in Manchuria, inflamed expansionist opinion. Not only did Japan's privileged position on the mainland seem threatened, but the United States could also be expected to gain economic advantages in China at the expense of Japan. Indeed, Japanese exports to China dropped by half between 1929 and 1931, and by the latter year the US had supplanted Japan as China's principal foreign supplier. The collapse of Japan's export trade in Asia, together with the sharp decline in Japanese–American commerce, provoked widespread anxiety among merchants, bankers, and government officials who feared losing access to the foreign exchange they needed to

pay for essential imports of coal, iron, oil, rubber, rice, and soybeans. Around the world, the deepening Depression led to increased protection for domestic markets in the industrialized nations, and even the non-industrialized Asian and African empires of the European powers were rapidly becoming inaccessible to Japanese commercial interests. The vast continental domains of the US and USSR, like Britain and France with their worldwide empires, had access to both the raw materials and the markets they needed to ride out the storm. Japan, by contrast, seemed isolated and economically vulnerable, with neither a market nor a resource base equal to its needs at a time when closed economic blocs were forming throughout the world.

Added to the fear of economic strangulation was a growing concern about Japan's security interests in the western Pacific. At the London Naval Conference of 1930, convened to reduce naval competition in categories of ships not covered by the Five Power Treaty (destroyers, cruisers, and submarines), the Japanese delegation was persuaded to accept a compromise agreement that some saw as a serious threat to Japan's naval superiority in its region. Patriotic organizations in Japan denounced the agreement as a 'sellout', while military critics of the civilian government exploited the widespread social discontent caused by falling farm incomes and growing urban unemployment to suggest ominous connections between the economic and security problems that the empire was facing. Many believed that a global war was inevitable in the not-so-distant future and that Japan's only hope of defending its interests lay in creating a self-sufficient strategic–economic bloc in East Asia controlled from Tokyo. In short, for critics of the civilian leadership in Tokyo, this conciliatory, pro-Western orientation was leading Japan down the path of national suicide.

MILITARY EXPANSION (1931–1941)

The collapse of Japan's democratic political institutions and the abandonment of its moderate foreign policy did not happen overnight. The transformation from a Western-type parliamentary system into a military dictatorship took place gradually, in almost imperceptible increments, between 1931 and 1936. There were many domestic reasons for the collapse of Japanese democracy amid the social tensions and economic distress caused by the Depression. The deepening agricultural crisis made the peasants particularly susceptible to demogogic appeals from political groups promising deliverance. Nevertheless, the militaristic critics of the government concentrated on foreign policy because the world outside was seen as both the cause of Japan's economic problems and the most promising source of relief. If the weak, vacillating policy of the government was to blame for the current crisis, relief would come with the rediscovery of Japanese pride at home and the reassertion of Japanese power abroad.

The spearhead of the revolt against the established political order was a group of army officers known as the 'Imperial Way' faction (so called because of their devotion to the emperor), consisting mainly of younger men stationed in Manchuria to guard the Japanese-owned railway and their supporters and promoters at home. They saw foreign conquest as the most effective way of promoting the spiritual regeneration of a Japan corrupted by Western cultural and commercial influences and threatened by Western naval power. Intent on purifying their society and restoring its glory, the young zealots of the Imperial Way launched a number of violent challenges to the political leadership and its foreign policy that prepared the way for the collapse of the parliamentary regime and the abandonment of its conciliatory foreign policy.

The first of these challenges came in September 1931, when middle-echelon officers on duty in Manchuria blew up a section of the railway, then blamed the attack on unnamed Chinese terrorists and used it as a pretext for occupying the rest of the province. This plot, which had been hatched in consultation with sympathetic officers in Tokyo's war ministry, represented a response to the encroachments in Manchuria by

the reinvigorated Chinese government of Chiang Kai-shek. Although the emperor, business leaders, and high government officials continued to preach caution and restraint in relations with the mainland, an outpouring of public support for the army's independent action forced the political authorities to accept the military *fait accompli*. In March 1932, a Manchurian independence movement, financed and controlled by the Japanese occupation army, established the sovereign state of Manchukuo, which was detached from China and placed under Japanese military protection. This virtually bloodless subjugation of Manchuria—a region with a land area greater than that of Japan, a population of 30 million, and valuable agricultural and mineral resources—had profound repercussions in Japanese domestic politics. The wave of euphoria that swept the country confirmed the army's predominance in political affairs and relegated elected officials to a subordinate role, particularly in the formulation of foreign policy.

The Western response to this flagrant violation of the principle of collective security was timid and vacillating. The American president, Herbert Hoover, was reluctant to impose economic sanctions against Japan, fearing that they would lead to war (an attitude evidently shared by most Americans at the time). Instead, Secretary of State Henry Stimson dispatched a note to Tokyo in January 1932, refusing US recognition to any 'treaty or agreement' brought about by means contrary to the Kellogg–Briand Pact. This nonrecognition doctrine allowed the Hoover administration to uphold the sanctity of international law without the risks involved in economic sanctions.

This cautious response was dictated by a number of considerations. First, American economic and strategic interests in northern China were minimal—certainly not important enough to warrant retaliatory measures that might result in a diplomatic and perhaps even military showdown. Second, American commercial and financial concerns with trade and investment interests in Japan were understandably reluctant to jeopardize them (not to speak of future opportunities), and did not hesitate to make their views known to Washington. Third, the US Congress had refused the funding required to bring American naval strength up to the Washington and London treaty limits, and as a result the United States lacked a credible force in the western Pacific to back up a strong diplomatic response to the Japanese action.

The cautious policy of the Hoover administration was continued following the presidential inauguration of Franklin Delano Roosevelt in March 1933. Economic reconstruction absorbed most of the new administration's energy, leaving little room for bold initiatives in foreign affairs, and the advent of the Nazi regime in Germany distracted world attention from the expansion of Japanese power in East Asia. Thus rumours of clandestine Japanese efforts to fortify the mandated Pacific islands, in violation of the Five Power Treaty, went uninvestigated. The State Department continued to discourage American trade with and investment in the vulnerable remnant of China under Kuomintang control, and American exports of strategic materials to Japan continued unabated throughout the rest of the 1930s.

Britain was even less inclined to risk antagonizing Japan by trying to dislodge it from a region of no particular importance to British national interests. Some officials in London even welcomed Tokyo's increasing military involvement in northern China as a convenient diversion from the region of East Asia—from Hong Kong south to Singapore—that was of much more concern to Britain on economic and strategic grounds. Throughout the Manchurian episode British policy regarding East Asia was dominated by the desire to divide the entire region into British and Japanese spheres of commercial and strategic interest. London's inclination to placate Tokyo was reflected in the tame condemnation of Japanese aggression in Manchuria by a League of Nations commission headed by Britain's Lord Lytton. On the basis of its report, the League's 'sanctions' against Japan were confined to symbolic gestures such as refusal to recognize the passports and postage of the Japanese puppet state, 'Manchukuo', that Tokyo had just imposed on the Manchurians.

It soon became evident that the Japanese military's appetite for foreign conquest could not be satisfied by the de facto absorption of Manchuria. The collapse of parliamentary democracy in many nations of Europe and the heightening of the Depression had undermined the credibility of those members of Japan's ruling elite who had tried to transplant Western-type political and economic practices to Japan and to co-operate with the Western powers in fostering international stability and prosperity. In their place emerged the dynamic young men of the Imperial Way faction. Gradually the power of the political parties and the Diet (the lower house of parliament) waned, while real authority was assumed by a small group of cabinet ministers who were beholden to the military chiefs. Army and naval officers infiltrated the middle and upper echelons of the civil service in increasing numbers, pressuring the surviving members of the old governing elite to adopt more authoritarian measures at home and more aggressive policies abroad. Internal repression intensified. Leftist politicians and labour leaders were imprisoned, newspapers were censored, and Western cultural influences came under attack from proponents of the new nationalism.

But the beneficiaries of Japan's political transformation were not to be the fanatical young officers of the Imperial Way. Their romantic dream of a purified Japanese society, untainted by the industrialized West, was clearly incompatible with the war of conquest that all significant parts of the ruling elite had come to favour by the mid-1930s. The more sober and practical-minded members of the military establishment recognized that spiritual virtues were no longer enough either to win wars or to promote the economic growth on which military success depended. The more conservative modernizers among the army leaders, while equally committed to military grandeur, realized that discipline, organization, and technological innovation were the best means of achieving that end. The so-called 'Control Faction' of older, more mature officers therefore resolved to harness the energies of their exuberant younger colleagues and redirect them into more effective channels. The opportunity to co-opt the program of the Imperial Way arose in February 1936, when 1,500 junior officers and soldiers in Tokyo seized government buildings and assassinated several current and former government leaders, along with a high-ranking general, before being captured by loyalist forces in the military. In response to this abortive putsch, the modernizing faction of the army high command hastened to restore discipline in the armed forces and to suppress the Imperial Way.

Even so, this modernizing faction had been converted to the cause of foreign conquest that the Imperial Way so energetically espoused. They endorsed domestic authoritarianism and foreign expansion not for purposes of spiritual renewal but rather to mobilize domestic support for military modernization and an increase in the political power of the army high command. Similarly, the business and financial leaders who had headed up Japan's industrial revolution were gradually won over to the cause of rearmament and foreign expansion for reasons of economic self-interest. The Zaibatsu elite—made up of the conglomerates Mitsui, Mitsubishi, Sumitomo, and Yasuda—which had previously co-operated with the civilian governments' policy of domestic liberalization and peaceful economic expansion abroad, joined forces with the modernizing sector of the army to form a vast military–industrial cadre devoted to massive rearmament in preparation for overseas conquest. The army leaders recognized the necessity of obtaining the services of this business elite in order to exploit the economic resources of Manchukuo.

Japanese heavy industry in turn reaped lavish rewards from the remilitarization of Japanese society and the increased economic penetration of the mainland. Industrial production skyrocketed from 6 billion yen in 1930 to 30 billion in 1941. The four Zaibatsu conglomerates more than tripled their total assets during the same period. It is ironic that a movement of national regeneration inspired by a nostalgic vision of the pre-industrial way of life was appropriated by the technologically minded elite of the army and heavy industry.

Historians have drawn parallels between the abortive coup of February 1936 in Japan and the 'Night of Long Knives' in Nazi Germany two years earlier, when Hitler turned against the anti-capitalist, romantic youth of the Sturm Abteilung and forged an alliance with conservative military and business elites.

Once the military technocrats and their allies in the Zaibatsu industrial and financial empires consolidated their authority in Tokyo, plans were laid for the further extension of Japanese power in East Asia. In August 1936, the cabinet adopted as 'Fundamental Principles of National Policy' the economic integration of Japan, Manchukuo, and northern China; the economic penetration of Southeast Asia; and the acquisition of undisputed naval primacy in the western Pacific. Then, to deter the Soviet Union from interfering in the north, the Japanese government in November 1936 signed the Anti-Comintern Pact with Nazi Germany.

The first stage of Japan's plan for regional hegemony was put into operation in July 1937, when an accidental clash between Chinese and Japanese troops on manoeuvres near Beijing escalated into a full-fledged (though undeclared) war. Japanese military forces swept south and west from their bases in northern China, defeating the Kuomintang army around Shanghai and capturing Chiang's capital city of Nanking in December. Hankow and Canton fell in the autumn of 1938, by which time all the major cities, ports, rail lines, and productive parts of northern and central China had fallen under Japanese control. On the heels of the victorious armies followed industrial officials who organized 'development companies' to exploit the mineral resources and run the basic industries of the newly occupied regions. In December 1938, the Nationalist government retreated to the mountain redoubt of Chungking in the west to carry on the fight, while a guerrilla resistance was organized by the Communist Party in Yenan in the northwest. The Japanese occupation authorities established a puppet government in northern China and in March 1940 formed a collaborationist regime in Nanking to rival the Nationalist stronghold in Chungking.

THE NANJING MASSACRE

On 13 December 1937, the Chinese Nationalist capital city, Nanjing, was occupied by the Japanese Imperial Army.[1] Apart from its importance as Chiang Kai-shek's capital, Nanjing had been serving as a refuge for tens of thousands of Chinese civilians who had escaped the rapid Japanese advances during the summer and autumn of 1937. Departing Nationalist soldiers had locked two of the city's gates in order to delay the Japanese advance, a move that also trapped hundreds of thousands of civilians within the city. According to a detailed post-war report, systematic torture and massacres began as the Japanese army entered the city. 'The people in one assembled group—including groups of the elderly, women and children, and wounded and sick soldiers—were toppled over in succession in the wake of echoing gunfire. . . . Suddenly, the roads and alleyways were awash with blood and flesh, and corpses were strewn throughout the streets. Devoid of all humanity, the Japanese forces continued to shoot and kill the unarmed people in the crowd.'

The killing of both civilians and military personnel continued for at least six weeks (other accounts argue that the killings actually lasted until March 1938), producing between 100,000 and 300,000 casualties. Japanese soldiers also committed an estimated 20,000 rapes. Although the veracity of such reports has frequently been challenged by revisionist commentators, some claim that the number was as high as 80,000. For example, one foreign correspondent wrote of 1,000 rapes over the course of a 24-hour period on 16–17 December. In the years after the war Japanese government officials consistently downplayed the events in Nanjing, as well as subsequent actions directed against civilians elsewhere in occupied areas of China. Given Japan's importance as a US ally in East Asia during the Cold War years, Washington was hardly inclined to prod the Japanese into acknowledging or atoning for their wartime crimes. Only in the 1990s was some effort made to come to terms with the crimes of the past.

Surprisingly, the US government took a wait-and-see attitude towards these events. After the expiry of the London Treaty in 1936, Japan had launched an ambitious program of naval construction that unmistakably upset the balance of naval power in the western Pacific. Japan's economic penetration of north and central China clearly endangered American commercial interests there. Yet Washington rebuffed British requests for joint diplomatic pressure against Tokyo to force a halt to the southward advance in China. Roosevelt was content to issue stern verbal warnings such as his vaguely worded 'Quarantine the Aggressor' speech in October 1937, in which he called for 'positive endeavors to preserve peace'. This phrase, in conjunction with the quarantine metaphor, was taken to imply that Washington was prepared to consider imposing economic sanctions against Japan—until the outcry from isolationists in the

United States forced the president to beat a hasty retreat. Within a year, the Japanese onslaught in China brought a change in American policy regarding the undeclared war in the Far East. This amendment was evident in a number of moves by Washington. For example, the US supported the Chinese cause by purchasing Chinese silver, which supplied the hard-pressed Nationalist government with the dollars that it needed in order to buy US military equipment. In addition, Secretary of State Hull announced a 'moral embargo' on aircraft sales to Japan, and Congress authorized the construction of two new aircraft carriers, as well as a twofold increase in the number of naval aircraft.

Still, the United States' greatest leverage consisted in its ability to mount a full-scale campaign of economic retaliation. Even though Japanese exports to the US declined in the 1930s, Japan remained that country's third best customer (behind Britain and Canada), receiving more than 40 per cent of its imports from the US. We have already noted that the risk to markets was one of the main reasons for Washington's reluctance to impose economic sanctions on Japan. But this commercial dependence worked both ways: heavy reliance on US suppliers for strategic materials such as petroleum, iron, copper, steel, and industrial machinery made Japan vulnerable to US economic pressure. Cutting off these supplies would seriously jeopardize Tokyo's plans for economic expansion and rearmament.

After a fierce struggle within the Roosevelt cabinet between supporters and opponents of sanctions, the former prevailed. On 26 July 1939, the United States gave Japan the required six months' notice of its intention to abrogate the commercial treaty of 1911, thereby removing the legal obstacles to trade restrictions. Before those six months were up, the outbreak of the war in Europe presented the Japanese with an opportunity similar to the one they had enjoyed in 1914, when events on the other side of the world diverted attention from Tokyo's expansionist designs in the Far East. The Asian colonies of Britain, France, and the Netherlands were left virtually undefended as most available forces were redeployed to Europe. Then the fall of the Netherlands and France in May–June 1940 made it possible for Japan to extort significant economic and strategic concessions from those countries, the Dutch government removing many restrictions on petroleum exports from the Dutch East Indies to Japan and the Vichy government of France closing the supply route through Indochina to Chiang Kai-shek's besieged regime in Chongqing. In September, Japanese forces occupied the northern half of French Indochina for the ostensible purpose of ensuring the isolation of the Chinese Nationalists' stronghold. Recognizing that further expansion southward would risk a confrontation with the US, Tokyo sought and obtained a Tripartite Pact with Germany and Italy, in the hope of intimidating Roosevelt into granting Japan a free hand in Asia.

Confronted with this unmistakable bid for primacy in the Far East, Washington mounted a campaign of retaliation that unfolded in graduated stages in response to each Japanese move. Reports of Japanese efforts to corner the market on American oil exports prompted an embargo on aviation fuel and the highest grades of iron and scrap steel in July 1940. As Japanese troops poured into northern Indochina in September, the embargo was extended to include all scrap metals. While Japan consolidated its position in northern Indochina, Roosevelt finally agreed in October 1940 to authorize joint Anglo–American naval staff talks (though he resisted London's suggestion that the American Pacific Fleet be transferred from Pearl Harbor to Singapore to bolster British naval power in the Far East).

Japan's objectives in the south were both economic and strategic. The economic planners in Tokyo hoped to achieve self-sufficiency in strategic materials by gaining control of the oil, rubber, tin, and nickel resources located in the European colonial possessions in Southeast Asia (British Malaya, French Indochina, and the Dutch East Indies). When the Dutch government refused Japanese demands for the right to import unlimited quantities of oil from the East Indies, the Imperial Council adopted a grandiose scheme in July 1941 for the expulsion of European power from Asia and the establishment of a confederation of Asian nations under the economic control, political tutelage, and military protection of Japan. In the minds of officials in Tokyo, this 'Greater East Asia Co-Prosperity Sphere' would give concrete form to the Asian version of the Monroe Doctrine suggested by earlier Japanese officials. The vacuum left by the withdrawal of European power from East Asia, like the vacuum left by the withdrawal of European power from Latin America in the nineteenth century, would be filled by the regional power whose cultural, economic, and military superiority entitled it to hegemony in its geographical sphere.

In pursuit of this objective, Japanese troops advanced into southern Indochina on 24 July 1941, seizing naval and air bases on the coast and thus threatening the British naval base at Singapore and the petroleum reserves of the

Dutch East Indies. Washington's response to this dramatic extension of Japanese power marked the decisive turn in its relationship with Tokyo: Roosevelt froze Japanese assets in the United States and imposed an embargo on high-octane gasoline, effectively ending all trade between the two countries and depriving Japan of the fuel it needed to resume mechanized military operations on the Asian mainland.

The mounting concern in Washington about the situation in the Far East was accompanied by growing public support for the embattled people of China. Pearl S. Buck's best-selling novel *The Good Earth* (1931) evoked widespread sympathy for the sturdy, virtuous Chinese peasantry. This image stood in glaring contrast to news stories and photographs of Japanese troops looting and pillaging throughout China. American support for the Chinese had taken the form of both official government loans (US$20 million in the spring of 1940 and $100 million in November 1940) and unofficial expressions of solidarity. In 1937, Captain Claire Chennault, a retired Army Air Corps officer who had become the chief adviser to the Chinese Air Force, took with him the 'Flying Tigers', a group of mercenary American pilots whose services on behalf of a foreign power were tacitly tolerated by Washington. In April 1941, Roosevelt signed an executive order legalizing this mercenary activity and in October dispatched an official American military mission to Chiang's government in Chungking.

The American embargo, together with stepped-up American economic and military support for the Chinese resistance, left Japanese officials in a quandary: Japan possessed less than two years' worth of oil at a time when the seemingly endless struggle on the mainland was absorbing huge quantities of fuel. In light of severe shortages of other vital minerals, the cutoff of US oil exports forced Tokyo to consider seeking a negotiated settlement with China and evacuating Indochina—the two conditions on which the resumption of American oil shipments depended. Such a reversal would have constituted a return to Japan's 1914–18 policy of peacefully seeking advantages in Asia while capitalizing on the Western powers' involvement in the European war.

This option was unmistakably the most promising one from a purely economic point of view. But withdrawal from the mainland would have meant a humiliating loss of face for the army officers who had spearheaded the expansionist policy of the 1930s. It would also have weakened the domestic position of the military and abruptly halted the momentum of the national regeneration movement launched in the aftermath of the Manchurian expedition.

The second option available to Japan was a southward thrust to break the US embargo by seizing the petroleum reserves of the Dutch East Indies and the other raw materials of Southeast Asia. In the end the lure of the extensive natural resources and territory in Southeast Asia left unprotected by the European colonial powers induced the military party in Japan to risk war with the United States.

Conflicting pressures were at play in both Tokyo and Washington in this period. Whereas Tokyo was preoccupied with Japan's traditional victim (China) and traditional rival (Russia) on the Asian mainland, Japanese military leaders, together with most civilian leaders, wanted to preserve normal relations with the United States. What they failed to realize, or realized too late, was that aggression in China was likely to alienate the American public and provoke retaliation from Washington. Even after the decision to expand toward Southeast Asia had been taken, high-ranking generals in Tokyo did not intend to include the American-owned Philippines in the new Asian economic bloc to be formed, under Japanese leadership, out of the former British, French, and Dutch possessions in the region. Rather, they hoped that the new East Asia bloc would compete peacefully with the Russian, American, and European economic systems on relatively equal terms.

The Japanese navy, on the other hand, had regarded the United States as Japan's most probable enemy ever since the end of the First World War. After the London Naval Conference of 1930, naval authorities in Tokyo pressed for parity with the US in order to ensure undisputed Japanese control of the western Pacific and permit an eventual advance southward. The army's lack of enthusiasm for this 'southern' strategy reflected its obsession with protecting the newly acquired empire on the Chinese mainland from the predatory grasp of the Soviet Union. An advance toward the South Seas would draw troops away from the north and might tempt Moscow to intervene in that region.

Two developments in the spring and summer of 1941 relieved this anxiety about Soviet intentions. In April 1941, the Japanese government signed a neutrality treaty with the Soviet Union in order to avert the possibility of a two-front war. Two months later, Hitler launched his full-scale military assault on Russia from occupied Europe, compelling Stalin to transfer several divisions from Siberia to European Russia to repel the Nazi advance against its major metropolitan areas. These two developments removed the threat of Soviet pressure in Manchuria and helped to gain the support of the Japanese military for the southern strategy championed by the navy. This confluence of strategic opinion was reflected in the cabinet's decision in July 1941 to acquire the bases in Indochina in preparation for a strike against Singapore and the East Indies.

American policy concerning East Asia was subject to similar pressures from different sections of Roosevelt's entourage. The struggle in the cabinet between advocates and opponents of economic sanctions was re-enacted within the leadership of the armed services. Naval authorities had targeted Japan as America's most likely enemy since the early 1920s. War plan 'Orange', formulated in 1924, envisioned the American battle fleet moving west from Pearl Harbor to liberate the lightly defended Philippines, destroy the Japanese navy, and blockade the home islands. But the spectacular increase in German naval power in the North Atlantic, threatening the critical trade route to Western Europe, forced a reversal in the thinking of US naval officials. Thus in the spring of 1939, they began shifting towards a defensive strategy in the Pacific, taking it for granted that

economic pressure would be enough to deter Japanese aggression.

On 4 November 1940, a revised war plan, dubbed 'Plan Dog', became the official basis of American naval strategy. It identified Germany as the foremost naval threat and assumed that Japan would never risk war with the United States by attacking its possessions in the Pacific. Even in the event that Japan did invade the Philippines, economic warfare and a defensive naval task force together would surely be enough to protect the United States' interests in the region while the bulk of its military power was deployed against Germany. As Roosevelt himself explained to those who argued for a hardline policy toward Japan: 'I simply have not got enough navy to go around— and every little episode in the Pacific means fewer ships in the Atlantic'.

By the time Japan seized the Indochinese bases and the United States imposed its oil embargo, negotiations were already underway between Tokyo and Washington. In the course of these talks, which had begun in February 1941, the incompatability of Japanese and American demands became apparent. The US insisted on the prior withdrawal of Japanese forces from all the territories occupied since 1931 as a precondition to a settlement in East Asia. Certain sections of official opinion in Tokyo—aware of the increasing naval co-operation between Britain and the US, disheartened by Germany's failure to deliver the knockout blow against the USSR, and anxious about Japan's dwindling oil reserves—were prepared to support a retreat from Indochina in exchange for a resumption of trade with the US and the promise of an adequate flow of strategic raw materials. However, no Japanese leader was prepared to relinquish the special position in Manchukuo and China that had been acquired at such great cost. And the United States continued to demand total Japanese withdrawal from the Asian mainland.

By the autumn of 1941, the Japanese naval forces in the western Pacific had attained virtual parity with the combined fleets of the United States and Britain in the region. At the same time, the productive capacity—and, therefore, the war-making potential—of the Western powers was far greater than that of the island empire. Moreover, the US had recently embarked on a massive naval construction program that threatened to erase Japan's margin of safety in the western Pacific within a few years. Together, as in the case of imperial Germany in the years before 1914, hopes of short-term advantage and fears of long-term inferiority can make the idea of a preventive war very tempting.

While the Japanese diplomats sought to moderate the more extreme demands of the American negotiators in the fall of 1941, the military and naval commands prepared for the worst. On 16 October, General Hideki Tojo replaced the civilian Prince Fumumaro Konoe as prime minister and proceeded to set a deadline for a settlement with Washington that would lift the embargo on strategic materials. When that deadline, after two extensions, expired on 30 November, a task force of six aircraft carriers and two battleships steamed eastward toward the headquarters of the American Pacific Fleet at Pearl Harbor. A few minutes before 8:00 a.m. (Hawaiian time) on Sunday 7 December, planes transported by this flotilla struck the American vessels moored in the harbour. Within two hours, eight battleships had sunk to the bottom, and the United States had lost the bulk of its Pacific fleet.

Since the Japanese code had been cracked in August 1940, American intelligence had been aware of Tokyo's plans to move against Singapore, the Dutch East Indies, and Thailand. There was also some evidence that Japan planned an assault on the Philippines. But no one in a position of authority in Washington expected an attack on Pearl Harbor, and even though the Japanese government's instructions to its consul in Honolulu contained strong hints of an impending attack against the nearby naval base, code machines (which had been dispatched to the Philippines) had unaccountably not been sent to Hawaii. Intercepted instructions cabled to Japanese negotiators in Washington contained sufficiently menacing language that the chief of staff, General George Marshall, dispatched a last-minute warning to Pearl Harbor on 7 December, but he sent it by Western Union rather than the overloaded government cable, and the messenger boy carrying the news was pedalling his bicycle toward the American military compound when the Japanese planes struck. That there were numerous examples of mistaken judgment on the part of US officials in the affair is indisputable. Still, there is no hard evidence to support the conspiracy-minded critics who claim that Roosevelt knew in advance of the plan and deliberately exposed the Pacific fleet to destruction in order to force the United States into a war against Japan and its European allies.

It is safe to conclude that neither Washington nor Tokyo looked forward to a war in the Pacific. Influential sections of the governing elites in both countries had good reason to press for restoration of the friendly diplomatic relations and profitable economic exchange of the 1920s. It is also true, though, that the two governments developed foreign policies in the course of the following decade that made confrontation inevitable. Despite the spectacular economic advances made by Japan in the inter-war period, the ruling elite in Tokyo regarded hegemony over China and the French, British, and Dutch empires in East Asia as the only alternative to economic decline and subservience to the European powers. Conversely, a consensus gradually developed in Washington that if Japan gained control of China and the European possessions in Asia, the balance of forces in the western Pacific would be unacceptably altered, and American economic interests in the region would be at risk. Once these incompatible perceptions of national interest came to the fore, it was only a matter of time before the two powers on opposite sides of the Pacific would come to blows.

THE WAR IN ASIA (1941–1945)

Japan's surprise raid on Pearl Harbor effectively erased the naval power of the United States in the western Pacific. Three days later, land-based Japanese planes sank two of Britain's premier battleships off the coast of Malaya. Japan soon followed those crippling blows to Anglo–American naval strength in East Asia with military advances against Western imperial outposts, including Hong Kong—where nearly 2,000 Canadian soldiers were killed or captured—and Singapore, where the British naval base was taken from behind by a land army that had advanced down the jungles of the Malay peninsula. By the spring of 1942 the major Western possessions in Asia—the Philippines, Malaya, most of the Dutch East Indies, and Burma—were occupied by Japanese forces, while the nominally independent Thailand became an ally and subservient client state of Tokyo.

An area encompassing 100 million people and sufficient food-producing land, strategic minerals, and petroleum reserves to give Japan the economic self-sufficiency it so desperately sought was organized as the Greater East Asia Co-Prosperity Sphere. With Japanese forces advancing west toward India and south toward Australia, the remnants of the British Empire in Asia were in mortal danger, as Britain's power was concentrated in the North Atlantic and the Mediterranean, combatting the German threat closer to home. The United States' only ally in Asia, the Chinese Nationalist government, was confined to a mountain redoubt in Chungking, cut off from land communications with the outside world when the Japanese closed the Burma road to India.

From the beginning of the Pacific War it was clear that Japan could pose no serious threat to the national existence of Britain and the United States. Britain's lifeline to Asia had been superseded in importance by its lifeline to North America. Not even the most fanatical warlord in Tokyo could have persuaded himself that Japan was capable of projecting its power across the Pacific to the American west coast. Such delusions were confined to North America, where California politicians persuaded the Roosevelt administration to authorize the forced evacuation and internment of 120,000 Japanese Americans in California, Oregon, and Washington in February 1942 on the grounds that they represented a fifth column of potential value to a Japanese invasion force. Similarly in Canada, thousands of Japanese Canadians were interned in British Columbia and Alberta.

Even in the aftermath of Pearl Harbor, the American and British governments agreed that Germany was still the main enemy. Relegating the Pacific war to the background, they continued to concentrate on preparing for a cross-Channel assault on Hitler's Fortress Europe, while the Soviet Union honoured its non-aggression pact with Japan in order to concentrate its forces against the German armies in the western part of the USSR.

The expanding Japanese empire reached its limit within the first year of the Pacific war. In June 1942, the Japanese fleet suffered its first major defeat when the US navy frustrated its attempt to seize Midway Island, west of Hawaii. From September 1942 to February 1943, Japanese efforts to reach Australia, the principal base of Anglo–American operations in the South Pacific, were turned back in a fierce jungle campaign in New Guinea and Guadalcanal. The American counter-offensive against Japan depended on a two-pronged strategy: first an island-hopping campaign across the central Pacific, spearheaded by the aircraft carriers that Japanese bombers had missed at Pearl Harbor and, second, a drive by the American army under General Douglas MacArthur along the northern coast of New Guinea and other islands in the vicinity of the Philippines.

By the summer of 1944, American naval forces advancing westward had reached the island of Saipan in the Marianas, from which the first land-based bombing raids of Japanese cities were soon to be launched. In October, MacArthur's forces landed on Leyte Island in the Philippines, and in February they retook Manila. The two prongs of the American counter-offensive converged on the island of Okinawa in April; just as the defeat of Germany permitted the redeployment of Allied troops and materiel to the Pacific, the Americans used the Okinawa base to launch the greatest air offensive in history against the major cities of Japan. During the spring and summer of 1945, these bombing raids from land- and carrier-based aircraft, supported by shelling from US battleships operating off the Japanese coast, destroyed or immobilized the remnants of Japan's navy,

THE INTERNMENT OF JAPANESE-CANADIANS

When war with Japan broke out in 1941, Canada had approximately 23,000 residents of Japanese descent, most of them Canadian citizens living in coastal British Columbia. Members of the Japanese community had long faced systemic discrimination in Canada, but the war fuelled new racist fears that they posed a threat to the nation's security.

Initially, in accordance with the War Measures Act, the Royal Canadian Mounted Police arrested and interned 38 suspected subversives of Japanese descent. But there was growing political pressure in British Columbia to follow the American example and relocate or intern every member of the Japanese community along the entire west coast. Neither the RCMP nor the Army's chief of staff considered such large-scale action to be necessary for national security. Nonetheless, in February 1942 the Liberal government of Mackenzie King announced that it would remove nearly 22,000 people of Japanese ancestry (nearly three-quarters of whom had been born in Canada or were naturalized Canadians) from the coastal areas of British Columbia. Beginning that year, thousands of Japanese-Canadian families were torn apart and their property was confiscated. Able-bodied men were sent to work camps, while women, children, and the elderly were relocated to communities in the BC interior.

In the spring of 1945, the government gave Japanese-Canadians a choice between moving somewhere east of the Rockies and accepting 'voluntary repatriation' to Japan. Some 10,000

agreed to the latter, and by 1947 (when the program was cancelled in response to public protests) almost 4,000 men, women, and children had been deported to what for many was not their homeland but a foreign country.

Although there was no evidence of widespread sedition, and no one was charged with treason, Japanese-Canadians did not reclaim their civil rights until 1949, at which time they were finally permitted to return to the BC coast, though their property was never returned. In 1988, Prime Minister Brian Mulroney formally apologized to Japanese-Canadians for their mistreatment and offered financial compensation to the survivors of wartime internment.

Japanese Canadians wait to be relocated to camps in the interior of British Columbia, 1942. Library and Archives Canada/British Columbia Securities Commission collection/C-046355.

shattered its industry, and cut off the home islands from their supplies and military forces abroad.

Acknowledging the certainty of defeat, the emperor formally urged the Supreme Council in June to approach the Allied governments for peace terms. The military and naval leaders in power refused to recognize the collapse of their dreams. Instead they vainly tried to arrange for Soviet mediation in favour of a conditional surrender that would enable them to keep their

positions of prestige and authority. In the meantime, a peace faction within Japan cautiously advocated ending the war on the sole condition that the titular authority of the emperor be preserved. But Washington reaffirmed the demand for unconditional surrender that had been formulated at the wartime conferences in Casablanca and Cairo in 1943. The formal definition of this unconditional surrender was issued on 26 July, in the so-called Potsdam Declaration. Japan was to be stripped of its empire and occupied militarily until it had been transformed into a peaceful nation. The future status of the emperor—a point of great symbolic importance to the Japanese people—was left ambiguous, but the penalty if Japan refused to surrender was plain: 'prompt and utter destruction'.

The government in Tokyo did not respond to this ultimatum, probably because such threats were common in the propaganda warfare of the time. In any case, the military and naval policy-makers with decisive authority in Japan were determined to fight to the finish, while the position of the moderate peace faction had been undermined by the uncompromising language of the Potsdam Declaration. The United States thereupon unleashed a weapon that had been developed in total secrecy by American and European émigré scientists in the course of the war. On 6 August, the first atomic bomb was detonated over Hiroshima—Japan's eighth largest city, with a population of 200,000—instantly killing over 70,000 people, seriously injuring as many more, and levelling 1,000 hectares of homes and factories. Three days later, a second bomb was dropped on Nagasaki with similar results. In the meantime the Soviet Union—honouring the pledge it had made at Yalta to enter the conflict in the Far East within three months of Germany's surrender—declared war on Japan and dispatched military forces to Japanese-occupied Manchuria.

Spurred by these devastating events into assuming an authority he had previously shrunk from exercising, Emperor Hirohito broke a deadlock in the Supreme Council on 10 August by voting to accept the Potsdam Declaration as the basis for Japan's surrender. The sole condition specified by Tokyo was that the emperor retain his throne as the titular leader of his people. Upon receiving American assurances to this effect, the Japanese government accepted the terms of surrender and formally capitulated to General MacArthur on 2 September aboard the American battleship *Missouri* in Tokyo Bay.

President Harry Truman's decision to drop two atomic bombs on Japan in August 1945 ushered in the nuclear age. It was the first and, so far, the only time that nuclear weapons have been used in combat. The question of whether, once they existed, they would be put to use seems never to have been raised by officials in Washington, from the advent of the US$2 billion nuclear weapons research program in August 1942—known as the Manhattan Project—to the first successful test explosion in the desert near Alamogordo, New Mexico, on 16 July 1945. The Manhattan Project had involved over 120,000 physicists, chemists, engineers, doctors, and technicians and had co-operated with Montreal Atomic Laboratory, where a team of Canadian, British, and European scientists had begun conducting atomic research under the aegis of the National Research Council, while the federal government worked to develop the country's uranium resources. A policy committee consisting of three Americans, two Britons, and one Canadian oversaw the crucial production of uranium for the project.

Military advisers had warned Truman that an amphibious invasion of Japan would cost almost 50,000 American casualties and prolong the war for another six months. The temptation to end the conflict immediately without sacrificing American lives outweighed any moral qualms that American policy-makers might have had about the nature of the weapon used. In any case, the indiscriminate slaughter of civilian populations by conventional aerial bombardment had become a standard practice since 1940. More people perished in the conventional bombing raids on Dresden and Tokyo than at Hiroshima or Nagasaki.

Subsequent critics have argued that the same military objective could have been achieved by unveiling the new weapon in a demonstration test on an uninhabited Pacific atoll in the presence of Japanese observers. Defenders point out that the scientists who had developed the two bombs were unable to guarantee that they would detonate and that, at the time the Nagasaki bomb was dropped, no others were available; the highly publicized testing of a 'dud' would have seriously damaged the credibility of American military power, stiffened Japanese resistance, and prolonged the war. These hypothetical disagreements aside, it seems clear that Japan could have been forced to surrender within a few months by a total naval blockade coupled with precision bombing of its internal transportation network. In those few months, however, the United States might well have been compelled to share with the USSR the prerogative of filling the post-war power vacuum in Japan, as it had been in Europe. By the end of the war, the Red Army had swept into Manchuria and into Korea down to the 38th parallel and had occupied the Kurile Islands and the southern half of Sakhalin Island. Stalin's conditions for complying with Washington's early (pre-bomb) desire that the USSR join the war against Japan had included the recovery of all the territory and privileges that his country had lost after its defeat by Japan in 1905.

In addition to the obvious advantages of avoiding a costly invasion of Japan, a diplomatic factor may have reinforced Washington's determination to use its new weapon as soon as it was proved operational by the test explosion in New Mexico. The diplomatic tug-of-war between the United States and its Soviet ally concerning the political reorganization of the post-war world had already begun. Upon learning of the test during the Potsdam Conference of the Big Three wartime leaders, Truman informed Stalin that the US had developed a new weapon 'of unusual destructive force'—a fact already known to Stalin through his espionage network. Some historians have suggested that Truman was eager to use the bomb on Japan for two reasons: to intimidate Stalin into granting political concessions in Europe and to end the war in the Far East before the Soviets had a chance to take part in the victory and therefore claim a role in the post-war occupation of Japan. In the defeated Japan—unlike the defeated Germany—the US enjoyed unchallenged primacy.

Beginning on 28 August, American military forces arrived to occupy Japan's key cities and supervise the disarmament of Japanese military forces. With the formal surrender a few days later, supreme authority passed to General Douglas MacArthur in the name of the Allied powers. Soviet requests to share in the occupation of the northern Japanese island of Hokkaido, only 40 kilometres from the Soviet-occupied Sakhalin Island, were turned aside. Although ostensibly acting on behalf of the victorious coalition, the United States proclaimed its intention to manage the occupation of Japan without the assistance of its wartime allies, and to administer it as a single political unit. The acrimonious Soviet–American disputes over the treatment of post-war Germany would not be re-enacted over the treatment of post-war Japan. The overwhelming American air and naval superiority in the western Pacific gave Washington, through its powerful proconsul in Tokyo, undisputed supremacy.

SUMMARY

Between 1914 and 1930, Japan emerged as the first industrial power in the Far East. As an island nation with a rapidly growing population and limited primary resources, it needed to maximize its access to raw materials and export markets. To that end it pursued a strategy of peaceful economic expansion and co-operation with the United States, which was both its largest export market and its main supplier of raw materials. To maintain good relations with the West, Japan attended the Washington Naval Conference of 1921–2 and pledged not to expand its sphere of interest in China.

By the early 1930s, however, several Western countries had taken steps to limit Japanese immigration. Economic depression had reduced American demand for Japanese imports while increasing American protectionism, and the United States was developing significant ties with China, to the detriment of Japanese interests there. Some Japanese, particularly in the military, began to question the value of the 'peaceful penetration' strategy. Military officers began to exert a stronger political influence in Tokyo, and Japan embarked on a program of military expansion, taking control of Manchuria in 1932. When Japan launched a full-scale invasion of China in 1937, the US imposed economic sanctions and, in 1940, an embargo on aviation fuel and iron. The following year, after the US refused to lift the embargo, Japan attacked the US base at Pearl Harbor, Hawaii, and proceeded to conquer much of the South Pacific before the US was able to rebuild its Pacific fleet and launch a counter-attack. The American victory at Midway in 1942 proved to be a turning point in the war. After a gruelling campaign against Japanese forces in the South Pacific, the US dropped atomic bombs on Hiroshima and Nagasaki in August 1945, forcing Japan into unconditional surrender.

NOTES

1.   With the imminent fall of Nanjing to Japanese forces, Chiang transferred the seat of the Chinese Nationalist government to Chongqing.

QUESTIONS FOR CRITICAL THOUGHT

1.   What were the major obstacles to Japanese power in the early part of the twentieth century?
2.   What is the measure of a great power? Does Japan in the early 1930s meet this criterion?
3.   Why were the Western nations so reluctant to oppose Japanese expansionism?
4.   Was Japan's vision of a 'Greater East Asia Co-Prosperity Sphere' attainable? Why or why not?
5.   Consider the political circumstances of December 1941 and discuss whether Japan had any other option than to attack the United States.
6.   Besides Japan, what country could have been a possible primary target for the American atomic bombs?

WEBSITES FOR FURTHER REFERENCE

Historical Text Archive: Japan
    http://historicaltextarchive.com/links.php?action=links&cid=5&sid=13

Internet East Asia Sourcebook
    www.fordham.edu/halsall/eastasia/eastasiasbook.html#Japan%20as%20a%20World%20Power

Internet Modern History Sourcebook: Asia since 1900
    www.fordham.edu/halsall/mod/modsbook52.html

World History Archives: The History of East Asia
    www.hartford-hwp.com/archives/55/index.html

PART TWO

THE COLD WAR BETWEEN THE SUPERPOWERS (1945–1985)

On 17 May 1961, US President John F. Kennedy made a landmark speech to the Canadian Parliament. Kennedy had been in office for only three months, and his trip to Ottawa was seen as an important step in establishing a strong relationship with the government of Prime Minister John Diefenbaker. The highly anticipated two-day visit received extensive coverage in Canadian newspapers, which printed detailed reports of not just the political discussions but also the attire of the popular, charismatic president and the first lady. An estimated crowd of 50,000 greeted Kennedy as he entered the House of Commons to give his address, which was broadcast on television. 'Nothing is more vital than the unity of the United States and Canada,' Kennedy declared in an eloquent speech that, despite its lighthearted charm, delivered a serious political message: Canada and the United States should maintain a strong strategic military alliance. American officials had become increasingly concerned about Diefenbaker's indecision over whether Canada should acquire nuclear weapons. In a lengthy foreign policy meeting between the two leaders before the Parliamentary address, Kennedy had already raised the issue of the perceived threats posed by Cuba and the Soviet Union.

From a public relations perspective, the visit was a success. Kennedy charmed the Canadian public by asserting his belief in the importance of maintaining a strong bond between Canada and the United States, a relationship he characterized famously when he stated, 'Geography has made us neighbours; history has made us friends.' But Kennedy failed to establish a friendly relationship with Diefenbaker, and his appeal for a closer military alliance failed to spur the prime minister to make an unequivocal commitment to deploy nuclear weapons on Canadian soil. Kennedy's speech to Parliament marked a high point in the political rhetoric of the Cold War era, but the reality of international relations remained more complex than Kennedy's aphorisms indicated.

✧ US President John F. Kennedy (left), Governor General George Vanier, and Prime Minister John Diefenbaker, followed by Jacqueline Kennedy and Olive Diefenbaker, leave Government House during the President's visit to Ottawa, May 1961. Library and Archives Canada/Credit Duncan Cameron/Duncan Cameron fonds/PA-154665.

CHAPTER 7

THE FORMATION OF THE BIPOLAR WORLD IN THE TRUMAN–STALIN ERA (1945–1953)

CANADA'S EMERGENCE AS A 'MIDDLE POWER'

More than a million Canadians served in the Second World War. On VE ('Victory in Europe') Day—8 May 1945—the Canadian army alone numbered almost half a million men and women, and for a brief period Canada ranked as the fourth strongest military power in the world. But Ottawa had no intention of maintaining such a large military after the war, and it ordered a massive demobilization. By the end of 1946, Canada had withdrawn its ground troops from Europe and reduced its standing army to 30,000. Recognizing that it was not destined to become a major power like Britain or the United States, Canada began to position itself as a 'middle power', capable of working effectively with various nations and playing an international role when called upon.

Many political observers considered the decade after 1945 to be the 'golden age' of Canadian diplomacy. As the Cold War began, Canadian officials were among the first to advocate a collective defence alliance for the West. Canada's interest reflected the fear of a communist threat sparked in part in September 1945 by the Gouzenko affair (see p. 193). In a 1947 speech in New York, Louis St Laurent, Canada's secretary of state for External Affairs, criticized the new United Nations Security Council as ineffective and argued that member states had the right to make additional security arrangements to protect their vital interests. American and British officials expressed interest in creating an alliance among the Western powers, and negotiations to that end began in 1948. Although the United States favoured an exclusively military pact, Canada lobbied for a clause covering general economic and social aims. Accordingly, when the final NATO Treaty was signed the next year, it included as Article 2 the following provision (also known as the 'Canadian article'):

The Parties will contribute toward the further development of peaceful and friendly international relations by strengthening their free institutions, by bringing about a better understanding of the principles upon which these institutions are founded, and by promoting conditions of stability and well-being. They will seek to eliminate conflict in their international economic policies and will encourage economic collaboration between any or all of them.

THE GOUZENKO AFFAIR

The 'Gouzenko Affair' began in September 1945, when a cipher clerk working in Ottawa's Soviet embassy defected and presented Canadian authorities with documents showing that the USSR was running espionage operations in Canada. No one took Igor Gouzenko seriously until Soviet officials attempted to recapture him. Placed in protective custody by the RCMP, Gouzenko revealed that during the Second World War, Soviet agents had penetrated sensitive government departments as well as the atomic research facility at Chalk River, Ontario.

When Gouzenko's revelations became public the following year, they created a sensation both across Canada and throughout the West, as other governments were alerted to Soviet spies operating in their nations. By that time the RCMP had already made several arrests, and two people—Sam Carr and Fred Rose, Canada's only Communist MP—were convicted of passing information on weapons research to the Soviet embassy. Prime Minister Mackenzie King established a royal commission to determine whether charges should be brought against the individuals listed in Gouzenko's files. The commission recommended charges against 22 people, and its sensational proceedings received more publicity than any of the court cases that eventually followed.

Viewed by some as marking the start of the Cold War, the Gouzenko Affair helped to harden public opinion toward the Soviet Union and fuelled fears of communist subversion as Canada entered the Cold War era. Igor Gouzenko remained in Canada until his death in 1982.

Igor Gouzenko holds a copy of his novel *The Fall of a Titan*, 15 October 1954. Library and Archives Canada, PA-129625/CP Images.

Canada continued to play a notable role in international affairs in the early 1950s, contributing an army brigade to the United Nations force (led by the United States) in Korea and cautioning the Americans against expanding their military commitment when the war there moved toward a stalemate. Canada also worked with the US to protect North America by establishing radar defence systems, including the Distant Early Warning (DEW) line, which stretched from Alaska to Baffin Island. Throughout this period, Canada followed two paths, taking significant steps to strengthen its bilateral relationship with the US and at the same time supporting multilateral peacekeeping efforts sponsored by the UN. These two approaches culminated in 1957, when Canada entered the North American Air Defence (NORAD) agreement with the United States and External Affairs Minister Lester B. Pearson received the Nobel Peace Prize for his efforts to defuse the Suez Crisis.

THE POLITICAL DIVISION OF EUROPE

When the advancing armies of the United States and the Soviet Union met at Germany's Elbe River, in April 1945, the exhilaration of certain victory momentarily eclipsed the political disagreements that had surfaced at the Crimea Conference two-and-a-half months earlier. Within a week, word had arrived of Hitler's suicide and the capitulation of the German armies in Italy and Austria.

The formal surrender by German military authorities on 7 May simply confirmed what had been a foregone conclusion for months: the collapse of the Nazi empire in Europe. The Allied soldiers camped along the Elbe and in other liberated regions of the continent still expected to be sent to the Far East for the final drive against Japan, but the end was finally in sight. The prospect of home was euphoric, and for a brief moment, in the afterglow of triumph in what was universally felt to be a worthy cause, the two pre-eminent powers in the victorious coalition could celebrate the dawn of a new era of world peace.

But this convergence of American and Russian military power had critical significance for the future of the world. Despite the universal relief on VE Day, the way the war was brought to a close created problems that prevented the restoration of the desired peacetime conditions. Foremost among these difficulties was the absence of any form of indigenous political authority or military power in Central Europe—the consequence of the decision to impose an unconditional surrender that meant the instantaneous destruction of all German political and military institutions. The brutality of the Nazi regime was such that the war had come to be seen as a moral crusade against a monstrous evil that had to be permanently eliminated. In striking contrast to Woodrow Wilson at the end of the First World War, Franklin Roosevelt did not distinguish between the enemy regime and the civilian population it had ruled. Hitler was seen as merely the agent of a people whose aggressive instincts disqualified them from any role in the post-war reorganization of Europe.

This moralistic justification of the war effort, intended to rationalize the sacrifices required of the American public, camouflaged the main reason for the United States' intervention in Europe: to correct the balance of power that had been disturbed by Germany's bid for dominance. But in dismantling the Nazi administrative and military apparatus and refusing to permit the formation of a new German regime, the Allied powers produced a vacuum in Central Europe that Churchill had foreseen before the Yalta Conference. Inevitably,

that vacuum would be filled by the military powers that converged on the centre of the continent in the spring of 1945.

The military situation at the moment of Germany's collapse dictated that the newly liberated continent should be informally partitioned into pro-Western and pro-Soviet spheres. Each of the two zones eventually adopted political institutions, economic practices, and foreign policies that reflected the preferences of its liberator. Despite the presence of powerful communist movements that had played significant roles in resisting the German occupation of their countries, France, Belgium, Greece, and Italy all re-established Western-style parliamentary systems and capitalist economic structures and adapted their foreign policies to fit the Anglo–American vision of the post-war world. By contrast, the states on the eastern half of the continent—despite their general hostility to communism and nationalistic antipathy for the USSR—adopted Soviet political and economic models and supported the foreign policy goals of the Kremlin under the watchful eyes of the Soviet occupation armies and their civilian collaborators among the local populations.

The ideological division of Europe did not take place overnight. In the Soviet sphere, non-Communist political parties were allowed to operate and non-Communist leaders to participate in coalition governments for a few years after the war; similarly, the Communist parties of France, Italy, and Belgium were tolerated and their members were allowed to hold cabinet posts in the early post-war coalitions. What eventually caused Europe to be divided into two mutually antagonistic blocs of states was the determination of the Soviet Union to establish a protective ring of subservient client states along the broad route—from the western shore of the Black Sea to the eastern shore of the Baltic—that had brought invading armies to the heart of the motherland twice within the memory of most of the citizens still alive in 1945.

The Western powers had reluctantly agreed to the border changes demanded by Joseph Stalin to secure the USSR's western frontier at the expense of Finland, Poland, and Romania. But Washington increasingly opposed the Kremlin's subsequent attempt to promote, through political intimidation backed by the Red Army, the installation of pro-Soviet regimes in the states of Eastern Europe beyond the newly expanded frontiers. In time, strategic thinking within Harry S. Truman's administration underwent a momentous evolution as policy-makers began to ponder the implications of events in Eastern Europe in the light of historical precedent and geographical context. Britain and, belatedly, the United States had intervened in the two world wars to restore the balance of power that had been upset by Germany. The temporary elimination of German power at the end of the First World War had been preceded a year earlier by the temporary disappearance of Russian power. The simultaneous weakness of Germany and the Soviet Union in the 1920s had enabled the small states of Eastern Europe to preserve their independence from both of their potentially powerful neighbours, with the support and encouragement of France. Hitler's subsequent bid for German hegemony in Europe had also resulted in the erasure of German power, but this time Soviet power had been projected into the political and military void of Eastern Europe at a time when no nation or coalition of nations on the western half of the continent was strong enough to balance it. As Truman's foreign policy advisers perceived that the Soviet Union was gaining control of the heartland of Eurasia and that the militarily exhausted, economically distressed nations along the western rim of Europe were also vulnerable to Soviet domination, Roosevelt's Wilsonian dreams were replaced with the tough-minded realism of geopolitics so familiar to European strategists and statesmen. A Soviet-controlled empire stretching from the Sea of Japan to the Atlantic and from the Arctic to the Aegean would be better positioned to mount a drive for world domination than even Nazi Germany had been at the height of its power. What Stalin may have seen as a legitimate effort to secure his country's western frontier was

increasingly interpreted by Washington as the beginning of a drive for continental hegemony on the road to global supremacy.

The USSR was able to establish its dominance over Eastern Europe from 1945 through 1948 because the only nation capable of preventing it had disengaged militarily from the European continent. At the time of Germany's defeat, the numerical strength of the US armed forces exceeded 12 million; by the end of 1947 that number had fallen to 1.4 million. While the United States demobilized its forces and dismantled its war industries, the Soviet Union kept more than 4 million seasoned veterans under arms and retained the formidable arsenal it had used to drive the German army from Moscow to Berlin.

From left, British Prime Minister Winston Churchill, US President Harry S. Truman, and Soviet Premier Joseph Stalin, at the Potsdam Conference, 23 July 1945. US Army Signal Corps, Courtesy of Harry S. Truman Library.

The reasons for the disengagement of US military power from Europe after 1945 are easy to understand. Americans were accustomed to small volunteer armies in peacetime and had no desire to keep their soldiers in post-war Europe beyond the token forces required for occupation duty in Germany, Austria, and Italy.[1] Once the United States had achieved its objectives regarding the war, it would have needed superhuman powers to persuade a war-weary public to bear the enormous costs of maintaining a large military force across the Atlantic solely to balance the forces of a nation that had so recently been hailed as a trusted ally against Hitler.

The American public's desire to 'bring the boys home' was entirely consistent with the Roosevelt administration's master plan for the political organization of the post-war world. Roosevelt shared the optimistic expectation of Wilson during the First World War that with the defeat of Germany, international conciliation would supplant the balance of power as the key to the preservation of world order.

These hopes were embodied in the new United Nations Organization (UN). Conceived by American, British, and Soviet representatives at the Dumbarton Oaks Conference in the fall of 1944 and formally established by the delegates of 50 states meeting in San Francisco in the spring of 1945, the UN was designed to replace the discredited League of Nations. Since both the United States and the Soviet Union shared—with Britain, France, and China—permanent representation on the new organization's decision-making body, the Security Council, it was widely assumed that any disagreements over post-war political arrangements could be settled in the UN without recourse to the power politics and regional alliance systems that had been discredited over the previous decade.

Furthermore, a monopoly on nuclear weapons in the early post-war years reinforced the sense of invulnerability to external aggression that had made the American tradition of isolationism possible. In the first few years after Hiroshima and Nagasaki, Washington's ability to devastate the principal cities of any potential aggressor without the slightest risk of retaliation against US territory seemed to give it more protection than even the Atlantic Ocean could. In short, the sense of national insecurity required to generate public support for new military commitments abroad was lacking. Roosevelt's tacit endorsement, at Yalta, of Soviet predominance in Eastern Europe made it difficult for his successor to complain about the Kremlin's exercise of that prerogative.

The Truman administration did not forcefully challenge the expansion of Soviet power until it appeared to cross the line that the wartime Allied leaders had tacitly recognized as separating the two spheres of influence. In 1946–7, a series of political developments along the southern rim of Eurasia was seen by Western leaders as evidence of a coordinated Soviet effort to attain one of Russia's traditional objectives: expansion southward into the eastern Mediterranean and the Persian Gulf—a region historically under the sway of British power.

The first direct confrontation between the Soviet Union and the Western powers took place in Iran, a country whose strategic location had made it the object of Anglo–Russian rivalry by the end of the nineteenth century. The two imperial powers had partitioned the country into spheres of influence in the decade before the First World War. Then, when the collapse of the tsarist empire and the advent of the communist regime temporarily reduced the Kremlin's influence in Iran, Britain proceeded to organize and supervise the exploitation of the vast reserves of petroleum that had recently been discovered there while striving to establish itself as the predominant political influence over the government in Tehran. In August 1941, as Hitler's armies advanced deep into the USSR, Soviet and British military forces simultaneously entered Iran and replaced the increasingly pro-German regime of Reza Shah with a more compliant government nominally headed by his young son, Mohammed Reza Pahlavi. According to an Anglo–Russian–Iranian treaty of January 1942, Russian troops were stationed in northern Iran and British troops in the south to protect the vital supply route from the Persian Gulf to the Soviet frontier along which British and American arms were transported to the USSR.

Both foreign occupation forces, as well as the American contingent that later joined the British, were to be withdrawn within six months of the end of the war. Shortly after the cessation of hostilities, the communist-controlled Tudeh Party supported a separatist revolt in the province of Azerbaijan, in northwestern Iran on the border with the Soviet Union. The Soviet occupation army prevented the Iranian government from suppressing the insurgency by denying its military forces access to the rebellious province. In November, a provincial assembly dominated by the Tudeh Party was elected in Azerbaijan and promptly declared its autonomy—a move widely regarded as the first step towards union with its neighbour, the Soviet Republic of Azerbaijan. The Iranian prime minister received a set of demands from Moscow that included indefinite retention of Soviet troops in northern Iran, recognition of the autonomy of Azerbaijan, and formation of a Soviet–Iranian joint stock company to exploit petroleum reserves in the northern part of the country.

Interpreting these moves as part of a campaign to gain effective control of the entire country, including its petroleum and its ports on the Persian Gulf, London and Washington applied vigorous diplomatic pressure on the Kremlin to desist. Tough speeches by British and US officials in February 1946 signalled the intention of their governments to resist further Soviet advances in the region. When the Red Army, alone among the three wartime occupation forces, delayed its evacuation beyond the deadline of 2 March, a firestorm of criticism from Britain and the United States compelled the Kremlin to withdraw its forces before the agreement on Azerbaijan's autonomy and the joint oil venture had been ratified. After the Red Army completed its evacuation that May, the Iranian parliament—apparently emboldened by the vigorous expressions of Anglo–American support—refused to ratify the agreement with the Kremlin that had been made under duress. In the meantime, an American military mission had

arrived in Tehran, and arrangements had been made for the Iranian government to purchase American military equipment.

The diplomatic setback suffered by the Soviet Union in Iran was a direct consequence of the Truman administration's decision to join Britain in protecting this historic object of the Kremlin's expansionist ambition. Washington's determination to bolster the Pahlavi regime set the stage for the establishment, seven years later, of a security link between Washington and Tehran that was to last for a quarter of a century. In a more general sense, it also heralded Washington's determination to resist the expansion of Soviet influence in Eurasia.

US suspicions were reinforced by Soviet pressures on Iran's neighbour Turkey in the same period. In March 1945, Moscow had formally denounced the Turko–Soviet friendship treaty of 1925, which had established close political and economic collaboration between these two historic enemies and included reciprocal pledges of non-aggression. In June 1945, Foreign Commissar Vyacheslav Molotov presented the Turkish ambassador to Moscow with a set of demands that together constituted a substantial infringement on Turkish sovereignty: cession of territory in the Caucasus annexed by Russia in 1878 and reacquired by Turkey after the First World War, revision of the Montreux Convention of 1936 governing the Turkish Straits so as to establish joint Soviet–Turkish jurisdiction over this vital waterway, and the leasing of Soviet bases on its shores to ensure its defence.

To the United States, these demands represented the revival of the Kremlin's old dream of breaking through to the Mediterranean at Turkey's expense; therefore, it had to be resisted with the same firmness that Britain had shown in the days when it was still capable of playing such a role. To Washington, as to London in the past, Soviet control of the Straits meant Soviet domination of the eastern Mediterranean. This in turn would give the USSR control of the vital commercial waterway linking Europe to the East, as well as easy access to the valuable mineral resources of North

Africa and the Middle East. Accordingly, when Ankara's rejection of its demands led Moscow to deploy 25 Soviet divisions on the Caucasian frontier, the Truman administration worked to bolster the beleaguered Turkish regime. In response to a harshly worded Soviet note in August 1946, reiterating the Kremlin's claims, Washington dispatched a naval task force to the eastern Mediterranean as a show of force and in September announced that a portion of the US fleet would be permanently stationed there. In the face of this ostentatious display of naval power, which was implicitly reinforced by the American monopoly on atomic weapons, the USSR backed down at the Turkish Straits just as it was being dislodged from northern Iran, although the extent of its retrenchment was not apparent until much later.

Meanwhile, across the Aegean, Greece was facing acute domestic unrest, in which London and Washington saw evidence of a third prong in the supposed Soviet campaign of southward expansion. After the German occupation forces had left Greece in November 1944, a fierce internal struggle had erupted between the conservative faction of the Greek resistance movement loyal to the monarchy and the communist partisans. The intervention of British military forces in the winter of 1944–5 led to a truce and an agreement for national elections to be held under Allied supervision, as well as a referendum on the restoration of the monarchy. The elections of March 1946 were boycotted by the left and therefore produced a comfortable majority for the royalist party, which was actively supported by the British. In the summer of 1946, at the height of the Turkish crisis, thousands of Greek communists concentrated in the north—with the encouragement and material assistance of the newly installed communist regimes across Greece's borders in Yugoslavia, Albania, and Bulgaria—renewed their guerrilla warfare against the pro-Western government in Athens. When the referendum in September showed a large majority in favour of restoring the monarchy, the internal conflict took on the character of an ideological confrontation between the British-backed

royalist regime in Athens and the communist-backed guerrilla movement in the north.

In this sense the Greek drama was reminiscent of the struggle between the pro-Western and pro-Soviet factions of the Polish resistance. But there were two critical differences between the Greek and Polish situations. First, the geographical position of Greece was decisively favourable to the pro-Western government and its British protectors. Whereas Poland's common border with the USSR and its forbidding distance from the Western powers worked in favour of the pro-Soviet Poles backed by the Red Army, the proximity of the Greek peninsula to the British bases in the Mediterranean was a major liability for the communists in their struggle with the Athens regime. Second, in his wartime bargain with Churchill, Stalin had excluded Greece from the Soviet sphere of influence, and he had shown no enthusiasm for the communist insurrection there in the winter of 1944–5. On the contrary, he instructed the Greek communists to co-operate with the British-backed government in the same way that he had urged the communist parties of France and Italy to co-operate with the pro-Western groups that dominated post-war coalition governments. The principal foreign supporter and supplier of the Greek communist insurgency was Yugoslavia, which—under the leadership of its charismatic leader, Marshal Tito—was already displaying the taste for independent activity that was soon to result in a total break with Moscow.

It may be supposed, from what is now known about the Kremlin's post-war foreign policy goals, that there were two reasons behind its caution in the Greek Civil War. First, Stalin was reluctant to help indigenous partisan forces establish an independent communist state beyond the effective control of the Kremlin; in the same way, he was reluctant to offer unqualified support to the communist forces of Tito in Yugoslavia and Mao Zedong in China. Second, it seems to have been feared that a communist takeover in a country specifically allotted to the Western sphere of influence would provoke sharp reactions from Washington and London, with potentially unpleasant consequences for the Soviet Union.

As it turned out, Britain's capacity to safeguard Greece's independence had been severely impaired by the economic crisis that followed the Second World War. The financial costs of the war had been partially offset by lend–lease assistance from the United States, and in 1946 Washington had provided an emergency loan of US$3.75 billion on the assumption that this would cover Britain's short-term needs until its export trade could be restored. But the loan money was promptly spent on food and fuel rather than invested in productive enterprises that would revive export capability. As a result, British reserves were quickly exhausted, and this potentially catastrophic situation was exacerbated by the worst weather conditions in recorded history during the winter of 1946–7. The national transportation system ground to a halt, the shortage of coal forced the closing of factories and temporary cutoffs of electricity, and the freezing of winter crops meant that the rationing begun during the war had to continue.

A nation in such dire straits was in no position to help the Greek government quell the communist insurrection, and the United Nations was prevented from intervening by the Soviet veto in the Security Council. Accordingly, the government in Athens appealed to Washington several times in 1946 for financial aid and military equipment. The Truman administration furnished such meagre economic assistance as it could, under existing authority, but by the beginning of 1947 it was clear that only large-scale, long-term assistance would avert a total collapse of the Greek economy and probable seizure of power by the communist guerrillas. To provide such massive aid to a financially unstable regime seemed inconceivable in the domestic political climate. The Republican Party, which had recently won control of the US Congress, had consistently opposed all the major foreign economic aid programs undertaken by Democratic presidents, up to and including the British loan in 1946. Having rallied to the cause of internationalism during the period of US participation in the Second World War,

the Republicans seemed poised to return to their pre-war traditions of isolationism and economic nationalism, which meant support for high tariffs and hostility to foreign loans that did not directly promote American exports.

Then in February 1947, the British Foreign Office officially informed Washington of its intention to terminate all financial assistance to Greece and Turkey and to remove the 40,000 British troops from Greece on account of Britain's own economic trauma. Remarking that Greece and Turkey alike were in desperate need of foreign loans, both to stave off economic collapse and to preserve their security, the British government expressed its hope that the United States would be able to take up the obligation Britain was about to relinquish.

Thus the government of the greatest empire the world has ever seen conceded the beginning of its demise. The recession of British power along its imperial lifeline, from Gibraltar to Singapore, had produced a vacuum along the southern shores of Eurasia comparable in importance to the vacuum in Eastern Europe produced by the crumbling of German power there. Now that Britain could no longer afford to maintain its far-flung garrisons and bolster friendly regimes along the lifeline, the United States had to choose between substituting its own power in that region and passively permitting the Soviet Union to fill the void.

President Truman took up the challenge in a speech to a special joint session of Congress in March 1947, declaring that the United States would replace Britain as the guarantor of the economic viability and military security of Greece and Turkey. The governments of Athens and Ankara would receive US$250 million and $150 million, respectively, in military and economic assistance, as well as American advisers to assist in their economic stabilization and military reorganization. The Soviet Union backed down from its claims on Turkey after the American show of force in the eastern Mediterranean, and in Greece the civil war petered out in 1948–9 as the Royal Greek Army, with US assistance, swept northward to occupy all the rebel strongholds in the mountains and force the communist partisans into exile in Bulgaria and Albania. (The Greek communists' chief benefactor, Yugoslavia, had sealed their fate by closing its frontier and terminating all assistance to them in July 1948, after Tito broke with Stalin and his party was expelled from the international communist movement.)

Embedded in Truman's March speech was a sentence clearly stating that the American government would not confine its foreign assistance to the narrow objective of helping Greece and Turkey to overcome their immediate difficulties: 'I believe that it must be the policy of the United States to support free peoples who are resisting subjugation by armed minorities or by outside pressures.' Implicit in this presidential declaration, which came to be known as the 'Truman Doctrine', was a pledge to use American economic resources to bolster nations bordering the Soviet bloc that appeared susceptible either to pressure from their powerful neighbour or to insurgency by domestic communist movements. Thus when the collapse of the Pax Britannica in the Balkans and South Asia created a power vacuum that the Soviet Union might fill, the Truman administration sent assistance to the governments of Greece, Turkey, and Iran. There remained two other power vacuums, however, in Europe (after the collapse of Germany) and East Asia (after the defeat of Japan), which represented even more serious threats in the eyes of some officials in the Truman administration.

It therefore became the task of those officials to persuade both the Republican-controlled Congress and the American public to abandon the tradition of peacetime isolationism. The most articulate and influential statement of the case for an activist foreign policy appeared anonymously in the July 1947 issue of the journal *Foreign Affairs* under the heading 'The Sources of Soviet Conduct'. Composed by George Kennan, director of the newly created Policy Planning Staff of the State Department, it summarized Washington's policy as follows:[2] the Soviet Union—for reasons having more to do with traditional Russian insecurity than with the messianic goals of

Marxist–Leninist ideology—could be expected to probe the weak points beyond its frontiers in an effort to extend its power in the world. It was in the national interest of the United States to contain any such expansion by strengthening the political, social, and economic institutions of countries subject to such expansionist pressures. Through the application of such counter-pressure the Kremlin would gradually be brought to realize that the cost of aggression would greatly outweigh any benefits that it might yield. The ultimate result, Kennan confidently predicted, would be the attenuation of the Soviet threat to the vital interests of both the US and the frontline nations.

THE MARSHALL PLAN

Shortly before this bold reformulation of American policy was published, US Secretary of State George C. Marshall delivered a speech at the Harvard University graduation ceremonies in June 1947 that directly addressed a problem that had preoccupied Kennan as he drafted the doctrine of containment: the fact that war-induced economic dislocations made the Western European countries vulnerable to Soviet domination. We have already seen how the post-war financial crisis affected Britain's ability to recover its industrial productivity and resume its foreign trade. Economic conditions were far worse in those nations on the continent that had been economically exploited by Germany and had served as the final battleground for the war in Europe. The continued impoverishment of countries such as France, Italy, and Belgium seemed an open invitation to the Soviet Union to extend its political dominion over them with the assistance of their powerful communist parties and communist-controlled labour organizations. To meet this presumed threat, Marshall invited the nations of Europe, including the Soviet Union and its satellites, to draw up a plan for European economic recovery with massive American assistance on the basis of permanent economic co-operation among themselves.

The inclusion of the Soviet Union in this unprecedented offer led the French and British governments to solicit the Kremlin's participation in a conference in Paris to draw up a collective response to the American initiative. On 26 June, Soviet Foreign Commissar Molotov arrived in Paris accompanied by 89 economic specialists, apparently prepared to give serious consideration to the proposal. Yet after a few days of fruitless talks the delegation abandoned the conference, while the Soviet government denounced the project and forbade the governments of its Eastern European protégés to have anything to do with it.

The grounds for the Soviet rejection of what came to be known as the Marshall Plan were two-fold. First, in order to collect the relevant economic statistics and to ensure that funds were spent for the purposes intended, Washington had insisted on having access to, and some degree of advisory authority over, the internal budgets of the recipient states. Foreign bankers impose similar conditions on any impoverished country. But it was too much to expect a victorious great power, particularly one as secretive and suspicious as the Soviet Union, to open its books to American officials and adjust its budgetary policies to priorities established in Washington. No doubt those officials would have revealed how vulnerable the post-war economy of the Soviet Union was—a reality that the Kremlin preferred to conceal for reasons of communist ideology as well as national pride. Thus Moscow denounced this requirement as an intolerable infringement on the national sovereignty of the participating states.

Second, Washington had stipulated that most of the Marshall aid be used for the purchase of American exports. This condition prompted the Soviets to suspect an ulterior motive beneath the facade of humanitarian largesse and seemed to confirm Leninist predictions of both the impending collapse of capitalism and the determination of capitalists to prevent it: American corporate monopolies, squeezed by declining domestic demand for their products as war-related orders dried up, were seeking new markets among the shattered economies of Europe. This interpretation received some confirmation from American officials themselves, who tried to sell the Marshall

program to Congress by warning that Europe's huge trade deficit with the United States would cause serious difficulties for American exporters unless the chronic 'dollar shortage' across the Atlantic were rectified through the granting of government credits.

In July 1947, representatives of all but one of the European nations outside the Soviet sphere (Spain[3]) assembled in Paris to lay the groundwork for a coordinated response to the Marshall proposal. In September, a plan for a four-year recovery program was submitted, specifying the anticipated combined budget deficit of the 16 participating states. On the basis of that plan, the US Congress voted in April 1948 to cover the combined deficit for the first year and agreed to make grants for three more years, in amounts to be determined. In mid-April, the recipient nations established the Organization for European Economic Co-operation to supervise the allocation of the aid and promote coordination among themselves. Between 1948 and 1952, the European Recovery Program (as Marshall's brainchild was officially known) supplied grants and credits totalling US$13.2 billion. The largest amounts went to Britain and its dependencies ($3.2 billion), France ($2.7 billion), Italy ($1.5 billion), and what was in 1949 to become West Germany ($1.4 billion).

The economic consequences of the Marshall Plan surpassed the most optimistic expectations of its authors. When the program ended in 1952, European industrial production had risen to 35 per cent and agricultural production to 10 per cent above pre-war levels. From the depths of economic despair, Western Europe embarked on a period of economic expansion that was to bring a prosperity unimaginable in 1947. In the meantime, the United States derived great commercial benefits from its financial benevolence, just as its Soviet critics had forecast: more than two-thirds of the goods and services imported to Europe under the plan came from the US, increasing profits for American firms and jobs for American workers. It is doubtful that the phenomenal economic growth that the US was to experience in the 1950s and early 1960s would have occurred without the stimulus provided by orders from the industrial nations that were rebuilding their war-torn economies across the Atlantic.

Yet we should not exaggerate the extent of the American economy's export dependence in the early post-war years. With a huge internal market capable of absorbing most of its industrial production and a considerable proportion of its agricultural output, the United States still exported less than 10 per cent of its gross national product—far less than the genuinely export-dependent nations of Western Europe and Japan. Even so, the post-war period was the first time in its history that the US began to develop an important stake in international trade. In 1946, total US exports were almost four times the pre-war average of $4 billion per year, and certain sectors of the economy had come to depend on foreign sales for a major part of their earnings. The dollars lent or given to Western Europe by the US were repaid many times over in the form of mutually beneficial commercial links that complemented their increasingly intimate political ties. (Canada also benefitted from the Marshall Plan, as trading agreements with the US enhanced the market for Canadian commodities.)

The post-war recovery of the industrialized West was facilitated by the relatively efficient operation of a new international monetary system established in 1944, at a meeting of financial representatives from 44 allied nations at the Bretton Woods resort in New Hampshire. Recognizing that low levels of international trade and investment represented a serious impediment to post-war economic growth in all countries, the delegates at Bretton Woods took a number of steps to promote the resumption of world trade and capital movements. To restore the system of multilateral international payments that had broken down in the 1930s, they created the International Monetary Fund (IMF), a pool of currencies contributed by member states upon which any member could draw in order to correct temporary balance-of-payments difficulties without resorting to exchange controls or devaluation.

The chronic problem of exchange instability was addressed by re-establishing a modified system of fixed exchange rates. The US dollar became the world's principal reserve currency and was made freely convertible into gold at a fixed price. The exchange rates in operation at the opening of the Bretton Woods conference were recognized as the par values for the new system, and any subsequent adjustment of the exchange value of a member country's currency required the prior approval of the IMF's governing board. Many of the Western European economies were not strong enough to accept convertibility of their fixed-rate currencies until the late 1950s, and there were occasional exchange problems for Britain and France. Nonetheless, Bretton Woods ushered in a quarter-century of relative exchange stability, which enabled exporters, importers, lenders, and borrowers to transact their foreign business without too much concern for the differences between currencies.

An additional stimulus to the post-war recovery of world trade was the creation of a multinational institution empowered to replace the beggar-thy-neighbour protectionism of the 1930s with rules for the international exchange of goods and services. As the United States became increasingly involved in world trade after the war, it pressed other nations, particularly those wartime allies that were deeply in debt to it and therefore particularly susceptible, to dismantle the 1930s trade barriers that blocked American access to their markets. Finally, in the summer of 1947, the US induced the major trading nations of the world to sign on to the General Agreement on Tariffs and Trade (GATT).

In subsequent years GATT became a forum for periodic negotiations to reduce the bewildering array of trade restrictions that had accumulated over the years. A fundamental clause concerned the 'most-favoured-nation' principle, according to which any trade concession negotiated between two members would automatically be extended to all. The reduction of tariffs and other trade barriers at GATT bargaining sessions led to unprecedented increases in the international exchange of goods and services. After almost two decades of stagnation, world trade grew at an annual rate of almost 7 per cent in real terms between 1948 and 1970, and many pre-war trade restrictions were scrapped.

The principal disappointment of the Marshall Plan was its failure to promote the economic integration of Western Europe along the lines originally envisaged by its architects. Even though one-sixth of Marshall aid was used to finance trade within Western Europe itself, and trade among the recipient countries did increase by 70 per cent, few efforts were made to remove impediments to the free movement of goods, capital, and labour across national frontiers during the life of the program. Creative efforts in the direction of economic integration would only come later, from disappointed European administrators of Marshall aid, such as France's Jean Monnet and Belgium's Paul-Henri Spaak, working independent of, and in a certain measure at the expense of, the United States.

The political consequences of the Marshall Plan were as far-reaching as the economic ones. The Soviet bloc's repudiation of the program not only foreclosed the possibility of restoring pre-war economic, and therefore political, relations between eastern and Western Europe, but it also accelerated the ideological polarization within each European state. The deterioration of political relations between Communist and non-Communist parties across the continent had already begun before the Marshall Plan was proposed. In the spring of 1947, the communist ministers in the coalition governments of France, Italy, and Belgium either were excluded from office or chose to leave it because of mounting ideological differences with the dominant pro-American parties. In the meantime, the communist parties of Eastern Europe were systematically removing all non-communist organizations from positions of power.

The trend towards ideological bifurcation was hastened by the Marshall Plan, for in facilitating the US penetration of Europe, it spurred the Soviet leadership to strengthen its

position by calling for a formal organization of European communist parties. Thus in September 1947, the Communist Information Bureau (or COMINFORM) was created, the successor to the COMINTERN (dissolved by Stalin in 1943 to allay the fears of his capitalist allies in the war against Hitler). Although it succeeded in liquidating all non-communist political forces in Eastern Europe that might prove susceptible to American influence, the COMINFORM was unable to generate effective opposition to the Marshall Plan in Western Europe. In the fall of 1947, strikes and disorders fomented by the communist-controlled labour organizations of France and Italy failed miserably. The governing coalitions in those two countries, from which the communist parties had been expelled the previous spring, resumed their eager quest for American economic assistance, actively supporting Washington's new anti-Soviet foreign policy.

Thus by the beginning of 1948, the European continent had been reorganized into two political and economic blocs, one dependent on the United States, the other on the Soviet Union. Soon the nations of Europe were also divided into two military blocs, each committed to common defence against the other and backed by the armed might of their respective patrons. Since the end of the war, Western and Soviet representatives had engaged in regular if not cordial communication at the foreign-minister level, in the Allied Control Council for Germany and in the United Nations, working to settle disputes through diplomatic negotiation. In February 1948, however, the communist takeover in Czechoslovakia—symbolically and literally the last major link between East and West in Europe—precipitated the final rupture in relations between the two. Thereafter, the effort at economic reconstruction in the western European nations seemed futile unless they could protect themselves against what, in the aftermath of the communist-inspired unrest in France, Italy, and the Prague coup, had come to be seen as the USSR's imminent bid to project its power westward beyond the sphere of interest informally allocated to it at the end of the war.

On 17 March 1948, two events that occurred on opposite sides of the Atlantic marked the determination of the Western nations to supplement their emerging transatlantic economic partnership with a commitment to collective self-defence. The first was the signing of the Brussels Pact and the subsequent formation of the Brussels Pact Organization, a military alliance binding Britain, France, and the three small countries now collectively known as Benelux (Belgium, the Netherlands, and Luxembourg) in a joint pledge to repel 'an armed attack' against any one of the signatories. The second was President Truman's special message to the US Congress requesting authorization to reinstate conscription and universal military training, which—in keeping with the traditional American preference for a small volunteer army in peacetime—had been allowed to expire after the war. These simultaneous actions were not unrelated: the Brussels Pact was designed to demonstrate the Western European nations' willingness to co-operate in their own defence and thereby to help Truman secure congressional approval of American participation in that effort.

The Soviet response to these first tentative steps toward US rearmament and Western European collective defence would confirm the worst fears of the Western leaders, accelerating the trend towards military preparedness and transatlantic co-operation in security matters. The site of the first direct confrontation between the two power blocs was, appropriately, the region of Europe where they collided head-on: occupied Germany. The partition of Germany, Austria, and their respective capitals into four military occupation zones under American, British, French, and Soviet jurisdiction had been intended as a temporary measure pending the emergence of indigenous political elites, untainted by Nazi connections, that would be able to govern their reunified sovereign state. In the meantime Germany (like Austria) was to be administered as a single political and economic unit by the Allied Control Council sitting in its capital, Berlin, which was also divided into four occupation sectors and was to be governed as a single municipal unit.

Several developments in the three years after the end of the war converged to sabotage this plan. Most were related to the Soviet Union's determination to take advantage of its control of eastern Germany as compensation for the damages it suffered during the war. The Soviet occupation authorities requisitioned German machinery, power plants, railway track, and rolling stock, as well as substantial quantities of coal and other raw materials for delivery to the USSR. They also repudiated their pledge to supply agricultural products from their zone to the three Western zones in exchange for the industrial equipment they had already received from them. These unilateral measures were understandable, given the desperate economic conditions caused by the German invasion of the USSR. But Washington had no intention of permitting the Soviets to strip the US zone of all its portable economic assets and continue receiving reparation deliveries from the Western zones while the United States footed the bill to support the impoverished Germans.

Convinced that Germany's recovery was vital to that of Europe as a whole, the United States unsuccessfully pressed the Soviet Union to treat reparations as part of a comprehensive plan for the German economy. Thus in May 1946, the US terminated the transfer of reparations to the Soviet zone. In the meantime, the Soviets had introduced economic measures in their own zone—such as confiscation (without compensation) and redistribution of all large landholdings—that clearly contradicted the free market principles of the US and further undermined the original policy of treating all of Germany as a single economic entity.

Then, in an abrupt shift in strategy, the Kremlin adopted a conciliatory approach towards Germany. At the Paris meeting of Allied foreign ministers in July, Molotov accused the United States of reintroducing a rejected plan (originally proposed by Roosevelt's secretary of the Treasury, Henry Morgenthau, Jr) that had called for the deindustrialization of Germany. Proposing the establishment of a single German government, Molotov also denounced a French plan for the separation of the Ruhr from Germany. These remarks were apparently intended to appeal to the starving and suffering German masses by portraying the Soviets as their friends and the Western occupying powers as their tormentors.

Not to be outbid in the 'struggle for Germany', US Secretary of State James Byrnes announced in September that Washington intended to promote the economic rehabilitation of Germany so that it might contribute to the recovery of Europe. He rejected the idea of splitting off the Ruhr from the rest of the country and called for the prompt formation of a provisional government with authority to administer the entire country so that Germans could once again manage their own affairs. Most important of all, in the context of German public attitudes, Byrnes specifically refused to recognize the Oder–Neisse frontier between Germany and Poland, which deprived Germany of a considerable portion of its pre-war territory and had been unilaterally established by the Soviets in 1945 in order to compensate Poland for the territory it had been forced to cede to the Soviet Union. By throwing US support behind German demands for the restoration of that lost land, Byrnes forced the Kremlin to choose between its client state in Poland and its prospective friends in Germany. Stalin sided with Poland, and in so doing irretrievably lost whatever chance he might have had to woo the Germans away from the West.

THE DIVISION OF GERMANY

The Truman administration made good on the commitments sketched by Byrnes, promoting greater coordination of the occupation policies in the three Western zones and granting more economic and political authority to the pro-Western German elites that were emerging there. On 1 January 1947, the Americans and the British formally merged their two zones into a single economic unit and in the following May established an economic advisory committee of 52 delegates from the regional (*Land*) assemblies that the two occupying powers had permitted to be elected in their zones. In July, the United States decided to extend Marshall Plan aid to the Western zones.

The French, who had at first opposed all measures favouring German political or economic integration (for obvious historical reasons), gave in to Anglo–American pressure in the summer of 1947 and began to participate in a common economic policy for the three Western zones.

Soon the rudiments of a West German administration appeared in the form of the Supreme Economic Council, which adopted a bold plan for industrial recovery that was to pave the way for the West German economic 'miracle' of the 1950s. On 1 March 1948, a central bank serving all three Western zones came into being; on 18 June, France finally agreed to fuse its zone with the Anglo–American zone ('Bizonia') to create a 'Trizonia'; and two days later, an all-West German currency, the Deutsche Mark, was established to cure inflation, curb black-market activities, and restore faith in paper money after three years of quasi-barter in which the hardest currency had been cigarettes. These reforms signified the allies' acknowledgement that Western European prosperity depended on Germany's economic recovery, that reunification of the entire country was impossible under current circumstances, and that the best alternative was to amalgamate the three zones and to integrate the new entity into a Western European community linked to the United States.

To Moscow, the process of economic integration in western Germany must have looked like what it indeed proved to be: a prelude to the political integration of the three Western zones in the form of a West German state dependent on and loyal to the United States. Since the newly consolidated zones contained three-quarters of Germany's population as well as the most productive industrial region of pre-war Europe (the Ruhr–Rhineland–Westphalia complex), the prospect of a politically unified, economically advanced west German state associated with the US was a troubling one for the Kremlin. Such a state might exert a magnetic attraction on German nationals within the eastern zone, which was being drained of its resources and subjected to acute economic privation by its Soviet occupiers.

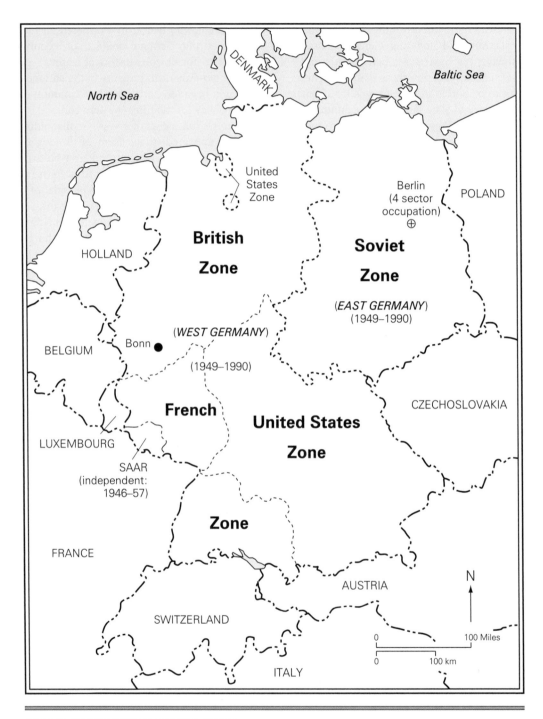

GERMANY BETWEEN EAST AND WEST

It might serve as a centre of Western intrigue against the Eastern European satellites. Worst of all, in light of Truman's request for the restoration of conscription in the US and the formation of a Western European military alliance, it might become a launching pad for aggression against the USSR by the US and its Western European clients in the Brussels Pact.

In response to these threats, Moscow chose to apply pressure at the point of greatest Western vulnerability: the Western sectors of Berlin, situated 177 kilometres inside the Soviet zone and tenuously linked to the Western zone by a highway and a railroad. On 24 June 1948, the Soviet authorities in Germany halted all surface traffic crossing from the Western zone through the Soviet zone to West Berlin, whose 2.4 million inhabitants had food stocks for only 36 days and thereafter faced the prospect of starvation. Though ostensibly undertaken in retaliation against the establishment of a strong currency in the Western zone (which was bound to destroy the weak German currency in the Soviet zone), the real purpose of the Berlin blockade was to expel the Western occupation forces from the city. If the formation of a West German state could not be prevented, at least the last open hole in the 'Iron Curtain' that Churchill had decried in his famous address in March 1946 could be plugged.

But the US and British governments organized an airlift to supply Berlin with food, fuel, and other basic commodities, and on 12 May 1949, Stalin terminated the blockade with a face-saving gesture that fooled no one. (The Kremlin announced that the roads and railroads, which had been closed 'for repairs' for a year, would be reopened to traffic from the West.) The Soviet Union's failure to remove this anomalous island of Western influence within a region firmly under its control and subject to its overwhelming military superiority was due to a single overriding fact: the United States possessed nuclear weapons that could be dropped on Soviet cities. The Berlin blockade accelerated the American involvement in the defence of Western Europe that had begun on the rhetorical level with the proclamation of

the Truman Doctrine and the adoption of the containment policy during the Greek and Turkish crises of 1947. On 23 April 1948, a few weeks after Truman's request for the reintroduction of conscription and the simultaneous formation of the Brussels Pact in Europe, British Foreign Secretary Ernest Bevin had sounded out the State Department about the possibility of linking the US, Canada, and the five signatories of the Brussels Pact in a North Atlantic security system. The imposition of the Berlin blockade in June strengthened the position of those in Washington who believed that the US had to break with its isolationist heritage and supplement its support for European economic recovery with a concrete commitment to European defence.

The two decisions required for the United States to take on such a commitment were both in the hands of the Congress—as had been the case three decades earlier, when Wilson's plans for the US to assume its global responsibilities were dashed on Capitol Hill. The US would need a sufficiently powerful military force to ensure the credibility of its commitment as well as legislative authorization to adhere to whatever system of regional defence Bevin and his European colleagues had in mind. As it turned out, congressional Republicans who had been converted to the 'internationalist' cause outnumbered the remaining isolationists by a wide margin. On 24 June 1948, the US Congress adopted the euphemistically named Selective Service Act, which laid the groundwork for a sharp increase in military manpower by subjecting all able-bodied males between 19 and 35 years of age to 21 months of compulsory military service. Like their counterparts in the Brussels Pact nations, which had also reinstituted conscription after the war, millions of young American men would receive military training not to fight a war in Europe, but to deter the Soviet Union from starting one there.

The concept of extending US military protection to the European signatories of the Brussels Pact seemed to contradict the essential purpose of the United Nations, which was to provide a global network of collective security that would render such regional defence arrangements unnecessary. When the British wartime government had pressed for a decentralized organization made up of regional associations, Roosevelt had insisted on the Wilsonian concept of a single universal organization without regional subdivisions. Shortly after Roosevelt's death, however, as delegates from 50 countries assembled in San Francisco to draw up a charter for the new world body, US officials concerned with Latin American affairs had expressed the fear that the projected global system of collective security might endanger Washington's special relationship with its clients south of the border. Just as the Wilson administration had insisted on exempting the region covered by the Monroe Doctrine from the purview of the League of Nations covenant, so the Truman administration arranged for the insertion of Article 51 in the United Nations Charter, which preserved the right of member states to establish regional security organizations outside the UN.

The first such regional agreement was the Rio Pact of September 1947, which established the principle of collective self-defence for the western hemisphere by defining an attack against one of the American republics as an attack on them all and providing for a joint response to aggression. The Brussels Pact was also based on the provisions of Article 51. Armed with the precedent of both pacts, Republican Senator Arthur Vandenberg introduced a resolution in the US Senate that was designed to circumvent the Soviet veto in the UN Security Council on matters relating to European security without violating the UN charter. The Vandenberg resolution in effect repudiated the US tradition of giving priority to the western hemisphere in times of peace by affirming Washington's willingness to join the nascent Western European regional security system.

Acting under the authority of the Vandenberg resolution, which easily passed the Senate, the United States opened discussions with the Brussels Pact countries on 5 July, and by the end of the year Canada, Italy, Norway, Denmark, Iceland, and Portugal had joined the talks. On 4 April 1949,

after months of intensive negotiations, delegates of these 12 nations signed the North Atlantic Treaty, a regional security arrangement, modelled on the Rio Pact, that obligated each signatory to assist any of the others that sustained an armed attack. A large majority of US senators ratified the treaty, and Truman signed it on 25 July. On the same day he requested congressional approval of the Mutual Defense Assistance Program, a one-year military aid package of US$1.5 billion that provided the financial underpinning of the US military commitment to the North Atlantic Treaty Organization (NATO).

In this way, and for these reasons, the mythical 'North Atlantic community' was born. It was a myth because it included countries that were nowhere near the Atlantic Ocean, such as Italy (and later Greece and Turkey, which joined in 1952). It was a myth because it did not include geographically eligible states such as Spain (on account of its Facist form of government and its past associations with the Axis powers)[4] and Sweden and Ireland (which insisted on retaining their traditional neutrality). And it was a myth because it did not represent any long-standing spirit of co-operation, given how recently most of its members had been at war with Italy, not to mention West Germany (which joined in 1955).

The new myth of Atlanticism superseded—at least for its American proponents—the older myth of hemispheric solidarity that had governed US diplomatic behaviour from the time of the Monroe Doctrine to that of Roosevelt's Good Neighbor Policy. Now the Atlantic Ocean was no longer regarded as an aquatic buffer between two distinctly separate (if not incompatible) civilizations, protecting the 'new world' from the nefarious influences of the 'old'. Instead, the sea was seen as uniting the peoples of European heritage, those whose forebears had traversed it and those whose forebears had remained at home, in a community of shared principles and values. In truth, the Atlantic alliance was forged not by a common devotion to a shared set of beliefs but by a shared fear of Soviet aggression, which had been exacerbated by the Berlin blockade. Another important consequence of the blockade was the formal partition of Germany into two political entities, each of them closely linked to one of the two superpowers. Shortly after the formation of the North Atlantic alliance and during the final week of the blockade, in May 1949, the three Western occupation powers permitted the establishment of the Federal Republic of Germany with its capital in the Rhenish city of Bonn. The first post-war elections were held throughout the three Western zones on 14 August and resulted in a plurality for the conservative, pro-Western Christian Democrats, whose leader, Konrad Adenauer,

became chancellor of the new Federal Republic. Resolutely anti-communist, profoundly suspicious of Soviet intentions, and firmly committed to free market principles, this shrewd Catholic politician from the Rhineland was ideally suited to guiding his fledgling state towards closer cooperation with the United States and to support its policy of containment and economic recovery in the non-communist half of Europe.

Although formally it was still an occupied country with several restrictions on its political sovereignty, the Federal Republic in fact ceased to be treated as a former enemy from the day it was

THE FIRST WAVE OF DECOLONIZATION IN THE COLD WAR ERA

As the nations of Europe struggled to come to terms with the new bipolar world order, it was evident to many that the age of imperialism would be another casualty of the devastating world war so recently ended. Though the will to colonize remained strong in many quarters, the economic realities of the post-war world dictated that it would be virtually impossible for the former great powers to retain far-flung colonial empires while simultaneously responding to domestic demands for rebuilding. As well, American rhetoric was also strongly anti-colonial during the immediate post-war years. Given such circumstances, on 15 March 1946 British Prime Minister Clement Attlee announced that Britain would no longer oppose Indian calls for independence. In a speech before the House of Commons, Attlee commented on the strength of Asian nationalism, its mass appeal, and the futility of continuing to oppose the inevitable. Citing India's wartime contributions, he observed that 'India herself must choose what will be her future Constitution; what will be her position in the world. I hope that the Indian people may elect to remain within the British Commonwealth. . . . But if she does so elect, it must be by her own free will.' The formal announcement of Britain's intent to leave India followed in February 1947 and, by the summer of the same year, the decision was reached to

partition India into the two sovereign states of India and Pakistan, with the latter divided into eastern and western halves. On 15 August 1947 India formally gained its independence. Ceylon (now Sri Lanka) and Burma quickly followed suit in 1948, initiating a wave of support for independence which would spread from Asia to Africa in the 1950s and 1960s. Coming to terms with the loss of empire was not nearly so easy for France and the Netherlands. Both nations exited the Second World War determined to reassert control over their former colonial territories. The result was a series of costly wars of independence— in Algeria, Indochina, and Indonesia, among others—which further diminished the power of the mother countries.

Even as the first colonies gained full independence, the ongoing Cold War had an immediate and obvious impact. Military, economic, and social assistance would be offered by both superpowers, but almost always with strings attached. Financial and military aid was often dispensed without adequate preparation or supervision. In the end, dictatorial governments grew wealthy while the local population continued to suffer, much as they had done under the recently departed colonial regimes. Only a fortunate few nations would manage to prosper, often by choosing non-alignment.

born. Instead, it came to be regarded as a bulwark against the Communist bloc and as a potentially valuable contributor to the economic reconstruction of Western Europe as a whole. Thus restrictions on Germany's economic sovereignty were relaxed and Marshall Plan assistance to Bonn was increased. By promoting savings, investment, and the revival of industrial production and foreign trade, Adenauer's minister of economics, Ludwig Erhard, generated a phenomenal economic boom in this war-ravaged country. By November 1949, the pre-war level of production was attained, and by the beginning of the 1950s West Germany had entered a period of sustained economic growth that was to restore it to the front rank of the world's industrial powers by the end of the decade.

Meanwhile, in October 1949, the eastern zone was transformed by its Soviet occupiers into the nominally independent state of the German Democratic Republic without the formalities of an election. In this way the eastern and western parts of Germany achieved separate statehood by the end of the 1940s, each adopting the political and economic systems of its protector. Hitler had set out to unify all of Europe under German auspices. Instead, his policies led to the division not only of Europe but also of Germany and even the city in which he had ruled and finally met his own end.

THE KOREAN WAR AND WESTERN REARMAMENT

It may be tempting to see the Berlin blockade and the formation of NATO as the decisive events that led to the rearmament, remobilization, and remilitarization of the United States and its allies in Western Europe. But the North Atlantic Treaty represented merely a statement of intention, and a rather vague one at that. Although it obliged members to take up arms 'immediately' in the event of an armed attack on any of them, it left each one to decide for itself whether an armed attack had in fact occurred, whether it threatened the security of the region covered by the treaty, and what responses (if any) were called for. In light of the overwhelming superiority that the Soviet Union

and its clients were thought to enjoy in terms of conventional military power in Europe at the time—175 divisions compared with 14 divisions for the Western powers[5]—it was unclear how the promised American assistance would be delivered to Europe in the event of a Soviet attack.

It was originally assumed that the United States could dissuade Moscow from interfering with Western Europe simply by throwing a 'nuclear cloak' over the region. The armed forces of the European members of NATO might be grossly outnumbered, but they would serve as a 'shield' that would slow a conventional Soviet assault until the 'sword' represented by the American nuclear arsenal could be unsheathed and plunged into the heart of the Soviet Union. But the deterrent power of America's ultimate weapon was compromised even before the ink on the North Atlantic Treaty was dry. On 29 August 1949, the USSR exploded its first atomic bomb, signalling the end of the nuclear monopoly that American intelligence experts had expected to last for several years.

Shocked by the Soviet nuclear test and apprehensive about its implications, President Truman ordered a comprehensive re-evaluation of US policy toward the Communist bloc. In April 1950, the National Security Council submitted a top-secret report, known as NSC-68, which portrayed the Soviet Union as inherently aggressive, fired by a messianic faith that was antithetical to the American way of life, with an unquenchable thirst for expansion that had led to the subjugation of Eastern Europe and China and threatened to engulf the remainder of the Eurasian land mass. Moscow's acquisition of atomic weapons would enable it to browbeat its non-nuclear neighbours into submission unless the United States took immediate steps to remedy this potentially catastrophic imbalance of power. The containment policy adopted in 1947 was no longer sufficient. The economic reconstruction of Western Europe and Japan, and the stockpiling of American atomic weapons thousands of kilometres away from the flashpoints of East–West confrontation, had failed to stem the advance of communism in the world. What was needed was a global offensive against the Soviet bloc that would restore the initiative to the non-communist world.

Among the specific recommendations of NSC-68 were prompt development of the thermonuclear (hydrogen) bomb, expansion of American and West European conventional forces, mobilization of America's economic resources to sustain this military buildup, and tightened bonds between the member states of the Western alliance system. Three proposals designed to strengthen NATO and give more concrete form to the US military commitment to Western Europe had been under active consideration ever since the explosion of the Soviet bomb. The first was to station large numbers of American ground forces in Europe (beyond the two divisions in West Germany), in order to supplement Allied manpower and enhance the credibility of Washington's pledge to participate in the defence of the western half of the continent. The second was to install air bases on the continent to accommodate the bombers that would carry the American nuclear deterrent. The third was to integrate the national armies of the alliance more closely and to develop procedures for joint military planning in order to remove the logistical inefficiencies that are endemic to a loosely organized coalition of sovereign states.

The general proposals included in NSC-68, together with its specific prescriptions for the buildup and projection of American military power abroad, implied nothing less than a revolution in the management of American national defence in peacetime. Predictably, the proposals gave rise to a fierce internal debate within the the Truman administration, from which Secretary of State Dean Acheson emerged as the staunchest proponent of the new approach. The prospect of sharp tax increases to finance this massive rearmament program alarmed a number of officials, including even Secretary of Defense Louis Johnson, who opposed the recommendations of NSC-68 on the grounds that they would undermine the economic health of the country. The State Department's two senior specialists on Soviet affairs, George Kennan and Charles Bohlen, argued that the project was based on a simplistic view of Soviet foreign policy goals and risked imposing an excessively rigid form on US policy toward the Communist bloc.

While Acheson strove to overcome mounting internal opposition to the new approach implied by NSC-68, the Kremlin launched a propaganda campaign in Western Europe that threatened to dampen Allied enthusiasm for the massive program of rearmament under consideration. In early 1950, a 'peace offensive'—organized by the West European Communist parties and endorsed by public figures of various political persuasions—denounced the Atlantic alliance as a US-inspired plot to intimidate the Soviet Union, one that was likely to result in the nuclear devastation of the very region that the alliance was supposed to protect. For the first time since the beginning of the Cold War, the non-communist left in France, Italy, and West Germany began to advocate neutrality for Western Europe in the global contest between the two superpowers. Neutrality was advertised as a way not only of avoiding total nuclear destruction but also of preserving for Western Europe a margin of choice between the antithetical ideologies competing for its favour.

What prevented the West Europeans from enjoying that choice was the unexpected outbreak of hostilities between communist and anti-communist armies on the Korean peninsula in the summer of 1950. Although Korea was *terra incognita* to most Europeans, enough was known about the similarities between its political situation and that of Germany to cause widespread uneasiness. Formerly a part of the Axis coalition, Korea had been partitioned in 1945 between the United States and the Soviet Union. After three years of fruitless negotiations regarding reunification, each occupying power had established a government in its own zone that claimed authority over the entire country. Now the communist North, armed and presumably encouraged by the Soviet Union, had attacked the non-communist South. Like South Korea, West Germany confronted an adversary who enjoyed decisive military superiority. The Soviet command in East Germany had recruited more than 50,000 'military police' from its occupation zone and had reorganized these paramilitary units into a powerful force that could be hurled against the disarmed Federal Republic. Consequently, the diffuse anxiety about the theoretical possibility of nuclear annihilation aroused by the Soviet atomic test in the summer of 1949 was instantaneously replaced by a more precisely focused fear regarding the prospect of a Korea-style conventional attack across the north German plain that could radically transform the balance of power in Europe.

Whether the Kremlin ever seriously considered making such an aggressive move in Europe—and no evidence has ever surfaced to indicate that it did—is beside the point. What mattered was that the governing elites of the NATO powers made the mental connection between Korea and Germany at the height of the Korean emergency. Moreover, Washington's response to the North Korean invasion removed any lingering doubts in Europe about the likelihood that the United States would honour its commitments abroad. A nation ready to fight a war in an obscure country that had been excluded from its defence perimeter in the western Pacific could scarcely be suspected of reluctance to defend the European members of the Western alliance system to which it had enthusiastically adhered.

The long-range geopolitical implications of the war in Korea were felt less on that strife-torn peninsula—where a permanent military stalemate developed in the summer of 1951 roughly along the original line separating North from South—than in the United States and Western Europe. The transformation of the Cold War into a shooting war in Asia led to the militarization of the containment policy in Europe. The Truman administration seized on the alarm caused by the Soviet aggression in Korea to push forward the ambitious program of military spending and security pledges to Western Europe that had been contemplated in discussions of the NSC-68 report. The NATO treaty was little more than a vaguely worded commitment to common defence, implicitly fortified by the existence of the US atomic arsenal and the large pool of US

military manpower produced by the introduction of peacetime conscription.

Initially, the concrete American contributions to European defence were supposed to be confined to munitions and matériel, and even those were in short supply because of the reduction in US military spending in the years after the Second World War. The Korean War abruptly changed all of that. In September 1950, the council of NATO foreign ministers assembled in New York and unanimously adopted a 'forward-looking strategy' for the defence of Western Europe, which was to be facilitated by the formation of an integrated military force under a unified command. In the same month, President Truman sent four divisions of combat troops to Europe and announced plans to increase even further the size of the US military contingent on the continent. On 19 December, the NATO foreign ministers announced the creation of an integrated defence system under the supreme command of General Dwight D. Eisenhower. When the US Senate endorsed the principle of an integrated command and approved Eisenhower's nomination on 4 April 1951—two years to the day after the signing of the NATO Pact—it also endorsed the transfer of the four divisions of American ground troops to Europe.

In the meantime, Washington had undertaken a massive military buildup designed both to increase America's nuclear and conventional capability and to furnish the European allies with the military equipment that they required. At the beginning of 1951, Truman submitted a US$50 billion defence budget—almost four times the amount proposed six months before—and increased the size of the standing army by half, to 3.5 million troops. In the last year of his presidency, the institutional structure of the Western alliance system was rationalized. The Lisbon conference of the Atlantic Council in February 1952 created a NATO secretariat, under a secretary general, and centralized all alliance activities in headquarters located in and around Paris. Plans were made to increase the number of divisions from 14 to 50, the combat readiness of existing forces was improved, and concrete steps were taken to centralize the command structure and integrate the national armies of the alliance. Negotiations were begun, and a number of agreements with various European states for the establishment of bases for American ground, air, and naval forces were concluded.

It is impossible to exaggerate the significance of the new American defence policy that gradually unfolded from the formulation of the Truman Doctrine in 1947 to the establishment of a full-fledged American military presence in Europe by 1952. By assuming the supreme command of NATO, furnishing armaments to its allies, and stationing its own ground forces on the other side of the Atlantic, the US had undertaken the task of preserving the post-war political status quo in Europe. The original emphasis on preventing the westward expansion of the USSR by promoting the economic recovery and political stability of Western Europe was superseded by the commitment to project American military power to the very heart of the continent in an effort to achieve the same objective.

But the assumption of such unprecedented global responsibilities was not without cost. The American economy, notwithstanding its spectacular rate of growth in the early 1950s, could not have been expected to sustain unlimited demands on its productive capacity. Particularly during the Korean War, when the American public had to endure wage and price controls and various restrictions on consumption, it was not surprising that Washington began to press its European allies to contribute more to their own defence. In July 1950, the five signatories of the Brussels Pact consented to increases in arms spending and the length of military service. But there were limits to what they could do at a time when their economic recovery was not yet complete. Moreover, France, Britain, Belgium, and the Netherlands were still obliged to maintain large military forces abroad to preserve order in the remnants of their colonial empires, while tiny Luxembourg's contribution was insignificant. Europe's greatest reserve of potential military strength was West Germany, with its large labour force and latent economic

capacity. It was unrealistic to expect the United States, which had assumed the major obligation to defend the Federal Republic, to continue its military buildup in that country without requiring the Germans themselves to contribute to their own protection, especially since any conceivable Soviet military advance in Europe would take place on German territory.

At the height of the Korean emergency, US officials began to prod the Western European governments to confront the issue they had preferred to postpone: the rearmament of West Germany and its admission to NATO. The increased pressure from Washington had its effect on Germany's apprehensive neighbours in the West. Particularly in France, public opinion began to accommodate itself to the idea of Germany's reintegration into the Western European system. Many French people had ceased to regard Germany as the hereditary enemy as they began to view Russia as the principal threat to national security. Moreover, the portion of Germany under Western influence, which contained more than three-quarters of the country's industrial plant, came to be seen as a valuable economic asset to Western Europe as a whole. The enormous productive potential of the Federal Republic, if permitted to develop to its full capacity, could serve as the engine of economic recovery for the entire western half of the continent. All that remained was to devise some means of assuring that West Germany's economic recovery would be managed without endangering the security of its non-communist neighbours.

Even before the stimulus provided by the Korean War, the French government had launched a bold initiative that was eventually to provide such assurance. On 9 May 1950, French Foreign Minister Robert Schuman formally proposed that the coal and steel production of France and West Germany be combined and supervised by a supranational authority, which would be open to the participation of the other countries of western Europe. Britain declined the invitation to join in discussions of this proposal because it was reluctant to compromise its privileged relationship with North America and the Commonwealth. But representatives of West Germany, Italy, and the Benelux nations joined French officials in negotiations that in 1951 produced an agreement to form a European Coal and Steel Community. When the Schuman Plan officially went into effect in the summer of 1952, the new supranational entity had been endowed with a political organization to complement its economic apparatus: an executive body, a parliamentary assembly, and a court of justice. Moreover, the specified objective of gradually abolishing all politically imposed obstacles to trade within the community (such as tariffs, quantitative restrictions, and import quotas) in coal and steel products implicitly established a precedent that could, and would, be extended to other and eventually all sectors of the economy. Thus the Schuman Plan contained the seeds of European economic integration that would germinate in the second half of the 1950s.

The Schuman Plan contained strategic implications as well, seeming to offer a solution to the question of German rearmament that had been insistently raised by the United States since the beginning of the Korean War. Schuman's proposal, like the abortive scheme for European union advanced a generation earlier by another French foreign minister, Aristide Briand, had been prompted by the hope of enmeshing Germany in a web of European economic integration that would forever remove both the incentive and the opportunity to make war on its partners in such a co-operative enterprise. It was inevitable that a proposal to domesticate Germany's industrial power by integrating it into a European economic community would give rise to the idea that Germany's warmaking potential could similarly be harnessed to the cause of joint European defence. Schuman's original hope was that an economically integrated, politically unified Europe, led by France and its junior partner across the Rhine, could emerge as a 'third force' capable of managing its own defence without depending on either of the two superpowers or becoming embroiled in their global struggle for hegemony. But the outbreak of the Korean War, five days after representatives of the

six interested states had assembled in Paris to consider the French proposal, abruptly transformed the nature of the discussion.

The concept of Franco–German partnership within a Europe disengaged from the two superpowers was eclipsed by the prospect of all-out war with the Communist bloc. On 24 October 1950, as the governments of Western Europe groped for a constructive response to Acheson's proposal for the addition of West German divisions to NATO, French Premier René Pleven unveiled a plan designed to satisfy the US demand for German rearmament while allaying the fears that such a development was bound to arouse in Germany's West European neighbours. The Pleven Plan provided for the formation of an integrated European military force, equipped and financed by the member states, with the integration of national contingents at the lowest possible level. In other words, German soldiers would be integrated with their French, Italian, and Benelux counterparts. There would be no German army or German high command; instead, German soldiers would be thinly diffused through the ranks of a genuinely European army, under the jurisdiction of a European defence minister who would be responsible to a European parliament.

The American government initially hesitated to endorse the French proposal for a unified European military force for fear it was merely a diversionary manoeuvre to delay or prevent Germany's entry into NATO. But Washington was gradually won over to the Pleven Plan as the best way of including Germany in the common European defence effort without inspiring apprehension in the other allied countries. At a time when the conflict in Korea was widely regarded as a prelude to a general war, the governments of Western Europe were uncharacteristically willing to accept the restrictions on their national sovereignty implied by the Pleven Plan. In May 1952, after long and arduous negotiations, representatives of the six nations concerned signed the treaty establishing the European Defence Community (EDC).

Thus was born the concept, if not yet the reality, of a supranational military organization under the supreme command of NATO, with common armed forces, a common European uniform, a common defence budget, and common political institutions including a council of ministers, an assembly, and a court of justice. The EDC treaty diverged from the original Pleven Plan in one important respect: instead of providing for the dispersion of national forces in small units throughout the military organization, it established national contingents on a divisional scale (ostensibly for reasons of efficiency). This meant that German divisions would contribute to the defence of Western Europe after all, although as part of a multinational force and under the direction of 'European' commanders. In recognition of West Germany's proposed adherence to the military alliance directed against the USSR, the three Western occupying powers took the necessary steps to eliminate the anomalous reminders of its status as a vanquished enemy. A day before the signing of the EDC pact in Paris, the American, British, and French governments concluded an agreement with the Adenauer regime in Bonn providing for the end of the military occupation and the restoration of political sovereignty to the Federal Republic.

As the parliaments of the six member states of the EDC ratified or debated ratification of the treaty to create a European army, two momentous political changes took place within weeks of one another in Washington and Moscow. In January 1953, the Democratic administration of Harry S. Truman, which had inaugurated the policy of containing the Soviet Union and took the United States into the Atlantic alliance, turned over the reins of power to the Republican administration of Dwight D. Eisenhower. And on 6 March, the Kremlin announced that Joseph Stalin had died the previous day. It soon became clear that a cadre of political and military personalities would rule the USSR on the basis of collective leadership and that the upper echelons of the Soviet government and Communist Party had undergone the most sweeping reorganization since the purges of the late 1930s. The simultaneous disappearance of the two elites that had between them presided over the destiny of the entire globe since the end

of the Second World War provoked a universal sense of uncertainty. This feeling increased once it became evident that the new US administration would resemble its Soviet counterpart in the degree to which power and responsibility would be delegated and diffused rather than centralized at the top. No one could predict with confidence whether the foreign policies of Truman and Stalin would be perpetuated by their unfamiliar and untested successors.

What was certain was that Truman had left an extraordinary legacy in the realm of foreign policy. The underlying objective of that policy— to prevent Soviet expansion beyond the regions under Soviet military domination at the end of the war—had been met everywhere. In Iran, Turkey, Greece, West Berlin, South Korea—wherever the Soviet Union had been perceived as probing Western intentions—the United States had exercised its diplomatic, economic, or military power to preserve the non-communist character and pro-Western inclinations of those disputed regions. The countries of Western Europe, on the brink of economic collapse and vulnerable to Soviet military pressure in 1947, had made spectacular strides toward economic recovery and collective defence.

In view of the remarkable success of that containment policy, it seems ironic that the Republican Party's victory of 1952 was in large part due to its success in portraying the Truman administration as 'soft on communism' in allowing the advance of Soviet power in Asia. China, the most populous country on earth, was widely thought to have been absorbed into the Soviet empire. American soldiers continued to die as the Korean War dragged on inconclusively. The communist insurgents in Indochina threatened to dislodge America's French allies and open all of Southeast Asia to the domination of the Kremlin and its puppets in the region. Added to this perception of Soviet gains across the Pacific was the widespread suspicion, incited by legislative demagogues such as Wisconsin Senator Joseph R. McCarthy, that communist agents had infiltrated America's domestic political institutions and were promoting Soviet interests there. The new US administration promised, in ill-defined ways, to remedy these defects in US policy concerning the Soviet bloc and to halt what the Republicans saw as the trend toward retrenchment and retreat.

SUMMARY

The end of the Second World War ushered in a new era in world history. Hopes were high that peace would bring stability, but serious disputes among the Allies had already surfaced during the war. The Soviet Union clashed with Britain and the United States over the future of Germany and Eastern Europe, and agreements made at war-time summit meetings could not prevent tensions from rising after 1945. The Western powers were alarmed at the Communist takeover of governments in countries under Soviet occupation, which divided Europe into two opposing blocs. By 1946 Winston Churchill had introduced the idea of an 'Iron Curtain' between the Communist bloc and the West, and commentators were describing the emerging ideological conflict as a 'Cold War'.

In response to the perceived Soviet threat, the United States launched two important initiatives in 1947: the Truman Doctrine and the Marshall Plan. Whereas the former was designed to prevent the spread of communism by supporting pro-Western countries that might otherwise be vulnerable to pressure, the latter was designed to promote economic growth and political stability by providing massive aid to European nations. The Soviet Union and its allies viewed the Truman Doctrine as a declaration of hostility and refused to participate in the Marshall Plan. The East–West rivalry escalated in 1948, when a Soviet blockade of Berlin forced the US to airlift supplies into the Western sectors of the city. In 1949, the US and Canada joined the major Western European powers in forming the North Atlantic Treaty

Organization (NATO), a military pact designed to protect against Soviet aggression. A new phase in the Cold War began the following year, when North Korea launched a surprise attack on South Korea. What had begun as a dispute over Europe was now a global conflict, and bipolarity became the dominant feature of international relations.

NOTES

1. Allied military forces remained in occupation of northern Italy until December 1945, notwithstanding that country's status as a 'cobelligerent' after the overthrow of Mussolini in 1943.

2. Though apparently not sufficiently clear to prevent its being misrepresented in subsequent years by advocates of policies that Kennan lived to abhor, such as the American intervention in the Vietnamese civil war to 'contain' Soviet (or Chinese) expansion.

3. Spain was excluded from participation in the Marshall Plan on account of its autocratic political system as well as its pro-Axis sympathies during the Second World War.

4. Although Franco's Spain was denied membership in NATO largely at the insistence of the British Labour government, the United States and Spain concluded a bilateral agreement in September 1953 that provided for the establishment of American naval and air bases on Spanish territory as well as American military and economic assistance to Franco. After the dictator's death and the restoration of a constitutional monarchy, Spain was admitted to NATO in 1982.

5. Intelligence estimates of Eastern bloc strength at this time were grossly exaggerated, as the American government itself conceded many years later. But the disparity between the two blocs was still significant.

QUESTIONS FOR CRITICAL THOUGHT

1. Discuss whether the United States was correct in its assessment that Stalin was about to make a bid for continental hegemony.
2. To what degree did Stalin violate the limits on Soviet expansion agreed to at Yalta?
3. When did the Cold War begin?
4. Why did Soviet specialists in the United States oppose NSC-68?
5. Why do many analysts view the ECSC to be the most important development in post-war Western Europe?
6. How should we assess Truman's legacy?

WEBSITES FOR FURTHER REFERENCE

The Avalon Project: World War II Conferences
    http://avalon.law.yale.edu/subject_menus/wwii.asp

Diefenbunker: Canada's Cold War Museum
    www.diefenbunker.ca

Harry S. Truman Library & Museum: Ideological Foundations of the Cold War
    www.trumanlibrary.org/whistlestop/study_collections/coldwar

History of the Atomic Age
    www.atomicarchive.com

CHAPTER 8

COEXISTENCE AND CONFRONTATION (1953–1962)

EISENHOWER'S 'NEW LOOK'

After 20 years in political opposition, the Republican Party, led by General Dwight Eisenhower, took control of the White House in January 1953 ostensibly committed to reversing the foreign policy of its Democratic predecessor. But the direction of this reversal was not towards isolationism and 'America first'. That wing of the party, led by Senator Robert Taft, had been decisively defeated by the 'internationalist' faction that had adopted Eisenhower as its standard-bearer and chosen as its foreign-policy spokesman John Foster Dulles, who was to become secretary of state. Before the election, Dulles had denounced

the Truman administration's containment doctrine as excessively passive and immoral in its abandonment of the populations of Eastern Europe that had been permitted to fall under Soviet domination. Instead of striving to preserve the balance of power that had been established in Europe at the end of the war, Dulles asserted, the United States should make every effort to liberate the satellite states and 'roll back' Soviet power to the boundaries of the USSR. He challenged all foreign nations to choose between enlisting in the American crusade for global righteousness and submitting to Soviet domination. Observers at the time did not fail to detect the parallels between this ideologically charged conception of American foreign policy and its Marxist–Leninist counterpart. Each regarded the other as so intrinsically evil as to preclude any accommodation, and each appeared unshakable in its confidence that, eventually, it would triumph over the other.

Such a dynamic vision of Washington's relationship with its principal rival in the world obviously implied a considerable increase in US military power. Yet a huge rise in defence spending would contradict the orthodox economic platform of the Eisenhower presidential campaign, which promised tax relief, reductions in government spending, and a balanced budget. The paradox was resolved by a high-level decision to inaugurate what was called a 'new look' in US defence policy. In January 1954, Dulles unveiled a strategic doctrine designed to increase military power while reducing defence expenditures. Since the most costly part of the defence budget was the money spent on conventional forces (mainly in pay and equipment for the army and navy), this would be reduced. The old idea of increasing NATO's troop strength to 50 divisions, which had been formally adopted by the alliance in 1952 but was never taken seriously because of the enormous costs involved, would be abandoned. Instead, the United States would place greater reliance on its nuclear arsenal and delivery system (which at the time consisted of powerful bomber forces based in the US and abroad).

In this way the Republican administration planned to hold down the costs of defence without sacrificing the security interests of the Atlantic alliance. To compensate for the inferiority of the Western allies' conventional forces in Europe, American strategic airpower would be upgraded to the point where it would be able to deliver a retaliatory nuclear blow 'instantly, by means and at places of our own choosing', as Dulles put it. While Dulles advertised this new approach as a way of providing 'more basic security at less cost', one of his colleagues in the administration described it more bluntly as 'more bang for the buck'.

The strategy of 'massive retaliation', as it came to be known, could remain a credible deterrent to aggression only so long as the Soviet Union lacked the means to retaliate in kind. When Dulles proclaimed the policy, the United States possessed the wherewithal to inflict extensive damage on Soviet territory by means of long-range bombers based at home or medium-range bombers deployed in allied countries along the periphery of the Soviet empire. The USSR had exploded its own hydrogen bomb in August 1953, only nine months after the first successful American test. But it possessed neither long-range bombers (capable of the round-trip flight from Soviet territory to North American targets) nor air bases in the western hemisphere. Thus the US could count on devastating the major urban areas and industrial sectors of its enemy without fear of reprisal.

The deterrent value of massive retaliation also depended on the ability of the United States to convince its adversary that aggressive activity in certain areas of the globe would automatically trigger nuclear response. The dynamic military strategy associated with Dulles therefore also gave birth to an equally aggressive diplomatic strategy intended to ring the Soviet bloc with hostile powers linked to and protected by the US through a series of mutual defence treaties. The Atlantic alliance and its emerging regional subgroup, the European Defence Community—both inherited from the Truman administration—formed the keystone of the global security system that Dulles was striving to construct. Confronted with a rearmed West Germany within a rearmed Western Europe backed by the invulnerable US nuclear deterrent, the Soviet Union would be dissuaded from risking further probes of the soft spots beyond the Western borders of its empire.

But the Dulles strategy for Europe was dealt a devastating blow in August 1954, when the French parliament refused to ratify the treaty establishing the EDC, two years after it had been signed by the leaders of the six member states. Ironically, the project for a supranational West European military force came to an end at the hands of the very nation that had originally proposed it. French opposition to EDC sprang from several considerations apart from the predictable hostility to the restrictions on national sovereignty implied by the treaty. Foremost among them was the fact that Britain was not to be a full participant (although it did pledge to assign one armoured division as a token of its involvement), which prompted fears that a return to Britain's traditional stance of aloofness from European affairs would leave France in a lonely and vulnerable position of inferiority on the continent.

Another reason for France's dwindling enthusiasm was a mounting hope of détente with the Soviet Union, sparked by the death of Stalin and the increasingly amicable behaviour of his successors. It had been easier to preserve the cohesion of the Western bloc when relations with the USSR were tense; now, Soviet and Western statesmen were able to meet cordially in Geneva to negotiate a settlement to the Indochinese War, and Winston Churchill himself was urging East–West discussions to settle the world's problems.

The French rejection of the EDC briefly threatened the unity of the Atlantic alliance, upset the plan to integrate West Germany into the system of European defence, and derailed the movement toward European unity. But after an initial flurry of recriminations, the interested parties settled down to explore other ways of ensuring Europe's common defence. This time the initiative came from London. As an alternative to the supranational defence organization that the EDC would have been, British Foreign Secretary Anthony Eden suggested that the more conventional military alliance created by the Brussels Pact of 1948 be enlarged to include Germany and Italy. As a charter member of the Brussels Pact, Britain already maintained four infantry divisions and air force units on the continent, and these would provide the counterweight to German power that France was seeking.

In October 1954, representatives of the Brussels Pact nations plus Germany and Italy signed an agreement enlarging the six-member Brussels Pact organization into the eight-member Western European Union (WEU). Britain, France, and the United States formally agreed to terminate their occupation of the Federal Republic (West Germany) and restore full sovereignty to it (including the right to rearm, on the sole condition that it promise never to manufacture atomic, biological, or chemical weapons on its territory). Thus West Germany finally ceased to be treated as an 'enemy' by the three powers that had occupied it since 1945, even though, in the absence of a formal peace treaty, the 'state of war' technically continued. Installed as a full-fledged member of the expanded WEU, West Germany was forthwith proposed for membership in NATO, which it officially joined in May 1955.

The Soviet Union responded to these momentous events by assembling representatives of its seven East European satellites in Warsaw to sign a 20-year mutual defence treaty that established a formal military alliance as a counterpart to NATO. This multinational 'Warsaw Pact Organization' superseded the separate bilateral arrangements concluded between the Kremlin and its clients during the Stalin era. Though formally a military alliance protecting the Eastern bloc against threats from NATO (and particularly from its newest member), for the rest of the 1950s the Warsaw Pact functioned mainly to assist in the Soviet political domination of Eastern Europe. Joint military exercises were not conducted until 1961, and even after that date the pact served more as a means of promoting political cohesion within the bloc and ensuring the members' subservience to Soviet foreign policy objectives than as a military alliance on the NATO model.

Thus only a few months after the collapse of the EDC scheme, joint European defences had been strengthened and the Western alliance system reinvigorated—contrary to every expectation—with the addition of a rearmed West Germany as an equal member. Those such as France's Jean Monnet who had hoped that the EDC would further the cause of European unity were chastened by this setback, but they redirected their energies toward promoting economic integration as a basis for political collaboration by strengthening and expanding the sole survivor of their earlier attempt at co-operation, the European Coal and Steel Community. The relative ease with which the six member states of the ECSC (France, West Germany, Italy, and Benelux) had consented to the removal of most restrictions on the exchange of coal and steel products within the community inspired optimism that the concept could be extended to other economic sectors. Intensive negotiations to that end were conducted during the mid-1950s. Finally, in March 1957, representatives of the ECSC states signed the Treaty of Rome establishing the European Economic Community (EEC), which formally began operations in January 1958.

The EEC had two overriding purposes: the gradual elimination of all legal restrictions on trade, capital movements, and labour migration within the community, and the establishment of a common external tariff to protect member states from foreign competition during the difficult transition to a genuine free trade zone. As had been the case during the formation of the ECSC, Britain declined to join the emerging economic bloc on

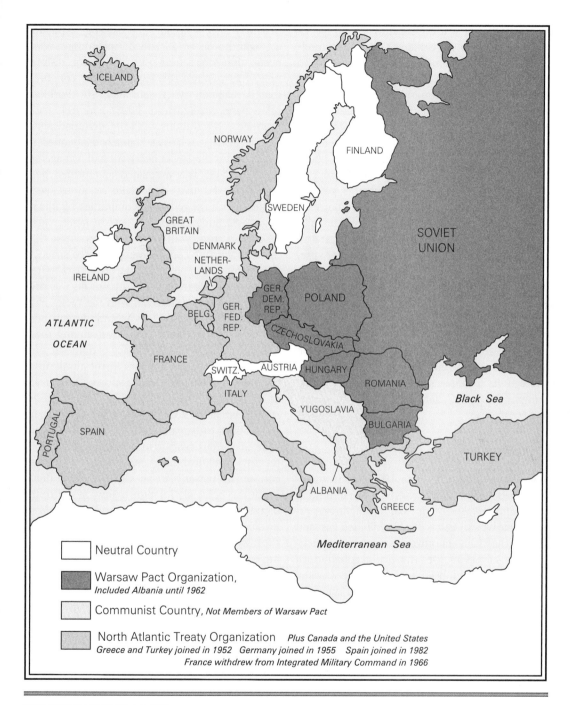

Neutral Country

Warsaw Pact Organization, *Included Albania until 1962*

Communist Country, *Not Members of Warsaw Pact*

North Atlantic Treaty Organization   *Plus Canada and the United States*
Greece and Turkey joined in 1952   Germany joined in 1955   Spain joined in 1982
France withdrew from Integrated Military Command in 1966

Europe in the Cold War

the continent for fear of jeopardizing its 'special relationship' with the United States and its preferential trade arrangements with Commonwealth countries (which enabled it to import food duty-free). To facilitate the long-range goal of political integration, a complex apparatus of embryonic political institutions was created as well. The most important of these organizations were the Council of Ministers, representing the six countries; the Commission, consisting of 13 'European' civil servants appointed by the member governments; and a 'European' parliament, empowered to oversee the Commission's activities. Initially, these institutions had minimal administrative authority and budgetary autonomy, but they presided over a process of economic integration that was to survive all efforts (especially by France) to reassert the old prerogatives of national sovereignty. Although the goal of political federation proved much more elusive, the 'idea' of Europe continued to exercise a powerful attraction on people weary of the old national antagonisms and aware of the advantages that political unity would bring in the global contest for power, influence, and prosperity.

THE POST-STALIN 'THAW'

Since Stalin's death in March 1953, the new collegial leadership in the Kremlin had been hinting that compromise and conciliation might be possible. One by one, issues that had divided East and West in the Stalin era proved susceptible to settlement. In July 1953, the armistice negotiations in Korea, which had been hopelessly deadlocked for two years, were quickly completed on terms that denied the Soviet client state in the north the political gains it had sought in the south. A year later, the victorious Vietnamese nationalist movement was compelled by its Soviet patron to accept a ceasefire agreement (at the Geneva Conference on Indochina) that left it in control of only the northern half of Vietnam.

In the spring of 1955, the Kremlin astonished even its fiercest opponents with a flurry of conciliatory gestures. The Austrian State Treaty, signed that May after a decade of bickering, stipulated the withdrawal of all Allied (including Soviet) occupation forces from Austria and the restoration of its political sovereignty on the condition that it maintain strict neutrality. The Porkkala naval base, wrested from Finland in 1947, was returned to that country. The Manchurian naval base at Port Arthur that Stalin had obtained in exchange for the Soviet declaration of war against Japan in 1945 was evacuated and turned over to China. Normal diplomatic relations were restored with the renegade communist regime of Yugoslavia, and steps were taken to establish them for the first time with West Germany. These dramatic diplomatic concessions prompted speculation in Western capitals that the Soviet Union had renounced its aggressive intentions and was prepared to settle its differences with the West.

There were several factors behind this new posture of accommodation. Foremost among them was the uncharacteristic primacy of domestic politics over international affairs in the thinking of the governing elite during the succession struggle of 1953–7. As Nikita Khrushchev worked to outmanoeuvre half a dozen rivals for the top post, he was obliged to bargain with and sometimes concede to various blocs and constituencies within the Soviet political hierarchy in order to gain and consolidate power.[1] At the same time, the fluidity of the political situation following the death of a despot in a country with no institutionalized mechanism for succession permitted the public expression of demands for improvements in living conditions and relaxation of the stifling political repression inherited from Stalin. In such an uncertain domestic political environment, the Soviet leadership was understandably inclined to avoid conflict with the West, particularly after failing to prevent the alliance of a rearmed Germany with the United States and its European partners.

It is also possible that the Kremlin's quest for stability in Europe during the mid-1950s reflected a positive consideration as well: the opportunity to profit from the revolutionary agitation in those parts of Africa and Asia that remained under European control. A Soviet diplomatic offensive on behalf of populations struggling to free themselves of British or French rule would certainly have dictated a defensive strategy in Europe, to avoid antagonizing either the colonial powers or the United States and its continental protégés. The high point of the trend towards relaxation of East–West tensions in Europe came in Geneva in July 1955, at the first post-war meeting of the Soviet and Western heads of government. Over four days, the four leaders—US President Eisenhower, Soviet Premier Nikolai Bulganin, British Prime Minister Anthony Eden, and French Premier Edgar Faure—engaged in friendly conversations that contrasted dramatically with the rhetorical fulminations of the previous decade. As head of the Western coalition, Eisenhower set the tone with an earnest appeal for a co-operative new approach to the problems of European security that would obviate the arms race and dispel the fear of nuclear annihilation.

Designed to get around the traditional Soviet objection to on-site inspection, Eisenhower's 'open skies' proposal envisioned a full exchange of blueprints of US and Soviet military installations, along with aerial photo-reconnaissance on both sides. Bulganin in turn unveiled a plan for disarmament that would prohibit both fabrication and use of atomic weapons and impose a ceiling on the size of the conventional forces of the world's leading military powers. The heads of government even agreed on an innocuous pledge to seek a solution to the touchiest issue of all—the political future of Germany—based on the principle of reunification of the two German states by means of free elections.

None of this discussion meant anything in practical terms. Neither arms-limitation proposal was acceptable to the other side, for the usual reasons. The Soviets were not about to expose their military secrets, nor were the Americans prepared to accept any reciprocal limitations of military capability without adequate provisions for inspection. Bulganin's vaguely worded endorsement of 'the reunification of Germany by means of free elections' was diluted by all sorts of qualifications, including the condition that any

such development be compatible with 'the interests of European security'. Both the Soviet prime minister and the behind-the-scenes master of the Kremlin, party boss Nikita Khrushchev, returned to Moscow by way of East Berlin in order to reassure the leaders of the German Democratic Republic that their nation's sovereignty would never be sacrificed.

Despite the absence of any concrete achievements, the very fact that the leaders were bargaining politely and face to face represented a significant departure from the confrontational style of the past. Eisenhower won accolades at home and abroad as a 'man of peace', while the Soviets conveyed an uncharacteristic image of sincerity and trust. To Eisenhower's earnest pledge that 'the United States will never take part in an aggressive war,' Bulganin solemnly replied, 'We believe that statement.' Newspaper columnists in the West spoke with wistful optimism about the 'spirit of Geneva', while the Soviet press repeated the catchphrase of the early post-Stalin years: 'peaceful coexistence'.

After the conclusion of the summit, the foreign ministers of the great powers were scheduled to assemble in October 1955 for a more intensive and prolonged exchange of views in an effort to give concrete form to the vague generalities advanced by the heads of government. But before the opening of the foreign ministers' conference, US Secretary of State Dulles made it clear that he had no intention of granting the Soviets the concessions in Europe that they sought as the price for relaxation of East–West tensions. Convinced that the Soviets had come to the conference out of weakness, Dulles chose to increase the pressure rather than resume the conciliatory initiatives of President Eisenhower (who was convalescing from a heart attack). Dulles lost no opportunity, before and during the conference, to berate the Soviet Union for its oppression of Eastern Europe and to demand that the German problem be settled before the questions of disarmament and East–West security were taken up—a reversal of the Kremlin's well-publicized set of priorities. The meeting dragged on for three weeks, but its fate was sealed by the provocative behaviour of the American secretary, who interpreted the Kremlin's uncharacteristically co-operative manner at Geneva and elsewhere as nothing more than a tactical ploy to lull the West into a false sense of security while it continued to pursue its aggressive goals in secret.

Yet in fact the conciliatory gestures emanating from Moscow in the mid-1950s reflected the beginning of what appears to have been a genuine change of attitude at the highest levels of the Soviet hierarchy. As Khrushchev began his bid for uncontested authority towards the end of 1955, he inaugurated a fundamental reassessment of Soviet policy, foreign as well as domestic. This reassessment rapidly developed into a full-scale indictment of the Stalinist legacy and those who sought to perpetuate it. The ambitious party secretary, sensing the chance for political victory, eagerly embraced the cause of 'de-Stalinization' as a weapon in his campaign for primacy within the collective leadership.

When the new Soviet line was displayed in public, the communist world was shaken to its very foundations. At a closed meeting of the Twentieth Congress of the Communist Party of the Soviet Union in February 1956, Khrushchev delivered a long, rambling address berating Stalin for his repressive policies and calling for the establishment of less arbitrary rules of political procedure in the Soviet Union. Implicit also in his speech was an endorsement of liberalization in the satellite states of Eastern Europe and a relaxation of the Soviet Union's tight grip over their domestic politics. This impression was confirmed two months later by the dissolution of the COMINFORM, which had been created by Stalin at the beginning of the Cold War to promote the unity of the communist parties of Europe and to ensure their subservience to the Soviet state.

It seems likely that Khrushchev's desecration of Stalin's image and his implicit endorsement of liberalization were motivated primarily by his desire to win the internal power struggle against the unreconstructed Stalinists within the Soviet hierarchy; however, the campaign also reflected considerations of foreign and domestic policy beyond the realm of political infighting. Clearly, the leadership faction identified with Khrushchev had come to regard the domestic political repression of the Stalin years as economically counterproductive. In the realm of foreign affairs, this faction had evidently concluded that Stalin's postwar policies had dangerously overextended Soviet power, to the detriment of the USSR's national interests. This was particularly true in Eastern Europe, where his obsession with creating a satellite empire as a protective buffer had united the West in armed opposition to the USSR, incited the defection of Yugoslavia, and led to violent anti-Soviet outbursts within the bloc (including riots in East Berlin in 1953).

Even before Khrushchev's denunciation of Stalin and the dissolution of the COMINFORM, the post-Stalinist leadership had taken tentative steps to relax the economic and political constraints on the Eastern European satellites in an effort to placate their discontented populations. Apparently the objective was to set in motion a gradual, orderly process of retrenchment and liberalization that would remove the most objectionable features of life under Soviet control without changing the satellites' status as ideological confreres and military allies of the Soviet Union. But Khrushchev's dramatic repudiation of the Stalinist legacy nearly transformed this cautious retreat into a rout. The new leader had shattered the myth on which the monolithic unity of the Communist bloc was based—namely, the infallibility of the Soviet Communist Party as the interpreter of Marxist–Leninist doctrine and keystone of the international communist movement. The challenge of communist pluralism that Tito had hurled at Stalin in 1948 now seemed to have gained the tacit endorsement of Stalin's successor, who invited the renegade Yugoslav leader to Moscow and received a lecture from him on the necessity for liberalization in the satellites.

The anti-Stalinist reaction inside the USSR quickly spread to Eastern Europe and became a source of acute danger to Soviet interests there, first in Poland and then in Hungary. In June 1956, labour unrest engulfed the Polish city of Poznań as thousands of workers demonstrated for better economic conditions. By October, this isolated outbreak of social protest had evolved into a nationwide expression of resistance to Soviet interference in Poland's internal affairs. The trials of the Poznań rioters abruptly ended; several communist leaders publicly urged that Soviet officers be removed from the Polish army; and Władysław Gomułka, a proponent of nationalist communism who had been jailed in 1951 by the pro-Soviet puppet regime, rejoined the central committee of the Polish Communist Party.

In October 1956, Khrushchev hastily flew to Warsaw to plead for the continuation of pro-Soviet policies but was rebuffed by Gomułka, whose election as first secretary of the Polish Communist Party the following day marked the advent of 'national communism' in Poland. As Soviet tanks rolled toward Warsaw and the Polish government began to distribute arms to the city's workers, Khrushchev recognized that a larger conflict was imminent and abruptly capitulated. He announced full support for Gomułka, arranged for the return of Soviet troops stationed in Poland to their barracks, and flew back to Moscow. Among the consequences of the 'Polish October' were the removal of many restrictions on individual liberties, the curtailment of Soviet military authority within Poland, and the formation of a de facto alliance between the 'national' Communist Party of Gomułka and the Polish Catholic church headed by Stefen Cardinal Wyszyński, who, like Gomułka, had been released from prison during the upsurge of political unrest. Recognizing that Poland's geographic position between Germany and Russia precluded a totally independent course, Gomułka prudently sought to consolidate the gains of October while affirming his country's loyalty to the Soviet bloc. By preventing the domestic liberalization from getting out of hand and by remaining committed to the goals of Soviet foreign policy, this shrewd Polish nationalist patriot secured a considerable measure of independence for his country and dissuaded the Kremlin from using military means to enforce its will.

Not so prudent, and not so fortunate, was the political leadership of communist Hungary, which had assumed power in October amid circumstances superficially similar to those in Poland. Hungary had been one of the last Eastern European states to succumb to Soviet domination, and the communist system had never succeeded in gaining mass support there. The Communist Party barely managed to cling to power, as its economic policies lowered living standards, provoking widespread resentment. The anti-Stalinist revelations at the Soviet Communist Party congress in 1956 undermined the authority of the hardline pro-Soviet leadership in Budapest; then the events in Poland inspired a popular insurrection in Hungary that rapidly exceeded the limits to dissent that Gomułka had imposed. The new Hungarian prime minister, liberal communist Imre Nagy, promptly formed a coalition government that, for the first time since the advent of the Cold War, included non-communist elements. He then announced his intention to conduct free elections, which were certain to result in the defeat of the unpopular Communist Party. On 30 October, Nagy obtained from the Kremlin a remarkable public pledge of support for Hungary's national independence, which included promises for the immediate removal of the Soviet troops that had been sent to Budapest to quell the incipient insurrection and the eventual evacuation all Soviet military forces from Hungarian territory. For a fleeting moment it appeared that the trend of the previous decade had been reversed, that the liberal policies of Stalin's successors would actually mean a significant degree of political independence for the Soviet Union's East European satellite empire.

But as Soviet troops streamed out of Budapest on 1 November, Nagy took the extraordinarily provocative step of announcing Hungary's withdrawal from the Warsaw Pact. The prospect of a politically independent and militarily neutral Hungary was too much for the Soviet leadership to tolerate. It would establish a dangerous precedent that, if followed by the other East European states, would destroy the buffer zone between the USSR and the West that Moscow had been so determined to establish after the collapse of Hitler's Reich. The 'liberation' of the Soviet East European empire and the 'rollback' of communist power to the Soviet frontier suddenly seemed imminent not because of Western pressure, but because of the explosion of unrestrained nationalism in Hungary.

Thus on 4 November, 250,000 Soviet soldiers returned to Budapest with 5,000 tanks and began a reign of terror. Everything that had been accomplished during the previous month was undone. The Nagy regime was forcibly replaced by a puppet government under János Kádár, whose authority rested entirely on the presence of Soviet troops. In the face of Soviet occupation, some 200,000 Hungarians fled to Western countries such as Canada, which received thousands of the refugees in the autumn of 1956.

The Kremlin abandoned its policy of gradual retrenchment in Eastern Europe, in part because of the dangerous precedent set by Hungary, but also because the simultaneous eruption of a crisis concerning the Suez Canal presented a tempting opportunity. With the United States and its allies preoccupied in Egypt, the Soviet Union could risk a military intervention in Hungary without facing heavy opposition from the Western powers.

THE SUEZ CRISIS

The relaxation of Moscow's grip on Eastern Europe and the recession of its power in the Far East in the years after Stalin's death coincided with the revival of its ambitions in those regions of the Middle East and Southern Asia that were liberating themselves from the colonial domination of Britain and France. Efforts in the 1920s to establish an ideological affinity between Soviet communism and the cause of colonial liberation had met with failure and were virtually abandoned during the Stalin years. But the Leninist doctrine of imperialism—according to which the capitalist nations of the West were driven by the dynamics of their own internal economic development to seek cheap sources of raw materials as well as markets for surplus production in the non-white

regions of the earth—remained a potentially powerful weapon in the ideological arsenal of the Soviet leadership.

In November 1955, this long-dormant policy of anti-imperialism was revived by Khrushchev and Bulganin during an extended sojourn in Southern Asia. The two Soviet leaders denounced the evils of European imperialism, endorsed the principle of national liberation, and promised economic, technical, and military assistance to the newly independent nations that were struggling to overcome the debilitating legacy of European rule. Together, this new Soviet ideological offensive and Washington's efforts to counter it were destined to drag a vast new region—from the eastern Mediterranean to the Indian Ocean—into the Cold War. Just as the collapse of German power in Europe and Japanese power in Asia in 1945 had left power vacuums that invited Soviet–US competition for influence in those areas, the retreat of British and French power in the Middle East and Asia during the 1950s created conditions of political instability that inevitably tempted the two superpowers to intervene and promote their respective interests.

The ruling elites of the newly independent post-colonial nations were confronted with a choice: declare their allegiance to one or the other of the two global coalitions or remain formally non-aligned in the East–West struggle. None of them chose to align themselves with the Soviet bloc, despite determined efforts on the part of the Kremlin. On the other hand, several were induced by the United States and its European allies to join Western-oriented regional security systems that were specifically directed against the Soviet Union and its allies. In the aftermath of France's military defeat in Indochina in 1954, Secretary of State Dulles masterminded a collective defence system for Southeast Asia to prevent Soviet and Chinese expansion in that region. Established on the NATO model (though without provisions for automatic defence collaboration), the Southeast Asia Treaty Organization (SEATO) embraced the US, Britain, France, Australia, New Zealand,[2] Pakistan, Thailand, and the Philippines.[3]

To bridge the geographical gap between NATO in the west and SEATO in the east, the British government responded favourably to a Turkish initiative in the spring of 1955 and joined the Baghdad Pact. The pact was reorganized in 1959 as the Central Treaty Organization (CENTO), after a revolution in Iraq brought an anti-Western regime to power. This regional security organization included Turkey, Iraq, Iran, Pakistan, and Britain (which remained a power in the region by virtue of its military and naval bases in the Persian Gulf). The formation of this Southwest Asian defence system was actively encouraged by the United States, which acquired observer status in its policy-making body. Thus by the mid-1950s, the Atlantic powers had forged a network of alliances around the southern rim of Eurasia that linked many of their former dependencies or client states in the common purpose of containing the Soviet Union in that area. The states of the Middle East and of southwestern and Southeastern Asia that adhered to these Western-sponsored regional pacts received not only the pledge of protection in the event of an external threat but also technical assistance to promote their economic development and enhance their military capability.

The alternative policy of non-alignment in the Cold War was most articulately expressed by the principal spokesman for the developing world, the prime minister of India, Jawaharlal Nehru. Long regarded as Britain's most valuable colonial possession, the Indian subcontinent had obtained its independence in August 1947, following its partition into the predominantly Hindu state of India and the separate predominantly Muslim state of Pakistan. Though embroiled in a costly regional conflict with its Muslim neighbour over the disputed province of Kashmir and plagued by religious strife between its Hindu majority and Muslim minority, Nehru's India aspired to a world role commensurate with its size and population. Its remarkable prime minister, who acted as his own foreign minister throughout his long tenure in office, pursued a policy of non-alignment in the East–West struggle and urged the other newly

independent nations of the southern hemisphere to do likewise.

Nehru did not hesitate to use the Soviet–American competition for influence to extract tangible benefits for his own poverty-stricken country, so long as it was understood that no political strings were attached. In January 1952, he concluded a five-year agreement with Washington for development aid for the subcontinent. Then in December 1953, he signed a five-year trade pact with Moscow, and in June 1955 a long-term agreement for Soviet economic and technical assistance to India. But Nehru's brand of neutralism, which stemmed in large part from his Gandhian abhorrence of war, kept his country out of the game of East–West global rivalry, except insofar as its pacifist influence could be projected as a sort of moral force on the world. The ultimate objective of Nehru and his disciples was to form a cohesive bloc of Third World nations recently emancipated from European rule that would promote the cause of world peace by declining all participation in the Cold War. Such was the message emanating from the first international conference of independent African and Asian nations, held at Bandung, Indonesia, in April 1955.

A very different version of Third World neutralism was espoused by Colonel Gamal Abdel Nasser, the charismatic military officer who had acquired dictatorial power in Egypt by the mid-1950s. Whereas the pacifist Nehru preached non-alignment as a virtuous end in itself, the soldier Nasser saw non-alignment as a means to two objectives, one short-term and the other long-term. His immediate goal was to promote a crash program of economic development and military rearmament for his own country in order to establish it as the dominant power in North Africa and the Middle East in the wake of the Anglo–French withdrawal from that region. His long-term goal was to establish a vast pan-Arab empire, from the Atlantic to the Persian Gulf, under his own leadership.

In pursuit of these objectives Nasser openly played the two superpowers off against one another, soliciting economic and military assistance from both while hinting to each that he was about to strike a bargain with its rival, in order to increase the amount it would offer. In September 1955, he procured from the Communist bloc a pledge of military supplies to equip the Egyptian army in exchange for cotton and rice. From the United States and Britain came a joint offer of financial assistance in the amount of US$70 million for Nasser's pet project: the construction of a new dam at Aswan on the Nile, which would increase Egypt's cultivable land by one-third and its electric power by one-half. Egypt rapidly developed into a microcosm of the East–West competition for influence in the Third World, with American and Soviet missions vying for the privilege of providing the funds that Nasser sought to modernize his country and its backward armed forces.

At the same time the Egyptian leader sought to remove three political forces that blocked the realization of his pan-Arab dreams. The first was French colonial authority in Algeria, which had been forcefully contested since the autumn of 1954 by a guerrilla movement dedicated to the cause of national independence. Unlike France's other overseas territories, Algeria contained a large French colonial population—estimated at more than one million by the 1950s—that had crossed the Mediterranean as early as the mid-nineteenth century to settle in the coastal cities and their agricultural hinterlands. These Christian, Caucasian 'French Algerians' dominated the economic life of the country through their ownership of its urban businesses and its fertile agricultural land, and their monopoly of political power was assured by a complicated electoral system that, although granting legal equality to all citizens, had the practical effect of disenfranchising most of the Arab Muslim majority.

Thus the insurrection against French rule that erupted in 1954 took on the character of a bloody civil war between two peoples of different ethnic and religious heritage, both claiming the right to control the political and economic life of their homeland. To the Muslim Arab insurgents, Nasser furnished all manner of assistance, including sanctuary for their political leaders, thereby acquiring immense prestige in the Arab world as the champion of its liberation from European colonial rule. The granting of independence to France's two other North African possessions, Morocco and Tunisia, in March 1956 appeared to confirm the inevitability of decolonization in the region.

A second obstacle to Nasser's dream was a vestige of colonialism that existed in his own country. Thus in October 1954, he had obtained from Britain a pledge to relinquish its right to maintain a military base on the Suez Canal and to evacuate the canal zone entirely within 20 months. In exchange, Egypt guaranteed freedom of navigation through the waterway and promised to permit the re-entry of British military forces in the canal zone in the event of an armed attack by an outside power against any Arab state or Turkey. By the summer of 1956, therefore, Anglo–French colonial authority in the Arab world had largely disappeared, and the remnant in Algeria was clearly nearing its end. The future seemed to hold the promise of Arab self-determination and unity after so many years of subservience and disunity under various European masters and their strategy of divide and conquer; such, at least, was the vision of the ambitious soldier-statesman in Cairo.

The third impediment to the realization of Nasser's pan-Arabist dream was the state of Israel, formed in May 1948 out of the territory of Palestine, a territory that, since 1920, had been administered by Britain under a mandate from the League of Nations. A resolution by the UN General Assembly in November 1947 proposing the partition of Palestine into two sovereign political entities, one Jewish and the other Arab, had been rejected by the neighbouring Arab states. Thus the proclamation of the Jewish state of Israel, upon the termination of the British directive, had resulted in a war between Israel and the Arab states, which in the summer of 1949 was temporarily interrupted by an uneasy truce.

To its Jewish inhabitants and their coreligionists abroad, the new state of Israel represented the fulfillment of a 2,000-year-old dream of returning to the land of their ancestors. In more concrete terms, it offered a haven from the persecution they had faced in Europe. The political movement of Zionism, founded in the 1890s by Austrian journalist Theodor Herzl in response to the resurgence of European anti-Semitism, was based on a single principle that guided the creators of Israel in 1948 and its defenders thereafter: the conviction, reinforced by the indelible memory of the Holocaust, that the Jews scattered throughout the world would never enjoy security in any nation where they constituted an ethnic minority. Their only hope lay in the establishment of a state populated, controlled, and defended by Jews. But to the proponents of pan-Arabism, the emergence of a state dominated by citizens of European descent in the very heart of the Arab world signified a return to the colonial past and posed a serious challenge to the cause of Arab unity. Thus Nasser took the lead in organizing the Arab states in opposition to Israel, barring Israeli ships from passing through the Suez Canal or using the Straits of Tiran, and providing bases for the Arab refugees from Palestine who launched hit-and-run raids across the Israeli border.

In the summer and fall of 1956, these disparate developments—Soviet–American competition for influence in the Middle East, Egyptian efforts to hasten the departure of Anglo–French power from the Arab world, and the Arab–Israeli conflict—converged in an international crisis that was to damage the solidarity of the Western alliance at the very moment when the unity of the Soviet bloc was being shaken by the events in Poland and Hungary. In June 1956, Britain formally terminated its 74-year military occupation of the Suez Canal as stipulated in the agreement of October 1954, leaving Egypt with full responsibility for the canal's defence. On 20 July, the US government, annoyed at Nasser's increasing dependence on military assistance from the Soviet bloc and attentive to pro-Israel sentiment in the Congress, abruptly withdrew its offer to finance the construction of the Aswan Dam. Stung by this threat to his personal prestige and his plans for Egypt's economic development, Nasser retaliated six days later by nationalizing the Suez Canal Company (which remained under the financial control of British banking interests) and by announcing his

intention to use the revenue from the canal to defray the costs of building the dam. After three months of fruitless diplomatic efforts to persuade Nasser to accept multinational control of this vital artery, through which the bulk of European trade and Middle Eastern oil shipments passed, the British prime minister, Anthony Eden, concluded that the only recourse was military force.

Eden also hoped to topple Nasser, whom he had come to see as a second Hitler. Nasser's prior support for the Algerian rebellion against France and the Palestinian guerrilla campaign against Israel guaranteed that Eden's scheme would find sympathetic audiences in Paris and Tel Aviv. Without consulting their American ally in advance, the British and French governments arranged an elaborate hoax involving three nations and designed to achieve for each its own objectives at Egypt's expense. First, by prior arrangement the Israeli army attacked Egypt on 29 October 1956, and within a few days had routed the Egyptian army on the Sinai peninsula and ominously approached the Suez Canal. On 5 November, British and French paratroops were dropped in Suez and Port Said for the ostensible purpose of separating the two armies and protecting the canal in the interests of its international clientele. But the real goal was the forcible replacement of the Nasser regime with one that would not threaten British interests in the canal, French authority in Algeria, or Israel's security along its western frontier.

The Suez intervention failed not because of Egyptian military resistance—which crumbled in the face of Israeli tanks in the Sinai and Anglo–French paratroopers along the canal—but rather because of the unexpected and vigorous opposition of the United States. For reasons related as much to personality conflicts between Eden and US Secretary of State Dulles as to divergent national interests, Washington exerted sufficient pressure on its two European allies to compel a humiliating withdrawal of the three military forces that had converged on the Suez Canal. Perhaps more surprising was the opposition of the government in Ottawa, which abandoned its traditional support for Britain and joined the US (albeit more quietly) in censuring the invasion. Helping to bring about the swift end to the crisis was Canadian Minister of External Affairs Lester B. Pearson, who lobbied tirelessly for the creation of a United Nations emergency peacekeeping force to be dispatched to the region. Advance members of the UN Emergency Force (UNEF), led by Canadian General E.L.M. Burns and containing a number of Canadian soldiers, arrived in mid-November, shortly after the ceasefire was reached on 6 November. Pearson later received the Nobel Peace Prize in recognition of his pivotal role in settling the crisis.

The Suez fiasco had long-range consequences for the future of the international balance of power. It spelled the end of Anglo–French pretensions to an imperial role in the Middle East. It undermined the political cohesion of the Atlantic alliance by showing Europe that it could no longer pursue

foreign policies without Washington's blessing. It bolstered the prestige of Nasser in the Arab world and solidified his reputation as the spokesman for the developing nations in their struggle to eradicate the last vestiges of European colonialism. The Soviet Union—which had intervened on Egypt's behalf to the point of threatening nuclear retaliation against Britain and France at the height of the crisis—acquired a reputation as the champion of Arab aspirations at the expense of the Western powers and their Israeli ally. Thus, just as the Soviet Union's undisputed predominance in Eastern Europe appeared threatened by nationalist agitation in Poland and Hungary, the Suez affair enabled the Kremlin to renew its ideological offensive in the Third World under the most favourable of circumstances. Moreover, while the liberalizing tendencies within the Communist

Canadian members of the United Nations Emergency Force watch over the border between Egypt and Israel. Department of National Defence/Library and Archives Canada/PA-122737.

bloc were abruptly curbed in Eastern Europe (through Polish prudence in Warsaw and Soviet repression in Budapest), Washington's abandonment of its allies at Suez strengthened those Western European forces—particularly strong in France—that favoured the pursuit of military, diplomatic, and economic policies independent of the United States.

The transatlantic tensions generated by the Suez Crisis were fed by Western Europe's mounting anxiety about the reliability of US military protection against the Soviet menace. The nuclear deterrence strategy embraced by the Eisenhower administration consisted of the threat of a massive nuclear strike against Soviet population centres in the event of a conventional Soviet military advance

THE CONGO CRISIS

Like the Suez Crisis, the Congo Crisis tested the ability of the United Nations to resolve regional conflicts fuelled by resistance to imperialism, competing economic interests, and Cold War rivalries. The imperial power in this case was Belgium, which had been involved in the region since the 1870s. King Leopold established the Congo Free State as his personal territory in 1885, and (even by contemporary standards) his administration was terribly oppressive. In response to reports of widespread atrocities, the Belgian government designated the Congo an official Belgian colony in 1908; however, this did little to improve social conditions, as Belgian officials focused on extracting the Congo's enormous mineral wealth and neglected its people. Colonial authority crumbled in the face of clashes between Congolese nationalists and government forces in 1959 and early 1960. As a result, Belgian authorities agreed to independence in June 1960.

The leaders of the new Republic of Congo, President Joseph Kasavubu and Prime Minister Patrice Lumumba, made preparations for a national government, but they were unable to establish control over the entire nation. In July 1960 the army mutinied, and the province of Katanga declared independence. Led by Moise Tshombe, secessionist forces requested military assistance from Belgium. Belgian troops were dispatched to Katanga to protect Belgian citizens and property, while Western companies worked to protect their economic interests. In response, Kasavubu and Lumumba appealed to the United Nations for military aid. With the support of the

Security Council, UN Secretary-General Dag Hammarskjöld authorized the creation of the United Nations Organization in the Congo (ONUC), a military force supplied by non-aligned countries.

In the meantime, the Soviets worked to increase their influence in the region, and Prime Minister Lumumba accepted their military aid. In August 1960 Lumumba's forces failed to capture Katanga, and Kasavubu dismissed the prime minister from office. Lumumba was arrested in December, and in January 1961 soldiers loyal to Congolese Army Chief of Staff Colonel Joseph Mobutu tortured and murdered him. Viewing Lumumba as a threat to Western interests, Belgium and the United States supported Mobutu, while forces loyal to Lumumba continued to fight in the north of the country, assisted by the Soviets. As the Congo teetered on the brink of civil war, the UN authorized ONUC to use offensive military force. When peace negotiations stalled in August 1961, ONUC launched an offensive against Katangan troops and Belgian mercenaries, eventually forcing Tshombe into temporary exile. After the Congolese government regained control over Katanga, ONUC troops were withdrawn in 1964. In 1965 Joseph Mobutu took power through a coup d'état, and over the next three decades Mobutu's pro-Western regime became notorious for widespread corruption and mismanagement. In 1971 he named the country Zaire and himself Mobutu Sese Seko. The Congo Crisis bequeathed a troubled legacy: although the country remained intact, the Congolese people continued to suffer under authoritarian rule.

into Western Europe. The credibility of this plan rested on the capability of the United States to unleash its nuclear arsenal without fear of a Soviet counterblow against its own cities. During the first decade of the Cold War the Soviet Union had made considerable progress in narrowing the lead of the United States in the nuclear arms race; it exploded its first atomic bomb in 1949 (four years after the US) and its first hydrogen bomb in 1953 (only nine months after the US).

Despite these achievements, the USSR lacked both a network of bases in the western hemisphere from which to threaten American territory with nuclear bombardment and an intercontinental delivery system to transport nuclear weapons from Soviet territory to targets in North America. During the second half of the 1950s, however, the Soviet Union did acquire such a delivery system, and it promised to neutralize the American deterrent. By mid-1955 it had perfected a long-range bomber with the round-trip capacity to strike at American territory, but the United States possessed five times as many such planes, as well as an efficient radar system to detect enemy aircraft. The major Soviet breakthrough in nuclear delivery systems came as a consequence of advances in rocketry associated with the early efforts at space exploration. On 4 October 1957, the Kremlin astonished the world with its announcement that Soviet scientists had successfully launched the first human-made space satellite, the Sputnik. A rocket capable of projecting a metal object into orbit around the earth would obviously be capable of delivering a nuclear warhead to a target anywhere on the surface of the globe. Already in August of the same year the Soviet news agency Tass had announced the first successful test of an intercontinental ballistic missile (ICBM). The US quickly followed suit, successfully testing a 5,000-mile range Atlas ICBM in December 1957 and then launching its first space satellite, the Explorer, in February 1958. But until the Americans could construct a large number of ICBMs, they would be forced to rely on obsolete long-range bombers (which, unlike the ICBMs, were vulnerable to interception by enemy aircraft before reaching

their targets) and on intermediate-range ballistic missiles (ICBMs) launched from bases in friendly countries close to the Soviet Union.

As it turned out, the United States soon erased the Soviet lead in the technology of nuclear delivery systems. By the early 1960s, it had begun to deploy its own ICBM system, had upgraded its long-range bomber force, and had expanded its arsenal of medium-range bombers and ICBMs based in allied countries. Anxiety in Washington about a 'missile gap' during the presidential campaign of 1960 proved to be unwarranted, largely because Soviet nuclear technology was not up to the ambitious task assigned to it by the Kremlin. But the fact remained that, for the first time since the advent of the atomic age, the United States was vulnerable to a massive nuclear attack using missiles launched from Soviet territory. A US nuclear response to a conventional Soviet thrust in Western Europe (whether by means of long-range bombers and ICBMs on American territory or medium-range bombers and ICBMs based on Allied soil) could severely threaten the United States by leaving its principal population centres exposed to annihilation.

From this ominous transformation of the nuclear balance, Washington's European partners drew two conclusions, both of which were destined to create serious tensions in the Atlantic partnership. The first was the growing suspicion that in a genuine crisis the United States would be unlikely to sacrifice its own cities for the sake of defending Western Europe against a conventional Soviet attack. The second was that by consenting to the deployment of medium-range US missiles and bombers on their own territory, as several of the NATO allies had been persuaded to do by the end of the 1950s, the nations of Western Europe would be exposing their own populations to total nuclear destruction in the event of a Soviet–American nuclear exchange. The realization that the densely populated countries of Western Europe that hosted American bomber bases or missile installations would be automatic targets for any surprise attack by the Soviet Union provoked widespread discontent within the Western bloc.

In England, which had launched its own modest nuclear armament program in the mid-1950s and integrated it with the much larger American deterrent force, groups such as the Campaign for Nuclear Disarmament and the Committee of 100 loudly demanded withdrawal from NATO, the removal of American air bases and missile sites, and the abandonment of British nuclear weapons. On the continent, official voices were raised in favour of a reciprocal disengagement of US and Soviet forces from their forward positions in Central Europe in order to avert a superpower confrontation in that region that could lead to a nuclear holocaust. At the same time, skepticism about the reliability of the American 'nuclear umbrella' prompted some Western leaders to call for greater European efforts towards self-defence and independence from the United States.

THE PROBLEM OF BERLIN

The disarray of the Western alliance in the wake of Suez and Sputnik emboldened the recently entrenched leadership group in the Kremlin to test the resolve of the United States and its European partners at their most vulnerable point. That point was West Berlin—a perpetual irritant for the Soviet Union and its East European satellites and militarily indefensible by the small US, British, and French garrisons stationed there. The former capital of Hitler's Reich once again became the focus of East–West tension in November 1958, when Khrushchev abruptly demanded the evacuation of all four occupation forces from Berlin within six months, failing which the Soviet Union would unilaterally transfer its functions in the city to its East German puppets sitting in the Berlin suburb of Pankow.

Since the Allies had neither diplomatic relations nor an agreement regarding access to Berlin with the Pankow regime, acceptance of the Soviet ultimatum would have isolated the Western enclave from its protectors and doubtless led to its absorption by East Germany. The Kremlin reopened the 'Berlin question' that had lain dormant for a decade after the abortive blockade of 1948–9

because of its uneasiness about the growing military power of West Germany, which was well on its way to possessing the strongest European military contingent within NATO. The enthusiasm with which the fervently anti-communist chancellor of the Federal Republic, Konrad Adenauer, and his aggressive young defence minister, Franz-Josef Strauss, endorsed the tough line of Dulles and welcomed the presence of US ground forces and nuclear weapons on West German territory provoked alarm in Moscow. Added to the ominous implications of the German–American military partnership for the Soviet Union were the devastating consequences of the West German economic 'miracle' for the economically depressed East German state. The prospect of a much higher standard of living, not to mention a less repressive political climate, had induced more than two million East Germans to escape to the Federal Republic during the first decade of its existence. The inordinately large proportion of highly skilled professionals in this mass migration jeopardized the economic recovery of the German Democratic Republic. By 1958, the long border separating the two Germanies had been effectively sealed. But the brain drain continued through the last remaining hole in the Iron Curtain: the unobstructed passage between the eastern and western sectors of Berlin.

The Khrushchev ultimatum on Berlin was intended in part to remove this challenge to Soviet control over its East European satellite empire and East German opportunities for economic development. But it was also designed to serve two more ambitious purposes. The first was to disrupt the increasingly intimate connection between the United States and West Germany. The Adenauer regime had come to regard Berlin as the pre-eminent test of Washington's determination to defend the security interests of Bonn. The Western allies had only token garrisons in Berlin, outnumbered five to one by communist forces nearby, and if they could be pressured into surrendering, the emergent Washington–Bonn axis would be severely damaged, perhaps beyond repair. The second objective was the disengagement of the other NATO allies from Washington's embrace. At the height of the Berlin crisis, in the winter of 1958–9, Moscow explicitly warned half a dozen western European nations that their military partnership with the United States guaranteed their total destruction in the event of a nuclear war between the two superpowers. This warning was unmistakably intended to discourage the European members of NATO from agreeing to the establishment of medium-range missile bases on their own soil.

The Western powers unanimously rejected the Soviet ultimatum, reaffirming their access rights to Berlin and refusing to recognize the transfer of Moscow's authority to the East German regime. Faced with this united front, the Kremlin finally backed down in March 1959. Khrushchev revoked the deadline for the transfer of sovereignty to East Germany, acknowledged Allied rights in Berlin, and proposed a summit meeting to settle the Berlin issue once and for all. By the summer of 1959, Britain, Italy, and Greece had formally authorized the establishment of bases for medium-range US missiles on their territory. At a conference of foreign ministers in Geneva that August, the US and Soviet governments announced that Chairman Khrushchev and President Eisenhower had agreed to exchange state visits. Apparently the Berlin crisis had been resolved by the Soviet government's unilateral retreat.

During the last two weeks of September 1959, Khrushchev became the first Soviet leader to visit the United States. After a whirlwind tour of the hinterland, he met with Eisenhower for a series of private discussions at Camp David, the presidential retreat in the Maryland mountains. Nothing of substance seems to have come from these confidential talks, except for a tacit agreement to put the Berlin problem on ice pending a summit conference of the great powers the following year. Nevertheless, the state-controlled Soviet press began to wax lyrical about the 'spirit of Camp David', just as it had celebrated the 'spirit of Geneva' after the inconsequential exchange of pleasantries at the summit four years earlier.

The new tenor of cordiality between East and West greatly improved the prospects for genuine détente as the 1950s drew to a close. The death of Dulles—the pre-eminent representative of the Cold War mentality in Washington—in May 1959 seemed to signify the end of the era of Soviet–American confrontation. The moratorium on the Berlin question provided a welcome respite from a tension-filled dispute. In a speech to the UN General Assembly in New York, Khrushchev unveiled a proposal for general and complete disarmament within four years—an appealing, if unrealistic, solution to the arms race that the Kremlin would periodically reiterate—and a few months later, in an apparent gesture of goodwill, announced that the Soviet Union would reduce its standing armed forces by a third. From the brink of conflict over Berlin, the two superpowers had advanced a considerable distance toward mutual accommodation.

The summit conference that was to turn the conciliatory spirit of Camp David into a comprehensive settlement of the remaining Cold War issues was scheduled to open in Paris in the spring of 1960. On 5 May, however, 11 days before the discussions were to begin, the Kremlin announced that a high-altitude US spy plane had been shot down over Soviet territory on the first of the month. After a clumsy effort by the State Department to deny the intelligence-gathering purposes of the U-2 flight, President Eisenhower accepted full responsibility for the incident. Khrushchev thereupon announced that he would not participate in the Paris meeting unless Eisenhower formally apologized for the violation of Soviet air space, punished those responsible, and promised to discontinue the flights. Since the intelligence-gathering function of these high-altitude flights was soon to be taken over by satellites orbiting the earth, it was not difficult for the president to agree to the last of those demands. But for reasons of domestic politics in an election year, as well as international prestige, Eisenhower refused to apologize, let alone to penalize subordinates who had merely followed instructions. This gave Khrushchev the pretext he had apparently sought to close down the Paris summit on the day it opened, and to revoke Eisenhower's invitation to the Soviet Union.

The Kremlin had been aware of the U-2 reconnaissance flights across Soviet territory since their inception in the summer of 1956, but had been unable to prevent them because their altitude put them beyond the range of Soviet fighters and surface-to-air missiles (SAMs).[4] Why, then, did Khrushchev seize on this relatively trivial incident as an excuse to sabotage the summit and cancel Eisenhower's goodwill visit to Moscow, both of which he had actively promoted? Khrushchev had come under intense pressure from the communist camp to reverse the policy of rapprochement with the West that he had inaugurated in the late 1950s. A hard-line faction within the Politburo strongly opposed a negotiated settlement of the German problem in general and the Berlin issue in particular, for fear that any concessions would further undermine the USSR's hegemonic position in Eastern Europe, which had been challenged four years earlier in Warsaw and Budapest. At the same time, the communist regime in China had become openly critical of Khrushchev's conciliatory posture in world affairs. In the eyes of the Maoist leadership in Beijing, the prospect of a Soviet–American rapprochement in Europe violated the Marxist–Leninist revolutionary principles, of which the Chinese communists had become the most orthodox defenders. Instead of pursuing the struggle for the triumph of world communism, Khrushchev was seeking peaceful coexistence through disarmament negotiations and summit talks with the enemy.

To counter this apparent renunciation of the messianic goals of world communism, Beijing let it be known after the Camp David talks that it would not be bound by any international agreements that the two superpowers and their partners might make. Reinforcing this ideological dispute was Beijing's perception that Moscow had failed to give it adequate support on several important issues, including its border dispute with India (a country with which the USSR maintained excellent relations); its campaign to take back the Chinese Nationalist offshore haven of Formosa (which enjoyed the military protection of the United States); and its goal of acquiring

nuclear weapons (the Soviets had promised in 1957 to supply a prototype, but Khrushchev had reneged in June 1959). Herein lay the beginnings of the 'Sino–Soviet split' that was soon to shatter the unity of the Communist bloc.

The opposition of Soviet hardliners, combined with the Chinese threat to challenge the Soviet leadership of the Communist bloc, had placed Khrushchev in a vulnerable position as the Paris summit conference approached. The U-2 incident fortuitously played into the hands of those in Moscow and Beijing who had been resisting a comprehensive settlement in Europe. Eisenhower, whom Khrushchev had praised on his return from Camp David as a man who 'sincerely wants, like us, to end the Cold War', was suddenly exposed as an organizer of spy missions for which, when caught red-handed, he lacked the grace to apologize. In light of Eisenhower's damaged credibility, it is also probable that Khrushchev preferred to await the change of administration in Washington that was due the following winter. In any case, within a week of the Paris meeting's premature demise, the man who during his US tour had virtually declared the Cold War to be over was threatening to make a separate peace treaty with East Germany, warning European nations hosting American bases that they were inviting nuclear destruction, and flying to Beijing to reassure his Chinese critics.

Khrushchev maintained his aggressive posture for the rest of Eisenhower's tenure in office. He seemed to take every opportunity to challenge the West, no doubt to disarm his critics at home and in Beijing but perhaps also to confront the incoming administration in Washington, whoever might be at its head, with a set of foreign-policy crises from the start. Once again, the temptation to fish in the troubled waters of the Third World proved irresistible. In Laos—a landlocked kingdom in Southeast Asia formerly attached to the French Indochinese empire—the Soviet Union sent massive military supplies to the pro-communist guerrillas then challenging the authority of the right-wing government forces trained and equipped by the United States. Khrushchev even took the gamble of extending Soviet influence to the heart of Sub-Saharan Africa, large portions of which were in the process of obtaining national independence from the European colonial powers.

By 1960, the membership of the United Nations had doubled, as newly independent states emerged from the ashes of the European colonial empires in the southern hemisphere. No longer was it an exclusive club dominated by the powerful white nations of the West; the world organization was becoming a forum for newly sovereign political entities from Africa and Asia. Combined with the nations of the Communist bloc, these former victims of European imperialism formed a solid majority in the General Assembly that might prove useful in forthcoming diplomatic contests with the United States and its allies in that forum of world opinion.

Despite the emergence of the post-colonial developing world as an arena for Soviet–US competition, the centre of the Cold War remained in Europe; the centre of Europe remained Germany; and the centre of Germany remained Berlin. Accordingly, it was in Berlin that Khrushchev strove to regain the initiative in foreign affairs that had been lost amid the abortive efforts to establish a foothold in Africa and to reorganize the United Nations. We know enough about the simmering discontent within the Soviet leadership and the increasingly bitter recriminations from Beijing to surmise that Khrushchev urgently needed a triumph in foreign policy to shore up his faltering position at home and within the international communist movement. The hemorrhage of East Germany's skilled labour force through the Berlin gap would continue so long as the Western allies occupied the western sector of the city. With the new, untested administration of John F. Kennedy recently installed in Washington, Khrushchev resolved once and for all to settle the Berlin issue on Moscow's terms. He took the occasion of a Soviet–American summit conference at Vienna in June 1961—the fourth such face-to-face meeting since the start of the Cold War—to confront the new US president with another ultimatum demanding a German peace treaty, an end to the

occupation regime, and the transformation of West Berlin into a free city. Upon his return to Moscow he set the end of the year as the deadline and announced a one-third increase in the military budget, to underline his determination to dislodge the Allied garrisons from Berlin.

On 25 July, Kennedy responded in kind, reaffirming the US commitment to defend West Berlin by armed force if necessary and requesting congressional authorization for an additional US$3 billion increase in defence expenditures and the doubling of draft calls. At the end of the tension-filled summer of 1961, the Kremlin announced that it was resuming the nuclear tests that had been suspended—by mutual agreement of the USSR, the United States, and Britain—since the fall of 1958. A series of Soviet nuclear tests in the autumn was capped by the detonation of a 58-megaton device—3,500 times more powerful than the Hiroshima bomb. American entrepreneurs advertised family-size fallout shelters to protect against the nuclear radiation that was sure to come, and to avoid falling behind in the arms race, the US and Britain resumed testing their own nuclear weapons.

In the meantime, however, the Soviets and their East German clients had improvised a temporary solution to the Berlin problem that avoided the risk of a nuclear showdown. On the morning of 13 August, East German police sealed the border separating the two sectors of the city and began constructing a concrete-and-barbed-wire barrier that eventually blocked all movement between East and West Berlin except through a handful of closely guarded checkpoints. The Western response to this unilateral nullification of intercity access arrangements was confined to diplomatic protests and a token reinforcement of Allied garrisons in the western sector. No attempt was made to remove the wall, which, though an embarrassing symbol of East Germany's prison-like status, served its purpose admirably: the torrent of East German refugees pouring through Berlin to the West was reduced to a trickle. More than 103,000 had fled during the first six months of 1961 alone. In succeeding years the annual outflow averaged 6,000.

It soon became clear that the Western allies had acquiesced in the *fait accompli* of the Berlin Wall, and on 17 October, Khrushchev again lifted his deadline for the resolution of the related issues of Germany and Berlin. Soviet and East German authorities would allow the Allied military forces in the Western sector to remain unharassed and would not interfere with their access to the Federal Republic across the East German autobahn. On 12 June 1964, the Soviet Union concluded a bilateral treaty with East Germany formally recognizing its sovereignty but without challenging the special status of West Berlin or the presence of the Allied military forces stationed there. Never again would the anomalous position of Germany and Berlin seriously disturb relations between the two superpowers. In order to avoid a nuclear confrontation, Washington and Moscow had become reconciled to what now seemed to be the permanent partition of the German nation and its former capital.

But the Berlin solution fell far short of the spectacular success in foreign policy that Khrushchev needed in order to stifle the discontents within the Communist bloc. Although the problem of East German emigration had been resolved, the Americans had stood firm in Berlin, with the unqualified support of their NATO allies (including even the increasingly independent-minded French regime of President Charles de Gaulle). The Kremlin's resumption of nuclear testing may be seen as serving two purposes: to compensate for the USSR's obvious strategic inferiority and vulnerability to the United States (as revealed by the U-2 flights over Soviet territory and later confirmed when the Pentagon revealed the small number of ICBMs the Soviets had managed to produce since Sputnik) and to intimidate the increasingly hard-headed Kennedy and the increasingly recalcitrant Mao Zedong. The resumption of nuclear testing in the fall of 1961 shattered the hopes for strategic arms control that had been nurtured by the 1958 moratorium and kept alive by the atomic disarmament negotiations conducted in Geneva. Thus instead of beginning a comprehensive resolution of East–West differences, the stalemate over Berlin heightened international tensions and rekindled Soviet–American competition in nuclear weaponry.

It was in this context of strategic rivalry that Khrushchev took his most reckless gamble in foreign policy, one that brought the two superpowers to the brink of a nuclear exchange that would surely have annihilated large proportions of the people inside and outside both countries. In one of the most notable ironies in the history of international relations, the confrontation that came closest to transforming the Cold War into a nuclear Armageddon took place not in Europe or the Far East, but in the one region of the world that had been entirely off-limits to Soviet influence because of its proximity to and historic connections with the United States.

THE UNITED STATES AND LATIN AMERICA IN THE CRISIS YEARS

From 1945 to the beginning of the 1960s, the position of the United States vis-à-vis the 20 independent republics of Latin America was one of undisputed domination. The Second World War and its aftermath had confirmed the economic pre-eminence of the US in the western hemisphere. Europe's commercial and financial stake in Latin America had declined dramatically as Britain, Germany, and France were depleted of human and material resources during the war and thereafter struggled to rebuild their shattered economies. In the meantime, the economic systems of most Latin American countries had been closely tied to the expanding economy of the US as it geared up for and eventually fought the global war against Germany and Japan. American military power was projected southward with the explicit consent of the Latin American states to protect them from Axis aggression. As the end of the war approached, many Latin American governments expressed concern that Washington's new global responsibilities, and its sponsorship of a new international organization for the maintenance of peace and security, would undermine the solidarity as well as the effectiveness of the inter-American regional security system that had been forged during the war. To allay Latin American anxieties on this score, US delegates at the founding conference of the United Nations in the spring of 1945 inserted a provision in the UN charter authorizing the formation of regional security organizations with powers of enforcement that would not be subject to the approval of the Security Council.

With the advent of the Cold War in Europe, the United States and its Latin American clients moved to give concrete form to the informal regional security arrangements agreed to during the war. The Inter-American Treaty of Reciprocal Assistance, signed in Rio de Janeiro in September 1947 and eventually ratified by all 21 American republics, established a permanent defensive alliance against aggression originating both outside and inside the hemisphere. In the spring of 1948, this military alliance gained a formal political structure when the loosely organized Pan-American Union was transformed into the Organization of American States (OAS). Thereafter, the peacekeeping machinery of the OAS proved unexpectedly effective in settling a number of disputes between member states such as Nicaragua and Costa Rica (in 1949, 1955, and 1959) and Nicaragua and Honduras (in 1957).

While the Latin American members of the OAS regarded the inter-American system as a multilateral mechanism for the maintenance of regional peace and security, the United States came to see it in much narrower and more explicit terms, particularly after the outbreak of the Korean War sparked a new American preoccupation with the spread of communism throughout the world. From Washington's perspective, the OAS–Rio Pact structure was designed to serve the same purpose as the other regional security systems that the US had sponsored: to defend the non-communist world against the expansionist ambitions of the Soviet bloc.

We have seen how the fear of communist insurgency in the war-ravaged countries of Western Europe had led the United States to provide large amounts of aid intended to cure the socio-economic ills on which communism was thought to thrive. Similar problems had existed much longer in Latin America, on a much larger scale, and its countries' governments had urgently requested help to address them; yet there was to be no Marshall Plan for the western hemisphere in the early post-war years. Although Secretary Marshall had pledged at the Rio Conference that serious attention would be given to Latin American pleas for development assistance, no progress was made in the few discussions of inter-American economic affairs in subsequent years. Whereas the Latin American countries hoped to secure US government assistance after the fashion of the European Recovery Program, Washington insisted that any development aid would have to come from private sources. Whereas the Latin states called for international agreements to stabilize world commodity prices in order to halt the drastic price fluctuations of the region's principal exports, the US consistently opposed any measures that would interfere with the operation of the free market as a price-setting mechanism.

All the Latin American countries experienced economic stagnation after the Second World War, partly because of long-term structural problems and partly because the war-induced demand for their raw materials came to an abrupt end after 1945. Economic problems exacerbated the acute social tensions that stemmed from extreme inequalities in the distribution of land and capital. The landowning, commercial, and financial oligarchies, in alliance with the military caste and the hierarchy of the Roman Catholic Church, maintained a monopoly on political authority and resisted social and economic reforms that would curtail their wealth and power to the benefit of the landless, impoverished *campesinos* in the countryside and the small but growing working class in the cities. Together, these conditions formed a classic prescription for social instability, and many of the Latin American republics suffered a seemingly endless cycle of popular upheaval and repressive conservative reaction in the years after 1945. Given the extensive involvement of US firms in the economies of Latin America, not to mention the US government's expanded security commitments in the region, it is scarcely surprising that the domestic turmoil to the south eventually engaged Washington's attention .

This situation is precisely what happened in the Central American republic of Guatemala. After the 13-year dictatorship of General Jorge Ubico was overthrown in 1944, a mild-mannered university professor named Juan Arevélo was elected president on a program of sweeping social renovation. From 1945 to 1951, Arevélo undertook to narrow the gap between rich and poor as well as to improve the educational and economic conditions of the large indigenous population through a series of government-sponsored reforms that antagonized landowners, foreign investors, and military officers alike. In March 1951, Arevélo was succeeded by the fiery spokesman for his party's left wing, Colonel Jacobo Arbenz Guzmán. After pushing a far-reaching program of agrarian reform through the Guatemalan parliament, Arbenz announced his intention to expropriate 90,000 hectares of undeveloped land belonging to the American-owned United Fruit Company and redistribute it to the peasantry. As United Fruit solicited the support of the US government against the Guatemalan regime, the new Eisenhower administration was becoming alarmed at what its ambassador in Guatemala City described as the mounting influence of communists in Arbenz's entourage.

By the beginning of 1954, representatives of United Fruit as well as agents of the United States' Central Intelligence Agency (CIA) were approaching right-wing Guatemalan exiles in Nicaragua and Honduras with schemes to overthrow Arbenz while Washington organized a boycott of arms to his country. When evidence surfaced that the Guatemalan leader had tried to circumvent the boycott by contracting for a shipment of 2,000 tonnes of light arms from Czechoslovakia, Washington had the pretext it needed to prevent the spread of Communist bloc influence to its own backyard. In June, the American-backed Guatemalan exiles re-entered the country (with air support from planes piloted by CIA operatives)

and instigated a military coup that toppled Arbenz and sent him into exile. The new military junta promptly revoked most of the land reforms enacted by its predecessor and launched a campaign of repression against left-wing organizations in the country.

The United States had intervened in Guatemala with the tacit acquiescence of the OAS, which had issued a declaration during the Caracas Conference in March 1954 condemning the domination of any member state by 'the international communist movement' as a 'threat to the sovereignty and political independence' of them all. But most of the civilian-ruled republics opposed the inclusion of anti-communism in the definition of pan-Americanism, and even some of the military dictatorships had to be threatened with American economic reprisals before they would vote. The prospect of US interference in Latin America, notwithstanding the principle of non-intervention enshrined in the OAS charter, remained a much greater source of concern to the Latin republics than the remote danger of a communist takeover. The CIA-sponsored coup in Guatemala suggested that the principle of non-intervention, for which Latin American governments had fought so hard and so long, had become a casualty of the Cold War.

As a symbol of the resurgence of unilateral, if covert, US interference in the internal affairs of Latin American states, the overthrow of Arbenz sparked widespread resentment among nationalist groups throughout the region. Left-wing political agitators pointed to the central role played by United Fruit in the Guatemalan episode to mobilize mass support by attributing Latin America's chronic economic problems to the nefarious influence of US corporations operating there. The extent of Latin American discontent with Washington came to light in dramatic fashion when Vice-President Richard Nixon, on a goodwill tour to eight Latin American countries in May 1958, was confronted by hostile demonstrations at every stop. In Caracas, Venezuela, his motorcade was almost overwhelmed by angry, stone-throwing mobs hissing: 'Yankee go home.'

The Nixon tour alerted Washington to the simmering grievances that the Latin American masses harboured against the United States. A few weeks later, an imaginative proposal by Brazilian President Juscelino Kubitschek, suggesting a joint program of economic development for the hemisphere, caught the eye of US officials alarmed by the upsurge of anti-American sentiments south of the border. The final year of the Eisenhower presidency was marked by a notable modification of US economic policy in relation to Latin America. Washington finally withdrew its opposition to the formation of a government-funded regional financing agency (a long-standing objective of several Latin American states). In October 1960, the Inter-American Development Bank (IADB) was established to disburse development loans to Latin American countries. Though a mere drop in the bucket compared to the region's enormous financing requirements, the advent of IADB lending was an important symbolic departure from Washington's previous insistence on referring Latin American borrowers to the private capital markets.

The Kennedy administration promptly transformed this tentative Eisenhower initiative into a full-fledged program of hemispheric economic development along the lines originally proposed by Kubitschek in 1958. In his inaugural address on 20 January 1961, the new president spoke of forming an 'alliance for progress' with the republics to the south, and in March he presented representatives from the Latin American states with a detailed proposal for US assistance to the region. The Alliance for Progress was formally brought into existence at the Inter-American Economic and Social Conference in Punta del Este, Uruguay, the following August. As originally conceived, the plan responded to two concerns that the Latin American countries had been voicing for decades. First, and by far most important, it pledged US$20 billion in US government aid over 10 years to promote the economic development of Latin America and to raise its per capita income by 2.5 per cent annually. Second, the United States agreed to seek means of preventing the wild fluctuation of foreign exchange earnings from commodity exports that had plagued the Latin American economies for so long.

This radical reversal of US policy concerning Latin America was undertaken with the enthusiastic support of all but one of the 20 republics to the south. Ironically, the exception was Cuba, the country that had over the years been most closely linked—economically, politically, and militarily—to the Colossus of the North. In January 1959, the autocratic Batista regime in Havana, which had preserved Cuba's traditionally subservient relationship with the United States and with the private American sugar companies that controlled its single-crop economy, had been toppled by an insurrectionary movement headed by a charismatic revolutionary named Fidel Castro.

Amid a flurry of rhetorical outbursts against 'Yankee imperialism', the new Cuban ruler took a number of steps to eliminate American economic influence in his country. In June 1960, he expropriated the extensive landholdings of the US sugar firms. The following October, he nationalized all the banks and large industrial enterprises on the island, a considerable proportion of which were American-owned. This challenge to US economic interests in Cuba provoked a graduated response from Washington, beginning with economic penalties such as a 95 per cent reduction of the sugar quota (by which Cuba's exports of its major cash crop were allowed to enter the United States at prices above those available on the world market) in July and in October an embargo on all exports to the island except medical supplies and most foodstuffs.

As the once-intimate economic relationship between the United States and Cuba approached the breaking point during 1960, the Soviet Union grasped this unprecedented opportunity to contest Washington's hegemonic position in the Western hemisphere. In February 1960, the USSR agreed to purchase one-fifth of Cuba's sugar, and in December it raised the proportion to a half. It also granted US$200 million in low-interest loans to the financially hard-pressed Havana regime. By the end of the year, Cuba was receiving substantial arms shipments from the Soviet bloc.

As President Eisenhower prepared to leave the White House in the winter of 1960–1, it was clear that efforts to use economic pressure against the Castro regime were futile, given the Soviet Union's eagerness to replace the United States as the primary customer for Cuba's sugar and the principal supplier of its foreign credits. Moreover, Castro had explicitly endorsed the general foreign policy goals of Cuba's new benefactors, most dramatically during a four-and-a-half hour address to the UN General Assembly in September 1960. The numbers of US diplomats in Havana were systematically reduced, at Cuba's insistence, to the point where relations broke off in January 1961. Meanwhile, thousands of Soviet technicians, military advisers, and diplomatic personnel poured into the country to lend their assistance to the revolutionary regime. The island that Washington had long regarded, in strategic and economic terms, as an extension of the Florida Keys seemed to be on the verge of becoming a client state of the Soviet Union.

In view of this situation, the outgoing Eisenhower administration left its successor a plan for the forcible overthrow of the Castro government. Under the supervision of the CIA, an army of refugees from Cuba had been armed and trained at clandestine camps in Florida, Guatemala, and Nicaragua in preparation for an invasion of the island. The organizers of the expedition were confident that the mere appearance of these paramilitary freedom fighters would incite an internal uprising by the victims of Castro's oppression. Although skeptical about its chances of success, Kennedy authorized the projected invasion. On 17 April, roughly 1,500 Cuban exiles established a beachhead at the Bay of Pigs (*Bahía de Cochinos*), an inlet on the southern coast of Cuba. But the anticipated revolt against Castro failed to materialize, and within three days the entire invasion force had been either killed or captured by Castro's forces.

As embarrassing as this episode was for Kennedy, its most important consequences were felt in Cuba itself. Convinced that the abortive

landing at the Bay of Pigs was merely the first move in Washington's campaign to dislodge him, Castro once again asked Moscow for what it had previously refused: the promise of military protection against the United States. Although Khrushchev had earlier threatened reprisals for any American effort to unseat Castro, the threat had not been taken seriously. In the aftermath of the Bay of Pigs fiasco, he once again refused protection to Castro, apparently reluctant to challenge the US militarily in a region so vital to that country's security. But sometime in the spring of 1962, as US plans to destabilize the Castro regime proceeded, the Kremlin decided to grant Castro's request after all and to deploy ballistic missiles in Cuba to deter another American-sponsored invasion by Cuban exile commandos, who were still being trained on American territory with no effort at concealment.

Cuban exiles in a US training camp prepare for the Bay of Pigs invasion. Lynn Pelham/Time Life Pictures/Getty Images.

Despite its professions of concern for the security of its new client state in the Caribbean, Moscow's decision to begin the construction of sites for 48 medium-range ballistic missiles (MRBMs) and 24 intermediate-range ballistic missiles (IRBMs) in Cuba in October 1962 must have been prompted by considerations more directly related to the Soviet national interest. Some have speculated that the missiles were intended to serve as bargaining chips in the global poker game that the Cold War had become. Perhaps Khrushchev envisioned a Cuba-for-Berlin deal that would finally remove the embarrassing showcase of Western economic prosperity and political liberty from the centre of East Germany. Or perhaps the Soviet leadership genuinely expected Washington to acquiesce in the *fait accompli* of nuclear weapons in its own backyard, just as Moscow had learned to live with the American intermediate-range missiles across the border in Turkey. In that case Khrushchev stood to regain for his country the strategic advantage that had been lost by the impressive buildup of American ICBMs since Sputnik, for missiles based in Cuba with ranges of 1,770 to 3,540 kilometres would have reduced the American warning time to virtually nothing and exposed much of the continental United States to a Soviet nuclear attack.

In any case, in mid-October 1962, the Soviet missile sites were discovered by US reconnaissance planes overflying Cuba, and Washington's response was firm. Smarting from partisan criticism of his failure to act against the Soviet military buildup in Cuba, Kennedy flung down the gauntlet to Khrushchev in a nationally televised address on 22 October. After citing the irrefutable evidence of the missile sites in the process of installation, he announced that the United States would impose an air and naval 'quarantine'—avoiding the term 'blockade' because it signified an act of war according to international law—to prevent the arrival of additional nuclear armaments in Cuba. He warned Moscow that any nuclear missile launched from Cuba against any nation in the western hemisphere would be considered a Soviet attack on the US and would trigger nuclear retaliation against the USSR, and he demanded the prompt removal of the missile sites already completed or in the process of construction.

After obtaining the unanimous support of the United States' allies in NATO and in the OAS, Kennedy ordered the naval quarantine into effect on 24 October. Nineteen US warships took their stations along the arc of an 800-kilometre radius around the eastern tip of Cuba with instructions to intercept and search all vessels suspected of carrying the proscribed missiles to the island. On the same day, 25 Russian cargo ships were steaming across the Atlantic for Cuba while construction work on the missile sites continued at a hastily increased pace. Suddenly, after a decade of careless rhetoric about 'massive retaliation' in Washington and 'winnable nuclear war' in Moscow, the two superpowers appeared poised for an epic confrontation from which neither seemed able to back down.

The first break in the impasse came on the evening of the 24th, when 12 of the 25 Soviet ships en route to Cuba (presumably those carrying the contraband) either altered or reversed course. The remaining problem of the missile sites already in place was resolved in the following few days through an exchange of written communications between Kennedy and Khrushchev. Confronted with the genuine possibility of all-out nuclear war, the Soviet leader capitulated to the Kennedy ultimatum on the basis of a single condition: the missile installations would be dismantled and returned to the Soviet Union in exchange for a promise from Washington not to invade Cuba. By the end of the year, the Soviet missile sites had been removed from Cuban soil, the US naval quarantine had been lifted, and Moscow had signalled to Washington its desire to settle all the outstanding disputes between the two superpowers across the globe.

Both sides recognized the necessity of sustaining the spirit of co-operation forged in the fire of the Cuban crisis. The Soviet Union, which could easily have blockaded Berlin in revenge for the US blockade of Cuba, refrained from even the slightest provocation in that vulnerable region. In the following year the United States quietly dismantled its Jupiter missiles based in Turkey—a step proposed by Khrushchev during the Cuban crisis as a quid pro quo for the removal of Soviet missiles from Cuba. (Washington had refused at the time on the grounds that, though the Jupiters were obsolete and had been slated for removal in the near future, the acceptance of such an exchange under duress would have undermined the credibility of the American commitment to its allies.)

The Kremlin gamely attempted to put the best possible light on the setback it had suffered in Cuba in order to reassure allies and prospective clients of its reliability as a patron. By extracting the no-invasion pledge from Kennedy, Khrushchev had rescued Castro from a terrible fate. The missiles were therefore no longer required as protection against Yankee aggression. But the American secretary of state, Dean Rusk, offered the most accurate assessment of the Cuban missile incident, in a line that typified the spirit of machismo that animated the Kennedy administration: 'Eyeball to eyeball, they blinked first.'

CANADA AND THE COLD WAR

In the decade leading up to the Cuban Missile Crisis, Canada and the United States had developed an exceptionally close military and security relationship. The North American Air Defence (NORAD) plan of 1957 was in many respects a successor to the 1940 Ogdensburg agreement that had established the Permanent Joint Board for defence of the northern half of the western hemisphere, except that NORAD was designed for peacetime. NORAD placed the air forces of both countries under a joint strategic command with its headquarters in Colorado. In 1958, the two countries signed the Development and Production Sharing Program, which enabled Canadian companies to bid on American defence contracts. Canada pursued its own military programs—most notably the development of the AVRO Arrow, a state-of-the-art supersonic fighter—but its defence industry remained closely tied to the United States. In 1959, the Tory government of John Diefenbaker

cancelled the AVRO Arrow project, largely because of cost overruns, and instead ordered the American-made F-101 Voodoo fighter-bomber and Bomarc anti-aircraft missile system. Intended to intercept Soviet long-range bombers, the Bomarcs were specifically designed to carry nuclear warheads.

The decision to purchase the Bomarc system appeared to mean that Canada would become a nuclear power, though Diefenbaker insisted that his government had not made any decision on whether Canada would actually deploy nuclear weapons. Nevertheless, the Canadian military continued to acquire weapons systems (such as the Honest John missiles obtained by Canada's NATO ground forces in 1962) designed to carry

An editorial cartoon by John Collins that appeared in the *Montreal Gazette* comments on the relationship between Canadian Prime Minister John Diefenbaker and US President John F. Kennedy. Library and Archives Canada/Credit: John Collins/John Collins fonds/C-133990.

nuclear payloads. Thus the missiles came to Canada unarmed and the warheads remained in the United States. Meanwhile, the international campaign for nuclear disarmanent was growing, and increasing numbers of Canadians opposed the acquisition of nuclear weapons.

By the time of the Cuban Missile Crisis, Canada's nuclear weapons remained unarmed, much to the displeasure of the United States. Diefenbaker and Kennedy disliked each other intensely, and relations between the two countries were further strained once the crisis began, when the Diefenbaker government initially refused both to place Canada's NORAD force on alert and to allow the United States to fly nuclear-armed fighters to arctic bases. Diefenbaker's decisions in these matters were intended to uphold the principle of Canadian independence, but they backfired. Not only were the Americans upset at Ottawa's lack of support, but members of Diefenbaker's own party were also dismayed by the absence of a clear national security policy. In a parliamentary vote of non-confidence in February 1963, Diefenbaker's government was defeated, and although he tried to focus his re-election campaign on Canadian nationalism, voters rejected his indecisive policies. When Lester Pearson became prime minister in 1963, the warheads question remained unresolved.

SUMMARY

The Cold War entered a new phase when the political leadership of the world's two superpowers changed in 1953. In the Soviet Union, Nikita Khrushchev became first secretary of the Communist Party following the death of Joseph Stalin, and in the United States, Dwight Eisenhower replaced Harry Truman as president. In 1955, in response to the formation of the Western European Union (WEU) and the restoration of full sovereignty to West Germany in 1955, the members of the Soviet bloc formed the Warsaw Pact military alliance. Despite these rival alliances, the Cold War appeared to be thawing. In a dramatic speech in 1956, Khrushchev launched an anti-Stalinist campaign that shattered the myth of communist unity and ideological infallibility. Conciliatory gestures on both sides led to a significant decrease in confrontational rhetoric.

This thaw did not last long. In the fall of 1956, the Soviet Union used military force to crush protest movements in Poland and Hungary. At the same time, the Suez Crisis renewed East–West tensions, pitting the Soviet Union and Egypt against Israel, Britain, and France. The United States took an increasingly hard line against the Soviet Union, depicting the free world as locked in a global struggle against the evils of communism. In October 1957, the Soviet Union stunned the West by successfully launching Sputnik, the world's first space satellite. In response, the US accelerated its own ballistic missile program, and the nuclear arms race continued to escalate. When the Soviet Union shot down an American spy plane in 1960, Khrushchev broke off diplomatic negotiations with Washington. With the construction of the Berlin Wall and the Bay of Pigs fiasco in 1961, relations between the East and West reached a new low. When the Cuban Missile Crisis provoked a showdown between the Soviet Union and the United States in 1962, the world came to the brink of nuclear war.

NOTES

1. Khrushchev acquired political primacy in June 1957 by engineering the expulsion of his three principal rivals—Malenkov, Molotov, and Kaganovitch—from the Presidium and the party Central Committee, though he did not become head of government until March 1958.

2. Australia, New Zealand, and the United States had already concluded a tripartite security treaty (ANZUS) in September 1951.

3. The United States had been granted a 99-year lease of Philippine military and naval bases in March 1947. The two countries concluded a bilateral mutual defence treaty in August 1951.

4. The U-2 was shot down by a Soviet SAM after it lost altitude because of engine trouble.

QUESTIONS FOR CRITICAL THOUGHT

1. Why did the promising period of détente following Stalin's death ultimately give way to a return to hostility and mutual suspicion?
2. What were the main factors motivating Khrushchev's quest for 'peaceful coexistence'?
3. Why did the Hungarian uprising of 1956 fail?
4. In what ways could the Kennedy administration have dealt with the crises of 1961 more effectively?
5. Why did Khrushchev take such a large risk in attempting to place missiles in Cuba?
6. Discuss the accuracy of Dean Rusk's assessment that the United States 'won' the Cuban Missile Crisis.

WEBSITES FOR FURTHER REFERENCE

The Harvard Project on Cold War Studies
   www.fas.harvard.edu/~hpcws/links.htm

The National Security Archive: George Washington University
   www.gwu.edu/~nsarchiv/

Research Guide to International Law on the Internet
   www2.spfo.unibo.it/spolfo/PEACE.htm

United Nations Website
   www.un.org/en/

CHAPTER 9

DÉTENTE AND MULTIPOLARITY (1962–1975)

CHAPTER OUTLINE

ARMS CONTROL AND STRATEGIC PARITY

If we define a global power as a state capable of exercising decisive influence anywhere in the world through economic, political, and military means, then the United States alone deserved that designation at the time of the Cuban Missile Crisis of 1962. Its economic preponderance was beyond dispute—its gross national product was three times that of its nearest competitor—as was its political influence in the non-communist world. America's political pre-eminence in Western Europe had been secured when President Truman assumed the leadership of the Atlantic bloc at the end of the 1940s, and in the 1950s President Eisenhower reaffirmed the ideological unity of

what he and Secretary of State Dulles liked to call the 'free world'. In the early 1960s, the political influence of the US was extended to the Third World through elaborate foreign assistance programs such as the Peace Corps, launched by President Kennedy. At the United Nations, the US occupied one of five permanent seats on the Security Council, with loyal allies in three more. Moreover, as the unchallenged protector and benefactor of the non-communist portions of the earth, it could—at least until the mid-1960s—be sure of commanding a comfortable majority for its policies in the General Assembly.

In sum, Washington's political standing in most of the non-communist part of the developing world had risen dramatically during the first half of the 1960s. The progressive rhetoric of the Kennedy administration gave US foreign policy a positive ideological component that it had lacked during the rigidly anti-communist Eisenhower years. The professed commitment to 'nation building' had a powerful attraction for the impoverished masses of the earth and their political leaders. The other part of the Kennedy policy regarding the developing world was a counter-insurgency feature designed to ensure that the sweeping socio-economic reforms that American aid programs were supposed to promote would be managed in an evolutionary rather than a revolutionary manner. This aspect of US policy naturally appealed to the ruling elites of the developing countries who feared insurrection and welcomed Washington's assistance in quelling it. Whereas Moscow had come out of the Cuban Missile Crisis with the tarnished reputation of a patron who could not or would not stand firm behind its client when the chips were down, the US was emerging as the champion of peaceful social reform and economic modernization in the developing world and appeared, however briefly, to be winning the contest for what President Kennedy called 'the hearts and minds of the underdeveloped and uncommitted peoples of the world'.

Only in the realm of military power was the Soviet Union widely thought capable of challenging the United States' supremacy, and even that threat proved to be illusory. The alarmist talk about a 'missile gap' that followed the firing of the first Soviet intercontinental ballistic missile in August 1957 and the launching of Sputnik two months later was based on a gross overestimation of the USSR's capacity to translate technological potential into strategic achievement. In December of the same year, the US launched its own 8,000-kilometre-range Atlas ICBM, and by 1960 the American nuclear arsenal consisted of roughly 50 strategic missile warheads to the Soviets' 35. Eisenhower's embarrassment over the U-2 affair of May 1960 was surpassed by Soviet Premier Khrushchev's own humiliation when the truth behind his inflated claims was exposed. The nation that had launched the world's first earth satellite and tested the first ICBM could not prevent US spy planes from overflying its territory for four years until engine trouble forced one to descend.

At the time of the showdown over Cuba, the United States outclassed the Soviet Union in every category of nuclear armament and delivery system. Moreover, while the US boasted a naval presence and base facilities all over the world, the USSR had neither. The Soviet Union remained the premier land power in Eurasia, capable of reaching the Rhine or the Mediterranean or the Persian Gulf in a few weeks by dint of its overwhelming conventional superiority. But it was dissuaded from seriously considering such a conventional military breakthrough both by the ICBMs and long-range bombers based on American soil and by the IRBMs, MRBMs, and medium-range bombers arrayed along the Soviet frontier in countries allied to the US.

In part, Khrushchev's attempt to leapfrog the American defence perimeter in Eurasia by implanting a Soviet nuclear armament system in Cuba may have represented a desperate gamble to correct this strategic imbalance. But the humiliating conditions of the Soviet retreat in Cuba had the opposite effect. Instead of establishing a more stable balance of nuclear power between the two superpowers, the Cuban crisis revealed to the world the extent of the Soviet Union's military inferiority. Instead of rallying the Communist bloc behind a newly invigorated USSR, it prompted China to accelerate the process of defection from the Soviet orbit that had begun two years earlier. Instead of enhancing Khrushchev's standing in the eyes of the Soviet military and civilian leadership, it aggravated the internal dissatisfaction that eventually led to his downfall.

The lessons learned from the Cuban fiasco led the Kremlin to adopt two strategies—one diplomatic and the other military—that were to remain the basis of Soviet policy after Khrushchev's departure. The first was to resume the quest for 'peaceful coexistence' with the West that had been initiated by Joseph Stalin's successors in the mid-1950s but had been interrupted by the bellicose Soviet probes in Berlin and Cuba during 1958–62. Its purpose was to minimize the possibility of a nuclear confrontation such as had almost occurred in 1962—a contest that the Soviet Union, in its current state of strategic inferiority, was bound to lose.

The second strategy was to accelerate a long-range program, also begun in the mid-1950s but postponed for domestic reasons, to transform the USSR from a Eurasian land power into a global sea and air power capable of defending its interests anywhere in the world. Its purpose was to achieve an approximate parity in nuclear and naval forces, so as to neutralize the strategic deterrent and naval superiority that the United States had exercised so effectively in the autumn of 1962.

The most dramatic consequences of the peaceful coexistence policy were to come in the realm of strategic arms control. Since the end of the Second World War, the United Nations had discussed nuclear disarmament, and proposals to that effect had periodically issued from Washington and Moscow. At the first meeting of the UN Atomic Energy Commission in June 1946, the United States, at the time enjoying a nuclear monopoly, offered to turn over its stockpile of atomic weapons to an international agency under UN auspices on the condition that all other countries pledge not to produce them and agree to an adequate system of inspection. But the Soviet Union, working to develop its own nuclear capability, rejected the so-called Baruch Plan on the grounds that the UN was dominated by the United States and its West European partners and therefore could not be trusted to exercise authority over atomic weaponry in an even-handed manner.

Once the Soviet Union became a nuclear power in September 1949, it began to take a greater interest in atomic arms control, particularly after the death of Stalin and the beginning of the pursuit of peaceful coexistence. At the 1954 session of the UN General Assembly, the Soviet delegate called for a moratorium on the manufacture of nuclear weapons and suggested creating a UN commission to consider means of controlling those already in existence. In May 1955, the Kremlin formally proposed that conventional forces be gradually reduced to fixed levels and that nuclear stockpiles be destroyed once those levels had been reached. In his speech to the UN General Assembly in 1959, Khrushchev advocated general and total disarmament within four years. But all the disarmament proposals that came out of the Soviet Union in the 1950s foundered on the question of verification. Washington insisted on inspection to certify compliance, while Moscow rejected the idea of foreign observers as an intolerable infringement of its national sovereignty. Even Eisenhower's 'open skies' proposal at the Geneva summit conference of 1955, which provided for each superpower to carry out aerial surveillance of the other's military installations, was denounced by the Soviet delegation as a ploy to legalize espionage against the USSR.

If superpower disarmament proved to be impossible, the nuclear alarm set off by the Cuban crisis prompted the two sides to focus on a more modest and attainable objective of limiting the testing, deployment, and proliferation of nuclear weapons in the future. In August 1963, the Soviet Union joined the United States and Great Britain in signing a treaty banning nuclear tests both in the atmosphere and in the sea. In January 1967, the same three nations, together with France—which had become the fourth nuclear power in 1960—agreed to keep outer space free of nuclear weapons. Later in the same year, Latin America was declared a nuclear-free zone by a majority of its member states, with the approval of both Washington and Moscow.[1]

CANADA IN THE 1960s

After emerging as a middle power in the 1950s, Canada was under increasing strain in the next decade as it tried to maintain both its diplomatic independence and its close relationship

Canada's first nuclear weapon, the Bomarc missile. Department of External Affairs/Library and Archives Canada/PA-122740.

The October Crisis

During a state visit to Canada in 1967, French President Charles de Gaulle made a fateful speech that sparked a major political controversy. Enthusiastic crowds greeted de Gaulle's arrival in Montreal. Though he was not scheduled to speak on the evening of 24 July, he decided to acknowledge the large gathering at city hall. From a balcony overlooking the crowd, de Gaulle gave a brief speech and uttered the phrase 'Vive le Québec,' adding, after a pause, the word 'libre'. The momentous significance of de Gaulle's remark was immediately recognized by the crowd, which broke into fervent applause. News of the event quickly spread to Ottawa, where Prime Minister Pearson went on television to declare that de Gaulle's actions were completely unacceptable to the Canadian people. The federal government protested strongly against the interference of the French president in Canada's domestic affairs, and de Gaulle cut his visit short. Although de Gaulle was widely criticized in English Canada and even in France, the speech was viewed differently in Quebec, where polls showed that a majority of people thought that Pearson had overreacted. The diplomatic feud eventually subsided, but the incident had important ramifications. De Gaulle had implicitly lent his international prestige to Quebec's independence movement, giving it a new level of political credibility. The following year, the Parti Québécois was formed, and in 1970 (by which time Pierre Elliott Trudeau was prime minister) the country was plunged into the October Crisis.

Triggered by the Front de libération du Québec (FLQ), the incident sparked a heated debate over the balance between civil liberties and national security. It began when the FLQ kidnapped James Cross, the British trade commissioner, in Montreal in early October 1970. Five days after Cross's abduction, another cell of the FLQ kidnapped Pierre Laporte, the Quebec minister of Labour and Immigration. In return for the release of the hostages, the kidnappers demanded a series of conditions that included the release of imprisoned FLQ members as well as the broadcasting of their political manifesto. After Cross was abducted, the government guaranteed safe passage for the kidnappers, and their manifesto was read on Radio-Canada. The kidnapping of Laporte, however, transformed the political climate and threw many officials into a panic. Unwilling to negotiate any further, authorities decided that drastic action was needed. On 16 October 1970 the federal government invoked, for only the third time in the twentieth century, the War Measures Act. The next day the body of Pierre Laporte was found in the trunk of a car.

With the imposition of martial law, the Trudeau government banned the FLQ, suspended civil rights, and ordered the Army to patrol the streets of Quebec. Authorities rounded up and detained over 450 people, most of whom were never charged with any offence. Prime Minister Trudeau argued that such extraordinary measures were needed in order to quell a full-scale insurrection by the FLQ. Initially, he enjoyed significant support among both anglophones and francophones—every French-speaking MP voted for the War Measures Act—but public opinion changed as evidence of a violent uprising failed to materialize. As in other countries with revolutionary movements, the deployment of military force by state authorities helped to inflame nationalist sentiment. In 1976 the Parti Québécois under René Lévesque won the provincial election. The use of the War Measures Act in 1970 remains controversial to the present day.

French President Charles de Gaulle addresses the crowd from a balcony at Montreal's city hall, 24 July 1967. CP Archives.

with the United States. By the end of 1962, the Diefenbaker government still had not decided whether to arm Canada's Bomarc missiles with the nuclear warheads they were specifically designed to carry. Diefenbaker's erratic foreign policy not only angered the American government but also undermined his own domestic support. As opposition mounted, Defence Minister Douglas Harkness resigned, accusing the government of anti-American posturing, and Liberal leader Lester B. Pearson promised that, if elected, his government would arm the Bomarcs. During the election campaign of early 1963, the US State Department took the unusual step of openly criticizing Diefenbaker's defence policy. Despite the ensuing controversy over the intervention of the US government in Canada's domestic politics, Pearson won the election and fulfilled his nuclear promise.

That decision helped to heal the rift with the United States, which had seen Canada's refusal to arm the Bomarcs as a failure to live up to its commitments to NATO and NORAD. Unlike Diefenbaker, Pearson was an accomplished diplomat who recognized the importance of maintaining good relations with the Americans, and he was extremely careful in his dealings with Kennedy.

Throughout the mid-1960s Canada continued to forge closer economic ties with the United States. In 1965, the two countries signed a landmark agreement regarding the production of automobiles. Under the 'Auto Pact', domestic car manufacturers were able to treat their assembly plants in Canada and the US as part of a single operation. The agreement not only allowed the 'Big Three' automakers to reduce their production costs but also facilitated the growth of factories in southern Ontario. The Auto Pact was seen by many observers as a victory for the type of 'quiet diplomacy' practised by Pearson.

Canada and the United States also made new commitments to strengthen their relationship. Shortly after the announcement of the Auto Pact, both governments released the results of a joint study commissioned in 1963 and authored by Arnold Heeney (representing Canada)

and Livingston Merchant (representing the US). Entitled 'Principles for Partnership', the study supported the view that the two countries shared fundamental values and interests that bound them together as inseparable allies.

Pearson's commitment to cultivating a stronger partnership with the United States coincided with his attempts to create stronger national unity in response to increasing separatist sentiment in Quebec. Parliament's approval of a new national flag, which became the official symbol of Canada in 1965, and of 'O Canada' as the national anthem in 1967 were important symbolic responses to the perceived need for greater nationalism. But as Canada celebrated its centennial year, the question of Canada's nuclear armament—which worried many Canadians and alienated some members of Pearson's own party—and the growing threat of Quebec separatism were troubling issues for Ottawa.

CONFRONTING THE PROLIFERATION OF NUCLEAR WEAPONS

The establishment of direct teletype communications between the White House and the Kremlin after the Cuban Missile Crisis—the 'hot line' agreement of June 1963—was an expression of the two countries' determination to reduce the risk of accidental nuclear war. But an even greater shared concern was the potential threat to the strategic balance posed by the acquisition of nuclear weapons by other countries. The United States had done its best to dissuade its Atlantic partners from developing nuclear capabilities of their own by refusing to share nuclear information while assuring them adequate protection under its own nuclear 'umbrella'. The Soviet Union had also adamantly refused to share its nuclear technology with its European satellites and its Asian allies or even to supply them with nuclear weapons under Soviet control. But the advance of scientific knowledge and the consciousness of national sovereignty were not limited to the US and USSR. What had been a nuclear duopoly at the beginning of the 1950s had become a nuclear club of ominously expanding membership by the middle of the 1960s. Britain had tested its first atomic device in 1952 and its first hydrogen (or thermonuclear) bomb in 1957. France and China, both of which began to pursue foreign and defence policies independent of their erstwhile superpower allies in the early 1960s, joined the nuclear club in 1960 and 1964, respectively.

Hoping to curb the further expansion of the nuclear fraternity, in July 1968 the United States, the Soviet Union, and Britain signed the Nuclear Non-Proliferation Treaty, which came into force in March 1970 after 97 countries had signed and 47 (including the original signatories) had ratified it. According to its provisions, the nuclear powers—except for China and France, both of which refused to sign—pledged never to furnish nuclear weapons or the technology to fabricate them to non-nuclear powers, while the non-nuclear countries promised never to produce or acquire them. An international inspection team was established in Vienna under the auspices of the UN's International Atomic Energy Administration to verify compliance with the treaty.

A spate of international agreements in the 1960s had the effect of forbidding the testing, development, or deployment of nuclear weapons by non-nuclear powers and by nuclear powers in certain specified regions. But they did nothing to limit the stockpiling of strategic weapons or the expansion and perfection of delivery systems by the two countries that alone possessed the capacity to unleash nuclear devastation on the world. It was in the realm of superpower arms control that the decision-makers in Washington and Moscow faced their greatest challenge. The USSR had had no incentive to endorse strategic arms control in the 20 years after 1945, when its nuclear capability remained decisively inferior to that of its principal adversary. To freeze the nuclear forces of the Soviet Union at a level of such strategic inferiority would have permanently relegated it to the position of military vulnerability that had enabled Dulles to threaten massive retaliation against conventional Soviet moves during the 1950s.

Even while the Soviet Union worked with other nations to impose limits on the nuclear arms race, it continued to pursue strategic parity with the United States. When the Brezhnev–Kosygin faction toppled Khrushchev in October 1964, it inherited an ambitious project for military expansion, launched in 1960 and aimed at erasing the Soviet Union's strategic inferiority by the end of the decade. This program included a buildup of Strategic Rocket Forces (created as an independent arm of the military forces), the development of medium- and intermediate-range ballistic missiles for deployment in Europe, and the upgrading of anti-aircraft and civil defence capabilities. In all of the categories of military strength, the new leadership in the Kremlin achieved its goals. During the second half of the 1960s, while Washington's costly conventional military operation in Indochina diverted funds that might otherwise have been spent on its nuclear arsenal, the Soviet Union tripled its land-based ICBMs and greatly expanded the number of its submarine-launched ballistic missiles (SLBMs).

Thus by the end of the decade the missile gap that had forced Khrushchev to back down during the Cuban crisis had been bridged. Whereas the United States had possessed 294 ICBMs compared to 75 for the Soviet Union in 1962, by 1969 the Soviet arsenal of long-range missiles numbered 1,050 against 1,054 for the US. During the same period, the Soviets had surpassed the American submarine force of 656 SLBMs and were challenging US superiority in long-range bombers. In short, the two superpowers had achieved what President Richard M. Nixon later termed 'essential equivalence' in their strategic forces. In the chilling language of defence analysts, they had acquired the capacity for 'mutual assured destruction' (MAD), the ability to destroy a quarter of the enemy's population and more than half its industry in a surprise attack.

During the same period, Moscow expanded its naval power with the intention of contesting America's hitherto undisputed supremacy on the high seas. Unlike the United States, the USSR had never developed a significant seaborne trade, and it was able to reach all its major allies by land. The Soviet leadership had therefore never felt the need of an ocean-going fleet and was content with a force geared to coastal defence. But in the course of the 1960s the Soviet navy acquired the capability to intervene far from its shores in defence of Moscow's interests. This feat was accomplished under the leadership of Admiral Sergei Gorshkov, who had been appointed head of the navy by Khrushchev in 1957. In 1964 a Soviet Mediterranean squadron made its first appearance, and in 1968 a regular and large Soviet naval presence was established in the Indian Ocean just as Britain was withdrawing its naval power from that region. By the early 1970s, the Soviet Union was able to project its naval power and its nuclear deterrent throughout the strategically important world. All that stood in the way of its becoming a global naval power was a lack of overseas bases and refuelling stations—that problem, as we shall see, was to be overcome in the course of the following decade.

This narrowing of the strategic gap between the two superpowers in the late 1960s provided the stimulus for the first successful effort at Soviet–American arms control since the advent of the Cold War. While there had been some serious discussion of convening talks in the mid-1960s, the American military escalation in Vietnam, the Arab–Israeli conflict in the Middle East, and the Soviet intervention in Czechoslovakia embittered relations between Washington and Moscow during the years when Lyndon Baines Johnson occupied the White House and Leonid Brezhnev and Alexei Kosygin jockeyed for primacy in the Kremlin. Not until 1969, after Richard Nixon had become president and Brezhnev had emerged as master of the Politburo, could the hopes of bilateral talks on strategic arms control be translated into reality. For complex reasons, both political and economic, Nixon and Brezhnev had simultaneously come to appreciate the many advantages that a relaxation of Soviet–American tensions offered both sides.

The military context of this movement towards improved relations was the rough parity in strategic weaponry that Moscow had now reached. In the face of the certainty of mutual destruction, the superpowers shared a common interest in curbing an arms race that neither side could hope to win. The economic advantages of a deceleration in military spending were obvious: swollen defence budgets had diverted financial resources that could otherwise have been spent on domestic social programs and productive enterprises in the Soviet Union and the United States alike. On 20 January 1969, the day of Nixon's inauguration, the Kremlin publicly proposed Soviet–American negotiations for the reciprocal limitation and reduction of nuclear delivery vehicles and defensive systems. A week later, the new US president endorsed the Soviet proposal and became the first American president to accept the principle of strategic parity. Formal talks between Soviet and American officials began in Helsinki in November, and six subsequent sessions were held alternately in Vienna and Helsinki under the formal title of Strategic Arms Limitation Talks (SALT).

After two years of tortuous negotiations, an interim arms control agreement was signed in May 1972, during an unprecedented official visit to Moscow by Nixon. Instead of attempting to impose limits on the size of the nuclear stockpiles acquired over the previous two decades, the SALT negotiators concentrated on two other components of the strategic balance that were more susceptible to agreement: the systems used to deliver warheads to their targets and to intercept incoming missiles. With respect to the first, a ceiling was placed on the number of ICBMs that each side could deploy for a period of five years (1972–7). The effect of this limitation was to freeze the number of existing American ICBMs at 1,054 while permitting the Soviet Union to expand its ICBM arsenal from 1,530 to 1,618. A moratorium of equivalent duration was declared on the construction of SLBMs, leaving the Soviet Union with 950 missiles in 62 submarines compared to 710 American missiles in 44 submarines. These two agreements represented the first successful effort by the two superpowers to establish quantitative limits on their strategic delivery systems.

The second issue to be addressed at the SALT I talks was the so-called Antiballistic Missile (ABM) System, designed to intercept and destroy incoming missiles before they reached their targets. The United States had been experimenting with a variety of anti-missile defence systems since 1956, a year before the Soviets launched their first ICBM. The first successful test of an interceptor missile was conducted in New Mexico in 1959. Between 1962 and 1967, Robert S. McNamara, the secretary of defense under Kennedy and Johnson, presided over the development of an ABM system with two principal components: a long-range, high-altitude missile (the Spartan) designed to intercept an incoming ICBM above the atmosphere, and a short-range missile (the Sprint) for use within the atmosphere against whatever might elude the Spartan. Shortly before leaving office in 1967, McNamara publicly described the purpose of this system—renamed 'Sentinel'—as that of defending cities against the relatively minor nuclear arsenal that China could be expected to deploy in the near future.

This description was a tacit admission that no anti-missile system could possibly provide an airtight defence of densely populated areas against the formidable nuclear arsenal of the Soviet Union. A single missile eluding interception could destroy Washington, New York, or Los Angeles. In recognition of this fact, Nixon in 1969 abandoned the idea of defending cities—except for Washington—in favour of protecting America's land-based retaliatory missiles, which (because they were housed in concrete underground silos) could be expected to survive damage that would be lethal for an unprotected urban area. The Nixon ABM system, renamed 'Safeguard' and partially operational by 1972, prompted great uneasiness in Moscow, while the simultaneous development of a Soviet ABM system ('Galosh') aroused similar apprehension in Washington.

The reason an apparently defensive system evoked such anxiety on both sides was that it threatened to upset the delicate balance of mutual deterrence that had been established by the end of the 1960s. The future deployment of an impenetrable ABM system by either side, capable of defending all of that side's large cities from nuclear attack, could be interpreted by the other side as a prelude to an attack launched without fear of retaliation. In recognition of this reality, the SALT I agreement limited each side to 100 ABM launchers and interceptor missiles at two sites. The logic underlying this feature of the SALT I agreement was that it preserved the stability of the strategic balance by reducing the incentive for either side to gamble on a first strike: as long as each side could protect its command centre[2] and one of its land-based ICBM sites, each would retain the capacity to retaliate, even if the rest of its nuclear arsenal were destroyed in a surprise attack.

Although, the Soviet Union retained superiority in total numbers of missiles covered by the SALT I agreement, Nixon was able to assure his domestic constituency that the United States enjoyed overall parity with the Soviet Union because of its superiority in strategic weapons systems not covered by the treaty limitations. First, the US retained considerably more long-range bombers. Second, the USSR had no equivalent in the Western hemisphere to the intermediate-range missiles (capable of reaching the western USSR) that the US had stationed in Europe. Third, the British and French nuclear forces, however inconsequential in comparison to those of the superpowers, represented an advantage to the US that the Soviet Union could not match, since it would not permit its East European satellites to develop independent nuclear forces and could scarcely count China's nuclear capability on the plus side of its strategic ledger.

The decisive advantage for the United States, however, was its technological superiority in the development of warheads. Many of its land-based (Minuteman) and submarine-based (Poseidon) missiles had been fitted with multiple warheads, each of which could be targeted for a different site. These so-called Multiple Independently Targetable Reentry Vehicles (MIRVs) greatly increased the destructive power and reduced the vulnerability to interception of each American missile included in the SALT I numerical limitations. Moreover, while satellite reconnaissance made it relatively easy to determine the number of land- and submarine-based missiles a nation possessed, it was virtually impossible to verify the number of independently targetable warheads each missile contained.

Overall, the two superpowers remained roughly equal in their strategic capability as a consequence of the SALT I Treaty, concluded in May 1972. Each side still had the ability to destroy the other many times over. The exclusion of long-range bombers, MIRVs, intermediate- and medium-range missiles, and other important components of the strategic balance left the two superpowers free to expand their nuclear capability by those and other means. Even so, the treaty represented the first successful effort to impose some restraints on the nuclear arms race, and it was specifically recognized as an interim agreement to be succeeded after five years by a more comprehensive treaty. The forced resignation of Nixon in August 1974 did not impede the ongoing Soviet–American negotiations for a new arms control treaty to replace the SALT I agreement. Continuity of policy was assured through the retention of Henry Kissinger as secretary of state by Nixon's successor, Gerald Ford. In November 1974, Ford and Brezhnev concluded an interim agreement at Vladivostok establishing guidelines for a SALT II treaty that would limit categories of strategic delivery vehicles not covered by SALT I (such as MIRVs and long-range bombers). For the first time since the beginning of the Cold War, officials in Washington and Moscow were confidently forecasting an end to the unrestrained competition for strategic superiority.

The co-operation required for the SALT talks would have been inconceivable without prior success in the reduction of political tensions between the two superpowers in those parts of the world where their interests directly collided. The most visible flashpoint at the time was Southeast Asia, where half a million US troops were fighting a North Vietnamese army supplied and supported by the Soviet Union. The Nixon administration's decision to terminate direct American

involvement in the war in Indochina removed a major irritant in Soviet–American relations. Even more important, however, was the gradual disintegration of the two rigid power blocs that had coalesced in the early years of the Cold War. Throughout the previous decade, a majority of the world's countries had been aligned in one of the two armed camps, which had both counted on the almost unswerving allegiance of those nations that remained under its tutelage and protection.

The dissolution of this bipolar international system during the 1960s was precipitated by three critical developments in the world. The first was the emergence of dozens of newly independent nations in the Third World, which swelled the ranks of the non-aligned bloc. The second was the increasingly assertive and independent posture of Washington's allies in Western Europe, who began to chafe at their position as pawns in the Cold War and eagerly sought a modus vivendi with the communist states to the east in the hope of reducing the risk of nuclear annihilation. The third was the defection of China from the communist camp and its emergence as an independent force in world affairs. These converging changes helped to make the international environment much more fluid than it had been at the beginning of the Cold War. In the end, the evolution of a multipolar international system would enable the United States and the Soviet Union to break the impasse of the Cold War and approach the hitherto impossible goals of arms control, disengagement, and détente.

FRANCE'S ASSAULT ON THE BIPOLAR WORLD

The first direct challenge to America's pre-eminent position in Western Europe came from France after the return to power in June 1958 of Charles de Gaulle, who had disappeared from the political scene in 1946. The occasion of his reappearance was France's costly, foredoomed struggle to retain control of its North African colony of Algeria in the face of an insurrection by the majority Arab population. Armed with emergency powers to settle this bitter dispute, which had brought his own country to the brink of civil war, de Gaulle proceeded to divest France not only of the albatross of Algeria but also of its remaining colonial possessions in Africa.

By 1962, France had virtually completed the painful process of post-war decolonization, and a fundamental constitutional reorganization had placed extensive authority in the hands of the president. These two developments freed France from the debilitating political and colonial burdens of the recent past and set the stage for a series of bold diplomatic initiatives aimed at a goal that had been dear to de Gaulle's heart since the end of the Second World War: the transformation of Europe into a political, economic, and strategic bloc independent of both the United States and the Soviet Union and capable of acting as a third force in world affairs. Although the outcome of this bid for Europe's independence fell far short of de Gaulle's ambition, the foreign policy of Gaullist France from 1962 to 1969 left a lasting imprint on East–West relations by loosening the ties that had bound the European members of NATO in subservience to Washington's authority and unqualified support for its global objectives.

De Gaulle was fundamentally dissatisfied with the international order envisioned by the leaders of the United States and Soviet Union at the wartime conferences in Yalta and Potsdam and formalized during the heyday of the Cold War. He regarded the post-war division first of Europe and then of the entire world into a bipolar system under the shared hegemony of the two non-European superpowers as an intolerable condition for France in particular and Europe in general, for several reasons.

To de Gaulle, the situation deprived once proud and independent states of the freedom of action: no nation dependent on the military protection of another, he declared, could ever aspire to the status of a great power. The understandable resentment engendered by such subservience was especially widespread in France, given the country's vivid memories of a glorious heritage as a power of the first rank. But de Gaulle's

blatant appeal to national pride struck a chord throughout Western Europe. By the 1960s, the European Economic Community was developing into the most formidable economic bloc in the world, with a combined gross national product approaching that of the United States. As they basked in economic prosperity and political stability, many Europeans began to wonder why they should adapt their foreign and defence policies to the global strategy of their transatlantic patron, particularly at a time when the Soviet threat to Western Europe seemed to have receded.

At the same time, de Gaulle exploited the fears aroused by the nuclear arms race. If Soviet–American tensions in regions of secondary concern to Europe were to erupt in a nuclear confrontation, Western Europe would inevitably suffer because of its alliance with the United States and the presence of US military bases and missile installations on its territory. Dulles's sabre-rattling during the Quemoy crisis (see p. 281) shortly after de Gaulle's return to power raised the prospect of a nuclear showdown over a worthless island thousands of kilometres from France. The Cuban Missile Crisis reinforced such apprehensions, as did the escalation of US military involvement in Vietnam a few years later.

The obverse of the fear of being dragged by the United States into a nuclear Armageddon over issues unrelated to Europe's vital interests was the fear of being abandoned by the superpower in the event of Soviet aggression on the continent. Ever since the development of Soviet intercontinental ballistic missiles in 1957, the credibility of Washington's pledge to deter a Soviet attack in Europe by threatening nuclear retaliation against the USSR itself had been viewed with mounting skepticism across the Atlantic. During the last years of the Eisenhower administration, European doubts about the future of the US commitment were fed by the writings of influential American defence theorists who rejected the 'all or nothing' strategy of massive retaliation in favour of a more discriminating approach that would permit a graduated response to a Soviet attack in Europe. Under the Kennedy administration, the outmoded doctrine of massive retaliation was formally replaced by a new policy called 'flexible response', in which a variety of military measures—conventional, tactical nuclear, or strategic nuclear—would be used to counter Soviet aggression in Western Europe.

This new strategy was a tacit acknowledgement that once American cities were within range of Soviet missiles, the threat of nuclear retaliation was no longer a credible deterrent. Its professed intention was to induce uncertainty, apprehension, and therefore caution in Moscow, since the precise nature of the US response to any attack could not be known in advance. However, by reserving maximum flexibility for the United States to determine the time, place, and manner of a military response to Soviet actions, this policy inevitably heightened insecurity among Europeans, who had become accustomed to depending on an unconditional US guarantee. Many observers in Europe interpreted the new approach as a thinly disguised effort to renege on the pledge of nuclear retaliation against a Soviet conventional attack.

Since the mid-1950s, French officials had anticipated a day when the risk of a Soviet nuclear response would weaken Washington's resolve to defend Western Europe and had considered alternative ways of providing for their country's defence. One possibility, broached by Prime Minister Pierre Mendès-France in 1954 and revived by de Gaulle in 1958, was to create a three-power directorate—consisting of the United States, Britain, and France—that would share control of NATO's nuclear force and jointly plan its political and military strategy. However, the Eisenhower administration rebuffed that idea both times it was proposed. In the meantime, the alternative solution of an independent French nuclear force was inherent in the ambitious nuclear energy program that France had launched in the mid-1950s. Shortly before the demise of the Fourth Republic in the spring of 1958, the French government authorized preparations for the testing of a nuclear device. De Gaulle accelerated this weapons-related research program,

and in February 1960 France became the fourth member of the nuclear club, having tested its first atomic bomb in the Algerian Sahara.

In 1946, a law called the McMahon Act had precluded the US government from assisting other countries—even its most trusted allies—in developing independent nuclear capabilities. This prohibition was modified 11 years later in order to permit the sharing of nuclear technology with Britain, which had exploded its first atomic bomb in 1952 and its first hydrogen bomb in 1957. But US support for the modest British nuclear force was offered on the unstated condition that it remain under indirect US control and conform to US strategic doctrine. By contrast, the nuclear capability that France had just acquired posed a serious challenge to the incoming Kennedy administration because of de Gaulle's undiguised intention to develop a fully independent nuclear strike force, or *force de frappe*. The prospect of a nuclear force operating under national rather than NATO (hence US) auspices directly contradicted the new strategic doctrine embraced by Kennedy and his defense secretary, Robert McNamara, which depended on a centrally controlled mechanism of retaliation against Soviet aggression.

The one component that the British and French nuclear forces lacked was a credible delivery system, and Kennedy sought to exploit this weakness in order to ensure American control over them. At the Nassau Conference between Kennedy and British Prime Minister Harold Macmillan in December 1962, the United States offered to supply Britain with Polaris missiles for use on British submarines as a replacement for its obsolete and vulnerable long-range bomber force. The offer was contingent on Macmillan's pledge that the modernized British force would be assigned to a projected Multilateral Nuclear Force (MLF) within NATO. Upon Macmillan's acceptance, Kennedy made a similar offer to de Gaulle on the same condition, but was rebuffed on the grounds that supranational control was incompatible with French military independence. In March 1963, the US spelled out its idea of an MLF for NATO in a proposal for a multinational fleet of surface ships armed with Polaris missiles under the joint supervision of the NATO member states. For Washington this plan represented a concession to European misgivings about the US monopoly of the alliance's nuclear decision-making authority. But for Paris it represented an attempt to dissuade France from its plans to deploy an independent nuclear force by raising the frightening possibility of West German participation in an all-European nuclear force. The other NATO powers were reluctant to antagonize France for fear of provoking a full-fledged crisis in the alliance, and as a result the MLF proposal finally died in December 1964. But by then France had already begun to put in place a rudimentary delivery system, which eventually included long-range bombers as well as land- and submarine-based missiles.

The incompatibility between the French and American perspectives was clear. Underlying the disagreement over technical matters of military strategy was a more fundamental divergence of views concerning the emerging supranational European entity. The formation of the European Economic Community in 1957 and the subsequent progress toward economic integration inevitably raised questions about future relations between the United States and this powerful West European economic bloc, with its potential for political and even military integration. The Kennedy administration had devised a 'grand design' for the improvement of those relations that hailed the emerging economic community as a welcome sign of vitality in valued allies, despite the potential threat to US commercial interests implied by the formation of an integrated, protectionist trading bloc. But in the realm of defence policy the US refused to give up its ultimate authority over the nuclear armament of the Western alliance. It was therefore on the sensitive issue of European military security that de Gaulle sought to mobilize his continental partners in support of his own 'grand design', which envisioned the disruption rather than the strengthening of the transatlantic partnership.

It seemed ironic that the French soldier-statesman would turn first to Germany—his country's traditional adversary—for assistance in freeing Europe from the grip of the United States. As head of France's provisional government in the immediate post-war years, de Gaulle had pressed for punitive measures against Germany, including political dismemberment and harsh economic penalties, to ensure that it would be forever subservient to France. After the establishment of the West German state, de Gaulle—then out of power—strongly opposed its reintegration into the Western European system on the basis of equality for fear that it would one day overshadow France.

But by the early 1960s, two aspects of the relationship between these historic adversaries were conducive to a political reconciliation. The first was the strengthening of the economic ties between them during the 1950s, to the point where each had become the other's most important trading partner. The hopes of integrationists like Jean Monnet in France and Walter Hallstein in West Germany were fulfilled as economic partnership and shared prosperity dissolved ancient grievances. The second factor favourable to rapprochement was France's newly acquired status as Western Europe's only nuclear power. Since, by agreement with its allies, West Germany was prohibited from acquiring a nuclear capability of its own, France was guaranteed a decisive advantage in military power, to compensate for its eastern neighbour's superior economic strength. From this position of strategic pre-eminence, de Gaulle felt secure enough to conclude a treaty of reconciliation with West German Chancellor Konrad Adenauer in January 1963.

But the Franco–German entente did not yield the benefits that de Gaulle had anticipated, and it lapsed into insignificance after Adenauer's replacement in October 1963 by Ludwig Erhard, who reaffirmed Bonn's close ties to Washington while holding Paris at arm's length. De Gaulle's project of a Paris–Bonn axis ultimately failed because he was unable to persuade the Germans that the independent French nuclear force, or any future European nuclear system that might evolve from it, would offer more reliable protection than the American strategic deterrent. As French criticism of the United States' pre-eminence in NATO intensified during 1964–5, West German officials began to fear that it might provoke an isolationist backlash in the United States that would lead it to withdraw from Europe. Such a prospect struck fear in the hearts of Germans, who recognized that the most reliable guarantee of their security against the Soviets was the one offered by the superpower across the Atlantic rather than the one proposed by the increasingly assertive but nonetheless second-rank power across the Rhine.

Frustrated in his effort to cement a Franco–German partnership as a prelude to the separation of Europe from the United States and its reorganization under French leadership, de Gaulle provoked a serious crisis within the Atlantic alliance in pursuit of the same goal. The central issue that he seized upon was the infringement on France's independence represented by the integration of its armed forces in a supranational military organization whose supreme commander had always to be a US general and whose nuclear arsenal was under the sole control of the American president. De Gaulle's dissatisfaction with the integrated command structure of NATO had been expressed in earlier gestures of non-cooperation, such as the refusal to permit the deployment of American-controlled tactical nuclear weapons on French territory in 1959, the removal of France's Mediterranean fleet from NATO jurisdiction in the same year, and the detachment of its Atlantic fleet from the alliance command in 1963. This incremental disengagement from NATO activities had prompted speculation that de Gaulle was laying the groundwork for a fundamental restructuring of the alliance that would transfer more decision-making authority to its European members.

Thus the 14 other NATO states were unprepared for the shock to allied unity administered by the French president in March 1966, when he announced the withdrawal of all French land and air forces from the NATO military command and demanded the removal not only of the alliance's military headquarters from the Paris region but of all American and Canadian military bases from French territory as well. As the Western governments reeled from these blows, de Gaulle provocatively embarked on a state visit to the Soviet Union in June 1966. In Moscow he was showered with honours, including an invitation to become the first Western leader to visit the top-secret space-launching site in Kazakhstan. Soviet Premier Kosygin returned the visit in December and received an equally cordial welcome in Paris. The Kremlin had actively encouraged France's estrangement from the United States in the expectation that it would benefit from the resulting turmoil in the Atlantic alliance. For his part, de Gaulle accompanied his broadsides against the US, which included harsh criticism of its interventions in Vietnam and the Dominican Republic, with an ostentatious bid for an improvement in France's bilateral relations with the Soviet Union.

By means of these two interrelated policies—disengagement from NATO and détente with Moscow—the French president evidently hoped to establish his nation as the spokesman for Western Europe in its relations with the Communist bloc. A French-dominated Western Europe detached from the United States would be in an advantageous position to negotiate directly with the Soviets to resolve the outstanding political disputes on the continent, particularly those concerning the status of divided Germany and its eastern frontiers. Since a French-led Europe unencumbered by the US nuclear guarantee would pose no threat to the USSR's security, the Kremlin could be induced to relax its iron grip on the Eastern European buffer states and reach an accommodation with West Germany. Conversely, Paris's privileged bilateral relationship with Moscow would give it sufficient leverage over Bonn to pressure the nervous Germans into settling the boundary disputes in Eastern Europe on terms acceptable to the Communist bloc. The ultimate goal of this ambitious project was a mutual disengagement in Europe that would leave the Soviet satellites in the east free to pursue their autonomous course as Western Europe resumed its evolution away from the United States. A continent partitioned into two rigid power blocs at Yalta and Potsdam would thereafter be emancipated from superpower domination and be free to reassert its authority and influence in the world.

The military consequences of France's withdrawal from NATO were trivial. The headquarters of the alliance were transferred from Paris to Brussels with relative ease. Neither the forced evacuation of US and Canadian military personnel nor the loss of French territory as a staging area for the provisioning and reinforcement of Allied troops in West Germany caused serious difficulties. The bases in France had always played a subsidiary, supportive role in NATO strategy, which saw West Germany as the main battlefield for conventional engagement with Warsaw Pact forces and presumed a nuclear response before they reached the Rhine. Supplies could be, and for years had been, channelled through Benelux and West German ports to the forward area in Central Europe. The only three indispensable French contributions to NATO's defence capability—the stationing of French ground and air forces in West Germany as a guarantee of French participation in its defence, access to the pipeline across France that carried oil and fuel to NATO forces in Germany, and overflight rights in French air—were all preserved by special agreement. Moreover, France retained representation on the exclusively political organs of the alliance (the North Atlantic Council and its subsidiary bodies) as well as liaison officers attached to some of the military organs. Thus the dire predictions of Western disarray in the wake of de Gaulle's disengagement were not borne out. The Atlantic alliance proved capable both of withstanding the assertion of French independence and of adapting to the increasingly pluralistic international environment that it heralded.

Similarly, the bid for a bilateral rapprochement with Moscow that accompanied the diplomatic warfare with Washington failed to produce the realignment of power in Europe that de Gaulle had expected. The monetary and financial crisis that engulfed France following the outbreak of student–worker unrest in the spring of 1968 revealed how poorly positioned France was to play the powerful independent role envisioned by its leader. The Soviet invasion of Czechoslovakia in the summer of the same year had the dual effect of strengthening the cohesion of the Western bloc and undermining the assumption of Soviet retrenchment in the east on which de Gaulle's hopes had rested. His abrupt abdication in April 1969 brought to an end the grand design that had overestimated both France's power and Europe's ability to defend itself without American assistance.

THE POLITICAL SETTLEMENT IN EUROPE

Although de Gaulle's conception of a new international system proved impractical, his vision of a new European order survived—with profound consequences for Europe, the Soviet Union, and the United States. De Gaulle was correct in his view that the outstanding matters of dispute between the Federal Republic of Germany and its communist neighbours to the east would have to be settled before the Cold War in Europe could be brought to a close and the superpowers' grip on their respective halves of the continent loosened. His mistake was to imagine that his own country, on the strength of its military supremacy and diplomatic influence in Western Europe, was capable of orchestrating that relaxation of tensions. The Gaullist strategy overlooked two fundamental elements of European power politics. The first was that the only continental state capable of granting the Soviet Union and its satellites the assurances that were the prerequisites for genuine détente in Europe was West Germany; the second was that Bonn, unlike Paris, would never dare to seek an accommodation with the Eastern bloc without obtaining the prior consent of Washington, on whose military protection and diplomatic support its security depended.

The Cold War in Europe had begun over the issues of Germany and Berlin and persisted into the mid-1960s because those two related questions remained unresolved. The main obstacle to resolution was West German Chancellor Adenauer's refusal to abandon the dream of the political reunification of the two German states. This cause had great emotional appeal for West German voters, but was anathema to the Soviet Union and its East European satellites, particularly the East German regime in Pankow, which understandably feared being submerged in the larger, more populous, and more prosperous West Germany. The West German denial of East Germany's sovereignty and insistence on Bonn's exclusive right to represent all Germans was formally expressed in December 1955 in the Hallstein Doctrine (named after the then-secretary of state of the West German foreign office), which affirmed Bonn's intention to regard diplomatic recognition of the East German regime as an unfriendly act because it implied acceptance of Germany's permanent division. Accordingly, West Germany severed diplomatic relations with all the Eastern European states that recognized Pankow, while prudently exempting the Soviet Union. A related source of antagonism between West Germany and its eastern neighbours was its refusal to recognize Germany's borders with Poland and Czechoslovakia, which had been redrawn in 1945 to the advantage of the latter two countries. To acknowledge the loss of those territories would be to antagonize the large and vocal political constituency of German refugees who had been expelled from them after the war and who dreamed of returning. The twin prospects of unification of the two Germanies and territorial revision in the east were understandably alarming for the East European states and their Soviet patron. No two issues had done more to keep the embers of the Cold War burning throughout the 1950s and into the following decade.

In December 1966, as de Gaulle was administering his shock treatment to the Western alliance, a governing coalition was formed in West Germany that brought to the foreign ministry Social Democratic leader Willy Brandt, a passionate proponent of world peace who was determined to normalize his country's relations with the Communist bloc even if that meant renouncing the cherished goals of national unification and recovery of the lost territories. Brandt's new 'eastern policy', or *Ostpolitik*, reflected a profound shift in West German attitudes towards those issues. Majority opinion within the two parties that formed the new coalition had concluded that the old 'policy of strength' regarding East Germany and Eastern Europe had failed to yield the desired results. Instead of weakening the communist system in Eastern Europe and promoting the reunification of the German peoples and the recovery of the former German territories, the unyielding approach inherited from the Adenauer years had left the Federal Republic isolated in the West as the last stronghold of Cold War orthodoxy amid a general evolution towards acceptance of the political status quo in Europe and the permanent division of the two Germanys.

The alternative that Brandt proposed was to normalize West Germany's relations with its East European neighbours in order to facilitate a continent-wide relaxation of tensions that might, in some distant future, lead to the peaceful reunification of the two German states. In short, the once-central component of Bonn's foreign policy—the insistence that all-German reunification was the precondition for détente—was abandoned, and détente became the means to the ultimate end of a united Germany on a peaceful continent. After informing and obtaining the tacit approval of his NATO allies (including the United States), Brandt embarked on a cautious campaign to improve West Germany's relations with Eastern Europe. In January 1967, Bonn restored diplomatic relations with the Romanian government in Bucharest, directly violating the Hallstein doctrine. By 1968, West German trade missions had been sent to several East European capitals to lay the groundwork for an unprecedented commercial penetration of the Communist bloc, financed by West German banks. The Soviet military intervention in Czechoslovakia in the summer of 1968 was a temporary setback, as Bonn joined other NATO nations in condemning the action. But the West German elections of October 1969 brought Brandt to power as chancellor in a coalition cabinet dominated by his Social Democratic Party. As head of government he renewed and intensified his efforts to reach a settlement with the East. In response to his earlier overtures, the Warsaw Pact states had specified that the price for such a rapprochement would be acknowledgement of the territorial status quo in Eastern Europe and recognition of East Germany's sovereignty.

Before tackling these difficult issues, Brandt paved the way for accommodation by signing the Nuclear Non-Proliferation Treaty in November 1969. He then concluded a non-aggression pact with the Soviet Union in August 1970 (31 years after the signing of the Hitler–Stalin pact), by which both parties affirmed the existing frontiers in Eastern Europe and forswore the use of force against one another. These two gestures helped to alleviate Moscow's fear of a revisionist West Germany armed with nuclear weapons. The festering dispute concerning Germany's border with Poland was disposed of with astonishing ease when, in December 1970, Brandt signed a non-aggression pact with Poland that formally renounced Germany's territorial claims by recognizing the German–Polish frontier at the Oder–Neisse line.

In September 1971, the four occupying powers in Berlin—the United States, the Soviet Union, Britain, and France—signed an agreement recognizing each other's existing rights in their respective sectors of the city and affirming the special political relationship between West Berlin and the Federal Republic. Thus for the sake of détente the Kremlin sacrificed the long-standing demand of its East German client for total control of access routes to the city—the very issue that had precipitated the Berlin crises of 1958–61. Finally, in December 1972, East Germany was compelled to accept and sign the Basic Treaty with the Federal Republic, in which Pankow did not receive the formal diplomatic recognition it had always demanded as a precondition for inter-German reconciliation. The Basic Treaty provided for increased commercial, cultural, and personal relations between the two German states as well as the exchange of permanent missions (rather than embassies). In September 1973, 24 years after they had emerged as de facto nations, the two Germanys were admitted into the United Nations as separate sovereign entities. Three months later, the last remaining issue in dispute between West Germany and the Eastern bloc—the border between Germany and Czechoslovakia—was resolved by mutual agreement. In December, Bonn signed a treaty with Prague that nullified the Munich Pact of 1938, thereby acknowledging the loss of the Sudetenland, whose German-speaking inhabitants had been forcibly repatriated after the collapse of the Third Reich.

In this piecemeal, ad hoc fashion, the unresolved issues of the Second World War were settled insofar as the countries of Central Europe were concerned. All that remained was for the two superpowers to give their approval to the European settlement negotiated bilaterally between West Germany and its eastern neighbours. Ever since the mid-1950s the post-Stalinist leaders in the Kremlin had issued periodic proposals for a European Security Conference to break the political impasse on the continent and reduce the likelihood of a military confrontation between NATO and the Warsaw Pact. The nations of Western Europe had consistently rebuffed these Soviet overtures on the grounds that political agreements were meaningless unless accompanied by a mutual reduction of military forces on the continent, an idea that had little appeal in Moscow (presumably because of Soviet apprehension about the political consequences in Eastern Europe).

By the early 1970s, however, two developments in the global balance of power forced the West European nations on the one hand and the Soviet Union on the other to reconsider their incompatible positions. An all-European conference now seemed advantageous to both sides. Western Europe's enthusiasm for an agreement to reduce the size of the military forces on the continent was increased by the ominous signs of retrenchment that had appeared in the United States in response to the traumatic experience of Vietnam. A resolution by a US senator calling for the withdrawal of most American military forces from Europe, though defeated in 1970, had attracted enough public and congressional support to cause anxiety in Europe about the future of the US military presence there. The abolition of conscription in the US after the Vietnam pullout foreshadowed a reduction in American military personnel that would require politically unpopular increases in European defence spending if the military forces of the two alliance systems were to remain at their current levels.

The key to Russia's newly conciliatory posture in Europe was to be found in Beijing. Soviet–Chinese border clashes in the Amur–Ussuri region in March 1969 highlighted the increasingly bitter territorial disputes between the two former communist allies; the spectacular visit to China in July 1971 by US National Security Advisor Henry Kissinger foreshadowed an improvement of Sino–American relations at the USSR's expense. Confronted by a hostile, independent China on its Asian frontier, the Soviet Union could not fail to recognize the advantages of détente and stability on its European flank.

Two months after Kissinger's trip, Brezhnev agreed in principle to participate in a conference on Mutual and Balanced Force Reductions (MBFR) in exchange for the Western nations' endorsement of the Soviet proposal for a European Security Conference (CSCE). After a year of preparation, the CSCE began in Helsinki in January 1973 and the MBFR in Vienna in October. Although the talks on military reductions became bogged down in technicalities, the political discussions in Helsinki achieved remarkable progress, largely because of the groundwork laid by the bilateral agreements between West Germany and the Communist bloc. Domestic scandals forced both Nixon and Brandt, the two Western architects of détente, from office in 1974, but their successors resumed their efforts to reach a comprehensive political settlement in Europe. What Moscow hoped to obtain at Helsinki was the West's formal recognition of the post-war political status quo in Europe, including the sovereignty of East Germany that Bonn had already conceded de facto through the Basic Treaty with Pankow.

In addition to these political goals, economic considerations played an important role in the Soviet Union's bid for détente in Europe. In Poland, riots sparked by food price increases in December 1970 toppled Gomułka's communist government and marked the culmination of a decade of growing economic unrest in Eastern Europe. In January 1949, Moscow had established the Council for Mutual Economic Assistance (COMECON) to develop an integrated economic bloc in Eastern Europe as a counterweight to the Marshall Plan and the Organization for European Economic Co-operation in the West. But as Western Europe edged towards genuine economic integration during the 1950s, COMECON remained little more than an instrument for perpetuating the USSR's stranglehold on the economic life of its satellites. The economies of Eastern Europe were exploited to accelerate the economic recovery of the Soviet Union through reparations from former enemy states, the formation of joint stock companies under Soviet control, and the forced diversion of trade on advantageous terms to the USSR. Khrushchev's efforts in 1962–3 to emulate the success of the European Economic Community by welding COMECON into a supranational integrated economic bloc with a division of production failed, largely because of Romania's refusal to accept its assigned role of grain and oil producer. As Romania pressed on with its plans for rapid industrialization in defiance of the COMECON blueprint, Czechoslovakia, Poland, and Hungary expressed discontent at having to pay for Soviet raw materials at prices far above those prevailing on the world market. There were also bitter complaints from the economically hard-pressed satellites that were compelled to supply, free of charge or on advantageous terms, military and industrial equipment to Third World countries where the Soviet Union was seeking political influence.

These rumblings within the Communist bloc reflected a growing awareness of the marked disparity between the prosperity of Western Europe and the economic stagnation of Eastern Europe. From Molotov's abandonment of the meetings on the Marshall Plan in 1947 through the 1960s, the Kremlin had strenuously opposed the one obvious solution to this problem—opening its satellite empire to trade and investment from the

West—for fear that economic penetration would bring ideological contamination and the threat of political unrest. But by the early 1970s, Brezhnev and his associates had come to believe that the only hope of satisfying the mounting consumer demands of the Eastern European peoples, and indeed of the Soviet population itself, was a massive influx of foreign industrial products, technology, and investment capital, which only the advanced economic powers of the non-communist world could provide.

Agreements on trade and technical co-operation made with France and West Germany in the early 1970s had set the stage for this economic opening to the West, which was given a tremendous boost on 1 August 1975, when representatives of 33 European countries (all but the perpetually isolated Albania), the United States, and Canada signed the Final Act of the two-year-long European Security Conference in Helsinki. Among its most important provisions were those that formally recognized the existing political frontiers of

1968

Even as events on the diplomatic front brought a measure of stability to the Cold War, a series of interconnected global developments triggered a massive anti-establishment backlash. Opposition to the ongoing war in Vietnam, to the presence of NATO troops and bases in Europe, and support for the civil rights struggle in the United States as well as the cause of the Palestinian people in the wake of the Six Day War, came together most starkly in 1968—the so-called 'year of the barricades'. Protests escalated across Western Europe and throughout North America (and to a lesser extent in Japan). In some cases the protests drew a large measure of public sympathy. Such was the case in Paris where, in May, a student-led protest at the Sorbonne gained the support of the major French unions, who urged their members to occupy factories and bring industrial production to a standstill. Soon the protests spread from Paris to a number of other centres, and, beginning on 13 May, a general strike paralyzed the nation. When the government of Charles de Gaulle threatened to declare a state of emergency the protests gradually subsided, but the authority of the government had been seriously weakened. Despite surviving an election in June 1968, de Gaulle would resign less than one year later.

Other European countries experienced similar upheavals. In West Germany students opposed to the conservative post-war social, economic, and political order, also took to the streets. After an assassination attempt against one of the student leaders, radical elements of the protest movement formed new groups such as the Red Army Faction (RAF) which adopted terrorist tactics to advance their cause. Between 1969 and 1977 the RAF was responsible for a series of kidnappings, assassinations, and bomb attacks. In North America protests spread across university campuses as the so-called New Left sought to draw attention to the ties between government, the military, and large corporations. Galvanized by revelations of the My Lai massacre and other atrocities committed by American troops in Vietnam and the assassinations of Martin Luther King Jr. and Robert Kennedy, the protesters occupied university administration offices, marched against the war, and demonstrated against corporate giants such as Dow Chemical Company. In Mexico, student unrest and violent government reprisals dominated the summer. But it would be a single event in Mexico City, host of the 1968 Summer Olympics, that made global headlines. During the playing of the US national anthem American sprinters Tommie Smith and John Carlos raised their fists in the Black Power salute, an act emblematic of the year's political activism. While there remains great disagreement regarding the achievements of the generation of 1968, most commentators agree that their actions marked the arrival of a new set of social and cultural values.

Europe (including the border separating the two Germanys); provided for an increase in economic and cultural relations between the two blocs; and specified prior notification of and the exchange of observers at large-scale military exercises conducted by the two alliance systems. The major concession made by Moscow in exchange for the West's implicit acknowledgement of its domination of Eastern Europe was the so-called basket three, which guaranteed respect for human rights and political freedoms in a manner reminiscent of the Yalta Declaration on Liberated Europe.

Thus three decades after the defeat of Hitler, the war he had started was brought to an end. This was done without the formalities of a peace treaty, since the Final Act of the Helsinki Conference was only a political statement of intent, not a legally binding document. The political division of Europe, which had precipitated the Cold War between the two victors in the struggle against Nazi Germany, was finally acknowledged as a *fait accompli*. By obtaining international recognition of its pre-eminence in the Eastern European buffer zone, as well as the de facto division of Germany, the Soviet Union now enjoyed a degree of political security to reinforce the military security that had resulted from its acquisition of strategic parity with the United States in the course of the 1960s.

Complementing the political and military détente of the mid-1970s was an informal economic détente in which commercial and financial channels between East and West were unclogged. The division of Europe into two closed economic blocs—both a cause and a consequence of the Cold War—came to an end as trade and investment between them increased. West German and French banks poured hard-currency loans into the economies of Eastern Europe, which enabled these states to purchase Western consumer goods and industrial products in unprecedented quantities. Italy opened a Fiat automobile plant in the heart of the USSR. The United States became the Soviet Union's principal foreign supplier of grain after the conclusion of a five-year sales agreement in October 1975. But as political and economic intercourse between the two blocs in Europe intensified and Soviet–American negotiations on strategic arms limitation progressed during the first half of the 1970s, the deteriorating situation in the Middle East threatened to nip the trend towards East–West reconciliation in the bud.

CONFLICT IN THE MIDDLE EAST

The Suez Crisis of 1956 marked a turning point in the history of foreign involvement in the Middle East. Chastened when Washington refused to support their efforts to retain their influence in the region, Britain and France were compelled to follow the lead of the United States as it worked to exclude the Soviet Union from this strategically located, oil-rich part of the world. The transfer of authority was formalized in January 1957 with the proclamation of the Eisenhower Doctrine, according to which the US was to assist any nation in the Middle East that it judged to be threatened by communist aggression. Since the Soviet Union at the time had neither the capacity nor, so far as anyone knew, the desire to expand militarily into the region, the Eisenhower Doctrine was used to justify American action against the one power there that did entertain expansionist ambitions at the expense of states friendly to the US and its European allies: Egypt.

In July 1958, Anglo–American troops intervened to rescue the pro-Western regimes of Jordan and Lebanon from the presumed threat of a pro-Nasser coup such as the one that had recently toppled the British-supported government of Iraq. It was President Nasser's professed goal to unite all the Arab states of the Middle East and North Africa under his leadership, and his increasingly intimate political and economic relations with the Communist bloc suggested to Washington that he was a stalking horse for the Kremlin in an area that the US now considered to be of vital interest.

Apart from the economic benefits that he obtained from the Soviet Union, such as development aid for the Aswan Dam project (replacing funds withheld by the United States and Britain),

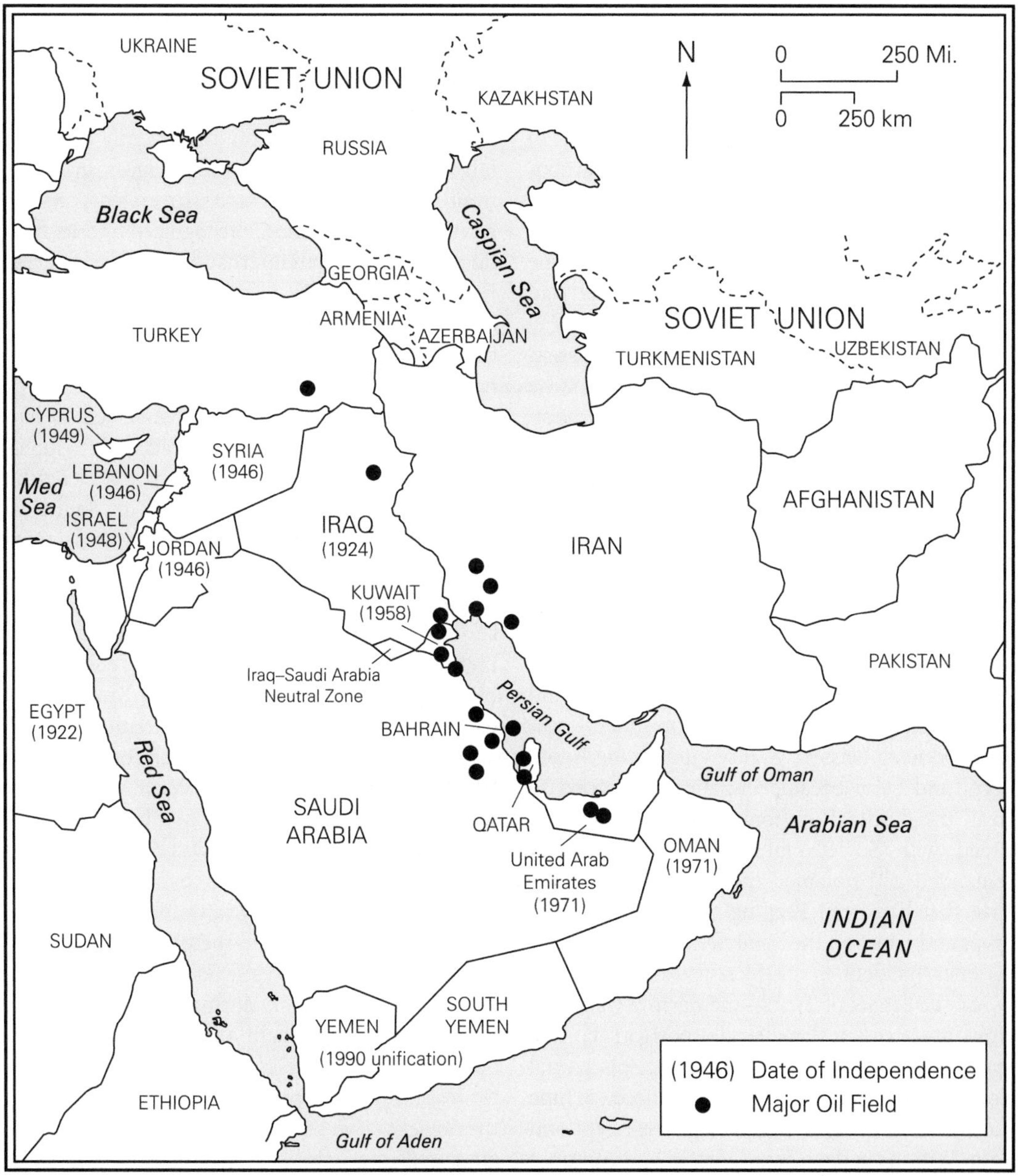
UKRAINE
SOVIET UNION
KAZAKHSTAN
RUSSIA
N
0 250 Mi.
0 250 km
Black Sea
Caspian Sea
GEORGIA
ARMENIA
AZERBAIJAN
TURKEY
SOVIET UNION
TURKMENISTAN
UZBEKISTAN
CYPRUS (1949)
SYRIA (1946)
LEBANON (1946)
Med Sea
ISRAEL (1948)
JORDAN (1946)
IRAQ (1924)
IRAN
AFGHANISTAN
KUWAIT (1958)
Iraq–Saudi Arabia Neutral Zone
PAKISTAN
Persian Gulf
EGYPT (1922)
BAHRAIN
Red Sea
Gulf of Oman
SAUDI ARABIA
QATAR
Arabian Sea
United Arab Emirates (1971)
OMAN (1971)
INDIAN OCEAN
SUDAN
SOUTH YEMEN
YEMEN
(1990 unification)
ETHIOPIA
Gulf of Aden
(1946) Date of Independence
Major Oil Field

THE MIDDLE EAST AFTER THE SECOND WORLD WAR

the Egyptian leader's main reason for cultivating friendship with the USSR was the hope that it would assist him, diplomatically and militarily, in removing what he saw as the major roadblock to the realization of his pan-Arab project: the state of Israel. In the aftermath of the Suez affair, particularly with the announcement of the Eisenhower Doctrine, the two superpowers had become indirectly embroiled in the dispute between the Jewish state and its Arab neighbours that had festered ever since the formation of Israel in May 1948. The Soviet Union furnished military assistance to Egypt and sent Soviet officers to train the army of Syria, Israel's northeastern neighbour, which was under the control of an anti-Western elite with close ties to Moscow. Fearing that a pro-communist Syria would also threaten the adjacent pro-Western regimes of Jordan, Lebanon, and Turkey, Washington stepped up its military assistance to those states, while supplying arms to Israel to counter the ominous buildup of Soviet weaponry in Egypt.

As the standoff between US-backed Israel and Soviet-backed Egypt and Syria continued without producing Nasser's goal of eliminating Israel, Egypt and Syria became impatient and tried to break the deadlock by force. On 17 May 1967, armed with Soviet tanks and planes, Nasser demanded and obtained the removal of the UN force that had been keeping the peace between Egypt and Israel on the Sinai peninsula ever since the Suez incident in 1956. A few days later, he closed the Straits of Tiran—the narrow waterway providing access to Israel's only port on the Red Sea—to Israeli shipping. Interpreting this partial blockade as a prelude to war, Israel on 5 June launched a pre-emptive strike against Egypt and Syria. Within six days, Israeli forces had captured the strategic buffer zone of the Golan Heights from Syria; the entire Sinai peninsula, including the east bank of the Suez Canal, from Egypt; and the west bank of the Jordan River, including the Jordanian sector of the holy city of Jerusalem (which had been partitioned after the 1948–9 war). By three bold strokes, Israel had decimated the forces of its most determined adversaries and

obtained defensible borders on all sides. It would cling to those borders for more than a decade, despite the entreaties of the UN Security Council, which in November 1967 passed a resolution calling for it to withdraw from the recently occupied territories in exchange for assurances from the frontline Arab states that its sovereignty within secure frontiers would be recognized and its freedom of navigation in international waters assured.

The Six Day War was a humiliating setback for the Soviet Union and its two client states in the Middle East. Moscow's credibility as a patron had been undermined. Its armaments in Egypt and military advisers in Syria had failed to halt the advance of the outnumbered Israeli forces on three fronts. The United States, distracted by its deepening military involvement in Southeast Asia and therefore reluctant to be drawn into a second conflict on the other side of the world, maintained a neutral posture in the Arab–Israeli showdown. For the first time since its establishment after the Cuban Missile Crisis, the hotline between the White House and the Kremlin was used to ensure that neither the Kremlin nor the White House would miscalculate the other's intentions in the Middle East. But Washington's prior military assistance to Israel was sufficient proof of where its sympathies lay, as was the ostentatious sale of 50 F-4 Phantom jets to Israel in December 1967, while Egypt and Syria were still licking the wounds they had suffered the previous June.

Half of the Arab states severed diplomatic relations with Washington during the Six Day War, and a number of them promptly granted the Soviet Union the use of their ports in retaliation for Washington's support of Israel. In early 1970, the Soviet Union sent Egypt some 300 surface-to-air missiles to help it counter Israel's air superiority, which had been decisively demonstrated in the war three years earlier and more recently in Israeli raids over the Suez Canal. Moscow also sent 20,000 advisers and technicians to staff the missile sites and reorganize Egypt's shattered military forces. In September 1970, Nasser died and was succeeded by Anwar Sadat. The completion of the Soviet-financed Aswan Dam in January

1971 was followed by new Soviet commitments of economic assistance to Cairo. In exchange the USSR obtained naval facilities at the Egyptian ports of Alexandria, Port Said, and Mersa Matrûh to accommodate its Mediterranean fleet as well as the use of Egyptian airfields for reconnaissance flights along NATO's southern flank. In March 1971, Sadat concluded a 15-year treaty of friendship and co-operation with the Soviet Union— the first Soviet military commitment to a Third World country—in the hope of obtaining the sophisticated weaponry his country needed to take back the Sinai territory it had lost to Israel four years earlier.

Egypt's hopes were to be disappointed, however, as were Israel's aspirations of gaining Washington's unqualified endorsement of its newly expanded borders. The two superpowers attempted to restrain their respective Middle Eastern protégés by restricting arms deliveries and prodding them to resolve their differences. Neither Washington nor Moscow wished to be dragged into a confrontation in this volatile part of the world at a time when their leaders, Nixon and Brezhnev, were striving to reduce East–West tensions. But neither was capable of controlling its client: for Cairo and Jerusalem alike the stakes had become too high. Sadat needed to recover at least a portion of the Sinai land lost to Israel in order to shore up his sagging domestic popularity and to divert public attention from the precarious state of the Egyptian economy. The leaders of Israel, for their part, were driven by mistrust and anxiety to refuse any concession that might undermine the security provided by the Sinai buffer. On the contrary, plans were made to populate the occupied territories with Jewish settlers—a policy that the Arab states bordering on Israel regarded as a prelude to de facto annexation.

The tension between Egypt and Israel, which boiled over in intermittent skirmishing along the Suez Canal in the early 1970s, was exacerbated by the presence of 2.75 million stateless Palestinian Arabs, half of them refugees from the territory incorporated into the new Jewish state after the 1948–9 war. The government of Israel had refused to repatriate them after the armistice, lest the Jewish citizens of the new state be numerically overwhelmed by a million discontented Arabs returning to a land they considered their own. Since no neighbouring Arab state was prepared to resettle them permanently within its own borders, the refugees had been 'temporarily' housed in camps located in Syria, Jordan, and the Egyptian-controlled Gaza Strip. In 1964, after a decade and a half of living in poverty while awaiting an uncertain resolution to their situation, the more politically active residents of the camps formed the Palestine Liberation Organization (PLO), which operated from Jordanian territory until it was expelled in 1970 by the military forces of King Hussein, who feared that his kingdom would be overwhelmed by its Palestinian majority. As the PLO reassembled in Lebanon in the early 1970s, its commandos staged a number of spectacular acts of terrorism to publicize the Palestinians' grievances, including airplane hijackings and the murder of Israeli athletes at the 1972 Olympic Games in Munich.

When Sadat failed to secure from the Soviet Union the offensive weapons that would have ensured Egypt's military superiority over Israel, he turned against his less-than-accommodating benefactors. In July 1972, shortly after the Nixon–Brezhnev summit talks in Moscow appeared to confirm the Kremlin's commitment to East–West détente at the expense of its clients in peripheral regions such as the Middle East, Sadat angrily ordered most of the Soviet advisers and technicians out of Egypt (although he continued to permit Soviet access to Egyptian naval facilities). Over the following months he came to believe that Egypt stood a good chance of recapturing at least some of the lost Sinai territory even without the sophisticated military hardware that Moscow had refused to provide. He also became convinced that a renewal of armed struggle in the Middle East was necessary in order to ensure the involvement of the two superpowers in the eventual peace settlement.

Thus in early October 1973, on the Jewish holy day of Yom Kippur, Egypt in concert with Syria

TABLE 9.1   UNOFFICIAL ESTIMATES OF PALESTINIAN RESIDENTS IN THE MIDDLE EAST AS OF MARCH 1973

Jordan	700,000
West Bank	675,000
Israel	350,000
Gaza	375,000
Lebanon	275,000
Syria	175,000
Egypt	25,000
Iraq	10,000
Persian Gulf countries	170,000
	2,755,000

Source: Dana A. Schmidt, *Armageddon in the Middle East* (New York, 1974), p. 148, © 1974 by the New York Times Company. Reprinted by permission.

launched a surprise attack against Israel. Egyptian forces drove across the Suez Canal into the Sinai, overrunning Israel's Bar-Lev defence installation with furious infantry and artillery assaults. In the meantime, a large Syrian force equipped with 800 tanks swarmed onto the Golan Heights overlooking Israeli settlements in the valley below. After two weeks of the fiercest tank battles since the Second World War, Israel gained the upper hand. One Israeli force mounted a counterattack on Syria and drove to within 30 kilometres of Damascus, while another landed on the west bank of the Suez Canal to encircle the Egyptian Third Army on the east bank in the Sinai, severing its supply lines and blocking its retreat.

The two superpowers were reluctant to become involved in another Middle East confrontation, but they did not want to be defeated by proxy. Therefore they supplied military equipment to their respective clients while vainly seeking to arrange a ceasefire in the United Nations. When Israeli forces crossed the Suez Canal on 16 October, facing Egypt with imminent defeat, the Kremlin endorsed Sadat's request that the United States and the Soviet Union jointly intervene to separate the belligerents. But Nixon refused to countenance the unprecedented deployment of

Soviet troops in a region of such strategic and economic importance to the US, and thus the Kremlin declared that it would introduce its own forces into the area unilaterally. In response, Nixon ordered a worldwide nuclear alert of American forces and the Soviet Union promptly followed suit. For a moment it seemed that the fourth Arab–Israeli war was about to become a global confrontation. That risk was averted by the UN Security Council, which passed a compromise resolution authorizing the interposition of 7,000 UN soldiers between the combatants to supervise a ceasefire. In December 1973, the Israelis and Arabs, under intense pressure from the superpowers (and with US and Soviet participation), conducted their first face-to-face negotiations in a quarter of a century at a peace conference in Geneva. Thereafter, US Secretary of State Henry Kissinger shuttled between Cairo and Tel Aviv intermittently for two years in an effort to bring Israel and Egypt together while freezing the Soviet Union out of the negotiating process.

In September 1975, the two sides finally agreed to a partial Israeli withdrawal in the Sinai, creating a buffer zone in which US and UN observers would use technological means to detect violations of the ceasefire. Although the Soviet Union did not recognize this US-sponsored interim solution, it refrained from interfering. Thus the superpower détente appeared to survive its first serious test, while the prospects for stability in the Middle East seemed more promising than ever before.

Nevertheless, the Western world's stake in the Middle East conflict had taken on an ominous new dimension. When Washington airlifted supplies to Israel to replace lost tanks and planes, the oil-producing cartel, the Organization of Petroleum Exporting Countries (OPEC), retaliated first by imposing a five-month embargo on petroleum shipments to the United States and then by quadrupling the price of crude oil between 1973 and 1975. Far more serious than the inconvenience of long lines at the gasoline pumps, these sharp and sudden price increases in an essential commodity produced the most serious economic downturn in the world economy since the Great Depression.

Together, the oil embargo and price increases exposed the prosperous nations of the industrialized world (the United States, Canada, the Western European countries, and Japan) to an unprecedented form of economic warfare waged by a coalition of impoverished nations in the developing world. OPEC's ability to raise at will the world price of its product highlighted the industrial world's dependence on foreign sources of energy: the US imported 40 per cent of its petroleum in the mid-1970s, while the Western European nations and Japan depended on imports for more than 80 per cent of their energy needs. The first commodity cartel to use its control of an essential raw material as an effective economic and political weapon, OPEC set a precedent that other primary producing nations could be expected to follow. The industrial world of the north depended on the non-industrial world of the south for more than half its supplies of a whole range of raw materials—cobalt, copper, chrome, manganese, tungsten, tin, bauxite, aluminum, and others—without which its economic growth would grind to a halt.

The prospect of Third World producers using the prices of essential commodities to forcibly redistribute the world's wealth haunted officials in the non-communist industrial world during the mid-1970s. Nervous statesmen in Western Europe began to call for a north–south dialogue to establish orderly procedures for the exchange of economic assets between the industrialized and commodity-producing regions of the earth. Others, especially naval and military strategists in the United States, once again emphasized the necessity of protecting the sea lanes to these vital mineral resources, and of ensuring both the security and the pro-Western orientation of the regimes that controlled them through increased military assistance and protection.

It was presumably in the interest of preserving East–West détente that the Kremlin decided not to interfere with the unilateral US effort to promote a reconciliation between Israel and Egypt. By the middle of the 1970s, that American campaign was well on its way to fulfillment as Kissinger, preserving the continuity of American foreign policy throughout the tumultuous transition from the disgraced Nixon to the untested Ford, established the United States as an ostensibly disinterested arbiter of the Arab–Israeli conflict. Apparently both superpowers had learned to appreciate the advantages of stability in the Middle East as a complement to the relaxation of tensions in Europe and the strategic arms control agreement recently achieved. Moscow seemed resigned to Washington's unilateral sponsorship of a Middle East peace, while the US prodded Israel into relinquishing the Egyptian territory it held in exchange for Cairo's pledge to respect the country's right to exist as a sovereign and secure state in the midst of the Arab world.

SUMMARY

The peaceful resolution of the Cuban Missile Crisis opened a period of détente between the United States and the Soviet Union. Both sides focused their efforts on arms control, beginning with the Nuclear Test Ban Treaty of 1963. But this did not put an end to the arms race between them. In the course of the 1960s, the nuclear arsenals on both sides expanded according to the doctrine of 'mutual assured destruction' (MAD), where each possessed enough weapons to withstand a first strike and to launch a massive counterattack—making it impossible for either side to 'win' a nuclear war. By the end of the decade, both nations were feeling the strain of heightened defence spending, and in 1972 they embarked on a first round of Strategic Arms Limitation Talks (SALT I). Another major achievement of détente was the Helsinki Conference of 1973–5, which produced a series of agreements between the European member states of NATO and the Warsaw Pact.

The détente between the two superpowers did not ease tensions in the Middle East. The formation of the Palestine Liberation Organization (PLO) in 1964 brought a new dimension to the Arab–Israeli conflict, which erupted into two regional wars: the Six Day War of 1967, and the Yom Kippur War of 1973. While the United States continued to support Israel, the Soviet Union provided aid to Egypt and other Arab regimes.

In retaliation for Western support of Israel, the Organization of Petroleum Exporting Countries (OPEC) imposed an embargo in 1973 and began a series of increases in the price of oil that sent shock waves through Western economies. These actions marked a new stage in the emerging global multi-polarity, in which non-aligned nations exerted greater international influence.

NOTES

1. The only precedent for regional nuclear demilitarization was a treaty in 1959 that declared Antarctica a nuclear-free zone.

2. A protocol signed in 1974 restricted each side to a single ABM deployment, thereby abandoning the original idea of protecting the two national capitals. Since then, even the plan to protect the American Minutemen silos has been scrapped, although President Reagan revived the idea in 1983 with his 'Strategic Defense Initiative' (see p. 306).

QUESTIONS FOR CRITICAL THOUGHT

1. What were the major obstacles to Kennedy's 'hearts and minds' policy?
2. Why did Lester Pearson place such importance on maintaining good relations with the United States?
3. What were the most important factors motivating de Gaulle to seek an independent nuclear deterrent?
4. Why was the Brandt era so important in terms of European foreign relations?
5. Discuss how the Six Day War represents a pivotal point in the Middle East.
6. Why did OPEC actions in the early 1970s have such a massive global impact?

WEBSITE FOR FURTHER REFERENCE

Canada: A People's History – The October Crisis
www.cbc.ca/history/EPISCONTENTSE1EP16CH1PA4LE.html

Documents from the Women's Liberation Movement
http://scriptorium.lib.duke.edu/wlm

Library of Congress: Civil Rights Resource Guide
www.loc.gov/rr/program/bib/civilrights/external.html

Sixties Project: Primary Document Archive
www2.iath.virginia.edu/sixties/HTML_docs/Resources/Primary.html

CHAPTER 10

THE RISE OF CHINA AND THE COLD WAR IN ASIA

THE COMMUNIST VICTORY IN THE CHINESE CIVIL WAR

The installation of a communist government in China in 1949 terminated a civil war that had raged intermittently since 1927 between the pro-Western government of Chiang Kai-shek and the communist guerrilla movement operating in the countryside. Since the communist victory in China followed the Soviet-inspired coup in Czechoslovakia and the USSR's attempt to dislodge the Western allies from Berlin, many in Washington regarded the new regime in Beijing as an Asian counterpart of the Soviet satellite empire in Eastern Europe. But the handful of American foreign-service officers who had spent time with the Chinese communist guerrillas during the war understood a basic fact that was entirely ignored in the United States amid the indiscriminate anti-communism of the 1950s: the Chinese Communist Party was a thoroughly indigenous organization. Its ideological affinity with and material dependence on the Soviet Union were both minimal, and its political relations with the Kremlin and its representatives in Asia had long been marked by stresses and strains.

From the mid-1930s to the spectacular triumph of 1949, the history of the Chinese Communist Party offered many examples of the ideological and tactical differences between the dedicated band of revolutionaries in China and the COMINTERN agents sent there by Moscow to organize an insurrection on the Soviet model. Prominent among those differences was the fact that whereas the Marxist–Leninist model emphasized the revolutionary role of the urban working class, the Chinese communist leadership recognized that in their pre-industrial country the revolution would depend on the landless peasantry. Although Lenin had relied on the impoverished rural masses of Russia to ensure the success of his revolution, he nevertheless regarded the peasantry as only an auxiliary force in the proletarian insurrection. In line with this theoretical conception, throughout the 1920s the Soviet COMINTERN agents in China and their protégés in the Chinese Communist Party concentrated their energies on organizing labour in preparation for a workers' insurrection that would begin in the cities and eventually spread to discontented peasants in the countryside.

But in China, where less than 1 per cent of the workforce toiled in factories, the workers' vanguard had no workers. The Chinese communists had learned this lesson at great cost in 1927, when, at the suggestion of its Soviet advisers, they incited proletarian uprisings in several cities that were easily suppressed by the government because of their isolation from the genuine class struggle that was brewing in the Chinese countryside. In the same year, a brilliant communist organizer named Mao Zedong had independently concluded that the only hope for social revolution in his country lay in mobilizing the hundreds of millions of oppressed peasants against their exploitative landlords and the political and military elites who sustained them. By the mid-1930s, Mao had effectively taken control of the

Communist Party apparatus. Though he adhered closely to the Stalinist line in international matters and did not dispute the relevance of Soviet communist ideology to his country, Mao charted an increasingly independent course for the Chinese variant of communism and began to assume the role of the infallible interpreter of Marxist–Leninist doctrine in China. This posture was anathema to Joseph Stalin, who was accustomed to dealing with foreign communist leaders who depended on the Kremlin for their positions and respected its absolute authority within the international communist movement.

The principal source of friction between the communist regime in Moscow and the communist revolutionary movement in the Chinese countryside was Stalin's determination to maintain

Chinese General Chiang Kai-shek inspects high-ranking officers of the Officers Training Corps at Lushan, Kinkiang, Jiangxi Sheng, *c.* 1937–43. Library of Congress, LC-USZ62-112372.

friendly relations with the very government that Mao was striving to overturn, that of the fervently anti-communist Chiang Kai-shek. The concern that the two strongmen shared in the 1930s was the increasing military menace that Japan posed to their respective countries. During Japan's undeclared war against China, from 1937 to 1945, the Kremlin pressured the communist guerrillas operating in northern Shensi province to observe a temporary truce in their challenge to Chiang's nationalist government in Nanking (and later Chungking) in order to present a united front to the foreign invaders. The Kremlin supplied considerable military and financial assistance to the Nationalist forces and persuaded Mao to place his Red Army under the nominal jurisdiction of the Chinese government.

The removal of the Japanese threat in 1945 did not dampen Stalin's desire to maintain cordial relations with Chiang. Nor did it produce any increase in direct Soviet support for the Chinese communist movement. On 14 August 1945, the day before Japan accepted the Allied terms of surrender, the Soviet Union concluded a treaty of friendship and alliance with the Chinese Nationalist government. By its terms Moscow formally recognized Chiang's regime as the legitimate government of China and pledged to send it military and economic aid in exchange for joint Sino–Soviet management of the Manchurian railway and the port of Dairen, the right to build a Soviet naval base at Port Arthur, and Chinese recognition of the 'independence' of the Soviet client state of Mongolia. In the meantime, the Kremlin advised the Chinese communists to dismantle their independent military apparatus and become junior partners in a political coalition with the Nationalists. By the time the Soviet military forces left Manchuria in 1946 (after stripping it of all portable industrial equipment), it was clear that Moscow was playing off the two rivals in the Chinese Civil War against each other in order to prevent the creation of a unified China under a single political authority. Thus the Soviet occupation forces turned over captured Japanese weapons to Mao's partisans in Manchuria while agreeing to Chiang's request that

the Soviet troops remain in the region until the Nationalist forces could arrive in sufficient numbers to prevent a communist takeover.

Moscow's equivocal policy regarding the Chinese Civil War continued after hostilities resumed in 1946 (following the failure of an American mediation mission headed by General George C. Marshall). As the Nationalist armies in the north disintegrated before the communist onslaught in 1948, Stalin urged Mao to halt his southward advance at the Yangtze River in order to let Chiang's forces regroup and create a non-communist enclave in the south. When the communists rejected that advice and burst into the southern cities in early 1949, the Soviet ambassador stayed with the retreating Nationalist government almost to the end. One reason behind the Kremlin's reluctance to give unqualified support to the communist insurrection in China was evidently the same one that had prompted it to exercise a restraining influence on the communist insurgents in Greece: the fear that a local communist triumph over forces supported by the West would provoke a response from the United States that could escalate into a global confrontation for which the Soviet Union was entirely unprepared. An additional reason may have been fear that a vigorous new communist regime, established without the assistance of the Red Army in a country with almost three times as many people as the Soviet Union, would inevitably become a competing pole of attraction within the world communist movement.

Ironically, while the Soviet Union attempted to restrain the Chinese communists and preserved its diplomatic contacts with the doomed Chinese Nationalist regime as it collapsed during the summer of 1949, Washington announced that it was terminating all economic and military assistance to Chiang Kai-shek on account of his government's corruption and inefficiency. As the People's Republic of China was established on 1 October 1949, Washington appeared prepared to accept the communist victory in the Chinese Civil War. In January 1950, a month after the last remnants of Chiang's military forces and political administration had retreated to the island of Taiwan (Formosa), US President Truman reaffirmed the Allied declarations of Cairo and Potsdam that Taiwan was to be regarded as an integral part of China and announced that he had no intention of resuming American military assistance to the Nationalist authorities that had been suspended the previous August. In effect, Washington implied that it would do nothing to prevent the new regime on the mainland from seizing the island from Chiang.

The economic conditions inherited by the new communist leaders in Beijing were so disastrous that, after winning their 22-year struggle without significant Soviet assistance and despite Soviet counsels of restraint, they had to look to Moscow for help in rebuilding. The damage done by the Japanese occupation and the civil war required massive infusions of foreign capital and technological expertise. Aware that anti-communist sentiment in the United States was increasing in response to events in Europe and that China's chances of receiving Marshall Plan-type assistance from Washington were therefore slight, Mao left his country, for the first time in his life, at the end of 1949 to visit the Soviet capital, carrying his hat in his hand. After being kept waiting for two months, the new ruler of the world's most populous nation was persuaded in February 1950 to sign a 30-year Treaty of Friendship, Alliance, and Mutual Assistance that was directed at Japan and, implicitly, at the United States.

By the terms of other agreements, Stalin secured China's recognition of the independence of Mongolia under Soviet tutelage as well as the continuation of Soviet participation in the management of the Manchurian railroad and Soviet base rights in the two Yellow Sea ports of Dairen and Port Arthur until 1952. Mao also had to consent to the formation of joint stock companies to develop the mineral resources of Manchuria and Xinjiang—two historic objects of Soviet economic ambition. Moscow thereby obtained the assurance of a friendly power on the Asian frontier, together with temporary naval privileges and long-term economic concessions that can only

be labelled imperialist in character. Such was the price that Mao had to pay for the Soviet economic assistance that turned out to be far less than he had hoped: US$300 million in long-term credits, which amounted to less than half a dollar for each Chinese citizen. Significantly, at a time when Chiang's armies were regrouping in Taiwan in preparation for an invasion of the mainland, there was no military assistance from Moscow.

These inauspicious beginnings of the Sino–Soviet entente, together with Stalin's earlier tendency to hold the Chinese communists at arm's length, raise an important question. Could Washington have disrupted the emerging partnership between Moscow and Beijing by extending diplomatic recognition and economic assistance to the communists once their authority on the mainland had been confirmed in the early months of 1950? The United States had traditionally considered itself the benefactor and protector of the Chinese people, and American export interests had long coveted China as a market for their goods. During the Second World War Franklin Roosevelt's overestimation of China's status as one of the world's five great powers had led him to secure for it, over the objections of a skeptical Winston Churchill, a permanent seat in the Security Council of the United Nations. We have also seen how the Truman administration, after the failure of its mediation efforts in the winter of 1945–6, had disengaged from the Chinese Civil War by withdrawing its support from the Nationalist regime.

There is some evidence, though sparse and inconclusive, that Mao entertained the possibility of establishing correct if not cordial relations with Washington at the end of the war, while he was still in close contact with American diplomatic and intelligence agents attached to the Chinese communist movement during the common struggle against Japan. The Truman administration's cultivation of friendly ties with Yugoslavia after Tito's defection from the Soviet bloc in 1948 offered an instructive precedent for Washington's willingness to temper its indiscriminate antipathy for communist regimes. The US government was in no hurry to join the East

European communist states, most of the Asian countries, Scandinavia, Switzerland, and Britain[1] in extending formal recognition to the Beijing government at a time when it was mistreating American citizens and seizing American property in China. But officials in the State Department were patiently preparing for a time when, after a suitable interval, the communist triumph in the Chinese Civil War would receive explicit recognition from the United States.

THE KOREAN WAR

Washington's acknowledgement of communist China was to be postponed for two-and-a-half decades because of the unforeseen outbreak of hostilities on the Korean peninsula in the summer of 1950. We have already noted the ways in which post-war Korea resembled post-war Germany. Temporarily partitioning the former along the 38th parallel of latitude into a northern Soviet zone and a southern American zone, the two superpowers failed to reach agreement on the conditions of reunification and thus permitted the establishment of two governments, one in each zone, that claimed sovereignty over the entire country. In August 1948, after free elections conducted under the supervision of the United Nations, the Republic of Korea was formed in the south with Seoul as its capital and conservative anti-communist Syngman Rhee as its president. In the following September, a People's Democratic Republic of Korea was established in the northern city of Pyongyang under the leadership of revolutionary communist militant Kim Il Sung.

Whereas the mutual disengagement of Soviet and American military power from divided Germany proved to be an impossible goal, the two superpowers had little difficulty withdrawing from divided Korea, the Soviets doing so by December 1948 and the Americans by June 1949. What they left behind was a bubbling cauldron of political instability: two separate Korean governments, each armed and supplied by one of the two contenders in the Cold War, each claiming authority over the territory ruled by the other.

On the early morning of 25 June 1950, this unstable political situation on the Korean peninsula boiled over into war when more than 100,000 North Korean troops launched a surprise attack across the 38th parallel against South Korea. Profiting from their numerical superiority and the element of surprise, the North Korean forces hurled back the South Korean army, capturing Seoul on 27 June. On the same day, the UN Security Council, meeting in the absence of the Soviet delegate (who had been boycotting its sessions since January 1950 to protest the UN's refusal to assign the Chinese seat to the newly established communist regime in Beijing), adopted a US-sponsored resolution requesting all member states 'to provide the Republic of Korea with all necessary aid to repel the aggressors'.

President Truman had already instructed the commander of the American occupation forces in Japan, General Douglas MacArthur, to furnish naval and air support to the South Korean army, and on 29 June, when South Korea's collapse seemed imminent, he ordered the transfer of two American infantry divisions from Japan to Korea. On 4 July, the Security Council, still without the Soviet delegate, established a UN expeditionary force for deployment in Korea, which the following day was placed under MacArthur's command with instructions 'to repel the armed attack and to restore international peace and security'. By the middle of September, 20 member states, including Canada, had contributed ground forces to the UN army. But the American troops stationed in Japan did most of the fighting, accounting for half of the ground forces (compared to 40 per cent contributed by South Korea), 86 per cent of the naval forces, and 93 per cent of the air forces.

It is evident from his remarks at the time that Truman's decision to intervene was prompted by his conviction that the North Korean attack was a Soviet-inspired probe of Western resolve in Asia similar to those that in Europe had given rise to the American doctrine of containment. 'This is the Greece of the Far East,' he told reporters on 25 June, pointing to the Korean peninsula on a large globe in his office. 'If we are tough enough

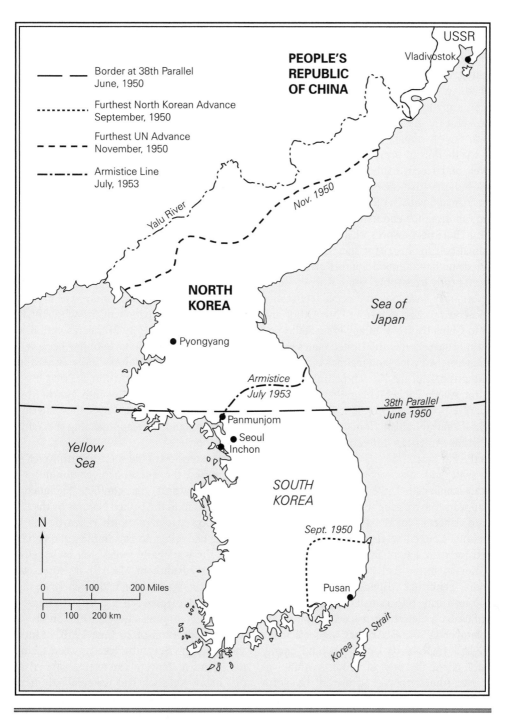

Border at 38th Parallel
June, 1950

Furthest North Korean Advance
September, 1950

Furthest UN Advance
November, 1950

Armistice Line
July, 1953

PEOPLE'S
REPUBLIC
OF CHINA

USSR

Vladivostok

Yalu River

Nov. 1950

NORTH
KOREA

Sea of
Japan

● Pyongyang

Armistice
July 1953

38th Parallel
June 1950

● Panmunjom

Yellow
Sea

● Seoul
Inchon

SOUTH
KOREA

N

Sept. 1950

0   100   200 Miles

0   100   200 km

Pusan

Korea Strait

THE KOREAN WAR, 1950–1953

now, there won't be any next step.' The evidence of Soviet inspiration for, if not collusion in, the North Korean aggression is circumstantial but compelling. Kim Il Sung had lived in the USSR for years, had returned to his country with the Soviet liberation army in 1945, and had been installed in power three years later on the express orders of Stalin. Soviet military advisers were attached to the North Korean army down to the battalion level, and recent evidence from the Soviet archives indicates that the North Korean invasion had been cleared with the Kremlin.

Stalin's motives for endorsing the invasion are less clear. But the prospect of a speedy victory at minimal cost for his client state over the outnumbered, under-equipped South Koreans must have been nearly irresistible. South Korea's warm-water ports may have looked especially attractive after Moscow's pledge to restore Port Arthur and Dairen to China by 1952. In any case, Stalin had no reason to suspect that the United States would interfere with the Pyongyang regime's bid to bring the southern part of the Korean peninsula under its control. After all, in a highly publicized speech in January 1950, Secretary of State Dean Acheson had specifically refrained from including South Korea within America's 'military defence perimeter' in the Far East.

The swift and massive intervention of the American-dominated United Nations army in Korea appears to have caught the Kremlin entirely off guard, since it could have used its veto in the Security Council to deny the authorization required for such action. By mid-September, the North Korean forces had conquered practically the entire peninsula, driving the demoralized South Korean army into a small corner around the port of Pusan on the southern coast. However, on 15 September 1950, MacArthur's UN force made a successful amphibious landing behind enemy lines at Inchon, the port of Seoul. Within two weeks MacArthur's troops had driven the North Korean army all the way north to the 38th parallel, killing or capturing half of its soldiers in the process. The daring landing at Inchon, and the liberation of South Korea that quickly followed,

had fulfilled the UN mandate to 'repel the armed attack' by restoring the military status quo ante. The accompanying instructions to 'restore international peace and security' seemed to suggest that the next step would be to negotiate with North Korea and secure its agreement to respect the sovereignty and security of its southern neighbour.

The disorganized retreat of the North Korean invaders, however, presented the Truman administration with an opportunity too tempting to pass up, that of forcibly reunifying the peninsula by erasing the artificial division that neither North nor South Korea had ever accepted as permanent and that had never been recognized by the UN. In pursuit of this objective, the United States on 7 October 1950 pushed through the UN General Assembly a resolution authorizing MacArthur to 'take all appropriate measures to insure a stable situation in the whole of Korea'. Acting on the authority of this resolution, which technically lacked the force of law because it had come from the General Assembly rather than the Security Council,[2] MacArthur ordered his troops to cross the 38th parallel into North Korea on 9 October. Within three weeks, they had captured Pyongyang and were approaching the Yalu River on the border.

The extension of the war to North Korea inevitably raised the question of communist China's attitude towards the conflict. Excluded from membership in the United Nations by the US veto and elbowed out of North Korea by the USSR, Beijing had taken no part in the diplomatic activity in the war's early stages. But even before the ominous advance of MacArthur's forces toward Manchuria, Washington had taken a step that was guaranteed to provoke a hostile response from the new communist government on the mainland: the decision of 26 June 1950, to interpose the American Seventh Fleet between China and the island of Taiwan, where the battered armies of Chiang Kai-shek had reassembled after their expulsion from the mainland.

This move was undertaken purely as a precaution—to prevent the communist and Nationalist Chinese from further complicating the situation by renewing their own bitter conflict—and its execution was scrupulously even-handed. But to Beijing it seemed a flagrant intervention in the Chinese Civil War that effectively prevented the communists from consolidating their triumph. Beijing's suspicions of Washington's motives were not allayed when MacArthur made a highly publicized visit to Chiang at the end of July, particularly in view of an earlier offer from the Nationalist leader to contribute 33,000 soldiers to the crusade against the communists in Korea.

It was MacArthur's counter-offensive deep into North Korea and rapid advance towards the Manchurian border that finally spurred Beijing into action. On 2 October, Premier Zhou Enlai warned Washington (through an intermediary) that if US forces crossed the 38th parallel, China might well be obliged to intervene in defence of its own interests. When that warning was ignored, almost 200,000 Chinese 'volunteers' quietly crossed the Yalu River into North Korea during the month of October, travelling at night to avoid detection by the UN forces then advancing northward. After a series of inconclusive engagements with MacArthur's troops, in late November the Chinese attacked along a broad front, forcing the UN troops to retreat southward. By the end of the year the counter-attacking Chinese and North Korean forces had crossed the 38th parallel, and on 4 January 1951, the southern capital of Seoul fell for the second time to the northern invaders.

The Truman administration had two equally unattractive options: to wage a protracted ground war on the Korean peninsula or to adopt MacArthur's strategy of extending the conflict to China itself by bombing Manchuria. Since China's alliance with the Soviet Union meant that the latter course would risk turning a regional conflict into a world war, Truman chose the former, deciding to confine UN military operations to Korea while simultaneously pursuing a negotiated settlement that would restore the political partition of the peninsula at the 38th parallel. By the beginning of April, the UN troops had halted the communists' spring offensive and counterattacked once again into North Korea. MacArthur then

issued on his own authority a provocative proclamation that in effect offered Beijing a choice: accept an armistice at the 38th parallel or endure attacks on its own territory across the Yalu. On 5 April, the Republican leader of the US House of Representatives caused a sensation by publishing a letter from MacArthur dated 20 March that revived the prospect of using Nationalist Chinese troops in Korea and advocated total victory in the war. Stung by this egregious challenge to his presidential authority, Truman dismissed MacArthur for insubordination and replaced him with General Matthew B. Ridgway.

The removal of MacArthur cleared the way for the United States to pursue a negotiated settlement in Korea. Both the US and the USSR realized that the risk of escalation was too great and that serious efforts to make peace were required. On 25 June, Truman accepted a Soviet suggestion for a ceasefire and the beginning of armistice discussions. The first meeting between representatives of the UN and the communists took place in July 1951. These talks dragged on intermittently for two more years until an armistice was finally signed on 6 July 1953, at the tiny farm village of Panmunjom near the 38th parallel. A demilitarized zone would be established along the redrawn border separating the two Korean states, and a joint UN–communist commission would meet periodically to resolve disputes. The new boundary line gained South Korea less than 400,000 hectares of territory—a paltry reward for a three-year conflict that cost a million South Korean, a million North Korean and Chinese, and 33,000 American lives.

The Korean War served as a catalyst for rearmament and remobilization in the West. No less dramatic were its effects on the political and military situation in the Far East. What had begun as a regional contest for sovereignty on the Korean peninsula had ended in the extension of the Cold War into the entire area of East Asia and the western Pacific. The United States, confronted by what it saw as a calculated bid by a monolithic Communist bloc to expand into the Asian power vacuum created by the defeat of Japan, hastened to extend military protection and economic assistance to the non-communist states of the region, just as it had done in non-communist Europe a few years earlier.

In addition to retaining military forces in South Korea and signing a mutual security agreement with that country, the United States made a number of other military agreements with island nations in the western Pacific to bolster their security against the presumed menace of communist aggression. In August 1951, a treaty with the Philippines (which had gained independence from the US in 1946) reaffirmed American air and naval base rights in that country and committed the United States to its defence. The following month, Washington concluded a tripartite security treaty with Australia and New Zealand (the ANZUS Pact), thereby taking over the role once played by Britain.

The most important addition to the new US-sponsored East Asian security system, however, was the country whose aggressive acts had brought the United States into the Far Eastern war a decade earlier. The United States' occupation of Japan, like its occupation of Germany, had originally been intended to prevent the defeated power from ever again threatening the security of its neighbours. In addition to total demilitarization, achieving this objective meant abolishing all nationalistic societies, purging public officials and business leaders who had co-operated with the military authorities in planning and waging the recent war, and dissolving the large industrial conglomerates that had promoted and profited from the seizure of the markets and resources of the 'Co-Prosperity Sphere' in East Asia.

It also meant imposing restraints on Japan's economic recovery and supervising its reparations payments. The commander of the occupation regime, General MacArthur, instructed his staff to draft a new constitution for Japan, which went into effect in May 1947. The document established parliamentary government on the British model, safeguarded civil liberties, and included a provision renouncing war as well as the maintenance of land, sea, and air forces. However, the

Soviet–American confrontation in Europe at the end of the 1940s led the Truman administration to reconsider and eventually to reverse its stern occupation policy in Asia for fear that an economically weak, militarily vulnerable Japan would become a tempting target for Soviet intimidation once the US occupation forces had been withdrawn. Thus in 1948–9, Washington removed all restrictions on Japan's economic recovery, halted the requisition of capital equipment for reparations, abandoned plans for the forced decentralization of Japanese industry, and began to provide financial assistance to promote Japan's economic growth and social stability.

The Korean War accelerated Japan's transformation from impoverished enemy to prosperous ally by demonstrating its value to the United States as a counterweight to Soviet and communist Chinese power in the Far East. American military spending during the war stimulated an economic boom in Japan that by the mid-1950s was to give its people the highest standard of living in Asia. Capital investment and technology transfers from the US increased sharply, enabling Japanese industry to replace its war-damaged equipment with the most up-to-date machinery. Japan's export trade rapidly recovered, first in textiles and other light industries, and later in advanced sectors such as electronics, automobiles, and shipbuilding.

This spectacular economic revival was accompanied by an expansion of Japan's defence capabilities. In the summer of 1950, the government in Tokyo secured US authorization to create the 75,000-member National Police Reserve to replace the American occupation troops that were being redeployed in Korea. A rudimentary Japanese navy was created in August 1952, and in February 1954 the existing ground and naval forces were expanded and a small air force was established. All of these were labelled 'self-defence' forces, in deference to the constitutional renunciation of war and the means of waging it. But whatever the designation, together they constituted the nucleus of Japan's rearmament during the period when the Cold War was being extended to Asia.

The rearmament and economic recovery of Japan, during and after the Korean War, took place behind the protective shield of the United States, which hastened to put an end to Japan's status as occupied enemy and restore it to full political sovereignty. In September 1951, the US and 48 other nations (excluding the Soviet Union and China) signed a peace treaty with Japan in San Francisco, which ended the state of war and brought the American occupation to end in April 1952. On the same day the treaty was signed, Washington and Tokyo concluded a security pact stipulating the indefinite retention of US military forces in Japan as well as the maintenance of a major base under direct US administration on the Japanese island of Okinawa. Thus the former enemy Japan, like the former enemy Germany at the other end of the Eurasian land mass, had come to be regarded by Washington as an indispensable asset in its campaign to contain the global expansion of Soviet power.

A similar function was soon to be performed by the outpost of the anti-communist Nationalist Chinese on the island of Taiwan. In the course of the Korean conflict, the United States had abandoned its even-handed policy toward the two sides in the Chinese Civil War, resuming the deliveries of economic and military assistance to Chiang's government in exile that had been discontinued in the final stage of the Nationalist collapse on the mainland. Throughout the 1950s, American assistance to Taiwan averaged US$250 million per year. In early 1953, President Eisenhower announced that the Seventh Fleet, which continued to patrol the Formosa Strait, would no longer interfere with Chiang's efforts to 'liberate' the mainland from communist rule. In time, Nationalist bombing raids were conducted against the Chinese coast and commandos were dispatched to the mainland. In December 1954, the US concluded a mutual defence treaty with Taiwan (which was still recognized by most non-communist countries as the 'Republic of China' and retained the Chinese seat in the United Nations). In 1955, the two houses of the US Congress voted by large majorities to authorize the president to commit military forces

to the defence of Taiwan. When China in 1954–5 and again in 1958 shelled Quemoy and Matsu—two small islands a few kilometres off its coast that had been occupied by Nationalist troops and used for commando raids against the mainland—the US pledged to defend them by force. Throughout the 1950s, Washington enforced a trade embargo on mainland China and forbade US citizens to travel there. The exotic land that had once exercised such an irresistible attraction for American merchants in search of markets and American missionaries in search of converts abruptly disappeared from the public consciousness of the United States.

THE USSR AND CHINA: FROM PARTNERSHIP TO RIVALRY

As Washington's support for the Nationalist regime in Taiwan poisoned Sino–American relations, Moscow and Beijing drew closer in the face of what they jointly saw as efforts to erect an anti-communist bastion in Asia composed of nations armed, assisted, and protected by the United States. The US-sponsored rehabilitation of Japan—the former enemy of both the USSR and China that had risen to power at their expense— was a particular source of common concern. Although prohibited by its own constitution from ever again becoming a first-rank military power, Japan's security pact with the US, its willingness to host American bases on its national territory, and its rapid progress toward economic recovery raised fears in the communist-controlled portion of East Asia that echoed the fears then being sparked in Eastern Europe by the revival of an economically powerful, US-supported West Germany.

The Sino–Soviet partnership that matured during the first half of the 1950s took the form of Soviet economic and diplomatic support for China in exchange for Beijing's continued recognition of Moscow's undisputed authority in the world communist movement. The Soviet Union had supplied China with roughly US$2 billion worth of military equipment during its undeclared war in Korea. Thereafter, by the terms of an agreement concluded in September 1953, Soviet economic aid and technical advisers poured into China to assist in its crash program of industrialization. By the middle of the decade, the Soviet Union had become China's principal trading partner, taking about half of its exports. In 1954, Moscow removed the last vestiges of Soviet imperialism in China by pledging to evacuate the Soviet naval base at Port Arthur by the end of the next year[3] and by transferring to Beijing the Soviet share of the joint stock companies that had been formed in 1950 to exploit the mineral resources of Xinjiang. This strengthening of bilateral ties between the two giants of the Communist bloc confirmed US fears of a monolithic communist conspiracy to conquer the world, fears that were aggravated by the spread of McCarthyite hysteria in the United States during the same period.

Yet even as some American officials bemoaned the 'loss of China', cracks were beginning to appear in the Sino–Soviet friendship. China had drawn close to the Soviet Union because it needed economic aid for its industrialization and diplomatic support in its disputes with hostile neighbours, particularly the US-backed Nationalist regime of Chiang Kai-shek in Taiwan. Throughout the entire period of the Soviet economic assistance program, however, Beijing authorities were disappointed by the amounts furnished and the strings attached to them. The military aid during the Korean conflict had to be repaid in full at a time when China was struggling to recover from the effects of its civil war and to launch its industrial takeoff.

The economic aid provided thereafter fell far short of Chinese expectations. Once Khrushchev mounted his campaign to extend Soviet influence in the non-aligned countries of the Third World in 1955, the USSR was supplying more development assistance to non-communist states such as India and Egypt than to its communist neighbour in Asia. Similarly, Soviet support for China's military preparedness was half-hearted and always conditional on Beijing's absolute subservience to Moscow. In October 1957, Khrushchev secretly agreed to furnish modest aid for the Chinese nuclear program that was about to get underway

and offered to supply China with a prototype of an atomic bomb—provided that Beijing consent to joint coordination of foreign policy and Soviet control of Chinese nuclear warheads. After two years of fruitless efforts to obtain Mao's consent to these infringements on China's freedom of action, Khrushchev unilaterally cancelled the agreement in June 1959.

These disagreements over Soviet aid to China were accompanied by a growing ideological dispute in the second half of the 1950s. At the root of this friction was Mao's insistence on reaffirming the orthodox Leninist belief in the inevitability of war with the capitalist powers at a time when Khrushchev, fearing the consequences for his own country of a nuclear exchange, was pursuing peaceful coexistence with the West in the form of arms-control negotiations and summit meetings with 'enemy' leaders. China's mounting dissatisfaction with the USSR's 'revisionist' pursuit of an accommodation with the capitalist world stemmed less from a divergence of ideological opinion than from a more practical concern involving Chinese national interests. Economically undeveloped, militarily weak, and diplomatically isolated, China depended on Soviet support for its security in East Asia. Thus each time Soviet and American chiefs of state met face-to-face—at Geneva in 1955, at Camp David in 1959, at Paris in 1960—Beijing feared a rapprochement between the superpowers that would leave China alone to face the threats posed by its unfriendly neighbours.

The most serious of these threats continued to come from the Nationalist regime in Taiwan. In May 1957, Chiang Kai-shek had agreed to Washington's installation of missiles, armed with nuclear warheads, that were capable of reaching the Chinese mainland. In the meantime, Chiang continued to fortify the coastal islands of Quemoy and Matsu and increased to almost 100,000 the number of Nationalist troops stationed there. When, in August 1958, China resumed its heavy shelling of Quemoy in an attempt to dislodge the Nationalists, President Eisenhower ordered US planes to airlift supplies to Chiang's troops and arranged for US ships to escort a Nationalist convoy to the beleaguered island, while the State Department issued a veiled threat of military intervention should China seek to recapture the areas. At the height of the Quemoy Crisis, Beijing was unhappy to find that Moscow did not offer the customary expressions of support; the silence was not broken until China agreed to participate in direct negotiations with representatives of the United States at Warsaw to seek a peaceful solution to the crisis.

In the following year, Khrushchev's meeting with Eisenhower at Camp David reignited Chinese fears of a Soviet–American accommodation at their expense. This suspicion was not allayed when Khrushchev, returning from his US tour via Beijing, publicly warned Mao to avoid a confrontation with Washington over Taiwan. Coming just three months after the Soviet leader had rescinded his pledge to help the Chinese develop a nuclear armament, and only a few days after his cordial meeting with Eisenhower, this warning cast doubt on the value of Soviet support for China's grievances against the the US-backed regime across the Taiwan Strait. Apparently Khrushchev had left Camp David expecting a prompt and amicable settlement of the Berlin issue, which could pave the way for a mutual recognition of the European status quo, and was not prepared to allow Sino–American tensions in the Far East to interfere with that development.

Another source of Sino–Soviet friction as the 1950s drew to a close was the conflict between China and India over Tibet. Once a Chinese province, the region had enjoyed de facto independence under its divine ruler, the Dalai Lama, from 1914 until 1950, when it was forcibly restored to China by the new communist regime. During the spring of 1959, China ruthlessly quelled an armed insurrection in favour of Tibetan independence and accused India, which had given sanctuary to the Dalai Lama and his entourage, of having incited it. Sino–Indian border clashes were accompanied by conflicting territorial claims along the rugged Himalayan frontier. Suddenly in September 1959, as Khrushchev prepared for his US visit, Moscow infuriated Beijing by declaring its neutrality in the Sino–Indian dispute and then announcing its intention to grant New Delhi a loan much larger than any it had ever furnished to its Chinese communist ally. Just as Khrushchev had placed a higher priority on reaching agreement with the West over Berlin and Europe than on supporting China at the Taiwan Strait, he was apparently willing to sacrifice China's security in the Himalayas in favour of cultivating closer relations with India, the titular leader of the nonaligned states of the developing world.

The Sino–Soviet quarrel first became public, albeit in disguised form, at the Third Congress of the Romanian Communist Party in June 1960. Responding to Khrushchev's defence of the policy of peaceful coexistence, and his implicit criticism of the Maoist claim that war with the capitalist states was both inevitable and winnable, the Chinese delegate asserted that the recent U-2 incident and the breakup of the Paris summit meeting (to which China had not been invited) revealed the evil nature of imperialism, and he indirectly chided the Kremlin for attempting to coexist with it. This seemingly fraternal debate over the interpretation of communist doctrine was soon followed up by direct action: three months later, Khrushchev abruptly recalled the 1,390 Soviet technicians who had been assisting China in its economic modernization, ordering them to return with their industrial blueprints. Then at the conference of world communist parties in Moscow in November 1960, the Chinese delegation accused the Soviet Union of betraying the cause of world revolution, and the Albanian delegation sided with China. The Kremlin retaliated in typically indirect fashion by striking at China's supporter. The following April, Khrushchev ordered the termination of all Soviet economic and technical assistance to Albania.

The deterioration of the Sino–Soviet relationship remained an internal affair within the Communist bloc until the fall of 1962, when a series of crises strained it to the breaking point. First, the outcome of the Cuban Missile Crisis led Beijing to denounce the Soviet Union for its humiliating retreat before the imperialist aggressor. The following summer, Mao attacked the Limited Nuclear Test Ban Treaty signed by the two superpowers and Britain as an attempt by the nuclear powers to frustrate the efforts of countries such as China to provide for their own defence. Refusing to sign the treaty, China would explode its first atomic bomb on 16 October 1964, without Soviet assistance (coincidentally, within a few hours of Khrushchev's fall from power).

The second source of conflict between Moscow and Beijing was the renewal of hostilities between China and India along their common frontier in the Himalayas, which coincided with the Cuban crisis. India had, the previous August, disclosed the conclusion of an agreement whereby the Soviet Union had promised engines for Indian jet planes. During the border skirmish, the Kremlin took pains to affirm its absolute neutrality, brushing aside Beijing's attempts to secure Moscow's endorsement of its position. The next year the Chinese Communist Party publicly denounced the Soviet Union for providing military assistance to China's enemy India after having cut off its aid to China in 1960.

The third occasion of Sino–Soviet tension was potentially the most ominous of all: a border dispute between the two communist powers in China's northwestern province of Xinjiang, which had formerly been within the Soviet sphere of interest. Little is known about this initial frontier clash, but it marked the beginning of China's assertion of territorial claims against the Soviet Union, which had retained possession of almost 260 million hectares of former Chinese territory in central Asia as well as the maritime provinces of Siberia that the tsars had forcibly acquired under treaties imposed on imperial China in 1858, 1860, and 1881. As overpopulation began to be recognized as a serious impediment to China's hopes for rapid industrialization in the course of the 1960s, the sparsely inhabited spaces of the former Chinese domains in the Soviet Far East exerted an understandable attraction on the economic modernizers in Beijing.

By the end of 1964, the Sino–Soviet rift had become embarrassingly public and apparently irreversible. China's entry into the nuclear club had given a tremendous boost to its prestige in the developing world, where it was by then avidly competing with the Soviet Union for influence. Within the international communist movement, pro-Chinese factions had broken away from the regular communist parties and professed a more radical brand of Marxist–Leninism in practically every country in the world. Although Albania remained the only Soviet satellite in Eastern Europe to repudiate Moscow's authority and transfer its allegiance to Beijing, China's defection presented the other satellites with the opportunity to pursue a more independent course by playing the two communist giants off against one another.

The two most notable beneficiaries of this trend were Romania and Czechoslovakia. Romania refused the role of agricultural and petrochemical producer assigned to it by the Eastern bloc's economic organization, COMECON, in 1962, and expanded its trade with the West to more than a third of its total. It also pursued an increasingly independent foreign policy, establishing diplomatic relations with West Germany and retaining them with Israel in 1967 in violation of Eastern bloc policy. Czechoslovakia during the first half of 1968 experimented with various forms of economic liberalism and political democracy that contradicted the basic tenets of communist doctrine.

Romania's assertion of independence was tolerated by Moscow because the harshly repressive regime of its leader, Nicolae Ceauşescu, prevented what the Kremlin feared most: the proliferation of liberal ideas that could infect Romania's partners in the Warsaw Pact. In Czechoslovakia it was the failure of the government of Alexander Dubček to keep the lid on domestic dissent during the 'Prague spring' of 1968 that precipitated the Soviet-led invasion the following August and the termination of Prague's brief flirtation with liberal communism and national independence.

The Soviet intervention in Czechoslovakia prompted a torrent of invective from Beijing against this blatant interference in the domestic affairs of a sovereign communist state. So did the enunciation by the Soviet first secretary in November 1968 of the Brezhnev Doctrine, which justified intervention by Communist bloc forces in any communist country threatened by internal or external elements 'hostile to socialism'. Though ostensibly directed at the Soviet satellites in Eastern Europe, this assertion of the right of intervention (or the 'Doctrine of Limited Sovereignty', as it was euphemistically called) could easily have been interpreted as a veiled threat to China, then in the midst of a domestic 'cultural revolution' with unmistakable anti-Soviet overtones.

From the vantage point of global power politics, the Sino–Soviet quarrel in the 1960s afforded the United States a rare opportunity. By playing the two rivals for leadership in the communist camp off against one another, as Romania was doing, Washington might have been in a position to exploit to its own advantage the divisions within the formerly monolithic Communist bloc. Instead, just as the divergence between China and the Soviet Union was approaching the breaking point in the middle of the decade, the United States became deeply involved, for the second time since 1945, in a military operation in Asia that temporarily reunited the entire communist world against it.

THE UNITED STATES AND INDOCHINA

Between 1862 and 1897, France had established political control over the region of southeastern Asia known as Indochina (which comprises present-day Vietnam, Laos, and Cambodia). As was frequently the case in late nineteenth-century imperial expansion, the motives for this colonization were mixed. Commercial interests were attracted by the valuable raw materials of the region—rubber, tin, tungsten, and rice—that could be shipped to European markets. Catholic missionaries flocked to this faraway outpost of the empire in search of converts. Military and naval officials envisioned garrisons and bases that would enable France to challenge Britain's pre-eminence in the Far East.

Indigenous resistance to French domination developed after the First World War under the leadership of a charismatic nationalist widely known by the pseudonym Ho Chi Minh. In 1919, Ho appeared at the Paris Peace Conference to argue that the Wilsonian principle of self-determination, invoked on behalf of the former subjects of the Austro–Hungarian Empire in Europe, should also be applied to the Indochinese victims of French colonial domination in Asia. On learning that the principle of liberal nationalism was to be restricted to white European peoples, Ho turned to the only other ideology that appeared to promise national liberation for his compatriots. After helping to found the French Communist Party in 1920, he travelled to Moscow to receive instruction in the techniques of revolutionary agitation, and in 1930 he formed the Vietnamese Communist Party.

After the fall of France in 1940, the Japanese had occupied Indochina with the tacit consent of the French puppet government in Vichy. Thus in China, Ho organized the League for the Independence of Vietnam, or Vietminh, a coalition of nationalist groups led by the Communist Party. In co-operation with the American intelligence organization called the Office of Strategic Services (forerunner of the Central Intelligence Agency, or CIA), the Vietminh spearheaded the underground resistance to the Japanese occupation. At the end of the war in the Far East, Ho appealed to Washington to support the independence of his country on the basis of the Wilsonian principle of national self-determination incorporated in the Atlantic Charter and reaffirmed in many of President Roosevelt's wartime pronouncements. In September 1945, following the surrender of Japan and the evacuation of its occupation forces from the Asian mainland, the Vietminh formally declared the independence of the Democratic Republic of Vietnam and established its capital in the northern city of Hanoi.

But Britain, whose military forces had temporarily occupied the southern portion of Vietnam, permitted French troops to re-enter the zone under its jurisdiction. Throughout 1946, the

Vietminh tried to negotiate national independence within the French empire along the lines of the self-governing dominions of the British Commonwealth, but France refused to relinquish its control. In November 1946, after the Vietminh refused to obey a French order to evacuate Hanoi and its port of Haiphong, the French military and naval forces in the vicinity bombarded the two cities, causing as many as 6,000 casualties. The Vietminh then took to the countryside, where they organized a guerrilla movement modelled on that of Mao Zedong in northern China, and engaged the French army in a full-fledged war of national liberation.

The policy of the United States regarding the Franco–Vietnamese conflict underwent a profound change during the second half of the 1940s. President Roosevelt had been personally opposed to the restoration of European colonial power in Asia after the war, and towards the end of that conflict he had toyed with the idea of placing Indochina under international trusteeship as a way of removing French authority from the region and preparing its constituent states for independence. Some historians have attributed Roosevelt's anti-colonialism to his desire to open the European possessions in Southeast Asia to American economic penetration. Others credit the American chief of state with a genuine desire to apply the progressive principles of the Atlantic Charter to the post-war world.

In any event, the Truman administration turned a deaf ear to Ho Chi Minh's post-war appeals for US economic assistance and diplomatic support for his country's political independence. Ho's communist affiliations became a matter of concern in Washington as the Soviet–American wartime partnership degenerated into the Cold War, despite the fact that Moscow had given little support or encouragement to the Vietminh. The victory of Mao's communists in the Chinese Civil War left the impression in Washington that all of Asia was under the threat of a coordinated communist advance masterminded by Moscow. France shrewdly played on these fears, arguing that its military operation in Vietnam, which shared a border with the newly communist China, was the Far Eastern counterpart to the containment policy that the United States and its non-communist partners were currently pursuing in Western Europe.

The first formal expression of US support for France's effort to retain control of Indochina came in February 1950. Following the diplomatic recognition of Ho Chi Minh's government by China and the Soviet Union in January, Washington established formal diplomatic relations with the puppet regime of Emperor Bao Dai in Saigon that had been established by the French in the previous year as a nominally independent state (along with Laos and Cambodia) within the French Union. However, it was the outbreak of the Korean War in June 1950 that prompted the United States to intervene actively on behalf of the French against the communist-led insurgency in Indochina. In the following autumn, Washington sent a team of military advisers and US$150 million in military equipment to assist the French effort in Vietnam.

By 1954, the United States was paying 78 per cent of the costs of the French military operations and had more than 300 military advisers on the spot. By the spring of that year, in spite of the increase in American support for the French forces, the Vietminh had gained effective control of the countryside using daring guerrilla tactics borrowed from Mao Zedong. The French military commander, General Henri Navarre, concluded that the only hope of crushing the guerillas, who struck from ambush only to disappear into the jungles, lay in luring them out into the open to fight a conventional war that the French, with their superiority in artillery and air power, fully expected to win. The French deployed 18,000 of their best troops in the fortress of Dien Bien Phu on the Laotian border in the hope of engaging the Vietminh in a fight to the finish on open terrain. A fight to the finish it was, after a 55-day siege of the fortress, but it was the French who were finished. Using artillery supplied by the Chinese to shell the French ground troops from the hills surrounding their self-made trap and Chinese anti-aircraft guns to neutralize French air power, the Vietminh killed approximately 1,200 French soldiers at Dien Bien Phu and captured the remaining 11,000.

During the siege of Dien Bien Phu, the leaders of the Big Four (Britain, France, the United States, and the Soviet Union), who were meeting in Geneva to discuss German affairs, were authorized to open negotiations for a ceasefire in Indochina. To this end, representatives of the three constituent states of Indochina, as well as China, were invited. By a tragic coincidence (from the French perspective), the talks on Indochina began on 8 May, the day after the fall of Dien Bien Phu. The US had consented to participate in the discussions in the hope of reaching a settlement that would preserve the non-communist character of Indochina, with or without a continuing French presence there. In a press conference in April, President Eisenhower had compared the situation in Southeast Asia to a line of dominoes. If Indochina were to fall to a communist insurrection, the rest of non-communist Asia would be gravely threatened, as would the United States' extensive security interests in the region.

The US public did not support a military intervention to rescue the French. Eisenhower turned down requests from Paris for the use of American bombers based in the Philippines because of congressional opposition and the absence of British approval for such an operation. Ironically, in light of subsequent events, one of the most outspoken opponents of intervention in Vietnam at the time was the Democratic leader in the Senate, Lyndon Baines Johnson.

The surrender of Dien Bien Phu dashed France's hopes of negotiating a settlement in Indochina from a position of strength, especially after US air support was ruled out. The final blow to France's imperial position in Southeast Asia came in mid-June, when a new government took office in Paris, headed by Pierre Mendès-France, a longtime critic of the war who had promised to obtain a ceasefire within a month or resign. Acting as his own foreign minister, Mendès-France hastened to Geneva and, ignoring the various factions jockeying for position in the Indochinese War, approached directly the representatives of the

powers that really counted. In conversations with the USSR's Molotov and China's Zhou Enlai he worked out the basis for a settlement that would give France the chance to make a graceful exit from a lost cause.

In July 1954, the Geneva Accords ending the eight-year war in Southeast Asia were signed. Vietnam was to be temporarily partitioned along the 17th parallel of latitude; the Vietminh would administer the northern zone, while the southern zone would be governed from Saigon, where the discredited Emperor Bao Dai had been replaced a month earlier by a US-educated Catholic mandarin named Ngo Dinh Diem. Neither sector was to join military alliances, permit foreign bases on its territory, or receive military assistance from abroad. Within two years the entire country was to be reunified on the basis of general elections conducted by secret ballot under the supervision of a UN Control Commission. The sovereignty of the royalist governments of Laos and Cambodia was formally recognized by all signatories.

The Geneva Accords concluded the French colonial adventure in Indochina that had begun in the 1860s under Napoleon III. They did not, however, ratify the independence of Vietnam under the auspices of the Vietminh. Ho Chi Minh had been persuaded by his Soviet and Chinese patrons to surrender roughly 20 per cent of the territory that he controlled to an anti-communist, US-backed regime in Saigon and to accept the temporary partition of his country. Why did Moscow and Beijing induce their fellow communist to accept a diplomatic settlement that denied his movement the fruits of the victory it was about to achieve? It may have been that Soviet Premier Malenkov was sufficiently alarmed by Dulles's loose talk about 'massive retaliation' in January 1954 to shrink from antagonizing the United States over a region of secondary strategic interest to the Kremlin, especially at a time when the post-Stalinist leadership was looking for ways to settle East–West differences in Europe. As for Beijing, it is possible that the long history of ethnic antagonism between the Chinese and Vietnamese tempered its enthusiasm for assisting in the formation of a politically unified Vietnam to its south, even one under a communist regime.

In any case, the United States promptly signalled its determination to prevent the unification of Vietnam and to protect the royalist regimes in Cambodia and Laos against any insurgencies mounted by their own communist movements. Having refused to sign the Geneva Accords, Washington felt under no obligation to honour its prohibition against foreign military involvement in Indochina. In September 1954, Dulles orchestrated the formation of the South East Asia Treaty Organization (SEATO), a regional security arrangement that committed its members not only to defend Laos and Cambodia against communist aggression or insurgency but also to protect South Vietnam against North Vietnam. By the end of 1954, Washington had replaced Paris as the anti-communist bastion in the region. American military advisers were sent to train the South Vietnamese army, while US economic assistance was supplied to the Saigon regime in ever-increasing amounts.

These egregious violations of the Geneva Accords were justified by the Eisenhower administration on the grounds that because the United States had not signed them it was not bound by them. In the same way, the South Vietnamese government had also refused to sign and thus did not consider itself obliged to hold the elections required for reunification of the country. In the summer of 1955, Hanoi twice formally asked Saigon to name representatives to the electoral commission required by the accords, but Diem refused, maintaining that elections would be pointless as long as North Vietnam refused to grant democratic liberties to its own citizens.

Convinced that the Vietminh would win an all-Vietnamese election, Washington publicly recommended cancellation of the electoral provisions of the Geneva Accords. As the date for the projected elections passed in the summer of 1956, the temporary demarcation line along the 17th parallel hardened into a de facto political frontier separating two ideologically antagonistic states. By the end of the decade, the number

of American military advisers attached to the South Vietnamese army had grown from 275 to 685, and about US$300 million worth of military aid was flowing into Diem's coffers annually. In the meantime, the Soviet Union and China had begun to furnish economic and military assistance to North Vietnam.

At the time of the ceasefire in 1954, thousands of Vietminh guerrillas had remained in the southern zone in anticipation of either a political victory in the unification election two years later or a renewal of the armed struggle in the event that the election plan failed. The cancellation of the elections prompted a renewal of the guerrilla campaign in the form of selective assassinations of officials appointed by the Saigon regime. In the meantime, the corruption, nepotism, and repressive policies of the Diem government had provoked widespread discontent among non-communist interest groups in the south. In 1960, a coalition of anti-Diem dissidents—communist and non-communist alike—formed the National Liberation Front, dedicated to social reform, political liberalization, and neutrality for South Vietnam. Capitalizing on this indigenous discontent, Hanoi extended support to this opposition group, which Diem contemptuously labelled 'Viet Cong' (Vietnamese communist).

In Washington, the new Kennedy administration had inherited a commitment to help the non-communist regimes of the former French Indochina—particularly Laos and South Vietnam—to preserve their independence from the communist regime in Hanoi and to protect them from indigenous communist insurgencies. Laos had been torn by civil strife for the rest of the decade, and in May 1961 the Geneva Conference was reconvened to find a solution. After a year of diplomatic wrangling, the Conference finally produced an agreement that ostensibly guaranteed the neutrality of Laos (with the same conditions contained in the Geneva Accords of 1954) under the authority of a coalition government composed of three factions: pro-Western, pro-communist, and neutralist. But by late 1962, the United States had resumed shipping arms to the

INDOCHINA, 1954–1975

coalition government, in violation of the neutrality provisions, and by 1964 American planes were conducting clandestine bombing raids against the Pathet Lao insurgents, who had abandoned the governing coalition as it turned increasingly to Washington for support.

The collapse of the Laos accords was inevitable: sharing a long border with Vietnam, Laos could not remain isolated from the escalation of violence there in the course of the 1960s. When Kennedy took office in January 1961, almost 900 American military advisers were stationed in South Vietnam, training its army in the techniques of both conventional and counter-insurgency warfare. By the end of the year, that number had increased to about 2,600; by the end of 1962, it stood at 11,000; and at the time of Kennedy's assassination in November 1963, it had swollen to 16,500. The amounts of military aid sent by Washington to Saigon had also increased dramatically.

The Kennedy administration tried in vain to prod the increasingly corrupt and dictatorial Diem to help the impoverished peasantry by instituting land reform; to give greater political freedom to the non-communist opposition groups, and to grant religious toleration to the Buddhist majority (which suffered systematic discrimination at the hands of the French-converted Catholic elite that dominated the government in Saigon). Diem, convinced that the mounting political and religious opposition to his rule was instigated by Hanoi and its agents in the south, rebuffed Washington's requests for conciliation in favour of even more repressive policies that only stimulated greater opposition to his regime. In 1963, as Vietnamese troops fired on unarmed protestors and stormed Buddhist temples, the United States publicly expressed its displeasure by reducing economic assistance to Saigon. Assuming this meant that Diem had lost Washington's favour, senior South Vietnamese military officers toppled his regime on 1 November with the tacit approval of the American ambassador in Saigon, Henry Cabot Lodge, and murdered Diem.

Between November 1963—when both Diem and Kennedy were killed—and the end of 1965,

South Vietnam experienced 12 changes of government. The succession of generals and marshals who occupied the top post in Saigon showed little interest in seeking public support by instituting land reforms or expanding political and religious liberties. Nevertheless, the new Johnson administration in Washington resumed and intensified the American military engagement on behalf of the anti-communist forces in South Vietnam. As the insurgents in the south began to receive large quantities of supplies from North Vietnam, China, and the Soviet Union, the character of the American involvement began to change.

In February 1964, the American-advised South Vietnamese launched covert commando raids into North Vietnam while using air strikes in neighbouring Laos to cut the supply line from north to south. In the summer, as President Johnson was facing intense criticism from his opponent in the forthcoming election, Senator Barry Goldwater, for waging a 'no win' military operation in Indochina, an incident off the coast of North Vietnam provided a convenient pretext to disarm the Republicans by escalating the US involvement. On the evening of 4 August, North Vietnamese torpedo boats allegedly fired on two US destroyers in international waters in the Gulf of Tonkin. Although the Vietnamese vessels promptly retreated and neither American ship was damaged, Johnson took the occasion to submit to Congress a previously drafted resolution requesting authorization to combat North Vietnamese aggression by all appropriate means. On 7 August, the Tonkin Gulf Resolution passed both houses with only two dissenting votes. In the absence of a formal declaration of war, this overwhelming expression of legislative approval gave Johnson the authority he needed to begin bombing North Vietnam and to send large numbers of ground troops to the south.

Following Johnson's landslide victory in the election of November 1964, his pre-established plans for the intensive bombardment of North Vietnam were implemented. In February 1965, when a Viet Cong night raid on the barracks of a US airfield at Pleiku resulted in nine American

PRIME MINISTER LESTER B. PEARSON'S SPEECH AT TEMPLE UNIVERSITY, 1965

As the United States escalated its military campaign in Vietnam, Canadian Prime Minister Lester Pearson became increasingly worried that, far from inducing the North Vietnamese to seek peace, this policy would only strengthen their determination to fight on. In April 1965, he decided to speak publicly about his concerns in a convocation address he was to give at Temple University in Philadelphia. When he showed a draft to his advisers, they warned against criticizing the Johnson administration's policy on American soil. But Pearson followed through with his plan: in the course of his address he called for a temporary halt to the bombing campaign, suggesting that 'a measured pause in one field of military action at the right time' might induce the North Vietnamese to save face by 'inject[ing] some flexibility into their policy without appearing to do so as the direct result of military pressure'.

Pearson afterwards met with the president, who, despite the fact that Pearson's comments had been carefully worded, was outraged. Grabbing the prime minister by the lapels and shouting 'You pissed on my rug!', Johnson declared that Canadians were not carrying their share of the free world's burden and had no right to criticize America. Apparently Pearson was too shocked to respond coherently. Though he considered Johnson a vulgar bully, Pearson knew that he had to apologize. However, the relationship between the two leaders was beyond repair. In future, they avoided meeting, and neither man would call the other by his first name.

The controversy surrounding Pearson's speech foreshadowed the larger political conflict generated by the Vietnam War. After 1965, the Canadian government tried to develop an independent foreign policy that would not alienate the United States, but its efforts to promote peace negotiations failed. Pearson was careful to never again publicly criticize American policy regarding Vietnam.

Canadian Prime Minister Lester B. Pearson and US President Lyndon B. Johnson give a joint news conference in Ottawa at the end of the president's visit to Canada in May 1967. CP Archives.

deaths and over a hundred casualties, Johnson ordered retaliatory air strikes against North Vietnam. Less than a month after these first large-scale bombings, Washington announced that two battalions of marines were being dispatched to South Vietnam. By the end of the year, the man who had promised during his election campaign that he was 'not going to send American boys 15,000 miles away from their homes to do what Asian boys should do for themselves' had sent more than 184,000 troops to Vietnam to shore up the sagging Saigon army. That number was to reach 385,000 by the end of 1966, 535,000 by the end of 1967, and a high point of 542,000 in February 1969. But neither the bombing of the north nor the influx of US troops in the south succeeded in quelling the insurrection against the South Vietnamese regime. Hanoi increased its flow of arms and men to the south while the indigenous forces of the Viet Cong gained effective control of almost all rural areas.

The turning point came on 30 January 1968, the first day of Tet, a Vietnamese holiday celebrating the beginning of the lunar New Year. On that day, Viet Cong guerrillas and North Vietnamese regulars launched a well-coordinated surprise offensive against 36 of the 44 provincial capitals of South Vietnam in addition to Saigon, where they penetrated the presidential palace, the radio station, the airport, and even the heavily fortified American embassy. The apparent goal of the 'Tet Offensive' was to spark an uprising in the South Vietnamese cities against the Saigon regime and its US protectors. In this strictly military sense it was a failure, and a costly one: more than 45,000 communist troops were killed, to 2,000 South Vietnamese and 1,000 Americans. The insurgents had failed to hold any of the cities they had overrun in the face of a furious US–South Vietnamese counterattack. But Hanoi and its supporters in the south had won a huge psychological victory by revealing that no part of South Vietnam was secure—not even the government buildings in the capital—and thus discrediting Washington's claims about the imminence of victory in a war that was becoming increasingly unpopular at home.

American opposition to the war in Vietnam had begun on a small scale in 1965, at the time of Johnson's escalation of the American military operations there. At that point, dissent was largely confined to university campuses, where 'teach-ins' were held to inform the public of the history and nature of the conflict. But as the numbers of conscripts increased, opposition began to surface in Congress. The casualty figures and 'body counts', reported on television directly from the battlefield, helped to fan the flames of discontent at home.

By 1966, Johnson faced opposition even from members of his own party, and he tried several times to induce Hanoi to negotiate an end to the conflict by temporarily suspending the bombing of North Vietnam. But the North Vietnamese government consistently refused to negotiate unless Washington agreed in advance to a permanent halt. After each bombing 'pause' failed to lure the North Vietnamese to the conference table on American terms, the bombing was resumed on an even greater scale in an effort to force them to talk. The Tet Offensive appeared to confirm that the ground war in the south was unwinnable, that the bombing of the north had done nothing to bring the contending forces closer to a negotiated settlement, and that the only way out of the quagmire was through a halt to the bombing, coupled with overtures to Hanoi.

The mounting public opposition to Johnson's Vietnam policy was symbolized by the strong showing of anti-war Senator Eugene McCarthy in the first of the Democratic primary elections leading up to the 1968 presidential campaign. When Senator Robert Kennedy, the younger brother of the slain president, entered the nomination race on an anti-war platform, the discouraged Johnson abruptly decided to reverse his course and leave the Vietnam mess to others. On 31 March 1968, he announced that he would not run for re-election, that future bombings of North Vietnam would be confined to the sparsely populated region below the 20th parallel, and that only token reinforcements of ground troops would be sent to the south. In return he asked Hanoi to enter into negotiations. On 3 May, the North Vietnamese government agreed to send a delegation to meet with US negotiators in Paris. For the rest of the year the two sides haggled over procedural issues, including the shape of the conference table, as Hanoi waited for the lame-duck Johnson administration to be replaced by one with the authority to end the war.

The new president, Richard Nixon, had spoken vaguely during his campaign of a 'peace plan'. Finally in July 1969, he unveiled what he touted as his country's new foreign policy for East Asia in general and Vietnam in particular. At the heart of this Nixon Doctrine was the concept of 'Vietnamization', the gradual strengthening of the South Vietnamese military forces to the point where they could assume the defence responsibilities that were to be gradually relinquished by the United States. The number of American military personnel in South Vietnam was reduced from 540,000 at the end of 1968 to 139,000 by the end of 1971 and 25,000 by the end of Nixon's first term. But in an effort to stall for enough time to help their ally become self-sufficient, the Nixon administration simultaneously escalated the level of violence in response to each North Vietnamese success on the battlefield.

In April 1970, US ground forces invaded neutral Cambodia with the intention of cutting off the supply routes to the south and driving the North Vietnamese regulars from their Cambodian sanctuaries. In the spring of 1972, North Vietnamese infantry units spearheaded by tanks burst through the demilitarized zone separating the two Vietnams and directly threatened Nixon's Vietnamization program. Nixon responded in May with orders to bomb transportation facilities and military installations in North Vietnam and to mine its principal harbours in order to cut off the flow of supplies from China and the Soviet Union. In December 1972, shortly after Henry Kissinger's announcement that a peace settlement was imminent, Nixon ordered a massive bombing raid on Hanoi and Haiphong to force North Vietnam closer to the American negotiating position.

Since assuming his position as national security adviser to the president, Kissinger had met secretly with North Vietnamese negotiator Le Duc Tho to explore the basis for an agreement to end the war. By the end of 1972, the United States made the crucial concession, agreeing to a ceasefire instead of the total withdrawal of North Vietnamese forces from the south that it had previously insisted on. Agreement was finally reached on 27 January 1973, shortly after Nixon began his second term. The US agreed to remove all of its armed forces from South Vietnam within two months, and the two sides agreed on an exchange of prisoners of war. The vague political terms of the accord provided for a coalition government in the south that would conduct free elections there. No serious discussions to that end were ever held, and within two years of the American evacuation

all three of Indochina's pro-Western regimes collapsed to communist-led insurgencies. The Saigon government fell to North Vietnamese forces in April 1975, two weeks after the Cambodian communist organization, the Khmer Rouge, toppled the pro-American government that had replaced the neutralist regime of Prince Norodom Sihanouk in 1970. The third domino fell in August, when the communist Pathet Lao dissolved the non-communist administration in Laos.

Between 1961 and 1973, a total of 57,939 Americans died in the Indochinese conflict—the longest and costliest foreign war in American history. The US Air Force dropped on Vietnam over three times the tonnage of bombs that had been dropped on Germany during the Second World War. The financial cost, including military aid to Saigon, has been estimated at US$150 billion, with another US$200 billion earmarked for the future in the form of veterans' benefits. In addition to these war-related costs, the escalation of the American military involvement in Vietnam coincided with a sharp increase in domestic spending to finance the social programs of Johnson's 'Great Society' project. As a result, while Johnson's administration could pride itself on having supported several progressive domestic policies, passing the Civil Rights Act of 1964 and the Voting Rights Act of 1965, the budget deficits of his presidency produced a rampant inflation, the damaging economic effects of which persisted for a generation.

The social and political consequences of America's long involvement in Indochina, though more difficult to gauge with precision, were scarcely less significant: skepticism bordering on cynicism towards government, fuelled by the enormous 'credibility gap' between the idealistic, optimistic pronouncements of administration officials and the sordid reality in the Vietnamese jungles that could be seen on the daily television newscasts; a public distaste for foreign entanglements that threatened to revive the isolationist tradition of the distant past; a host of war-related social and psychological afflictions among returning veterans. Of course, no one could have imagined what the ultimate costs of the US involvement in Indochina would be. Nevertheless, it is worth trying to understand what accounts for the extraordinary tenacity and persistence with which this endeavour was pursued by four successive administrations of divergent political tendencies.

Economic advantage was not a significant consideration because neither the raw materials of the region nor the potential markets for

THE KILLING FIELDS

Although the Vietnam War finally ended in 1975, the withdrawal of American forces did not bring peace to the people of Southeast Asia. As the North Vietnamese consolidated their power, neighbouring Cambodia descended into a tragic period of almost unimaginable horror. With the exception of the Japanese occupation of 1941–5, Cambodia had been a colonial protectorate of France from 1863 to 1953. After the Second World War, guerrilla forces challenged French colonial rule, and in 1953 Cambodia became an independent kingdom. In the 1960s the government of Prince Norodom Sihanouk faced resistance from leftist groups, including the armed wing of the Communist Party, known as the Khmer Rouge. At the same time, Sihanouk's regime had to manage relations with not only unstable neighbours, especially North and South Vietnam, but also Cold War rivals seeking to influence its foreign policy. Cambodia oscillated between supporting China and the United States; however, its relationship with the latter deteriorated in the 1960s as the fighting in Vietnam spilled over the Cambodian border. Suspecting that the Americans wanted to replace him with a more pro-Western leader, in 1965 Sihanouk threw his support behind China and allowed North Vietnamese forces to establish bases in Cambodia. He began a campaign of political repression which, along with his close ties with China, alienated many Cambodians. In 1969 the US began a secret bombing campaign against targets in Cambodia, and Sihanouk's position became increasingly untenable. In 1970 he was deposed while travelling outside the country and fled to China, where he announced his support for the Khmer Rouge.

Sihanouk's support provided an important boost to the party, which grew from a marginal force to a major threat to the Cambodian government. After five years of fighting, the Khmer Rouge and forces loyal to Sihanouk captured the capital, Phnom Penh, in April 1975 and renamed the country Democratic Kampuchea. Sihanouk became the head of state but was soon forced out of office, and in 1976 the Kampuchean Communist Party tightened its control under the leadership of Saloth Sar, known as Pol Pot. Declaring the communist takeover to mark 'Year Zero', Pol Pot embarked on a totalitarian campaign to re-engineer Cambodian society into a vast agrarian collective. The communists abolished private property, banned religion, and targeted Cambodia's urban population. While intellectuals and members of the middle class were murdered, millions of Cambodians were forcibly resettled in the countryside. From 1975 to 1978 at least 1.7 million and perhaps as many as 2.5 million people died of torture, starvation, exhaustion, and neglect. In response to cross-border attacks by the Khmer Rouge, Vietnam invaded Cambodia in 1978 and captured Phnom Penh the next year, ousting the Khmer Rouge from power. Forces loyal to Pol Pot and Sihanouk continued to operate from strongholds near the Thai border; in a twist on Cold War politics, they received support from both the United States and China, as neither country had made peace with Vietnam. In 1989 Vietnamese forces withdrew in the face of diplomatic pressure, and the country was renamed Cambodia. In 1994 thousands of Khmer Rouge members accepted a general amnesty, and four years later Pol Pot died while under house arrest. The 73-year-old former dictator had cheated justice, declaring before his death, 'My conscience is clear'.

American exports or investment played an important role in decision-making concerning Indochina. The military threat—actual or potential—posed by a unified communist Vietnam to the United States and its allies in Asia was nonexistent, given the strength of American naval and air power in the region. Imponderables such as bureaucratic inertia, personal involvement on the part of policy-makers, and concern about loss of prestige in the eyes of both allies and adversaries all likely played their part in preventing Washington from extricating itself from Indochina for so many years.

Inevitably, though, we are drawn to the conclusion that one important motivation was concern about China. In April 1965, President Johnson publicly accused Beijing of masterminding the North Vietnamese effort to absorb the south, and Secretary of State Dean Rusk repeated that allegation on several occasions during the legislative hearings on the Vietnam conflict conducted in 1966. Certainly Beijing did supply Hanoi with military equipment during the war with the United States. The main purpose of that assistance, however, was not to promote the establishment of a militarily powerful, politically unified Vietnam but to give China greater weight, relative to the Soviet Union, in the competition for influence in the north. Centuries of ethnic antagonism between the Chinese and Vietnamese peoples had left a legacy of mutual mistrust that even the common ideological bond of communism could not overcome. Although US officials seeking to justify their nation's intervention in Indochina often suggested that Vietnam was a stalking horse for an expansionist China bent on conquering all of Southeast Asia, the very idea was an absurdity that would have astonished specialists in the region's history—but by the 1960s there were precious few such specialists left in the State Department, owing in part to the McCarthyite purges of the previous decade following the 'loss' of China. In any case, even if the Vietnam intervention was motivated in part by the hope of containing Chinese communism in Asia, by the early 1970s Beijing itself was beginning to explore the possibility of improving its relations with Washington.

CANADA AND THE VIETNAM WAR

Officially, Canada was an impartial bystander throughout the Vietnam War. Canadian representatives served on two international commissions that sought to secure a truce in Vietnam, and Canadian officials were involved in attempts to mediate negotiations between Washington and Hanoi. In the wake of the controversy caused by his Temple University speech (see p. 291), Lester B. Pearson never issued another public statement on the subject. Pierre Elliott Trudeau, who succeeded Pearson as prime minister in 1968, did not get along with President Nixon, but he was careful not to openly criticize the American war effort. When the United States widened its bombing campaign against North Vietnam in 1972, Trudeau did not protest.

During the war, approximately 20,000 draft dodgers and 12,000 deserters found refuge in Canada, and many of them settled permanently. By 1971, there were more Americans coming to Canada than Canadians moving to the United States. When Washington increased its bombing of North Vietnam as a negotiating tactic, Trudeau came under tremendous political pressure to condemn the lack of progress towards a peaceful settlement, and in January 1973 the House of Commons passed a motion calling for an end to hostilities in Southeast Asia. The Nixon administration was outraged, but the war was in its final phase, and Washington wanted Canada to participate in the International Commission of Control and Supervision that would oversee the truce. During this time, Canadian public opinion regarding the US became increasingly negative: a national poll taken in 1974 found that over half of those interviewed felt that Americans exerted too much influence on Canada's way of life.

Despite its official stance of impartiality, Canada did contribute to the US war effort. At least 10,000 Canadians enlisted in the US armed forces and served in Vietnam, and Canadian

Anti–Vietnam War protesters make their way to the US Consulate in Montreal, 19 February 1966. *The Gazette* (Montreal) © 1966.

officials co-operated with the CIA in its covert operations against North Vietnam. Moreover, the infamous herbicide 'Agent Orange', used by American forces to destroy foliage so that it could not be used as cover by the attacking enemy, was produced in Ontario and tested at a military base in New Brunswick. In all, Canadian companies sold more than US$2 billion worth of munitions and military equipment to the United States and exported an additional $10 billion in provisions and supplies used by the American military in Vietnam. From an economic perspective, therefore, Canada clearly benefited from the war.

SINO–AMERICAN RAPPROCHEMENT

The split between the Soviet Union and China continued to widen during the second half of the 1960s. In the fall of 1966, Mao expelled all Soviet exchange students from China, and the Kremlin promptly responded in kind. By the end of the decade, the Sino–Soviet quarrel had escalated from a doctrinal dispute between rival claimants to leadership of the communist world into a fierce diplomatic and, briefly, even military clash between sovereign powers over territory and regional security. Into this breach between Moscow and Beijing plunged the new administration in Washington, which had taken office in January 1969. After initiating peace negotiations with North Vietnam, the Nixon government undertook to profit from the Sino–Soviet split by opening a dialogue with the communist regime of mainland China, which had been ostracized by successive American administrations for 20 years. The result was a transformation of the global relationship between the communist and non-communist worlds.

Sino–Soviet relations finally erupted in violence in March 1969, when Chinese troops ambushed a Soviet contingent near the disputed Damansky (or Chenpao) Island, at the confluence of the Amur and Ussuri rivers; 31 Soviet soldiers and an unknown number of Chinese died in this border clash. Subsequent skirmishes in the same region and along the frontier of Chinese Xinjiang during the spring and summer were accompanied by a renewal of Chinese territorial claims against the Soviet Union. In response to these provocations, Moscow took steps to reinforce its defences on the Chinese border. In April 1969, East European military contingents were detached from the Warsaw Pact command and transferred to the Far East. The number of Soviet divisions deployed along the Chinese frontier was increased from 15 in 1967 to 21 in 1969 and 30 in 1970. Tactical nuclear weapons were stockpiled in Soviet-controlled Mongolia, while officials in the Kremlin apparently considered launching a pre-emptive strike against China's infant nuclear installation at Lop Nor in Xinjiang.[4] And in the summer of 1969, Moscow sounded out the governments of India, Thailand, and Indonesia about the possibility of organizing an Asian defence pact directed against Beijing.

Although neither the pre-emptive strike nor the defence pact materialized, the nervous authorities in China ordered the construction of nuclear fallout shelters in anticipation of a Soviet attack. Negotiations over the disputed frontier, which had begun in September, broke down three months later. By 1972, there were 44 Soviet divisions standing guard along the 7,000-km border with China (compared to 31 divisions in Eastern Europe), while a quarter of the Soviet air force had been redeployed from west to east.

Meanwhile, the Nixon administration had undertaken a fundamental re-evaluation of US policy regarding China in the light of the Sino–Soviet split and the consequent breakup of the monolithic Communist bloc. In 1969, the White House made a first tentative gesture of reconciliation, relaxing certain trade and travel restrictions that dated from the Korean emergency. The Chinese reciprocated a year later by reopening the informal Sino–American talks in Warsaw, which had been suspended in early 1968 because of the US bombing campaign in Vietnam. In April 1971, the Chinese government caused a minor sensation when it invited an American table-tennis team competing in Japan to try its skills against the championship Chinese team. Newspaper columnists remarked on Beijing's circuitous 'Ping-Pong diplomacy', but Washington hastened to follow up this unofficial Chinese overture.

In June of that year, Nixon formally revoked the 21-year-old trade embargo on China. On 9 July, Kissinger, after establishing contact with Chinese authorities through the government of Pakistan (which enjoyed cordial relations with both the United States and China), secretly flew to Beijing. Six days later, Nixon astonished the world with the announcement that he would personally travel to China to 'seek the normalization of relations' between the two governments. To impress on his future hosts the seriousness of his quest for an improvement in Sino–American relations, Nixon made two changes in American foreign policy that were guaranteed to win approval in Beijing. For years the US had kept up a steady diplomatic pressure to prevent the United Nations from expelling the Chinese Nationalist government in Taiwan and transferring its seat on the Security Council to the communist regime in Beijing, but in October 1971 it put an end to that campaign. Then in December, Washington openly sided with Pakistan against India, China's perennial antagonist, in the war that led to the creation of the new state of Bangladesh out of former East Pakistan.

Having smoothed his path to Beijing with these goodwill gestures, Nixon journeyed more than 32,000 kilometres in February 1972 to become the first American president in history to set foot on Chinese soil. After several days of intensive negotiations, punctuated by an hour-long meeting between top US officials and the ailing 78-year-old Mao Zedong, the two governments issued a joint communiqué in Shanghai that candidly recorded the differences still separating the two countries. Beijing demanded the withdrawal of US military forces from Taiwan and reaffirmed its intention to support 'the struggles of all oppressed peoples' (presumably including the Vietnamese, who were then engaged in a bloody struggle with China's new friend in the capitalist world).

For its part the United States agreed to reduce its military installations in Taiwan, but it also insisted that only peaceful means be used to resolve the dispute between the two Chinas. While committing itself to the total withdrawal of US military forces from Indochina once a settlement could be negotiated in Paris, Washington reaffirmed its treaty commitments to South Korea and Japan. On a positive note, both governments agreed to abandon the pursuit of 'hegemony' in East Asia and to oppose any other nation's efforts to that end (an unmistakable warning to Moscow). The communiqué also endorsed the expansion of cultural and commercial contacts between the two nations, to complement the normalization of political relations that was underway.

That the pre-eminent representative of American anti-communism should visit the centre of militant revolutionary opposition to the capitalist world was in itself almost inconceivable. The respectful, almost deferential, behaviour of both delegations during the public ceremonies stood in glaring contrast to the mutual distrust and ideological antipathy that had characterized Sino–American relations since 1950. American reporters observing Nixon and Kissinger embracing their Chinese hosts remarked how far the two governments had progressed since the Geneva Conference of 1954, where Secretary of State Dulles had refused to shake the hand of Chinese Foreign Minister Zhou Enlai. It was evident that both Washington and Beijing had been prompted by the most compelling of motives to jettison the bitter legacy of two decades and seek a durable basis for rapprochement.

This concern, of course, was to restrain and contain the Soviet Union. Nixon and Kissinger hoped that the Kremlin's willingness to agree on strategic arms control and political détente in Europe would be hastened by the emerging Sino–American understanding in the Far East. Moscow's subsequent eagerness to conclude the SALT I Treaty and settle the remaining East–West

political differences in Europe was undeniably influenced by Nixon's willingness to 'play the China card' and confront the Soviets with a potential Chinese threat to their eastern borderlands. For their part, Mao and Zhou presumably welcomed the normalization of relations with Washington and the prospective US disengagement from Indochina and Taiwan for the same reason, allowing them to concentrate China's military strength in the north and counteract the massive Soviet buildup in Siberia, Mongolia, and the maritime provinces.

In addition to these overriding considerations of military strategy, the economic motivations for the Sino–American rapprochement must not be overlooked. It is hardly surprising that the idea of the China market asserted an almost magical attraction on US business interests in the early 1970s, when the spectacular post-war economic expansion of the United States had begun to peter out. Increased competition from Japan and the European Economic community had eaten into the US' share of the world market for manufactured goods, while the deficit financing of the Great Society at home and the military intervention in Southeast Asia during the previous decade had generated the highest rates of inflation the US had known since the Second World War.

In August 1971, the United States went off the gold standard, shattering the edifice of international monetary relations erected at Bretton Woods in 1944 and exposing the weaknesses of the United States' financial position in the world. The prospect of gaining access to a virtually untapped market comprising a quarter of the world's population fuelled extravagant expectations on the part of certain US export interests. Within months of Nixon's visit, US business executives were flocking to China. US exports to China increased from US$5 million in 1969 to $700 million in 1973.

From the Chinese perspective, the increase in trade both with the United States and with its ally Japan offered an attractive alternative to the economic connection with the Soviet Union that had been severed at Moscow's behest in the 1960s. By

January 1975, Chinese Premier Zhou Enlai was publicly advocating closer economic relations with Japan and the United States, and he took pains to dissuade Tokyo from succumbing to the allure of Siberian oil and raw materials, which could be exchanged for the Japanese technology that the Soviet Union desperately needed. At the same time, Chinese officials were urging the European Common Market to resist Soviet overtures for closer commercial and financial relations.

Neither the Nixon administration nor the interim successor government of Gerald Ford was eager to take the final step of establishing regular diplomatic relations with Beijing for fear of alarming the already nervous Nationalist regime in Taiwan. Following the exchange of 'liaison offices' in 1973, Washington was still not prepared to grant formal diplomatic recognition to Beijing and instead introduced a rather clumsy 'two Chinas policy'. But the remarkable increase in Sino–American trade, the influx of American journalists, scholars, and tourists to China, and numerous return visits by Kissinger, together with the Ford trip of 1975, confirmed that the United States was serious in its courtship of China. No longer would the world's most populous country be treated as a pariah by the most prosperous country. No longer would China be regarded in the US as the Far Eastern agent of a monolithic, Moscow-based communist conspiracy intent on absorbing the rest of non-communist Asia.

Instead, it would be viewed, and would come to view itself, as a middle-rank power of great potential but modest achievement, pursuing regional rather than global objectives. When the United States was militarily engaged on the mainland of Asia during the 1950s and 1960s, waging two wars against fraternal communist states bordering on China and protecting the Nationalist Chinese regime on an island that Beijing regarded as its own, China's vital interests seemed directly threatened by the capitalist superpower across the Pacific. But the US withdrawal from Asia and the simultaneous increase of Soviet military power along China's northern border during the first half of the 1970s brought the two communist behemoths into direct

conflict with one another and spelled the end of the Cold War in the Far East.

SUMMARY

The collapse of the Japanese empire in August 1945 left a vast power vacuum in Asia, comparable to the one created in Europe by the capitulation of Germany three months earlier. Politically, however, the two post-war situations differed significantly, for the United States had waged the war in the Far East without military assistance from the Soviet Union. By the time the Red Army had begun to consolidate control of its prescribed occupation zones in Asia, the predominance of the US and its European associates in the rest of Japan's former East Asian empire was assured. US forces under General Douglas MacArthur unilaterally undertook the military occupation and political administration of the Japanese home islands.

After 1945, British, French, and Dutch forces returned to their old imperial outposts in Southeast Asia either to reassert colonial authority or to grant political independence to successor regimes controlled by pro-Western indigenous elites. In either case, any communist ambitions were effectively blocked. In China, however, the long civil war between the communist forces of Mao Zedong and the Nationalist forces of Chiang Kai-shek ended with the establishment in October 1949 of the People's Republic of China, a communist state comprising one-quarter of the world's population that promptly became a military ally and economic beneficiary of the Soviet Union.

The bitter rivalry between the communist powers and the West led to two major conflicts, one in Korea and the other in Vietnam. As the Vietnam War escalated, the United States faced growing opposition to its policies both at home and abroad. Canada became a haven for American 'draft dodgers', who refused to serve in the war. Japan became a key Western ally and buffer state against communist expansion and by the mid-1950s was experiencing a remarkable economic recovery. Relations between China and the Soviet Union deteriorated in the late 1950s, and in the early 1970s the US took advantage of the Sino–Soviet rift to improve relations with China. The withdrawal of American troops from Vietnam in 1973 marked the beginning of the end of the Cold War in the Far East.

NOTES

1. London's hasty recognition of the People's Republic appears to have been prompted by concern about the status of the British Crown colony of Hong Kong, a coastal showcase of Western capitalism that was tolerated by Beijing because of its value as a 'window' to the non-communist world.

2. The General Assembly possesses no decision-making power, according to the UN Charter. Once the Soviet Union, realizing its error in boycotting the Security Council, resumed its seat on 1 August, it was in a position to veto any resolution presented to the body. Hence the United States was driven to endow the General Assembly with an authority it did not legally possess.

3. The Soviet withdrawal from Port Arthur, which had been scheduled to take place in 1952, was postponed by joint agreement because of the Korean War. The pullout finally took place in 1955.

4. China had exploded its first atomic bomb in October 1964 and its first hydrogen bomb in June 1967. But by the end of the 1960s its delivery system consisted only of missiles with a 3,218-km range and medium-range bombers, a circumstance that left it vulnerable to a Soviet pre-emptive strike.

QUESTIONS FOR CRITICAL THOUGHT

1. What were the major differences between Chinese and Soviet communism?
2. Did the United States miss an opportunity to establish favourable relations with Mao's China? How could it have achieved this goal?
3. In what ways did the Korean War impact the progress of the Cold War?
4. What were the primary causes of the Sino–Soviet split?
5. Why did the Truman administration elect to support French efforts to restore colonial control in Indochina?
6. What were the social and political consequences of American intervention in Indochina?

WEBSITES FOR FURTHER REFERENCE

The American Experience: Vietnam Online
   www.pbs.org/wgbh/amex/vietnam/index.html

John Fairbank Memorial Chinese History Virtual Library
   www.cnd.org/fairbank/

Mao Tse-tung (Zedong) Internet Library
   www.marx2mao.com/Mao/Index.html

The Pearson Peacekeeping Centre/Centre pour le Maintien de la Paix
   www.peaceoperations.org

CHAPTER 11

THE RESURGENCE OF EAST–WEST TENSIONS (1975–1985)

CANADA IN THE WORLD DURING THE TRUDEAU ERA

Canada's foreign policy developed significantly under Pierre Elliott Trudeau, who served as prime minister from 1968 to 1979 and from 1980 to 1984. Trudeau attracted more international attention than any of his prime ministerial predecessors, and he brought an independent and cosmopolitan style to diplomacy. Distrustful of bureaucrats in the Department of External Affairs, Trudeau in 1968 launched an extensive foreign policy review. He was openly critical of both NORAD and NATO, which he felt were too militaristic. In a 1969 speech Trudeau stated, 'It is a false perspective to have a military alliance determine your foreign policy.' Even before the foreign policy review was completed, he announced that Canada would begin reducing its commitment to NATO. Despite protests from the United States and from Europe, Canada's military contribution to the organization was cut in half, to 5,000 troops.

The policy review recommended that Canada adopt a realistic approach to external affairs based on national self-interest. Defining Canadian foreign policy as 'the extension abroad of national policies', the Trudeau government decided that Canada would no longer deploy nuclear weapons, and the Bomarc missile system was taken out of service by 1971. In 1972, the government published an External Affairs report recommending that Canada adopt a 'Third Option' by pursuing new economic and cultural partnerships in order to reduce Canada's dependence on its two traditional trading partners, Britain and the United States. As part of Trudeau's effort to distance Canada's foreign policy from that of its southern neighbour, his government extended diplomatic recognition to the People's Republic of China in 1970 (two years before Nixon visited Beijing), and in 1973 Trudeau visited China, where he had cordial meetings with Mao Zedong. Three years later, Trudeau made a controversial state visit to Cuba, where he received a warm welcome from Fidel Castro (Canada was one of only two nations in the western hemisphere to maintain diplomatic relations with Cuba following the 1959 revolution that brought Castro to power).

Despite these foreign-policy initiatives, domestic issues dominated Trudeau's period in office. An ardent federalist who vehemently opposed Quebec separatism, Trudeau invoked the War Measures Act in response to the terrorist campaign of the Front de liberation du Québec

(FLQ) during the October Crisis of 1970 (see p. 249), and 10 years later led the successful federalist effort to defeat the Quebec referendum on sovereignty-association. During this time, Trudeau also focused on negotiating a new constitutional framework. The result of this effort was the Constitution Act, which passed in 1982 and marked a watershed in the nation's development by severing many of the remnants of Canada's colonial ties to Great Britain, though the link to the British monarchy was retained.

Distressed by the increasingly antagonistic relationship between the superpowers—which was exacerbated in 1983, when Soviet fighter jets downed a Korean airliner in Soviet airspace—Trudeau dedicated the greater part of his final years in office to a personal peace mission, on which he visited several heads of state to lobby for the reduction of nuclear weapons. Although he was awarded the Albert Einstein Peace Prize for his diplomatic efforts, they did little to ease the growing East–West tensions that had prompted his mission.

Canada's role in international affairs changed during the Trudeau era, but its geopolitical position remained fundamentally unaltered. Canada continued as a member of NATO even though its commitment was reduced, and its membership in NORAD was renewed regularly under Trudeau. Despite Trudeau's political rhetoric, Canada still co-operated closely with the United States. In 1983, for example, in the face of stiff opposition from peace groups, the Trudeau government agreed to allow the American military to test cruise

Prime Minister Pierre Trudeau (right) enjoys a song with Cuban Prime Minister Fidel Castro in Cuba, January 1976. Library and Archives Canada/Credit: Duncan Cameron/Duncan Cameron fonds/PA-136976.

missiles at Canadian facilities. The US remained by far Canada's most important trading partner.

THE PROSPECTS FOR PLURALISM AND INTERDEPENDENCE

The 1975 Helsinki Conference marked the end of the Cold War in Europe. The Cold War in Asia drew to a close in the same year, as the pro-Western regimes in South Vietnam, Cambodia, and Laos succumbed in rapid succession to Communist-led insurgencies. In the meantime, the People's Republic of China and the United States accelerated the rapprochement that had begun in the early 1970s. Just as Washington tacitly recognized the permanence of Soviet dominance in Eastern Europe, it acknowledged the triumph of national communist movements in China and Indochina. The 33,000 ground forces in South Korea and the token air units stationed there and in Thailand constituted the sole remnants of the once formidable US military presence on the mainland of Asia that had been established for the ostensible purpose of containing Chinese expansion in that part of the world.

In the meantime, signs of progress toward regional détente had even begun to appear in the boiling cauldron of the Middle East. The Soviet Union refrained from interfering with US Secretary of State Henry Kissinger's successful efforts to lay the groundwork for an agreement between Israel and its principal antagonist, Egypt, that promised to bring a measure of peace and stability to that chronically unstable area. All the ghosts of the past three decades appeared to have been interred by the arms control agreements concluded between the two superpowers and the signs of political détente that surfaced almost simultaneously in Europe, Asia, and the Middle East—the three historic flashpoints of the Cold War.

Underlying Washington's pursuit of stable relations with the two quarrelling giants of the communist world and the simultaneous reduction of the United States' overseas role during the first half of the 1970s was the Nixon–Kissinger vision of a new global order that came to be called the 'pentagonal multipolar system'. In place of the rigid, ideologically defined bipolar system that had operated during the first quarter-century following the end of the Second World War, Nixon and Kissinger envisaged a looser multipolar system in which five rather than two power centres—the US, the USSR, Western Europe, China, and Japan—would function as the principal actors on the stage of world politics. The split within the Communist bloc and China's bid to play an independent role in the world, together with the impressive economic power of the newly enlarged Common Market[1] and Japan, all seemed to render obsolete the familiar conception of a world divided into two monolithic power blocs directed from Washington and Moscow (for the comparative economic power of the five poles of the pentagonal world order, see Table 11.1). By the time of his forced resignation in the summer of 1974, Nixon—an unabashed admirer of Charles de Gaulle—had put in place a foreign policy adapted to the new pluralistic international environment that had been prematurely heralded by the French president a decade earlier.

With regard to Europe, we have seen how the Final Act of the Helsinki Conference in 1975

TABLE 11.1 SHARES OF GROSS WORLD PRODUCT, 1960, 1970, 1980 (PERCENTAGES)

	1960	1970	1980
European Community	26.0	24.7	22.5
United States	25.9	23.0	21.5
Soviet Union	12.5	12.4	11.4
Japan	4.5	7.7	9.0
China	3.1	3.4	4.5
Less Developed Countries	11.1	12.3	14.8
Other	16.9	16.5	15.8

Source: 'International Systems Structure and American Foreign Policy' in Kenneth A. Oye, Robert J. Lieber, and Donald Rothchild, eds, *Eagle Defiant: United States Foreign Policy in the 1980s.* Copyright © 1983 Kenneth A. Oye. Reprinted by permission of Kenneth A. Oye.

resolved the disputes over borders and sovereignty that had poisoned East–West relations since 1945. The relaxation of political tensions had economic benefits for both sides, and trade contacts between East and West expanded significantly in the course of the 1970s. The new willingness on the part of Moscow and its satellites to embrace trading partners outside the communist world opened up markets and resources that had been virtually inaccessible to Western commercial interests.

Accompanying this expansion of inter-bloc commercial relations was a remarkable increase in Western European lending, both private and public, to the communist states to the east. Hard-currency loans helped the Soviet satellites to pay for their imports of Western technology and industrial products. At the same time, however, the industrial world's economic slowdown caused by the oil shocks of the 1970s shrank the markets for products from the Eastern bloc. Consequently, many COMECON countries had to borrow even more heavily to finance their growing trade deficits with the West. The combined foreign debt of the Soviet satellites increased from US$19 billion in 1975 to about $62 billion by the end of 1981. The government of Poland alone had run up a foreign debt of $28 billion, of which about $25 billion was held by West European banks and governments, while Romania, East Germany, and Hungary became deeply indebted to Western financial institutions. The result of these commercial and financial connections across the Iron Curtain was an unprecedented degree of economic interdependence between Western and Eastern Europe (including the Soviet Union).

According to the advocates of détente in the West, this web of interdependence would enhance the prospects for continued peace and stability in Europe by giving the West valuable leverage over the East. The economic benefits of trade, technology transfer, and hard-currency credits would demonstrate to the Communist bloc the value of co-operation with the non-communist world and thus discourage a reversion to Cold War policies. As Eastern bloc consumers came to depend on the economic resources of the West for their

rising standard of living, the argument ran, their political leaders would be obliged to maintain friendly relations with the West in order to ensure continued access to those resources; otherwise, they would risk widespread public discontent.

THE RENEWAL OF THE ARMS RACE

Europe's progress towards political conciliation and economic interdependence did not reduce tensions between the two superpowers. Nor did it do anything to further efforts to impose restraints on the nuclear arms rivalry between them. The retention of the Kissinger foreign policy team following Nixon's ignominious departure from office allowed the détente process to continue on schedule during the caretaker administration of Gerald Ford. The Ford–Brezhnev interim agreement signed at the Vladivostok Summit in November 1974 sketched the basic outlines of a replacement for the SALT I Treaty that was due to expire in 1977. But by then, the negotiations for a successor agreement had been thrown off track by a number of technological innovations in the Soviet nuclear arsenal that US congressional critics denounced as a threat to the delicate balance of strategic forces that had been confirmed by SALT I.

During the Ford interregnum, the USSR had tested a MIRVed missile for the first time and deployed a new long-range bomber called the 'Backfire'. These two developments seemed to suggest that Moscow was bent on competing with Washington in the two categories of delivery vehicles in which the United States enjoyed a lead that compensated for its inferiority in size and number of ICBMs. To meet the congressional criticism and offset the perceived threat posed by the Soviet Union's acquisition of qualitative superiority to match its quantitative superiority in delivery vehicles, the new administration headed by Jimmy Carter accelerated the development of several new weapons systems: the 'Missile Experimental' (MX), widely considered to be virtually invulnerable to attack because the ICBMs could be continually shuttled along 16,000 kilometres of rails in and out of 4,600 shelters in a kind of nuclear shell game; the small, inexpensive 'cruise' missile, a pilotless miniature aircraft with its own guidance system that could slide beneath radar and reach Soviet targets undetected; and the new Trident submarine intended to replace the aging Polaris, whose missiles would be within range of any important target in the Soviet Union.

Carter also authorized deployment of the B-1 bomber, an improved supersonic intercontinental aircraft designed to replace the obsolete B-52 bomber, and the so-called Enhanced Radiation Weapon, or neutron bomb—a tactical nuclear weapon that would supposedly minimize collateral damage to civilians in friendly states (such as West Germany) that might be subjected to a conventional Soviet attack. The threat to use the

B-1 and the neutron bomb was apparently little more than a bargaining ploy in the stalled negotiations on SALT II: Carter cancelled the former in June 1977 and deferred deployment of the latter in April 1978, presumably to allay Soviet fears of a US strategic buildup and make it easier for Brezhnev to persuade his colleagues in the Kremlin to accept the limitations imposed by the prospective agreement.

In any event, the US and Soviet chiefs of state signed the SALT II Treaty in Vienna in June 1979. The agreement limited each side to 2,250 delivery vehicles, of which no more than 1,320 could be MIRVed missiles. In theory, this permitted the Soviet Union approximately 9,000 warheads on land-based missiles—more than enough to

US President Jimmy Carter (left) and Soviet President Leonid Brezhnev sign the SALT II Treaty in Vienna, 18 June 1979. © CORBIS.

justify the Carter administration's determination to accelerate development of the mobile (and theoretically invulnerable) MX missile system.

As the second treaty on strategic arms control was being debated in Washington, the issue of nuclear weapons in Europe suddenly emerged as a matter of grave concern to the Atlantic alliance. The Soviet Union had begun to replace its obsolete intermediate-range missile force with powerful new land-based missiles whose 4,800-kilometre range put them within reach of any target in Western Europe. Accordingly, the NATO Council decided in December 1979 to deploy a new generation of intermediate-range missiles in Western Europe. In the absence of an arms control agreement, these new missiles would serve both as a counter to the new Soviet weapons and as a deterrent to a conventional assault against Western Europe by the Warsaw Pact.

NATO's decision to modernize the nuclear weapon force in Europe provoked an agitated response from the Kremlin as well as an outpouring of anti-nuclear sentiment in the West European countries slated to receive the new missiles. Public opposition increased after January 1981, when Ronald Reagan came to power in the United States. Reagan was widely perceived to be much less committed than Carter to removing the justification for deploying the controversial intermediate-range missiles.

But Reagan surprised allies and adversaries alike by bringing the United States into the Intermediate-range Nuclear Forces (INF) talks with the Soviet Union in Geneva in November 1981. He also upstaged Brezhnev—who had won widespread approval in NATO countries with his call for a moratorium on nuclear weapons in Europe—by proposing a simple, definitive solution to the nuclear arms race on the continent. Under the so-called 'zero option', the US would cancel deployment of its 572 cruise and Pershing II missiles in exchange for the dismantling of the 600 Soviet intermediate-range missiles. The Kremlin rejected this scheme, which would have required it to scrap a formidable missile force already in place in exchange for a US promise not

to deploy missiles whose effectiveness had yet to be demonstrated and whose deployment was strongly opposed by a significant segment of public opinion in Western Europe. Little progress was made in the INF negotiations, in part because the Soviets insisted on counting the 162 British and French intermediate-range missiles as part of the American atomic arsenal in Europe, while the US refused to negotiate on behalf of other sovereign states. At the end of 1983, the Soviet delegates walked out of the INF talks, and the US began to deploy the Pershing and cruise missiles at the designated European sites.

The complex issue of strategic arms control also continued to elude a mutually acceptable solution. The Reagan administration seemed ambivalent in its attitude towards strategic arms control. On the one hand, Reagan presided over the largest peacetime military buildup in history, and officials in his entourage indulged in bloodcurdling rhetoric about the necessity of preparing to fight a nuclear war. The administration pressed Congress to authorize construction of the MX missile system, and the president floated the idea of abandoning the existing defence arrangements based on reciprocal deterrence (or mutual assured destruction) in favour of an air-tight anti-ballistic missile system composed of satellite-launched laser beams that could intercept and destroy all Soviet missiles before they reached the territory of the United States or its allies. Such an innovation—dubbed the Strategic Defense Initiative by its proponents—would not only violate the ABM provisions of the 1972 SALT I Treaty but would also, according to many experts, promote acute instability in the strategic balance and therefore increase the risk of preventive nuclear war.

On the other hand, the Reagan administration took two steps that belied its reputation for Cold War zealotry. After denouncing the unratified SALT II agreement for freezing the United States into a dangerous position of strategic inferiority, Reagan pledged to continue the Carter policy of abiding by the treaty's limitations provided that the Soviet Union did likewise. He also surprised many observers by agreeing to resume strategic arms negotiations with the Soviet Union. In a May 1982 speech he suggested that the new round of discussions be called Strategic Arms Reduction Talks (START), to signify a break with the SALT II Treaty (which had languished unratified in the US Senate ever since it was signed by Carter and Brezhnev in June 1979) as well as to express his preference for deep reductions in, rather than limitations on, the nuclear arsenals of the two superpowers.

The START talks, which began in Geneva in June 1982, yielded no concrete results by the end of the first Reagan term, but at least they kept the process of arms control negotiations alive at a time when relations between the superpowers were deteriorating. The failure of arms control talks during Reagan's first term was due in no small measure to instability in the Soviet leadership: Yuri Andropov, who replaced Brezhnev in November 1982, died in February 1984, and his successor, Konstantin Chernenko, in turn died in March 1985, to be succeeded by the unknown, untested Mikhail Gorbachev.

The poisoning of relations between the United States and the Soviet Union had begun during the

THE DOWNING OF KAL FLIGHT 007

Although the Cold War was soon to enter its final phase, tensions between the superpowers escalated dramatically in 1983. The beginning of the US Strategic Defence Initiative (known popularly as the 'Star Wars' program), coupled with plans to deploy Pershing II missiles in Europe, raised fears in the Soviet Union that the United States was developing a new first-strike nuclear capability. In a cover story in early 1983, *Time* magazine called these developments 'nuclear poker'. President Ronald Reagan increasingly portrayed the Cold War as a stark struggle of good versus evil. In a now-famous speech in March 1983, he called the Soviet Union an 'evil empire'. Six months later, the downing of Korean Air Lines Flight 007 served as a tragic reminder of how the Cold War could affect people in almost any part of the world.

On 1 September 1983, KAL Flight 007 was en route from Anchorage, Alaska, to Seoul, South Korea. Deviating from its flight plan, the Boeing 747 entered Soviet airspace over militarily sensitive areas of the Kamchatka Peninsula and Sakhalin Island. Soviet fighters intercepted the plane and, with orders to force it to land, fired warning shots, but they received no response. One of the fighters then fired two missiles at the plane as it neared international airspace, sending it crashing into the sea. All 269 passengers were killed. Soviet officials initially denied responsibility for the attack but then admitted that their fighters had fired after the plane had violated Soviet airspace without notification and failed to heed warnings. While American officials expressed outrage, the USSR news agency claimed that KAL Flight 007 had deliberately entered Soviet airspace as part of an espionage mission. In response, Reagan declared that the incident showed the true nature of Communism: 'This was the Soviet Union against the world and the moral precepts which guide human relations everywhere. It was an act of barbarism, born of a society which wantonly disregards individual rights and the value of human life and seeks constantly to expand and dominate other nations.'

The incident sparked a series of elaborate conspiracy theories, though the International Civil Aviation Organization eventually concluded that pilot error was to blame for the deviation from the plane's flight plan. While the facts remained clouded in Cold War secrecy, the broader trend in international relations was clear. For the major powers of the Far East, concerns over Soviet military activity spurred regional co-operation. Relations between China and the United States steadily improved, fuelled by economic interests and a shared suspicion of the Soviet Union. The downing of KAL Flight 007 appeared to confirm that the Cold War would continue for the foreseeable future.

Carter administration, when a significant segment of American official opinion had concluded that détente was virtually dead. For many observers, the Soviet invasion of Afghanistan in 1979 underscored the fact that Moscow had reneged on its implicit pledge to pursue peaceful coexistence with the West and promote stability in the world. This shift in attitudes was prompted less by developments in the area of nuclear capabilities than by a succession of Soviet gains and US setbacks in the non-nuclear area during the second half of the 1970s that appeared to signal a return to the confrontational spirit of the Cold War era.

TURMOIL IN SOUTH ASIA

The Cold War would also be exacerbated by a series of geopolitical transformations, the first of which occurred in Iran. The regime of Shah Mohammed Reza Pahlavi had been installed by the British and Soviets in 1941 and rescued from a 1946 Soviet-backed insurgency in its northernmost province by Anglo–American pressure on Moscow. It had become Washington's staunchest ally in the region after 1953, when the Central Intelligence Agency masterminded a coup that restored the shah to power after his ouster by nationalist politician Mohammed Mossadegh. By the mid-1950s, American firms had acquired, along with the British-owned Anglo-Iranian Oil Company, equal control of Iran's rich petroleum reserves under an arrangement that supplied the government in Tehran with oil royalties, which it used to finance a crash program of industrialization. In the early 1970s, the Nixon administration began to equip the shah's military and naval forces with sophisticated weapons intended to enable Iran to replace Britain as the principal peacekeeping force of the anti-communist bloc in the Persian Gulf.

But by 1978, opposition to the Pahlavi dynasty was mounting among a broad-based coalition of Shi'ite Muslim fundamentalists who detested the Shah's secular policies and the Westernized lifestyle of his entourage; small merchants who

resented the distorting influence of US-based multinationals on the Iranian economy; and progressive opposition politicians disenchanted with the regime's repressive methods and corrupt practices. In January 1979, massive street demonstrations forced the Shah into exile, and the following month a fundamentalist Islamic movement loyal to Shi'ite clerical leader Ayatollah Ruhollah Khomeini took power in Tehran.

Neither the Soviet Union nor the small but influential Iranian Communist Party had played any significant role in these events. Nevertheless, the revolution took on an increasingly anti-American character, with devastating consequences for Western interests in this strategically and economically important region. Pro-American elements in the Iranian political and military elite were executed, the extensive American economic interests in the country were confiscated, and American military installations (including the radar network along the northern frontier intended to monitor Soviet military activity) were closed down. Iran's oil production was abruptly cut back by the continuing domestic unrest and the war with neighbouring Iraq that broke out in December 1980, and though this circumstance was of minimal concern to the United States (which received only 5 per cent of its oil imports from Iran), it produced serious economic difficulties for America's allies in Western Europe and Japan that were much more dependent on Persian Gulf oil. Moreover, the upsurge of Muslim fundamentalism in Iran threatened to spread throughout the Middle East, causing political instability and undermining pro-Western regimes in Saudi Arabia, Egypt, and elsewhere.

Concern over the Iranian Revolution deepened further in November 1979, when a group of several hundred Iranian students seized the American embassy in Tehran, taking 69 Americans hostages in an effort to force Washington to extradite the shah (who had been admitted to a New York hospital for treatment of the cancer that finally killed him in July 1980). The Iranian militants released female and black hostages the following month, and in January 1980, 6 hostages that had escaped with the help of Canadian Ambassador to Iran Ken Taylor returned to the United States. However, the remaining 53 were not freed until Carter vacated the White House in January 1981. In the meantime, fundamentalist attacks on the US consulate in Tripoli, Libya, and the US embassy in Islamabad, Pakistan, raised the spectre of a jihad, or holy war, against US interests throughout the Islamic world.

As the United States was watching its long-time client state transform into a centre of anti-American agitation, the Soviet Union in December 1979 embarked on its first overt military operation outside Eastern Europe since the end of the Second World War, dispatching paratroops and armoured columns to Afghanistan to quell a Muslim insurrection against the pro-Soviet government in Kabul. Afghanistan, like its neighbour Iran, had been the site of acute rivalry between tsarist Russia and Britain before the First World War, and in 1907 it was formally recognized as a neutral buffer between Russia and British India. During the Cold War it continued to occupy this non-aligned status between the Soviet Union and the newly created state of Pakistan, the West's principal ally in South Asia.

Unlike Iran, however, Afghanistan had gravitated towards the Soviet orbit in the 1950s, renewing an earlier non-aggression pact with Moscow and receiving substantial Soviet economic aid. Then in April 1978, Marxist Nur Mohammed Taraki led an insurrection that overthrew the leftist but nominally neutralist regime in Kabul and established an openly pro-Soviet government, which in turn was toppled by another Marxist, Hafizullah Amin in September 1979. In the meantime, a fundamentalist Muslim insurgency against the Soviet-backed regime, which received covert military assistance from the United States, China, and Pakistan, attracted such broad support among the Afghan population as to prompt the Soviet intervention of December 1979. By the following spring, almost 100,000 Soviet soldiers had poured into the country to bolster the new regime of Babrak Karmal, an Afghan exile in

Eastern Europe who had been brought in by the Soviets to replace the murdered Amin.

This military operation did not significantly alter the East–West balance of power in South Asia, since Afghanistan had always been recognized as lying within the Soviet sphere of influence and had already been ruled by a Soviet puppet government before the intervention. But Washington reacted to the Soviet action with unexpected harshness, leading observers to wonder whether the period of détente had definitively come to an end. President Carter increased the 1981 defence budget by 5 per cent in real terms, imposed an embargo on grain deliveries to the Soviet Union, restricted Soviet access to US fishing waters and high-technology exports, and organized a boycott of the Olympic Games scheduled to be held in Moscow in July 1980. Carter also advised the US Senate, which by then needed no prodding from the White House, to delay consideration of the SALT II Treaty that had been signed in 1979 but was still unratified.

In January 1980, Carter announced that the United States considered the Gulf region vital to its national interest and therefore would intervene directly to defend it against Soviet aggression. This move was due in large part to fears that the invasion of Afghanistan represented an attempt by the Soviets to position themselves for a future move towards the oil resources of the Persian Gulf and the Arabian peninsula as well as the warm waters of the Indian Ocean.

Carter then proceeded to take a number of steps to shore up the deteriorating American position in the region. Relations with the military regime of General Zia ul-Haq of Pakistan, which had cooled because of his repressive internal security policies and his apparent interest in acquiring an independent nuclear capability in violation of the non-proliferation treaty, were improved. Plans were made for the creation of a Rapid Deployment Force for use in the Persian Gulf–Red Sea region. Washington approached a number of pro-Western states in the vicinity in hopes of finding base facilities for US air and naval forces to compensate

THE RISE OF THE *MUJAHIDEEN*

In April 1978 the People's Democratic Party of Afghanistan (PDPA) took power and established a Soviet-backed Marxist regime. Land reform, new educational initiatives (often aimed at women), the elimination of traditional religious laws, and repression of political opponents soon followed. Internal revolts against the PDPA, most often motivated by the attempt to curtail religious practices, began almost immediately. Fearing for its survival the party appealed to the Soviet Union for assistance against the *mujahideen* (literally, 'one who struggles'). By January 1980 the Soviets had established a sizeable military presence in Afghanistan which, in turn, served to unite the ordinarily fragmented elements of the Afghan opposition—including some from outside the country. For the next nine years, *mujahideen* groups received funds, equipment, and training from the United States by way of the CIA and sympathetic officials in Pakistan. In addition, in order to prevent any challenges to the neighbouring regime—a key American ally during the Cold War—the US increased its military assistance to Pakistan, beginning with a shipment of anti-aircraft missiles.

Utilizing primarily guerrilla tactics, the *mujahideen* waged an effective campaign of harassment and ambush. Increasingly frustrated by their inability to launch a decisive strike against the opposition, the Soviet forces instead targeted Afghan civilians in the belief that popular support was enabling the rebels to continue their activities. By the time of the Soviet withdrawal in 1989 an estimated one million Afghans had died, another four million had been wounded, and at least one-third of the pre-invasion population had been displaced (both internally and externally). Further, the rapid Soviet withdrawal left a power vacuum in the country, paving the way for old factional rivalries among the *mujahideen* to re-emerge. Without US assistance after the fall of the Soviet Union, the country descended into an anarchic state as local warlords carved out regional enclaves of power. By 1994 the situation was so dire that a small group advocating stability through the re-establishment of pure Islamic law was able to gain some measure of public support. Taliban ('one who seeks knowledge') strength grew on the twin promises of eradicating corruption and re-establishing centralized rule, until they were able to take control of the government in Kabul in 1996.

---

for the loss of the formidable military and naval apparatus formerly controlled by the shah as the Western-backed policeman of the region. In June 1980, Oman and Kenya granted the US access to naval and air facilities at Masirah Island and the port of Mombasa, respectively. In August, Somalia agreed to receive US warships at its naval bases formerly used by the Soviet fleet. The American naval base on the British-owned island of Diego Garcia in the middle of the Indian Ocean was enlarged and upgraded to accommodate a larger US naval force to offset increased Soviet naval power there. Throughout the first half of the 1980s, the Reagan administration stepped up US military aid to the Afghan resistance.

PEACE AND WAR IN THE MIDDLE EAST

Even as the American position in the Red Sea, Persian Gulf, and Indian Ocean was challenged in the late 1970s, other developments enhanced Washington's political influence in the Middle East. Especially notable was the reversal of Egypt's policy toward the two superpowers after the Kremlin failed to deliver the military assistance its Arab clients needed to tip the balance against Israel, and Henry Kissinger succeeded in his overtures to Egyptian President Anwar Sadat. In March 1976, Sadat renounced the 1971 Soviet–Egyptian Friendship Treaty, and a month later he cancelled Soviet naval privileges in Egyptian ports. US President Carter, meanwhile, resumed the Kissinger policy of elbowing the Soviets out of the peace negotiations between Israel and Egypt. The prospects for resolving the remaining differences between the two countries were improved when Sadat travelled to Jerusalem in November 1977 in a bold attempt to break the deadlock in the stalled peace process. This symbolic gesture of goodwill, together with the appreciative response of the Israeli public, paved the way for a bilateral accord that Washington had been promoting since the Yom Kippur War in 1973.

In September 1978, at the Camp David presidential retreat, Sadat and Prime Minister Menachem Begin of Israel signed a remarkable agreement that called for Israel to return the Sinai peninsula to Egypt in two stages (in 1980 and 1982) and for Egypt to recognize Israel's right to exist as a sovereign nation. The agreement left the sensitive issue of Palestinian autonomy in the Gaza Strip and on the West Bank of the Jordan River for future negotiation. Egypt and Israel signed a peace treaty in March 1979, exchanged formal diplomatic recognition in February 1980, and resumed their bilateral efforts to restore stability to the Middle East in the face of the unremitting hostility of the Palestinian political organizations and their supporters in the Arab world. Syria, Iraq, Libya, and Algeria took the lead in opposing the Camp David Accords and received strong support from the Soviet Union. But the Israeli–Egyptian rapprochement survived the assassination of President Sadat in October 1981 by Egyptian opponents of Camp David. It also continued in spite of a number of belligerent actions by the Begin government, including the bombardment of PLO offices in Beirut in July, the annexation of the Golan Heights in December, and the continued construction of permanent Israeli settlements on the West Bank. The final Israeli withdrawal from the Sinai took place in April 1982, in accordance with the Camp David timetable, and Sadat's successor, President Hosni Mubarak, reaffirmed his predecessor's policy of peaceful relations with Israel.

But the negotiations concerning the West Bank and Gaza showed no sign of progress, and relations between the Palestinian populations of these areas and their Israeli occupiers continued to deteriorate. The Camp David Accords had been based on President Carter's assumption that removal of the Egyptian threat would make Israel more accommodating on the Palestinian issue. But Prime Minister Begin, who believed that Israel was entitled to perpetual control of the West Bank, was emboldened to strengthen his country's military position and deal harshly with the Palestinians.

In the meantime, the tense political and military situation in Lebanon set the stage for an explosion that almost derailed the peace process. The political leadership of the PLO and many of its military cadres had settled in Lebanon after they were expelled from Jordan in September 1970. Then, following a bloody clash between left- and right-wing Lebanese factions in the middle of the decade, a large contingent of Syrian troops moved into the Bekaa valley of northeastern Lebanon as part of an Arab peacekeeping force. The Syrians promptly introduced jet fighters and ground-to-air missiles in Lebanon and lent support to the Palestinian units that were using Soviet-built artillery to shell the Galilee area of northern Israel. In 1978, Israeli forces crossed into southern Lebanon and forced the PLO to fall back behind the Litani River, 29 kilometres from the Israeli frontier, while a United Nations peacekeeping force was dispatched to southern Lebanon to separate the belligerents. But once the Palestinians established positions in southern Lebanon outside the UN buffer zone and resumed the shelling of Galilee, the Begin government decided to profit from the instability in Lebanon to establish a secure northern border once and for all.

Apparently believing that he had been given the 'green light' by US Secretary of State Alexander Haig, Begin sent a large Israeli force across the Lebanese frontier in early June 1982. The ground forces and tank columns overwhelmed the PLO strongholds in southern Lebanon; the American-built jet fighters knocked out all of the

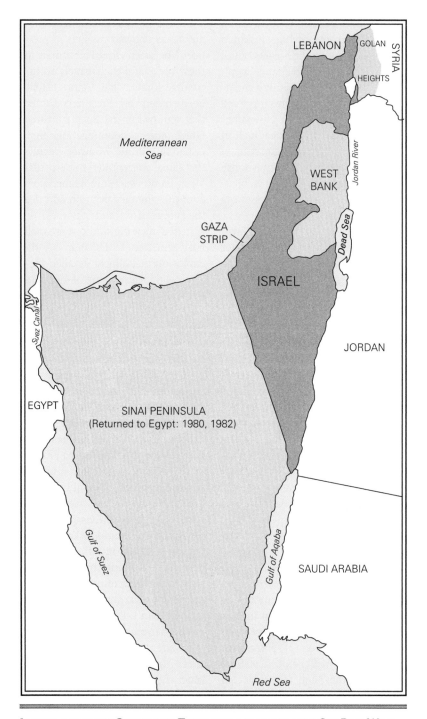

ISRAEL AND THE OCCUPIED TERRITORIES AFTER THE SIX DAY WAR

Soviet-built Syrian surface-to-air missile sites in the Bekaa valley; and the Israeli planes used their American-built missiles to destroy almost half of Syria's Soviet-built jet fighters. Israeli infantry and tank columns closed in on Beirut as Israeli planes bombed the western part of the city where PLO headquarters were located. By the end of the summer, a US-sponsored agreement was worked out whereby the Palestinian political leaders and military forces were evacuated from Lebanon under the protection of a multinational peace-keeping force consisting of American, French, and Italian marines.

The invasion of Lebanon achieved Israel's immediate objective: to eliminate the PLO as a military threat along its northern frontier. It also demonstrated that the Israelis' US-built weaponry was capable of defeating the Syrian arsenal of Soviet-built missiles and fighter planes, thereby tarnishing Moscow's reputation as an effective military patron for the hard-line Arab states. However, Israel's military triumph caused a deterioration of relations between the Begin government and the Reagan administration in Washington, which regarded the intervention as a threat to regional stability and expressed its displeasure by announcing an embargo on future sales of F-16 fighter planes to Israel.

A further indication of Washington's irritation with its Israeli client came in September 1982, when Reagan formally proposed his own compre-hensive solution to the Palestinian–Israeli conflict. The Reagan Plan, which had been formulated without consultation with Israel, contradicted the Begin government's policy of sponsoring Israeli settlements on the West Bank in preparation for the establishment of permanent Israeli authority over the region and its Palestinian majority. But neither did it support the idea of an independent Palestinian state. Instead, it called for the creation of a Palestinian–Jordanian federation that would administer the Israeli-occupied territories under the authority of King Hussein. Nothing ever came of this proposal, not only because of Israel's lack of enthusiasm but also because Hussein was unable to obtain the assent of the PLO and

the major hardline Arab states for the so-called Jordanian solution.

Two weeks after the unveiling of the abortive Reagan plan, developments in Lebanon served to dampen US interest in actively pursuing peace in that troubled country. In mid-September, Israeli military forces occupied the Muslim section of West Beirut after the assassination of Bashir Gemayel, the newly elected Christian president of Lebanon (whom Israel had strongly supported in the expectation that he would agree to a separate peace with the Jewish state along the lines of the Camp David Accords). Two days later, Gemayel's enraged followers burst into two Palestinian refu-gee camps in the Israeli-controlled area and mas-sacred approximately 800 civilians while Israeli military authorities looked the other way.

Washington had pledged to PLO leader Yasser Arafat that the Israelis would protect the Palestinian civilians remaining in Beirut after the evacuation of the PLO fighters. Thus Reagan hastily arranged for the return of the multinational military con-tingent to provide a semblance of security. But the indefinite presence of American, French, and Italian peacekeepers in Lebanon angered Muslims, who suspected the Westerners of favouring the Christians in the ongoing Lebanese Civil War. It also annoyed Syrian President Hafez al-Assad, whose own 'peacekeeping' units were deployed in the northeastern part of the country to promote Syrian ambitions. A succession of terrorist attacks on American personnel in Lebanon culminated in October 1983, when a suicide mission blew up the headquarters of the marines outside Beirut, killing 241 US servicemen as they slept. After a face-saving interval, Reagan pulled all US marines out of Lebanon and abandoned hope of mediat-ing a settlement there.

The only sign of progress in the Middle East came in the fall of 1984, when the newly estab-lished coalition government in Israel, headed by Labour Party leader Shimon Peres, began with-drawing Israeli troops from southern Lebanon. In the meantime, Shi'ite Muslims, Druze, and Palestinians resumed their violent quarrels while the Lebanese government of Amin Gemayel, brother of the slain Christian leader, saw its authority collapse. But the Syrian army, lavishly re-equipped by the Soviet Union, remained in northeastern Lebanon. Hafez al-Assad, who had come to power in Syria in 1970 just after the death of Egypt's Nasser, had built up his military forces with Soviet aid as Sadat turned from Moscow to Washington. With Egypt isolated by the Camp David Accords and Iraq distracted by its war with Iran, many Arabs had come to see Assad as the heir to Nasser, leading the Arab struggle against Israel.

Yet the larger aspiration associated with Nasser's name—the quest for Arab unity—had proved as elusive as ever in the years since his death. Despite the common linguistic and religious heritage that linked most of the Arab peoples in the Middle East, the political fragmentation of the region continued to prevent the realization of the pan-Arab ideal. The sharp contrast between secular ideologies (such as that of the Baathist[2] ruling elites then in power in Syria and Iraq) and Islamism was one cause of disunity. Another was the divergence in the positions taken by the various Arab states with regard to the Cold War: Egypt, Jordan, Saudi Arabia, and Oman maintained close ties with the United States, while Syria, Iraq, and South Yemen sought and received military and diplomatic support from the Soviet Union. Opposition to the existence of the state of Israel and support for Palestinian nationalism appeared to be the major sources of cohesion among the Arab states. But even that cohesion was undermined by Egypt's separate peace with the Jewish state, and Jordan's flirtation with the Reagan plan for a Palestinian–Jordanian federation.

The Iraq–Iran War of 1980–8 aggravated the disarray in the Arab world. From 1973 to 1979, Iraq's oil revenues had increased from US$2 billion to $21 billion, enabling that country to build a formidable military. After becoming president of Iraq in 1979, Saddam Hussein apparently assumed that he could profit from Iran's internal upheaval and international isolation by using his Soviet- and French-equipped army for a quick,

decisive victory over the tattered remnants of the Shah's military forces. But by 1982, a spirited Iranian counter-offensive together with a sharp decline in Iraqi oil revenues (the result of over-supply on world markets) had transformed the conflict into a long war of attrition. If Hussein's ultimate objective was to establish himself as Nasser's heir by mobilizing the Arab world against the two non-Arab states in the Middle East—Israel and Iran—he failed ignominiously. Syria's Assad, who presided over a secular Arab regime faced with an internal threat from Islamic fundamentalists, strongly supported the non-Arab Islamic regime of Khomeini against the secular Arab state of Iraq. The explanation of this apparent paradox was simple: Assad regarded his fellow Baathist Saddam Hussein as his most likely rival in the Arab world. Libya, Algeria, and South Yemen also backed Iran against Iraq for their own reasons, while the rest of the Arab world closed ranks behind Saddam Hussein.

By the mid-1980s, the optimism engendered by the Camp David accords had given way to a bleak pessimism. Not a single other Arab state had joined Egypt in acknowledging Israel's right to exist. On the contrary, Egypt was virtually drummed out of the Arab bloc in 1978, and Sadat was assassinated in 1981 precisely because he had been the first Arab leader to recognize the Jewish state. Hardline factions within the increasingly frustrated PLO began using terrorism to publicize their grievances against Israel; one notable incident was the murder of an elderly, disabled Jewish man after the highjacking of the Italian cruise ship *Achille Lauro* in 1985.

On the other hand, the Israeli government thumbed its nose at the Camp David principle of Palestinian autonomy in the occupied territories, establishing 90 new Jewish settlements on the West Bank between 1977 and 1984 and offering generous tax subsidies and low mortgage interest rates to entice Israeli citizens to relocate there. The negotiations on autonomy for the West Bank and Gaza, mandated by the Camp David Accords, had advanced at a snail's pace since August 1979 and were effectively killed by the Israeli invasion of Lebanon in 1982.

The goal of peace and stability was just as elusive outside the Israeli–Palestinian context. Lebanon had ceased to exist as a state in the proper sense of the term; roving bands of Christian and Muslim gunmen, together with Syrian military forces in the north and Israeli soldiers in the south, provided what passed for law and order. The armed struggle between Iraq and Iran had taken on the appearance of a First World War-type stalemate, with no end in sight as the casualty lists lengthened. In the meantime, the two superpowers continued to arm and support their clients in the region.

Despite occasional outbursts of irritation, the Reagan administration maintained intimate relations with Israel, which had become the world's largest recipient of US foreign economic aid and co-operated actively with US intelligence agencies in the Middle East and throughout the world. Egypt was number two on the list of US aid recipients, and in return shared intelligence and allowed the United States to use Egyptian ports and air space in emergencies. Washington also intensified its military ties to Saudi Arabia in return for Riyadh's help in stabilizing world oil prices by increasing production as needed. Meanwhile, although the Soviet Union had been ejected from its Egyptian bases and excluded from the Israeli–Palestinian peace process, it resupplied the Syrian army after its defeat in Lebanon in 1982, furnished economic and military assistance to Iraq and South Yemen, and diplomatically supported the PLO in various world forums. By the end of the 1980s, there was still no end in sight to the conflict in the Middle East.

SUMMARY

During the mid-1970s, it looked as though the Cold War was coming to an end. The Helsinki Conference of 1973–5 and a series of other agreements had eased tensions between the West and the Soviet bloc, and the Soviet Union was allowing more trade with Western nations in order to promote economic growth in Eastern Europe. In Asia, the end of the Vietnam War and the improvement of Sino–American relations seemed to signal a new era of stability. Meanwhile, in the Middle East, efforts to find a settlement to the Arab–Israeli conflict were renewed. Negotiations to this end resulted in a landmark agreement in 1978, when US President Jimmy Carter persuaded Egypt and Israel to sign the Camp David Accords. Progress was also made on international arms control, and the Strategic Arms Limitation Talks produced a second agreement in 1979 (SALT II).

By 1980, however, East–West tensions were again on the rise. After the Soviet Union invaded Afghanistan in 1979, the United States provided military assistance to Afghan resistance groups and led a boycott of the Moscow Olympics in 1980. The US Senate failed to ratify the SALT II Treaty, stalling arms control negotiations. In 1979, a revolution in Iran brought an Islamic fundamentalist regime to power, which threatened to destabilize the Gulf region, and the following year a war began between Iraq and Iran that was to continue until 1988. Israeli–Arab conflict continued in spite of the Camp David Accords, and in 1982 Israel invaded Lebanon. With the election of Ronald Reagan as president in 1981, the US geared up for confrontation with the Soviet Union by embarking on a program of massive military expansion. As a new generation of missiles was deployed in Europe in the early 1980s, fears of a third world war increased.

NOTES

1. In January 1973, Britain, Denmark, and Ireland joined the European Economic Community. Greece was admitted as the Community's tenth member in January 1981; Spain and Portugal followed in 1986.

2. The Baath Party (otherwise known as the Arab Socialist Renaissance Party) came to power in Iraq and Syria in 1963 and has been influential in many other Arab countries, advocating secularism, socialism, and Arab unity.

QUESTIONS FOR CRITICAL THOUGHT

1. Discuss the reasons why the rapprochement between the United States and China was important.
2. Why did Reagan support the resumption of arms limitation talks with the Soviet Union?
3. Why did the Iranian Revolution cause so much concern in the United States?
4. What were the most important factors facilitating the Camp David Accords of 1978?
5. Why has Arab unity been so difficult to secure?
6. Why did the United States back Iraq during the Iran–Iraq War?

WEBSITES FOR FURTHER REFERENCE

Cold War International History Project
   http://wilsoncenter.org/index.cfm?topic_id=1409&fuseaction=topics.home

The Cold War Museum
   www.coldwar.org

Library of Congress: Soviet Archives Exhibit
   www.ibiblio.org/expo/soviet.exhibit/entrance.html#tour

National Security Archive: Afghanistan – Lessons from the Last War
   www.gwu.edu/~nsarchiv/NSAEBB/NSAEBB57/soviet.html

CHAPTER 12

AFRICA: FROM INDEPENDENCE TO DEPENDENCY

DECOLONIZATION AND OPTIMISM

The achievement of national liberation in the second half of the 1950s and early 1960s generated a euphoric sense of optimism in the African colonies formally ruled by France, Britain, and Belgium. In May 1963, representatives of the liberated African states assembled in Addis Ababa, Ethiopia, to found the Organization of African Unity (OAU). Inspired by the ideology of pan-Africanism that had been popularized by the defiant, charismatic leader of Ghana, Kwame Nkrumah, the OAU's charter enunciated a set of goals designed to protect the recently won independence of the member states so that their peoples could thrive and prosper.

One of the cardinal principles of the charter was the recognition of the overriding need to prevent territorial conflicts both between rival African nations and among antagonistic groups within each nation. Such conflicts threatened to unravel the delicate fabric of African independence by tempting extracontinental powers to exploit for their own benefit the resulting political instability and economic chaos. Accordingly, the member states of the new organization solemnly affirmed the absolute inviolability of the political frontiers that had been inherited from the colonial era, notwithstanding the fact that these borders had been drawn to suit the administrative convenience of the colonizers rather than the economic, strategic, and ethnographic conditions of the colonies.

The second goal of the OAU was political unification of the entire continent under the aegis of a single sovereign authority. How such an ambitious program was to be carried out amid the bewildering diversity of languages, ethnic groups, and religions was not specified. But some African leaders regarded military co-operation as the most effective means to achieve the ultimate objective of continent-wide political integration. Nkrumah himself had first proposed the establishment of a multinational African army in the early 1960s to restore order during the Congo Crisis, and subsequent outbreaks of unrest prompted similar suggestions from other African heads of state. As with the principle of the inviolability of national borders, the prime motivation behind this enthusiasm for a multinational African military force was the desire to remove any pretext for foreign interference in Africa's internal affairs.

The same was true for the third axiom of the OAU's pan-African ideology: the need to remain neutral in the Cold War. The founders of the new organization were intent on avoiding the fate of other developing nations whose independence had been compromised by the spread to their regions of the rivalry between the superpowers. Delegates of the new African states had taken an active role in the first international conference of the non-aligned movement at Belgrade in 1961, and the principle of non-alignment was recorded in the OAU charter two years later. Throughout the first decade of independence, the absence of significant Soviet and American interests in Africa spared that continent the trauma of East–West conflict that afflicted Asia during the same period.

But political independence from Europe and military disengagement from the Soviet–American confrontation were not enough to guarantee post-colonial Africa a bright future. What Africa required above all else was a continent-wide program of economic development on a massive scale. Of all the poverty-stricken regions of the non-Western world, Africa indisputably occupied the most precarious position. Though exceptionally well endowed with a variety of raw materials and agricultural products, the continent was sorely deficient in capital, technology, entrepreneurial skills, managerial expertise, and adequate markets for the commodities (mainly foodstuffs and minerals) that represented the greatest part of its export trade. It also included the largest concentration of low-income, resource-poor, and landlocked countries on the face of the earth. Although 10 per cent of the world's population lived in Africa, its share of world industrial output was less than 1 per cent. Even by the mid-1980s, only 7 of the 45 African societies had a per capita income of US$1,000 or more. Unless this condition of extreme economic backwardness could be remedied, the optimistic plans for Africa's post-colonial future that had been generated in the early days of independence and non-alignment would be dashed.

As they launched their ambitious campaign for economic development during the 1960s, the new states of Africa confronted two divergent paths. They could integrate their national economies into the flourishing international economic system dominated by the United States, Western Europe, and Japan. Or they could strive to disengage Africa from the world economic order and pursue a development strategy based on the principle of self-reliance. In light of Africa's desperate need for foreign investment, loans, aid, trade, technology, and technical expertise, it is scarcely surprising that the ruling elites of the independent African states opted for membership in, rather than withdrawal from, the international economic order that alone could satisfy those requirements.

Consequently, post-colonial Africa promptly established strong links with the international monetary and trading system represented by such organizations as GATT, the IMF, and the World Bank. This involvement in the Western capitalist economic order yielded some notable benefits for the African countries during the first decade of independence. They became frequent customers at the soft loan windows of the IMF and World Bank. As well, by participating in tarrif negotiations sponsored by GATT they were able to develop trading relationships with the developed world on the basis of the exchange of their primary goods for its manufactured ones. The economic boom in the industrial world and the remarkable growth of international trade during the 1960s generated ample capital for investment, loans, and development aid to the developing world while stimulating demand in the industrialized countries for raw material and agricultural exports from Africa. During this time Africa also benefited from the large number of American Peace Corps volunteers who flocked to the continent to offer much-needed technical and managerial expertise. These volunteers made a notably strong contribution in countries such as Ghana, Liberia, and Ethiopia, where they held roughly 80 per cent of the secondary-school teaching posts in the 1960s.

Even amid the relative prosperity of the 1960s, some ominous trends had begun to give rise to pessimism about Africa's prospects for genuine independence and economic development. The first of these was the stubborn persistence of

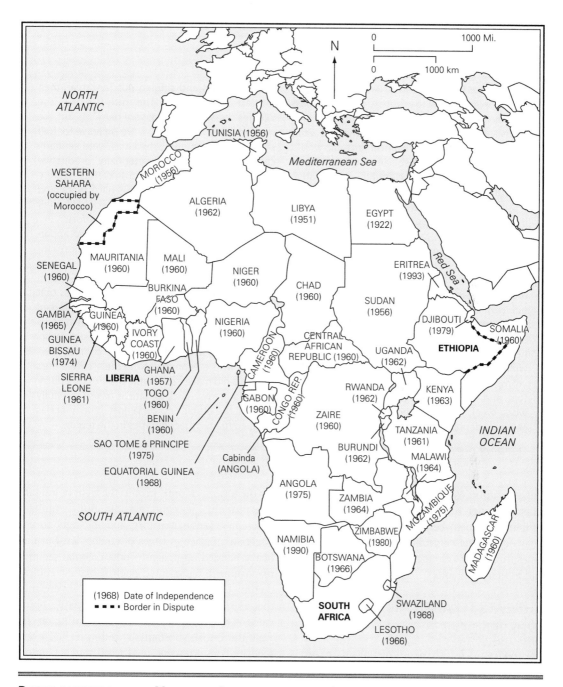

NORTH
ATLANTIC

TUNISIA (1956)

Mediterranean Sea

MOROCCO
(1956)

WESTERN
SAHARA
(occupied by
Morocco)

ALGERIA
(1962)

LIBYA
(1951)

EGYPT
(1922)

ERITREA
(1993)

Red Sea

MAURITANIA
(1960)

MALI
(1960)

NIGER
(1960)

CHAD
(1960)

SUDAN
(1956)

SENEGAL
(1960)

BURKINA
FASO
(1960)

DJIBOUTI
(1979)

SOMALIA
(1960)

GAMBIA
(1965)

GUINEA
(1960)

NIGERIA
(1960)

CENTRAL
AFRICAN
REPUBLIC (1960)

UGANDA
(1962)

ETHIOPIA

GUINEA
BISSAU
(1974)

IVORY
COAST
(1960)

CAMEROON
(1960)

GHANA
(1957)

KENYA
(1963)

SIERRA
LEONE
(1961)

LIBERIA

RWANDA
(1962)

TOGO
(1960)

GABON
(1960)

CONGO REP.
(1960)

ZAIRE
(1960)

BENIN
(1960)

TANZANIA
(1961)

INDIAN
OCEAN

SAO TOME & PRINCIPE
(1975)

Cabinda
(ANGOLA)

BURUNDI
(1962)

MALAWI
(1964)

EQUATORIAL GUINEA
(1968)

ANGOLA
(1975)

ZAMBIA
(1964)

MOZAMBIQUE
(1975)

SOUTH ATLANTIC

ZIMBABWE
(1980)

MADAGASCAR
(1960)

NAMIBIA
(1990)

BOTSWANA
(1966)

(1968) Date of Independence
Border in Dispute

SOUTH
AFRICA

SWAZILAND
(1968)

LESOTHO
(1966)

DECOLONIZATION AND NATIONAL INDEPENDENCE IN AFRICA

JULIUS NYERERE'S VISION

Whereas Ghana's Kwame Nkrumah remained convinced that the route to Africa's success lay in achieving his pan-African vision, Tanzania's Julius Nyerere gradually came to advocate a different path, that of self-reliance. Tanzania would become an egalitarian socialist society whose foundation rested on scientific, co-operative agriculture and the hard work of its people. Writing in 1967, Nyerere argued that Tanzania must break free of traditional economic models which focused on the development of heavy industry via foreign aid. Nyerere argued that 'indeed it is even more stupid, for us to imagine that we shall rid ourselves of our poverty through foreign financial assistance rather than our own financial resources.' Seeking to avoid the dependence that would inevitably follow the arrival of foreign technicians and advisors, he instead planned to develop those resources which Tanzania possessed in abundance: food crops, as well as cash crops such as coffee, cotton, and tea. Criticizing the average 45-hour work week of the average rural Tanzanian, Nyerere demanded a substantial increase in working hours and singled out Tanzanian men for particular criticism. 'The truth is that in the villages the women work very hard. . . . But the men who live in villages . . . are on leave for half of their life.' Women in the cities were similarly castigated for wasting potentially productive hours in 'gossip, dance, and drink'. Thus Nyerere came to believe that through hard work and education the people of Tanzania would lift their country out of poverty by their own effort.

Unfortunately the costly bureaucratic apparatus that supported this vision of a self-reliant socialist society, in combination with the rapid population growth endemic in Sub-Saharan Africa, gradually overwhelmed any progress that the state made. By the 1980s Nyerere was forced to admit that his vision of African socialism had a number of weaknesses, and he and his successors gradually began to reduce the level of state intervention in the economy. Nonetheless, Nyerere's Tanzania did make remarkable progress in education and literacy, and, to date, it has successfully avoided the ethnic and social instability that has plagued many other countries in the region.

---

imperial attitudes by countries such as Britain and France. Under this policy of 'neo-imperialism', as it has come to be known, European powers retained indirect control over their erstwhile colonies through the exercise of economic, political, and military influence.

THREATS TO AFRICAN INDEPENDENCE

The policy of British neo-imperialism in Africa developed in a subtle, covert manner. During the early period of African independence, London strove to retain a host of military privileges in many of the successor states of its African empire. The Anglo–Nigerian Pact of 1960, for instance, reserved three important prerogatives for the former colonial power: the right of military intervention, the right to retain British military bases on Nigerian territory, and the right to use Nigerian airspace in times of emergency. But this heavy-handed approach to post-colonial security management represented such a blatant contradiction to the principle of national sovereignty that the Nigerian government summarily abrogated it within a year. Reading the writing on the wall, the British substantially reduced their overt security commitments in Africa (though London did not hesitate to send troops to bolster friendly regimes in Uganda, Kenya, and Tanzania during the 1960s). Instead, Britain concentrated on preserving its considerable economic influence in the region through British-based multinational corporations and financial institutions that had retained significant interests there. Britain was also capable of exercising a degree of cultural influence through the Commonwealth, as the loosely affiliated association of former British dependencies was dominated by the anglophone African states.

France exercised a much more direct, overt form of neo-imperial power on the continent after its departure from the former territories of French West Africa and French Equatorial Africa in 1960. French security interests in tropical Africa were protected through a series of bilateral mutual defence pacts granting the former colonial power the right of military intervention. To bolster its position as Europe's 'gendarme' in the region, Paris obtained the right to maintain garrisons in half-a-dozen West and Central African states. By the mid-1960s, some 10,000 French military forces had been stationed in Africa and its offshore islands, and a large French naval force regularly patrolled the western shores of the Indian Ocean. Paris used the territories of Senegal and Gabon as bases for covert intelligence operations in Africa, while French counterinsurgency experts trained the security forces of many of its client states there.

This extensive network of security agreements, combat units, and military installations enabled France to launch a number of military interventions in Africa in support of its own interests or those of its African protégés. During the 1960s French units left their barracks in Cameroon, Gabon, Niger, and Chad to defend client regimes under attack from dissident elements. On other occasions, the French government exercised behind-the-scenes influence to hasten the downfall of long-time antagonists—such as Modibo Keita of Mali (1968)—or former protégés who had fallen from grace—such as N'garta Tombalbaye of

From left, Presidents Moktar Ould Daddah of Mauritania, Seyni Kountche of Nigeria, and Idi Amin Dada of Uganda, at the closing session of the 14th Summit Meeting of the Organization of African Unity, Libreville, Gabon, 5 June 1977. Associated Press.

Chad (1975), Moktar Ould Daddah of Mauritania (1978), and Jean-Bedel Bokassa of the Central African Republic (1979).

In March 1977 and May–June 1978, France intervened in Zaire's Shaba (formerly Katanga) province, ostensibly to rescue resident European nationals but also to protect Zairian leader Mobutu Sese Seko—the western power's most reliable ally in Africa—against exiled security forces that had returned from their Angolan sanctuary to challenge his authority. Eventually the French contingents in Zaire were replaced by an all-African peacekeeping force, but one that hardly satisfied Nkrumah's bold objective to prevent foreign intervention in African affairs. The brainchild of the francophile president of Senegal, Léopold Senghor, the multinational army was dominated by contingents from the pro-French states of Morocco, Gabon, and Senegal and depended heavily on French technical and logistical support.

Economic agreements reinforced France's privileged relationship with most of its former African colonies. At the time of the establishment of the European Economic Community (1957), France had insisted on several provisions preserving preferential trade terms for, and special financial relationships with, the overseas dependencies of member states. Since Britain did not join the EEC until 1973, the vast majority of African countries involved in the treaty at the time of decolonization were the successor states of French West Africa and French Equatorial Africa. The Yaoundé Convention of 1963 (which remained in force from 1964 until 1969) set up a European Development Fund (EDF) of US$800 million, subsequently increased to $1 billion in the second Yaoundé accord of 1969 (which operated from 1970 until 1975). The EDF was a foreign aid program (of which France and West Germany each bore roughly a third of the cost) that financed infrastructure and agricultural projects, with most of the appropriations going to sub-Saharan states with close ties to France, such as the Ivory Coast, Senegal, and Cameroon. Language ties ensured a preponderance of French technicians and advisers on most EDF-financed projects, and French

construction firms received a disproportionate share of the contracts based on EDF funds.

The preferential trade arrangements of the Yaoundé Accords proved extremely advantageous to the EEC in general and to France in particular. The vast bulk of EDF funds was earmarked for the purchase of manufactured products from Europe, and the former African colonies had to import grain from EEC countries at prices well above the going rate on world markets. In sum, the preferential commercial arrangements codified in the two Yaoundé conventions ensured that France's membership in the EEC would not entail the sacrifice of strategic African markets and traditional sources of raw materials (especially cobalt, uranium, phosphates, and bauxite) and tropical agricultural goods (mainly coffee and cocoa).

France solidified its strong financial connection with its former African possessions with the creation of the 'franc zone', a monetary association that tied the currencies of most sub-Saharan francophone African states to the French franc. The participating countries were collectively designated as the Communauté Financière Africaine (CFA), or African Financial Community. The franc zone in effect established a common monetary system by allowing the free convertibility between the currencies of CFA members and the French franc at fixed parity. This arrangement created an open channel through which French capital could flow in and out of the African countries within the franc zone without encountering the risks of exchange-rate instability or prohibitions against the repatriation of profits. This open invitation to French investors (at the expense of foreign competitors) yielded impressive results in French client states such as Senegal and the Ivory Coast, which became African havens for subsidiaries of multinational (but mainly French) corporations.

Just as France had insisted on the Yaoundé arrangement to preserve its preferential trade ties with francophone Africa after it joined the EEC, Britain demanded similar protection as it belatedly gained admission in 1973. In 1975, lengthy negotiations between the EEC and the OAU resulted in Lomé I, a convention which established preferential trade between the EEC and a newly established bloc of former European colonies designated as the Association of African, Caribbean, and Pacific States (ACP).

The Lomé Convention offered participating African nations many advantages over the two Yaoundé accords it replaced. Whereas the Yaoundé conventions had granted member states of the EEC (notably France) privileged access to African markets but excluded many African products from the European market, the Lomé system offered much more favourable terms of trade for the African states. While all ACP manufactured products and 96 per cent of ACP commodity exports were admitted duty-free in EEC Europe, the ACP states were permitted to impose their protectionist restrictions on imports from EEC countries. A second benefit of the Lomé agreement was the establishment of an aid program for the most impoverished of the African countries. But the most advantageous feature of Lomé I from the African perspective was the creation of a commodity stabilization fund (STABEX), which provided financial compensation to African states when the price of their commodity exports dropped below a stipulated level. This innovation was hailed as a long-overdue solution to the problem of commodity price fluctuations that had plagued those African countries that depended on the world market price of a single commodity for the major portion of their export earnings.

Though the Lomé regime conferred notable nonreciprocal advantages on the ACP countries, African officials waged a spirited campaign to rectify some its defects during the renegotiation of the original agreement toward the end of the 1970s. They complained bitterly about the inadequacy of the aid program, the rigorous conditions attached to it, and the absence of African voices in decisions concerning the disbursement of funds. Despite increased development assistance (which was largely cancelled out by inflation and population increases), Lomé II (in 1980) encountered widespread opposition in Africa.

Critics denounced the Lomé system as an instrument of neo-imperialism that perpetuated African dependency in the guise of 'Eurafrican' economic co-operation. The system, its critics argued, reinforced the continent's position of inferiority in an international division of labour dominated by high technology and automated manufacturing. And by promoting the export of African commodities in exchange for European manufactures as the basis of Africa's foreign trade, the 'Eurafrican nexus' inhibited the process of product and market diversification that had paved the way for the economic success of the newly industrializing countries (NICs) of East Asia. Instead of exploiting its abundance of cheap labour to produce low-quality, low-price manufactured goods and aggressively seek new markets abroad (like Taiwan and South Korea), Africa remained hopelessly locked in the neo-colonial embrace of Western Europe. The third renegotiation of the Lomé convention (Lomé III), in 1985, did not significantly alter this condition of increasing dependency and vulnerability.

RECESSION AND REORGANIZATION IN THE 1970s

Such advantages as Africa did obtain from its participation in the international economic system during the prosperity and expansion of the 1960s vanished as the world slid into deep recession in the 1970s. The two successive oil shocks of that decade devastated the economies of nearly all African nations, save those with substantial petroleum reserves (such as Algeria, Nigeria, Libya, Gabon, Congo, and Cameroon) and those with diversified economies (such as Senegal and South Africa) that were able to export and attract foreign investment. On the other end of the developmental scale, those landlocked, resource-poor, or drought-ridden states—such as Chad, Niger, Ethiopia, Uganda, and the Sudan—were plunged into socio-economic chaos.

At the same time, the problem of Africa's lopsided reliance on commodity exports returned to haunt it with a vengeance during the world recession. As prices of commodities other than petroleum sank to their lowest levels in three decades (reflecting the drop in demand in the recession-ridden industrial world), many African producers of primary products were driven to the wall. Unable to pay for essential imports of food and oil, most African nations had to rush to the IMF and the commercial banks of industrialized countries. Africa's foreign debt soared, from US$14.2 billion in 1973 to $42 billion in 1976 to over $150 billion by 1984, while the ratio of total debt to GNP of all the countries on the continent doubled (from under 20 per cent in 1973 to 40 per cent in 1984).

Africa was also hurt by a fatal combination of unchecked population growth, drought, and decline in food production (due in part to a frantic flight from the countryside to urban areas in search of higher living standards), which resulted in widespread famine and disease. The inevitable austerity measures imposed by the banks and the IMF as preconditions for future loans forced African countries to slash domestic spending and curtail imports. The consequence was negative economic growth for most of the non-oil-exporting states and the transformation of the post-independence dream of Africa's glorious future into the nightmare of dependency and decline.

The first signs of Africa's economic stagnation during the early 1970s prompted a radical proposal for relief. At its tenth annual conference, in Addis Ababa in 1973, the OAU formally called for the creation of a New International Economic Order (NIEO), an innocuous euphemism for a massive transfer of wealth from the developed countries of the northern hemisphere to the less developed countries (LDCs) of the south. The plan called for a drastic increase in development assistance from the industrial world, the cancellation of outstanding foreign debts, the establishment on a global basis of mechanisms to stabilize commodity prices, and the reduction of northern protectionism against LDC exports. This project for the reallocation of global economic resources based on need rather than the free market criteria of supply and demand received the enthusiastic endorsement of the non-aligned movement later in the year and that of the UN General Assembly in 1974.

But the proposal for an NIEO ran aground on the shoals of global recession by the end of the 1970s. The soaring rates of inflation and unemployment in the developed world were scarcely conducive to the spirit of altruism required for such a large-scale redistribution of global wealth. Instead, the industrial states responded to the economic downturn by adopting policies that merely aggravated Africa's economic crisis, such as the reduction of foreign aid commitments and the enactment of additional protectionist measures against imports from the developing world.

Faced with the unwillingness of wealthy industrial states to endure the reduced standard of living that the NIEO scheme for a global redistribution of resources would entail, Africa was forced to reconsider its earlier decision to join the world economic order. Africa's unenviable plight beginning in the mid-1970s was a direct consequence of the asymmetry of its international economic relationships. While the continent had only marginal importance to the world economic system, the impact of that system on the economic well-being of the African states (which had become highly dependent on the developed world for uninterrupted access to markets, investments, loans, and technical expertise) was devastating.

It was entirely understandable that some African leaders, their fragile economies battered by the global recession, began to have second thoughts about the discarded option of continental self-reliance and co-operation. In December 1976, a proposal to establish an African Economic Community, modelled on the EEC, received the support of a number of prominent African officials who regarded the political and economic balkanization of the African continent as a major obstacle to its economic development. But those who hoped to keep alive Nkrumah's ambitious project struggled to generate support among the more skeptical African leaders, who recalled the failures of earlier pan-African schemes, and the movement petered out.

African leaders found a middle ground between the bleak reality of balkanization and the utopian goal of continental unity in the prospect of regionalism. The emergence of the regionalist movement in Africa reflected the failure of several countries' economies to live up to expectations in the new era of independence. In 1980 the African states endorsed the so-called Lagos Plan of Action (LPA) as an emergency response to the deteriorating economic conditions on the continent. While paying lip service to the ultimate objective of African economic unity by the end of the century, the LPA called for the strengthening of existing regional economic units and the creation of new ones as the most practical means of fostering economic growth in the short term and full continental integration in the long term. The principal regional associations were the Economic Community of West African States (ECOWAS), the Economic Community for Central African States (ECCAS), the Southern African Development Coordination Conference (SADCC), and the Preferential Trade Area (PTA) for East and Southern Africa. These organizations, which together covered all of tropical Africa, were the only existing mechanisms for the kind of economic co-operation that might reverse the trend toward degeneration and decay.

The most promising of these regional associations was ECOWAS, founded in May 1975 in Lagos, Nigeria, by the representatives of 15 West African nations. Based on the principle of collective self-reliance and regional co-operation, ECOWAS rapidly developed into a test case in Africa's campaign to loosen the neo-colonial bonds with Europe that had been tightened in the Lomé system. In particular, Nigeria's dominant role in ECOWAS, together with its sponsorship of the LPA, signified a determined bid for regional leadership. The large, populous, resource-rich country had recently celebrated a triumph of national unity, when its national troops overwhelmed a secessionist uprising by the proclaimed state of Biafra in a civil war in the late 1960s. In the 1970s the country enjoyed a financial windfall from skyrocketing oil prices, which helped to fuel Nigeria's growth as a regional power.

But Nigeria's hegemonic aspirations in West Africa conflicted with France's neo-imperial relationship with its allies in the region. In the end, the anglophone nation's cultural and linguistic isolation amid predominantly francophone neighbours who preferred Paris to Lagos as a source of guidance (and financial assistance) hampered Nigeria's ambition to become the dominant regional power in West Africa. Furthermore, the sharp decline in oil prices due to oversupply during the 1980s exposed the error of Nigeria's development strategy of relying on a single, volatile export commodity and resulted in a severe drop in the country's foreign exchange reserves. Nigeria's economic problems during the glut in world oil supplies damaged ECOWAS's growing reputation as an alternative to the Eurafrican system in West Africa and as a model for regional integration for other parts of the continent.

REGIONAL RIVALRY AND COLD WAR

The economic crisis that gripped Africa in the 1970s was accompanied by an epidemic of armed conflict, both within and between a number of African societies, that aggravated the instability of the continent. Two of these confrontations—the civil war in Chad and the feud between Morocco and Algeria over the former Spanish Sahara—reduced to shambles the pan-African ideals of the sanctity of frontiers and the sovereignty of post-colonial states. Worse, the new outbreak of violence in the 1970s resulted in the very circumstance that the OAU had worked so hard (and so successfully) to prevent: the extension of the Cold War to Africa. The Soviet Union moved in suddenly, to be followed inevitably by the United States, and soon both superpowers were avidly courting allies and employing proxies as they extended their global rivalry to the continent.

The first of these developments occurred in July 1974, when the Kremlin concluded a pact with the East African state of Somalia. The agreement committed the Soviets to train and equip the Somali army in exchange for access to naval facilities at the port of Berbera on the Gulf of Aden as well as the use of two Soviet-constructed airfields in the country. The Russian navy had already acquired access to a former British base at Aden on the opposite shore of the gulf through an agreement with the revolutionary regime that had been established in South Yemen after the end of British colonial rule in 1967.

The escalating Soviet involvement in the northwest littoral of the Indian Ocean was complicated by a regional rivalry between the new Soviet client state of Somalia and the self-styled 'Marxist–Leninist' military regime in Ethiopia, which had overthrown the pro-Western Emperor Haile Selassie in 1974 and terminated the country's long-standing relationship with the United States in early 1977. When Somali President Mohamed Siad Barre launched a military invasion of Ethiopia with the intention of annexing the Ogaden region with its ethnic Somali inhabitants, he turned from Moscow to Washington for support while the leftist regime in Addis Ababa predictably approached the Kremlin. In November 1977 Siad Barre abrogated the 1974 treaty of friendship, expelled all Soviet military personnel, and revoked Soviet access to Somali naval and air facilities. In the meantime, Moscow began supplying Ethiopia with tanks, aircraft, and military advisers and air- and sea-lifted some 18,000 Cuban soldiers and their equipment to Ethiopia to relieve the beleaguered forces of Ethiopian President Mengistu Haile Mariam. By 1978 Ethiopia had defeated Somalia in the Ogaden and proceeded to reward its Soviet benefactor with naval facilities at the port of Massawa to compensate for its loss of the Somali port of Berbera.

Just as it had taken advantage of the collapse of Haile Selassie's 44-year-old monarchy in 1974 to establish a Soviet client state on the Horn of Africa, the Soviet Union capitalized on the overthrow in the same year of the 42-year-old dictatorship in Lisbon to extend its influence to the southern tip of the continent. In 1975–6 the Soviet Union transported 20,000 Cuban troops, together with tanks, armoured personnel carriers, and small arms, to the former Portuguese colony of Angola, on the west coast of Africa, where the Marxist-oriented Popular Movement for

the Liberation of Angola (MPLA) was struggling with an American-backed rival organization, the UNITA movement. The triumph of the pro-Soviet faction in the Angolan Civil War was assured in December 1975, when the US Congress, as part of a post-Vietnam reaction against overseas military entanglements, voted to cut off American aid to UNITA. The victorious MPLA proceeded to form a Marxist government in Luanda, and its president, Agostinho Neto, concluded a treaty of friendship and co-operation with the Soviet Union in October 1976.

After delivering the MPLA to victory in Angloa, Moscow appeared to have gained a foothold in an African country with substantial oil reserves, vast untapped mineral resources, and a strategic location astride the sea route around the Cape of Good Hope. In fact, Moscow's success was in some ways limited: the Soviets failed to obtain naval facilities on the Angolan coast; American multinational corporations such as Gulf Oil, General Tire, and Chase Manhattan Bank retained their large investments in the country; and Angolan President José Eduardo dos Santos (who assumed power after Neto's death in 1979) expressed an interest in reducing his country's dependence on the Soviet Union and in forging closer economic ties to the West.

Nevertheless, the Soviet Union had undeniably advanced its strategic interests in the Horn and Southern Africa during the second half of the 1970s. Several hundred Soviet military advisers and an estimated 41,000 Cuban troops operated in a dozen countries on a continent that had previously been immune to Communist-bloc influence. In addition to the Soviet client states in Ethiopia and Angola, regimes that called themselves Marxist were established with Soviet assistance in Mozambique, the Congo Republic, and Benin (known as Dahomey before 1975). In North Africa, the radical Arab regime of Colonel Mu'ammar al-Qaddafi in Libya, which had toppled the pro-Western monarchy in 1969, nationalized American oil properties, closed down the American and British air bases in the country, received substantial Soviet economic and military assistance, and generally supported Moscow's foreign policy goals. The ambitious Qaddafi also began to intervene in the internal affairs of the neighbouring pro-Western regimes of Chad, the Sudan, Somalia, and Liberia in what appeared to be a campaign to establish Libya as the dominant power in its subregion.

Up until the mid-1970s, Africa had been largely disengaged from the superpower rivalry that had drawn most other parts of the developing world into the Cold War. As Britain, France, and Belgium divested themselves of their African possessions, the newly independent states succeeded in avoiding having to choose between Moscow and Washington in the East–West struggle. The few instances of superpower engagement in Africa before the mid-1970s—the establishment of American military bases in pre-Qaddafi Libya and Morocco, the unsuccessful Soviet intervention in the Congo—merely prove the rule. Africa played a minor role in US foreign trade and investment and no role at all in American security concerns. Africa's former colonial masters in the European Community remained the most important economic partners of the newly independent African states, with France remaining the principal foreign military force in its former domains on the continent.

Prior to the mid-1970s the Soviet Union lacked the capacity and apparently the will to sustain a major campaign to extend its influence to Africa. But the belated collapse of the Portuguese and Ethiopian empires and the intensification of the struggle for black majority rule in Rhodesia (Zimbabwe) and South-West Africa (Namibia) permitted Moscow to make inroads into Africa. The Soviet Union was able to exploit this turbulence at a time when the Kremlin had acquired the logistical capability to extend its power to the African continent.

The United States' response to the escalating Soviet involvement in Africa changed gradually over the second half of the 1970s. The Ford–Kissinger administration was prevented from intervening in the Angolan Civil War by a Democratic-controlled Congress traumatized by the Vietnam experience. The Carter administration originally displayed an uncharacteristic sensitivity to African concerns and de-emphasized the global context of the regional conflicts that were sweeping the continent. It was the Carter administration that appointed a prominent civil rights leader, Andrew Young, as America's first black ambassador to the United Nations and repealed the 1971 Byrd Amendment, which authorized the importation of chrome from Rhodesia in violation of United Nations sanctions against that country's renegade white minority regime, which had declared its independence from Britain in 1965 rather than submit to black majority rule. And under Carter, the US worked hard to promote a negotiated settlement between South Africa and the South-West Africa People's Organization (SWAPO) with the goal of establishing black majority rule in South-West Africa. All of these actions signalled the determination of the new American president to identify his country with the liberationist aspirations of the African states rather than to see them as mere pawns in the East–West struggle.

The increasing Soviet–Cuban engagement in Africa forced the United States to adopt a tougher policy concerning the African states. This policy shift was indicated by the US's refusal to recognize the new Angolan regime unless Cuban troops were withdrawn from the country and by its decision to assist French military forces that were dispatched to Zaire in the spring of 1978 to help the pro-Western Mobutu regime repel an invasion of Shaba province by exiles allegedly trained in Angola by Cuban advisers. From 1978 on, President Carter and his anti-Soviet national security adviser, Zbigniew Brzezinski, periodically warned Moscow that its activities in Africa were having an adverse effect on the fragile East–West détente that both Carter and Brezhnev wished to preserve.

Washington's sharp reaction to the Soviet–Cuban activity in Africa reflected a concern that had been mounting ever since the oil embargo of 1973: apprehension about a possible cutoff of a whole range of strategic minerals that the United States imported from Africa in large quantities. These minerals included chrome, antimony, cobalt, vanadium, platinum, manganese, and ferromanganese, not to mention crude oil (of which Nigeria had become America's second largest supplier). The destabilizing activities of the Soviet-backed regime of Qaddafi in Libya, together with the Soviet-supported challenges to the autocratic American client state in Zaire, threatened to undermine the security of pro-Western regimes on the continent and jeopardize American access to their strategic resources.

In a more general sense, the Soviet Union's intervention in Africa, either directly or through its Cuban proxies, convinced American strategic thinkers that the country had transformed from a Eurasian land power to a global power with worldwide air and naval capabilities. The rapid deployment of Cuban troops, tanks, and military equipment to Angola and Ethiopia seemed to demonstrate Moscow's ability to leapfrog the ring of containment states that had been forged by the United States during the Cold War. The Soviet naval squadron that patrolled the Red Sea and the Indian Ocean from bases in Ethiopia and South Yemen was seen in Washington as a potential menace to the Western world's lifeline to the petroleum reserves of the Persian Gulf.

Thus, by the end of the 1970s, the OAU's hallowed maxims of African unity and non-alignment had been dealt a severe blow by the polarization of the continent along ideological lines. The francophone states of West and Central Africa, Zaire, Egypt, Morocco, the Sudan, Kenya, and Somalia had established or intensified security ties with the West. At the same time, Angola, Ethiopia, Guinea-Bissau, Libya, and Mozambique openly identified with the Socialist bloc, while Algeria, Guinea, and Uganda received Soviet aid. This East–West rivalry in Africa opened deep fissures within the OAU: when the insurgents in Angola invited the covert intervention of South Africa and the government in Luanda welcomed Cuban troops in the mid-1970s, the organization split down the middle on the question of which side to support. Later, when the embattled regimes in Zaire and Chad looked to Paris for

military assistance, they received encouragement from other pro-Western, conservative African leaders but aroused the ire of those African states that identified with the Eastern bloc.

But the Soviet–American competition in Africa that had emerged so unexpectedly during the second half of the 1970s proved to be short-lived because of Moscow's inability to supplement its military aid with significant economic support in the form of trade, loans, and investments. In particular, the inconvertibility of Eastern bloc currencies precluded the expansion of African trade with COMECON countries beyond the customary bilateral barter schemes.

By the time of Brezhnev's death in 1982, the Kremlin's bid for influence in Africa had failed ignominiously. In rapid succession, African countries that had once welcomed aid and advice from the Eastern bloc—Egypt, Somalia, the Sudan, and Guinea—broke with their former benefactors and dislodged the Soviets from their privileged positions. Even those African states that retained some of the rhetoric of Marxist–Leninism, such as Angola, Mozambique, and Guinea, declined to seek admission to COMECON for the pragmatic economic reasons cited above. When they looked abroad for financial relief, it was not to Moscow, but to New York, London, Tokyo, Paris, or Washington (home of the IMF and the World Bank). Thus the Western bloc, due to its dominant position in the international economic system from which Africa could not, or would not, shake free, continued to exercise the dominant external influence on the continent throughout the 1980s.

The persistence of Africa's dependence on external powers in the Western world was graphically demonstrated in the civil war in Chad. For 15 years this resource-poor, landlocked, ethnically divided country languished under the corrupt dictatorship of N'garta Tombalbaye, who displayed undisguised favouritism toward the settled Christian inhabitants of the south at the expense of the nomadic Islamic population in the north. In 1975 the overthrow and execution of Tombalbaye in a military coup plunged Chad into political chaos. Two years later the northern Muslims, fortified by links with Muslims in the

Arab world, issued a secessionist demand for the establishment of a separate Islamic republic.

In the meantime, the adjacent Islamic state of Libya to the north exploited this civil conflict by dispatching troops to bolster its historic claim to the northern portion of Chad known as the Aouzou strip. French military forces quickly intervened to counter the Libyans, and Paris eventually threw its support behind a Chadian leader named Hissène Habré, who waged a long campaign throughout the 1980s—interrupted by brief periodic truces—against Qaddafi's army and its indigenous allies in northern Chad. Efforts of the OAU to intervene in the dispute came to naught, and the intrusive French involvement in Habré's campaign to expel Libyan forces from Chad once again revealed the limits to Africa's ability to manage its own affairs. Habré was eventually overthrown by a disgruntled former associate, in 1990, as France declined to intervene in what was viewed as a quarrel between rival Chadian leaders.

Another blow to the cause of African unity and stability was the conflict that erupted during the same period in the territory known as the Spanish Sahara. In 1974 the government of Spain, weakened by the mortal illness of its longtime dictator, Francisco Franco, hastily unveiled plans for a plebiscite to enable the inhabitants of Spain's last remaining colonial possession to determine their political future. The contiguous states of Morocco and Mauritania simultaneously registered strenuous objections to this democratic method of decolonization, asserting their own historic claims to the territory (which coincidentally possessed one of the world's largest deposits of phosphates). The Moroccan monarch, Hassan II, personally led an expedition of 350,000 of his compatriots into the northern portion of the Spanish Sahara to demand its reincorporation into 'Greater Morocco', the twentieth-century reincarnation of an ancient Arab empire that once dominated the region.

Faced with the prospect of conflict with African states over a territory it had already decided to evacuate, Madrid prudently shelved the idea of a plebiscite and concluded a secret agreement to hand over the northern two-thirds of the Spanish Sahara to Morocco and the remaining territory to Mauritania. When the last Spanish forces withdrew in February 1976, Moroccan and Mauritanian troops promptly occupied the zones alloted to them by the departing colonial power, and the former Spanish possession disappeared within the expanding frontiers of its two neighbours.

However, this territorial transfer had occurred without the assent of its inhabitants. In 1973 they had founded a national independence movement named Polisario (a Spanish acronym for the Popular Front for the Liberation of the Western Sahara) to hasten the departure of the Spanish. As Spain withdrew, Polisario promptly proclaimed a 'Saharawi Republic', obtained diplomatic recognition from most member states of the OAU, and proceeded to wage guerrilla warfare against the occupation forces of Morocco and Mauritania. By 1979 the economically depressed, politically unstable Mauritania was compelled to withdraw its troops from, and renounce its territorial claims to, the southern third of the Western Sahara. Morocco thereupon moved its forces southward and proceeded to annex the area evacuated by the Mauritanians.

In the meantime Algeria (which had quarrelled with Morocco from 1962 to 1972 over their own post-colonial boundary) vigorously opposed Morocco's designs in the Western Sahara and furnished substantial diplomatic and economic support to Polisario. Throughout the 1980s, this rivalry in the Western Sahara remained another major impediment to the doomed cause of pan-African co-operation, splitting the OAU into pro-Morocco and pro-Algeria (and pro-Polisario) factions.

The struggle over the Western Sahara also dashed hopes for regional co-operation among the peoples inhabiting the area of North Africa commonly known as the Maghreb,[1] which includes the countries of Algeria, Morocco, Tunisia, Mauritania, and Libya. Linked by a common language (Arabic) and religion (Islam) that set them apart from other African states, the countries of the Maghreb had groped for some type of regional identity and collective purpose ever since their liberation from European colonial control. But their linguistic and religious affinities proved to be inadequate sources of cohesion amid the national rivalries and competing territorial ambitions that plagued the region. Bitter border disputes, such as those between Algeria and Morocco and between Libya and Tunisia, were aggravated by the sharp ideological contrast among the Maghreb's constituent states: Morocco (a conservative, pro-Western monarchy), Algeria and Libya (radical republics with close ties to the Eastern bloc), Tunisia (a conservative, pro-Western republic), and Mauritania (a military dictatorship). As a result, throughout the 1980s the Arabic-speaking states of North Africa were no more successful in forging a strong regional identity—as a less ambitious alternative to the elusive pan-African ideal—than were the francophone and anglophone countries south of the Sahara. The formation in 1991 of the Arab Maghreb Union by these five states seemed to some observers a promising step in the direction of regional co-operation, to others little more than a desperate effort to coordinate regional economic activities in the face of Europe's move toward a single market in 1992 (discussed in Chapter 15).

THE IMPACT OF APARTHEID

If post-independence Africa was being torn apart by the various disruptive tendencies—economic, ethnic, ideological—discussed above, there was one issue on which all of the African states agreed: the necessity of removing the last bastion of white supremacy on the continent, the system of racial separation, or apartheid, practised in the Republic of South Africa since 1948. While the white ruling elite in the British, French, and Belgian colonial possessions in Africa submitted to black majority rule at the beginning of the 1960s, the white minority government of South Africa cracked down on the restive indigenous population that sought to emulate their compatriots to the north. The massacre of over a hundred unarmed black demonstrators by the South African police at Sharpeville in March 1960 was Pretoria's defiant response to the growing opposition to apartheid in this mineral-rich country.

All attempts by the black majority to obtain the political rights that most other Africans had already acquired met with determined resistance from the ruling National Party, mouthpiece of the Afrikaner-speaking descendants of Dutch and French emigrants from seventeenth-century Europe. The African National Congress (ANC), an originally moderate organization founded in 1912 to promote the interests of South Africa's disenfranchised, exploited black majority, was brutally suppressed by South African security forces. In 1963, one of its prominent officials, an activist lawyer named Nelson Mandela, was arrested and sentenced to life imprisonment, while the remainder of its leadership fled into exile. Precluded from engaging in legal political activity, the ANC endorsed the only alternative: armed struggle. The first major outbreak of violence came in 1976, when student riots in the black township of Soweto, outside Johannesburg, resulted in at least 575 deaths. Organizations such as the OAU, the Commonwealth, and the UN continually denounced the South African regime, while the ruling elites of the newly independent states insistently demanded the end of apartheid and the advent of black majority rule. At the same time, international opposition to apartheid was growing, as the governments of Western countries began to take action to protest the policies of the South African government. One of the leading nations in this movement was Canada, which in 1977 adopted an arms embargo and other political measures to protest apartheid and civil rights abuses in South Africa.

Throughout the 1960s and well into the 1970s, South Africa profited from the presence of a protective shield across its northern border in the form of friendly, white-controlled states that had resisted the trend toward decolonization. These states included the Portuguese possessions of Angola and Mozambique, the white minority regime in Rhodesia, and the former German colony of South-West Africa (which had been administered by South Africa since the end of World War I under a long-expired mandate from the long-defunct League of Nations). But the emergence of the two self-professed Marxist–Leninist regimes in Angola and Mozambique in 1975, followed by the belated introduction of black majority rule in Rhodesia (renamed Zimbabwe) in 1980, confronted South Africa with antagonistic northern neighbours that were willing to lend aid and sanctuary to insurgents against the Pretoria regime.

Throughout the 1980s, South Africa clung tenaciously to South-West Africa (renamed Namibia) as its last remaining buffer against black Africa.

But an insurrection launched by SWAPO, together with diplomatic pressure from the world community (including gentle prodding from Washington) forced South Africa to enter into negotiations for a transfer of sovereignty in Namibia and to soften the harshness of apartheid at home. As the talks on Namibia's political future bogged down, South African President P.W. Botha took steps to broaden the electoral base of his country's rigidly racist political system. A new constitution approved

CANADA AND THE CAMPAIGN AGAINST APARTHEID

Canada took a prominent role in the international campaign against South Africa's apartheid regime during the 1970s and 1980s. In 1977 Canada's minister for External Affairs criticized the conventional policy of separating trade from politics as a 'cop-out', suggesting that it was Canada's moral responsibility to take a stronger stand on apartheid. The Canadian government subsequently announced a range of new measures that went much further than its ongoing arms embargo. Canada withdrew its trade commissioners from South Africa and closed its Consulate General in Johannesburg. It also joined the Commonwealth sports boycott, denying financial support to any Canadian athlete or team competing in South Africa. In 1978, the government adopted a code of conduct for Canadian companies doing business in South Africa, and the following year Prime Minister Joe Clark announced the end of Canada's preferential tariff agreement with the country.

Under Brian Mulroney the government significantly expanded Canada's campaign against apartheid. It strengthened the code of conduct for Canadian businesses, established a multimillion-dollar aid program for educating blacks in South Africa, and introduced a voluntary ban on all loans to the South African government. At a meeting of Commonwealth countries in August 1985, Canada joined Zimbabwe, Australia, India, Zambia, and the Bahamas in adopting a new set of sanctions against Botha's apartheid

government. These sanctions included a ban on air links, agricultural products, and a variety of commodities produced in South Africa. In 1987, Prime Minister Mulroney met with Oliver Tambo, the leader of the ANC. As international pressure on South Africa mounted, the Canadian government continued to take a leading role in targeting the Botha regime, setting the campaign against apartheid at the top of its foreign policy agenda. In January 1990, Canada's minister for External Affairs announced, 'The fight against apartheid is a central element of the foreign policy of this Government, both because the cause is so compelling, and because we believe this is so clearly one of those international issues where Canada can make a difference.'

Four months after he was finally released from prison in February 1990, Nelson Mandela visited Canada, where he received a hero's welcome. Mandela thanked Canada for its leadership in the international struggle against apartheid, and he asked Prime Minister Mulroney to maintain economic sanctions against Pretoria until the last vestiges of the apartheid regime were eliminated. In a speech to the House of Commons, Mandela stated, 'I would like to take this opportunity to salute the great Canadian people whom you represent and with whom we believe you are in full accord on the question of South Africa. They have proved themselves not only to be steadfast friends of our struggling people but great defenders of human rights and the idea of democracy itself.'

by referendum in November 1983 enfranchised the 'Coloured' (mixed-race) and Asian minorities, establishing a tricameral parliament with a separate legislative chamber for the white (4.5 million), Coloured (2.6 million), and Asian (800,000) citizens (but continuing to exclude the 25 million members of the black majority).

The dangling of the carrot, represented by the talks on independence for Namibia and by limited political reform within South Africa, was accompanied by the wielding of the stick against hostile states to the north. In 1980 South Africa began to apply strong pressure against neighbouring regimes that had given sanctuary to ANC guerrillas. Economic and military assistance flowed from Pretoria to insurgent organizations such as the Mozambique National Resistance Movement (MNR), UNITA in Angola, and the Lesotho Liberation Army in Lesotho. The unrelenting economic warfare and periodic search-and-destroy raids against Mozambique proved so successful in destabilizing the shaky regime of Samora Michel that it was obliged, in March 1984, to sign the Nkomati Agreement, whereby it agreed to control the activities of ANC guerrillas on its territory in exchange for South Africa's pledge to terminate its support for the MNR. A similar pact was foisted on Lesotho, which was totally dependent on South Africa for its economic viability.

But the internal challenge to the South African government continued, resulting in the declaration of a state of emergency in July 1985. With a handful of exceptions—including Hastings Banda of Malawi and Félix Houphouët-Boigny of the Ivory Coast—African leaders pursued a policy of economic sanctions, non-recognition, and support for the ANC-led armed resistance within South Africa in order to bring down this last bastion of white privilege on the continent. Following a meeting of Commonwealth leaders in 1986, British Prime Minister Margaret Thatcher imposed economic sanctions on South Africa. In Washington, the Reagan administration followed suit while pursuing its policy of 'constructive engagement', which was aimed at concluding an agreement between South Africa and Angola that would lead to the

simultaneous withdrawal of South African and Cuban forces from the latter country, as well as the eventual establishment of black majority rule in Namibia. Despite these efforts, the southern part of the African continent remained mired in violence and instability: insurgencies raged in Angola, Mozambique, Namibia, and South Africa, while the two superpowers observed the chaotic situation with interest and concern.

SUMMARY

Africa was the last region of the world to be liberated from European colonial domination in the twentieth century. During the late 1950s and the early 1960s—several years after the European powers had withdrawn from most of their imperial outposts in Asia and the Middle East—France, Britain, and Belgium relinquished control over their African possessions. The immediate consequence was the proliferation of independent political units in an area that had been administered from Europe since the period of imperial expansion before the First World War. In 1945 only four African states belonged to the newly established United Nations: Egypt, South Africa, Liberia, and Ethiopia. By the end of 1960, although Portugal and Spain clung tenaciously to their African colonies, 25 new African nations had joined the UN, representing a quarter of its entire membership.

In most African states, with the notable exceptions of Algeria and the Belgian Congo (subsequently renamed Zaire and now known as the Democratic Republic of the Congo), the transition to national independence during this first phase of decolonization was relatively smooth and peaceful. The British and French had been compelled to acknowledge that their continued presence in Africa was untenable when both the United States and the Soviet Union, together with the newly liberated states of the developing world, opposed colonialism in the post-war era.

The second phase of decolonization unofficially began in 1963, when the pan-African aspirations for the post-colonial era were embodied in the Organization of African Unity (OAU), which supported three goals: to prevent territorial conflicts between rival nations in Africa; to facilitate the political unification of the continent; and to remain neutral in the Cold War. Yet this second phase of decolonization failed to meet the expectations for economic prosperity and political stability. Most of Africa remained economically underdeveloped, with high levels of poverty, unemployment, and debt. In many countries, corruption and neo-imperialism undermined efforts to expand local infrastructures to meet the needs for improved education, health care, and other social services. While South Africa continued to enforce apartheid, much of the continent was plagued by outbreaks of war and insurrection. By 1984, 45 African countries operated as sovereign political units in the post-colonial world; nevertheless, the future of the continent was uncertain.

NOTES

1. The term 'Maghreb' means 'the Arab West' (literally 'where the sun sets'), that is, the Arabic-speaking region of North Africa. It is contrasted with the 'Mashreg' ('the Arab East'), which refers to the area known in the Western world as the Middle East.

QUESTIONS FOR CRITICAL THOUGHT

1. The OAU resolved to retain the frontiers established during the colonial era. Was this the correct decision? Why or why not?
2. Discuss the theory that African unity was key to the continent's post-colonial success.
3. To what extent was neo-colonialism an obstacle to African development in the post-colonial era?
4. To what extent did the Cold War shape post-colonial development on the African continent?
5. Consider ways for a country to end its dependency on cash crop production, keeping in mind the structure of the world economy.
6. How was the apartheid regime in South Africa able to maintain its power for so long?

WEBSITES FOR FURTHER REFERENCE

African History on the Internet: Colonial Period
    www-sul.stanford.edu/depts/ssrg/africa/history/hiscolonial.html

History in Focus: Empire
    www.history.ac.uk/ihr/Focus/Empire/index.html

Internet African History Sourcebook
    www.fordham.edu/halsall/africa/africasbook.html

Political Discourse: Theories of Colonialism and Postcolonialism
    www.postcolonialweb.org/poldiscourse/discourseov.html

CHAPTER 13

THE FAR EAST: THE ROAD TO THE NEW CO-PROSPERITY SPHERE

THE MIRACLE OF JAPAN

At the end of the summer of 1945, the Japanese Empire lay in ruins. This once proud society had suffered a humiliating defeat in war, the loss of its colonial possessions, and the destruction of a quarter of its infrastructure by American strategic bombing. During its military occupation of the Japanese islands between 1945 and 1952, the United States treated its former enemy with a combination of political firmness and economic leniency. By imposing on the defeated power a democratic political system and a constitution that renounced war and the development of the means to wage it, the occupying power banished the threat of Japanese militarism that had plagued East Asia for decades. But by encouraging the economic recovery of Japan, the US had set in motion the process whereby its former enemy was to become—within a generation of Hiroshima—its major commercial and financial competitor.

The United States made an enormous contribution to the economic recovery of Japan after the Second World War. The provision of almost US$2 billion in aid—mostly in the form of food and raw materials, which were in dangerously short supply—rescued Japanese society from the immediate consequences of its wartime devastation. Of greater long-term significance was the abandonment by the end of the 1940s of reparation requirements, which removed a potentially damaging claim on Japanese production that might well have discouraged domestic savings, investment, and entrepreneurial activity. Furthermore, the revocation of plans to dissolve the industrial conglomerates that had collaborated with the imperial government before and during the war paved the way for the re-emergence, in modified form, of old Zaibatsu powerhouses such as Mitsubishi, Mitsui, and Sumitomo.

This American willingness to tolerate the consolidation of Japanese industry in the interest of efficiency and economy of scale also facilitated the formation of huge new firms, such as Hitachi, Toshiba, Toyota, and Nissan. By 1949 Japan had already attained its pre-war level of productivity, owing in large part to the benevolent economic policy pursued by the US military occupation authorities. In the following year, the Korean War added a powerful stimulus to Japanese industrial production in the form of American military purchases of war-related goods and equipment. Another notable American contribution to Japan's post-war economic revival was the provision of

US military protection under the Mutual Defence Treaty of 1952. Post-war Japan never had to spend more than 1 per cent of its GNP on defence, and the resulting financial savings were channelled into industrial reconstruction and development.

It would be inaccurate, however, to attribute Japan's post-war economic recovery solely, or even primarily, to American encouragement and protection. US occupation policies between 1945 and 1952 may have laid the foundation for Japan's recuperation, but the subsequent 'Japanese miracle' was a product of trends intrinsic to the island nation itself. Foremost among these were such sociocultural factors as the Japanese people's renowned industriousness (which fostered a willingness to work long hours at low pay) and frugality (which resulted in one of the highest savings rates in the world, in some years approaching 25 per cent of disposable income). Japan's universal adoption of an ethic of austerity, emphasizing production over consumption and deferred indulgence over instant gratification, was in large part responsible for the low labour costs and high capital formation that afforded the Japanese economy its competitive advantage on the world market.

Another significant element in Japan's post-war economic revival was the active, interventionist role assumed by the state in promoting industrial production and foreign trade. The Japanese government, acting through bureaucratic agencies spearheaded by the powerful Ministry for International Trade and Industry (MITI), skilfully used monetary incentives, such as subsidized interest rates on loans and preferential tax treatment, to encourage the diversion of the country's productive factors—labour, capital, and raw materials—to firms engaged in the export trade. The state also looked with favour on the high degree of concentration that characterized Japanese industry in general and the export business in particular. The goals of achieving economies of scale, avoiding duplication, and discouraging destructive competition resulted in the establishment of 10 gigantic foreign trade cartels that collectively accounted for more than half of Japan's total exports.

This strategy of export-oriented growth reflected Japan's reduced geopolitical situation in the post-war world. Deprived of its colonial empire, which had previously provided economic resources to Japanese industry, the small island was now obliged to ship finished manufactured goods to foreign markets in order to pay for the imports of food, fuel, and raw materials that were sorely lacking at home. The results of this export drive were extraordinary: Japanese exports, which were negligible in 1949, had risen to 3.2 per cent of total world exports in 1961 and 10 per cent of the world total by 1986.

The remarkable expansion of Japan's export trade depended on two factors of the post-war international economic order. The first was the relatively free access to foreign markets that had been gained through periodic tariff reductions negotiated under the auspices of GATT. By targeting a handful of potentially lucrative markets and flooding them with manufactured goods priced slightly above—or, in some cases, even with—the cost of production, Japan succeeded in underselling foreign competitors in their own domains. As a consequence, North America became Japan's major foreign customer, taking more than a third of Japanese exports by 1984, with Europe occupying a distant second place. By 1986, an astonishing 22 per cent of all US imports came from Japan.

The second aspect behind Japan's export growth was the assured availability of relatively inexpensive raw materials, food, and, above all, energy. From the end of the Second World War through the early 1970s, commodity prices remained at bargain levels relative to the prices of finished manufactured products. This disparity was an enormous advantage to Japan, which was deeply dependent on foreign sources of minerals, agricultural products, and fuel. But it was a source of vexation to countries rich in raw materials, such as Canada, which found themselves frustrated by Japan's lack of interest in trading for manufactured goods.

In the 1970s, Canada was Japan's seventh-largest supplier of commodities such as wheat, lumber, ores, and coal; only 3 per cent of Canadian

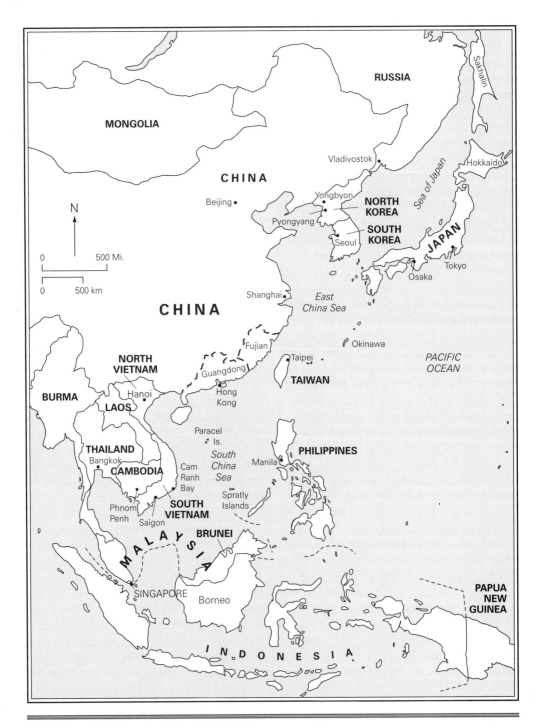

ASIA AFTER THE SECOND WORLD WAR

exports to Japan were finished manufactures. Japan was Canada's second-largest commercial partner (second only to the United States), but the Japanese exported primarily automobiles, communications equipment, and other manufactured products. Canada tried to improve its trading relationship with Japan through negotiated solutions, such as the Framework for Economic Cooperation, designed in 1976 to expand bilateral trade and investment. However, the Japanese government viewed such agreements as largely political rhetoric, and the economic relationship between Japan and Canada remained basically unchanged. By the end of the decade, less than 5 per cent of Japan's foreign investment went to Canada. Despite Ottawa's diplomatic efforts to improve bilateral trade, Japan continued to view Canada as a technologically unsophisticated country with an unproductive economy that relied too heavily on its natural resources.

Even when taken together, all of the aforementioned domestic and international conditions that favoured Japan's economic development fail to fully account for that country's phenomenal post-war recovery. A key requirement was a strategy for exploiting the advantages and compensating for the disadvantages of Japan's economic situation. In retrospect, it is difficult to recall a country with greater economic disabilities than Japan confronted in the years after the Second World War: for example, its shortage of arable land, raw materials, and energy, or its severe shortage of capital due to the destruction of manufacturing plants during the war and an epidemic of inflation after it. Japan also endured the curse of overpopulation, a situation that was aggravated by the return of six million soldiers and settlers from China, Korea, and the islands that had been conquered and colonized in the years of imperial expansion.

But what had appeared at first glance to be a severe disadvantage—a population too large for the available land, food, and fuel—came to represent, in the eyes of the economic planners in Tokyo, a veritable bonanza, a large and compliant workforce willing to endure working conditions and wage rates that would have been intolerable to organized labour in the Western industrialized countries. Japanese employers actually had the edge on competitors in other industrialized countries, where higher labour costs led to higher prices for the finished product. In short, Japan compensated for its comparative disadvantage of insufficient raw materials, food, fuel, and capital by successfully exploiting its comparative advantage of low labour costs to produce labour-intensive manufactured goods—mainly in the textile, iron, steel, and shipbuilding industries—which it exported at competitive prices to high-labour–cost markets in the West.

As the profits from foreign sales of these labour-intensive manufactured products accumulated, the second phase of Japan's post-war economic development began. The country's comparative advantage lay no longer in low labour costs, since other East Asian nations were beginning to produce labour-intensive goods at lower prices as Japanese workers demanded higher wages, but rather in the accumulation of capital for product development. The Japanese government shrewdly responded to this evolution in the country's comparative advantage by shifting resources from the labour-intensive to the capital-intensive sector of the economy. Accordingly, as Japanese exports of textiles, iron and steel goods, and ships declined, they were replaced by exports of new products such as petrochemicals, television sets, transistor radios, motorcycles and, finally, automobiles—of which Japan became the world's leading producer in 1980.

By the 1970s, another important development in Japan's comparative advantage prompted a further change in the structure of its export trade. Having produced an ample supply of well-educated, highly skilled technicians, scientists, and engineers, Japan began to redirect its economic resources from the capital-intensive to the technology-intensive sector. At first Japan concentrated on importing foreign technology and adapting it to its own particular requirements, but the country soon began to promote domestic research and development that would generate homegrown production techniques and technologies. As a result, the label 'made in Japan', once associated with cheap manufactured goods of dubious quality, came to designate state-of-the-art products of highly sophisticated design.

In the meantime, the old labour-intensive industries that had dominated the first phase of Japan's trade expansion had virtually disappeared. In the mid-1950s, textiles and clothing products had accounted for more than one-third of Japanese exports. By 1984, that proportion had declined to 3.6 per cent. A similar trend was evident in the iron, steel, and shipbuilding industries that Japan had once relied on. Instead, world markets were being saturated with technology-intensive products from Japan such as telecommunications equipment, office machines, electrical machinery, computers, and precision instruments. By the early 1980s, this small, resource-poor, over-populated island off the coast of China had surpassed its gigantic neighbour, the Soviet Union, as the second economic power of the world (as measured by GNP and most other universally recognized indices); by the middle of the decade, it would overtake the United States to become the world's first financial power.

As noted earlier, Japan's export-driven industrial growth depended to a large extent on the availability of cheap energy supplies and raw materials from abroad and on the unimpeded access to foreign markets for manufactured products that had been fostered by the post-war international trading system. In the 1970s and 1980s, both of these advantageous conditions were endangered, with serious consequences for Japan. The sharp increase in world oil prices—not to speak of the prospect of petroleum-producer cartels, embargoes, and supply disruptions—represented a serious threat to a country that possessed no oil reserves of its own. Equally ominous was the mounting threat of protectionism in the industrial world. Japan's enormous annual trade surplus with the European Community, which ballooned from US$506 million in 1970 to $12.2 billion in 1975 to $22.5 billion in 1986, generated angry charges of dumping and pleas for protection.

By the early 1980s, the European Community was erecting selective barriers against Japanese imports, while some member states, such as France, were shackling Japanese firms with cumbersome customs procedures. In the meantime, American manufacturers of automobiles, television sets, video equipment, and other products consistently undersold by their Japanese counterparts pressured Washington into insisting that Tokyo agree to voluntary export restraints. The combined result of the oil price increases and the emergence of protectionism in the developed world was a precipitous drop in Japan's growth rate, from an average of about 10 per cent (from the mid-1950s to the mid-1970s) to 5–6 per cent for the rest of the 1970s and 3–4 per cent in the early 1980s.

In the face of the rising cost of energy imports from the Middle East and the escalating protectionist threat to its export trade to the United States and Europe, Japan initiated a compensatory strategy of intensifying its economic ties to the developing countries within its own region. Tokyo began to target East Asian countries for massive development assistance as part of a policy to promote regional economic co-operation. Private Japanese firms followed the government's lead by making substantial investments in mining and petroleum facilities in Southeast Asian countries to secure reliable supplies of inexpensive raw materials and fossil fuels while developing new markets for Japanese manufactured products as a hedge against American and European protectionism. Meanwhile, Japanese companies that had abandoned labour-intensive production at home invested their retained earnings in light manufacturing concerns operating in low-wage East Asian countries in order to export low-priced goods to markets in the developed world.

The other nations of the region eagerly welcomed Japan's financial and commercial expansion along the western rim of the Pacific. They received desperately needed capital to finance their own industrial development and gained access to the Japanese market for their exports. Bitter memories of the wartime occupation combined with concerns about the influx of Japanese goods occasionally engendered expressions of ill will, such as the anti-Japanese demonstrations during Prime Minister Kakuei Tanaka's tour of Southeast Asia in 1974. But Prime Minister Takeo Fukuda repaired much of the damage during a subsequent visit to the region in 1977. His combination of tactful diplomacy and generous loan commitments won support in the region, and this benevolent policy was sustained by subsequent governments.

Japan had largely succeeded in dispelling the residual feelings of distrust in its neighbours by the 1980s. It had become not only the premier trading partner of many East Asian countries, but also, and more significantly, a model for economic development that many of them were successfully emulating. After decades of backwardness and third-class status in the international economic order dominated by the Western industrial powers, the countries of East Asia had made the crucial decision to 'look East', to profit from the lesson of the only non-Western country that had reached the highest level of economic performance. So well did they learn that lesson, and so successfully did they apply it to their own particular circumstances, that they became major trading powers in their own right.

THE ASIAN TIGERS AND ASEAN

The earliest Asian imitators of the Japanese example—South Korea, Taiwan, Singapore, and Hong Kong—acquired, in the lexicon of international economics, the nickname 'Asian Tigers'. Following the Japanese prototype, the four countries shared a set of characteristics—or what economists refer to as 'factor endowment'—that would scarcely be considered conducive to economic development. Like most other developing nations, they suffered from overpopulation and a shortage of capital, but unlike many Third World societies, they were deficient in natural resources such as minerals and fossil fuels as well as in arable land.

The Asian Tigers were able to turn these apparent disadvantages into advantages, to make a virtue out of necessity, as they resolutely followed the path of export-driven industrialization that Japan had blazed for them a generation earlier. The shortage of mineral wealth, energy sources, and fertile agricultural land—which precluded non-industrial alternatives, such as mining and farming, that were available to other developing countries in Africa and Latin America—provided a strong incentive to export finished manufactured products to pay for essential imports of raw materials, fuel, and food. As compensation for the shortage of capital, the excess population (as in Japan) yielded an abundant supply of cheap, docile, mobile labour to produce low-cost manufactured goods that did not require large infusions of capital or sophisticated technologies.

Another characteristic that the newly industrializing countries (NICs) of East Asia shared was a common cultural heritage, based on Confucianism, that emphasized the virtues of frugality, industry, self-discipline, and hierarchy. This cultural tradition offered a value system that was ideally suited to the type of production that the four industrializing societies had introduced. They all exploited—in both senses of the term—their overabundant, tractable workforce by specializing in those labour-intensive sectors of light industry that required a large number of low-skilled workers willing to toil long hours at tedious, low-paying tasks, such as fabricating ready-to-wear garments or assembling discrete components of intricate machines.

The Asian Tigers enjoyed the latecomer's advantage in their relationship with Japan. Once Japan had launched a new product and created a new market for it, South Korea, Taiwan, Hong Kong, and Singapore would move in and undercut the Japanese with their cheaper version of the original item. The NICs launched their earliest export drives in the 1960s with low-cost, low-quality textiles just as Japan was moving beyond the production of such labour-intensive products. In the following decade, as the profits generated by low labour costs enabled them (again, like Japan) to attract foreign capital to supplement domestic savings, they purchased more sophisticated machinery and equipment; in this way they followed Japan's model of making the shift in comparative advantage from labour-intensive to capital-intensive production. Their export trade advanced up the product scale to radios, televisions, sewing machines, motorcycles, and ships at the same time that Japan was moving into high-technology products. By the 1980s, the advanced educational systems and technical training programs of the Asian Tigers had begun to produce such a highly skilled, experienced workforce that some of them even began to encroach on the Japanese domain in technology-intensive industries such as computers and biotechnology.

Among the numerous shared characteristics of the four East Asian NICs, there was a notable difference between them in the relative extent of government participation in economic development. South Korea, at one end of the spectrum, developed a brand of 'state capitalism' in which the government actively intervened in the economy in a number of ways: by providing tax incentives and subsidies to encourage production in certain chosen sectors; by protecting favoured firms while allowing others to decline; and by maintaining direct state ownership and control of certain basic industries. The ruling elites of Taiwan and Singapore, though less committed to the principle of centralized control of the economy, stressed government planning and made lavish use of public funds to promote private economic development in selected sectors. At the other end of the spectrum was Hong Kong, which introduced an unfettered laissez-faire capitalism characterized by low taxes, minimal government spending (apart from creating the infrastructure necessary for economic development, such as roads, harbours, sanitation, and education), and private ownership of business. Whatever the differences in emphasis between government guidance and private enterprise, all four countries displayed a preference for letting the invisible hand of world market forces rather than the heavy hand of government planning dictate the allocation of resources within their economies.

The economic success of the four East Asian countries is revealed in the comparative growth statistics for all non-Western nations. With a combined population of only 3 per cent of the total population of the developing world, the Asian Tigers accounted for 60 per cent of its total manufactured exports in 1976. From 1963 to 1976, their combined growth rate exceeded 6 per cent, compared to less than 2 per cent for the South Asian countries of India, Bangladesh, Nepal, Sri Lanka, and Burma. In the decade after the Second World War, the United States and Britain had been obliged to supply economic aid to the resource- and food-poor countries of South Korea and Taiwan, and Singapore and Hong Kong, respectively. By the mid-1980s, the Western world could no longer sell manufactured goods to East Asia and faced stiff competition from East Asian manufactured exports in other markets. Canada, Australia, and the United States had settled into a peculiar kind of neo-colonial relationship with the region, importing its manufactured products in exchange for food and raw materials while running up huge annual trade deficits.

As had been the case in Japan, the crash program of industrialization in the four NICs depended on a number of conditions in the international system. In the security sphere, all four benefited in varying degrees from US military protection, with South Korea and Taiwan owing their very national existence to the projection of US military and naval power across the Pacific. In the financial realm, all four had received massive infusions of Western capital, originally in the form of American or British government aid, then through commercial loans from American and European banks or direct investments from Western-controlled multinational corporations. But it was in the sphere of international trade that the NICs were most dependent on extrinsic economic forces, as two-thirds of their manufactured exports went to industrialized countries (primarily the US, Canada, and the EC).

This dependence on the Western-dominated international economic system became a liability in the early 1980s as a result of three trends that endangered East Asia's continued growth. The first was the international debt crisis, with its flurry of defaults and reschedulings, which reduced the amount of capital available for foreign lending while inspiring caution in the foreign loan departments of Western banks. The second was the severe recession in the industrialized world, which caused a drop in demand for East Asian exports. The third was the upsurge in protectionist sentiment in North America and the European Community.

These three trends in the first half of the 1980s confirmed what had first come to light during the oil shocks of the previous decade: despite their remarkable records of economic growth, the NICs of Asia shared with other developing nations, such as those of Africa and Latin America, the disadvantage that international economists call 'extraregional bias'. This term means that the economic performance of each Asian country depended much more heavily on economic events outside the region than on those within it, leaving it vulnerable to trade disruptions caused by distant forces beyond its control.

A natural solution for avoiding extra-regional bias was to strengthen economic ties within East Asia as a way of forming an intraregional economic bloc that would serve as a buffer against adverse trends in the international economic order. But the overriding preference for trade and financial ties with developed countries outside of Asia precluded this possibility. Another obstacle to forging intraregional economic links was the intense commercial rivalry that had developed among the NICs and between the NICs and Japan. Since these five industrial dynamos possessed essentially the same factor endowment, produced the same products, and exported to the same markets, their economic relations with one another were characterized by fierce competition. However, the threat of interruptions in the delivery of raw materials and energy together with the protectionist barriers set up by the industrialized world obliged Japan and the Asian Tigers to look for markets and natural resources closer to home. What they found was a new possibility for intensive regional economic

co-operation with an organization known as the Association of Southeast Asian Nations (ASEAN).

Formed in August 1967 by the states of Indonesia, Malaysia, Thailand, and the Philippines—and later joined by Brunei after its independence from Britain in 1984—ASEAN comprised economies that effectively complemented those of Japan and the Asian Tigers. While deficient in capital and industrially undeveloped, the countries of ASEAN were richly endowed with many of the natural resources (such as petroleum, natural gas, wood, and foodstuffs) that Japan and the NICs lacked. Japan, South Korea, and Taiwan began to take advantage of this golden opportunity by exporting finished manufactured goods and technology to these Southeast Asian countries in exchange for raw materials and fuel and by investing heavily in the oil, mining, forestry, and agricultural sectors of their economies. The result of this intensified exchange of capital, manufactured products, and raw materials was a complementary economic subsystem in Asia that in some respects resembled the neo-colonial nexus between the United States and Latin America, or between the European Community and Africa. Or, as some observers recognized, it represented a benevolent version of the old imperial Japanese dream of the Greater East Asia Co-Prosperity Sphere, based on reciprocal economic interchange rather than unilateral military domination.

But by the end of the 1970s, the countries of ASEAN had grown dissatisfied with the role of commodity-producing junior partners of the dynamic industrialized economies to the north. They opted instead for the low-cost, low-skilled, labour-intensive, export-oriented strategy of industrialization that had previously enriched Japan and then the Asian Tigers. ASEAN was soon recording annual growth rates of between 6 and 8 per cent in a period when most developing countries reeled from the effects of recession and excessive indebtedness. They began to make significant inroads in markets for low-cost manufactures in the industrialized world by edging out the four NICs with cheaply made and cheaply priced textile products. Once again, the law of comparative advantage seemed to operate with predictable regularity on the Asian stage as ASEAN made its bid for rapid industrialization.

In contrast to the situation in Japan and the NICs, however, commodities continued to account for the largest proportion of export earnings in Indonesia, Malaysia, Thailand, and the Philippines. Consequently, the four members of ASEAN got the worst of both worlds in the 1970s and early 1980s. They were hit hard by the sharp decline in commodity prices (with the exception of Indonesian oil) that afflicted most primary producing countries and by the protectionist policies of the industrialized countries, which cut into their earnings from manufactured exports. To finance mounting trade deficits, especially with Japan, the countries of ASEAN were forced to borrow heavily from international lending agencies, substantially increasing their foreign debt.

In the meantime, the inevitable bill for the social costs of rapid industrialization came due. By attracting impoverished peasants from the countryside to the cities in order to depress wages and enhance their comparative advantage in labour-intensive manufactured exports, the fledgling industrial economies of ASEAN ignited a politically volatile situation. Anger over the inflation-induced decline in real wages, the widening gap between the urban wealth of the entrepreneurial few and the rural poverty of the multitude, and the age-old problem of the maldistribution of land sparked violent rural insurrections in Indonesia, Thailand, and the Philippines that were ruthlessly quelled by the authoritarian governments of the three countries.

The most formidable menace to ASEAN's ambitions to preserve its role as a supplier of raw materials, food, and fuel while following the path of industrial development set by Japan and the NICs was the emergence of a new regional rival with similar goals. It also happened to be the world's most populous country and a major military power, whose unexpected plunge into the free-for-all of East Asian economic development confronted its neighbours with a host of new opportunities and risks.

THE DENG REVOLUTION IN CHINA

The rapprochement between China and the United States during the first half of the 1970s was prompted primarily by their common concern about the expansion of Soviet military power and secondarily by the prospect of mutually profitable economic relations between the two countries. While the Sino–American entente may have served the purpose of counterbalancing Soviet military power during the second half of the decade, it proved to be a bitter disappointment for North American merchants eagerly eyeing the untapped Chinese market of 800 million consumers, and even more so for those Chinese officials allied with Premier Zhou Enlai who had anticipated bounteous economic benefits in the form of trade, aid, loans, investments, and technology transfer from the capitalist countries.

China's first foray into the international economic system, during the second half of the 1970s, proved to be a false start that resulted in a colossal failure. After the death of Mao Zedong in 1976, his heir-apparent, Hua Guofeng, launched an ill-conceived campaign to modernize the Chinese economy by reverting to the old practice of promoting heavy industry through intrusive government planning while simultaneously soliciting foreign investment and loans from the industrialized world. A combination of excessive foreign borrowing, unfavourable contracts signed with multinational firms, poor planning, and general waste resulted in industrial stagnation and low agricultural productivity. The lack of technical, managerial, and entrepreneurial expertise, together with the absence of a sufficient infrastructure, prevented the Chinese economy from successfully employing the capital and applying the technology that was flowing from Japan, the United States, and the European Community.

An almost unimaginable impediment to economic development in the world's most populous country was the absence of a sufficient internal market, owing to the fact that 80 per cent of the Chinese population lived and worked on the farm at a bare subsistence level. In fact, China's rural masses had sunk below that level during the period from 1974 to 1977, when the country's sluggish agricultural performance resulted in widespread famine that was overcome only with a substantial increase in food imports. China's inability to export manufactured products to pay for these essential food purchases abroad led to a fundamental reassessment of the first post-Mao development strategy and the cancellation or scaling back of most industrial projects in 1978.

The most important lesson learned from China's experience in the 1970s was that the country's best chance for economic modernization lay in discarding the remnants of the old Maoist plan of self-reliance and formulating a development strategy based on full integration in the international financial and trading system. The blueprints for such a scheme were readily at hand: the East Asian NICs and ASEAN countries had overcome their own substantial handicaps to establish impressive records of economic growth while China remained mired in industrial backwardness.

The Chinese leader who undertook to implement this new development strategy was Deng Xiaoping, a protégé of Mao's late second-in-command, Zhou Enlai. Between 1978 and 1981, Deng gradually purged those domestic opponents (including his rival for the succession, Hua Guofeng) who bitterly accused him of betraying orthodox Maoist principles by exposing China's economy to the exploitative forces of the international capitalist order.

Deng's ambitious program for China's modernization required a fundamental restructuring of the country's economic system. From 1950 to 1980, China had constructed a gigantic industrial system largely on its own. The only foreign assistance it had received was in the form of plant and equipment imports from the Soviet Union during the 1950s. In line with the Soviet prototype, resources had been channelled into state-run heavy industries such as defence, metallurgy, chemicals, and petroleum. Goods were allocated by government planning rather than by supply and demand, and production was earmarked for the domestic market rather than for export.

The path-breaking innovation of Deng, together with his protégé Zhao Ziyang, who replaced Hua Guofeng as prime minister in 1980, was to shift priorities from heavy to light industry and from import-substitution to export-oriented production. He also introduced into this long-time paragon of Marxist–Leninist orthodoxy a limited free market and private ownership of property. The result was the most spectacular transformation in China since the revolution of 1949. For better or for worse, the 1980s for China will be remembered as the Deng decade.

The Deng-Zhao development strategy was unabashedly based on the principle of the Open Door once associated with Western imperial domination. Through this open door would come foreign loans, investment, trade, technology, and tourists, while Chinese college students headed in the other direction in search of educational opportunities in the industrialized world that were unavailable at home. But the door to China would not be open to the entire country, which was divided into two separate regions for the purposes of foreign economic relations. The interior part of the country—backward, rural, and underdeveloped—would remain largely untouched by the outside world; it would perform the secondary role of nurturing infant inland industries to produce goods for the domestic market. The coastal region, with a population exceeding 200 million (or about a quarter of the country's people), would be tightly integrated with the international commercial and financial system in the hope that foreign trade and capital would serve as the engines of economic development for the entire country.

The first step in this coastal development strategy was taken in 1979 with the creation of four 'special economic zones' comprising the southern cities of Shenzhen, Zuhai, Shantou, and Xiamen. Foreign companies involved in light manufacturing were offered tax incentives to set up joint ventures with Chinese companies, or to create their own fully owned subsidiaries, for export-oriented production based in these designated economic zones. By the end of 1983, 188 equity

Chinese Premier Deng Xiaoping is greeted by workers at a Nippon Steel Corp. steel mill at Kimitsu, south east of Tokyo, 1978. Associated Press.

joint venture contracts had been concluded with multinational firms, mostly in the tourist, construction, textile, and oil exploration industries. In 1984, the Chinese government designated 14 additional coastal cities and Hainan Island as tax havens for foreign capital.

It is ironic that many of the same treaty ports from which Western trading interests had dominated the economy of imperial and republican China became the principal sites of foreign investment and commercial development in the People's Republic. The old imperialist city of Shanghai, for example, accounted for about 15 per cent of China's total exports and

70 per cent of its light industrial exports (such as clothing, textiles, bicycles, and sewing machines) during the 1980s. Its inhabitants enjoyed a per capita income of US$1,800, placing it on a par with Taiwan and South Korea (the two NICs on whose free export zones the Chinese special economic zones had been modelled). Other cities that benefited particularly from their designation as special economic zones included Shenzhen next to Hong Kong and Zuhai opposite Macao. The glaring contrast between the booming treaty port region and the backward hinterland left the impression of two separate countries, the one advancing into the industrialized world, the

other languishing in the Third, or what some economists now call the Fourth, World.

The most important foreign promoter and main beneficiary of China's entry into the world economic system was Japan, a fact that is scarcely surprising given the complementary nature of the two countries' economies. China possessed the oil, coal, and strategic raw materials that Japan required, while Japan had the capital, technology, and high-level manufactured goods that China needed. With almost 25 per cent of the world's population, China customarily received only about 1 per cent of the world's total export value. As Japan encountered protectionist pressures from its premier trading partner across the Pacific, the lure of the potentially vast market on the Asian mainland proved irresistible.

By 1985, China had replaced oil-exporting Saudi Arabia as Japan's second most important trading partner, behind only the United States. One-fourth of China's trade was with Japan, which remained China's top trading partner until 1987, when it was edged out by Hong Kong. These important commercial ties were matched by strong financial connections, as Japan supplied about half the foreign credits that China received from 1979 to 1983. After being extremely cautious with its direct investments during the first half of the 1980s (to Beijing's profound disappointment), Japanese direct investment in China soared from US$100 million in 1985 to $2.2 billion in 1987.

Behind Japan and Hong Kong, China's other great economic partner throughout the 1980s was the United States. Though the value of Sino–American trade remained half that of Sino–Japanese trade in the decade, the economic links between the two countries came to overshadow their shared concern about the Soviet Union as the Soviet threat to both began to subside. Sino–American trade increased from a paltry US$375 million in 1977—before the advent of the Deng export strategy—to $2.3 billion in 1979 and $5 billion in 1980. Exploiting its comparative advantage of abundant, cheap labour—Chinese wages averaged $0.60 an hour, compared to $12 in Japan and $20 in the US—China proceeded in

the 1980s to replace the East Asian NICs as the United States' major supplier of low-cost clothing and textile products.

This surge of Chinese exports to the United States provoked a furious response from American textile producers, as well as from competitors in Taiwan and South Korea. An arduous round of negotiations produced an agreement in 1987 to restrict annual increases in Chinese textile exports to the United States for the following four years. In exchange for its shipments of light industrial goods to the US market, China imported large quantities of agricultural commodities from the American Midwest.

Apart from food, the three most valuable commodities the United States supplied to China during the 1980s were capital, technology, and managerial and technical skills, all of which were exceedingly scarce. By 1988, US firms had investment commitments totalling over US$3 billion in nearly 400 joint ventures situated in the special economic zones on the southern coast. Unlike the first wave of quick-profit-seeking entrepreneurs of the 1970s, these US businesses had invested for the long haul.

A typical example is the set of contracts concluded with US oil companies to develop China's vast offshore oil reserves. By 1982, oil and oil products already accounted for 21 per cent of China's exports; six years later, China had become, with the help of American and Japanese direct investment, the world's fifth largest petroleum producer. In total, China attracted more than US$7 billion of direct foreign investment from 1979 to 1987, at a time when the flow of private foreign capital to other developing countries had virtually dried up.

China's policy of acquiring foreign technology underwent a significant change after 1978. During the 1950s, China had imported technology in the form of complete sets of equipment from the Soviet Union, largely for use in heavy industries such as metallurgy, electric power, and chemicals. But the cutoff of Soviet technology deliveries after the Sino–Soviet split during the 1960s thrust the country back on its own meagre technological resources. The new opening to the capitalist world in the early 1970s brought an expansion of foreign purchases, but the lack of a suitable infrastructure and properly trained managerial and technical personnel prevented China from adequately absorbing these technology imports.

During the 1980s, China abandoned the old practice of importing complete plants in favour of a more discriminating strategy of acquiring key technologies and selected equipment through licensing agreements and joint ventures from the United States, Japan, and the European Community. The long-term goal was to gradually reduce dependence on foreign sources and establish a domestic technology base. Though the new policy succeeded in bringing a significant amount of technology from the developed world, Beijing remained dissatisfied on two counts. First, the old Coordinating Committee (CoCom) regulations, dating from the early days of the Cold War, imposed restrictions on US technological exports to the People's Republic, and these were removed only gradually throughout the decade. Second, Japan displayed an irritating reluctance to transfer technology at a sufficiently high level to satisfy those Chinese officials who dreamed of their country's becoming a major power in high tech by the year 2000.

One of the main barriers to the successful application of technology imports in China, in addition to the inadequate infrastructure, was the shortage of managerial and technical expertise. The deficient Chinese educational system, which had been hurt by the outburst of anti-intellectualism during the Cultural Revolution of the 1960s, left China with a woefully insufficient supply of scientists, engineers, technicians, and managers to participate in the bold project of economic modernization that Deng had launched. China's only recourse was to send students abroad to acquire necessary skills and training. Between 1978 and 1988, almost 50,000 Chinese students were dispatched to foreign universities (two-thirds of them in North America) to learn subjects and skills that were inadequately taught at home. But the return of these educated young people

proved to be a mixed blessing for the authorities in Beijing. While the students had acquired the skills and training that were desperately needed by Chinese industry, they had been exposed to Western cultural influences and political ideas as well. The appearance on the streets of Chinese cities of women wearing makeup, young men in blue jeans, and teenagers of both genders with a taste for rock music, drugs, premarital sex, and other 'Western' practices clashed with the puritanical ethic of Maoism that still prevailed in spite of the revolutionary economic innovations. More seriously, the democratic principles that Chinese students had absorbed in North America and Western Europe undermined the authoritarian, one-party system that continued to operate in China, notwithstanding the new constitution, enacted by the National People's Congress in 1982, that ostensibly guaranteed civil liberties.

In addition to seeking bilateral loans and direct investments from countries of the developed world, China sought assistance from the various multinational organizations that ministered to the financial needs of the Third World. In November 1978, China formally requested assistance from the United Nations Development Program (UNDP), and within four years had become the largest recipient of UNDP funds (to the consternation of impoverished developing countries that were competing for the same scarce funds). A greater indication of China's reaching out to the West was its involvement with three Western-dominated international organizations, the International Monetary Fund, the World Bank, and GATT. China joined the IMF in 1980 and promptly borrowed from that organization to finance its balance of payments deficit in exchange for the customary pledges to check inflation, balance the budget, control the growth of the money supply, increase interest rates, and reduce the trade deficit by cutting imports and expanding exports. In the same year China also obtained membership in the World Bank; within seven years the country had received over US$5.5 billion in funds as well as expert advice on economic policy from the International Development Agency (IDA), a subsidiary of the organization. In 1982 Beijing gained observer status in GATT and in 1986 applied for formal membership (which would have brought the advantage of greater access to foreign markets, but also the obligation to disclose domestic economic practices to intrusive officials).

China's increasing interest in co-operating with these three Western-dominated international organizations, which had long been denounced by the Maoist leadership as instruments of imperialist hegemony, signified its total acceptance of—in fact, avid participation in—the capitalist world order. It also represented China's abandonment of the other developing nations in the Third World, whose interests it had championed against the superpowers during the Maoist years. By the end of the 1970s China had terminated its own economic assistance program to developing countries and was soon competing with these same countries for loans, aid, and direct investments from international agencies as well as Western banks and corporations. China's per capita GNP of US$280 in the mid-1980s placed it 130th among the world's 169 countries.

Yet the post-Mao leadership had decisively rejected the neo-Marxist dependency theory embraced by many intellectual defenders of Third World interests, which promoted national self-reliance and isolation from the world capitalist system. It had also rejected the radical concept, associated with the New International Economic Order, of the global transfer of wealth from north to south. Instead, it had unconditionally embraced the familiar Western liberal model of national economic development through global interdependence, the international division of labour, and the pursuit of comparative advantage, which required fuller integration with (rather than isolation from) the international trading and financial system.

The record of China's economic achievement during the 1980s was impressive. Its foreign trade grew from US$38.6 billion in 1980 to almost $80 billion in 1987, with petroleum and petroleum products as well as textiles and clothing earning the most in foreign exchange. China's productivity gains soared to three times as great as those of India—an Asian country with which it had been frequently compared—and its growth rates approached those of the Asian Tigers.

Simply put, China was becoming the latest NIC as its predecessors, on their way up the scale of comparative advantage, left behind a huge market for labour-intensive manufactured products. But China also held two trump cards that could be played in the future contest for economic primacy in Asia. The first was its endowment of raw materials and energy supplies, which represented a significant advantage over resource-poor competitors such as Japan and the Asian Tigers. The second was the potentially enormous (though undeveloped) Chinese domestic market, which could absorb part of the industrial production that might be cut off from markets in the United States and the European Community in the event of a global trade war. In any case, the long-sleeping giant of Asia had awakened, with incalculable consequences for its neighbours and the world.

THE TRANSFORMATION OF CHINA

The emergence of China raised a number of important questions. For instance, would China be capable of developing a mutually beneficial economic partnership with Japan that did not force the People's Republic into a neo-colonial form of dependency? If so, would a Beijing–Tokyo axis dominate the rest of Asia? Would China's exports of manufactured goods and raw materials (not to speak of its forthcoming acquisition of Hong Kong, its territorial claims against Taiwan, and its influence over Chinese minorities in Southeast Asian countries) stifle the development of the NICs and ASEAN and generate economic and political tensions in the region? Or could the western rim of the Pacific become a prosperous economic community characterized by a high degree of regional co-operation—a genuine 'co-prosperity sphere that might serve as a useful model for developing countries in other parts of the world? Finally, in light of the absence of deeply rooted traditions of democracy, civil liberties, and self-government, would China prove any more capable than the authoritarian regimes that presided over the industrialization of Taiwan, South Korea, Singapore, and the ASEAN countries of making Western-style political freedom compatible with a crash program of economic development in a Third World setting?

As China began its radical economic reorientation in the late 1970s, it simultaneously pursued new diplomatic and security policies that also diverged sharply from past practices. In the diplomatic realm, Deng Xiaoping decisively abandoned Mao's doctrine designating the two superpowers as equal adversaries of China in favour of a full-fledged rapprochement with the United States in the face of what he perceived as the greater threat from Moscow. The arrest (in 1976) and subsequent trial and imprisonment (in 1980) of the so-called Gang of Four, which included Mao's widow Jiang Qing and three associates, signified Deng's triumph over the faction within the Chinese ruling elite that opposed the opening to the West.

In the meantime, signs of China's increasing diplomatic co-operation with the United States were evident in virtually every region of the world, but were particularly striking in Africa. The Beijing regime that had once promoted and financed Marxist revolutions across the globe sided with the US and South Africa in support of the anti-communist insurgency against the Soviet-backed government in Angola in 1975–6. China also backed US and French efforts to rescue the pro-Western Mobutu regime in Zaire from a Soviet-supported insurrection in 1977–8 and denounced Cuba for its military interventions in a number of African states.

At the end of 1978, Deng Xiaoping achieved a long-awaited political breakthrough that confirmed the new direction of Chinese foreign policy. This was US President Jimmy Carter's announcement that formal diplomatic relations between the United States and China would begin on 1 January 1979 and that the United States–Taiwan Defence Treaty would expire a year beyond that date. Thereafter, the only security link between Washington and Taipei—long-time partners in

the war against communism in Asia—would be the sale by the former of defensive weaponry on a restricted basis. While this agreement represented a major compromise on the part of the US, it also signified a moderation of China's policy toward Taiwan. Though not explicitly renouncing the right to use force to reacquire its wayward province, Beijing increasingly appealed to Taipei for peaceful reconciliation out of respect for the island's special economic practices.

The alignment of American and Chinese foreign policies in Africa and the establishment of diplomatic relations between Washington and Beijing set the stage for close US–Chinese co-operation in Asia in the face of two developments that appeared to tip the balance of power in the region in favour of the common Soviet adversary. The first was the increasingly antagonistic activities of the communist state of Vietnam, which had been reunified in April 1976, a year after the defeat of the US-backed regime in Saigon. Throughout 1978, China's relations with its former ally against American imperialism in Asia had steadily deteriorated. The ostensible cause of this friction was the plight of the Chinese minority in Vietnam, which was heavily concentrated in urban areas and predominated among the merchant classes. Ethnic antagonism and socio-economic resentment combined with the suspicion that the Chinese nationals constituted a sort of fifth column to promote Beijing's interests in Vietnam prompted Hanoi to wage a pitiless campaign to relocate many of the Chinese urban dwellers to the countryside after confiscating their property. This policy understandably elicited sharp protests from Deng on behalf of his mistreated compatriots.

Beneath the veneer of humanitarian concern for the plight of ethnic Chinese in Vietnam lay the more deeply felt fear of encirclement by the Soviet Union and what Beijing had come to regard as Moscow's client state in Hanoi. In spite of receiving loyal support and military assistance from China during the war with the United States, Vietnam had taken several steps throughout 1978 to affirm its allegiance to the Soviet Union. In June, Hanoi obtained membership in the Soviet-controlled economic association COMECON, which prompted the retaliatory termination of all Chinese economic and technical assistance to Vietnam. In November, it signed a treaty of friendship with Moscow, which provided for the stationing of Soviet air and naval units in the country.

Reassured by these gestures of support from the Kremlin, Vietnam launched a military invasion of its newly established communist neighbour Kampuchea (now Cambodia) in December 1978. The purpose of the offensive, which was accomplished in short order, was the overthrow of the Chinese-backed regime of Khmer Rouge dictator Pol Pot and the installation of a Vietnamese puppet government in Phnom Penh. Hanoi's bid for regional dominance on the Indochinese peninsula confronted Beijing with an aggressive, hostile neighbour to the south allied with adversary number one to the north, with its massive troop buildup and missiles targeted on Chinese sites. China retaliated by dispatching its own military forces across the frontier into Vietnam in February 1979 but withdrew them a couple of months later.

If China derived any advantage from the Vietnamese invasion of Kampuchea it was the reinforcement of an increasingly co-operative diplomatic relationship with Washington. When Pol Pot and his Khmer Rouge followers retreated from Phnom Penh to harass the Vietnamese client government from guerrilla bases in the countryside, the United States and China jointly recognized him as the legitimate leader of Kampuchea and sent him military supplies through Thailand, even in the face of mounting evidence that his regime had perpetrated grisly acts of genocide against its own population after its accession in 1975.

The second important source of cohesion in the budding partnership between Washington and Beijing was the Soviet invasion of Afghanistan at the end of 1979, which aggravated Chinese fears of Soviet encirclement as well as American anxieties about the security of oil reserves in the Persian Gulf. The two governments co-operated in supplying the anti-Soviet resistance within Afghanistan, via Pakistan, and coordinated a tough diplomatic campaign in various world forums—including a boycott of the 1980 Olympic Games in Moscow—to pressure Moscow to withdraw.

The advent of the Reagan administration in 1981 introduced a discordant note in the Sino–American relationship over the issue of Taiwan. In 1979, as formal diplomatic relations were severed by Carter, US Congress had passed the Taiwan Relations Act in order to preserve an informal—and awkward—connection with Taiwan by establishing an American Institute on the island staffed by US foreign service officers on temporary leave. But during his presidential campaign, Reagan denounced Carter for abandoning America's trusted anti-communist ally and talked of restoring normal diplomatic relations with that government. In June 1981, President Reagan appeared to reverse the Carter policy of disengagement from Taiwan by authorizing the sale of defensive military equipment to the island, prompting an angry rejoinder from Beijing. But Reagan's anti-Soviet geopolitical objectives eventually overshadowed his sentimental attachment to the old Nationalist Chinese stronghold on Formosa.

In August 1982, Beijing and Washington reached a compromise arrangement, which called for a gradual reduction of American military aid to Taiwan in exchange for China's pledge to pursue its long-term goal of reunification through peaceful means. In 1986 President Chiang Ching-kuo, Chiang Kai-shek's son and heir, authorized unprecedented visits to the mainland for family reunions, and by the following year Chinese trade with Taiwan (mainly through Hong Kong) had surpassed US$1 billion in value.

China appeared to have a precedent for peaceful reunification with Taiwan with the 1984 agreement concluded between Beijing and London concerning the political future of Hong Kong. The pact specified that the old British crown colony would revert to Chinese sovereignty in 1997 as a special administrative region enjoying a high degree of autonomy (including its own separate, fully convertible currency) as well as the prerogative of retaining its capitalist economic system for at least 50 years after its absorption. The People's

Republic stood to gain many advantages from bringing the question of Hong Kong's future to a satisfactory resolution. By the end of the 1980s, the thriving little city-state had become China's largest trading partner, the entrepôt for over 10 per cent of its exports and a valuable source of foreign exchange in the form of remittances from Hong Kong Chinese to relatives in the People's Republic.

It would also afford China access to US economic interests, which were heavily engaged there.

China's conciliatory effort to promote a peaceful annexation of the two NICs, Hong Kong and Taiwan, was paralleled by a marked improvement in its relations with the rest of non-communist Asia. In an attempt to court the states of ASEAN, Beijing reduced its ties to communist insurgent

WARTIME ATROCITIES AND SINO-JAPANESE RELATIONS

China and Japan normalized diplomatic relations in 1972, at which time the Chinese government formally waived its right to war reparations from Japan. Since that time the economies of the two countries have become increasingly interconnected, and relations have generally remained positive. However, the question of wartime atrocities has never been fully resolved and periodically serves as a destabilizing issue between the two countries. In the 1990s attention focused on the rewriting of Japanese textbooks and what was perceived as a dangerous downplaying of wartime atrocities such as the Nanjing Massacre. At the same time, calls for individual restitution (as opposed to national reparations) became more prominent, especially after Japan issued apologies in 1992 and 1993 to 'comfort women' who had been taken as sex slaves by the Japanese Imperial Army during the war. Provision was made for the creation of a fund to assist with medical and welfare support, but this effort was widely deemed to be insufficient and was not, in any case, a reparation fund. As well, despite the public apologies, key members of government continued to deny that women had been forced into prostitution. As late as 2007, Prime Minister Shinzo Abe repeated the position of the revisionists—that the women were not coerced into sexual slavery (the resulting outrage led Abe to retract his statement).

The absence of formal reparations and the belief that many of the Japanese apologies were insincere led many Chinese victims of wartime aggression to seek redress through the legal system. Cases were heard relating not only to 'comfort women' but also to forced labourers and to victims of biological and chemical experimentation. The majority of these cases, however, were dismissed before they ever reached a courtroom; others remain on appeal. Nonetheless, there were some successes such as the Hanaoka forced labourers settlement, by which the Kajima Corporation was compelled to set up a fund of ¥500 million for the victims in 2000. Kajima, however, insisted that this was not a compensation fund and was, rather, to promote 'friendship between China and Japan'.

In 1998 Japanese Prime Minister Obuchi Keizō issued a formal, if vaguely worded, apology to Chinese President Jiang Zemin which stated that '[t]he Japanese side is keenly conscious of the responsibility for the serious distress and damage that Japan caused to the Chinese people through its aggression against China during a certain period in the past and expressed deep remorse for them.' In 2001 Japanese Prime Minister Junichiro Koizumi reiterated that sentiment by saying 'I express heartfelt apology and condolences to the Chinese people who fell victim to aggression.' Koizumi, however, renewed the controversy regarding wartime crimes when he made several visits to the Yasukuni Shrine where several convicted Japanese war criminals are honoured. In 2009, however, neither the prime minister nor the leader of the opposition (now prime minister-designate) visited the shrine, a decision commented upon favourably by newspapers in China.

groups in Thailand, Malasia, and the Philippines, and co-operated with Thailand in supplying aid to the Kampuchean resistance during the Vietnamese occupation.

Most importantly, China's expanding trade relationship with Japan during the early 1980s was reinforced by a diplomatic entente based on a shared concern about the Soviet military and naval buildup in the Far East and joint support for ASEAN's diplomatic initiative to persuade Vietnam to evacuate Kampuchea. The Sino–Japanese rapprochement was not immune to the resurgence of ethnic animosity based on historical memories, however.

Thus these problems did not disturb Sino–Japanese relations for very long. Some friction between Washington and Beijing continued over such issues as the residual restrictions on technology transfer, US textile protectionism, Chinese arms sales to various Middle Eastern regimes and staunch support for the Palestinian cause, and China's human rights abuses. But the Sino–American rapprochement appeared firmly established by the mid-1980s on the basis of mutually beneficial economic ties as well as a modest amount of diplomatic coordination, military co-operation, and sharing of intelligence on Soviet military activities.

SUMMARY

During the post-war period the Far East emerged as an economic power. Led by Japan, which experienced an 'economic miracle' in the decade after the Second World War, the region became a global force in manufacturing and finance. Japan's remarkable transformation was the product of state intervention, labour productivity, and managerial efficiency. To compensate for the country's lack of natural resources, Japan focused on manufacturing finished products that could be traded for raw materials. Its miracle also owed a lot to support from the United States.

The global recession of the mid-1970s had a significant impact on East Asia. In response to the downturn, Japan shifted the focus of its economic policy from labour-intensive manufacturing to the technology sector. Western countries such as Canada and the United States tried to capitalize on Japan's manufacturing boom by exporting raw materials in exchange for manufactured products from the region. But this strategy resulted in large trade deficits and a rise in protectionist sentiment in the West. As Western markets declined, Japan developed new trading links with other Asian nations, notably South Korea, Taiwan, Singapore, and Hong Kong. These four countries benefited enormously from the rise in Japanese trade and investment. By the 1980s, they were known as the 'Asian Tigers' as they became world leaders in a broad range of manufactured goods. As Western markets continued to shy away from such goods from the Far East, Japan and the Asian Tigers worked to expand trade within the Association of Southeast Asian Nations (ASEAN).

Another factor that contributed to the growth of the region was the dramatic economic expansion experienced by China in the 1980s. After the death of Mao Zedong in 1976 and the rise of Deng Xiaoping, China began to experiment with market reforms and to encourage foreign investment. Relations between the United States and China continued to improve in the 1980s, as mutually beneficial economic ties and shared suspicions of the Soviet Union outweighed their ideological differences.

QUESTIONS FOR CRITICAL THOUGHT

1. Discuss the influence of US intervention in Japan's post-war economic success.
2. What was the most important *domestic* factor facilitating the Japanese 'economic miracle'?
3. What are the flaws in the Japanese model of development? Are these problems evident in the so-called Asian Tigers?
4. What was Deng Xiaoping's most important contribution to Chinese development?
5. Why were the 'special economic zones' so effective?
6. What are the negative consequences of China's dramatic economic growth?

WEBSITES FOR FURTHER REFERENCE

Ministry of Economy, Trade, and Industry (Japan)
www.meti.go.jp/english/index.html

National Museum of Japanese History
www.rekihaku.ac.jp/english/index.html

Selected Works of Deng Xiaoping
http://web.peopledaily.com.cn/english/dengxp/home.html

Virtual Museum of the Cultural Revolution
www.cnd.org/CR/english

PART THREE

FROM COLD WAR TO NEW WORLD DISORDER (1985–2000)

In 1993, Canadian Lieutenant-General Roméo Dallaire was appointed Force Commander of the United Nations Assistance Mission in Rwanda. Responsible for overseeing implementation of a peace treaty between Rwanda's warring factions, General Dallaire instead found himself in the midst of a humanitarian crisis. As the country slid into chaos and civil strife in 1994, Hutu forces began systematic massacres of the Tutsi minority. Dallaire warned that stronger military intervention was needed to prevent an imminent genocide, but the UN rejected his appeals.

In May 1994, several weeks after the massacres began, Dallaire was driving to the capital, Kigali, when he came upon a child of about three wandering on the road. As Dallaire records in his book *Shake Hands with the Devil: The Failure of Humanity in Rwanda*, the incident left a lasting impression:

> I got out of the vehicle and walked toward him. Maybe it was the condition I was in, but to me this child had the face of an angel and eyes of pure innocence. I had seen so many children hacked to pieces that this small, whole, bewildered boy was a vision of hope. Surely he could not have survived all on his own? I motioned for my aide-de-camp to honk the horn, hoping to summon up his parents, but the sound echoed over the empty landscape, startling a few birds and little else. The boy remained transfixed. He did not speak or cry, just stood sucking on his biscuit and staring up at us with his huge, solemn eyes.[1]

As Dallaire and his aides searched for the boy's parents, they encountered a young Rwanda Patriotic Front solider, who said that the boy had no name and no family. When Dallaire offered to take the child to an orphanage in Kigali, the soldier asserted that his friends would look after him, insisting that the boy was better off among his own people. The soldier then yanked the child from Dallaire's arms, and Dallaire never saw him again. For Dallaire, the episode came to symbolize the tragedy in Rwanda: 'It's a memory that never lets me forget how ineffective and irresponsible we were when we promised the Rwandans that we would establish an atmosphere of security that would allow them to achieve a lasting peace.' Nearly 800,000 people were murdered before the massacres ended.

As the genocide in Rwanda demonstrated, the international community was unprepared for many of the bloody conflicts that erupted with the end of the Cold War. The need to provide effective international leadership to deal effectively with civil wars and humanitarian crises would be one of the defining features of the late twentieth century.

✧ Lieutenant-General Roméo Dallaire at the airport in Kigali, Rwanda, 1 August 1994. CP Archives (Ryan Remiorz).

---

[1]Excerpted from *Shake Hands with the Devil: The Failure of Humanity in Rwanda* by LGen. Roméo Dallaire. Copyright © 2003 Roméo Dallaire, LGen. (ret) Inc. Reprinted by permission of Random House Canada.

CHAPTER 14

MOSCOW, WASHINGTON, AND THE END OF THE SOVIET EMPIRE

THE GORBACHEV REVOLUTION

The political rise of Mikhail Gorbachev came at a time when the Soviet Union was struggling to cope with economic decline and military vulnerability. Gorbachev's plan to combat these twin problems was based on the only policy that offered a realistic chance of success: the settlement of his country's outstanding political disputes with its adversaries in the West, particularly its fellow superpower, the United States. The comparative international stability resulting from such a settlement would enable the Soviet Union to redirect its limited internal resources—together with whatever economic assistance it might gain from the non-communist developed world—to Gorbachev's pet project: a set of wide-ranging socio-economic reforms that included the decentralization of decision-making

and self-management in industry, the encouragement of private initiative, and the introduction of a modified market economy in order to boost productivity and eventually satisfy the long-suppressed demands of Soviet consumers.

The first dramatic instance of Gorbachev's campaign to improve Soviet–American relations occurred in the most complex and dangerous area of the superpowers' rivalry—the arms race. During the first half of the 1980s, the Reagan administration had undertaken a massive military buildup that included the deployment of intermediate-range nuclear weapons in Western Europe (Pershing II ballistic missiles and ground-launched cruise missiles), the continued search for a suitable delivery system for the MX ICBM missile, the expansion of research and development on the space-based anti-missile defence system designated as the Strategic Defense Initiative (SDI), the application of new technologies to the conventional defence capability of NATO, and the plan to create a 600-ship navy by the end of the 1980s.

Confronted with the impossible task of matching this formidable military buildup with his country's meagre technological assets, Gorbachev desperately sought to negotiate an end to a military competition that could only exacerbate the internal economic crisis of his country. President Reagan, facing a huge budget deficit caused by the attempt to combine increased military spending with reduced taxation and being squeezed by a congressional resolution requiring budgetary balance, was receptive to Gorbachev's overtures. As a result, the stalled arms-control negotiations resumed in 1985 at the behest of the two leaders.

GORBACHEV'S SPEECH TO THE 27TH CPSU CONGRESS IN 1986

By 1985 the situation in the Soviet Union was desperate. The aged leaders of the Communist Party had little choice but to move in a new direction under the leadership of the Politburo's youngest member, then 54-year-old Mikhail Gorbachev. Gorbachev had long since concluded that the time for small changes had passed and that only radical reforms could preserve the Leninist system while moving the USSR into the post-industrial age. Thus, in March 1986, Gorbachev delivered a blunt assessment of the problems facing the USSR in his closing address to the 27th Party Congress. Invoking Lenin's insistence that every revolutionary party must address its weaknesses, Gorbachev identified five challenges: the need to secure socio-economic growth, as well as scientific and technological development; the need to overcome bureaucratic inertia and localism; the quest for labour efficiency; the need for openness; and the threat of nuclear weapons. Aware that defence expenditures were crippling the Soviet ability to launch domestic reforms, Gorbachev announced that Soviet foreign policy would be 'oriented towards a search for mutual understanding, towards dialogue, and the establishment of peaceful coexistence as the universal norm in relations among states'. Arms control and reduction would be an essential step towards achieving peaceful coexistence.

Domestically Gorbachev laid out a multi-part plan to modernize the inadequate Soviet economic infrastructure. The principle of individual responsibility would be emphasized, and the Central Committee would move quickly to eliminate unnecessary or irrelevant function. Henceforth, every Soviet citizen would be required to demonstrate a new dedication to their own work and to the success of their work collective. People would be encouraged to submit their own ideas, and all ideas would be considered. To this end, 'sluggishness, formalism, indifference, the habit of letting good ideas get bogged down in empty, and endless roundabout discussions and attempts to "adjust to readjustment" must be completely overcome.' Gorbachev vowed that the party would remove all obstacles to reform by rationalizing the bureaucracy. Nonetheless, throughout his speech Gorbachev was careful to emphasize that reform would be carried out in the spirit of Leninism. These changes were intended to strengthen the Soviet system and to return to its pre-Stalinist roots; they were not planned to destroy that system in its entirety.

At a summit conference in Reykjavik, Iceland, in October 1986, Reagan and Gorbachev—without any prior consultation with their respective allies—came to the verge of endorsing a remarkable proposal that would have abolished all ballistic missiles and possibly set the stage for total nuclear disarmament. Although this idealistic scheme was never fulfilled, the two sides did make substantial progress on the more limited issue of intermediate-range nuclear forces (INF) in Europe. In February 1987, Gorbachev agreed for the first time to consider the INF matter separately from the rest of the comprehensive arms-control package that he had been promoting. Finally, on 8 December 1987, after almost a year of intensive diplomacy, both leaders signed a historic agreement eliminating all intermediate-range nuclear forces (that is, ground-based missiles with ranges from 500 to 5,500 kilometres) from the European theatre.

This agreement, which resembled Reagan's 1981 proposal for a 'zero option', involved a significant compromise by the Kremlin in a number of areas. First of all, it had abandoned its demand that the abolition of INF in Europe be accompanied by the termination of the American SDI, a program that Moscow considered a serious threat to its strategy of nuclear deterrence. Second, Gorbachev accepted a drastically asymmetrical reduction of theatre nuclear weapons, with the Soviet Union agreeing to destroy 851 launchers and 1,836 missiles by the end of 1991, compared to 283 launchers and 867 missiles by the United States. Third, Gorbachev agreed to eliminate not only those Soviet SS-20 missiles located in the European part of the country but also those that were deployed in Asia, thereby allaying the concerns of China, the country on which those missiles had been targeted. Finally, the Kremlin broke with past practice by accepting an extremely intrusive verification procedure, which called for the two parties to exchange extensive information about nuclear forces and to submit to short-notice, on-site inspections by the other signatory for 13 years after the ratification of the pact.

The INF Treaty was the first arms-control agreement in a decade. While it removed only about one-fifth of the existing nuclear weapons in the world, it marked an important departure from the cautious, incremental approach of arms-control negotiations in the 1970s. Unlike the two previous treaties dealing with strategic nuclear forces (SALT I and SALT II), the INF pact prescribed the elimination of an entire category of nuclear weapons instead of merely limiting the continued growth of existing forces. The Washington summit that produced the INF Treaty also drew the broad outline of a strategic arms limitation agreement, which had eluded negotiators ever since the two superpowers resumed the stalled SALT process under the new designation START (Strategic Arms Reduction Talks) in 1982.

After nine years of arduous negotiations, it fell to Reagan's successor, George H.W. Bush, to sign

US President Ronald Reagan (left) and Soviet President Mikhail Gorbachev meet at the White House during the Washington Summit, December 1987. Ronald Reagan Presidential Library C44169-16.

jointly with Gorbachev the historic agreement for strategic arms control in July 1991. The START Treaty placed strict restrictions on ballistic missile warheads and launchers, required deep reductions in the highly accurate land-based ICBMs, and (like the INF Treaty) provided for intrusive verification procedures. The practical effect of these provisions was to reduce US and Soviet strategic nuclear forces by about 30 per cent. While the exclusion from the START agreement of certain strategic weapons systems—such as ICBMs equipped with multiple independently targetable re-entry vehicles (MIRV) and sea-launched cruise missiles (SLCM)—left lots of work for future negotiators, the arms race in strategic nuclear weapons had decelerated significantly by the beginning of the 1990s.

In the meantime, both sides announced a number of unilateral cuts in spending on conventional arms. The budget that President Reagan submitted to Congress in early 1988 sacrificed the goal of a 600-ship navy that he had once enthusiastically endorsed. In a major speech at the United Nations that December, Gorbachev announced a substantial cut in Soviet military forces to be completed by 1991. The two sides also made great progress in reducing conventional forces in Europe. The Mutual and Balanced Force Reduction (MBFR) talks between NATO and the Warsaw Pact had droned on without result in Vienna since 1973, with the Soviets resisting any agreement that would reduce their numerical advantage in conventional military forces in Central Europe. In March 1989, these fruitless exchanges were replaced by a new negotiating forum, under the aegis of the 35-state Conference on Security and Cooperation in Europe (CSCE), that was designated as the Conventional Armed Forces in Europe (CFE) talks. After only 20 months of negotiations, the 22 members of the two alliance systems signed the CFE Treaty on 19 November 1990. This agreement established a balance of conventional forces in Europe by requiring the Soviet Union to remove a large proportion of its tanks, armoured vehicles, aircraft, heliocopters, and artillery from the region west

of the Ural Mountains. However, the success of the CFE talks was overshadowed by a spectacular series of political developments on the eastern half of the continent, which quickly diminished the significance of balanced conventional arms reductions between the two mutually antagonistic military blocs.

THE DISINTEGRATION OF THE EASTERN BLOC

As had been the case during Nikita Khrushchev's anti-Stalinist campaign in 1956, Gorbachev's denunciation of Leonid Brezhnev and his attempts to introduce economic and political reforms in the Soviet Union undermined the position of the hardline, orthodox communist bosses in Eastern Europe while inspiring reform-minded citizens to contest their authority. The difference between 1956 and 1989, however, lay in the Kremlin's attitude toward its client states in Eastern Europe. Whereas Khrushchev had regarded them as indispensable allies against NATO, Gorbachev had come to view them as liabilities that received enormous economic benefits from the USSR (in the form of trade subsidies, loans, cheap energy, and raw materials) while giving little in return. In light of the successful arms-control negotiations with the West, the strategic value of the satellites to Moscow appeared to diminish. Consequently, when the populations of Eastern Europe successively rejected their communist leaders in 1989, they were able to do so without fear of repeating Hungary's experience in 1956 or Czechoslovakia's in 1968. On the contrary, Gorbachev appeared to look with favour on, and even to take some credit for, the revolutionary political changes that swept Eastern Europe as the 1980s came to a close.

The pace of change in the Eastern bloc in 1989 was breathtaking, as the Soviet satellites dismissed their communist leadership in rapid succession. Poland, with a popular and powerful labour movement (Solidarity) and an influential religious institution (the Catholic Church) independent of government control, had the easiest time of it. In January 1989, the government of General Wojciech

Jaruzelski, which had declared martial law in 1981 and outlawed the Solidarity movement, agreed to enter into negotiations with representatives of the banned labour organization to resolve the country's serious economic and political problems. Solidarity's status as an opposition party was legalized that spring, and in the free elections held in June, its candidates won an overwhelming victory. In August, Tadeusz Mazowiecki, a devout Catholic and staunch Solidarity member, became prime minister of the first coalition government in the Eastern bloc in 41 years. He promptly introduced a number of free market economic reforms aimed at dismantling the communist system of centralized government control.

Also in January 1989, the Hungarian parliament authorized the formation of opposition parties. Within a few months, a special commission appointed by the Communist Party redefined the 1956 revolution as 'a popular uprising against an oligarchic rule that had debased the nation'. Imre Nagy, who had been the prime minister during the revolution and who had been overthrown and executed by the Soviets, was publicly praised, and the closed frontier with Austria was thrown open. In January 1990, the Hungarian government asked the Soviet Union to remove all of its military forces from Hungary, and in March the Kremlin agreed, promising to remove its troops by the summer of 1991.

In Czechoslovakia the threat of a nationwide strike in the fall of 1989 forced the hardline regime of Gustáv Husák to tolerate non-communist participation in a coalition government. When Husák resigned from the presidency in December, he was replaced by the country's most renowned dissident, playwright Václav Havel. The Czechoslovak parliament also elected as its speaker the elderly Alexander Dubček, whose political and economic reforms during the 'Prague Spring' of 1968 had led to the Soviet military intervention that summer. Like the Hungarians, the Czechs requested and received from Moscow the assurance that all Soviet troops would be withdrawn from their country by the summer of 1991.

The two Soviet satellites whose communist ruling elites staunchly resisted change were Romania and the German Democratic Republic. The Romanian dictator, Nicolae Ceauşescu, refused all compromise, even as his allies in the Warsaw Pact began to undertake dramatic domestic transformations. But the revolutionary tide flowing through Eastern Europe could not be stopped, even in Ceauşescu's retrograde police state. Facing hostile demonstrations on the streets of Bucharest in December 1989, the Romanian president attempted to flee the country but was caught and executed. The new government promptly planned free elections and purged supporters of the Ceauşescu regime.

As Ceauşescu's counterpart in East Germany, Erich Honecker, stubbornly resisted political reform and attempted in vain to organize the forces of repression in that country, tumultuous street demonstrations demanding radical reform broke out in Leipzig and other East German cities. In September 1989, the opening of the Hungarian frontier with Austria afforded East German citizens the opportunity to escape to the West, which they did in large numbers. Within a month the ailing Honecker had resigned, and on 9 November his successor lifted all travel restrictions to the West and, in a historic act, opened the Berlin Wall, which had been erected 38 years earlier to dam the torrent of émigrés from the East German state. In free elections held on 18 March 1990, a centre-right coalition won almost 49 per cent of the votes against 22 per cent for a centre-left group, and only 16 per cent for the renamed remnant of the old Socialist Unity (Communist) Party that had ruled the country for 40 years. In April, the parliament of the German Democratic Republic created a democratically elected government in the form of a coalition dominated by the centre-right bloc aligned with the Christian Democratic Party, which was the ruling party in West Germany.

The opening of the Berlin Wall, the collapse of the Communist regime, and the first free elections in East Germany unleashed a new political force that few observers had anticipated. Many of the East German refugees who streamed into the Federal Republic, as well as their compatriots who had remained behind to march in the streets against the Communist regime, openly called for the lifelong dream of many Germans on both sides of the Iron Curtain: the reunification of the two German states. By the time of the East German elections, all of the major political groups in both states had endorsed that long-dormant cause. With the disintegration of the East German political apparatus and the decline of the Socialist Unity (Communist) Party, the very rationale behind the German Democratic Republic had been gravely undermined. Even Moscow was calling for changes in East Germany.

Once liberated from the fear of Soviet military intervention and political repression by the communist apparatus, the populace of East Germany eagerly embraced reunification in the hope of reaping the economic and political benefits that would presumably flow from citizenship in a single Germany dominated by the capitalist, democratic institutions of the West. Conversely, the citizens of the Federal Republic had harboured the sentimental aspiration to be reunited with their compatriots in the east since 1949, when the goal of German unity had been enshrined in the constitution of the West German state.

German reunification introduced two complications in the otherwise smooth process of European détente unfolding in the late 1980s. First of all, West German Chancellor Helmut Kohl's hesitation to formally recognize the Oder–Neisse Line as the eastern frontier of a reunited Germany caused understandable concern in Poland that its newly gained independence from the Soviet Union would be threatened by the

East and West Berliners celebrate the fall of the Berlin Wall, November 1989. © STR/epa/CORBIS.

THE REDUCTION OF CANADIAN TROOPS IN EUROPE

German reunification and the end of the Cold War had important ramifications for countries of the NATO alliance, which were forced to reconsider their military commitments abroad. Canada, for example, had been a key early supporter of NATO, maintaining a sizable and well-respected military contingent in West Germany. By the mid-1960s, Canada's military presence in Germany peaked at 6,700 soldiers and included a full armoured regiment, three mechanized infantry battalions, an artillery regiment, and a reconnaissance squadron. However, under the government of Pierre Trudeau, Canada's armed forces entered a period of sustained decline. Canada's military presence in Europe increased when Brian Mulroney came to power in 1984, but it never returned to the pre-1970 levels. As the passing of the Cold War transformed Europe, Canada took advantage of the new strategic environment to announce that it would withdraw all of its troops from the continent by 1994.

revival of old territorial disputes with Germany. Second, Bonn's insistence (in concert with its partners in the Atlantic Alliance) that a reunified Germany be permitted to retain membership in NATO rather than reverting to neutrality (as demanded by the Soviet Union) generated serious misgivings in Moscow. But once Kohl accepted the permanence of the eastern frontiers and Gorbachev recognized that a united Germany within NATO would represent less of a menace to Soviet security than a united Germany cut loose from the constraints of alliance membership, the anxieties of Germany's neighbours were allayed.

Consequently, after a round of negotiations among representatives of the two German states and the four foreign powers that still enjoyed residual occupation rights (the United States, Britain, the Soviet Union, and France), the legal basis for German reunification was laid. On 3 October 1990, the frontier markers that had separated the two German states since 1949 were removed, and the most visible symbol of the Cold War had passed into history. With the disappearance of East Germany and the repudiation of communism and Moscow's authority by the remaining East European states, the dissolution of the Warsaw Pact in November 1990 and the abolition of the Soviet-led trading system Comecon in January 1991 came as no surprise.

DISENGAGEMENT AND TROOP WITHDRAWAL

Even before the Soviet Union's satellite system in Eastern Europe disintegrated at the end of the 1980s, Mikhail Gorbachev had begun to scale back Soviet military and political commitments abroad. His first move was to cut his country's losses in the costly war in Afghanistan, which had dragged on since 1979 with victory nowhere in sight, owing to the tenacious resistance of the Muslim *mujahideen* armed by the United States and China via Pakistan. In early 1988 the Kremlin announced that all Soviet troops would be withdrawn within 10 months, regardless of the fate of the Soviet-installed puppet regime in Kabul; in February 1989, the last retreating Soviet soldier crossed the frontier.

Gorbachev's abandonment of Afghanistan was soon followed by a settlement of the other conflict in Asia that had, since the late 1970s, poisoned relations between Moscow on the one hand and Washington and Beijing on the other. In December 1988, the new ruling elite in Hanoi, under persistent prodding from its Soviet patron, announced a major troop withdrawal from Cambodia. By the summer of 1989, most of the Vietnamese units had returned home, leaving the Hanoi-installed government in Phnom Penh to its own devices in its civil war with the rebel coalition, which included the Khmer Rouge organization. In exchange, the United States cut off military assistance and diplomatic support for the anti-government group. This was a remarkable instance of Soviet–American co-operation in disengaging from a bitter regional dispute inherited from the Cold War era. The USSR proceeded to withdraw its naval and air forces from Cam Ranh Bay in Vietnam, and in 1990 it announced a major withdrawal of ground troops and a sharp reduction in economic assistance to its old ally. The leadership in Hanoi followed Gorbachev's lead by renouncing the centralized economic planning learned from the Soviet Union in favour of a market-based economy, while starting to solicit Western investment.

As East–West rivalries in Asia dissipated, long-standing disputes between US and Soviet surrogates in Africa were settled with the help of skilful diplomacy. In December 1988, South Africa agreed to a ceasefire with the SWAPO rebel organization in Namibia and consented to a UN-supervised election there in exchange for the phased withdrawal of the 53,000 Cuban troops stationed in neighbouring Angola by July 1991. After winning the Namibia elections in November 1989, SWAPO leader Sam Nujoma, who had made overtures to Namibia's white businessmen and farmers, was installed in March 1990 as the country's first president.

Meanwhile, the termination of South African aid to the UNITA rebel movement and the withdrawal of all South African military forces from Angola in late November 1989, together with the evacuation of Cuban troops that had been protecting the Marxist MPLA government in that country, set the stage for negotiations to end the civil war in the former Portuguese colony. Further north, the Soviet–American proxy war on the Horn of Africa petered out as Washington and Moscow left their clients in the region, Somalia and Ethiopia respectively, to fend for themselves. In 1991, Ethiopia's president, Mengistu Haile Mariam, and Somalia's dictator, Mohammed Siad Barre, succumbed to internal insurrections. Both left their countries in economic chaos and political anarchy.

THE COLLAPSE OF THE SOVIET UNION

The upheaval caused when the Soviet Union lost control of its satellite system in Eastern Europe and abandoned its clients in the developing world at the end of the 1980s was mirrored by internal turmoil as the political structure of the country itself began to unravel. The severe crisis that Gorbachev confronted at home was, paradoxically, compounded by the very political reforms that he had initiated. In June 1988, the Nineteenth Party Congress replaced the old rubber-stamp Supreme Soviet with a new Congress of People's Deputies, with two-thirds of its members selected by democratic means. This body was to elect from its own members a new 450-person Supreme Soviet to function as a democratic parliament in the Western sense. The Supreme Soviet that emerged from the elected Congress of People's Deputies in May 1989 provided the Soviet people with their first taste of genuine democracy. Live television broadcasts of its proceedings showed a grim-faced Gorbachev, in his new capacity as president, subjected to harsh criticism from a variety of opposition groups. Grievances that had been ignored or suppressed in the pre-Gorbachev years became subjects of intense nationwide debate, with the whole world watching. The expectations that had been raised by the slogans of *glasnost* and *perestroika* now fell as the deteriorating political and economic conditions in the USSR became apparent.

Signs of the economic decline of the Soviet Union were ubiquitous. Agricultural production had fallen far below government targets, oil and coal production declined, GNP dropped 2 per cent in 1990 (the worst record since the Second World War), the foreign debt swelled, and trade deficits increased. In the summer of 1989, widespread strikes broke out in a number of cities in protest against severe shortages of basic consumer goods. Despite the government's efforts at fundamental economic reform, the fruits of *perestroika* scarcely represented an improvement over the period of stagnation under Brezhnev. Meanwhile, throughout 1990, long-suppressed nationalist discontent bubbled to the surface in many of the non-Russian republics: ethnic strife between Christian Armenians and the Muslims of Azerbaijan in the Caucasus; rioting by Muslims in the Central Asian republics of Uzbekistan, Kazakhstan, and Tajikistan; and declarations of independence or claims of political sovereignty by parliaments in Ukraine, Georgia, Armenia, and Moldavia.

The most vociferous resistance to Soviet authority came in the three Baltic states of Latvia, Lithuania, and Estonia, which had been annexed by the USSR in 1940. In November 1988 Estonia declared itself a sovereign state within the Soviet Union, with the right to fly its own flag, issue its own passports, and veto legislation passed by the Soviet parliament. In Lithuania, the anti-Soviet government that came to power in March 1990 went a step further, declaring its outright secession from the Soviet Union and instructing its young men to refuse to submit to Soviet military conscription. After similar developments in Latvia, Gorbachev determined that the trend toward the political disintegration of the Soviet system had gone far enough. In early 1991, Soviet military units intervened in the Baltic states, as Gorbachev, who had vastly increased his personal powers when he assumed the presidency the previous year, appeared to align himself with those forces hostile to further reform (such as the army, the Committee for State Security [KGB], and the Communist Party), which had formed the back-bone of the order that he had overthrown.

With the angry resignation of liberal Foreign Minister Eduard Shevardnadze in December 1990, reform advocates began to pin their hopes on one of Gorbachev's disillusioned collaborators, Boris Yeltsin. After his selection by the Supreme Soviet of the Russian Republic as its chairman in May 1990, Yeltsin insistently pressed for increased democratization, the introduction of a market economy, and greater autonomy for the Soviet republics. His election as president of the Russian Republic by popular vote in June 1991 gave him the mandate to push forward with his ambitious reform program. He promptly announced plans to liberalize the Russian economy and took the ultimate step of banning the Communist Party. It was evident that Yeltsin's plans for the Russian Republic went far beyond Gorbachev's cautious proposals.

During this time the Soviet president's nimble balancing act between the entrenched ruling elite and the impatient advocates of structural reform had run its course. Gorbachev's support of the army's intervention in the Baltics aligned him with those intent on quelling the forces of ethnic nationalism that threatened the very existence of the Soviet Union. But his ploy to consolidate his authority by securing public endorsement of a reformed union of sovereign republics backfired in March 1991, when 6 of the 15 constituent republics boycotted a nationwide referendum on the subject. Referendums in the three Baltic republics recorded huge majorities in favour of total independence, while Ukraine, Georgia, the Caucasus, the republics of Central Asia, and Russia itself seethed with secessionist discontent. By the summer of 1991, the three pillars of the Soviet system constructed by Lenin and Stalin in the early 1920s—the Communist Party, the command economy, and the multinational union—faced a formidable challenge from the emerging forces of democracy, free market capitalism, and ethnic nationalism. The man who had opened this Pandora's box by attempting to reform the communist system from within without challenging its legitimacy seemed to be overtaken by events.

The embattled defenders of the old order struck back on 19 August 1991, in a desperate bid to reverse the course of recent Soviet history. In a conspiracy involving the KGB, the army, and hardliners within Gorbachev's own entourage, the vacationing president was detained in his Crimean villa, while the leaders of the coup declared a six-month state of emergency and formed an interim government under Gorbachev's conservative vice-president, Gennady Yanayev. Within a few days the coup collapsed as a result of resolute action by Yeltsin, whose public opposition to the plot inspired massive public support and won over the rank and file of the military. Though Gorbachev returned to Moscow and attempted to re-assume his presidential duties, the creaky system he had tried to prop up through internal reform was beyond repair. The new president of the Russian Republic became the man of the hour as the political institutions of Gorbachev's refurbished union rapidly disintegrated in the fall of 1991.

One by one, each of the constituent republics declared its independence, obtained foreign recognition, and applied for membership in the United Nations as a sovereign state. Ukraine became one of the first republics to gain Western recognition of its sovereign status when Canada recognized its independence following a Ukrainian referendum in December 1991. On 21 December, 11 of the 15 new nations formed a loose-knit association called the Commonwealth of Independent States to replace the Union of Soviet Socialist Republics.[2] A few days earlier the Soviet president, seeing the writing on the wall, had transferred control of Soviet nuclear weapons to the president of Russia. On 25 December, Mikhail Gorbachev resigned the presidency of a political entity that had vanished from the world scene.

The collapse of the Soviet Union presented the international community with a complex set of legal, political, and security dilemmas. Some were promptly and effortlessly resolved: for example, the designation of Russia as the heir to the permanent Soviet seat on the United Nations Security Council. Two in particular proved to be far more challenging. The first question surrounded the formidable stockpile of nuclear weapons that had accumulated in the Soviet Union during the Cold War. The second concerned the political status of the numerous ethnic minorities that resided within the frontiers of the newly independent states. For the next several years, Yeltsin and his counterparts in a number of the non-Russian republics grappled with these two controversies as the outside world observed with intense interest.

TENSIONS IN THE FORMER SOVIET REPUBLICS

The international community was understandably anxious about the fate of the nuclear warheads that remained in four of the former Soviet Republics—Russia, Belarus, Ukraine, and Kazakhstan—after the USSR had ceased to exist at the end of 1991. The sudden and unanticipated appearance of these new nuclear states, together with the initial uncertainty concerning the custody of the weapons of mass destruction that they had inherited from the Soviet Union, became a matter of utmost concern to the rest of the world. (This topic will be addressed in detail in Chapter 20.)

During the same period, many of the 15 Soviet successor states wrestled with internal threats to their stability caused by powerful and competing strains of ethnic nationalism that had erupted with the demise of the old multinational union. Adopting the same divide-and-rule strategy employed by the European powers in Africa in the age of imperial expansion, Stalin had drawn the internal administrative borders of the Soviet Union to ensure the presence of at least one large minority group within each republic. This patchwork of ethnically diverse subnational political units enabled the Kremlin to play one group off against another, thereby preventing the emergence of a unified national consciousness in any region. The removal of Moscow's heavy hand resulted in an upsurge of acute ethnic antagonism between former subject peoples as they struggled to define and defend their national identities.

This ethnic antagonism was particularly evident in the Caucasus, which along with the Balkan peninsula was the historic intersection of Christianity and Islam at the southeastern gateway to Europe. The Christian Armenians inhabiting the enclave of Nagorno–Karabakh within Muslim Azerbaijan declined to recognize the sovereignty of the Azeris, who formed the majority population, and received diplomatic support and military aid from Armenia in their bid for secession. Georgia faced separatist challenges from the inhabitants of Abkhazia and South Ossetia, who sought unification with their northern compatriots inside the Russian Federation. In the autumn of 1993 the new Georgian head of state, Gorbachev's former foreign minister Eduard Shevardnadze, had to request Russian military assistance to restore order amid spreading economic chaos and political unrest.

The Russian Federation itself, which had been formed in March 1992, was buffeted by ethnic tensions all along its Caucasian frontier. The Ingush and North Ossetes violently disputed the border between them. The Muslim inhabitants of Chechnya, a mountainous region that had been annexed by the tsars in the 1870s after a long and bloody guerrilla war, declared its independence as the Soviet Union disintegrated at the end of 1991. Yeltsin promptly dispatched military forces to reassert Moscow's authority, but the combination of stiff resistance from Chechen partisans and vocal opposition to the intervention within Russia compelled him to withdraw.

After tolerating the secession of the rebellious province for three years, the Russian president finally yielded to his military and security advisers, who warned that the loss of Chechnya's important oil reserves, refineries, and pipeline would seriously jeopardize Russian security interests in the northern Caucasus and embolden other non-Slavic minorities within the multi-ethnic Russian Federation to break away. In December 1994, some 40,000 Russian infantrymen and hundreds of tanks poured into Chechnya in an effort to suppress the separatist rebellion led by President Dzhokhar Dudayev. It took the disorganized, undisciplined Russian army two months to capture the Chechen capital of Grozny, which it later lost to returning Chechen forces. After a ceasefire was negotiated in the summer of 1996, Russia lost control of Chechnya. But the breakaway regime in Grozny failed to obtain international recognition as foreign powers, led by the United States, dismissed the conflict as an internal Russian affair. In 1999, Islamic militants in Chechnya crossed into the neighbouring Russian province of Dagestan to incite rebellion there and were accused by Russian authorities of organizing terrorist bombings in Moscow that killed several civilians. At the end of the year Russian military units again poured into the breakaway province to suppress the defiant Chechen resistance in Grozny. After Yeltsin was replaced by his

protégé Vladimir Putin at the beginning of 2000, Moscow tightened the screws on Chechnya with the full support of the Russian public.

Beyond the combustible Caucasus, territorial disputes flared up all across the former Soviet Union. West of the Urals, Ukraine and Russia wrangled over control of the Crimean peninsula, which had been transferred from Russian to Ukrainian sovereignty in the mid-1950s despite its Russian-speaking majority. Of particular interest to Russia were the strategically located Black Sea ports of Sevastapol and Odessa, along with the Black Sea fleet based in these two Crimean ports. An agreement signed in the spring of 1997 divided the fleet between the two countries. Meanwhile, 12 million Russians residing in eastern Ukraine grew restless under Kiev's rule. The Russians in Estonia and Latvia, constituting 30 per cent and 34 per cent of the population respectively, reacted against discriminatory political treatment at the hands of their new Baltic masters, and their vigorous protests evoked a sympathetic response from Moscow. In the former Soviet Republic of Moldavia (renamed Moldova after achieving independence in 1991), the Russian-speaking minority established a breakaway republic on a strip of territory east of the Dniester River in reaction to indications that the Romanian-speaking Moldovans were contemplating unification with Romania.

Unable to reassert its authority east of the Dniester, the Moldovan government had to accept a 'peacekeeping' force in the form of the Russian Fourteenth Army, whose soldiers openly sided with their rebellious ethnic compatriots. Though in 1994 an agreement was reached for a phased withdrawal of the Russian troops over three years, the circumstances surrounding the establishment and preservation of the 'Dniester Republic' reflected Moscow's apparent willingness to protect the interests of the Russian diaspora in the Soviet successor states.

Ethnic tensions also boiled over in the five newly independent republics of Central Asia: Kazakhstan, Kyrgyzstan (previously Kirghizia), Tajikistan, Turkmenistan (previously Turkmenia), and Uzbekistan. The disappearance of Soviet

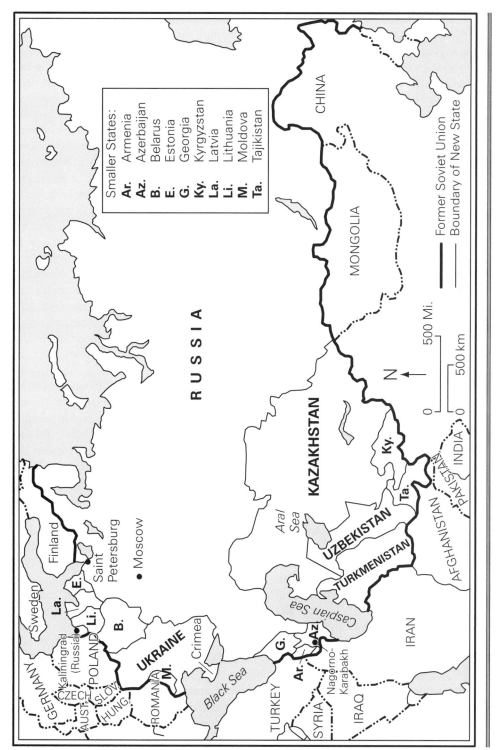

Smaller States:
Ar. Armenia
Az. Azerbaijan
B. Belarus
E. Estonia
G. Georgia
Ky. Kyrgyzstan
La. Latvia
Li. Lithuania
M. Moldova
Ta. Tajikistan

Former Soviet Union
Boundary of New State

500 Mi.
500 km

N

THE SUCCESSOR STATES OF THE FORMER SOVIET UNION

military power and Marxist–Leninist ideology from this region in the early 1990s had set loose linguistic and religious groups that attracted the attention of ambitious regional powers intent on filling the vacuum. Turkey avidly courted the Turkic-speaking Kyrgyz, Turkmen, and Uzbeks, while Iran forged ties with the Persian-speaking Tajiks.

Powerful religious forces also exercised an influence on the post-Soviet destiny of Central Asia as a result of the final victory of the Muslim *mujahideen* over the Soviet-backed regime in nearby Afghanistan. After the departure of Soviet troops in February 1989, the Afghan government of Mohammed Najibullah clung to power for the next three years, profiting from the revival of ethnic and tribal rivalries that shattered the cohesion of the resistance movement. However, the collapse of the Soviet Union sealed the fate of its puppet state in Kabul. On 25 April 1992, the *mujahideen* seized control of the capital city and established an Islamic state in place of the defunct Marxist regime. The fall of Kabul gave inspiration to the Islamic movements that had sprouted in all five Central Asian republics to challenge the ex-communist, secular ruling elites that retained political power after independence. Pakistan, the long-time patron of the Islamic resistance in Afghanistan, cultivated close links with the Islamic opposition in the Central Asian republics in the hope of exploiting its shared devotion to the teachings of the Koran to replace Russia as the dominant foreign influence in the region.

Incapable of coping with the growing domestic threat of Islamic fundamentalism (whose advocates often allied with pro-democracy opposition forces), the governments of the Central Asian republics appealed to Moscow for help in the fall of 1992. Russian military units, operating under the aegis of the Commonwealth of Independent States, in conjunction with troops dispatched by the secular government of Uzbekistan intervened in Tajikistan at the request of that country's embattled regime. After ruthlessly crushing the opposition coalition in the winter of 1992–3, some 25,000 Russian soldiers together with token forces from the other Central Asian republics remained on duty in Tajikistan to protect Moscow's traditional clients among the clans that ruled the country.

In the meantime, the Islamic section of the Tajiki opposition movement had regrouped in neighbouring Afghanistan to resume its insurgency. But Afghanistan had already begun its headlong slide into anarchy following the *mujahideen*'s liberation of Kabul in April 1992. The coalition of guerrilla organizations that had ousted the Soviet client regime rapidly degenerated into a bewildering array of ethnic and linguistic factions struggling for supremacy. The most important squabble pitted the Pashto-speaking Pathans of the southeast against a perpetually shifting alliance of rival linguistic and tribal groups to the north and west, including Persian-speaking Tajikis and Turkic-speaking Uzbeks. The mountainous country that had long been considered a convenient buffer between Russian Central Asia and whatever power dominated the Indian subcontinent appeared on the verge of disintegration along ethnic lines.

The ongoing civil war in Afghanistan, which devastated its capital city throughout 1993–5, predictably piqued the interest of aspiring regional powers once Moscow and Washington had washed their hands of the affair. Pakistan, Iran, and Uzbekistan all sought to expand their influence by patronizing rival factions. Russia, meanwhile, remained concerned that the ethnic and religious turmoil in Afghanistan might infect the republics of Central Asia and even spill over its own southern frontier. As a result, it retained its peacekeeping forces in Tajikistan, with the full support of its Central Asian clients. While Tajikistan was becoming a Russian protectorate, Kazakhstan (the largest and most economically advanced of the five republics in the region) remained on exceedingly cordial terms with Moscow. The large number of Russian-speaking Slavs that had migrated there from European Russia actually outnumbered the indigenous Kazakhs and proudly clung to their linguistic and cultural identity. The Kazakh government felt obliged to accommodate its Russian-speaking economic elite lest it become subversive.

THE CENTRAL ASIAN REPUBLICS OF THE FORMER SOVIET UNION

Compared to neighbouring Afghanistan and the Caucasian countries across the Caspian Sea, the five Central Asian republics collectively enjoyed a period of relative peace and stability after achieving independence from Moscow. This harmony reflects Russia's interest in bringing peace to the region without attempting to reassert its former authority. Nevertheless, Central Asia has never enjoyed a prolonged period of freedom from foreign domination. A revival of Russian chauvinism and neo-imperial aspirations, the emergence of Iran as an aggressive patron of Islamic insurgencies against secular regimes, or some other unforseen development in the years to come could undermine that stability and jeopardize the independence of these fledgling republics.

The upsurge in nationalist agitation within and beyond the frontiers of Russia during the early 1990s coincided with a severe economic crisis that gripped the country during its rapid and painful transition to a free market economy. Yeltsin and his team relentlessly pursued policies of economic liberalization by such measures as privatizing over half of the state enterprises, legalizing land ownership, reducing government subsidies to inefficient firms, and abolishing price controls that caused severe short-term dislocations in Russian society. The combination of raging inflation, declining production, speculation, corruption, and shortages of consumer goods eroded much of the goodwill that Yeltsin had accumulated in the aftermath of the 1991 coup. The crisis spawned a vocal political opposition that comprised an unlikely alliance between hard-line communists opposed to Yeltsin's economic and political reforms and a new breed of Russian nationalists who deplored the decline of Russian power and prestige in the world.

Yeltsin and his opponents waged a bitter political battle in the Russian parliament throughout 1993 until September, when the Russian president dissolved the legislative body, assumed emergency powers to defend his program of democratic political reform and economic liberalization, and announced new parliamentary elections to gauge public sentiment. Later that month Yeltsin ordered a military assault on the parliament building where his political enemies, including his former vice-president, General Alexander Rutskoi, and the speaker of the parliament, Ruslan Khasbulatov, were meeting to plot his political demise. The sight of the parliament in flames and his opponents being led off to prison seemed to signal a definitive victory for Yeltsin.

But the results of the December 1993 elections told a different story. To the surprise of most observers of the Russian political scene, the neo-fascist Liberal Democratic Party of Vladimir Zhirinovsky won almost a quarter of the votes and 64 seats in the lower house of the parliament. The flamboyant Zhirinovsky, who had raised eyebrows by calling for the restoration of the Russian Empire to its historic borders (a move that would have included rescinding the 1867 sale of Alaska to the United States), expressed a nostalgic yearning for an idealized past on the part of military officers humiliated by the Red Army's retreat from its imperial outposts and civilians traumatized by Yeltsin's economic shock therapy.

For the non-Russian republics, it became apparent, after the initial wave of post-independence euphoria, that the dissolution of the Soviet Union was a mixed blessing. Many of the new republics welcomed the restoration of closer ties with Moscow once Russia began assuming a greater assertiveness in its relations with the non-Russian successor states. Most suffered severe economic hardships as Moscow terminated the system of credits and subsidies to which they had become accustomed in the Soviet era. Others faced ethnic and religious threats to their stability and territorial integrity that they could not handle by themselves. Apart from the fiercely independent Baltics and Ukraine, the non-Russian successor states sought to strengthen their economic and security ties with Russia in order to cope more effectively with their daunting domestic difficulties and organize their national defence.

The Russian military presence in Belarus, Georgia, Moldova, Tajikistan, and Turkmenistan with the approval of those governments, together with a military basing agreement with Armenia, served as reminders of Moscow's continuing influence beyond the frontiers of the Russian Federation. Belarus's bid in 1993–4 for a privileged monetary and commercial arrangement with Russia reflected the sombre reality of its desperate economic dependence on its mammoth neighbour. The simmering discontent of the large Russian minorities in several of the non-Russian republics, the bogey of pan-Turkism in the Caucasus and Islamic fundamentalism in Central Asia, and the deteriorating economic conditions at home all represented potential pretexts for a revival of Russian expansionist ambition.

SUMMARY

The most significant global developments from the mid-1980s to the early 1990s were the definitive and entirely unanticipated end of the Cold War and the disappearance of the Soviet Union. These two momentous events came about as a result of policies inaugurated by Mikhail Gorbachev. Unlike his predecessors, Gorbachev had developed an appreciation of two realities about the USSR. The first was that the deterioration of the nation's economic system during the Brezhnev years had imperilled its capability to exercise power and influence in the world proportionate to its enormous size and population. The second was that the large and ever-increasing technological advantage enjoyed by the United States over the Soviet Union ensured an American victory in the arms race that had escalated after the period of détente in the 1970s. To rectify these problems, Gorbachev initiated a new system of political openness, or *glasnost*, accompanied by economic restructuring, or *perestroika*. Although

Gorbachev intended to save the Soviet Union, his reforms actually hastened its destruction.

The year 1989 marked a turning point in the history of the twentieth century. The withdrawal of Soviet forces from Afghanistan greatly improved East–West relations. In January, political reforms in Hungary touched off a series of popular democratic movements within the Soviet bloc. By September, communist rule had collapsed in Poland and Hungary. In November, the East German government opened its border, and the Berlin Wall came down amid massive celebrations. Within a month, the communist regimes in Czechoslovakia and Romania were ousted. During a summit meeting in December, Gorbachev and US President George H.W. Bush announced that the Cold War had officially ended. Over the next two years, Germany became unified, the Warsaw Pact was annulled, and the USSR was dissolved. By 1992, the world had entered a new era in international relations.

NOTES

1. Extracted from *Shake Hands with the Devil: The Failure of Humanity in Rwanda* by LGen Roméo Dallaire. Copyright © 2003 Roméo Dallaire (ret.) Inc. Reprinted by permission of Random House Canada.

2. The three Baltic republics and Georgia originally declined to join the Russian-dominated Commonwealth of Independent States (CIS). In the fall of 1993, Georgian President Eduard Shevardnadze reluctantly brought his country into the CIS in exchange for Russian military assistance against separatist movements that were threatening to tear the country apart in the early 1990s.

QUESTIONS FOR CRITICAL THOUGHT

1. What was the biggest problem facing Mikhail Gorbachev when he gained power in 1985?
2. To what extent did arms reduction benefit both the United States and the Soviet Union?
3. What steps could Gorbachev have taken to save the Soviet Union from collapse?
4. Which areas gained the most from the changes unleashed by Gorbachev's reforms?
5. How might nationalist agitation be contained for a prolonged period of time?
6. Discuss whether Yeltsin's unfettered economic liberalization was the best way to transform the Russian economy.

WEBSITES FOR FURTHER REFERENCE

Cold War International History Project: End of the Cold War
www.wilsoncenter.org/index.cfm?topic_id=1409&fuseaction=va2.browse&sort=
Collection&item=End%20of%20the%20Cold%20War

Communism: End of an Era
http://news.bbc.co.uk/hi/english/static/special_report/1999/09/99/iron_curtain/default.htm

Ronald Reagan Presidential Library – Archives
www.reagan.utexas.edu/

US Intelligence and the End of the Cold War
www.cia.gov/library/center-for-the-study-of-intelligence/csi-publications/books-
and-monographs/at-cold-wars-end-us-intelligence-on-the-soviet-union-and-eastern-
europe-1989-1991/art-1.html

CHAPTER 15

EUROPE: INTEGRATION AND DISINTEGRATION

THE RESURRECTION OF THE EUROPEAN IDEA

The unexpected disintegration of the East European Communist bloc at the end of the 1980s coincided with the less sensational but equally significant progress toward integration by the countries of Western Europe. The impulse toward West European economic co-operation that had originated with the Treaty of Rome in 1957 enjoyed a revival in the mid-1980s after many years of false starts and unfulfilled expectations. The Single European Act of 1985 stipulated that by the beginning of 1993, all barriers to the free movement of goods, services, capital, and labour among the 12 member states of the European Community (EC)[1] would be removed, enabling firms within the group to reduce costs by expanding production to meet the demands of this enormous market of 380 million consumers. This revitalized campaign for European economic integration retained its momentum for the rest of the decade under the resolute leadership of the European Commission's new president, Jacques Delors.[2] In the spring of 1989 he unveiled an ambitious plan for a European Monetary Union (EMU), which in the short term would coordinate exchange rates more effectively and in the long term was expected to serve as the nucleus of a European central bank that would issue a common currency.

The sudden and unexpected collapse of the Soviet empire in Eastern Europe, together with the end of the Cold War and the reunification of Germany in 1989–90, presented the proponents of European unity with a new set of challenges. Foremost among these was how to define the future relationship between the European Community and the former Soviet satellites. When the members of the recently defunct Comecon eagerly applied for membership in the EC, the governments of Western Europe were placed in an exceedingly awkward position. Did the recently emancipated citizens of Budapest, Prague, and Warsaw, who avidly embraced the principles of political democracy and free market capitalism and proudly reaffirmed their historic links to the common cultural heritage of the West, deserve to participate in the emerging supranational European entity as much as their counterparts in London, Paris, and Berlin?

The recurrent issue of enlarging the EC's membership had always provoked intense debate, and the candidacy of the former Soviet satellites was no exception. Some member states feared that premature admission of the untested, underdeveloped countries of the former Eastern bloc would overburden the EC's institutions and sap its economic base. Others worried that their own products would encounter stiff competition from exports from the low-wage East European states, which were eagerly redirecting their foreign trade from Russia to Western Europe.

Though the EC made overtures to these eastern countries by establishing the European Reconstruction Development Bank in December 1989 to provide emergency financial assistance to the fledgling democracies, it remained hesitant to welcome them into the fold. Instead, the West Europeans sought to placate them with a series of 'association agreements' that prescribed the gradual removal of trade barriers over a 10-year period and vaguely alluded to the possibility of eventual membership. After turning the cold shoulder to the indigent refugees from Comecon, the European Community readily agreed to consider applications from the affluent members of the European Free Trade Association (Austria, Finland, Norway, and Sweden). Negotiations with those four countries began in 1993, and on 1 January 1995, all of them but Norway (whose citizens rejected membership in a November 1994 referendum) formally joined the organization.

In the meantime, the lengthy discussions among existing members to accelerate the progress of economic and political integration finally produced a landmark agreement in December 1991. The Treaty on European Union (often called the Maastricht Treaty, after the Dutch city where its final provisions were worked out) formally endorsed the objective of a common European currency by 1999. The provision for monetary union, which concluded a decade-long behind-the-scenes skirmish among technocrats over such arcane details as managing exchange rates, interest rates, and money supply, was indisputably the most far-reaching of all the policies adopted at Maastricht. The goal was to achieve a rough convergence of monetary and fiscal policies among the participating countries by creating an institution to manage such matters as inflation rates and budget deficits free from political interference from EC member governments. This concept implied nothing less than the eventual transfer of monetary authority—one of the traditional hallmarks of national sovereignty—from the finance ministries of the individual EC countries to an organ of the emerging supranational entity.

Though the Single European Market would go into effect on schedule at the beginning of 1993, the Maastricht Pact encountered problems as the governments of the member states prepared to submit it for popular or parliamentary approval. The deepening recession in Europe caused those in many EC countries to reconsider the wisdom of sacrificing national control of domestic economic policy to that elusive entity called 'Europe'. Public resentment against anonymous, meddling Eurocrats from Brussels mounted in Britain, as the full extent of Maastricht's intrusiveness became apparent to the general public. Shrill critics in France blamed that country's high unemployment rate on the influx of cheap goods and labour permitted under the single market arrangement. Germans, already suffering from inflationary pressures caused by the emergency expenditures required to absorb the inhabitants of the former German Democratic Republic, fretted that the Deutschemark would continually be called on to bail out the weaker currencies under the European Monetary Union's exchange rate mechanism.

These manifold anxieties reached a fever pitch in June 1992, when Denmark unexpectedly rejected the Maastricht Treaty in a nationwide referendum. The British government jumped at the opportunity presented by this refusal and postponed its own acceptance of the pact, while German opponents challenged the treaty's compatibility with their federal constitution. But public appreciation of the long-term advantages of economic integration remained a powerful countervailing force that ensured an eventual compromise. One by one the principal obstacles to acceptance

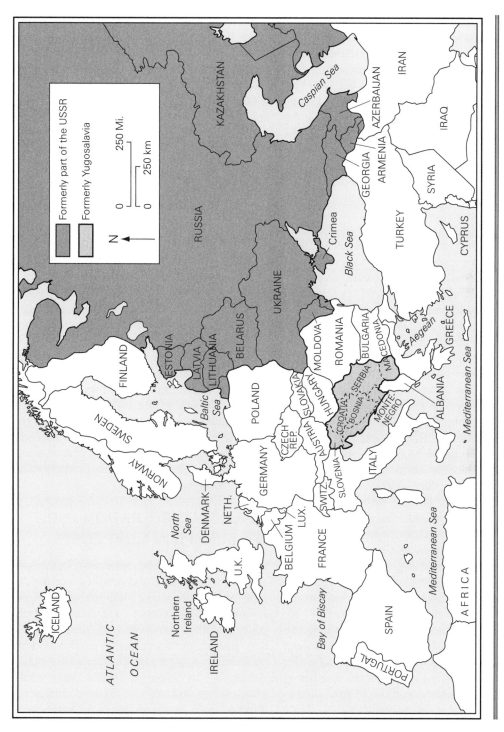

EUROPE AFTER THE COLD WAR

vanished in the course of intense bargaining, as a number of escape clauses were prudently added to those already embedded in Maastricht in order to allay the concerns of various member states. In May 1993, Denmark approved the Treaty on European Union in a second referendum, and the British parliament tendered its approval. As the treaty took effect the following November, the 'European Community' was transformed into the more integrationist-sounding 'European Union'.

THE EUROPEAN MONETARY UNION

At a conference in Madrid in December 1995, the 15 finance ministers of the newly expanded European Union took a number of bold steps toward full economic integration. They reaffirmed the Maastricht commitment to creating a common European currency by 1999; they established a precise timetable for achieving full monetary union; and they finally gave the new European currency a name—the 'euro'. Since Maastricht had established strict conditions for membership in the proposed European Monetary Union (EMU)—including the reduction of annual public deficits below 3 per cent and a total public debt below 60 per cent of gross domestic product—it became clear that not all 15 members of the EU would be willing or able to join the EMU by the target date. But the momentum toward monetary union persisted in spite of the serious economic difficulties experienced by several would-be members as a result of the severe economic downturn that gripped Europe in the closing years of the century. In March 1998, the European Commission issued a recommendation, approved by the European Council in May, that 11 of the 15 EU members be admitted to the EMU in 1999. The exceptions were Britain, Denmark, and Sweden (which had all opted, for various reasons, to remain out for the time being) and Greece (the only one of the 15 that failed to meet the Maastricht entry criteria).

To the surprise of many skeptics, the other 11 members of the EU adopted the single currency at the prescribed deadline of 1 January 1999. From this date, all bank and credit card transactions were conducted in euros, though newly minted coins and newly printed bank notes would not replace the national currencies until 2002. The European Central Bank assumed control over the money supply, interest rates, and other responsibilities traditionally managed by the central banks of the individual member states. However, the adoption of the euro did not result in the total integration of the 11 economic systems. One of the remaining obstacles was the discrepancy in tax rates and social welfare costs among the countries, which gave the firms of some states a competitive advantage over those of others. Another was the de facto immobility of labour owing to linguistic, ethnic, and cultural considerations that inhibited workers in countries with high unemployment from exercising their right of unrestricted migration to seek jobs in EU countries with better opportunities.

Despite these residual roadblocks to full integration, the establishment of a common currency under the jurisdiction of a Europe-wide central bank by the end of the twentieth century was a monumental achievement. It vindicated the unshakable vision of the small band of post-war reformers who saw economic co-operation as the most effective means of assuring prosperity and security for the old continent.

DEFENCE CO-OPERATION AND THE EUROPEAN ARMY CORPS

While the sections of the Maastricht Treaty dealing with social and economic policy received the most public attention, a little-noticed provision endorsed the objective of a common security policy and the creation of a multinational military instrument to implement it. This important innovation represented an insurance policy against the day when the United States would withdraw its military forces from Europe in response to the disappearance of the Soviet menace that 40 years earlier had brought American troops to the continent in the first place.

Previous European (and particularly French) proposals for West European defence co-operation had provoked opposition in the United States on the grounds that an exclusively European defence entity would (at best) duplicate tasks already performed by NATO and (at worst) undermine the cohesion of the alliance. But the coincidence of the end of the Cold War and the start of a severe recession in 1989 prompted Americans to clamour for military retrenchment in order to address domestic economic problems. Consequently, traditional US concerns about an exclusively European security system rapidly dissipated. President Bush's unilateral proposal in 1991 to remove all short-range, ground-based nuclear weapons from Europe, Canada's announcement in the following year that it would withdraw all of its troops from the continent by 1994, and President Bill Clinton's decision in 1993 to reduce the US contingent in NATO to 100,000 by the end of 1996 seemed to convey the same message: the Europeans would be expected to bear a much greater share of the defence burden.

Reading the writing on the wall, French President François Mitterrand and German Chancellor Helmut Kohl dusted off their old scheme for a Franco–German military force as the nucleus of a European army under the aegis of the West European Union (WEU). In May 1992, France and Germany concluded an agreement to create a 35,000-person European Army Corps (Eurocorps) with forces from their own militaries. After Belgium agreed to contribute a mechanized division, the three nations established an organizational headquarters in Strasbourg in November 1993. Spain and Luxembourg subsequently joined, and the Netherlands dispatched military observers as an explicit expression of interest. Despite all the rhetoric about European defence co-operation, the renovated European Union failed the first test of its capacity to manage regional security in the post-Cold War environment. Faced with the first outbreak of large-scale violence on the continent since 1945, in the former Yugoslavia, Europe proved incapable of devising a diplomatic or a military solution to the conflagration in its own backyard.

The efforts to forge a framework for European security co-operation in the first half of the 1990s coincided with a profound identity crisis within NATO itself, as the United States and its European partners pondered the future role of the Atlantic alliance in a world without the Warsaw Pact and the Soviet Union. One of many items on the agenda of the Atlantic alliance was the issue of NATO's relationship to the rudimentary military structure of the WEU. In their first combined meeting, in June 1993, the two organizations attempted to resolve logistical problems related to their combined enforcement of the UN economic sanctions against Serbia in the Adriatic and to establish ground rules for future collaboration.

Even though it was given a high priority after the end of the Cold War and the reduction of American military personnel in NATO, plans for European defence co-operation remained vague. The highly touted Eurocorps became operational in 1995 and conducted its first official exercises with French, German, Spanish, and Belgian units and observers from Luxembourg (which had recently joined). But the Eurocorps manoeuvres seemed largely ceremonial. The WEU, once thought to be the nucleus for a common European defence force, laboured in vain to define a special role for itself within the EU. When Germany and France formally proposed the gradual merger of the two organizations in 1997, Britain and the EU's neutral states (Austria, Finland, Sweden, and Ireland) blocked the proposal. It was later agreed that the WEU would remain a defence organization separate from the EU, which was entitled merely to request rather than to order WEU military operations such as peacekeeping and humanitarian interventions.

When fighting broke out in the Balkans, it was neither the Eurocorps nor the WEU but NATO that employed its air power to force peace negotiations in Bosnia and then assumed the role of implementing the Dayton Accords on the ground in that troubled region. Individual European countries made important contributions to peacemaking in the Balkans—the German *Bundeswehr* played a major role in the stabilization force

(SFOR) in Bosnia, while France and Britain were active members of the Contact Group that sought a settlement in Bosnia and in December 1998 co-sponsored the effort at Rambouillet to forge a peace agreement for Kosovo. However, these national undertakings were outside the EU structure, and they merely confirmed the Union's failure to forge a common security policy to match its common monetary policy.

From the time President Mitterrand and Chancellor Kohl revived the long-moribund WEU in the early 1980s, the push to develop a separate European defence corps had come from France and Germany. But at an EU summit in Austria in October 1998, the recently elected British Prime Minister Tony Blair, dismayed by the Union's embarrassing military unpreparedness during the Balkan crisis, withdrew the traditional British objection to military co-operation within the EU. Blair and French President Jacques Chirac then issued a joint declaration in Saint-Malo in December 1998, challenging the EU to adopt an autonomous military capability separate from NATO, a goal that was endorsed at the June 1999 EU summit in Cologne. Fifty years after France had first broached the plan for a European Defence Community, Europe finally seemed prepared to make a serious effort to create a multinational army of its own.

THE EU AND THE QUESTION OF EXPANSION

Amid the success of monetary integration and the failure of military integration during the last half of the 1990s, the EU confronted the controversial issue of expanding its membership. In the summer of 1997, the European Commission issued a document called 'Agenda 2000', which advised applicant states that they would have to meet a set of stringent criteria adopted in 1993, including democratic political institutions, a market economy, and a willingness to accept the EU's regulations. On reviewing the various applications, the Commission designated six countries—Cyprus, the Czech Republic, Estonia, Hungary, Slovenia,

and Poland—as suitable candidates. After the European Council endorsed the Commission's recommendation in December 1997, enlargement talks with the approved countries opened in March 1998. The rejected suitors—Bulgaria, Latvia, Lithuania, Romania, and Slovakia—had to settle for vaguely worded Accession Partnerships, which included guidelines for how to improve their chances for future acceptance. Turkey, a loyal NATO ally that had applied for EU membership in 1987, deeply resented its exclusion (which had been engineered by its old adversary, Greece) as the EC opened accession negotiations with Cyprus and the five former communist countries.

The Turkish government was particularly outraged at the EU's handling of the candidacy of Cyprus, which in 1974 had been partitioned into Greek and Turkish sectors. The EU announced that if the Turkish portion of the divided island refused to participate—which it would do until it received the international recognition that no foreign power was prepared to give—the accession negotiations would be conducted with the Greek Cypriot delegation alone. The prospect of the Greek sector of Cyprus entering the EU while the Turkish sector (and Turkey proper) remained outside the Union generated acute bitterness in the Turkish capital of Ankara. Many Turks perceived the ulterior motive of religious and cultural prejudice as being behind the EU's refusal to admit what would be Europe's first predominantly Muslim member state.

In addition to launching the new wave of expansion, the EU Commission's Agenda 2000 proposed fundamental reforms of two controversial programs that had long consumed most of the Union's annual budget. The first was the Common Agricultural Policy (CAP), an elaborate set of subsidies that guaranteed farmers fixed prices for their goods. The CAP had been a long-standing source of friction within the EU, pitting members with large agricultural sectors (such as France), which benefited from the price supports, against those with small farming populations (such as Britain), which had to finance the subsidies as well as pay higher prices for agricultural products. The second program under review was one calling for sectoral funds to be earmarked to promote economic growth in less developed member states (such as Portugal and Greece).

The prospect of accepting predominantly agricultural, underdeveloped countries from Central and Eastern Europe in the new century threatened to overwhelm the EU's budgets for both the CAP and the sectoral funds unless both programs were radically recast. But France blocked all attempts to reform the CAP at the expense of its politically powerful farmers, while the poorer member states in Southern Europe pressed for an increase in the sectoral fund portion to protect the share of the money they would receive when the Central and Eastern European states began asserting their claims to development assistance. In sum, the prospects for genuine reform of the EU's complex budget seemed dim as the twenty-first century began.

As the EU considered admitting the former communist states of Eastern Europe, the question of those countries' relationship with NATO became a topic of intense controversy. Though the Soviet Union and then the Russian Federation scrupulously honoured Mikhail Gorbachev's pledges to remove all Red army units from the former Soviet satellites, these fledgling democracies of Eastern Europe felt exposed, unprotected, and in need of reliable allies during periods of regional instability. This sense of insecurity intensified at each sign of political turmoil or outburst of nationalistic rhetoric in Russia. As former members of Comecon, Czechoslovakia (later the Czech Republic and Slovakia), Hungary, and Poland had sought admission to the EC to solve their economic problems; as former signatories of the Warsaw Pact, the same three countries applied for membership in NATO in order to obtain protection against a possible future security threat from Russia.

When Moscow expressed displeasure at the prospect of its former clients joining a US-dominated military alliance that might well be construed as an anti-Russian coalition, NATO planners devised various innocuous alternatives to allay East European apprehensions without offending the Russians. After rebuffing the three bids for prompt admission, NATO, in late 1991, established a new entity called the North Atlantic Cooperation Council (NACC), which comprised all members of NATO, all former members of the Warsaw Pact, and all Soviet successor states. President Clinton subsequently unveiled, in January 1994, a Partnership for Peace plan, which envisaged various modes of military co-operation between NATO and the armies of the former Communist bloc in Europe, as well as with any former Soviet republics or neutral countries that would wish to join. At every hint by NATO that the former Warsaw Pact satellites' applications for admission would be considered, Russian President Boris Yeltsin issued dire warnings and proposed instead that the exclusive Atlantic Alliance be replaced by the all-inclusive Conference on (later renamed Organization for) Security and Cooperation in Europe as the guardian of continental peace and stability. The governments of Poland, Hungary, and the Czech Republic persevered and finally, in March 1999, gained admission to the Atlantic Alliance. Mired in economic crisis and dependent on the American-dominated imf for financial assistance, Russia could do nothing to prevent the extension of NATO into its traditional sphere of influence.

The historic curses of economic backwardness and ethnic antagonism remained sources of potential instability in Central and Eastern Europe towards the close of the twentieth century. The rapid transition from command to market economies, which involved the privatization of nationalized enterprises, the reduction of government subsidies, and the removal of price controls, caused painful adjustments in these societies. The short-term costs of higher unemployment and diminished purchasing power seemed to many citizens of the former communist states too high a price to pay for the promised long-term benefits of increased productivity, higher incomes, and greater competitiveness in world markets.

West European lending and investment in the East also fell far short of expectations, a circumstance that was due in part to the severe recession that gripped the industrialized world during the early 1990s. Though the European Union replaced the Soviet Union as Eastern Europe's largest trading partner between 1989 and 1994, the benefits for the former communist countries were not immediately apparent. They collectively ran a huge trade deficit with the West due to the high tariffs and stringent quotas imposed by the protectionist EC.

The resulting disillusionment that set in after the euphoria of 1989–90 generated a certain amount of nostalgia for the good old days and amnesia about what they had really been like. The ex-Communist parties in Poland and Hungary capitalized on this public backlash against market-oriented economic reform to regain power throughout nationwide elections in 1994, though they dared not attempt to restore the Marxist–Leninist model. The tepid response of Western Europe to Eastern Europe's desperate appeals for financial assistance and commercial co-operation aggravated the socio-economic tensions that had been brought on by these unfulfilled hopes.

Another trend that was visible in the newly liberated states of Eastern Europe following the end of the Cold War was the resurfacing of ancient nationalist antagonisms that had been submerged during the four decades of enforced communist solidarity. The country that managed to cope most effectively with this problem was the multi-ethnic state of Czechslovakia. As the Red Army withdrew in 1991, it became evident that a substantial proportion of the Slovaks in the eastern half of the country preferred self-rule to subordinate status within the Czech-dominated state. Intent on terminating the endless ethnic bickering that had plagued the country since its liberation, President Vaclav Havel chose the path of least resistance. After a remarkably cordial series of negotiations concerning the appropriate division of the country's economic and military assets, the country split into the Czech Republic and Slovakia in January 1993.

This amicable separation left the new state of Slovakia with a potentially disruptive separatist problem of its own in the form of half a million discontented Hungarians. Nor were the Czechoslovakian successor states the only countries in Eastern Europe to face this predicament. Two million Hungarians in the Transylvanian region of Romania, an indeterminate number of Belorussians and Ukrainians in eastern Poland, and other discontented minorities represented latent threats to stability in the region.

THE BALKAN TRAGEDY

The most poignant casualty of this resurgence of ethnic nationalism in Europe was the population of Yugoslavia. The death in 1980 of Josip Broz Tito, whose 35-year rule had successfully kept the lid on the multi-ethnic cauldron in this renegade communist country on the Balkan peninsula, had ushered in a decade of rising tension among the inhabitants of Yugoslavia's six federated republics and two autonomous regions.[3] In the summer of 1991, Slovenia and Croatia, the two most Westernized, anti-communist, and economically advanced republics in the federation, declared their independence amid sporadic clashes between the partisans of secession and the Yugoslav federal army. This army had long been under the effective control of Serbia, the largest and most populous of the Yugoslav republics, whose citizens were widely scattered throughout the disintegrating state. The Serb minority in Croatia and Slovenia, in collusion with the remnants of the Serb-dominated Yugoslav federal army, took up arms against the new states, whose claim to sovereignty signified the demise of the federation in which they had long enjoyed a privileged status.

Peace was mercifully restored to Croatia and Slovenia by early 1992, through a ceasefire agreement brokered by UN mediators and monitored by a UN peacekeeping force. This force included a large contingent from Canada, which had been one of the leading supporters of previous UN missions, having contributed more than 80,000 soldiers to UN peacekeeping operations over the years.

The peaceful end to the conflict in Croatia and Slovenia set the stage for the bloodiest conflict in

CANADIAN PEACEKEEPERS IN CROATIA

Canada played a key role in the United Nations peacekeeping operations in the former Republic of Yugoslavia. As Yugoslavia descended into a bloody civil war in the early 1990s, the United Nations Protection Force (UNPROFOR) was sent to enforce a peace agreement brokered between the new Croatian government and the minority Serbs who sought independence from Zagreb. In 1992, UNPROFOR was asked to patrol the buffer zone between the warring factions, and Canada contributed a mixed force of 875 soldiers from the Princess Patricia's Canadian Light Infantry and a variety of militia units. Commanded by Lieutenant-Colonel James Calvin, the Canadian troops were responsible for the UN Protected Area in the northwestern corner of Croatia, where they gained a reputation for being fair but firm peacekeepers. Unlike most of the peacekeeping units from other countries, Canadian battalions were deployed with the full complement of heavy weaponry and equipment, giving them an advantage when dealing with challenges to the area.

The civil strife in the former Yugoslavia involved many paramilitaries that had little understanding of, or respect for, the peace treaties signed by the political leaders in the region. As a result, Canadian peacekeepers often faced unstable and hostile conditions as they worked to fulfill their mission. In the summer of 1993 they were ordered, along with French troops, to enforce a new ceasefire in the volatile southern sector of Croatia, and in September they moved to an area known as the 'Medak Pocket', where fighting had renewed between Serbian and Croatian units. During the night of 15 September, Canadian soldiers engaged in a prolonged firefight with Croatian forces. After a tense standoff the next day, the Canadians moved into the local Serbian villages, which had been subjected to 'ethnic cleansing' by Croatian forces. Canadian soldiers searched for survivors and recorded evidence of the atrocities that littered the area. The peacekeepers' forceful actions in September 1993 marked an important step in establishing the authority of UNPROFOR, contributing significantly to the eventual success of the efforts to end the civil war.

Europe since the end of the Second World War. After the European Community formally recognized the independence of the two secessionist republics in January 1992, a request for recognition arrived from the neighbouring republic of Bosnia–Herzegovina, an ethnically diverse region composed of roughly 44 per cent Muslim Slavs, 33 per cent Orthodox Serbs, and 17 per cent Croats, who were mostly Roman Catholic. At the same time, the Serbs of Bosnia, unwilling to be submerged in a state certain to be controlled by its Muslim majority, declared the independence of their own ethnic enclave and boycotted a referendum that resulted in the declaration of Bosnia–Herzegovina's independence in March. Though the federal Yugoslav army evacuated Bosnia in the spring of 1992, many of its Serbian members stayed behind to assist their ethnic compatriots in the breakaway republic as they took up arms against its Muslim-dominated government with the covert support of the Serbian regime in Belgrade.

In the ensuing months, the Serb forces in Bosnia–Herzegovina placed the capital city of Sarajevo under siege, subjected its starving population to continuous mortar fire, and inaugurated a pitiless campaign to expel Muslim civilians from Serb-controlled areas that contributed a new term to the vocabulary of international politics: ethnic cleansing. The Red Cross eventually found all three factions guilty of violating the Geneva Convention governing appropriate conduct of warfare, as television screens throughout the world carried graphic reports of wholesale looting, gang rape, and slaughter of innocent civilians.

The international community responded to the carnage in Bosnia through a variety of channels. The European Community failed to reach consensus on an appropriate policy toward the crisis apart from according prompt recognition to the Yugoslav successor states as the federal republic disintegrated in 1992, co-operating in the enforcement of economic sanctions against Serbia, and dispatching envoys to conduct fruitless negotiations with the warring factions. NATO exerted a modicum of direct influence on the tragic situation after its decision in the spring of 1993 to enforce a UN-authorized 'no-fly' zone over Bosnia to prevent the Serbs from supplementing their artillery barrages against Muslim positions with air strikes. In February 1994, US aircraft shot down a few Serb planes that had bombed Muslim targets in violation of the no-fly zone. The threat of NATO air strikes against Serb forces besieging Sarajevo brought a suspension of the random mortar attacks on that city's defenceless population.

In Washington, the Clinton administration, preoccupied with domestic issues and wary of foreign entanglements after its chastening experience in Somalia, sent only a token contingent of 300 troops to join the UN peacekeeping force in Macedonia, where there was little likelihood of armed conflict. As a means of avoiding the commitment of a greater number of ground troops to the Balkan quagmire, the United States resorted to air power. In the spring of 1993, Secretary of State Warren Christopher attempted in vain to persuade the European powers to join the US in launching air strikes against Bosnian Serb artillery

A Bosnian special forces soldier and civilians in downtown Sarajevo come under fire from Serbian snipers, April 1992. AFP/Getty.

positions and supply lines. The European members of NATO rejected this initiative because of fears that air strikes would endanger their own troops, which were actively participating in the only peacekeeping forces stationed on former Yugoslav territory. These were the two United Nations Protection Forces, UNPROFOR I and II, established in 1992 to shield humanitarian aid missions dispatched from abroad and to police designated 'protected areas' in Croatia and Bosnia–Herzegovina.

The UN had no more success than the European and US-led coalitions in promoting the re-establishment of peace and stability in the former Yugoslavia, as none of the belligerents displayed much willingness to co-operate with the blue-helmeted peacekeeping forces from the world organization. At the beginning of 1993, Cyrus Vance, on behalf of the UN, and Lord Owen, on behalf of the EC, presented a joint proposal that would have set up 10 autonomous provinces within Bosnia–Herzegovina. But Bosnian Serbs overwhelmingly rejected the peace plan, which would have deprived them of the 70 per cent of Serbian territory they had won on the battlefield. A second plan, put forward in July 1994 by the so-called contact group, comprising the United States, Russia, Britain, France, and Germany, proposed assigning the Bosnian Serbs half of a partitioned country and failed for the same reason.

The stubbornness of Bosnian Serbs eventually antagonized even the Serbian government itself. In August 1994, a month after the Contact Group plan was rejected, Belgrade angrily ended its political and economic support for the faction and closed the Serbian border with Bosnia–Herzegovina in order to cut off the flow of supplies to the Serb forces still fighting there. The failure of all efforts to negotiate an end to the conflict and the inability of either side to achieve a decisive military breakthrough condemned the populace of Bosnia–Herzegovina, combatants and civilians alike, to a seemingly endless cycle of stalemate and slaughter.

The Bosnian nightmare also generated acute strains within NATO, revealing a wide divergence of strategic interests between the United States and its major European allies. In was an ironic turn of events that the 45-year-old military alliance, which had been created to combat the perceived threat of Soviet agression but had never had to engage in battle with its designated adversary, launched its first post-Cold War military operation in a region far removed from the historic flashpoint along the old inter-German frontier. In the fall of 1994, a string of Bosnian Serb military successes prompted the US to abandon the arms embargo against Muslim forces and to renew its pressure on Britain and France to endorse NATO air strikes. But by that time, London and Paris vigorously opposed Washington's attempt to shore up the faltering Muslims as a recipe for prolonging a conflict that they desperately wanted to end and in which their own ground forces operated for impartial humanitarian purposes.

In the spring of 1995, intensive Bosnian Serb shelling of Sarajevo finally spurred NATO to action. When the Bosnian Serb leadership ignored an ultimatum to halt the artillery attacks and remove its heavy weapons from protected territory in the so-called 'exclusion zone', NATO aircraft bombed the Bosnian Serb stronghold of Pale. The Bosnian Serb leader Radovan Karadžić and his military commander General Ratko Mladić responded to the NATO raids by ordering their troops to take hundreds of UNPROFOR personnel hostage and hold them near potential bombing targets to dissuade NATO from resuming its air campaign. Though Serbian President Slobodan Milošević pressured the Bosnian Serbs into releasing the hostages within a few weeks, the event had demonstrated the impotence of the UN in the region and prompted the Clinton administration to press for an extensive NATO air campaign to counter Bosnian Serb assaults against the designated 'safe areas'.

In the meantime the Bosnian Muslim regime in Sarajevo had joined forces with the government of Croatia in March 1994 to forge a Bosnian–Croat Federation to cope with the increasingly bellicose Serbian populations within their respective territories. The Croatian regime of Franjo Tudjman,

N

0   100 Miles

0   100 km

- **——** Former Yugoslavia
- **——** New National Boundary
- **- - - - -** Autonomous Region within Serbia

SLOVAKIA

UKRAINE

MOLDOVA

AUSTRIA

HUNGARY

ROMANIA

SLOVENIA

Zagreb

CROATIA

VOJVODINA

Novi Sad

Belgrade

BOSNIA-
HERZEGOVINA

Sarajevo

S E R B I A

Black
Sea

Adriatic Sea

MONTE-
NEGRO

Dubrovnik

Pristina

KOSOVO

BULGARIA

Titograd

Skopje

ITALY

ALBANIA

MACEDONIA

TURKEY

GREECE

Aegean Sea

THE BALKAN PENINSULA AFTER THE BREAKUP OF YUGOSLAVIA

which had received substantial military assistance and advice from the United States, launched a military operation in the Krajina region adjacent to Bosnia, which had been occupied by Croatian Serb forces since the end of the brief Serb–Croat War in 1991. The immediate result of the offensive was a brutal campaign of ethnic cleansing, as Croatian military units massacred Croatian Serbs, destroyed their villages, and expelled some 150,000 of them to Serb-controlled territory in Bosnia and even to Serbia itself.

During the retreat of Croatian Serbs from the Krajina, a Bosnian Serb mortar attack on a Sarajevo marketplace on 28 August 1995 killed 37 shoppers. This brutal act against civilians in a designated safe area provoked a massive

NATO air assault against ethnic Serb positions throughout Bosnia, with two important consequences. First, the Bosnian Serb leadership finally consented to move its artillery out of range of the Bosnian Muslim capital. Second, the Bosnian Serbs agreed to join a negotiating team headed by Milošević to seek a diplomatic settlement to the bloody conflict. American envoy Richard Holbrooke brokered a 60-day ceasefire starting 12 October 1995, during which peace talks were conducted in Dayton, Ohio, to flesh out an informal understanding reached earlier in Geneva.

The Dayton Agreement was initialled on 21 November by Milošević, Croatian President Tuđman, and Bosnian President Alija Izetbegović and was formally signed by the three leaders at the Elysée Palace in Paris on 14 December. The agreement preserved the sovereignty of Bosnia but formally recognized two distinct 'entities' within its borders: the Bosnian–Croat Federation and a Bosnian Serb Republic. A federal government

PROGRESS OF THE INTERNATIONAL CRIMINAL TRIBUNAL FOR THE FORMER YUGOSLAVIA

The International Criminal Tribunal for the former Yugoslavia (ICTY), located in The Hague, was created in 1993 by UN Security Council Resolution 827. The Resolution empowered the tribunal to prosecute those persons responsible for 'serious violations of international humanitarian law' in the territory of the former Yugoslavia, dating back to 1991. These violations included ethnic cleansing, the systematic mass detention and rape of women, and mass killings. The tribunal, involving over 1,100 staff members, has commenced proceedings against 161 individuals (only two of whom—Ratko Mladić and Goran Hadžić—remain at large at the time of this writing). By August 2009, 60 people had been sentenced, 11 acquitted (often because the motivation to commit either genocide or ethnic cleansing could not be definitively proven), and 18 cases, involving 41 accused, remained in process. Several cases were referred back to Yugoslav courts given the nature of the offences. The current president of the ICTY, Patrick Robinson of Jamaica, estimates that all of the proceedings will conclude by 2013—some 22 years after the earliest of the offences was committed. Between 1993 and 2009 the UN budgeted just under US$1.6 billion to fund the operations of the tribunal.

Although the tribunal received a relatively specific mandate from the UN Security Council, it has now established six core goals: holding leaders accountable, bringing justice to victims, giving victims a voice, establishing the facts, developing effective and broadly applicable standards of international law, and strengthening the rule of law. The tribunal's judges have consistently sought to demonstrate that an individual's senior political position cannot protect him or her from prosecution and that 'those suspected of bearing the greatest responsibility for atrocities committed can be called to account, as well as that guilt should be individualised, protecting entire communities from being labelled as "collectively responsible".

The highest ranking official to be brought before the tribunal was former Yugoslavian leader Slobodan Milošević who was charged in 1999 with four counts of deportation, two counts of murder, and persecutions based on political, racial, and religious grounds. In 2006, however, Milošević was found dead in his cell at the tribunal's detention centre. Radovan Karadžić, the leader of Bosnia's Serb Democratic Party, was finally arrested in 2008. An amended indictment against Karadžić lists 11 counts, including genocide, crimes against humanity, violations of the laws or customs of war, and breaches of the Geneva Conventions. His prosecution is currently in the pre-trial phase and will likely be the last case concluded by the ICTY.

representing the three principal ethnic groups would wield supreme political authority, while a NATO controlled multinational peace implementation force (IFOR) of 60,000 troops (scaled down to about 20,000 by the end of the century) would replace the departing UNPROFOR as the country's supreme security organization.

The Dayton Accord thus established a NATO protectorate in a war-ravaged country that, though ostensibly held together by a superficial federal structure under a weak central government, had in effect been partitioned into three ethnic-based regions. Of the 2.3 million people who had been displaced by the war, less than a fifth returned to their country of origin, and most of those settled in territory protected by the military forces of their own ethnic group. The rest were accorded temporary asylum in foreign countries, with Germany taking in the largest number. The International Criminal Tribunal for the Former Yugoslavia (ICTY), which had been established in The Hague, indicted several alleged war criminals for their participation in the Balkan blood bath.

The United States trained and equipped the army of the Bosnian–Croat Federation in order to build it up to twice the armed strength of the Bosnian Serb Republic, assuming that Serbia would fight alongside its ethnic brethren in any future conflict between the two Bosnian political entities. The original objective was to create a rough balance of power in the country that would allow the US-dominated NATO peace implementation force to withdraw. But Clinton soon recognized the fragility of the political situation in Bosnia and revoked his earlier deadline of June 1998 for the removal of US troops from the country, leaving them to remain indefinitely.

The partition of Bosnia became more permanent, as neither the Bosnian Croats nor the Bosnian Serbs were willing to co-operate with the Muslim-dominated government in Sarajevo. The only possible alternative to the division into ethnically homogenous sectors was the return and resettlement of refugees throughout the country. Such an ambitious operation would require the indefinite presence of a NATO ground force that was large enough to protect the returning refugees, a costly and risky commitment that no alliance country was prepared to make.

As the political situation in Bosnia stabilized under the watchful eyes of the IFOR peace implementation force, another long-simmering ethnic conflict boiled over within Serbia itself. Its autonomous southern province of Kosovo contained a 90 per cent ethnic Albanian majority that had become increasingly resentful of its discriminatory treatment by the Serb-dominated government in Belgrade. When the financial collapse of Albania in 1997 (caused by a fraudulent investment scheme) led to the disintegration of that country's national army, large quantities of its weapons were acquired by the Kosovo Liberation Army (KLA), a radical wing of ethnic Albanians in Kosovo. As the KLA openly called for secession, President Milošević sought to crush the rebellion by encouraging Serb paramilitary forces in Kosovo to terrorize Kosovar Albanians into leaving the country.

In October 1998, American negotiator Richard Holbrooke patched together a temporary arrangement with Milošević, which led to the withdrawal of Serbian regular army units from Kosovo but left the ethnic Serb paramilitary forces behind to resume their work of intimidation. The Holbrooke–Milošević deal temporarily ended the violence in Kosovo, while Serbian officials and Kosovar Albanian leaders negotiated a formal agreement at a conference jointly sponsored by France and Britain in Rambouillet, France, in February 1999. The two antagonists had been forced to the conference table by the joint pressure of the United States and Russia, which at that stage were co-operating in the Contact Group of foreign powers to promote a peaceful settlement of the latest eruption of communal violence in the Balkans.

At Rambouillet, Milošević acceded to Albanian demands for a referendum in Kosovo to determine the territory's political future, a concession that would doubtless have resulted in a vote for independence in light of the huge Albanian majority in the province and its growing resentment of Serbian domination. But the Serbian president rejected the military stipulations of the accord, which prescribed the deployment of Western ground forces to monitor the agreement. Milošević apparently assumed that, in the absence of foreign troops, he would be able to manipulate the projected referendum in Kosovo to prevent a vote for independence. When Russia supported Serbia's rejection of the military protocol, Milošević exploited this division within the ranks of the Contact Group, seizing the opportunity to settle the matter by force. Serbian infantry and armour poured into the northern part of Kosovo, evicting ethnic Albanians from their homes, burning their villages, and forcing many of them to flee across the Albanian frontier. This latest instance of ethnic cleansing in the Balkans seemed designed to partition the province into two ethnic entities, with the southern, Albanian part left to fend for itself.

After Holbrooke and representatives of the European Union failed to persuade Milošević to sign the Rambouillet Agreement containing the military protocol, which the Kosovar Albanians had signed, NATO mounted a retaliatory air assault against Serbia (still formally known as the Federal Republic of Yugoslavia) in March 1999. While NATO planes carried out almost 10,000 bombing missions against military targets and civilian infrastructure thoughout the country for 79 straight days, the Serb paramilitaries in Kosovo accelerated their ruthless campaign of ethnic cleansing against the Kosovar Albanians.

The air campaign was terminated on 10 June, after Milošević's government agreed to withdraw all Yugoslav forces from Kosovo and to permit the deployment of a NATO-led multinational ground force (KFOR) to oversee the return of Albanian refugees and provide security for the province. Once the multinational force replaced the departed Yugoslav forces, over 70 per cent of the one million Albanian refugees returned to Kosovo. Some of them took revenge against the Serb minority for the deaths of about 10,000 of their countrymen during Milošević's campaign by undertaking their own ethnic cleansing, destroying the homes of Kosovar Serbs and forcing many of them to seek refuge in Serbia. At the beginning of the new century, KFOR faced the daunting task of restoring law and order to a devastated land.

SUMMARY

During the 1990s, Western Europe entered a new phase of integration. The principles of this alliance were laid down in the Treaty on European Union (often called the Maastricht Treaty), signed in 1992. Its goals included the creation of a common currency, the harmonization of social and welfare policies, and the eventual establishment of a European military force to provide security across the continent. The Single European Market came into effect on schedule in 1993, but other elements of integration encountered serious opposition in some countries. The end of the Cold War raised difficult questions about the role of the United States and the future of NATO, and no consensus was reached on how to create a new framework for European security. To deal with such uncertainties, in 1991 the North Atlantic Cooperation Council (NACC) was established to facilitate negotiations among the member states of NATO, the European Community, and the now-defunct Warsaw Pact.

As leaders discussed the future of Europe, a bitter ethnic conflict broke out in Yugoslavia in 1991. Following the secession of Slovenia and Croatia from the Yugoslav federation, members of the Serbian minority took up arms against the breakaway states. Although a brief peace was negotiated in 1992, it failed to prevent the spread of violence between rival groups of Croats, Serbs, and Muslims in Bosnia–Herzegovina. This conflict produced a new term, 'ethnic cleansing', which was used to describe the barbaric crimes perpetrated by factions divided by religion and nationality. The European Community avoided military intervention, and the United Nations Protection Forces failed to stop the escalating civil war. In 1995, NATO began conducting air assaults to prevent attacks by Serbian units on Muslim areas, and later that year the United States brokered the Dayton Accord, which finally ended the conflict in Bosnia. When ethnic cleansing broke out in the neighbouring province of Kosovo in 1999, NATO again used air power to subdue Serbian forces. The atrocities committed in the former Yugoslavia demonstrated that the end of the Cold War did not create lasting peace or social justice in many parts of the world.

NOTES

1. The original six signatories of the Treaty of Rome (France, Germany, Italy, Belgium, the Netherlands, and Luxembourg) plus Britain, Ireland, Denmark, Greece, Spain, and Portugal. The term 'European Community' refers to the association of countries formed in 1967 from the European Economic Community (EEC), the European Coal and Steel Community (ECSC), and the European Atomic Energy Community (Euratom).

2. The European Commission, with its headquarters in Brussels, exercises the executive power of the European Community (now the European Union). The European Parliament in Strasbourg, comprising 526 members elected for 5-year terms by universal adult suffrage in the member countries, constitutes the embryonic legislative body of the Union.

3. The six federated republics included Bosnia–Herzegovina, Croatia, Macedonia, Montenegro, Serbia, and Slovenia. The two autonomous regions (within Serbia) were Kosovo and Vojvodina.

QUESTIONS FOR CRITICAL THOUGHT

1. To what extent does closer European integration through such organizations as the European Union benefit member nations? What are the negative consequences?
2. Why have some nations consistently opposed greater integration? Discuss whether such concerns are justified.
3. What factors most contributed to the collapse of the former Yugoslavia?
4. Why was the UN unable to deal effectively with the crises in the Balkans?
5. Are tribunals such as the ICTY an effective way to deal with crimes against humanity and war crimes? What other methods might be more successful?
6. Why was the use of NATO forces in the Balkan conflict so controversial?

WEBSITES FOR FURTHER REFERENCE

Europa—Gateway to the European Union
  http://europa.eu/index_en.htm

European Union Internet Resources
  www.lib.berkeley.edu/doemoff/govinfo/intl/gov_eu.html

Frontline: The World's Most Wanted Man
  www.pbs.org/wgbh/pages/frontline/shows/karadzic/bosnia/eindex.html

The World Bank: Europe and Central Asia
  http://web.worldbank.org/WBSITE/EXTERNAL/COUNTRIES/ECAEXT/0,,contentMDK:2072
  3133~pagePK:146736~piPK:146830~theSitePK:258599,00.html

CHAPTER 16

ASIA AT THE CROSSROADS

ECONOMIC GROWTH AND SECURITY DILEMMAS IN EAST ASIA

By the mid-1990s East Asia was enjoying the dual advantage of sustained economic growth and regional stability. With the notable exception of Japan (whose long and spectacular advancement had slowed), the export-oriented economies of the region continued to flourish owing to their comparative advantages in labour and production costs. In 1993, the combined gross domestic product of East Asia increased by 7 per cent, compared to less than 1 per cent for the rest of the world. During the same period the region basked in an unprecedented period of peace. For the first time since the 1930s, East Asia was spared the trauma of war or civil conflict.

Within this increasingly favourable environment the national success story was the spectacular economic performance of the People's Republic of China. While the rest of the world languished in recession, China recorded annual GNP increases of 7, 12, and 13 per cent between 1991 and 1993. This impressive performance vindicated the reformers allied with Deng Xiaoping, who had abandoned the economic principles of Marxism–Leninism in the face of bitter opposition from orthodox defenders of the communist faith.

The ruling elite in Beijing responded to the collapse of communism in the Soviet Union by accelerating China's economic transformation in the hope of avoiding the fate of their counterparts in Moscow. In the process they outmanoeuvred their orthodox critics, who criticized Deng as a Chinese Gorbachev whose radical economic reforms threatened to stimulate the same kind of political opposition to the communist dictatorship. Unlike the former Soviet leader, however, Deng and his prime minister, Li Peng, steadfastly refused to permit the kind of political liberalization that would threaten the party's monopoly on power.

The first, and most shocking, demonstration of this hardline policy was the government's response to protests in Beijing's Tinanmen Square. In the spring of 1989, at least 100,000 students converged on the square to dramatize their demands for greater political freedom by staging hunger strikes, chanting democratic slogans in front of the ubiquitous Western television cameras, and wheeling around a replica of the Statue of Liberty as the symbol of their cause. The Chinese government called in the People's Liberation Army to suppress the peaceful protest in early June. The resulting massacre of about 1,300 unarmed civilians curtailed public dissent within the People's Republic. The imprisonment of domestic dissidents, even as foreign trade representatives and investment bankers came calling, signified that Beijing's policy of opening the country's economy to the outside world would not be accompanied by a liberalization of its internal political system.

Though the Tiananmen Square massacre sparked public outrage in many countries, foreign governments and business interests reacted with caution. China enjoyed virtual immunity from international criticism of its repressive political system because of its value as a potential trading partner and investment market for the industrial powers of the world. This fact helps account for the divergent political paths of the two communist powers—the Soviet Union and China—after widespread popular unrest buffeted both societies at the end of the 1980s. The disintegrating Soviet economy rendered the reforming regime in Moscow utterly dependent on foreign assistance, thereby making it vulnerable to foreign pressure for political reform. The booming economy of China dissuaded Western nations that eagerly eyed China's markets for their exports and capital investment from jeopardizing these prospects with offensive criticism of the country's political practices.

After a brief interval following the Tiananmen Square massacre, Japan and the Western industrial nations restored normal economic relations with China. In response to China's annual applications for most-favoured-nation (MFN) trade status in the early 1990s, the administration of George H.W. Bush concluded that the advantages of preserving profitable economic links with China outweighed concerns about that country's blatant violation of its own citizens' human rights. Washington therefore refrained from using the threat of revoking preferential trade status as a means of promoting democratization in China. The Clinton administration continued this policy by granting Beijing annual renewals of MFN in 1993 and 1994 in spite of the absence of evidence that China had curtailed its repressive policies.

Canada was another Western country that set aside its humanitarian concerns in order to expand its economic relationship with China. By 1992 the value of trade between these two countries had reached CAD$4.6 billion. But while the Canadian government maintained a foreign policy that aimed to balance concerns over human rights with opportunities for economic partnerships, it remained focused primarily on bilateral trade. In 1994 Prime Minister Jean Chrétien visited Beijing and Shanghai with a delegation that included two federal ministers, nine provincial premiers, and the territorial leaders. During the visit, Chrétien and Chinese Premier Li Peng signed a nuclear co-operation agreement and a letter of intent for several other development projects. The 'Team Canada' trade mission was so successful that Chrétien returned to China in 1996 and 1998, and in 2001 he assembled the largest trade delegation in Canadian history. The 2001 Team Canada mission to China included not only Chrétien and an array of political leaders, but also more than 500 business participants from Canada.

THE IMPACT OF CHINA'S ECONOMIC GROWTH

Though Gorbachev-style political liberalization had been ruled out by the economic reformers in Beijing, China's crash program of market-based modernization could not avoid creating dislocations in the country's social and political order. The promotion of capitalist enterprise in the coastal regions predictably spawned an entrepreneurial class whose interests increasingly diverged from those of the entrenched communist managerial elite. The burgeoning private sector that produced goods for the export market competed for scarce capital and resources with the parochial, inefficient state-run sector that continued to turn out goods for domestic consumption, generating a certain degree of social friction and political factionalism.

China's increasing integration with the international economic order had other important

A lone demonstrator stands down a column of tanks at the entrance to Tiananmen Square, June 1989. Getty Images.

domestic consequences as well. Neighbouring capitalist countries such as Taiwan and South Korea relocated labour-intensive manufacturing operations to the China coast in order to take advantage of China's comparatively low labour costs, while Japan and the Association of Southeast Asian Nations (ASEAN) countries expanded their trade with coastal China. As that economically booming region tightened its links to the world economy, the government in Beijing had to loosen its grip on the domestic economy, where world market forces were beginning to influence domestic wages, prices, and interest rates. In short, China's adoption of the free market as the engine of its economic growth led to

decentralization and regionalism, an unfamiliar and unintended development in a country long accustomed to centralized control.

While coastal provinces such as Guangdong (opposite Hong Kong) and Fujian (opposite Taiwan) exploited their foreign economic connections to contest Beijing's absolute authority, signs of religious and ethnic discontent appeared in areas along China's landlocked western periphery. The long-running agitation of Tibetan separatists was accompanied by other sources of regional dissidence. Islamic militants in the western province of Xinjiang drew inspiration from fellow Muslims in the Central Asian republics that had recently achieved national independence, while the peoples of Inner Mongolia took notice as the Republic of Mongolia, across the northern frontier, shook off the authority of Moscow. Though nothing of immediate consequence resulted from these faint rumblings of opposition to central authority, they served as reminders of that country's status as one of the world's last great multinational states after the disintegration of the Soviet Union into its constituent ethnic components.

China's spectacular economic growth in the early 1990s coincided with its acquisition of absolute military security in East Asia for the first time since the establishment of the People's Republic in 1949. The collapse of the Soviet Union and the reduction of American naval power in the western Pacific eliminated the only impediments to China's strategic superiority in its region. This unprecedented condition of invulnerability emboldened Beijing to pursue, rather aggressively, some traditional as well as some more recently acquired foreign policy goals. One target of China's foreign policy objectives was the British dependency of Hong Kong, where, in 1992, the British governor general had introduced a set of democratic reforms. Concerned that these reforms might contaminate the increasingly independent-minded coastal provinces on the mainland, Beijing condemned the reform measures and preemptively pronounced them null and void upon the expiration of British sovereignty over the colony. When Hong Kong was formally absorbed by China in July 1997, it retained a considerable degree of autonomy from the communist government in Beijing. However, it was clear that China was firmly in control of Hong Kong and could tighten the screws whenever it wished to do so.

As the date for China's recovery of Hong Kong approached, the indigenous inhabitants of the island of Taiwan began to discuss the taboo topic of declaring independence from the mainland in order to preclude a similar fate. In March 1995, China reacted to this political rhetoric by testfiring several missiles off the Taiwan coast. When Taiwanese president Lee Teng-hui paid a private visit to the United States in June, Beijing angrily broke off the largely meaningless talks on reunification that it had been conducting with Taipei. Provocative Chinese military exercises in the Taiwan Strait in March 1996 prompted the dispatch of two US aircraft carrier battle groups to the region as a signal of Washington's determination to prevent Taiwan's forcible reunification with the mainland. Joint naval exercises conducted by the US and India (China's long-time adversary) in the Indian Ocean that same year, together with the tightening security partnership between Washington and Tokyo, confirmed Washington's commitment to containing China's ambitions in Asia.

Before he died of a long and debilitating illness in February 1997, Deng Xiaoping, the architect of China's economic reform in the post-Mao era, mounted an assault on the principal roadblock to full-scale modernization in China: the inefficient, money-losing, state-owned industries inherited from the Maoist era. Deng's hand-picked successor, Jiang Zemin, announced his intention to resume the reformist campaign of his mentor by removing from the regime's ruling circles the last of the old-guard defenders of communist orthodoxy. The new president then attempted to restructure the unproductive nationalized firms and the financially troubled state-run banks, which had squandered a fortune in unproductive loans and investments. This restructuring of the old state-run industrial and financial enterprises resulted in the dismissal of millions of workers who had grown accustomed not only to guaranteed lifetime employment but also to a wide range of employer-sponsored social services.

By the summer of 1998, the communist regime in China faced the unfamiliar challenge of worker protests, as many of those dismissed from their jobs in the interests of greater efficiency and productivity took to the streets to publicize their opposition to the new policies. This socio-economic unrest coincided with mounting demands from religious groups for greater freedom to practise their faith and with hints of separatist agitation in Tibet, Xinjiang, and other regions with non-Chinese majorities. Though a crackdown by the authorities kept the lid on this simmering discontent, Jiang's new government was confronted with the possibility that its bold campaign of economic modernization could generate tensions within Chinese society that would be difficult to contain.

Meanwhile, in the United States, the Clinton administration attempted to expand Sino–American trade while working out an acceptable arrangement to liberalize China's trading practices so that it could enter the new World Trade Organization (WTO), which replaced GATT in 1995. China's bid to join the WTO had been thwarted by its inordinately high tariff rates and its egregious violation of intellectual property rights through pirated computer software and compact disc sales. In the fall of 1999, Beijing and Washington finally reached an agreement, paving the way for China's entry into the world body. But the two countries' economic co-operation contrasted with a set of political disagreements. Beijing was alarmed by American plans to develop a theatre missile defence system in Asia, which, though ostensibly intended to protect Japan from nuclear attack, threatened to limit the political effectiveness of the nuclear threat China was exerting over Taiwan. Evidence of alleged Chinese espionage at American nuclear research facilities, uncovered in 1999, contributed to anti-Chinese sentiment in the US, as did Beijing's harsh treatment of political and religious dissidents and its continued crackdown in Tibet. Conversely, the accidental bombing of the Chinese embassy in Belgrade during the NATO air campaign against Serbia in the spring of 1999 sparked anti-American sentiment in China.

Throughout the 1990s Beijing advanced new territorial claims in the South China Sea. Their claim to the Spratly and Paracel island groups, which are believed to possess substantial oil and natural gas reserves, pitted China against its old adversary Vietnam, as well as the ASEAN states Indonesia, Malaysia, and the Philippines, which had hired oil companies to prospect on their behalf within the territorial limits of some of the islands. In the mid-1990s China began to construct buildings that could be used for military purposes on the aptly named Mischief Reef in the Spratlys, provoking sharp protests from the Philippines at this apparent southward extension of Chinese power. China's increasing assertiveness in the Taiwan Strait and the South China Sea occasioned considerable anxiety among its neighbours in East Asia, where the disappearance of the Soviet Union and the reduced American military and naval presence had created a power vacuum. None of these political and territorial disputes degenerated into the type of confrontation that spells regional instability.

TROUBLE ON THE KOREAN PENINSULA

The only genuine trouble spot in East Asia during the 1990s was the Korean peninsula, where North Korea, in an apparent bid to compensate for its diminished political and economic position caused by the collapse of the Soviet bloc and the disappearance of its Soviet patron, endeavoured to acquire a nuclear capability. Though it had, with some reluctance, signed the Nuclear Non-Proliferation Treaty (NPT) in 1985, North Korea refused to sign an agreement with the International Atomic Energy Agency (IAEA) to permit on-site inspections to verify compliance with the treaty provisions. By the end of the 1980s, the communist regime of Kim Il Sung was widely suspected of having extracted enough weapons-grade plutonium from the waste products of its commercial nuclear reactors in the city of Yongbyon to produce several atomic bombs.

Responding to diplomatic pressure from its traditional allies, Russia and China, as well as to economic incentives from its long-time antagonists, Japan and the United States, North Korea finally agreed to open its nuclear facilities to international inspection in the summer of 1991. For the next three years, however, the North Korean dictator placed every conceivable obstacle in the path of the frustrated IAEA inspectors. After numerous instances of stalling and reneging on agreements, Kim's refusal to permit inspection of specified sites finally triggered a declaration of non-compliance from the agency, in the spring of 1994, and Washington pressed for United Nations trade sanctions.

This threat prompted North Korea's agreement to seek a solution through direct exchanges with the United States. The death in July 1994 of the 82-year-old North Korean leader, who had ruled his country since its creation in 1948, briefly interrupted the progress of these negotiations, but talks resumed with the succession of Kim Il Sung's son and hand-picked political heir, Kim Jong Il. In the autumn of 1994 North Korea finally consented to freeze its nuclear weapons development program, gradually dismantle its existing nuclear facilities, and permit international inspection of the two suspect sites. In exchange the Clinton administration agreed to establish a diplomatic liaison office in the North Korean capital, Pyongyang—a requirement for establishing the formal political ties that would facilitate the foreign investment North Korea desperately needed. The US also agreed to supply North Korea with oil for factories and homes as compensation for the energy production it agreed to forego by closing its nuclear plants. An international consortium led by Japan and South Korea was formed to finance the construction of two light-water reactors—which produce far less plutonium than the graphite-core reactors at Yongbyon—to meet North Korea's long-term energy requirements.

The question of North Korea's motives in this long international drama prompted intense speculation by experts in the field. One interpretation focused on what may be called the 'cornered animal' syndrome. The already hermit-like country had been plunged into even greater international isolation after the breakup of the Soviet Union and the decision by the Chinese communist leadership to follow the capitalist road to economic development. In the early 1990s North Korea's traditional economic benefactors in Moscow and Beijing terminated the lavish subsidies they had bestowed on Pyongyang during the Cold War, demanding hard currency payments for their exports at prices to be determined by the world market.

Another likely source of anxiety in Pyongyang had to do with China's diplomatic recognition of, and expanding trade contacts with, North Korea's bitter rival on the peninsula. The reunification of the two Germanies in 1990 represented an ominous precedent for the indigent, isolated communist state in the north as it faced a prosperous society in the south. The only trump card left in Kim Il Sung's (and then Kim Jong Il's) hand was the nuclear card, which could be played at the appropriate moment to forestall a German-style reunification under South Korean auspices. Since the mid-1990s, North Korea's growth rate had declined precipitously, while a virtual breakdown in food production had led to acute malnutrition and, according to some reports, the starvation of about two million people. South Korea sent food shipments northward as a gesture of good will as it intensified its efforts to reach a final settlement with its old rival. At the urging of the United States and South Korea, North Korea finally agreed to attend so-called Four Party Talks (involving the two Korean states, the US, and China) to discuss means of reaching a peace settlement on the peninsula. Two rounds of negotiations were held in Geneva in 1998, but they stalled when North Korea insisted the US withdraw all its military forces from South Korea and sign a separate bilateral treaty with North Korea.

A breakthrough of sorts occurred in November 1998 when South Korean tourists were permitted to visit North Korea for the first time since the two governments were established 50 years earlier. While some South Korean government officials were having second thoughts about reunification with a starving, economically backward population in the north, South Korean corporations eagerly developed plans for joint ventures that would give them access to North Korea's cheap labour and abundant raw materials.

North Korea's starving population and increasing economic turmoil lent an air of urgency to concerns about its capacity to become a nuclear state. The international consortium created to build the two light-water reactors began construction in the summer of 1997. A cost-sharing arrangement to finance the project was finally reached in November 1998 among South Korea, Japan, the European Union, and the United States. The IAEA had certified that the North Korean nuclear site at Yongbyon remained inactive and that the specified amount of the spent fuel from its plutonium-producing reactor had been prepared for shipment out of the country. But in 1998 evidence surfaced of other underground sites suspected of housing reactors capable of producing weapons-grade plutonium, in violation of the 1994 agreement.

The North Korean government rejected all US requests for unrestricted inspection of the suspected sites. Amid the growing concerns about a possible clandestine nuclear weapons program in North Korea, Pyongyang made significant progress in developing a delivery system for whatever nuclear weapons it might produce. Without warning it launched a rocket over Japanese territory on 31 August 1998. What North Korea later claimed was an attempted satellite launch, Japanese intelligence concluded was a test of the new Taepodong 1 ballistic missile. Kim Jong Il seemed intent on impressing upon neighbours such as Japan and South Korea that the isolated communist regime on the northern half of the Korean peninsula, despite its debilitating economic difficulties at home, remained a force to be reckoned with in the region.

CHANGES IN JAPANESE FOREIGN POLICY

Amid the remarkable economic growth of China and the ominous nuclear ambitions of North Korea, the historical regional adversary of those two communist countries had fallen on uncharacteristically hard times. Japan, whose model for economic expansion had been the envy of the world and had spawned imitators throughout East Asia, suffered its worst economic slowdown since 1945. The social tensions that inevitably resulted from a long and severe recession were exacerbated by two controversies in Japan's relations with the United States.

The first was the long-standing trans-Pacific conflict over trade policy, which erupted into strongly worded American complaints about Japanese protectionism, particularly concerning exports of automobiles and automobile parts, semiconductors, and rice. The second source of tension was the dispute over what is known in the lexicon of defence policy as 'burden sharing'. Many Americans had begun to express reservations about continuing to provide military protection to Japan while that country flooded the US market with its products and shielded its domestic farms and factories from American competition. Though Tokyo reluctantly bowed to American pressure and consented to increase its share of the costs of maintaining US military forces on its territory to 70 per cent by 1995, the issue caused resentment on both sides of the Pacific.

The debate over sharing the cost of Japan's defence in East Asia coincided with a wide-ranging reassessment of the future of the country's international military role in the post–Cold War era. The principal question was whether Tokyo should revoke its long-standing prohibition against participation by the Japanese military forces in overseas operations. Japan had contributed financially to the military campaign against Iraq in 1991, but parliamentary opposition prevented the government of Toshiki Kaifu from dispatching units of the Japanese army (or Self-Defence Force, as it is euphemistically named) to join the multinational contingent in the Persian Gulf.

In the spring of 1991, Kaifu sent Japanese naval minesweepers to the Gulf as part of a post-war operation to secure the sea lanes for oil tankers. This was the first time since World War II that Japanese naval forces had been sent overseas. In October 1992, Kaifu's successor, Kiichi Miyazawa, furnished a small contingent of Japanese military engineers to the United Nations peacekeeping operation in Cambodia to assist in construction projects. This seemingly harmless contribution shattered another precedent: it was the first foreign assignment of Japanese ground troops since the war (though the engineers were expressly prohibited from engaging in combat-related activities). The bitter memories of earlier Japanese transgressions abroad were periodically rekindled by public relations gaffes such as the Japanese Diet's refusal to issue a formal apology on the fiftieth anniversary of the attack on Pearl Harbor and its refusal to provide financial compensation to surviving Korean women who had been forced into prostitution by Japanese military units during the war. But a half-century of Japanese military passivity and diplomatic prudence seemed to have allayed those anxieties. In light of the expanding military and economic might of China, many of Japan's neighbours began to appreciate its potential role as a countervailing force in the evolving balance of power in East Asia.

After reaffirming the Japanese–American Security Treaty in April 1996, Tokyo and Washington redefined that bilateral security relationship in September 1997. Among other things, the new agreement obliged Japan to provide logistical support to US military forces in the event of conflict in the Far East, though the precise geographical area covered by the agreement was left ambiguous. It was evident that the target of this enhanced security co-operation between Japan and the United States was North Korea, whose apparent determination to acquire nuclear weapons was causing considerable alarm in Tokyo. The North Korean ballistic missile test across Japanese territory in August 1998 was the last straw. It led directly to

THE END OF THE POST-WAR ORDER IN JAPAN?

Post-war Japanese politics was dominated by the right-of-centre Liberal Democratic Party (LDP). The LDP lost power only once, very briefly, in 63 years. However, at the end of August 2009 Japanese voters frustrated with ongoing economic problems, a bloated bureaucracy, and a weak social safety net overwhelmingly voted to defeat the LDP and install a majority Democratic Party (DPJ) government. With 308 out of 430 seats in the lower house of the Japanese parliament, the Democratic Party was handed a strong mandate to introduce major changes in the direction of Japanese politics and foreign policy. The DPJ campaigned on a platform of strengthening the social welfare system; reorienting Japan towards Asia; re-evaluating elements of Japan's traditionally close relationship with the United States; and reconsidering the American military presence on Okinawa—a cornerstone of the post-war US commitment to Japanese defence, but an ongoing source of irritation to others.

Many analysts have predicted that Japan will now move closer to China, given the steadily increasing economic connections between the two nations. Yukio Hatoyama, the prime minister-designate, has assailed globalization in its current form, arguing that American free market policies have not benefited Japan. The Democrats have also been critical of the powerful bureaucracy which laid the foundation both for Japan's tremendous success in the 1960s and 1970s and the crises of the 1990s. The interconnections among the bureaucracy, business, banking, and government have increasingly given rise to accusations of nepotism and corruption. The new government has indicated that it intends to move quickly to break up the *amakudari* system, whereby retired bureaucrats move in and out of government and private sector positions, perpetuating their own power and blocking attempts to reform the political system and to change the direction of the economy.

Even before the Democrats officially took power in mid-September 2009, however, commentators predicted that any attempt to reform the bureaucracy is doomed to failure for the simple reason that the newly elected party needs to work with the bureaucracy in order to accomplish its other election promises, most importantly the promise to create a strong social welfare system. Nonetheless, it seems clear that Japan stands ready to undertake a fundamental reassessment of the country's direction in the post-war era.

Japan's endorsement of an American proposal to begin joint research on a theatre missile defence system in East Asia. The system would employ satellites, radar, and sea-based missiles to identify and intercept incoming ballistic missiles.

The most notable source of dissension in the Japanese–American alliance was the presence of US military personnel on Japanese territory in general and on the island of Okinawa in particular. While the Japanese government consistently favoured keeping American forces in Japan (in spite of domestic opposition) because of their contribution to stability in the region, it faced intense political pressure from Okinawa to reduce the conspicuous and overbearing American military presence there. Though a compromise of sorts was reached in 1996, when the two countries agreed to convert the large US Marine base on the small island into a heliport, resentment against the intrusive presence of foreign military units continued to brew.

Japan's relations with the two other great powers in Northeastern Asia were complicated by largely symbolic issues left unresolved from the Second World War. Japanese Prime Minister Keizo Obuchi's refusal to issue a written apology to China for Japanese transgressions during the war, particularly after he had offered just such a statement to South Korea in 1998, caused great annoyance in Beijing. Meanwhile, Japan's relationship with Russia continued to suffer because of Tokyo's refusal to recognize Russian sovereignty over the Kurile Islands, which had been unilaterally seized by Soviet troops at the end of the war. The Soviet Union under Mikhail Gorbachev and Russia under Boris Yeltsin had implied on more than one occasion that a compromise settlement of the dispute over the islands was possible in exchange for Japanese investment in Siberia. But the downward slide of the Soviet, and then the Russian, economy made Japanese investors wary of sinking their funds into such a risky venture. The prospect of a massive flow of Japanese capital into Russia was rendered even less likely by Japan's own economic difficulties that began in 1997, when many banks and insurance companies failed or suffered huge losses because of defaulted loans. As a result, the dispute remained unresolved at the close of the twentieth century.

SECURITY CONCERNS AND FINANCIAL CRISIS IN EAST ASIA

The relationship between the United States and Asia saw fundamental changes in the aftermath of the Cold War. While the US retained important trade and investment stakes across the Pacific, the recession of Soviet power in the Far East and the economic difficulties of the early 1990s prompted a reassessment of American security interests in the region. As domestic issues increasingly dominated the political agenda in the US, American public opinion began to question the wisdom of maintaining a massive and costly military presence in a part of the world where the enemy had vanished and the allies were running up huge trade surpluses with their transpacific protector.

The most conspicuous consequence of this reappraisal of America's future security role in Asia was the closure in 1992 of the American naval base at Subic Bay in the Philippines, the principal supply and repair centre for the Seventh Fleet. Although the evacuation of Subic Bay and Clark Air Base in the Philippines did not represent the disappearance of US naval and air power from the western Pacific—compensatory arrangements for emergency access to base facilities in Malaysia, Indonesia, Singapore, and Brunei were promptly negotiated, and the Seventh Fleet retained its home port at Yokosuka on the Japanese island of Honshu—the withdrawal from the Philippines seemed to some observers the symbol of a subtle shift in American priorities in East Asia. Economic interests would receive greater attention than security concerns in a comparatively stable and secure area whose combined gross national product was approaching that of North America and where it was increasingly difficult to identify even hypothetical enemies.

Yet the preservation of this state of regional stability could hardly be taken for granted in a part of the world that had been torn by international and civil strife from the early 1930s to the end of the Cold War. This reality was all the more evident in light of the sharp increase in arms purchases by the rapidly industrializing countries in the region during the early 1990s. For this reason, organizing a multilateral body to ensure Asian regional security in the post–Cold War era became a matter of considerable urgency for the nations concerned, lest an individual power such as China (with its nuclear arsenal, expanding naval power, and booming economy) be tempted to unilaterally fill the strategic vacuum left by the disintegration of the Soviet Union and the recession of American power. Unlike Europe and the western hemisphere, though, Asia lacked an existing security mechanism such as NATO, the WEU, the CSCE, or the OAS that could be adapted to the new strategic circumstances. Dulles's old brainchild SEATO had never amounted to much more than a cover for America's military engagement in Indochina and had disappeared without fanfare after the Vietnamese triumph in the mid-1970s.

In the early 1990s, two alternative but potentially complementary initiatives emerged as options to address the dilemma of organizing East Asian security. The first of these emanated from ASEAN, an initially loose-knit organization that sought to expand its role as a multilateral force for stability in the region. In May 1993, ASEAN officials proposed that the diplomatic machinery set out in the organization's Treaty of Amity and Co-operation be used as a means of settling regional disputes. In July of the same year, the organization's foreign ministers hosted a meeting in Singapore, inviting representatives of all powers with interests in Asia and the Pacific. This unprecedented official gathering decided to convene a summit the following year to review the entire question of Asian security in light of the new geopolitical realities. The 18-nation ASEAN Regional Forum held its inaugural meeting in July 1994 in Bangkok, with high hopes for future co-operation to ensure East Asian peace and stability; however, nothing of any significance resulted from the meeting.

The ASEAN security initiative ran into competition from an unexpected overture from Washington, which presented a second option for addressing security concerns in East Asia. In July 1993, President Clinton invited Asian leaders to assemble in Seattle after the annual meeting of the Asia-Pacific Economic Co-operation Conference (APEC), an informal organization established in 1989 at Australia's suggestion to discuss economic issues of interest to nations on the Pacific rim. Some Southeast Asian leaders expressed concern that the US initiative might impede the development of an ASEAN-sponsored security dialogue in Asia, while others worried that APEC might evolve into a vehicle for US domination of a future Pacific community in which Asian countries would be relegated to a subordinate role. Though the Seattle meeting produced nothing more than innocuous declarations, the question became whether ASEAN and its new Regional Forum or the US-dominated APEC would serve as the nucleus for a post–Cold War security arrangement in Asia.

At the November 1994 APEC summit in Jakarta, Indonesia, Clinton pressed the leaders of the 18 Pacific rim nations to endorse a vaguely worded commitment to free trade within the region by the year 2010 for industrialized countries and 2020 for developing ones. Skeptical signatories such as China and Malaysia fretted about the possible consequences of prematurely exposing their protected domestic markets to foreign competition. Repressive dictatorships such as the conference's host anticipated with some annoyance embarrassing questions about democratic procedures and human rights that would inevitably be raised in the context of such a trade agreement. In the end, however, all participants signed the nonbinding declaration, establishing at least the concept of a Pacific economic community in which the United States would play a leading role. APEC set up a working group, under Japanese leadership, that was instructed to draft a blueprint for implementing the agreed-on free trade goals by the 1996 summit in Osaka. The breakthrough at the Jakarta Conference overshadowed the earlier meeting of the ASEAN Regional Forum, which had reissued an appeal to Asian countries to play a more active role in regional collective defence.

ASEAN's attempts to forge a regional security system in Southeast Asia proved disappointing for the rest of the decade. In 1995, the organization admitted Vietnam into the fold and formally resolved to incorporate all other countries in the region by the end of the decade. Myanmar (formerly Burma) and Laos joined in 1997, followed by Cambodia in 1999. At its 1995 summit, in Bangkok, the ASEAN states had also concluded a treaty designating South East Asia as a nuclear weapons–free zone, obliging each signatory to refrain from producing or testing nuclear weapons. The expansion of its membership and

its commitment to regional nuclear disarmament were seen by some observers as proof that ASEAN would enter the twenty-first century poised to become a regional collective security system worthy of the name. But the apparent trend toward multilateral co-operation was contradicted by Indonesia's announcement on the eve of the Bangkok Summit that it had concluded a bilateral security treaty with Australia. This agreement reflected Jakarta's disappointment with the ASEAN Regional Forum, which though it had been established as an embryonic collective security system for Southeast Asia, had proved totally ineffectual amid the escalating tension in the region's two trouble spots in the Taiwan Strait and the South China Sea.

THE APEC AFFAIR

When protesters clashed with the RCMP during the 1997 meeting of the Asia-Pacific Economic Cooperation (APEC) forum in Vancouver, it touched off a political crisis in Canada. Known as the 'APEC Affair', the incident illustrated how international issues could become enmeshed with domestic politics. APEC was designed not as a political or diplomatic forum but rather a loose club of countries that met to discuss ways to foster trade and commerce. However, due to the attendance of President Suharto, the dictator of Indonesia, this summit became highly controversial. A number of groups, including many university students, organized protests against the presence of Suharto, whose government was widely condemned for human rights abuses. For Prime Minister Jean Chrétien, the APEC summit was an important political event, and the federal government sought to prevent protesters from disrupting the meeting or embarrassing leaders such as Suharto. The RCMP laid down strict rules for protesters, requiring that they remain in approved demonstration sites well away from the meeting. When a group of protesters confronted the police at the University of British Columbia,

RCMP officers used pepper spray to disperse the crowd. Dozens of people were arrested, and many protesters were temporarily blinded. Television cameras captured one officer emptying his canister of pepper spray on a small group of people, including the cameraman who recorded the incident. This image became a powerful focal point, as the RCMP came under heavy public criticism for its harsh treatment of student protesters.

After the summit, the news media reported that evidence indicated that the RCMP had acted under the direction of the Prime Minister's Office. In the face of serious allegations of police brutality and political interference, the RCMP Public Complaints Commission launched an inquiry. The RCMP later admitted that it made errors in its handling of the APEC protests, but the Chrétien government denied any wrongdoing. When asked about the incident at a news conference, the Prime Minister said, 'For me pepper, I put it on my plate.' Like the televised image of protesters being pepper-sprayed, Chrétien's comments became a symbol in the debate over whether the Canadian government had sacrificed democratic principles in favour of international trade.

The long-time prime minister of Malaysia, Mahathir Mohamad, became the leading exponent of a coherent political, social, and cultural ideology that was designed to unite the diverse population groups within ASEAN. Borrowing heavily from the policies and pronouncements of Kee Kuan Yew, former prime minister of Singapore, Mahathir and his followers preached a return to 'Asian values' as the basis for a successful program of development for the countries of the region. These Asian values included authoritarian government, hierarchical social order, and state control of economic life, which were preferable to the 'Western values' of political democracy, civic culture, and market capitalism. But in 1997, the miraculous economic growth of East Asia, which had impressed the world for more than three decades, suffered a sharp setback when the currencies and financial markets of Thailand, South Korea, Indonesia, and Malaysia collapsed.

None of the renowned Asian 'Tigers' were immune to the spreading economic crisis. Two of South Korea's largest steel companies and its third-largest automobile firm went bankrupt. When the South Korean won plunged to record lows, in November 1997, the government rushed to the IMF and secured a loan of US$57 billion, the largest amount ever provided to a single country by the international lending organization. The IMF attached its customary stiff conditions to the bailout, including demands that the highly protected South Korean economy be opened to foreign imports and that the country's notoriously restrictive financial markets be made more accessible to foreign investors. The new government of the reforming President Kim Dae Jung, which took power in 1998, undertook a radical economic restructuring by closing money-losing banks, investment firms, and industrial conglomerates while streamlining those that survived and forcing them to adapt to foreign competition. These measures led to bankruptcies of inefficient firms and increasing unemployment and generated widespread protests throughout the century.

The regional financial crisis of 1997–8 severely tested the concept of Asian values that Malaysia's Mahathir had advertised as the recipe for future progress. While most of the battered economies of the region were forced to adopt Western policies of economic liberalization to ensure the flow of IMF funds, the he defiantly refused to capitulate. Mahathir blamed the Asian financial crisis on foreign exchange speculators from the developed world, and he imposed exchange controls to shield Malaysia from the sinister influence of globalization. As the other countries in the region dutifully bowed to the requirements of the IMF and other multinational financial institutions in order to shore up their battered treasuries, Malaysia was left as an isolated champion of Asian values amid a global economic order dominated by the developed countries of the West.

When the Asian financial crisis hit Indonesia, it aggravated the domestic political crisis that had been simmering there for some time and led to the forced resignation in May 1998 of President Suharto, who had ruled with an iron hand for 32 years. A sprawling nation with a population of 200 million people and over 17,000 islands, Indonesia casts a long shadow over Southeast Asia. Under Suharto's predecessor, President Sukarno, the country had pursued an aggressive policy of regional expansion. One of the principal reasons for the establishment of ASEAN in August 1967 had been to enmesh Indonesia in a multilateral system of regional co-operation that would curb its expansionist ambitions, just as the European Economic Community had been set up in part to harness West Germany's energies for the greater good of the region.

Apart from its occupation and annexation of the former Portuguese territory of East Timor in 1975, Suharto's regime had maintained a relatively low profile in Southeast Asia, as it turned inward to concentrate on a crash program of economic development. By the beginning of the 1990s Indonesia had recorded impressive growth rates and seemed poised to become the next 'Asian Tiger'. The onset of the regional financial crisis, however, sent the economy into a tailspin. The rupiah lost almost three-quarters of its value, widespread food shortages developed, and poverty and unemployment spread. The crisis led to a revival of xenophobic violence against the ethnic Chinese minority that dominated the commercial life of the country.

Suharto was replaced by his vice-president and long-time supporter, Baharuddin Habibie, who faced not only the continued economic disaster but also a revival of separatist agitation in East Timor. In January 1999, the Habibie government caved in to Timorese pressure by promising a referendum that would permit the East Timorese to choose between autonomy within Indonesia and independence. The remainder of the year was marked by an escalation of violence between the pro-independence faction and pro-Indonesian groups backed by the Indonesian military, which had opposed the government's decision to hold a referendum. The referendum, which was finally held under the auspices of the United Nations in 1999, recorded a majority for independence.

As East Timor seceded from Indonesia, that sprawling country faced what Suharto had feared most: the resurgence of separatism in other provinces that resented being dominated by Java, the most populous of the Indonesian islands and home to the capital, Jakarta. Well-armed separatist movements in Irian Jaya and in the Sumatran province of Aceh eagerly sought to follow the East Timorese precedent, threatening to unravel the multi-ethnic, multilingual, multi-religious collection of islands that Sukarno had unified after World War II. In November 1999, the National Assembly repudiated Habibie, whose links to the reviled Suharto alienated the public and whose abandonment of East Timor had antagonized the army. It named as president Abdurrahman Wahid, leader of the country's largest organization of Muslims (who constitute 88 per cent of the population). Wahid faced the challenge of preventing the artificial state of Indonesia from degenerating into a series of debilitating, ethnic-based civil wars.

The one example of a successful bid to end armed conflict in Southeast Asia during the 1990s was the termination of the 14-year civil war in Cambodia. This remnant of the Cold War was brought to an end by the intervention of the United Nations together with some old-fashioned great-power diplomacy by Beijing and Washington. Pressure from the Kremlin had induced Vietnam to withdraw troops from Cambodia at the same time that the United States was urging the coalition of resistance groups to seek a negotiated settlement. As the last Vietnamese troops left Cambodia in the summer of 1989, the regime in Phnom Penh opened peace talks in Paris with the three rebel factions that had recently coalesced under the titular authority of Prince Norodom Sihanouk. In the following year, the United Nations Security Council assumed an active role in promoting a resolution of the Cambodian conflict. In the meantime the political crisis in the Soviet Union left Moscow's protégés in Hanoi vulnerable to the intense pressure exerted by China and the United States—the two most vigorous foreign supporters of the Cambodian rebels—to induce the puppet state in Phnom Penh to accept a compromise settlement.

Finally, in October 1991, after two years of intensive negotiations and several abortive cease-fires, the four parties to the dispute signed a peace accord in Paris. The Paris Agreement established a United Nations Transitional Authority in Cambodia (UNTAC) to operate in partnership with a supreme national council chaired by Sihanouk and comprising representatives of the three insurgent groups and the Vietnamese-backed government. By the end of the year, Sihanouk and the Khmer Rouge officials had returned to Phnom Penh from their havens in China and Thailand, respectively. UNTAC, whose 22,000 military and civilian personnel from 45 countries (including Canada) represented the most formidable peacekeeping force ever deployed by the United Nations, began to arrive in the spring of 1992 to enforce the ceasefire, supervise the disarmament of the contending military forces, and prepare for nationwide elections scheduled for the following May.

Though abandoned by their long-time sponsors in Beijing, the Khmer Rouge refused to disarm and prevented UNTAC personnel from registering voters in the areas under their control. In November 1992, the Khmer Rouge announced their intention to boycott the forthcoming elections in protest against the favouritism allegedly shown by UNTAC toward the government. The May 1993 elections, which were certified as free and fair by the UN observers, resulted in a plurality for the party headed by Sihanouk's eldest son, Prince Norodom Ranariddh. In the following month he formed a provisional government in coalition with the former head of the Vietnamese puppet regime, Hun Sen. Sihanouk mounted his former throne as head of a constitutional monarchy in September, the remaining UNTAC troops departed in November, and by early 1994 the two former rebel factions had joined forces with military units of the former government against the Khmer Rouge. In June of that year, after renewing their campaign of intimidation and violence, the Khmer Rouge representatives in Phnom Penh were expelled from the capital.

Though Khmer Rouge guerrilla forces continued to harass the governing coalition's troops from their enclaves along the Thai border, the once-bloody civil war in Cambodia had dwindled to the type of low-level insurgency that many countries in the Third World have long had to endure. A traumatized society that had suffered one of the most grisly outbreaks of genocide in the twentieth century embarked on a period of relative peace and stability. This benign outcome was facilitated by the fundamental shift in the Asian balance of power occasioned by the decline of the Soviet Union. Vietnam, relegated to a position of political isolation and military vulnerability by the loss of its traditional protector, was driven to seek an accommodation with its old adversaries in Washington and Beijing at the expense of its grandiose dreams of dominion over all of Indochina. With the end of the Cold War, the United Nations was able to devise a settlement that proved satisfactory to all but the recalcitrant partisans of Pol Pot.

TENSIONS IN SOUTH ASIA

While most of Asia enjoyed a period of relative peace, stability, and economic growth during the final decade of the twentieth century, the three principal countries on the Indian subcontinent—India, Pakistan, and Bangladesh—had to cope with a set of economic, demographic, and ethnic problems whose international significance was magnified by a conventional arms race that escalated, eventually, into a nuclear arms race.

Much of the tension in South Asia stemmed from the rancorous rivalry between India and Pakistan that had persisted since their emergence as independent states after the Second World War. That antagonism may in turn be traced to the uneasy coexistence on the Indian subcontinent of two ancient religious faiths and their devoted followers. The partition in 1947 of the British Empire's 'crown jewel' into a predominantly Hindu (though ostensibly secular) India and a devoutly Muslim Pakistan, together with the exchange of almost two million refugees, had been undertaken for the purpose of forming two states that were as ethnically homogeneous as possible in order to minimize friction between members of these historically antipathetic religious groups.

The process of partition was accompanied by appalling atrocities that left a legacy of bitterness on both sides, while the massive population transfers had left substantial discontented minorities within the frontiers of each state. The Sikhs of the Punjab, embracing an eclectic faith combining elements of both Hinduism and Islam, insistently challenged the authority of the Indian state. The Muslims who predominated in India's northernmost state of Jammu and Kashmir displayed a conspicuously zealous spirit of defiance toward the Hindu-dominated government in Delhi, for which they received strong encouragement and considerable financial support from the Islamic government of Pakistan. India's experimental schemes of autonomy for Kashmir,

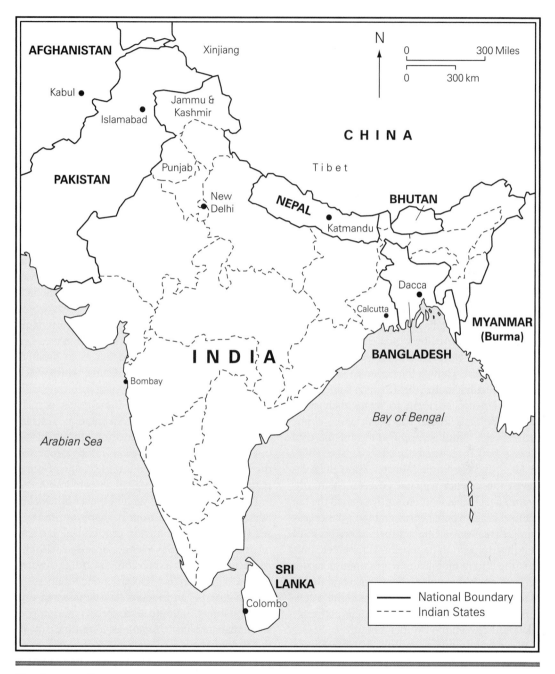

THE INDIAN SUBCONTINENT

undertaken periodically in order to assuage the secessionist ardour of the state's Muslim citizens and to thereby deprive Pakistan of any pretext for interfering in India's internal affairs, came to naught. In 1989 Kashmir saw an upsurge of Muslim secessionist insurgency that continued through the 1990s and into the twenty-first century. Two major wars, perennial border skirmishes, and fiery political rhetoric in Delhi and Islamabad poisoned relations between the two successor states of British India.

India's relentless quarrel with Pakistan over Kashmir was rivalled in intensity by two long-standing controversies with the People's Republic of China. The first was a border dispute that had flared up sporadically since the autumn of 1962, when Indian and Chinese forces battled over contested territory along the Himalayan frontier. The second concerned Tibet, an isolated, mountainous kingdom to India's north, which had been invaded and annexed by China in the autumn of 1950 while the world's attention was distracted by the Korean War. Though the communist regime in Beijing initially granted the Tibetans some autonomy and permitted them to retain their spiritual and political leader, the Dalai Lama, clashes between the Buddhist population and the communist police recurred throughout the 1950s. In 1959 Chinese Prime Minister Zhou Enlai dissolved the Tibetan regional government headed by the Dalai Lama, who promptly crossed the border into India, where he was granted political asylum. Thereafter, as China strove to eradicate the Buddhist religion in its rebellious province, India took the lead in mobilizing world opinion against Beijing's repressive policy there. The combination of the Sino–Indian border dispute and the controversy over Tibet caused a notable deterioration of relations between the two neighbours.

While continuing to affirm its commitment to the non-aligned movement, which Pandit Jawaharlal Nehru himself had helped to found, India became increasingly apprehensive about the practical consequences of its isolated position in the Cold War world and recognized the need for allies. After Nehru's death in 1964,

India accelerated its orientation toward the Soviet Union, which had already begun to furnish it with diplomatic support and economic assistance in Nehru's final years. The rapprochement between Delhi and Moscow was directly related to the Sino–Soviet split, as each country came to regard China as its principal antagonist.

In the meantime the United States sought to counter what some in the State Department decried as the embryonic Moscow–Delhi axis in South Asia by cultivating increasingly warm relations with India's regional rival, Pakistan. The Nixon administration openly sided with that country in its brief, ill-fated war with India in 1971, in which Pakistan's defeat resulted in the loss of East Pakistan (now the independent state of Bangladesh). In the aftermath of the war, Washington undertook to bolster the military capability of Pakistan to match that of India, which the US increasingly regarded as the Kremlin's client state on the subcontinent. Pakistan returned the favour by using its good offices to promote the US's reconciliation with China (with which Pakistan maintained cordial relations on the basis of their common hostility to India). This intimate Sino–Pakistani–American collaboration reached its height after the Soviet invasion of Afghanistan in 1979, when the three powers jointly supported the Islamic resistance to the Soviet military occupation forces and their Afghan allies in Kabul.

The end of the Cold War and the withdrawal of Soviet military forces from Afghanistan in 1990 set the stage for a major geopolitical realignment in South Asia. No longer obsessed with the menace of Soviet expansion toward the warm waters of the Indian Ocean, policy-makers in Washington began to focus on two other threats to the stability of South Asia, threats that, ironically, emanated from America's long-time ally in the region.

The first of these threats was the looming phenomenon of Islamism. In the early 1990s, Pakistan, whose citizens were subjected to the legal provisions of the *Sharia*—the Islamic code of religious law based on the teachings of the Koran and the traditional sayings of Mohammed—began to cultivate closer relations with other Muslim states, including Iran, Afghanistan, and the newly independent republics of Soviet Central Asia.

Islamabad's shift from an anti-Soviet to what might be called a pro-Islamic foreign policy coincided with the second development that caused strains in the US–Pakistani partnership. Since 1974, when India first tested an atomic weapon, Pakistan had been suspected of undertaking a clandestine nuclear program of its own to match that of its regional rival. Alarmed at the prospect of nuclear proliferation on the Indian subcontinent, the US Senate passed a resolution in 1986 calling for an end to Washington's generous economic and military assistance program to Pakistan unless the State Department could certify that Pakistan was not engaged in developing nuclear weapons. When, in 1990, the State Department acknowledged that it could no longer give such assurances, the US aid program abruptly stopped. The cutoff of this military support obliged Pakistan to shop for its hardware and spare parts on the international arms market, while the removal of whatever restraining influence Washington may have exercised quite possibly strengthened Islamabad's determination to join the nuclear club.

The loosening of US ties with Pakistan coincided with an improvement of Washington's relationship with Delhi, whose traditional foreign policy had been thrown into disarray by the demise of its patron and benefactor in Moscow. Pleased by the termination of US aid to Pakistan and sharing America's concern about the prospect of Pakistan's 'Islamic bomb', India proved receptive to US initiatives in 1991–2 for closer military and naval co-operation. The warmth in relations between the two countries had been helped by an ideological evolution that started in India in the late 1980s with Prime Minister Rajiv Gandhi's campaign to liberalize the state-controlled economic system. By cutting off government subsidies, reducing protective tariffs, and abolishing restrictions on foreign investment, India seemed prepared to join the international economic system from which it had long sought to insulate itself.

By the middle of the 1990s the hopes of closer co-operation between the United States and India in the post–Cold War era had fallen short of expectations. Repressive measures undertaken by the Indian government in 1993 to cope with a resurgence of unrest in Kashmir provoked criticism from the Clinton administration on the grounds of human rights. While the conventional arms race between India and Pakistan continued to escalate, the two sides failed to reach an agreement on a long-planned affirmation of the subcontinent's status as a nuclear-free zone. The sole sign of progress in reducing regional tensions in South Asia was an agreement between India and China providing for the gradual demilitarization of their frontier, which had been the site of sporadic clashes in the past. Here was yet another case of the demise of the Soviet Union paving the way for a rapprochement between former antagonists. The loss of its supporters in the Kremlin left India isolated and therefore more tractable; the disappearance of its Soviet antagonist rendered China more secure and therefore more amenable to compromise.

The stakes in the Indo–Pakistani conflict rose with the progress of nuclear weapons programs in both countries. Since its original test of a nuclear device India had continually denied possessing atomic bombs, insisting on the peaceful commercial intent of its research and development efforts. But India steadfastly refused to sign the Nuclear Non-Proliferation Treaty (NPT) unless it became *universal* (that is, all countries signed) and *nondiscriminatory* (that is, the five powers with nuclear weapons agreed to dispose of them). Pakistan also refused to sign the NPT in light of the refusal of its regional rival. Both countries began to develop delivery systems in the form of short- and medium-range missiles, raising the spectre of a nuclear arms race on the subcontinent.

The covert nuclear competition suddenly became overt in May 1998, when India announced that it had conducted five underground nuclear tests. The purpose of the tests was twofold: first, to counter the formidable nuclear arsenal of its other archrival, China; second, to match the nuclear capability that Pakistan had been developing (with Chinese assistance) for more than two decades. Jolted into action by the Indian tests, Pakistan withstood intense pressure from the United States and defiantly conducted two underground tests of its own toward the end of the same month. The US, Japan, and other countries promptly imposed sanctions on the two countries, but when financially strapped Pakistan was about to default on its foreign debt, the Clinton administration rescinded most of the sanctions and the IMF rushed in with a rescue package.

The nuclearization of the Indian subcontinent therefore became an accomplished fact. It dealt a serious blow to the cause of non-proliferation, prompting other non-nuclear states to reconsider their willingness to forego membership in a club of states possessing weapons of mass destruction that had expanded from five to seven.

SUMMARY

From the 1980s to the end of the twentieth century, East Asia appeared to be going in two directions. On the one hand, the end of the Cold War eased tensions and facilitated international co-operation throughout the region. Led by Japan, East Asia continued to grow as a global economic powerhouse. In the wake of Deng Xiaoping's economic reforms, China enjoyed a period of spectacular economic growth and was granted 'most-favoured-nation' trade status by the American government. In the post–Cold War era, the United States reduced its military presence in Asia, closing large naval bases. ASEAN worked to provide a new framework for regional trade and security, creating a free trade area in 1992. The peaceful transfer of Hong Kong from Britain to China in 1997 underscored the rise of Asian power and the decline of Western imperialism.

On the other hand, East Asia continued to experience conflict and instability. The massacre of protesters in Tiananmen Square in 1989 demonstrated that China's economic progress did not improve its poor record on human rights. China was also heavily criticized for human rights abuses in Tibet, and it continued to clash with Taiwan. In the early 1990s, Japan entered a prolonged economic recession, and in 1997–8 East Asia was plunged into a serious financial crisis. At the same time, the region also endured persistent threats of war on the Korean Peninsula and the Indian subcontinent. While there were fears that North Korea would develop nuclear weapons, both India and Pakistan tested nuclear devices in 1998. These regional conflicts represented enough of a threat to global stability that they attracted mediation from powers outside the East Asian community, particularly from the United States; however, negotiations failed to secure a lasting settlement.

QUESTIONS FOR CRITICAL THOUGHT

1. Was Deng's determination to prevent political liberalization necessary to ensure the success of his economic reforms? Why or why not?
2. Construct an argument for why North Korea should have been prevented from developing a nuclear program.
3. What were the most important factors leading to the Asian financial crisis of the late 1990s?
4. Why did India gravitate towards the Soviet Union in the 1970s?
5. Why has the United States maintained such a close relationship with Pakistan over the years?
6. Discuss the effect that India's and Pakistan's possession of nuclear weapons has on further efforts at non-proliferation. Are such efforts rendered pointless?

WEBSITES FOR FURTHER REFERENCE

Asia-Pacific Economic Cooperation – Official Site
www.apec.org

China and the WTO
www.wto.org/english/theWTO_e/countries_e/china_e.htm

Government of the PRC – Official Site
http://english.gov.cn/chinatoday.htm

World History Archives: Asian Economic Crisis 1990s
www.hartford-hwp.com/archives/50/index-a.html

CHAPTER 17

AFRICA ON ITS OWN: ETHNIC CONFLICT, AUTOCRACY, AND UNDERDEVELOPMENT

AFRICA AFTER THE COLD WAR

The disengagement of the two superpowers from Africa at the end of the 1980s set the stage for unprecedented international involvement on the continent. The appearance of multinational peacekeeping missions under the auspices of the United Nations and its designated representatives were intended not to promote the national interests of the participating countries (as had always been the case in the past) but to promote the stability and protect the civilian populations of the subject country. Never before had foreign intervention in Africa been inspired by such seemingly altruistic motives, and never before had the United Nations played such an activist role on the continent. But these operations represented belated,

piecemeal efforts to limit the immediate consequences of anarchy, poverty, and civil war. What was desperately needed—and entirely lacking—were comprehensive solutions to Africa's long-term problems.

The Horn of Africa had been one of the most hotly contested sites of superpower rivalry in the latter stages of the Cold War, when Washington and Moscow lavished economic and military aid on their respective client states in order to advance their own interests. With the breakup of the Soviet Union and the resulting decline in the strategic value of the Horn to the United States, the countries that had formerly benefited from this superpower patronage were abruptly left to their own devices. The first two casualties of this disengagement were the corrupt, repressive regimes in Somalia and Ethiopia that had been avidly courted by Washington and Moscow in the period of East–West global rivalry. This collapse of the dictatorships in Mogadishu and Addis Ababa resulted not in stable governments based on popular consent but in anarchical conditions in which public loyalty was to tribe and clan, not to nation.

In May 1991, the 14-year despotism of Mengistu Haile Mariam in Ethiopia was overthrown by an insurgent group dominated by inhabitants of the northern province of Tigre and known as the Ethiopian People's Revolutionary Democratic Front. Following US-sponsored peace talks in London, the front's leader, Meles Senawi, assumed power of the country, which was scarcely a country at all. It was splintered into 64 different ethnic groups that shared nothing but a common determination to resist the authority of the central government in Addis Ababa. In order to placate these dissident factions, Meles granted each a high degree of autonomy within its region, including the all-important prerogative of speaking the local language or dialect.

Autonomy was not enough to satisfy the militants in two of the most powerful ethnic groups in the polyglot country. The Oromos, who constituted approximately 40 per cent of the population, grew increasingly dissatisfied with the new Tigrayan-dominated government and began to consider the alternative of secession. Meanwhile, the inhabitants of the former Italian colony of Eritrea, which had been federated with Ethiopia in 1952, had been fighting for their own separate state since 1971. After the demise of the Mengistu dictatorship, the Eritreans demanded and obtained a referendum on full independence. In May 1993, they voted overwhelmingly to sever their ties with Ethiopia, and a new African state was born.

Though the secession of Ethiopia's northern province on the Red Sea transpired without bloodshed, it set an ominous precedent not only for the other restless ethnic groups in that country but also for dissident minorities elsewhere in Africa. It was the first violation of the Organization of African Unity's solemn dictum that the territorial integrity of the post-colonial states be preserved at all costs lest the principle of self-determination become an agent of political disintegration throughout the continent. Though it was successful in gaining prompt recognition from foreign powers, Africa's newest nation was plagued from its inception by a disruptive religious schism that perfectly illustrated the problem that prompted the OAU's original admonition. The country is equally divided between Christians and Muslims, a combination that (as we shall see) gravely impaired the stability of neighbouring Sudan. Eritrea also experienced continual conflicts with Ethiopia, which had lost its ports on the Red Sea when Eritrea seceded. The resulting friction over the payments Ethiopia was obliged to make for access to these ports, aggravated by a border dispute between the two countries, erupted in May 1998 in an armed conflict that continued into the next century.

Somalia, Ethiopia's perennial antagonist on the Horn of Africa, faced an even more tragic fate after the fall of Mohamed Siad Barre, in 1991. As in Ethiopia, the concept of national identity vanished amid the resurgence of particularist sentiments. Although the Somalis (unlike the Ethiopians) constitute a relatively homogeneous ethnic and religious population, clans and subclans exert the strongest claim on popular loyalty. When Ali Mahdi Mohamed, Siad Barre's successor from a branch of the Hawiye clan, failed to establish his authority over rival clans and subclans, the central administrative structure of the Somali state disintegrated and the fragile economy collapsed. General Mohamed Farah Aideed, from a rival Hawiye subclan, forcefully contested the authority of the central government in Mogadishu, while other local warlords took up arms to defend their turf. In May, the Issaq clan declared an independent 'Somaliland Republic' in the northern portion of the country, which had been a British protectorate before uniting with the former Italian Somaliland to form the post-colonial state in 1960.

Unlike the Eritreans, the Issaqs failed to secure foreign recognition of their statehood. But they faced little interference from what passed for the central government in Mogadishu, which after the overthrow of 'interim president' Ali Mahdi Mohamed in the fall of 1992, proved incapable of exercising even a modicum of authority anywhere in the country. Throughout 1992, Somalia degenerated into a nightmare of starvation, disease, and violence. Over 400,000 Somalis starved to death as 14 private armies jockeyed for power, extorting protection money from relief workers and plundering food shipments from international humanitarian agencies and foreign governments.

In response to the heart-rending news reports and pictures of the widespread suffering caused by this human-engineered famine, the United Nations decided to take action. Prodded by its energetic new secretary-general, Boutros Boutros Ghali, who had taken office in January 1992, the Security Council declared an arms embargo on Somalia in order to stem the flow of weapons to the bickering warlords and established an international peacekeeping force called the United Nations Operation in Somalia (UNOSOM I). Hampered by bureaucratic roadblocks and legal constraints that prevented it from employing force against the warlords and their armed gangs, UNOSOM failed in its mission to protect relief convoys delivering food and medicine to Somalia's starving, disease-ridden population.

At the end of 1992, the Security Council authorized the United States to assume control of a much larger international force empowered to use 'all necessary means' to facilitate relief operations. This 40,000-person task force (UNITAF) of soldiers from more than 20 countries—the first genuinely humanitarian military operation in the history of the United Nations—succeeded in opening up most of the supply routes and reducing the incidence of looting throughout the winter

and spring of 1993. In May of that year, UNITAF turned over its peacekeeping responsibilities to a revamped United Nations force (UNOSOM II) that—unlike its predecessor—was armed with the authority to use force where required. A unit of 4,000 American personnel remained with the UN mission until mounting casualties prompted President Clinton to begin withdrawing US troops in early 1994. Though the incidence of violence and starvation declined markedly after the catastrophic years of 1991–2, sporadic clashes between UN troops and local militias continued as Somalia remained mired in anarchy and unrest. When the UN mandate expired in March 1995 and the last blue-helmeted units withdrew, Somalia was left to its own devices.

The failure of peacekeeping efforts in Somalia had ramifications for many of the countries that

Somali women wait in a food line supervised by Nigerian soldiers, May 1993. © Peter Turnley/ CORBIS.

contributed soldiers to the effort, including the United States and Canada. Graphic television images of the mutilated bodies of US soldiers being dragged through the streets of Mogadishu in 1993 shocked the American public and undermined political support for the UN mission. After its experience in Somalia, the US became increasingly wary of deploying ground troops on peacekeeping missions. For Canada, the Somalia mission shook public confidence in peacekeeping for different reasons. News that members of the Canadian Airborne Regiment had tortured and murdered a Somali teenager in 1993 created a national scandal. An investigation into the killing revealed a larger pattern of serious misconduct among some of the Airborne soldiers serving in Somalia, and the government was pressured into launching a full inquiry. The Canadian government disbanded the Airborne Regiment and took measures to reform the military, but the revelations of the inquiry tainted Canada's image as a leader in international peacekeeping.

While peacekeepers struggled to restore order in clan-divided Somalia, another country of Northeastern Africa was being plagued by acute ethnic violence. In Sudan, the military regime of General Omar Hassan Ahmed al-Bashir, which had seized power in the summer of 1989, came under the domination of a fundamentalist Muslim movement called the National Islamic Front. The Muslim ruling elite from the northern part of the country intensified a long-standing campaign to apply the Islamic legal system (the *Sharia*) to the predominantly Christian south. Southern rebels in the Sudan People's Liberation Army (SPLA), which had been resisting the application of Islamic law to their region since the early 1980s, stepped up their attacks against the military forces of the regime in Khartoum. The civil war between rebel contingents from the Christian south (supported by predominantly Christian Ethiopia) and government forces from the Muslim north (backed by the Islamist regime in Iran as well as the secular Arab states of Iraq and Libya) raged throughout the 1990s, interrupted by periodic ceasefires.

The struggle in Sudan was complicated by the outbreak of violence among various rival factions within the SPLA. In May 1993, the government placated the major rebel groups by finally agreeing to exempt the southern Christians from the application of the *Sharia*. But the continuing tension in Sudan demonstrated that religion must be added to ethnicity, clan loyalty, and regional identity as potential threats to national unity and state sovereignty in Africa. The internal struggle acquired an international significance when the Sudanese government allegedly began to sponsor terrorist acts on behalf of Islamism abroad, including an assassination attempt against Egyptian President Hosni Mubarak (who had cracked down on radical Islamists in his own country) while he was in Addis Ababa for the OAU summit meeting in June 1995. Egypt accused Sudan of establishing training camps for radical Islamic militants, including thousands of battle-seasoned veterans from Afghanistan, while the United States took the lead in denouncing the Sudanese government's alleged support for international terrorism. Washington imposed economic sanctions against Khartoum in November 1997 and furnished military aid to Uganda, Eritrea, and Ethiopia, three countries that shared a border with Sudan and were strongly opposed to its radical Islamist government.

In Angola, the difficulty of terminating the country's civil war revealed that the end of intervention by the superpowers and their partners did not guarantee a return to regional stability in Africa. Foreign involvement in the bitter conflict dividing the former Portuguese colony had ceased in the late 1980s with the simultaneous withdrawal of South African forces backing the anti-communist rebel faction and Cuban troops assisting the self-proclaimed Marxist government. Intensive negotiations had produced a historic peace agreement signed in 1991 in Bicesse, Portugal, by Jonas Savimbi of UNITA (the Ovimbundu-dominated rebel movement) and Angolan President José Eduardo dos Santos of the ruling MPLA (representing the non-Ovimbundu majority).

The Bicesse Accord provided for a ceasefire leading up to the country's first free elections, to be held in the autumn of 1992 under the supervision of United Nations personnel. After the two factions agreed to form a coalition government and combine their military forces in a joint national army, the elections were held on schedule at the end of September with over 90 per cent of eligible voters participating. The MPLA, which had jettisoned its Marxist program and cultivated cordial relations with the West after the departure of its Cuban mercenaries and Soviet advisers, won 54 per cent of the vote compared to UNITA's 34 per cent.

Refusing to accept the electoral results, Savimbi withdrew his troops from the integrated national army and resumed his guerrilla warfare against the MPLA. Within a few months, UNITA had regained control of more than two-thirds of the country. After the United States cut off all subsidies to UNITA and recognized the legally elected Angolan government, Savimbi was forced to finance his military effort with illegal diamond-mining operations in the northern regions of Angola that were under UNITA control. He smuggled the precious stones to foreign customers through neighbouring Zaire with the co-operation of Zairean President Mobutu Sese Seko, who had served as the main conduit for US aid to UNITA before the peace agreement.

On-again, off-again peace talks and truces amid a continuing military stalemate characterized the volatile situation in Angola. The United Nations exerted pressure on UNITA to terminate its insurgency and abide by the peace accords. In the fall of 1994, a new UN-brokered power-sharing agreement was finally reached. The Lusaka Accords called for a ceasefire, the disarmament of the UNITA rebels, and the creation of a national army composed of soldiers from both sides. As we shall see, the hopes that the 19-year civil war would come to an end were premature.

The other former Portuguese colony that had been struggling with civil war and superpower intervention since the mid-1970s was Mozambique, where the reconciliation between former enemies was also a long and difficult process, though in this case, one that was ultimately

successful. In October 1992, Mozambiquan President Joaquim Alberto Chissano and Afonso Dhlakama, head of the Mozambique National Resistance (RENAMO) rebel movement, signed a peace accord in Rome. The ceasefire in the long civil war held, in spite of occasional violations, and the two sides recorded substantial progress in negotiations over political power sharing, mutual disarmament, and the drafting of electoral law. In December the United Nations Security Council established a 7,500-person peacekeeping mission designated as the United Nations Operations in Mozambique (ONUMOZ) to monitor the demobilization and amalgamation of the two armies. A joint defence force equally divided between former government and RENAMO soldiers began operation in the first half of 1994. For the rest of the decade, an uneasy truce in this long and bitter civil conflict brought a modicum of normality to this impoverished, devastated land.

The most tragic manifestation of interethnic tension in Africa was the resumption of strife between the Tutsi and Hutu in Rwanda. After the country gained independence in 1962, periodic insurrections against the Tutsi ruling elite by the disenfranchised Hutu majority resulted in the systematic annihilation of hundreds of thousands of innocent civilians in both groups. During the spring and summer of 1994, the military forces of the Rwandan Hutu massacred at least 800,000 Tutsis and moderate Hutus in a campaign of genocide. When the Tutsi-controlled Rwandan Patriotic Front, led by Paul Kagame, gained the upper hand in the conflict, some 1.7 million diseased and destitute Hutu fled to refugee camps in neighbouring Zaire and several thousand more to Tanzania. Vigorous efforts by the United Nations High Commission for Refugees to repatriate the Rwandan Hutu were hampered by their fear of revenge at the hands of the surviving Tutsi population, despite the Rwandan government's solemn assurances of protection for the innocent and fair judicial proceedings for those accused of genocide.

The political crises that culminated in the Rwandan genocide could be seen in equal measure throughout Central Africa. Civil and interstate conflict spread through the region during the second half of the 1990s. The first of these was prompted by the disintegration of Mobutu Sese Seko's corrupt autocracy in Zaire. In 1991, Mobutu was persuaded by the United States, France, Belgium, and other foreign supporters to call a national conference to draft a democratic constitution and to form a coalition government with the opposition leader, Etienne Tshisekedi, as prime minister. In April 1992, after dismissing his rival in a bid to regain absolute authority, Mobutu again bowed to foreign pressure to reconvene the national conference. This time, the opposition-dominated institution attempted to exercise sovereignty by reinstating Tshisekedi as head of government, asserting supreme legislative authority under the new title High Council of the Republic (HCR), and drafting an interim constitution that reduced Mobutu's position to a ceremonial one. Amid inflation raging at an annual rate of 1,000 per cent, widespread rioting and looting by soldiers unwilling to receive monthly salaries in the worthless national currency, and interventions by French and Belgian paratroop units landing to protect their countries' nationals, Mobutu, then ill with cancer, gradually lost his iron grip.

In May 1997, Laurent Kabila's Alliance of the Democratic Forces for the Liberation of Congo-Zaire finally ousted the 32-year-old dictatorship in Zaire and promptly renamed the country the Democratic Republic of the Congo (not to be confused with the neighbouring Republic of the Congo). Once in power, Kabila's army, which had received contributions of troops and military advice from Rwanda during its successful offensive against Mobutu's security forces, repaid its Rwandan Tutsi supporters by attacking the Rwandan Hutu who had sought refuge in eastern Zaire/Congo rather than risk retribution for the 1994 genocide by returning to their homeland. During this period Kabila managed to receive continued support from the United States, which had supported the insurrection against Mobutu once the Congolese leader had lost his usefulness

as a bastion of anti-communism in Central Africa after the end of the Cold War. Though expressing stern disapproval of the violence against the Hutu, Washington was careful to maintain cordial relations with the new regime in Kinshasa, which controlled an abundant supply of copper, cobalt, gold, and diamonds.

In the summer of 1998, an abrupt policy change executed by Kabila plunged the Democratic Republic of the Congo into a war that eventually drew in seven of its neighbours. The multilateral conflict reflected the increasing willingness of African states to violate national borders in the defence of their vital interests. Kabila's first policy shift involved suspending his campaign in the eastern part of the country against the Hutu refugees, whom his Rwandan allies regarded as a potential threat to the security of their Tutsi-dominated state. The new Congolese president then dismissed most of the Rwandan Tutsi military advisers who had come to Kinshasa to help reorganize the Congolese army. Taking advantage of a mutiny among Congolese military units and the emergence of an insurgent movement in the eastern region, Rwanda and Uganda (which also feared incursions from the Hutu refugee camps) sent military forces into the Congo in an all-out bid to topple Kabila's government. Angola, Namibia, and Zimbabwe rallied to Kabila's support from the south, while Chad and Sudan lent assistance to the embattled Congolese government from the north. Efforts by the United States, France, and Belgium to organize peace talks came to nought.

Soon after Kabila had toppled Mobutu in Zaire/Congo, a civil war erupted in the neighbouring Republic of the Congo (or Congo-Brazzaville) between the legally elected government of President Pascal Lissouba and forces loyal to former president Denis Nguesso. In October 1997, military forces from the Angolan enclave of Cabinda poured into Congo-Brazzaville to support Nguesso's rebel forces, which succeeded in overthrowing Lissouba and re-installing Nguesso. The Angolan government of President José Eduardo dos Santos intervened in

Congo-Brazzaville as part of its own campaign against the Angolan rebel movement UNITA, which had been conducting an insurgency since the mid-1970s. While in power, Lissouba had permitted UNITA to use Congo-Brazzaville as a base of operations and a source of weapons and military supplies, which Savimbi purchased with profits from his diamond sales.

The Angolan-backed overthrow of Lissouba and the fall of Mobutu (who had allowed UNITA forces access to Congo-Brazzaville across Zaire's territory) strengthened dos Santos's position against UNITA. Under the Lusaka Accords of 1994, Savimbi had pledged to demobilize his armed forces and convert his guerrilla movement into a political party by February 1998. This deadline passed without any evidence of demobilization, while harsh criticism of UNITA from Portugal and the United States had no effect. The spreading civil unrest in the two Congos and Angola generated acute concern in the industrial world because of the threat to the productive oil fields in Angola's northern region and its Cabinda enclave as well as to the French-owned Gulf-Aquitaine's huge installation in Congo-Brazzaville's Pointe Noire.

The ferocious tribal conflict between Hutu and Tutsi in Rwanda in 1994 was re-enacted in the small neighbouring country of Burundi, where (as in Rwanda) the Hutu constituted the majority while the Tutsi controlled the military and the government. In 1993, Melchior Ndadaye became Burundi's first Hutu president after a free and fair election, only to be overthrown and executed a few months later by a dissident faction of the Tutsi-dominated army. Though the coup failed, it unleashed a wave of Hutu attacks against Tutsis that forced thousands of refugees to seek asylum in Rwanda, Zaire, and Tanzania while plunging the little country into political and economic chaos. In the summer of 1996, a group of Tutsi officers finally succeeded in toppling the Hutu president, Sylvestre Ntibantunganya, and later organized a campaign to destroy the political power of the Hutu by forcibly resettling them in rural areas. As in Rwanda, this African variant of genocide and ethnic cleansing transpired amid an attitude of relative indifference on the part of the international community.

NIGERIA: WEST AFRICA'S STABILIZING FORCE

With the spread of conflict in Africa during the 1990s many looked to Nigeria—West Africa's wealthiest and most powerful country, with a quarter of the continent's population—as a nation with the potential to enforce regional stability. After nine years of military rule, Nigeria took what seemed to be a major step toward democratization by conducting free and fair presidential elections in June 1993. But when the popular opposition leader, Chief Moshood K.O. Abiola from western Nigeria, appeared to have won at the polls, President Ibrahim Babangida, the army general representing the northern military elite that had long dominated the country's political system, declared the election null and void on the grounds of voting irregularities. A nationwide protest movement, reinforced by American and British pressure, forced General Babangida to step down. After a brief transitional period, power was assumed by his former defence minister and protégé, General Sani Abacha. This development continued the pattern of Nigerian political behaviour since 1965, when the military seized power five years after independence and continued to rule either directly or through civilian surrogates for the next three decades.

Though Nigeria's vast oil reserves afforded the potential for substantial economic development, the country suffered a set of disadvantages that prevented it from fulfilling its great promise. Three of these disadvantages proved particularly difficult to overcome: the hodgepodge of some 250 ethnic groups inhibiting the development of national loyalties; the endemic political corruption flowing from the hope of instant wealth from oil sales; and the decline in oil revenues (which account for over 90 per cent of Nigeria's export earnings) caused by the low world price for crude after the dramatic increases of the 1970s. By the mid-1990s, this oil-rich country had defaulted on most of its foreign debt and was obliged to adopt the usual strict conditions of economic liberalization in exchange for emergency loans from the IMF and the World Bank.

In June 1998, General Abacha died and was replaced by General Abdusalam Abubakar, who immediately took steps to dismantle the edifice of authoritarian military rule by allowing political parties to operate and by freeing hundreds of political prisoners. The presidential election of February 1999 was won by the reform-minded General Olusegun Obasanjo, a former president who held the distinction of being the only Nigerian military leader to have voluntarily relinquished power to a civilian successor. Even so, the military continued to exercise strong influence on the government, raising questions about the future of democracy in this important African country.

Nigeria possessed the largest, best-equipped army in West Africa, which enabled it to serve as the principal force for regional stability in the 1990s. Nigerian military units dominated the Economic Community of West African States Ceasefire Monitoring Group (ECOMOG), the peacekeeping force that had been dispatched to Liberia in 1990 by the Economic Community of West African States (ECOWAS). ECOMOG had originally intervened in Liberia to prevent the insurgent leader Charles Taylor (who represented the Gao and Mano ethnic groups) from seizing power after the murder in 1990 of President Samuel Doe (whose government was dominated by the Krahns).

For the next seven years a bloody civil war destroyed the economy and caused more than 150,000 deaths as the contending factions fought to a stalemate before finally agreeing to a ceasefire. Elections conducted under ECOMOG's supervision in July 1997 brought to power, through democratic means, the Patriotic National Front of Liberia of Charles Taylor, the very man whose insurgency had caused the civil war and precipitated the ECOMOG intervention in the first place. Nigerian-dominated ECOMOG units remained in Liberia not only to supervise the disarmament and demobilization of the various armed factions operating

throughout the devastated country but also (many observers suspected) to look after Nigeria's strategic and economic interests in Liberia.

The next opportunity for Nigeria to expand its regional influence occurred in Sierra Leone, where a dissident military faction called the Armed Forces Revolutionary Council had joined with Revolutionary United Front rebels to overthrow the government of President Ahmed Tejan Kabbah in May 1997. In February 1998, Nigerian military units were dispatched to the small West African country, where they promptly expelled the rebel forces from the capital and reinstalled the civilian government. A month later, the 16 member states of ECOWAS endorsed the unilateral Nigerian operation in Sierra Leone and voted to transform its Nigerian-dominated military wing ECOMOG into a permanent West African security organization.

The Nigerian military government's intervention in Liberia and Sierra Leone on behalf of democratic rule smacked of hypocrisy in light of its refusal to tolerate democracy at home, which had prompted harsh criticism from Western countries and its expulsion from the Commonwealth in 1995. However, its willingness to employ military force to cope with instability in neighbouring countries, together with its dominant position in ECOWAS and ECOMOG, enhanced Nigeria's position as the regional hegemon in West Africa and enabled it to fend off the challenge of those francophone states in the region that had traditionally opposed its ambitions. By the end of the twentieth century it seemed to be emerging as the only African power capable of assuming peacekeeping functions on an increasingly volatile and violent continent.

PROGRESS TOWARDS POWER SHARING AND MULTIPARTY DEMOCRACY

The 1990s in Africa were marked by the persistence of entrenched autocracies, which managed to remain in power through the suppression of opposition parties or the blatant manipulation of the electoral process in countries such as Cameroon, the Central African Republic, Congo,

Guinea, and Togo. Military juntas took power in Gambia in 1994 and in Niger in 1996. In East Africa the governments of Uganda, Kenya, and Tanzania, though paying lip service to the principle of multiparty democracy in order to satisfy donor countries, remained one-party states under authoritarian ruling elites. The persistence of these authoritarian political structures in Africa paradoxically coincided with the revival of tribal and clan loyalties that cut across national frontiers and weakened the power of central governments. The Organization of African Unity, the traditional defender of the sanctity of borders that had been inherited from the colonial era, lost its status as a symbol of interstate co-operation amid these trends toward national disintegration.

Despite this situation, progress toward multiparty democracy was evident in a few African states. Zambia's Kenneth Kaunda and Benin's Mathieu Kerekou yielded to pressure from external aid donors and domestic public opinion to allow free elections, and both willingly handed over power to the leaders of victorious opposition parties. Hastings Banda, the long-time autocrat in Malawi, was peacefully driven into opposition. Robert Mugabe of Zimbabwe, who had once extolled the virtues of a one-party state, successfully co-opted his rival Joshua Nkomo by installing him in the vice-presidency. In the Ivory Coast, the death in December 1993 of President Félix Houphouët-Boigny, who had ruled the former French colony as a benevolent despot since its independence in 1960, resulted in multiparty elections.

The most dramatic instance of democratization and political power sharing on the continent during the 1990s occurred in the Republic of South Africa, where the white-only government of F.W. de Klerk that took office in 1989 began to initiate a number of political reforms designed to promote racial reconciliation in the land of apartheid. De Klerk surprised international observers by abolishing the racial segregation of beaches, parks, and libraries and by permitting mass demonstrations by dissidents. In February 1990, the government legalized the African National Congress (ANC) and released the ANC's deputy leader, Nelson Mandela,

after 27 years in prison. The ANC, deprived of its sanctuaries in Angola and its military aid from the Soviet Union (following Mikhail Gorbachev's decision to terminate support for resistance movements in the developing world), was prepared to de-emphasize its commitment to revolutionary violence in favour of negotiations.

In 1991, the de Klerk government took several bold steps toward the pursuit of a dialogue with the ANC (represented by Mandela, who was elected president in July of that year) concerning political power sharing with the black majority. In December, delegations representing all the major black and white political factions met in Johannesburg at the Convention for a Democratic South Africa (CODESA) to discuss means of implementing the general goals of multiracial adult suffrage and multiparty democracy that had already been embraced by most of the parties. Faced with bitter opposition from the Conservative Party and the neo-Nazi Afrikaner Resistance Movement on his extreme right, de Klerk submitted his policy to the white citizens of South Africa in the form of a referendum accompanied by his vow to resign if it were rejected. In March 1992, two-thirds of the white voters endorsed the prime minister's policy of resuming negotiations with the ANC, thereby sealing the fate of the white minority's political monopoly. In the meantime, the abolition of the last vestiges of apartheid—for example, the racially determined residency requirement and the obligation of birth registry by race—led to the removal of most of the international sanctions that had been imposed on South Africa in the mid-1980s.

The multiracial CODESA negotiations for an interim constitution and transitional government temporarily broke down in early 1992 amid mutual recrimination but were relaunched in April 1993, and representatives of 21 political groups bargained intensively for the remainder of the year. In November, the negotiators formally adopted an interim constitution for the country pending the drafting of a permanent one in 1999. The interim constitution abolished the pseudo-independent black homelands and established a democratically elected National Assembly, which would choose the president and function both as a legislature and a constituent assembly empowered to draft the permanent constitution. In the meantime, the first multiracial national elections with universal adult suffrage were scheduled for April 1994.

Vigorous opposition to the negotiating process came from the white Afrikaner extremist movement, which attacked several participants in the multiparty negotiations. At the same time, much more ominous rumblings of discontent were emanating from Chief Mangosuthu Buthelezi's Inkatha Freedom Party, which claimed to represent the Zulu population of the KwaZulu-Natal region on the east coast. Inkatha had forged links with the Afrikaner extremists on the basis of a common hostility to Mandela and his program. The party obtained covert subsidies and training from dissident members of the South African security service who opposed de Klerk's policy of racial reconciliation, and waged a violent campaign against ANC supporters in Natal. As the movement toward a settlement gathered momentum, Buthelezi threatened to withdraw the predominantly Zulu lands from the proposed new South African state that would be controlled by an ANC dominated by officials from the Xhosa tribe.

In the end, both of these threats to a peaceful rapprochement dissipated. Afrikaner extremism was blunted with vague promises to study the feasibility of carving a 'white homeland' out of the new South Africa (though it was unclear where such an entity would be situated without violating

ANC leader Nelson Mandela casts his vote in the first free elections in post-apartheid South Africa.
© CSI Productions/Alamy.

the rights of the black majority). And after making substantial inroads into Buthelezi's base of support among his fellow Zulus, the ANC succeeded in co-opting the recalcitrant Zulu leader with concessions of a substantial degree of regional autonomy to KwaZulu-Natal. The elections transpired peacefully and on schedule at the end of April 1994. To no one's surprise, the ANC won a sizable majority (though short of the 75 per cent that would have enabled it to make unilateral changes in the country's constitution). Control of the state was transferred by scrupulously legal means from the white ruling elite that had reigned unchecked for almost three-and-a-half centuries to the representatives of the formerly disenfranchised black majority. Former revolutionary Mandela assumed the presidency of the new multiracial, democratic state, with de Klerk serving as deputy president and Buthelezi as minister of home affairs. Mandela and de Klerk subsequently shared the Nobel Peace Prize for their successful resolution of independent Africa's longest and most intractable conflict.

From Mandela to Mbeki

The inauguration of Nelson Mandela, in 1994, seemed to usher in a new era of growth and prosperity for South Africa. Shortly after being sworn into office, Mandela laid out an ambitious program of reforms to address the most serious consequences of the apartheid era. Within its first 100 days in office, the new government pledged to address systemic barriers to education, healthcare, housing, and clean water. Efforts would be made to restore services to the townships, and public works programs would provide training and jobs for unemployed youth. Particular attention was to be paid to education because '[e]verywhere we must reinculcate the culture of learning and of teaching and make it possible for this culture to thrive.' Finally, Mandela pledged to ensure that the security forces and the criminal justice system would operate in a democratic, non-racist, and non-sexist manner. While no one would have anticipated that these changes would take place over night, South Africa seemed to be making genuine progress towards these goals during his tenure.

In June 1999 Mandela retired from office, handing power to Thabo Mbeki, who began to move South Africa away from the semi-socialist doctrines of the ANC and towards a more liberal, market-oriented economic focus. International commentators saw this as a positive step, necessary to link South Africa to the world economy; critics, however, decried the resulting lack of progress in reducing unemployment (which remained over 20 per cent in 2008) and economic inequalities. Statistics from 2007 revealed that South Africa was home to the greatest gap between rich and poor in the world, and even Archbishop Desmond Tutu criticized Mbeki for creating policies which benefited only a small black elite—just as the apartheid leaders of the past had enriched themselves at the cost of the masses.

In the years leading up to Mbeki's resignation, in 2008, accusations of corruption and fraud were increasingly common. Critics pointed to the continuation of high crime rates in South Africa, a charge Mbeki vehemently denied, even when corroborated by statistics from his own police forces. He argued that claims regarding an increase in violence against women were unfounded and motivated by lingering racism. He was also accused of rejecting scientific evidence regarding HIV/AIDS and of delaying access to anti-retroviral drugs, thereby worsening the epidemic in his country (5.5 million South Africans are HIV-positive). In 2002, Mandela personally criticized Mbeki's stance on this issue; three years later, in an attempt to remove the veil of shame and secrecy regarding the disease, he took the unprecedented step of announcing that one of his sons had died of AIDS. Despite all of these problems, the ANC received 65.9 per cent of the vote in April 2009 elections, an indicator of the enormous reservoir of support, which the party still retains.

The prospects for peace, prosperity, and security in South Africa seemed brighter in 1994 than ever before, as whites, blacks, and people of mixed heritage optimistically enlisted in this bold experiment in multiracial harmony. A striking symbol of the new rapport between groups that had fought bitterly for decades was the plan to combine the formerly white-controlled army (the South African Defence Force) and the military wing of the African National Congress (Umkhontowe Sizwe) into a new South African National Defence Force. The 1994 agreement that terminated white rule was designed to encourage the white minority, especially businesspeople and farmers, to remain in South Africa rather than follow the precedent of white minorities in the rest of the continent by fleeing to Europe with their valuable skills and portable financial assets. While there was some white emigration and capital flight, caused in part by an increase in violent crime and a steep slump in the economy during the second half of the decade, Mandela's conciliatory policies produced a remarkable degree of racial harmony in the former bastion of apartheid. Though some neighbouring countries feared an era of economic domination by South Africa, many observers looked forward to its adopting a leadership role in its region.

DEVELOPMENTS IN NORTH AFRICA

In the early 1990s, while Iran began to tailor the rigid Islamic orthodoxy inherited from the Khomeini era to the practical requirements of a modern state aspiring to regional supremacy and economic modernization, the Arab societies along the Mediterranean shore of Africa experienced an explosive upsurge of Islamic violence with potentially significant consequences for that region's future stability. All across North Africa, unemployed or underpaid young people who faced bleak economic futures proved susceptible to the allure of Islamic protest movements that denounced the corruption and culturally decadent practices of the secular regimes that had held power for the entire post-colonial period. If

there is any truth to Marx's definition of religion as the opiate of the people, then the Maghreb in the first half of the 1990s represented a perfect case study of a messianic religious movement furnishing comfort to destitute populations without hope of improvement and resentful of the political authorities held responsible for their plight.

The phenomenon began in Algeria, the former French possession in North Africa that had been ruled by a one-party, secular socialist regime since independence in 1962. In 1989, President Chadli Bendjedid launched a bold reform program designed to soften the autocratic structure of the Algerian state in the hope of promoting solutions to the country's acute economic difficulties. One of the early results of this internal liberalization was the emergence of political opposition groups that challenged the political authority of the National Liberation Front (widely known by its French acronym, FLN), which had engineered the successful rebellion against the French colonial system and controlled the state apparatus after independence.

The most popular of those dissident organizations was the Islamic Salvation Front (FIS), which denounced the secular policies of the government in Algiers and demanded the establishment of a state based on orthodox Islamic principles as a means to social as well as spiritual salvation. After recording impressive political gains in the municipal elections of June 1990, the FIS routed the FLN in the first round of national legislative elections in December 1991 and appeared poised to assume power as anti-government demonstrations swept the country. But in January 1992, Bendjedid abruptly resigned, making way for a government dominated by high-ranking military officers, who proceeded to declare martial law, cancel the second round of elections, ban the FIS, and arrest its leaders.

The years following Bendjedid's resignation were marked by violent clashes between the army, which took direct control of the Algerian state in January 1994, and the increasingly vociferous advocates of the potent new political force of 'Islamism'. In 1995, former general Lamine

Zeroual was elected president in ostensibly free elections, but he proceeded to rule in close consultation with the officer corps and its civilian allies. In the meantime, a group of armed Islamist groups had responded to the cancellation of elections by inaugurating a campaign of terror that included kidnapping, bombing, murder, and mutilation carried out against hundreds of innocent civilians. Compounding Algeria's problems was a severe economic crisis, caused by an overdependence on oil as a source of export earnings during a decade of declining world petroleum prices, which forced the country to reschedule its foreign debt and appeal for a massive influx of loans from the International Monetary Fund and the World Bank.

Secular regimes elsewhere in North Africa applauded the Algerian government's crackdown on the FIS and took steps to curb their own Islamist opposition. Egyptian President Hosni Mubarek waged a relentless campaign against the Muslim Brotherhood, which had survived earlier attempts by Nasser and Sadat to eradicate it as a political force. The governments of Tunisia (a secular one-party state like Algeria) and Morocco (a conservative monarchy) severely restricted the activities of Islamist groups in their respective countries in the hope of inoculating themselves against 'the Algerian disease'. Western Europe faced something of a dilemma as it observed the mounting tension between secular Arab governments and their Islamist opponents. On the one hand, it was difficult for Western countries promoting the spread of democratic principles and practices to support the repressive methods used by the embattled regimes in the Maghreb to stifle Islamic dissent. On the other hand, European leaders worried about a massive trans-Mediterranean exodus of refugees from an Islamicized North Africa that would severely strain their social welfare systems and fan the already smouldering fires of domestic racism.

The Islamist challenge did not prevent the countries of Africa north of the Sahara from achieving notable progress toward greater regional stability and co-operation after a tumultuous decade. One of the two sources of conflict in North Africa during the 1980s was the civil war in Chad, involving a strong Muslim secessionist movement in the north (supported by neighbouring Libya) and the central government (backed by France, the former colonial power). At the end of the decade, Muammar al-Qaddafi, who at one point had asserted territorial claims to the northern part of Chad, withdrew his military forces from the territory, and France reduced its support for the central government. The decrease of foreign involvement in the affair allowed the civil war to dwindle to a low-intensity conflict punctuated by sporadic clashes between the two factions. At the same time, Libya gained a measure of international respect for its hands-off policy towards its vulnerable southern neighbour.

The other regional conflict involved Morocco's annexation of the former Spanish Sahara, which had been abandoned by Spain (and renamed Western Sahara) in the mid-1970s. Throughout the 1980s Morocco's King Hassan laboured in vain to obtain recognition of this annexation from the neighbouring countries. In the face of bitter opposition led by Algeria, the Moroccan monarch finally agreed to consult the indigenous population of the phosphate-rich territory to determine their wishes. The United Nations dispatched a task force to the Western Sahara in 1991 to lay the groundwork for an eventual referendum. But Morocco refused to deal with the indigious national liberation movement Polisario, which resumed its low-intensity guerilla war against the Moroccan forces.

While Rabat and Algiers were struggling to reach a peaceful solution to their dispute in the Western Sahara, all of the countries in the Maghreb were exploring ways to coordinate their economic activities in the face of Europe's rapid progress toward a single market in 1993. The post-colonial African states had failed to make any headway toward the ambitious goal of pan-African economic integration, and even more modest proposals for economic co-operation at the subregional level had proved elusive. The five states of North Africa finally took a significant step in that direction in 1991, when they established a subregional organization called the Arab Maghreb Union. Two years later they worked out the rudiments of an institutional apparatus, including a permanent secretariat and a development bank, and engaged in far-reaching discussions about the possibility of creating a customs union by 1995. The bitter, long-standing rivalry between Morocco and Algeria, which could revive if the proposed referendum on the future of Western Sahara does not transpire according to plan (disputes about how and when such a referendum would occur have lasted into the twenty-first century), represents a potential obstacle to closer integration in the Maghreb. The transformation of any of the five states, peacefully or otherwise, into a radical Islamic republic like Sudan would also be likely to generate extreme tension in neighbouring countries and undermine these efforts at regional co-operation.

AFRICA: INDEPENDENT OR ALONE?

The political events in Europe at the close of the Cold War had a critical impact on Africa. As Gorbachev's Soviet Union sharply curtailed its foreign aid programs to the Third World at the end of the 1980s, the United States and Western Europe began to receive urgent requests from the newly liberated states of Eastern Europe for credits, investment, and aid for their struggling economies. The preoccupation with promoting democracy and market-based economies in the former Soviet satellites and republics inevitably diverted Western attention from Africa's desperate economic plight. Already burdened with an enormous foreign debt, African countries were able to attract very little new commercial lending. Since banks in the developed world tended to shun the impoverished countries of the continent as poor credit risks, over 90 per cent of Africa's foreign loans derived from foreign governments or multinational lending agencies such as the IMF and the World Bank. International investors also hesitated to sink their funds into African projects. After the mid-1980s, direct private investment declined in Africa while

tripling in Latin America and increasing fivefold in East Asia. The result of this shift in foreign lending and investment has been Africa's virtual absence from the emerging global trading system. By the mid-1990s, the continent accounted for a paltry 2 per cent of total world trade.

The one notable aberration in this trend was the West African nation of Ghana, which experienced a remarkable economic rebirth after decades of stagnation and destitution. In 1957, Ghana became one of the first African nations to gain independence, under the leadership of Kwame Nkrumah. He instituted a brand of state socialism involving government control of the traditional industries of cocoa farming and gold and diamond mining combined with tariff protectionism that effectively insulated the Ghanaian economy from the global trading system. During the mid-1980s, Ghanaian President Jerry J. Rawlings abandoned the statist legacy of the Nkrumah years in favour of a free market strategy of economic development similar to that pursued by the newly industrializing countries of East Asia and, later, of Latin America. By the middle of the 1990s, the government had sold off most of the nationalized companies that had traditionally dominated the economy. Ghana opened the door to foreign investment and basked in a decade-long average annual growth rate of 5 per cent.

Ghana's extraordinary record predictably attracted the interest of major international corporations that had shown little enthusiasm for commitments elsewhere on the continent, while making Ghana the darling of the stone-faced, tight-fisted officials of the IMF and the World Bank responsible for distributing development loans to Third World countries. But to most observers, Ghana's experience of market-based growth seemed the conspicuous exception that proved the general rule that Africa was a continent mired in economic backwardness, cut off from the emerging international trading system that many previously underdeveloped countries in Asia and Latin America had avidly joined.

In sum, the end of the Cold War proved to be a mixed blessing for Africa. On the one hand, it reduced the amount of external interference in the affairs of the continent. On the other, the decline in Africa's strategic importance to the Western bloc brought a return of the traditional attitude of relative indifference that had characterized the policies of the United States and most European countries before the East–West rivalry spilled into Africa in the mid-1970s. The tragedies in Somalia and Rwanda in the 1990s inspired an outpouring of humanitarian assistance from the developed world and a flurry of activity in the United Nations. However, the absence of significant economic or strategic interests in the region on the part of the world's major powers limited the scope of that involvement, particularly in a period of budget cutting and preoccupation with domestic problems. The United States, France, and Britain all developed programs to train and equip African military forces to serve in peacekeeping operations in order to avoid being drawn into African conflicts, in which their own vital interests were not at stake. These external powers applauded the peacekeeping operations of Nigeria and ECOMOG in West Africa, but they stopped short of providing financial support to back up their rhetoric.

The developed country that had taken the most active role in African affairs since independence was France. The principal donor of foreign aid to the continent, it did not hesitate to wield economic influence and military power on behalf of its interests and those of its African clients. Yet even France began to loosen its historically intimate ties to the continent during the 1990s. It reduced its military involvement in Africa once the civil war in Chad wound down in 1990. Its humanitarian interventions in the civil conflicts in Somalia (under UN auspices) and Rwanda (with UN approval) involved small numbers of troops and were of limited duration. While garrisons of the Foreign Legion remained in half-a-dozen African countries as tangible symbols of Paris's commitment to its francophone clients on the continent, the end of the Cold War and the mounting preoccupation with European economic integration pushed African security concerns into the background. In December 1997, France announced plans to cut by almost 40 per cent the size of its armed forces stationed in its former African colonies and to close several French military bases by the end of the century.

France also took steps to loosen the privileged economic links that it had continued to enjoy with its former possessions in West Africa. The cornerstone of this special relationship was the complex set of monetary arrangements governing the so-called African Financial Community (CFA). By guaranteeing a fixed parity of 1 French franc to 50 CFA francs, Paris ensured that the 14 countries in the franc zone[1] would enjoy the privilege of possessing Africa's only readily convertible currencies. While this commitment to maintain the fixed parity of the CFA franc cost the French treasury several billion dollars a year, it served to cement France's ties to its former African empire and yielded substantial economic advantages to the former colonial power. French industry enjoyed preferential access to African commodities, especially oil and minerals; French export firms enjoyed guaranteed markets for their manufactured products; and French investors found lucrative outlets for their savings. The major benefit for the African countries was the monetary discipline imposed on them, which resulted in lower inflation and more sustained growth than in the rest of Africa during the first two decades after independence.

The cozy relationship between France and its former colonies in Sub-Saharan Africa began to fray in the mid-1980s as the economies of the CFA countries declined and the French government focused its attention on Europe. Other Western nations and international financial institutions had criticized France's subsidy to the franc zone countries as a vehicle for French financial influence that discriminated against foreign competitors and inhibited West African economic growth by encouraging waste and inefficiency. France finally bowed to this foreign pressure in January 1994 by abruptly cutting the African franc's parity value from 50:1 to 100:1. Though the IMF and the World Bank confidently predicted that the long-overdue devaluation would encourage new foreign investment and stimulate exports in francophone Africa, the short-term consequences were exceedingly painful for many of the CFA countries. The instantaneous doubling of domestic prices combined with government-imposed wage freezes led to widespread labour unrest and acute popular discontent as peoples' ability to purchase food, medicine, and other essential goods was reduced. What appeared to some observers as the moderation of France's regional ambitions in Africa left that continent (for better or for worse) more isolated and alone at the end of the twentieth century than it had ever been.

SUMMARY

As in all other parts of the world, the end of the Cold War influenced developments in Africa in a number of important ways. The end of the East–West rivalry made it possible to settle those conflicts in which the two superpowers had been indirectly involved since the mid-1970s. The disappearance of the Soviet threat also enabled Western nations to apply greater pressure on friendly regimes in Africa to reform autocratic political systems that they had previously tolerated in the interests of combating communism. However, the end of the ideological antagonism between Moscow and Washington and their respective regional clients brought neither peace nor prosperity to Africa. Instead, an eruption of ethnic and religious violence throughout the 1990s fuelled wars that killed hundreds of thousands of people and produced millions of refugees.

Serious economic problems in Africa also undermined the goals of stability and democratization that had seemed attainable during the 1980s. The heavy burden of international indebtedness, the desperate need for foreign investment, and disadvantageous terms of trade continued to inhibit Africa's economic development. Most of these problems were largely ignored in the West, though an outbreak of famine in Ethiopia in 1984–7 galvanized public opinion to support aid projects. The prosperous nations of the industrialized West soon lost interest in courting African regimes with aid programs when the collapse of the Communist bloc removed the need for foreign allies in the East–West struggle. The end of apartheid in South Africa and the election of Nelson Mandela as president raised great hopes for progress in 1994. But in that same year the genocide perpetrated in Rwanda showed the tragic depths of the continent's problems. The failure of the United Nations mission in Somalia in the mid-1990s significantly increased the reluctance of Western powers to intervene in Africa.

NOTES

1. Benin, Burkina Faso, Cameroon, Central African Republic, Chad, Congo, the Comoros, Gabon, Ivory Coast, Mali, Niger, Senegal, and Togo are the former French colonies in the franc zone. Equatorial Guinea, a former Spanish colony, joined in 1985.

QUESTIONS FOR CRITICAL THOUGHT

1. Discuss the superpowers' role in creating the current condition of African nations.
2. Why have peacekeeping missions in African nations frequently failed? How could these failures have been avoided?
3. Why has Central Africa been a particular focus of political and cultural violence?
4. What form of government seems to have been effective in post-colonial Africa? Why has it been more successful than other forms?
5. How can the nations of Africa attract foreign investment?
6. Outline ways that the nations of post-colonial Africa can prosper in the current world economy.

WEBSITES FOR FURTHER REFERENCE

Colonial and Postcolonial Studies Resources
  http://myweb.uiowa.edu/sessions/ColStudies.htm

Internet Archive: 'Postcolonial'
  www.archive.org/search.php?query=subject%3A%22postcolonial%22

Postcolonial (and Colonial) Studies
  http://vos.ucsb.edu/browse.asp?id=2089

Vistas Internet Links
  www.smith.edu/vistas/vistas_web/links.htm

CHAPTER 18

THE MIDDLE EAST: THE ROCKY ROAD TO RECONCILIATION

THE GULF WAR OF 1991

Baghdad justified its August 1990 seizure of Kuwait not only on the basis of territorial claims dating to the time of the Ottoman Empire but also on a set of more recent grievances. Iraqi dictator Saddam Hussein charged that the royal family of the oil-rich emirate had jeopardized Iraq's economic situation by expanding oil production to depress the world price, by illegally diverting oil from Iraqi wells, and by refusing to write off the huge debt Iraq had incurred during its eight-year war with Iran.

When the US administration of George H.W. Bush promptly persuaded the United Nations Security Council to approve extensive economic sanctions against Iraq and later to authorize the use of military force to expel Iraqi forces from Kuwait if they did not withdraw before 15 January 1991, Saddam Hussein redefined the impending confrontation as an Arab–Muslim 'Holy War' against the West and its ally in the region, Israel. After securing the diplomatic backing of its former adversary (and Iraq's former patron and supplier) in Moscow, the United States assembled a military force in Saudi Arabia consisting of NATO allies—such as Britain, France, and Canada—together with those Arab states—such as Egypt, Saudi Arabia, and Syria—that feared the consequences of Iraq's invasion. After the UN deadline for the evacuation of Kuwait expired, the US-led coalition launched a devastating air campaign against Iraqi military targets followed by a ground offensive into Kuwait and southern Iraq. The coalition secured a swift military triumph that ejected Iraqi forces from Kuwait and thwarted Hussein's aspirations for territorial expansion in the Persian Gulf and political leadership in the Arab world.

For many of the 34 nations that participated in the US-led coalition, the war in the Persian Gulf marked the first deployment of troops in combat since the end of the Second World War. The Canadian government of Brian Mulroney, which strongly supported the Bush administration and was one of the first governments to condemn Iraq's invasion of Kuwait, ordered Canada's troops into action for the first time since the Korean War. Canada contributed three navy ships, a squadron of CF-18 fighters, and a field hospital. It did not send a contingent of ground

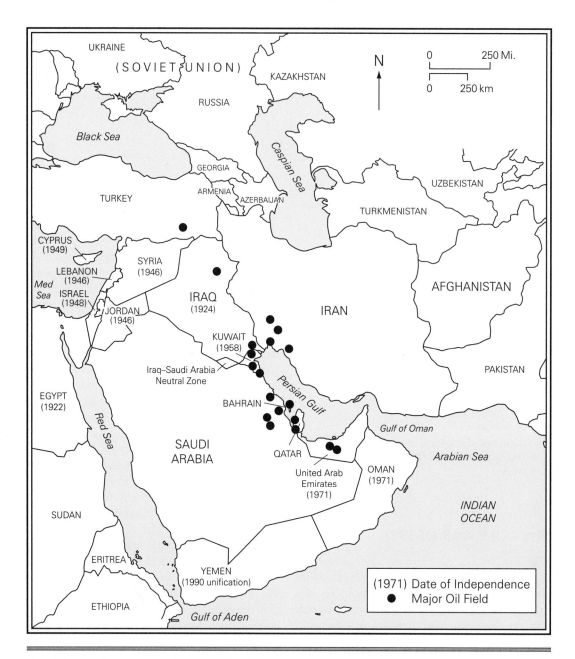

The Middle East at the End of the Twentieth Century

troops, and the 4,500 Canadians serving in the Gulf War suffered no combat fatalities. Despite the fact that Canada played a minor role in the war, the cost of its military contribution totalled well over CAD$500 million.

For the United States, the outcome of the Gulf War vastly enhanced Washington's credibility as patron and protector in the Middle East. Though Saudi Arabia, Kuwait, and the other Gulf states paid about two-thirds of the US$71 billion cost of the war compared to $7.4 billion from the US,[1] it was American diplomacy that assembled the victorious coalition and US military power that routed the Iraqi army. The disintegration of the Soviet Union at the end of the year left the United States in an unrivalled position of supremacy in this oil-rich, strategically significant part of the world. Iraq had been among the world's foremost military powers, but it was now decisively defeated and faced total diplomatic isolation in the United Nations. Saddam Hussein's regime was subjected to a set of costly financial penalties and humiliating infringements on Iraqi sovereignty. The Security Council extracted from Iraq a pledge to pay billions of dollars in war reparations to Kuwait for the damage caused during its occupation. An international embargo on Iraqi oil denied Hussein funds to finance essential imports for his shattered economy. In May 1991, UN inspection teams entered Iraq to supervise the dismantling of the arsenal of nuclear, chemical, and biological weapons that Hussein had accumulated over the previous decade.

Yet defeated Iraq had not been completely displaced as a regional power on the Persian Gulf. The ceasefire that had ended the land war after only 100 hours of combat had enabled Hussein's elite personal army, the Republican Guard, to escape virtually unscathed. This formidable military force enabled Hussein to preserve his country's territorial integrity and retain his own political authority by ruthlessly quelling insurrections of Kurdish separatists in the north, Shiite rebels in the south, and dissident elements within his own military.

For the remainder of the decade Saddam Hussein played a game of cat and mouse with the United Nations inspection team (UNSCOM) as it attempted to uncover evidence of Iraq's arsenal of proscribed weapons of mass destruction (WMDs). Baghdad's uncooperativeness coincided with a disintegration of the consensus that the Security Council's five permanent members had managed to achieve. When UNSCOM requested UN action to compel compliance after Iraq attempted to obstruct its weapon inspections in the fall of 1997, Russia, China, and France raised objections to an Anglo–American proposal for an extension of the economic sanctions that prevented all imports except food and medicine from reaching Iraq. Hussein exploited this split by expelling all American members of UNSCOM, whom he accused of conducting espionage for their own nation, a move that brought the inspection team's operation to a halt. As the United States and Britain beefed up their military and naval presence in the Gulf and threatened military action if the inspections were not permitted to resume, the Iraqi leader defiantly denied UNSCOM access to certain 'presidential sites', where UN technicians believed biological and chemical materials were located. UN Secretary-General Kofi Annan intervened in this tense standoff in February 1998 with a hastily organized visit to Baghdad, where he persuaded the Iraqi government to grant unrestricted access to all sites in exchange for his pledge to raise the issue of discontinuing sanctions against Iraq in the Security Council.

While endorsing the Secretary-General's deal with Baghdad, the Security Council explicitly threatened the use of military force if Iraq failed to reopen all sites to inspection. But in the summer and fall of 1998, Iraq, feeling threatened by UNSCOM's discovery of data about the Iraqi chemical weapons program and by the aggressive investigatory practices of the Australian head of the inspection team, resumed its policy of defiance. In December the United States and Britain finally lost patience and unleashed a four-day attack against Iraq with bombers and cruise missiles.

Operation Desert Fox targeted not just suspected sites of weapons development but also the
political and military infrastructure of the regime,
reflecting Washington and London's determination to topple the Iraqi government. This military
strategy was complemented by an expansion of
political warfare, which included the creation of
Radio Free Iraq to broadcast criticism of Saddam
Hussein's regime as well as the provision of financial and military aid to Iraqi opposition movements and the two main Kurdish political parties.

Hussein responded to the Anglo–American air
campaign and political warfare by ending all co-
operation with the weapons inspection team and
evicting UNSCOM from the country. American
and British warplanes continued to patrol the no-
fly zones that had been established in the north
and south after the Gulf War, while economic
sanctions on Iraq remained in force. However,
weapons inspections had come to an end without dispelling the strong suspicion that Iraq still
possessed WMDs or, at least, the capability to
produce them.

As the post-war economic and military sanctions tamed—at least temporarily—the Baathist
regime in Baghdad, the immediate threat to
regional stability from the fundamentalist Islamic
regime in Tehran dissipated as well. The death
of Ayatollah Ruhollah Khomeini in June 1989
left an immense power vacuum in the Islamic
Republic. President Ayatollah Ali Khamenei succeeded Khomeini as supreme leader, but effective control of the state apparatus devolved on
the former parliamentary speaker, Hojatoleslam
Hashemi Rafsanjani, who succeeded Khamenei
as president. The pragmatic Rafsanjani and his
new cabinet of technocrats abandoned many of
the orthodox Islamic principles of Khomeini in
order to pursue policies appropriate to a modernizing state intent on expanding its regional
influence and achieving economic growth. When
principles in the Koran or the *Sharia* clashed with
the practical requirements of modern life—as
with the prohibition against charging interest in
money lending—theological doctrine at times
succumbed to the demands of modernization.

This shift in priorities, which antagonized dog-
matic supporters of the late ayatollah's strict Shiite
theocracy, lessened the militancy that had characterized Iran's relations with foreign states since
the revolution of 1978–9. Rafsanjani maintained
a policy of scrupulous neutrality during the Gulf
War instead of exploiting the distress of his country's former enemy in Baghdad to expand Iran's
power in the region and complicate the US-led
coalition's post-war peacekeeping plans. In the
hope of attracting foreign investment and lending
to rebuild Iran's war-ravaged economy, he sought
to improve relations with the West by inducing the
Iranian-backed Hezbollah movement in Lebanon
to release several American and British hostages.

The reformist forces in Iran won a stunning
victory over the guardians of the old orthodoxy in May 1997, when the progressive cleric
Mohammed Khatami was unexpectedly elected
president with almost 70 per cent of the vote. The
new head of state boldly proposed reconciliation with the West and gained a popular following among discontented groups within Iranian
society (notably youth and women) by advocating the rule of law, respect for individual liberties, and openness to foreign cultural influences.
The president's progressive rhetoric placed him
in opposition to the conservative, anti-Western
supreme leader Ayatollah Khamenei and his
fellow defenders of the Khomeini legacy.

Amid this internal debate over the future
direction of the country, Iran was drawn into a
regional conflict in South Asia after the end of
the long civil war in Afghanistan. In 1996, a faction of Sunni Muslim Pashtuns known as the
Taliban, led by Mullah Mohammed Omar, seized
the Afghan capital of Kabul and began to subject the country to a strict Islamic code, which
included the suppression of 'decadent' Western
influences. Supported by neighbouring Pakistan,
the Taliban consolidated its control of the country and spent the next two years suppressing an
Iranian-backed faction of Farsi-speaking Shiite
Afghans known as the Hazara.

In 1997 Omar established the Islamic Republic
of Afghanistan, with himself as 'Commander

of the Believers'. The regime combined a rigid interpretation of Islam with older, Pashtun traditions. With the founding of the new Afghan state, schools were closed to females, women's employment was prohibited, and the wearing of the burqa was mandated. New statutes followed in 1998 which closed home schools for girls and proscribed both music and dancing. These new injunctions were enforced with draconian efficiency by the Ministry for the Promotion of Virtue and the Suppression of Vice. Subsequently, in 2000 and 2001 the Ministry also moved to ban poppy growing by Afghan farmers, even though the Taliban had in the past drawn considerable revenue from the opium trade.

Iran suffered a humiliating setback in Afghanistan in the summer of 1998, when the pro-Pakistani Taliban decimated its Hazara protégés. But Iran's opposition to the Taliban regime received strong support from Russia and the former Soviet Republics of Central Asia bordering on Afghanistan, all of which worried about the effects that the fanatical brand of Islam practised by the puritanical rulers in Kabul might have on their own Muslim citizens. China, anxious about the threat of Islamic separatism in its eastern province of Xinjiang, broke with its long-time ally Pakistan and joined the emerging regional coalition against the Taliban regime. At the same time, however, pro-Taliban forces were drawing considerable

THE POLITICS OF OIL

Traditionally the United States endeavoured to secure safe and reliable access to Middle East oil by manipulating the balance of power in the region. Either Iran or Iraq would be backed as the situation dictated. Thus, prior to the Iranian Revolution in 1979, the pro-western regime of Shah Mohammed Reza Pahlavi received considerable financial and military aid from the West. Twice the Shah's regime had been rescued from defeat by western intervention—once in 1946 while facing a threat from the USSR, and again in 1953 after Prime Minister Mohammed Mossadegh attempted to limit the powers of the monarchy. However, in the aftermath of the Iranian Revolution the US looked to Iran's traditional rival, Iraq, providing financial and logistical support to the forces of Saddam Hussein. A Senate staff report for the Committee on Foreign Relations identified a number of ongoing initiatives to support Iraq, including '(1)"Operation Staunch," an active US diplomatic effort to identify and halt arms shipments to Iran; (2) the provision of Commodity Credit Corporation credits to Iraq for . . . purchases in the United States; (3) vocal condemnation of Iran at the United Nations and other arenas; and, (4) the provision of military intelligence to Iraq'.

However, in the wake of the Gulf War, US policy shifted towards what has been called 'dual containment'—an effort to isolate both Iran and Iraq. This objective would be accomplished by limits on trade and investment in Iran, enforced by sanctions against any foreign companies considering investing in the country, theoretically limiting its ability to purchase WMDs. Simultaneously, harsh economic sanctions would be enforced against Iraq, even as a United Nations inspection team ensured compliance with post-Gulf War disarmament provisions. Both initiatives were reinforced by a continued US naval presence in the Gulf and a permanent troop presence in Saudi Arabia. In the final analysis the American 'dual containment' strategy had a number of unintended consequences. European companies were angered by the threatened sanctions for trading with Iran; the more moderate Iranian regime of Mohammed Khatami received little encouragement from the United States; in 1998 UN inspectors were forced out of Iraq, rendering the process of verifying compliance increasingly difficult; and, finally, the US presence in Saudi Arabia, close to many Islamic holy sites, became an enduring catalyst for Islamist resentment.

financial support from Pakistan, in addition to money and equipment from Saudi Arabia. The new Taliban regime provided an ideal headquarters for radical Islamist movements such as that of Osama bin Laden, who by this time was entrenched in Afghanistan, building support for his movement and its Wahhabist interpretation of Islam.

NEGOTIATIONS BETWEEN ISRAEL AND THE PALESTINIANS

The 1987 Palestinian uprising (or *Intifada*) in the West Bank and Gaza Strip revealed that many Palestinians had lost faith in the Palestine Liberation Organization's ability to end the Israeli occupation and felt driven to take matters into their own hands. Israel responded to the civilian insurrection, which consisted largely of rock throwing, with disproportionately harsh countermeasures that provoked international condemnation. With Moscow curtailing its support for Syria and the PLO while permitting Soviet Jews to emigrate to Israel in record numbers, the Bush administration grew impatient with the Israeli government of Yitzhak Shamir, which refused to negotiate with the PLO or envision any kind of Palestinian political entity on the West Bank. After the PLO formally endorsed UN Resolution 242, recognizing Israel's right to exist in peace and security and renouncing terrorism, the United States ended its boycott of the Palestinian organization and opened talks with PLO representatives in Tunis.

Towards the end of the 1980s, there were other signs that peace in the Middle East might not be far off. When Egypt was officially readmitted to the Arab League at its Casablanca summit in 1989 without being obliged to renounce its 1979 peace treaty with Israel, it was seen as an implicit acceptance by the other Arab states of the legitimacy of negotiation with the Jewish state. Syria, isolated in the Arab world and abandoned by its Soviet benefactor, was driven to seek a rapprochement with Egypt and tone down its anti-Israel rhetoric. By the opening of the new decade, the end of the Iran–Iraq War, the re-entry of Egypt into the Arab

camp, and the isolation of hard-line Syria made the prospects for peace and stability in the region seem better than they had been since 1982–3.

An unforeseen consequence of the multinational military operation against Iraq in January 1991 was its beneficial effect on the peace negotiations between Israel and its Arab neighbours, which had stagnated since the Israeli invasion of Lebanon in 1982. One such gain was its effect on solidarity among Arab states. Arab unity had been shattered by the war, with the PLO joining Jordan and Libya in support of Baghdad while Syria, Egypt, Saudi Arabia, and the smaller Gulf states enlisted in the Western-led coalition against Iraq. Saudi Arabia and Kuwait retaliated for Yasser Arafat's support of Saddam Hussein by abruptly cutting off their financial subsidies to the PLO. The rift among Arab states, the financial weakness of the PLO without its Gulf oil money, and the discontinuation of military and economic support for Syria and Iraq from the disintegrating Communist bloc all afforded the state of Israel an unprecedented margin of security.

This more favourable geopolitical environment did not alter the inflexible attitudes of the hard-line Likud government of Prime Minister Yitzhak Shamir. On the contrary, Israel quickly perceived the opportunities afforded by the disarray in an Arab world that had seemed monolithically menacing for so long. The PLO, hurt by the simultaneous loss of its benefactors in the Gulf and its sponsors in the Kremlin, became more amenable to compromise than it had ever been. Syrian President Hafez al-Assad, also chastened by the loss of Soviet economic aid and political patronage, became increasingly susceptible to American pressure as he turned to the only remaining superpower for compensatory support.

One of the reasons that President Bush and his secretary of state, James Baker, were able to assemble and sustain the improbable coalition that humbled Iraq in 1991 was their implicit pledge to press for a mutually satisfactory resolution of the Arab–Israeli conflict after the Gulf War. Israel had long shunned the PLO leadership in Tunis, considering it irredeemably committed to violence as the means of achieving its political objectives and suspecting it of harbouring the ultimate hope of removing the Jewish state from the map of the Middle East. Arafat's steadfast support for Saddam Hussein's position during the Gulf War as Iraqi Scud missiles fell on Israeli cities appeared to confirm that assessment. But the PLO's political strength declined in the aftermath of the war, enhancing the prestige of the local Palestinian leadership in the Israeli-occupied territories. Accordingly, the Bush administration approached a group of relatively moderate Palestinians unaffiliated with the PLO and persuaded them to meet with Israeli negotiators as part of the official Jordanian delegation to Middle East peace talks in Madrid in October 1991. Throughout the winter and spring of 1992 Baker coordinated a complex set of bilateral encounters between Arab and Israeli representatives in Washington in a bold attempt to broker the type of comprehensive settlement that had eluded American administrations since Jimmy Carter's preliminary and partial breakthrough at Camp David in 1978.

In spite of this strenuous American diplomatic effort, the sessions in Madrid and Washington were hampered by two irksome problems, one substantive and the other procedural. The substantive obstacle to a Palestinian–Israeli agreement was the familiar question of the political status of the West Bank and the Gaza Strip. Ever since the withdrawal of the Labour Party from the Israeli governing coalition in March 1990, the Likud government had sponsored a housing construction program for Jewish settlers in those two occupied territories, which was bound to complicate all proposals involving autonomy for the predominantly Arab populations living there. Shamir obstinately forbade serious discussion of territorial compromises since he had no intention of sacrificing a square inch of land that he considered an integral part of historic Israel.

The procedural stumbling block to progress in these peace negotiations was the absence of the PLO. Despite its temporary decline after the Gulf War, Arafat's organization remained the most popular advocate of the Palestinian national cause

in the eyes of the people it presumed to represent. However much Shamir and his associates might have abhorred the movement and its flamboyant chief, a lasting peace settlement between Israel and the Palestinians was unimaginable without the PLO's seal of approval.

In 1992, a dramatic shift in the political situation in the Middle East put the derailed peace talks back on track. The first significant breakthrough occurred as a result of the unprecedented participation of Syria in serious peace talks with Israel. This development seemed to signify Assad's heightened interest in a land-for-peace deal that would return the Golan Heights to Syria (as Sadat had regained the Sinai peninsula for Egypt 15 years earlier) in exchange for recognition of and security guarantees for the Jewish state. It also may have reflected his expectation that a conciliatory policy toward Israel would enhance the prospects for the American economic assistance that Syria coveted.

The second breakthrough was the triumph of the Labour Party in the Israeli parliamentary elections in June, which ended 15 years of rule by the right-wing Likud coalition. The new Labour prime minister, Yitzhak Rabin, abruptly reversed Shamir's policy of housing construction in the West Bank and Gaza Strip by imposing a partial freeze on Jewish settlements there. This goodwill gesture paved the way for more productive exchanges with the Arab delegates at the US-sponsored peace talks that had resumed in Washington at the end of August. It also had the effect of unblocking US$10 billion worth of American government loan guarantees to resettle recent Russian Jewish emigrés to Israel, which had been withheld by the Bush administration as punishment for Likud's provocative house-building program in the occupied territories.

The momentum of the peace process was interrupted by a change in US administrations in 1993. At the same time, opposition to a land-for-peace exchange was emanating from the 115,000 Israeli settlers in the occupied territories, who feared for the future of the communities that they had been encouraged to establish by Likud officials over the previous decade and a half. From the other extreme, Islamic groups operating in the West Bank and Gaza, such as Hamas and Islamic Jihad, vociferously denounced the Arab meetings with representatives of the Jewish state then underway in Washington as a disgraceful betrayal of the Palestinian cause.

The influence of these Islamic extremists in the occupied territories grew at the expense of the PLO leadership in Tunis. Syria's decision to join the Middle East negotiations sent shock waves through the PLO high command. What Arafat feared most of all from Assad—though this fear proved unfounded—was a bilateral bargain with Israel (like the one Anwar Sadat had negotiated years before) that would restore Syrian sovereignty over the Golan Heights at the expense of

Palestinian claims in the West Bank and Gaza. Israel's insistence on negotiating with the various Arab delegations separately and sequentially rather than in a multilateral forum increased the risk that the PLO would be sacrificed by Arab states more intent on pursuing their particular national interests than on altruistically supporting the campaign to secure a homeland for the stateless Palestinians.

This fear of being left out of negotiations prompted Arafat to launch a pre-emptive campaign to reach his own accommodation with the Jewish state. And for a number of reasons, the evolving political situation in Israel was quite conducive to negotiations with the perennial enemy. First, the Labour Party had long favoured the type of territorial compromise with the Palestinians that Shamir and the Likud had

With US President Bill Clinton looking on, Israeli Prime Minister Yitzhak Rabin (left) and PLO leader Yasser Arafat shake hands after signing the Oslo Peace Accord at the White House, 13 September 1993. William J. Clinton Presidential Library, P7291-10a.

steadfastly opposed, and Rabin had periodically expressed his new government's interest in a land-for-peace arrangement after assuming power in June 1992. Second, Israelis of various ideological persuasions had grown weary of the political as well as financial burdens of the occupation in the West Bank and Gaza. While the *Intifada* had failed to undermine Israeli military authority in the territories, it revealed the perpetual menace of domestic unrest that could only intensify amid the unmistakable demographic trend of dramatic population increases among Palestinians under Israeli rule. Finally, the emergence in the territories of radical Islamic groups that denounced the PLO for its caution and moderation transformed Arafat's reputation in Israel from enemy number one to a preferable alternative to the zealots of Hamas and Islamic Jihad.

FROM OSLO TO THE WYE RIVER ACCORD: NEGOTIATIONS IN THE 1990s

The Middle East peace negotiations in Washington had been stalled not only by the absence of the PLO (which retained effective veto power over any agreement reached there), but also by the cumbersome procedures and excessive publicity that inevitably accompany talks between large, unwieldy delegations. These impediments vanished once Israeli Prime Minister Rabin decided to respond to Arafat's overtures by making Palestine a priority over Syria. Top-secret talks between small, tight-knit delegations from Israel and the PLO were organized in Oslo not by the new US administration of Bill Clinton but by Norwegian Foreign Minister Johan Jørgen Holst. On 20 August 1993, Israeli and PLO representatives initialled the so-called Oslo Declaration of Principles, and on 13 September Arafat and Rabin signed the historic Oslo Peace Accord in Washington under the benevolent gaze of President Clinton. US officials had known about the secret exchanges in Norway but learned of the actual terms only after the negotiations were completed. Five days before the signing ceremony,

Rabin and Arafat exchanged letters confirming Israel's recognition of the PLO as the official representative of the Palestinian people and the PLO's affirmation of Israel's right to exist and its rejection of violence as a means of achieving its political goals. The poignant spectacle of the chairman of the Palestine Liberation Organization and the prime minister of Israel shaking hands on the White House lawn marked (if only temporarily) the end of an era in the melancholy recent history of the Middle East.

The crux of the 1993 pact between Israel and the PLO was in the section covering the political future of the two occupied territories and their Palestinian majorities. The agreement established a five-year transitional procedure for the transfer to Palestinian sovereignty of the entire Gaza Strip and of the city of Jericho and its environs in the West Bank. During this interim period, the so-called Palestinian Authority, created in May 1994, would gradually acquire control of all internal affairs in the two specified regions, while Israel would retain authority over their foreign relations as well as over all matters affecting the security of any remaining Jewish settlements there.

In spite of bureaucratic foot-dragging and isolated outbursts of violent opposition from hardliners on both sides—such as the massacre by a fanatical Jewish settler of 29 Arabs during prayers in a Hebron mosque and sporadic suicide bombings and assaults on Israeli soldiers by radical Islamic opponents of the pact—the two sides proceeded to implement the agreement throughout 1994. The departing Israeli military units and civil servants turned over their functions to newly re-established Palestinian police forces and administrative agencies. Arafat later paid a historic visit to the squalid refugee camps in Gaza, where he received the ardent acclamation of his people. By the end of the year the Israeli military government on the West Bank had transferred responsibility for education, tourism, social services, health, and taxation to the Palestinian authority. International donors led by the World Bank supplied funds to balance the Palestinian Authority's budget until sufficient tax revenues

could be raised. As this first phase of the transfer of power came to an end, Arafat, Rabin, and
Israeli Foreign Minister Shimon Peres shared the
1994 Nobel Peace Prize for their path-breaking
efforts at reaching a durable Middle East peace.

The issues left unresolved by the PLO–Israel
Peace Accord were predictably the most intractable of all. One was the question of the future
of Jerusalem, the holy city of both Jewish and
Muslim faiths, which had been partitioned
between Israel and Jordan in 1948 and then unified under Israeli control after the Six Day War in
1967. Another was the long-standing grievance of
the Palestinian refugees and their offspring who
had fled during the first Arab–Israeli war in 1948
and resettled—temporarily, as many of them
believed—in half a dozen countries throughout
the Middle East. Would they obtain the right to
return to their homeland and, if so, under what
conditions? And what political future lay in store
for the West Bank beyond the confines of the
Palestinian enclave in Jericho? How far could
the principle of autonomy be extended without depriving the citizens of Israel of a credible
assurance of safety and security? Future negotiators would have to determine the fate of the
numerous Jewish settlements scattered throughout the predominantly Arab populations of the
West Bank, which were hailed by some Israelis
as the vanguard of the campaign to restore the
Greater Israel of Biblical times but denounced
by most Arabs as impediments to Palestinian
self-determination.

In addition to these pending matters between
Israel and the PLO, the question of the Jewish state's
relationship with Jordan and Syria also remained
unresolved. A major breakthrough occurred in
August 1994, when King Hussein hastily followed in Arafat's footsteps to Washington for a
handshaking ceremony with Rabin, during which
the two leaders signed a nonbelligerency pact.
The following October they joined President
Clinton at the Jordanian–Israeli border to proclaim the end of the 46-year state of war between
the two neighbouring countries and to approve
procedures for settling disputes over water rights.

Jordan thus became the second Arab country
in the region, after Egypt in 1979, to agree to full
diplomatic and economic ties with Israel. Having
earlier relinquished Jordan's claim to the West
Bank that it had lost in the 1967 war, Hussein
issued no territorial demands and was therefore
able to reach a quick understanding with Rabin.
Jordan's principal reward for making peace with
Israel (apart from the complex arrangement on
water access) was the prerogative of protecting
Muslim holy sites in Jerusalem, a provision that
infuriated Arafat because it undermined PLO
plans to designate East Jerusalem as the capital of
a future Palestinian state.

In spite of the dramatic breakthrough represented by Israel's agreements with the PLO and
Jordan, it was clear that a comprehensive and
durable peace in the Middle East was inconceivable without the participation of Syria. President
Assad had been trumped by Arafat (who had
asked the Syrian leader not to sign a separate
agreement with Israel while he secretly prepared
his own bilateral deal with the Jewish state) and
upstaged by King Hussein. Syria's participation in
the unfolding Middle East settlement continued to
hinge on a satisfactory arrangement for the Golan
Heights. Israel's claim to the buffer zone lacked
the sentimental fervour of what Menachem Begin
and his followers used to insist on calling Judea
and Samaria. The interests of the 15,000 Israelis
in the Golan *kibbutzim* could be sacrificed for a
general peace agreement with far fewer political
costs than those of the 100,000 settlers in towns
with recognizable Biblical names on the West
Bank. But practical considerations precluded a
simple solution. The Golan's strategic importance to Israel derived from its pre-1967 status
as a highland from which Syria could shell with
impunity Israeli settlements in the valleys below.
As the site of the headwaters of the Jordan River,
the source of 40 per cent of Israel's water supply, it assumed an economic significance as well.
These two issues, together with the multitude of
matters in dispute between Israel and Jordan and
Israel and the PLO, were enough to keep negotiators from all sides busy for the rest of the decade.

Under persistent prodding by the United States, Israel and the Palestine Liberation Organization signed an Interim Agreement in 1995 to implement the crucial provisions of the 1993 Oslo Agreement within four years. While Israeli and Palestinian negotiators haggled over the details, extremist opponents of reconciliation in both camps did their best to sabotage the effort to reach a mutually acceptable compromise. On 4 November 1995, amid the harsh rhetorical campaign in Israel mounted by the Likud opposition against the ruling Labour Party's concessions to the PLO, Israeli Prime Minister Yitzhak Rabin was assassinated by a Jewish opponent of the peace settlement. Thus was the architect of Israel's military victory in 1967, who had spent more than a quarter of a century defending the Jewish state, cut down in his pursuit of a diplomatic settlement of the Arab–Israeli conflict.

In the spring of 1996, Hamas did its part to undermine Arafat's new conciliatory policy and derail the peace process by unleashing a number of terrorist attacks that killed almost 60 civilians in several Israeli cities. Despite this upsurge in violence, Rabin's successor, Shimon Peres, honoured an important provision of the agreement reached with Arafat in September 1995, which provided for the transfer of military authority in six West Bank towns (including Ramallah and Bethlehem) from the Israeli army to the Palestinian Authority by the end of the year. After this first stage of the Israeli withdrawal from the West Bank, Arafat's supporters won an overwhelming victory in the first ever Palestinian elections for a Legislative Council on 20 January 1996. Arafat's electoral triumph over his critics appeared to reveal strong Palestinian support for a negotiated settlement. However, the PLO chairman failed to make good on his pledge, tendered in exchange for the Israeli military withdrawal, to persuade the Palestinian National Council (PNC) to repeal the provision of the PLO charter that endorsed armed struggle against the Jewish state. Hamas, Hezbollah, and their sympathizers in the PNC clung to their opposition to the peace agreement with Israel, accusing Arafat of betraying the cause of a Palestinian state

for the financial and political rewards of 'collaborating' with the 'Zionist entity'.

With Egypt and Jordan on record in support of the peace process, Syria (which continued to wield control of Lebanon) remained the only holdout among the front-line Arab states bordering Israel. Syrian President Hafez al-Assad held a trump card in his relentless quest to recover the Golan Heights, one that might reconcile Syria to the existence of the Jewish state. This prize was his ability to suppress hardline rejectionist groups such as Hezbollah, which he had allowed to operate from Damascus and to use Syrian-controlled Lebanon as a base for terrorist operations against Israel. However, preliminary talks between Israeli and Syrian officials led nowhere, with Jerusalem insisting on additional security guarantees that Damascus was unwilling to offer and Syria demanding the unconditional withdrawal from the Golan that no Israeli government was prepared to risk.

Though Israeli–Syrian negotiations remained bogged down throughout the 1990s, successive Israeli governments tried their hand at reaching an accommodation with the government of Lebanon to enable Israeli military forces to withdraw from the 'security zone' in the southern tenth of that country that had been created in 1985. So eager was Israel to extricate itself from the Lebanese quagmire that, in 1996, it offered for the first time to withdraw without the customary precondition of a formal peace agreement between the two states. In exchange, the Israelis demanded assurances that Beirut would prevent armed attacks against northern Israel that Hezbollah fighters operating in southern Lebanon had been launching for years with the support of Syria and Iran. Israel's bid to terminate its politically unpopular occupation of southern Lebanon was blocked when Syria vetoed any compromise that would leave Israel in possession of the Golan.

While Syria consolidated its hegemonic position in Lebanon and avoided substantive negotiations with Israel, Assad faced a new threat from Syria's long-time antagonist to the north. In the summer and fall of 1998, Turkey exerted strong (and eventually successful) pressure on Syria to cut off its support for the Kurdish separatist movement PKK, which had used havens in Syria and in Syrian-controlled territory in Lebanon since the mid-1980s to conduct a guerrilla campaign on behalf of a separate Kurdish state in western Turkey. Turkey's position in the region was bolstered by a close security partnership with Israel, which was established in 1996 and strongly supported by the two countries' American ally. The new alliance between Ankara and Jerusalem confronted Assad with the nightmare of a two-front war in the event of conflict with either of these two countries with which Syria had territorial disputes.

With Egypt, Jordan, and the PLO engaged in peace negotiations with Israel and Syria weakened by the Turkish–Israeli security partnership, some optimistic observers in the Middle East entertained visions of an ultimate peace accord based on shared economic self-interest that might allow the parties involved to forget, once and for all, their old military conflicts and regional political rivalries. If France and Germany could overcome their ancient tribal hatreds and jointly spearhead a successful movement of supranational co-operation in Europe, the argument went, why should Israel and its Arab neighbours not be able to find common ground based on a mutually beneficial commitment to economic development and regional integration?

Such optimism was dealt a severe setback with the election of a Likud government in Israel in May 1996. The new prime minister, Binyamin Netanyahu, had ousted the Labour government of Shimon Peres by winning a razor-thin majority on a campaign pledge to revise the 1993 Oslo Agreement in Israel's favour. Netanyahu's dependence on religious and right-wing nationalist parties in his ruling coalition led the new government to permit and provide financial incentives for a major expansion of Jewish settlements in the West Bank, where the Jewish population swelled to more than 150,000 by the end of 1996. This aggressive settlement policy predictably antagonized the Palestinians, damaged Arafat's credibility among his constituency, and strengthened

the position of Hamas and other opponents of the peace settlement. The head of the Palestinian Authority was unable to curb the increasing number of violent acts committed by these rejectionist groups, both in Palestinian-controlled parts of the West Bank and in Israel itself. Netanyahu responded to each Palestinian suicide bombing by closing Israel's borders to Palestinian workers (causing economic hardship for the people concerned) and accelerating the construction of new Jewish settlements (further undermining Arafat's claim that the peace process would yield tangible benefits for the Palestinian residents of the West Bank). Both leaders seemed constrained by their political constituencies from taking the necessary risks to achieve a lasting peace. The Palestinian Authority chairman did not dare to suppress Hamas for fear of sparking an internecine struggle within the Palestinian movement that might threaten the dominant position of his own organization, which had already come under intense criticism for its rampant corruption and authoritarian practices. The Israeli prime minister was continually required by the narrowness of his majority to cater to the groups within his governing coalition that favoured the expansion of West Bank settlements.

In exasperation with the snail's pace of peace negotiations, Arafat attempted to jump-start the process in 1998 by threatening a unilateral declaration of Palestinian statehood when the interim period of the peace agreement expired on 4 May 1999. This threat, together with strong pressure from the Clinton administration in Washington, brought the Likud government of Israel back to the conference table. After nine days of talks near the US capital, Arafat and Netanyahu concluded the Wye River Memorandum. It stipulated a series of Israeli withdrawals from the West Bank (which would bring about 20 per cent of the territory under full Palestinian control) in exchange for Arafat's pledge to implement a number of security measures and to remove the anti-Israeli language from the Palestinian National Charter. The Wye Memorandum directly involved the United States in the peace process by arranging for the Central Intelligence Agency to monitor the agreed-upon security arrangements in order to allay Israeli concerns.

After carrying out the first stage of the withdrawal from West Bank areas in November 1998, Israel accused the Palestinian Authority of violating the Wye agreement and abruptly suspended further implementation of its provisions. Within a month Netanyahu's enemies patched together a majority to dissolve the Knesset and hold new elections in May 1999. In order to avoid generating public support in Israel for Netanyahu's bid to remain in office, Arafat prudently withdrew his threat of a unilateral declaration of Palestinian statehood. Labour won the elections, bringing its new head, former general Ehud Barak, to power on a pledge to breathe new life into the dormant peace process. Barak promptly attempted to revive the stalled talks with the Palestinian Authority over the West Bank and the moribund negotiations with Syria over the Golan Heights.

BEYOND WYE RIVER

In May 2000, Ehud Barak ended the Israeli occupation of southern Lebanon, paving the way for further progress in the Israeli–Palestinian peace talks. However, subsequent discussions at Camp David in July failed to produce any concrete progress. The key stumbling blocks remained the status of Jerusalem and the issue of the right of return for Palestinian refugees. Though blame for the failure of this round of negotiations was initially placed on Yasser Arafat's intransigence, more recent analyses have apportioned the blame to all parties.

Following the failure of the Camp David talks, violence escalated dramatically within the region. In September 2000 Israel's opposition leader Ariel Sharon and a delegation of Likud officials visited the site of the Temple Mount in Jerusalem (since the eighth century the site of the al-Aqsa mosque, one of the holiest sites in the Islamic world). Sharon's visit was interpreted by many as a provocative act, given the frustration already existing due to the failed summer peace talks. Palestinians

reacted by launching a second *Intifada*, though this time, the stone-throwing of the late-1980s were replaced by much more violent tactics which cost the movement much of its international support. Retaliatory violence by Israeli settlers and radical factions on all sides served to only increase the bloodshed.

In January 2001 a near-breakthrough on the diplomatic front, at the Taba Summit, once again ended in failure. The next month Ehud Barak was defeated by Ariel Sharon in the prime ministerial election. In forming a new government out of the over 30 parties with representation in the Knesset, Sharon was forced to build a new coalition which included several far-right parties whose platforms promoted increased Israeli settlement in Palestinian territories.

The second *Intifada* continued into 2002 when the Israeli military reoccupied the West Bank and Gaza Strip and imposed an internal closure of the former. This move had a direct economic impact on the 125,000 Palestinian day-labourers who had been working in Israel. By the summer of 2003 the death toll from this renewed wave of violence stood at 2,400 Palestinians and 780 Israelis. Yasser Arafat's support dropped from 32 to 21 per cent among Palestinian voters; meanwhile, polls showed that support for radical Islamist parties had risen from 12 to 30 per cent. Arafat's death, in November 2004, did little to heal the factional divisions among the Palestinian peoples.

By 2005, Sharon opted to remove a number of Israeli settlements from Gaza, in accordance with earlier agreements. However, he also announced that a 'security barrier' would be erected to seal off Israeli territory from suicide attacks. Thus, even with the return of some Israeli settlements, the construction of the barrier meant that the Palestinians had lost additional land overall. Given the situation by the mid-2000s, it was hardly surprising that, in the 2006 elections to the Palestinian Authority, the Fatah Party experienced a sweeping defeat. Hamas increased its representation from 43 to 76 seats in an election judged by international monitoring agencies to be free and fair. Hamas also extended its influence from Gaza into the traditionally more moderate West Bank.

Following these elections the United States and a number of other western governments cut off assistance to the Palestinian Authority in protest against the rise of Hamas. However, this action led to accusations that the US was interested only in the rhetoric of promoting democracy in the Middle East. When a government that was unfriendly to US interests was elected, aid was immediately diverted. Thus, the twenty-first century began much as the previous century had ended in the Middle East, with only halting progress towards peace, punctuated by frequent outbursts of deadly violence.

SUMMARY

The last two decades of the twentieth century saw renewed attempts by the international community to secure a lasting peace in the Middle East, focused primarily on the perennial problem of the Arab–Israeli conflict. As the Cold War wound down in the late 1980s, Moscow and Washington tried to dampen regional rivalries in the Middle East. The Soviet Union pressured Syria and the PLO to seek a negotiated settlement with Israel, while the United States urged the Jewish state to renounce its annexation of the occupied territories and halt settlement activity on the West Bank. A complicating factor was the unanticipated Palestinian uprising (or *Intifada*) on the West Bank and Gaza Strip, which began in 1987 as a spontaneous popular reaction to the failure of peace talks. Pressure mounted on both sides to find an

end to the conflict, but negotiations dragged on until the Oslo Peace Accord was signed in 1993. Despite this landmark agreement, peace remained elusive, and new waves of violence broke out in the mid-1990s. In the wake of another round of stalled negotiations in 1998–9, a second *Intifada* began in 2000.

Two other factors dominated events in the Middle East. The first was the Gulf War of 1991, when the United States led a large international coalition to liberate Kuwait from Iraqi occupation. The American allies included both European and Arab states, and the defeat of Iraq altered the balance of power in the region. Yet the survival of Saddam Hussein's regime in Iraq (and its reputed weapons programs) remained a major issue for the rest of the decade. The second factor in the Middle East was the growth of terrorist groups based on Islamic fundamentalism. In the late 1990s, al-Qaeda emerged as a major terrorist organization, sponsoring a series of high-profile attacks against American targets. The US responded by launching an unsuccessful missile strike on a terrorist camp in Afghanistan in 1998, and its subsequent failure to neutralize al-Qaeda would have momentous repercussions in the twenty-first century.

NOTES

1. Japan and Germany, two great powers that were precluded by the lingering legacy of World War II from participating militarily in the operation, contributed to the UN effort by footing the rest of the bill.

QUESTIONS FOR CRITICAL THOUGHT

1. Why was Washington able to sustain an effective coalition during the course of the first Gulf War?
2. What factors allowed the Taliban to take power in Afghanistan?
3. Which global developments contributed to the resumption of Israeli–Palestinian negotiations in the late 1980s and early 1990s?
4. What are the key obstacles to a definitive Israeli–Palestinian peace accord?
5. Discuss whether foreign aid and assistance should be denied to the democratically elected Hamas.
6. How can the United States secure 'safe and reliable' access to Middle East oil?

WEBSITES FOR FURTHER REFERENCE

Columbia University Libraries: Middle East and Islamic Studies
  www.columbia.edu/cu/lweb/indiv/mideast/cuvlm

Harvard University Center for Middle Eastern Studies
  http://cmes.hmdc.harvard.edu/resources

University of Exeter: Arabic, Islamic, and Middle Eastern Resources
  http://as.exeter.ac.uk/library/about/awdu/resources/

Yale University Library: Research Guide to Middle East Politics
  www.library.yale.edu/neareast/politics2.html

CHAPTER 19

LATIN AMERICA: DEMOCRACY, FREE MARKETS, AND REGIONAL STABILITY

NORTH AMERICAN FREE TRADE AND ITS IMPACT ON LATIN AMERICA

The newly acquired propensity for pursuing free market principles in Latin America predictably evoked an appreciative response in Washington; this favourable reaction in turn engendered hopes among Latin American leaders of developing closer trade and investment ties with the United States. In June 1990, the administration of George H.W. Bush encouraged such hopes by floating the concept of a free trade zone for the entire western hemisphere—an initiative dubbed 'Enterprise for the Americas'—seen by some observers as an insurance policy taken out by the US in anticipation of formidable economic blocs forming in Europe and East Asia. But Latin American plans to join a hemispheric trading system suffered a temporary setback when Washington retreated to the more circumscribed objective of strengthening commercial links among the three countries of North America alone.

The origins of what was to become known as the North American Free Trade Agreement (NAFTA) lay in the bilateral treaty signed by the United States and Canada in October 1987. This pact aimed to eliminate, by 1 January 1989, all tariffs and other trade barriers between the two countries, which had long been each other's most important trading partner and had largely complementary exports. Canada had entered into negotiations with the United States following the 1985 report of the Macdonald Commission, which concluded that free trade was the only viable route to sustained economic growth, given that over 75 per cent of Canada's exports went to the US. But as American and Canadian negotiators ironed out the details of the agreement, a variety of Canadian organizations, including labour unions and nationalist groups, argued that the Free Trade Agreement (FTA) would result in layoffs and lower wages while undermining Canadian cultural industries and eroding the country's political sovereignty. In spite of this growing public opposition, Conservative Prime Minister Brian Mulroney, seeking a mandate to ratify Ottawa's agreement with the United States, was re-elected in the 1988 federal election, in which free trade was the dominant campaign issue. Although the parties opposed to free trade won a majority of the popular vote, Mulroney won enough seats to

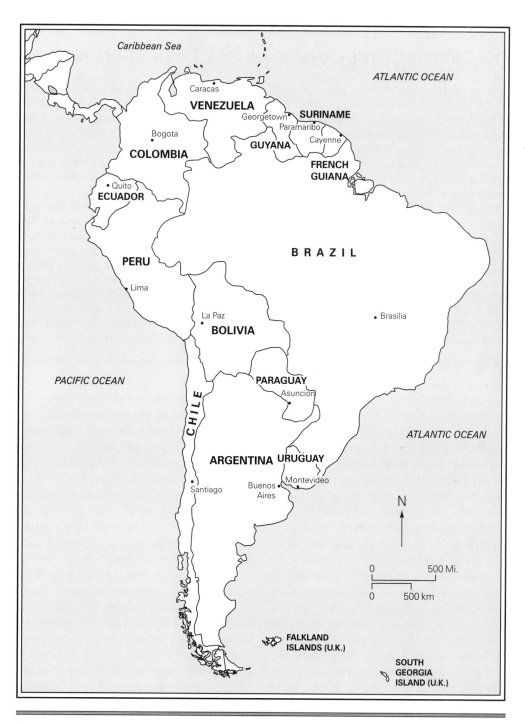

SOUTH AMERICA AT THE END OF THE TWENTIETH CENTURY

The Origins of the Canada–US Free Trade Agreement

Prime Minister Brian Mulroney's meeting with US President Ronald Reagan in Quebec City in March 1985 marked a turning point in Canada's trading partnership with the United States. The meeting was dubbed the 'Shamrock Summit' after Reagan and Mulroney celebrated their Irish heritage by singing 'When Irish Eyes are Smiling' on stage with their wives. The famous televised image of Reagan and Mulroney crooning together became a symbol of the close relationship between the two leaders, as the new Conservative government transformed Canada's foreign policy.

Elected to office seven months earlier, Mulroney sought to move away from Pierre Trudeau's 'Third Option' approach to foreign policy by aligning Canada much more closely with the United States. In particular, Mulroney hoped to negotiate a new trade agreement with the Reagan administration,

and Canadian and American delegates worked on the details of an agreement in advance of the president's 1985 visit. Although Ottawa failed to persuade Washington to accede to a military trade accord to be unveiled at the March summit, the two countries did agree to a declaration of intent to liberalize trade before Reagan travelled to Canada.

The Canadian media portrayed the Shamrock Summit as more of a political spectacle than a serious policy meeting, but it had important long-term ramifications, paving the way for negotiations that produced the Free Trade Agreement with the United States in 1988. As one American official put it, 'We have what amounts to a revolution in US–Canadian relations.' For the next eight years, Mulroney presided over arguably the most pro-US government in Canadian history.

pass the free trade bill in Parliament just before the ratification deadline.

In the year that the US–Canada treaty came into force, President Carlos Salinas de Gotari of Mexico (who had recently secured an advantageous debt settlement with his country's foreign creditors and begun to implement a free market economic program) pressed Washington for a free trade arrangement modelled on the US–Canada pact. Both governments recognized the short- and long-term importance of the economic ties between the two countries. Mexico had already become the third largest trading partner of the United States. Its 90 million citizens represented a huge potential market for American exports as well as an abundant source of comparatively cheap labour for American manufacturing industries willing to transfer their production facilities south of the Rio Grande. From Mexico's point of view, the US accounted for almost 85 per cent of its total foreign trade and offered the opportunity for both an expanded market for its emerging

export industries and a massive infusion of investment capital for its economic development.

Persuaded of the advantages that both countries stood to reap by removing the remaining barriers to each other's exports, the administrations of presidents Salinas and Bush, in March 1990, initiated bilateral talks that were later expanded to include America's new free trade partner, Canada. In October 1992, the leaders of the three North American countries signed a complex trilateral treaty to phase out all tariffs, quotas, and other impediments to free trade among the three parties within 20 years. NAFTA was ratified by the legislatures of the signatory states in the following year and went into effect on 1 January 1994.

The trilateral arrangement was not without anomalies and complications. In Mexico, a combination of social tensions, political turmoil, and finanacial instability resulted in the devaluation of the peso, casting doubt on the sunny optimism of the Salinas presidency. In Canada, separatist agitation in Quebec threatened to destabilize the country and seriously damage its economy. The movement for Quebec separtism intensified in 1994, when the provincial Parti Québécois, led by Jacques Parizeau, came to power in Quebec while the federal Bloc Québécois, led by Lucien Bouchard, remained the second largest party in the House of Commons. In 1995, the Quebec government called a referendum, and Parizeau and Bouchard led a strong campaign promoting Quebec sovereignty. A narrow victory by the federalist 'No' campaign, which won with only 50.6 per cent of the vote, managed to cool some of the separatist sentiment. Ultimately, the lure of economic growth promised by NAFTA overshadowed anxieties about the future.

With a deal for North American free trade in place, the political and business elites of the other states in the hemisphere worried that the diversion of American foreign trade and investment to Mexico would leave them at a distinct disadvantage. The Latin American nations scrambled to patch together subregional trading arrangements to compensate for their exclusion from the NAFTA behemoth, with its 370 million consumers and US$6 trillion in annual production. Many Latin American officials and business people also harboured the hope that by phasing out protectionism among themselves, they were preparing their economies for the day when the North American trade zone expanded southward. In 1991, four countries situated on the so-called southern cone of South America—Argentina, Brazil, Paraguay, and Uruguay—established a regional common market (Mercado Comun del Sur, or Mercosur) with the ultimate goal of removing all intraregional tariffs. The advantages of the new duty-free customs union had already become apparent in 1993, when trade within the region had increased by two-thirds in three years. In 1992, the Andean Group—Bolivia, Colombia, Ecuador, Peru, and Venezuela—which had recorded minimal progress toward economic co-operation since its formation in 1971, cut almost all regional tariffs to zero and saw Andean trade surge by 30 per cent the following year. Thirteen islands in the Caribbean

developed plans for a regional common market (Caricom) in 1992, and in 1993, the six member nations of the Central American Common Market, which had been stillborn since 1964, signed an agreement to work toward the elimination of trade barriers among themselves. This surge in free trade activity led experts to predict that most trade within Latin America would become tariff-free in the first decade of the twenty-first century.

The phenomenal growth of free trade within Latin America during the 1990s was accompanied by a new openness in trade with the outside world. The average tariff imposed by Latin American nations on foreign goods declined from 56 per cent in 1985 to 15 per cent in 1993. The principal beneficiary of this decline of protectionism was the United States, with which Latin America was conducting half of its foreign trade by the mid-1990s. This dramatic trend in Latin American tariff cutting, together with the region's expanding trade connections with North America that had made Latin America the world's fastest growing market for US exports, gave new life to President Bush's original concept of a free trade zone from Alaska to Argentina.

Throughout the first year of NAFTA's operation, the Latin American states lobbied intensively in Ottawa, Washington, and Mexico City to gain admission to the fledgling regional trading system. At a summit meeting of the 34 nations of the western hemisphere in Miami in December 1994—the first such gathering since 1967—President Clinton responded to the insistent entreaties of the Latin American free marketeers by unveiling a modified version of the Bush scheme for a hemispheric trading system. As a practical step in that direction, the United States, Canada, and Mexico announced their willingness to consider enlarging NAFTA to include Chile, Latin America's free market showcase with its decade of impressive growth. The invitation to Chile was a subtle call to the other Latin American states to accelerate their already remarkable opening to the world trading system or risk falling behind in the race to gain access to the huge and expanding North American market. It

Mexican President Carlos Salinas de Gotari (standing at left), US President George H.W. Bush, and Canadian Prime Minister Brian Mulroney stand behind their respective trade representatives Jamie Serra Puche, Carla Hills, and Michael Wilson as they sign the North American Free Trade Agreement on 7 October 1992 in San Antonio, Texas. CP Archives (Pat Sullivan).

was also an indirect signal to the economic power-houses in East Asia and the integrating economies of the European Union that they would have to liberalize their trading practices or face an economic bloc of potentially hemispheric proportions.

THE POLITICAL CONSEQUENCES OF ECONOMIC REFORMS IN LATIN AMERICA

Latin America's enthusiastic adoption of free market domestic principles and liberal foreign economic policies did not transpire without painful political consequences. By abandoning the traditional strategies of protectionism, import substitution, and government subsidies in favour of free trade and export-driven growth, Latin American governments had deliberately exposed the less productive sectors of their domestic economies to potentially destructive foreign competition. In doing so, they ran the risk of increasing the disparity in income and wealth that was already the worst in the world, as the influx of cheap foreign goods and the reduction of government subsidies forced marginal enterprises into bankruptcy and their workers into unemployment.

The uprising of impoverished Indian peasants in Mexico's Chiapas province when NAFTA took effect on New Year's Day 1994 perfectly symbolized the human costs of applying free market principles to societies accustomed to economic protection from the government. The limitless opportunity for entrepreneurial success, which classical liberal economic theory hailed as the engine of national economic growth, threatened (at least in the short run) to inflame social tensions and generate political conflict between the haves and have-nots of the region.

The evolution toward a market economy in Latin America during the early 1990s was accompanied by a turn toward political democracy in a region long accustomed to various types of authoritarian rule. The transition from military to civilian rule in countries such as Argentina, Brazil, and Chile had already begun in the 1980s, when the end of the Cold War reinforced this trend by removing the incentive for Washington to support repressive regimes in the name of anti-communism. The leaders of the earlier authoritarian era, such as Augusto Pinochet of Chile, Alfredo Stroessner of Paraguay, and the military officers of the juntas that had ruled Argentina and Brazil, were succeeded by civilian politicians who obtained power by peaceful, legal means and wielded it with proper respect for human rights and parliamentary procedures.

Three conspicuous exceptions to this general trend toward democratization are worth noting because each represents an important theme in contemporary Latin American political culture. The first is Fidel Castro's Cuba, a country that, because of its economic dependence on the Kremlin, was the western hemisphere's principal casualty of the collapse of the Soviet Union. The Cuban economy had already begun a steep slide into depression in the mid-1980s when the cutoff of subsidies and low-interest loans and the decline in oil imports from Moscow in the early 1990s accelerated the decline. The situation was worsened by the continuing US trade embargo, which contributed to severe shortages of food, fuel, and other essential commodities.

Castro reacted to the loss of his principal foreign benefactor and the breakup of the Communist bloc by defiantly reaffirming the Marxist–Leninist ideology that he had appropriated as a youthful revolutionary leader 30 years earlier. He did, however, make one notable concession to the capitalist ideology he so despised. In 1995, Cuba passed legislation designed to attract foreign investment by allowing full ownership of domestic firms and the repatriation of profits. This policy led to some European and Canadian business deals, which ran afoul of US legislation that imposed sanctions on foreign companies investing in Cuban properties that had been confiscated from American owners after the revolution. Apart from this somewhat progressive policy, Cuba remained an embargoed, destitute, outcast relic of the Cold War, occupying an anomalous position in a region increasingly enamoured of the free market path to economic development.

Cuba's condition of extreme political and economic isolation, together with the unwavering animosity of the million-odd emigrés concentrated in the nearby US state of Florida and the growing discontent among those who had remained behind to endure acute economic deprivation, continued to pose a serious challenge to Castro's authority. As in the past, Castro attempted to relieve his domestic pressures by encouraging dissidents to emigrate to the United States, a manoeuvre that ended when the Clinton administration closed the border. In spite of Washington's continued boycott, Cuba has managed to expand its trade and political relationships with a number of its neighbours in the western hemisphere, including Canada. At the end of the century, Castro, the aging revolutionary who had weathered political storms, economic crises, military invasions, and assassination attempts in the course of his long and eventful career, continued to meet the threats to his political position.

Less than a hundred miles east of Cuba lay another exception to the trend. François 'Papa Doc' Duvalier had ruled impoverished Haiti with a toxic combination of corruption and brutality from 1957 until 1971, when, shortly before his death, he transferred power to his son Jean-Claude 'Baby Doc'. Though inheriting his father's ability to intimidate his opponents and lavishly reward his loyal supporters among the Haitian elite, the younger Duvalier succumbed to an insurgency in 1986 and slipped into exile on the French Riviera. After three decades of the Duvalier dictatorship, Haiti was the poorest country in the western hemisphere. Three out of four adults were illiterate, one out of five children died before the age of five, and wealth was concentrated in the hands of an oligarchy residing in a few of the small country's major cities. In February 1991, a charismatic Catholic priest, Father Jean-Bertrand Aristide, assumed the presidency after winning the country's first free elections in decades on a platform of sweeping social and political reform. The following September, the upper echelon of the Haitian military—closely linked to the socio-economic elite, whose privileged position was threatened by the distributive program of the popular new chief executive—deposed Aristide and forced him into exile in the United States.

Washington's forceful reaction to this blatant violation of the popular will, which included vigorous diplomatic pressure and economic sanctions in conjunction with the Organization of American States and the United Nations, moved the Haitian military authorities to sign the so-called Governors' Island Agreement in July 1993, allowing Aristide to return to power by the end of October. But the leader of the coup and de facto ruler of Haiti, Lieutenant General Raoul Cédras, dragged his feet on procedural matters related to the reinstatement of the ousted president. The specified deadline passed with the irate Aristide still languishing in his American exile while his supporters pressed the US government to take stronger action to dislodge the recalcitrant junta and restore the legally elected president.

In the meantime, the Clinton administration was forcibly repatriating the almost 50,000 Haitian refugees who had fled the country to escape the military regime's brutal treatment of suspected Aristide sympathizers. When it became evident that the economic sanctions were punishing the Haitian masses without having any appreciable effect on the brazen generals in Port-au-Prince, US troops occupied the country and forcibly reinstated Aristide in the fall of 1994. Just as five years earlier, when the US military overthrew, captured, and returned Panamanian dictator Manuel Noriega to the United States to face drug-smuggling charges, democracy had to be imposed externally by force of arms.

The third exception was Peru. In April 1992, its democratically elected president, Alberto Fujimori, suspended the constitution, dissolved the parliament, and placed opposition politicians under house arrest on the pretext of coping more effectively with the country's rampant inflation, drug trafficking, and terrorism. After rewriting the Peruvian constitution to allow himself to run for office again, Fujimori was re-elected in 1995 with over 65 per cent of the vote. Although Fujimori's undemocratic methods provoked criticism at home and abroad, the achievements of his government won widespread domestic and international support: inflation was cut in half; the country recorded impressive rates of economic growth; the leader of Sendero Luminoso (Shining Path), a terrorist organization allegedly financed by sales of narcotics, was captured and jailed; both the Shining Path and the Tupac Amaru revolutionary movement declined in influence; and incidents of political and drug-related violence dropped for the rest of the decade. Peru's apparent success in curing its ruinous domestic ills by what might be called mildly authoritarian means represented an alluring alternative to parliamentary democracy in a region long vulnerable to the appeal of the leader.

Latin America's great success story during the 1990s was the termination of the two bloody civil wars that had wracked Central America throughout the previous decade. The return of stability to the region was helped by the disengagement of the Soviet Union and the United States from the civil war in Nicaragua. As Moscow reduced oil deliveries to the capital, Managua, and urged restraint on the Sandinistas, Washington suspended aid to the Contras in 1987, thereby shifting the burden of peacemaking to the countries of the region. Attempts at a regional settlement had failed ever since the Contadora group's attempts at mediation in 1983. But a peace plan drafted by Costa Rican President Oscar Arias Sanchez and endorsed by five Central American heads of state in August 1987 offered a solution in the form of a ceasefire, a discontinuation of all external military aid to the belligerents, and free democratic elections in Nicaragua.

Weakened by the reduction of Soviet aid, the government of Sandinista President Daniel Ortega Saavedra instituted a unilateral ceasefire in March 1988. In February 1989, amid the deteriorating economic conditions of the country, which included an inflation rate of over 3,000 per cent, severe shortages of many essential commodities, a sharp decline in GNP, massive unemployment, and a defence burden that consumed over half of the national budget, the government announced its decision to conduct the free elections called for in the Arias Plan on 25 February 1990. The Contras, deprived of their US aid, agreed to demobilize their military forces and participate in the electoral process, as Washington ended its economic embargo of Nicaragua.

The Sandinista regime's willingness to hold elections was fuelled in part by the optimistic expectation, reinforced by most opinion polls, that the Sandinista Party would win handily against its political opposition. To the surprise of most observers, however, the free elections resulted in the triumph of a ragtag coalition of opposition groups ranging from Somoza supporters on the extreme right to democratic socialists, calling themselves the National Opposition Union (UNO), on the left. In April 1990, Violeta Barrios de Chamorro, who had served in the Sandinista ruling junta in the first nine months of the revolution before resigning in disillusionment, replaced Ortega as president of Nicaragua in the first democratic, peaceful transfer of power in that country in recent memory. The Sandinistas honoured their pledge to preserve the ceasefire in the civil war, while the Contras continued to disband in the expectation of participating in the political system now controlled by their ideological allies.

The tenuous truce between Chamorro's centre-right governing coalition and the Sandinista-controlled military survived despite periodic clashes between reconstituted Contra and Sandinista guerrilla groups in the countryside and continual verbal sniping from parliamentary critics at both extremes of the political spectrum. Chamorro's inclusion of Sandinistas in her cabinet and her retention of Humberto Ortega, brother of the former Sandinista president, as army chief alienated her right-wing allies in Parliament and antagonized the United States. When she finally yielded to right-wing and US pressure in the fall of 1993 by promising to replace Ortega within a year, she predictably enraged her Sandinista coalition partners. Ortega eventually relinquished his post in February 1995. Despite ongoing political tensions, the two sides did not revert to the type of violent behaviour that had devastated the country during the 1980s.

The political defeat of the Sandinistas in Nicaragua dealt a crushing blow to their ideological allies in El Salvador, the Democratic Revolutionary Front (FDR), and its military wing, the Farabundo Marti National Liberation Front (FMLN), which had been engaged in an insurgency against the central government throughout the 1980s. In federal elections in March 1989, pro-American businessman Alfredo Cristiani, leader of the victorious Nationalist Republican Alliance (ARENA), replaced the ailing Christian Democratic President José Napoleon Duarte (who had attempted in vain to steer a middle course between ARENA on the right and the FMLN on the left). The ARENA government expanded and intensified its predecessor's counterinsurgency campaign against the rebels. But pressure from the United States to seek a negotiated peace and curb its hardliners in the military forced the Salvadoran government to the conference table, just as the collapse of the Sandinistas and the crisis in the Soviet Union deprived the FMLN of external support.

Peace talks to end the struggle between the Salvadoran government and the FMLN began under the auspices of the United Nations in April

1990, and in January 1992 they produced a cease-fire. By the end of that year the reciprocal demobilization of government and rebel forces under the supervision of a United Nations observer force (ONUSAL) formally ended the 14-year civil war, which had caused 75,000 deaths and massive socio-economic dislocation. Despite occasional instances of rebel terrorism and government repression, the ceasefire held. The FMLN began to operate as a political party rather than a revolutionary movement, and the Cristiani regime abandoned the excesses of its predecessors. In elections in 1997, the FMLN and the ruling ARENA party each won a third of the seats in the parliament, so that these two former enemies became political competitors willing to play by the rules of the game. As the bloody civil wars in Nicaragua and El Salvador faded into sporadic spasms of violence, Central America, after a decade and a half of ideological strife, entered into a period of relative peace and stability.

In December 1999, a historic event took place when the American flag was lowered for the last time in the Panama Canal Zone and the famous waterway reverted to full Panamanian control, in conformity with the agreement signed in 1977 by US President Jimmy Carter and Panamanian President Omar Torrijos. The United States Southern Command, the emblem of US military dominance in the Central America–Carribbean region, was relocated to Miami. With this, the end of the century marked, at least symbolically, the end of United States hegemony in Latin America, an era that had begun with the American victory over Spain at the end of the previous century.

SUMMARY

In the 1990s, Latin America, like most other parts of the world, experienced the spread of political democracy and economic liberalism. The ruling elites of most Latin American countries were converted to the belief that salvation lay in adopting the market-oriented strategy for growth that had been successfully employed by the newly industrialized countries of East Asia.

The North American Free Trade Agreement, signed by Canada, the United States, and Mexico in 1992, paved the way for a number of separate treaties that reduced regional tarrifs and increased trade in the region. Latin American governments began selling off state-owned firms to private investors, ostensibly to eliminate the inefficient practices of protected, subsidized state firms by subjecting them to the competitive conditions of the free market but also to generate revenue for hard-pressed state treasuries. By the mid-1990s, most of the Latin American states had jumped on the free market bandwagon, slashing government subsidies, reducing tarrifs, and promoting export-oriented growth.

At the same time, countries in the region faced the damaging legacy of the Cold War era, which included heavy foreign debts, social inequalities, and political corruption. Colombia and Bolivia continued to be sites of large-scale narcotics production, while Mexico remained a key transit point for narcotics distribution to North American consumers. The transition to democracy was uneven: dictatorships were eliminated in countries such as Brazil, Chile, Argentina, and Panama, but insurrections plagued Colombia, Venezuela, Haiti, and Peru.

The end of the Cold War also brought a further decline in direct American imperialism in Latin America, as well as greater regional integration. Following the US invasion of Panama in 1989 to depose Manuel Noriega, the 1990s saw a decrease in unilateral American intervention in the region. When the United States led a multinational force to stabilize Haiti in 1994, military authority was handed over to the United Nations the following year. The final transfer of full control over the Panama Canal Zone to the Panamanian government in 1999 ended one of the most notable examples of American imperialism in Latin America. Yet by the end of the century, American intelligence services and military units were still involved in the domestic affairs of some countries—particularly Colombia—and American economic power remained a pervasive force in the region.

QUESTIONS FOR CRITICAL THOUGHT

1. Outline the pros and cons of having large economic blocs in the Americas.
2. What are the negative consequences of free market economic principles and liberal foreign economic policies?
3. What were the primary factors facilitating the transition from military to civilian rule in Latin America?
4. Is 'mildly authoritarian government' the only way forward for Latin America? What other possibilities exist and how successful would they be in the region?
5. Considering the contemporary world economy, discuss the likelihood of Cuba surviving in its current form.
6. Have we seen the end of US hegemony in Latin America? If not, where and in what form might it reappear?

WEBSITES FOR FURTHER REFERENCE

Internet Resources for Latin America
  http://lib.nmsu.edu/subject/bord/laguia

Latin American Network Information Center
  www1.lanic.utexas.edu

Sources and General Resources on Latin America
  www.oberlin.edu/faculty/svolk/latinam.htm

University of Washington Libraries: Latin American History
  www.lib.washington.edu/subject/History/tm/latin.html

CHAPTER 20

A UNIPOLAR WORLD OR A NEW MULTILATERALISM?

THE AFTERMATH OF THE COLD WAR

The power and resilience of nationalism have been demonstrated across the globe since the end of the Cold War. Not only within the defunct Soviet Union and the former Communist bloc but throughout the Third World as well, long-dormant sentiments of ethnic identity have resurfaced to challenge the legitimacy of existing territorial arrangements. In its benign, neo-Wilsonian version, the principle of national self-determination led to a peaceful realignment of old frontiers or the delineation of new ones, as in the former Czechoslovakia and former Soviet republics, such as Belarus. In its malignant form (as in the cases of the former Yugoslavia and Soviet

successor states, such as Georgia and Tajikistan), the awareness of ethnic individuality has incited animosities among neighbouring peoples with painful consequences for all concerned.

Amid this renaissance of nationalism in the post–Cold War era, however, the antithetical trend of multilateralism has persisted as an important force in world affairs. The elusive quest for international co-operation in the management of global problems has a long history. Before the Second World War, there were several attempts to institutionalize multilateral mechanisms for promoting global peace and security, including the Hague Peace Conference, the League of Nations, the Washington Naval Conference, the Geneva Protocol, and the Kellogg–Briand Pact. Informal collaborative arrangements among the world's major central banks on behalf of international monetary stability in addition to various bilateral and regional agreements to reduce trade barriers during the inter-war period set precedents for subsequent efforts at international economic co-operation. During the Cold War, the multilateral approach to global economic issues survived in the non-communist world with varying degrees of success in such institutions as the IMF, the World Bank, and GATT. The management of international security problems was hampered by the intense global rivalry between the two Cold War blocs. Yet proof that the multilateralist spirit persisted could be found in the sporadic peace-keeping operations by the United Nations in the Middle East during the 1950s and 1960s, and in the Nuclear Non-Proliferation Treaty, the Limited Nuclear Test Ban Treaty, and so forth.

In the post–Cold War era, the revival of nationalist sentiment and the emergence of several new nations throughout the world guaranteed that the nation-state would continue to be the principal unit of political sovereignty. To some observers this renewal seemed unfavourable to the determined but futile pursuit of internationalism that had endured throughout the twentieth century, with its sorry record of global warfare, genocide, and economic distress. Nevertheless, it is worth examining a number of developments that suggest that the announcement of internationalism's demise may have been premature.

THE MANAGEMENT OF THE GLOBAL ECONOMY

The earliest and most successful example of international co-operation in the post–Second World War era was the series of multilateral negotiations to promote the expansion of world trade. GATT had been established in 1947 as a forum for negotiating the reduction of tariffs and other barriers to the free exchange of goods across national boundaries. In a series of eight international meetings (or 'rounds'[1] as they were called) since its founding year, GATT coordinated a substantial reduction of world tariff levels among the major trading nations of the non-communist world. The first seven GATT negotiations had focused primarily on reducing tariffs on manufactured goods. The Uruguay Round, a complex set of negotiations involving 123 nations that began in 1986 and was finally completed in 1994, delved into a number of other areas, including the politically sensitive problem of trade barriers in the agricultural sector.

The Uruguay Round proved to be much more acrimonious than any of the participants had anticipated. GATT's earlier success in lowering tariffs had not produced the free trade paradise championed in classical liberal economic theory. On the contrary, the earlier tariff reductions and the growing interdependence of the world economies had generated a new clamour for protectionism once inefficient industries and farms felt the sting of foreign competition. Governments responded to these pressures by adopting informal measures to exclude foreign products without violating GATT guidelines. For example, Japan, because of the formidable political power of its farmers' lobby, insulated its domestic agriculture from foreign competition with high tariffs and stringent quotas; it reduced its tariffs on manufactured goods below the level of most advanced industrial countries while relying on a set of covert barriers to manufactured imports. These included a tight-knit internal distribution system that effectively discriminated against foreign companies, preferential government purchasing arrangements with domestic firms, and legal roadblocks to the purchase of Japanese firms by foreign interests.

The European Community wielded a very effective non-tariff barrier to food imports known as the Common Agricultural Policy (CAP). Originally created as a bilateral bargain between France and Germany to protect their relatively inefficient but politically powerful farmers from foreign competition, the CAP developed into a formidable bureaucratic mechanism to provide price supports for European food products when domestic prices fell below world levels and to subsidize the export of foodstuffs when surpluses accumulated. European farmers were thus able to sell their food domestically at artificially high prices and export it at artificially low ones, at the expense of both European consumers and foreign competitors.

US trade negotiators, responding to complaints from American farmers and exporters, insistently pressed Japan and the European Community to open up their markets or risk retaliation as the Uruguay Round dragged on into the 1990s. In December 1990, the talks were suspended amid recriminations and angry complaints from all sides. It was ironic that just as the Cold War was winding down, many observers worried that it would be replaced by a trade war among the former members of the anti-communist coalition. The bitter disputes that erupted during the Uruguay Round between the United States and its European and Japanese trading partners revealed that the once-dominant economic power in the world had lost the ability to impose its will.

The North American Free Trade Agreement (NAFTA) was designed in part to rectify this perceived erosion of American economic power. American and Canadian motivations for forging the Free Trade Agreement, later expanded to include Mexico with the much bolder possibility of incorporating the entire western hemisphere, reflected a defensive reaction against what some North American policy-makers saw as the ominous emergence of protectionist commercial blocs across the Atlantic and the Pacific. The signing of the GATT Treaty in April 1994 concluded the Uruguay Round of negotiations and paved the way for the gradual implementation of the multilateral agreement that would cut global tariffs by an average of one-third. Other sweeping features of the agreement included the elimination of a number of notorious import quotas (such as Japan's rice quota and the US sugar and textile quota) and the extension of protection to intellectual property such as patents, copyrights, and trademarks in order to curb the rampant piracy of movies, compact discs, computer software, and prescription drugs. Since American tariffs were already relatively low compared to those of most of its principal competitors and since most of the newly protected intellectual property was produced by American companies, the United States derived the greatest benefit from these new trading rules.

The World Trade Organization (WTO) formally replaced GATT as the governing body of world trade rules on 1 January 1995. Notwithstanding the various conditions and caveats that some signatory countries insisted on, the successful completion of the Uruguay Round and the creation of the WTO appeared to reduce the possibility of global commercial warfare and the international political tensions that trade wars inevitably generate. As the provisions of the Uruguay Round were phased in, world trade faced fewer politically imposed obstacles than at any time since the Second World War. The parallel development of the EU, NAFTA, and other regional (and potentially discriminatory) trading systems that might appear on the world scene represented the only significant potential threat to the multilateral, nondiscriminatory recipe for trade expansion represented by the WTO philosophy.

The Uruguay Round of trade negotiations was dominated by the advanced industrial nations in North America, Europe, and East Asia. The less developed countries of Africa and Latin America found it difficult to participate effectively in the international trading system until they could overcome the major obstacle to their economic development: an acute shortage of working capital. The only readily available sources of such capital were the savings that had accumulated in the wealthy countries of the industrialized world. During the first two decades after the Second World War, a small proportion of those savings reached the developing countries via two types of capital transfer. The first type was government foreign aid, which was provided either as an outright gift or as a low- or no-interest loan. The second was direct investment in Third World countries by private firms, which often resulted in the repatriation of profits but at least left the host country with the physical assets, technology, and skills that the capital had helped to develop. Though meagre in comparison to these countries' desperate needs, the transfers proved relatively advantageous to the recipients.

During the 1970s and 1980s, the volume of both government foreign aid to and private direct investment in the developing world declined significantly. To compensate, these capital-starved countries increasingly sought loans from commercial banks (most of which were based in Europe, North America, and Japan) as well as from the International Monetary Fund and the World Bank. While the banks and the international agencies had committed funds to the Third World before, they increased the scale of their lending dramatically in these two decades to replace the shrinking government aid and direct investment.

The principal cause of this expansion of commercial bank loans to the Third World was the sudden quadrupling of world oil prices in 1973, which left the OPEC countries awash in oil profits that they promptly deposited in American and European banks to ensure their safety and earn the highest rate of interest. The only way that the banks could turn a profit on this money was by lending it out at a higher interest rate than that paid to their depositors. To the banks' dismay, however, the deep economic slump caused by the oil price increases had dampened demand for loans in the industrialized world, as businesses and private individuals cut back spending. Unable to find sufficient business in Europe and the United States, the commercial banks cultivated business with the treasury officials of developing countries, particularly those in Africa and Latin America. The IMF and the World Bank complemented the commercial banks' quest for profitable lending opportunities in the Third World by sharply increasing their own lending operations for the broader purpose of promoting economic growth in the recipient countries.

Underlying the strategy of both the commercial banks and the official lending organizations was the expectation that this massive flow of capital would generate a spurt in exports from developing countries that would earn sufficient foreign exchange to service their burgeoning foreign debt. In this way, loans to Third World countries would pay for themselves, while the export earnings in excess of the payments the developing countries were required to make to service their debt would be available to finance further domestic economic growth. The expanding economies of the Third World would in turn generate demand for products from the industrialized countries, forging a mutually advantageous financial nexus between north and south. It was a multi-billion dollar bet that none of the players could lose. The results of this new wave of lending were astonishing. The total medium- and long-term debt of developing countries skyrocketed from US$70 billion in 1970 to $400 billion in 1979 and to $1.3 trillion in 1989.

THE MOVEMENT AGAINST GLOBALIZATION

By the turn of the twenty-first century, the movement against economic globalization had become a significant international force. The creation of the WTO in 1995 sparked a growing reaction by activists who argued that the elimination of trade barriers produced poorer living conditions and worse environmental standards in developing countries.

When the WTO convened in Seattle in 1999, tens of thousands of well-organized protesters filled the city streets to voice their opposition to what they regarded as an undemocratic organization dominated by corporate interests. Although the overwhelming majority of activists were peaceful, the news media focused on the relatively few who damaged property and confronted local police.

While Quebec City prepared in 2001 to host the Summit of the Americas (which was held to discuss the expansion of free trade), government officials feared a repeat of the Seattle disturbances. To keep the activists well away from the summit, a four-kilometre steel fence was erected around the Old City. But even before the meetings began, protesters attacked the fence, breached the security perimeter, and clashed with police. Police officers responded with tear gas, water cannons, and rubber bullets. As the summit continued, running battles between police and protesters produced approximately 400 arrests and dozens of serious injuries on both sides. Prime Minister Jean Chrétien condemned the outbreak of violence, but members of the New Democratic Party argued that the police had overreacted. Some of the people arrested later alleged that they had been stripped naked, hosed down with water, and denied food.

As the images of violent conflict were televised around the world, the security fence came to epitomize the ideological gulf between those who supported international free trade and those who saw it as a tool of economic oppression.

Police clash with protesters who have broken through the fence surrounding Old Quebec City during the Summit of the Americas, 20 April 2001. CP Archives (Paul Chiasson).

On a superficial level this influx of capital seemed a godsend to those on the receiving end of the transactions. It supplied countries already in possession of abundant natural resources, land, and labour with the one essential ingredient for production—investment capital—that they were incapable of generating on their own because of their low rate of domestic savings. As the recipient countries were to learn very quickly, though, the money from the commercial banks carried a high price tag. Unlike government aid programs, the loans were tendered at market rates; worse, instead of running for a fixed term, most of them carried variable interest rates, which tied them to the changing cost of funds in the industrialized world. And unlike direct investments, principal and interest had to be repaid at regular intervals regardless of whether the loan was producing

sufficient income for its recipients. During the early 1980s, as global interest rates rose to historic levels and a deep recession in the industrialized world reduced demand for (and therefore depressed the prices of) Third World commodities, many of the developing countries that had borrowed heavily from the commercial banks and international financial institutions found that they were unable to produce sufficient export earnings to service their foreign debt. The world faced the prospect of a massive default that would severely undermine the international financial system and cause economic chaos in many countries.

The task of devising a solution to the Third World debt crisis of the 1980s fell principally on the IMF, the international agency that had been established to help countries experiencing financial difficulties. The long campaign to restore international financial stability unfolded in three stages. The initial response of the IMF, and of the banks and governments of the industrialized world that were closely linked to it, reflected the widespread presumption that full responsibility for the debt crisis lay with the recipient governments. By indulging in such politically popular but extravagant policies as maintaining over-valued currencies that encouraged imports at the expense of exports, running up huge budget deficits, and subsidizing food, fuel, and other basic commodities, these states had brought the problem on themselves and therefore had to swallow a bitter pill to cure the disease. That cure was to be an austerity program that would enable the offending countries to resume payments on their foreign debts and begin their economic recovery. The IMF loan packages required currency devaluation, cuts in government spending, and the reduction of subsidies on basic commodities to balance budgets. While this belt-tightening produced the desired result of reducing the debtor countries' trade deficits, the domestic price increases and cuts in government spending provoked widespread social unrest that brought with it the threat of political instability. The cure also did not seem to be working, as many countries, especially in Latin America and Africa, continued to fall behind on their debt payments while some teetered on the brink of financial collapse.

The second phase of the multinational effort to solve the Third World debt crisis began in 1985, when the US Treasury Department floated a proposal based on premises different from those that had inspired what many critics were beginning to denounce as the heartless policy of the IMF. The Baker Plan (named after then US Treasury Secretary James Baker) de-emphasized the need for austerity among the debtor countries, suggesting instead substantial new foreign loans to stimulate economic growth in those countries, which would help them restore their ability to service their foreign debt. But by the mid-1980s the balance sheets of the multinational banks had been battered so heavily by the 'nonperforming' loans to the Third World that they refused to risk

further losses by making new financial commitments. During the second half of the decade, many of the banks unloaded their Third World debt instruments on the secondary bond market for prices far below their face value. Others sold discounted loans to companies that resold them in the debtor country to finance a direct investment there (a complex arrangement known as a 'debt-for-equity swap'). Very few were willing to risk further exposure to Third World debt, so the Baker Plan failed to generate much support within financial circles.

In the meantime, many Third World debtors had rejected the idea that their own mismanagement was solely responsible for the debt crisis. They demanded that the creditor countries bear part of the burden of remedying the deteriorating situation by agreeing to forgive a significant portion of their debt. Some of them even considered banding together in 'debtors' cartels' to threaten their creditors with a joint rejection of their financial obligations that would undermine the already shaky foundations of the international banking system. Though no such deliberate, coordinated default ever took place, concern about such a calamity prompted the administration of US President George H.W. Bush to issue a new proposal, known as the Brady Plan (after Treasury Secretary Nicholas Brady), in March 1989.

The Brady Plan differed from the two previous remedial efforts by acknowledging for the first time that debt reduction represented a necessary part of any successful strategy for managing the debt crisis. The novelty of this approach was that it contained a set of incentives as well as sacrifices for both parties in the dispute. The banks were offered the opportunity to exchange their current bonds for new ones with either a reduced principal or lower interest rate. Repayment of the new bonds would be guaranteed by special earmarked funds to be raised through a new round of borrowing by the IMF, the World Bank, and the governments of several advanced industrial states. The commercial banks thus avoided the risk of default by sacrificing a portion of their anticipated foreign loan profits. In exchange for this reduction of existing debt and the possibility of future loans, the Third World countries were required to implement a series of austerity measures devised by the IMF to restore their financial stability.

During the early 1990s, a number of Latin American states concluded multi-billion dollar debt reduction agreements with their creditors based on the Brady Plan. This debt relief helped some of these countries record impressive economic growth and afforded others some much-needed breathing space as they struggled to overcome intrinsic impediments to development. The principal long-term significance of these Brady bargains is that they led to the replacement of an increasing proportion of commercial bank debt with debt held by multilateral lending institutions, especially the IMF and the World Bank. The increasing global influence of these two vestiges of the Bretton Woods system, together with the progress in trade liberalization under the auspices of GATT and its successor, the WTO, represented an intriguing paradox: in an era of privatization in the economic sphere and heightened national consciousness in the political sphere, these publicly financed multilateral agencies expanded their role in managing the trading and monetary systems of the world.

THE PROGRESS OF ARMS CONTROL

The most spectacular instance of multilateral co-operation in the post–Cold War era occurred in the area of arms control. For four decades, the massive buildup of weaponry in all categories—conventional, biological, chemical, and nuclear—had drained funds from domestic programs and increased international insecurity. The few successful efforts to restrain the arms race had required years of labourious negotiation and produced only limited results. By the middle of the 1980s, the two superpowers possessed the capability to destroy each other and most of the world's population. On the continent of Europe two enormous armies equipped with a formidable array of military hardware faced each other along what was ominously called the 'central

front'. Many countries were stockpiling chemical and biological weapons in anticipation of an exotic new type of warfare whose devastating consequences for humankind and its natural environment could scarcely be imagined. Yet as the Cold War came to an end and the Communist bloc disintegrated at the end of the decade, the major military powers of the world achieved breathtaking progress in arms control agreements that had eluded them for so many years. Despite the continuation of many violent, long-standing quarrels, and the emergence of some new ones, the world at the turn of the century seemed in many ways a much safer place than at any time since the end of the Second World War.

The continent of Europe had become the most highly militarized region of the world in the course of the Cold War. While NATO was preparing to deploy a new generation of conventional weapons of stunning technological sophistication, the two alliance systems signed the Treaty on Conventional Armed Forces in Europe (CFE) in November 1990. The CFE pact rectified the imbalance in conventional forces on the continent by requiring deep cuts on the Soviet side, a requirement that became unnecessary when the Warsaw Pact disbanded in 1990 and the Soviet Union disintegrated into 15 independent republics at the end of 1991. The eight Soviet successor states located in the treaty zone divided up the military equipment of the defunct USSR and promptly consented to abide by the agreed-upon limits on conventional arms. After the CFE Treaty officially entered into effect in July 1992, the eight European republics of the former Soviet Union scrupulously complied with its provisions, as revealed by inspections carried out by multinational verification teams.

The abortive Soviet coup in the summer of 1991 sparked a series of sweeping reductions in US and Soviet nuclear forces and the cancellation of nuclear modernization programs initiated in the final years of the Cold War. This rapid succession of nuclear arms reductions began in September 1991, when President Bush proposed that both sides dismantle all of their ground-launched tactical nuclear weapons (TNWs). When Soviet President Gorbachev reciprocated a week later, all such short-range nuclear weapons in Europe were targeted to be destroyed. Following the collapse of the Soviet Union in December, the new republics readily agreed to transfer all of the roughly 17,000 TNWs to Russian territory for eventual destruction.

The remarkable progress in strategic arms control during the Gorbachev years (1985–91) had already substantially reduced the long-range nuclear forces of the United States and the Soviet Union when, in 1991, Gorbachev and Bush signed the Strategic Arms Reduction Treaty (START I), which had been under consideration since 1982. The legality of this landmark agreement, seen by many as the pinnacle of achievement in arms control, was brought into question just a few months later by the fall of the Soviet Union. The approximately 12,000 warheads constituting the former Soviet Union's land-based strategic nuclear forces—the ICBMs capable of reaching foreign targets anywhere in the world—were dispersed among the four successor states of Russia, Ukraine, Belarus (previously Belorussia), and Kazakhstan, where they had been located. The three non-Russian republics possessed almost a third of the former USSR's strategic nuclear arsenal.

In the spring of 1992, the four former Soviet nuclear states, under pressure from Washington, resolved the legal predicament of the warheads' status by joining the United States in signing the Lisbon Protocol to START I. Through this arrangement they formally assumed all of the former Soviet Union's obligations under the arms control agreement. Recognizing Russia as the rightful heir to the defunct superpower's nuclear arsenal, Ukraine, Belarus, and Kazakhstan also pledged to sign the Nuclear Non-Proliferation Treaty as non-nuclear states and to transfer all of their nuclear warheads to the Russian Federation within seven years.

President Bush had meanwhile renewed his campaign for steep reductions in strategic arms, unilaterally cancelling virtually the entire US nuclear modernization program (including the MX, Midgetman, and advanced cruise missiles) and proposing drastic reductions in the number of warheads on existing ground- and sea-launched weapons systems. Russian President Boris Yeltsin quickly responded to these American initiatives by confirming the earlier reductions agreed to by Gorbachev and expressing strong interest in maintaining the momentum of reciprocal strategic arms cuts. At their first summit meeting, in the summer of 1992, Bush and Yeltsin reached agreement on a successor to START I. In January 1993, in Moscow, the two presidents signed START II, which provided for a 25 per cent reduction of each country's strategic forces to between 3,000 and 3,500 warheads over 10 years. The treaty also called for the total elimination of the notorious multiwarhead (MIRV) ICBMs that had been the focus of the strategic arms negotiations from their beginning in November 1969.

The implementation of START II was delayed while all parties waited for the START I agreement to officially take effect. For though the United States, Russia, Belarus, and Kazakhstan had dutifully ratified the treaty and the protocol, the Ukrainian government had decided to exploit its advantage as an instant nuclear power by stalling ratification in the hope of obtaining both US aid to finance the removal of its warheads and adequate security guarantees to compensate for its voluntary resignation from the nuclear club. The security issue became paramount as ultranationalist firebrands in Russia openly spoke of regaining the old Soviet frontiers, while the continuing deterioration of the Ukrainian economy rendered the costly procedure of denuclearization impossible without substantial foreign assistance.

A tentative settlement was finally reached at the Moscow Summit, in January 1994, when Yeltsin and US President Clinton provided Ukraine with security guarantees and financial compensation, though the Ukrainian parliament did not take all of the required actions until the end of the year. This arrangement removed the last obstacle to transferring all of the former Soviet Union's nuclear material to Russian custody. At the same meeting, the two presidents issued the dramatic announcement that beginning 30 May 1994, their countries would no longer be targeting their long-range missiles on each other's territory. Though a purely symbolic gesture—since re-targeting can be accomplished in a matter of minutes—the joint declaration revealed how far the world had progressed toward strategic arms limitation since the heydey of the Cold War.

As the START I Treaty took effect in 1994 and inspections of the two nuclear arsenals began in 1995, the START II Treaty sparked intense opposition in the Russian parliament, preventing its ratification. One of the issues was Russian resentment at the expansion of NATO to include the former Warsaw Pact states of Poland, Hungary, and the Czech Republic. Another was Russia's growing reliance on nuclear weapons for national defence to compensate for the woeful state of the country's conventional forces, which was demonstrated during the war in Chechnya in 1994–6. Despite the Russian foot dragging on START II, the once menacing nuclear arsenals of the Cold War era had been substantially reduced during the last decade of the century.

Significant strides were also made in the decades-long campaign to limit nuclear testing. In 1992, the United States, Russia, and France unilaterally declared moratoriums on nuclear tests, and their leaders publicly endorsed a comprehensive nuclear test ban. The two other nuclear powers, Britain and China, continued to insist that the threat of nuclear proliferation required them to maintain an effective deterrent, which periodic testing alone could ensure. But the US removed one of the impediments to a worldwide test ban in the summer of 1993 by cancelling Britain's access to the site in Nevada where it had been conducting all of its nuclear tests. In August 1993, in Geneva, the Conference on Disarmament decided to open formal negotiations on a Comprehensive Test Ban Treaty (CTBT), which would extend the old Limited Test Ban Treaty (banning tests in the atmosphere and in the sea) to include underground tests.

In the meantime the United States, Russia, France, and Britain extended their existing moratoriums on testing. China alone refused to fall in step with the other nuclear powers, breaking its self-imposed moratorium in the fall of 1993 and again in the summer and fall of 1994 with underground tests at its Lop Nor testing site in Xinjiang. Some Western analysts suspected that those underground blasts were tests of warheads for a new generation of long-range ballistic missiles that China was developing. Beijing justified the tests—of which it had conducted 41, compared to about 1,000 by the US—on the grounds that China lagged far behind the other nuclear powers in the sophistication of its nuclear weaponry and needed to bridge the gap before the anticipated CTBT became effective. Possessing only a limited number of nuclear-powered submarines capable of firing SLBMs, China seemed intent on building a larger fleet and developing a new 7,723-km range in order to maintain the credibility of its nuclear deterrent. France also resumed its nuclear testing program after a three-and-a-half-year moratorium with six tests at its site on the Mururoa Atoll in the South Pacific in 1995–6. However, it was American rather than Chinese or French recalcitrance that shattered the hopes of ending all nuclear testing in the world. Dissatisfied with existing inspection procedures to verify compliance, the US Senate rejected the CTBT in November 1999.

As the world's nuclear states sought to reduce their arsenals and curb nuclear testing during the 1990s, the issue of nuclear proliferation became an important item on the arms control agenda. The international mechanism for preventing the spread of nuclear weapons is the Nuclear Non-Proliferation Treaty (NPT). It was unveiled in Geneva in July 1968, brought into force in March 1970, and eventually signed by most countries of the world. The NPT forbade those signatories that did not already possess nuclear weapons from ever acquiring them and obligated those that did—the United States, the Soviet Union, and Britain—to pledge never to assist other countries to join the nuclear club. The other two nuclear powers, France and China, which had long declined to sign the NPT, finally agreed to do so in 1992. By that year, therefore, all five countries that were capable of initiating a nuclear war were committed to preventing the spread of these weapons of mass destruction to other states. A further step towards preventing the spread of nuclear weapons came in 1994, when Argentina, Brazil, and Chile finally signed the Treaty of Tlatelolco of 1967, which had declared all of Latin America a nuclear-free zone. Cuba, the last holdout, signed the treaty in March 1995.

It had been evident for some time, however, that many other countries were capable of manufacturing nuclear weapons if they chose to do so. This was true not only of industrial societies blessed with an advanced technological base and an abundant supply of scientists and engineers, but it was also true of less developed countries with substantial financial assets (such as some of the oil-producing nations in the Middle East and North Africa) that could purchase the necessary technology and expertise from foreign sources. The countries thought to possess or be capable of producing nuclear weapons that had refused to sign the NPT included South Africa, India, Pakistan, and Israel. It was no coincidence that all four had been engaged in recurrent conflicts with regional antagonists: white-ruled South Africa with virtually all of the other countries on its continent, Israel with its Arab neighbours, and India and Pakistan with each other. All of these embattled states may have regarded their putative ability to produce nuclear weapons at a moment's notice—or, in Israel's case, its alleged possession of warheads and a delivery system—as an effective deterrent to aggression by hostile neighbours. South Africa later acknowledged that it had produced six nuclear warheads in the course of the 1980s before destroying them in 1990 and signed the NPT in 1991. India, which had tested an atomic device in 1974 but denied possessing nuclear weapons, confirmed its possession of a nuclear arsenal when it carried out tests in May 1998, which prompted Pakistan to follow suit.

The threat of nuclear proliferation posed by this handful of nonsignatories was compounded by the problem of those signatories that had long been suspected of violating the treaty and concealing their clandestine nuclear programs from the agency charged with its enforcement, the Vienna-based International Atomic Energy Agency (IAEA). The list of suspects included Iran, Iraq, Libya, and North Korea. While little was known of the nuclear ambitions and capabilities of Iran and Libya, a great deal of such information came to light in the early 1990s about North Korea and Iraq. North Korea became the first signatory to renounce the Nuclear Non-Proliferation Treaty and overtly challenge the IAEA's investigatory authority to verify compliance in 1993. Though a minimally satisfactory resolution of that controversy was achieved, the precedent of North Korea's defiance of the treaty and its enforcement agency remains for other aspiring nuclear powers to ponder. The full extent of Iraq's nuclear aspirations became known to the world in the aftermath of the Gulf War in 1991. The UN inspection team that was dispatched to the defeated country discovered a clandestine nuclear weapons program more advanced than anticipated, together with a rudimentary delivery system comprising hundreds of ballistic missiles. As a consequence, Iraq became the first state to undergo compulsory denuclearization under the supervision of inspectors from the UN and the IAEA, though inspections were suspended indefinitely in December 1998.

These experiences caused concerned observers to speculate about how many other aspirants to nuclear status may exist in the world. The end of the Cold War and the substantial reductions in the nuclear forces of the two countries that had waged it paradoxically resulted in increased anxiety about the spread of nuclear weapons to renegade states and even non-governmental entities (such as terrorist groups or drug cartels) beyond the purview of international law and arms control agencies. When the next five-year NPT review conference met in New York City in the spring of 1995 to discuss terms for the renewal of the treaty, representatives of the 5 nuclear and 160 nonnuclear powers addressed the proposal issued by the United States in September 1994 (and supported by Britain and France) that the NPT remain operational permanently rather than for the 25-year period stipulated in the original treaty. In May 1995, the NPT was extended indefinitely, on the condition that the existing nuclear states agree to a Comprehensive Test Ban Treaty (CTBT) and work toward total nuclear disarmament. The US Senate's rejection of the CTBT in the fall of 1999, together with a lack of progress in the reduction of existing nuclear arsenals, strengthened the position of those non-nuclear states that accepted the NPT with great reluctance and hoped to see its demise.

The frightful prospect of impoverished but entrepreneurial laboratory technicians smuggling stolen supplies of weapons-grade uranium or plutonium out of one of the four nuclear republics and selling them abroad to the highest bidder became a major worry to the international community. Pressure from Washington and other foreign powers induced these states to tighten their procedures for ensuring the security of the nuclear waste materials stored on their territory. In November 1994, the United States secretly airlifted from Kazakhstan (with the full approval of its government) enough enriched uranium to make two dozen atomic bombs[2] for fear that the inadequately monitored weapons-grade material would fall into the hands of eager purchasers such as Iran, Iraq, or North Korea.

Another source of international concern was the widespread unemployment in Russia's nuclear weapons industry caused by the country's general economic decline and the massive cuts in its defence budget after the various arms control agreements began to be implemented. This situation sparked anxious speculation in the West that highly skilled but unemployed or underpaid nuclear scientists and engineers would be tempted to sell their valuable services to the governments of aspiring nuclear powers, just as expatriate German scientists had helped to develop the nuclear programs of both superpowers during and after World War II. As a partial solution to this problem, the US government offered to provide financial subsidies to research centres in Russia to employ scientists laid off by the nuclear weapons

industry. Despite this provision, the clandestine spread of nuclear expertise and material remained a sobering possibility as long as the Russian economy continued to deteriorate.

The progress in limiting the development, testing, and proliferation of nuclear weapons during the 1990s was accompanied by even greater success in the campaign to eliminate two other categories of military hardware. Whereas the five nuclear powers stopped short of surrendering all of their warheads and dismantling all of their delivery systems, most countries eagerly embraced the campaign to banish for all time the frightful scourge of biological and chemical warfare. Though the Biological Weapons Convention of 1972, which entered into force in 1975, prohibited the production and possession of biological weapons, efforts to enforce it were continually hampered by the impossibility of devising foolproof verification procedures. In 1992, Russia, after conceding that it had violated the provisions of the treaty from the very beginning by secretly stockpiling bacteriological weapons, joined the United States and Britain in agreeing to permit unrestricted access to biological facilities for international inspection teams. Each periodic review of the 1972 convention revealed the same melancholy but incontrovertible truth: any competent biologist working with standard equipment can breed bacteriological agents with lethal properties that could be placed at the disposal of renegade governments, terrorist groups, or simply individuals with a score to settle. In addition to Russia, 11 other nations (including China, Iran, Iraq, and North Korea) were widely suspected of possessing the capability of producing germ-warfare agents.

The prospects for abolishing chemical weaponry proved considerably brighter. The Geneva Protocol of 1925, reflecting the widespread revulsion against the poison gas attacks of World War I, had prohibited the use—but not the possession—of chemical weapons. The two superpowers, as well as many other countries that had accumulated enormous stockpiles of chemical weapons during the Cold War, were therefore technically in compliance with that old international agreement.

The disappearance of the Soviet threat provided President George H.W. Bush an opportunity to attempt to close this gaping loophole in international law. In the spring of 1991, he offered to destroy all American stocks of chemical weapons within 10 years after an agreement banning their possession entered into force. The Chemical Weapons Convention, which had been under discussion in the United Nations for two decades, was finally completed and opened for signature at the beginning of 1993; it entered into force in 1997. This landmark agreement replaced the Geneva Protocol by prohibiting the production, acquisition, and exportation of chemical weapons and requiring the destruction of all stocks of such weapons within 10 years of the agreement's entry into force. Since a civilian chemical industry can shift to weapons production on very short notice, stringent verification procedures (including challenge inspections and immediate access to all chemical production facilities) were stipulated and accepted by all the signatories. However, several of the countries known to possess chemical weapons declined to sign the convention. Those that did and admitted to having chemical weapons programs, including India, China, and South Korea, accepted intrusive inspections of their facilities. One of the conspicuous holdouts was Iraq, whose indiscriminate use of chemicals during the war with Iran in the 1980s had helped to stimulate public support for the ban in the first place.

THE NEW WORLD ROLE OF THE UNITED NATIONS IN THE 1990s

The original expectation that the United Nations organization would play a prominent role in enforcing international security was cut short by the Cold War. The global rivalry between the Communist and anti-Communist blocs during the 40 years after the Second World War precluded the kind of co-operative spirit that would have been required for the UN to function as anything more than a forum for the international exchange of opinion. Its only significant operation on behalf of collective security during that period, the military intervention in Korea in 1950, had depended on an exceptional circumstance that would never recur: the Soviet boycott of the Security Council, which permitted a unique display of unanimity in support of the use of force to repel an armed attack. The few other instances of UN intervention in military conflicts were of limited scope and minimal consequence. Most were related to monitoring the periodic ceasefires that punctuated the continuous war in the Middle East.

As the Cold War wound down toward the end of the 1980s and Soviet–American hostilities eased, the world body was afforded its first opportunity to rediscover the global peacekeeping role that its architects had originally envisioned for it. Its initial foray into post–Cold War peacekeeping proved to be its most successful and therefore became a model for future operations. As world attention was riveted on the dramatic events unfolding in Eastern Europe and the Soviet Union in 1990–1, the decade-long civil war in El Salvador came to an end through the good offices of the United Nations. The Security Council then dispatched an observer mission (ONUSAL) to the country to monitor the ceasefire and collect the weapons that the rebel movement had consented to turn in. In this way the world body helped to defuse a long and bitter civil dispute that had become swept up in the East–West struggle during the previous decade.

During the first half of the 1990s, the task of facilitating demobilization and reconciliation after civil wars became a hallmark of United Nations' policy-making in the aftermath of the Cold War. In addition to the operation in El Salvador, UN peacekeeping forces intervened in civil conflicts in Angola, Bosnia–Herzegovina, Cambodia, Croatia, El Salvador, Macedonia, Mozambique, Rwanda, Somalia, and the Western Sahara. The diverse objectives of these operations included protecting civilian populations, assuring the delivery of relief supplies, supervising ceasefires, disarming combatants, and preparing and monitoring elections or referendums. The balance sheet for these United

Nations activities includes the notable successes in El Salvador and Cambodia as well as the disappointing failures in Angola and Somalia. But the most remarkable feature of the sudden upsurge of UN involvement in hotspots across the globe was what appeared to be the resuscitation of the world organization as an influential actor on the international stage in the post–Cold War world.

This new activism on the part of the United Nations increased markedly after the accession, in early 1992, of the new secretary-general, Dr Boutros Boutros-Ghali of Egypt. Within a few months of taking office, Boutros-Ghali presented the Security Council his Agenda for Peace, which proposed a set of fundamental reforms of the organization to enable it to expand its peacekeeping mission throughout the world. The principal obstacle to prompt and effective UN peacemaking operations—apart from the squabbling between the two superpowers that had recently come to an end—had always been the absence of a permanent military organization capable of responding quickly to a crisis. Boutros-Ghali sought to rectify this deficiency by imploring the member states to designate permanent military units, composed of volunteers, that would be available on short notice for UN peacekeeping operations. By the mid-1990s, several countries had indicated their willingness to supply such standby forces.

The Security Council had also enlisted the cooperation of existing regional and national military units to bolster its peacemaking activities pending the availability of the forces earmarked for UN service. Examples of this assistance include the reliance on NATO and WEU naval units to enforce the UN trade embargo imposed on Serbia in 1992, the authorization of NATO aircraft to police the no-fly zone over Bosnia declared by the UN in the same year, and the Security Council's approval of the French military intervention in Rwanda in 1994 to establish protected areas for refugees fleeing the civil war in that country. To enhance the UN's peacekeeping capability the secretary-general's office inaugurated a number of important institutional changes, which included increasing the size of the military advisory staff in New York, emphasizing long-range planning and intelligence operations, and improving the coordination between UN headquarters and officers in the field. Some reformers even began to suggest that the world body take the much bolder step of forming a multinational volunteer army under its own jurisdiction for deployment in the world's troublespots, a sort of French Foreign Legion in blue helmets.

The multilateralist vision of a permanent international military organization to enforce peace and security in the world, whether in the form of earmarked national units on call or through the establishment of a permanent UN peacekeeping instrument, proved utopian. The project involved too great a sacrifice of national sovereignty by the member states contributing the personnel and equipment. The numerous UN peacekeeping operations in the 1990s were conducted in destitute developing countries for universally recognized humanitarian purposes and did not directly engage the vital interests of the participating countries. There seemed to be no likelihood of unified and effective action by the United Nations in conflicts impinging on the national interests of great powers.

The other problem was that peacekeeping operations, especially those of indefinite duration, placed heavy strains on the UN budget. The failure of several countries (including the United States and Russia) to pay their assessed dues in a timely fashion, which caused the international organization occasional financial embarrassment, was not an auspicious sign for subsequent multilateral peacekeeping. Particularly in times of economic hardship, member states find it politically difficult to justify increased expenditures for UN operations in distant conflicts of peripheral concern to their domestic constituencies. Boutros-Ghali's failure to win a second term as secretary-general because of the adamant opposition of the US spelled the end, at least for the foreseeable future, of the trend toward a more aggressive and interventionist policy for the United Nations.

SUMMARY

At the end of the twentieth century, three global issues dominated the international landscape. The first was a rise in sectarian violence associated with a resurgence of ethnic nationalism. The collapse of the Soviet Union in 1991 spawned a number of ethnic conflicts, especially in the Caucasian region. Religious fundamentalism accompanied the surge of nationalism in a number of areas, such as the Indian subcontinent, producing a volatile mix of intolerant ideologies and sectarian violence. Second, the late twentieth century saw a movement towards a global system for economic management. After lengthy debates involving 123 nations, the Uruguay Round of negotiations was completed in 1994, making world trade freer than it had been at any time since 1945. In 1995, the WTO replaced the General Agreement on Tariffs and Trade GATT. The new system was designed to promote the integration of national economies, but foreign indebtedness remained a crucial problem for developing countries. In the late 1990s, an increasing number of international protests targeted the IMF and the World Bank. Critics argued that the fiscal policies of the IMF and the World Bank served only to deepen economic disparities and social inequities in the Third World.

The third trend in international relations at the end of the twentieth century was the effort to control the spread of weapons of mass destruction. Following the dissolution of the Soviet Union, the United States and the Russian Federation negotiated several agreements, most notably START II, signed in 1993. But negotiations for CTBT stalled when several countries, including the US, failed to support the agreement. Although progress was made toward expanding NPT, it was rejected by Israel, India, Pakistan, and North Korea. Negotiations to control chemical weapons were more successful, and the Chemical Weapons Convention came into force in 1997. Tests of nuclear weapons by India and Pakistan in 1998, together with North Korea's ongoing nuclear program, ensured that arms control would continue to be a pressing global concern.

NOTES

1. The eight rounds were the first Geneva Round (1947), the Annecy Round (1949), the Torquay Round (1950–1), the Second Geneva Round (1955–6), the Third Geneva (Dillon) Round (1959–62), the Fourth Geneva (Kennedy) Round (1963–7), the Tokyo Round (1973–9), and the Uruguay Round (1986–94).
2. Approximately 591 kilograms. A nuclear bomb can be made with 15 kilograms of weapons-grade uranium or 5 kilograms of plutonium.

QUESTIONS FOR CRITICAL THOUGHT

1. How can developing nations overcome the burden of debt and still secure the capital necessary to modernize?
2. Create one argument supporting and one refuting the following statement: Globalization operates primarily to the advantage of the wealthy, developed nations.
3. What steps can be taken to remedy the threat of nuclear proliferation?
4. How can the UN become a genuinely effective agent of collective security?
5. Can the UN operate as a peace*making* force? Why or why not?
6. Discuss whether unilateralism or multilateralism held sway at the end of the twentieth century.

WEBSITES FOR FURTHER REFERENCE

Global Gateway: World Culture and Resources
  http://international.loc.gov/intldl/intldlhome.html

UNESCO
  http://portal.unesco.org/

University of Hawai'i at Manoa Library: Resources on Globalization
  http://hawaii.edu/emailref/internet_resources/Globalization.html

Women and Development Resources
  www.gdrc.org/gender/link-resources.html

CHAPTER 21

THE TWENTY-FIRST CENTURY

THE TURN-OF-THE-CENTURY WORLD

At the 1893 World's Columbian Exposition, massive crowds were dazzled by the technologies that would shape the coming century. Thomas Edison's kinetoscope ran a short film clip of British Prime Minister William Gladstone speaking before the House of Commons; the first paying motion picture hall utilized Eadweard Muybridge's zoopraxiscope. Machinery Hall and the Electricity Building showcased the latest advances in electrification, including Nikola Tesla's revolutionary alternating-current powering, massive Westinghouse generators which allowed the exposition grounds to be flooded with light. Elisha Gray's teleautograph machine provided an early glimpse of the technology that, in the 1970s, would become the modern fax machine. Karl Benz's quadricycle, powered by an internal combustion engine was also on display. Meanwhile, Friedrich Krupp spent an estimated US$1.5 million on a pavilion to present the latest in his company's metal manufacturing and arms, including a gun with a firing range of nearly 21 kilometres and the latest in high-carbon armour plate which was capable of stopping the newest and most powerful shells, also produced by the Krupp works. However, the impact of such weapons on the nature of warfare seems to have been lost in the outpouring of public enthusiasm for all of the technological marvels on display.

The tension between the destructive capacity generated by technological innovation and the enormous potential such inventions held to improve human life would define the twentieth century. By the end of the 1990s, technology had apparently swept away geographical and temporal boundaries and had made available, via the Internet, an overwhelming amount of information. However, nuclear weapons had already raised the spectre of human annihilation, and even the relatively innocuous personal computer was viewed as a possible threat to global order and stability as the last moments of the century ticked away.

Although predictions of a global meltdown caused by the Y2K bug were not realized, numerous uncertainties remained as the twenty-first century dawned. Had the bipolar international system of the Cold War era been replaced by a unipolar world where the United States would operate as the delegated enforcer of global rules and regulations (as in the Persian Gulf in 1991

THE Y2K PANIC

To save computer memory, which was extremely limited in computers of the 1950s and 1960s, the technology industry commonly used two digits to represent the year (e.g. '81' rather than '1981'). By the 1990s, concerns surfaced that the transition from 1999 to the year 2000 could cause catastrophic problems for older computer systems, which might read '00' as '2000' or as '100', '1,000', or '4,000'. Nowhere would this hit harder than in the financial sector, where the passing of one day might be electronically interpreted as a step backwards or forwards of one hundred or one thousand years. An economist from Deutsche Bank Securities predicted a 70 per cent chance that the world would be forced into a recession because of the financial damage caused by what was soon labelled the 'Y2K bug'; other analysts claimed that the cost of responding to the potential crisis could reach US$2 trillion. In 1997 the head of the Y2K Cooperation Team, a project funded by the World Bank, wrote that '[w]e have never gone through a global event like this in which all the world is affected by one thing at the same time, something that has the potential to disrupt commerce.' Millennial celebrations[1] were tempered by incessant discussions of the possible meltdown. The BBC and many other broadcasters opened special websites devoted to providing readers with the very latest information, noting that there were 'fears of disruption on a massive scale, with predictions of aeroplanes falling out of the sky, nuclear bombs going off or people's bank accounts being cleared of funds'.

In the end, the cost of patches, fixes, and equipment replacement was estimated at between US$300 and $500 billion and the feared global communications and transportation meltdown did not materialize. The largest glitches reported were a US spy satellite which shut down for several hours due to the date error and a Japanese nuclear facility in which a false alarm sounded for many hours. Nonetheless, the Y2K bug had clearly seized the popular imagination in a way that few other events had ever done, an initiation into the truly globalized nature of the twenty-first-century world.

and in Kosovo in 1999)? Would economic superpowers such as Japan, China, and the European Union develop military capabilities that would be independent of (and even to a certain extent competitive with) America's formidable military might, to confirm the trend toward a genuinely multipolar international system? Or would the elusive dream of one world without regional poles of attraction finally become a reality through the strengthening of the supranational mechanisms of collective security in the United Nations and other agencies? Would the power of global commerce and technology to bring the world closer overcome the fragmenting forces of ethnic nationalism which had recently destroyed the Yugoslav and Czechoslovakian states? Finally, would the state of the natural environment turn out to be the biggest challenge of all in the twenty-first century?

These questions were temporarily forgotten in late 2001, in the wake of a coordinated series of terrorist attacks on the United States. On the morning of 11 September, terrorists hijacked four US airliners: two of the planes were flown into the twin towers of the World Trade Center in New York; a third plane crashed into the west wing of the Pentagon in Washington; and the fourth, apparently bound for either the White House or the Capitol Building, crashed into a field in Pennsylvania. As millions of television viewers watched in horror, the twin towers collapsed. Nearly 2,800 people had died before the day was over, including everyone on the four planes. Almost immediately, evidence indicated that al-Qaeda, the Islamist terrorist organization established by Osama bin Laden in the late 1980s, was responsible for the attacks. The group had conducted a series of attacks on Western targets in the 1990s, but efforts by the Clinton administration to destroy its training camps in Afghanistan had failed to neutralize its operations.

The attacks of 11 September sent shockwaves around the world, and the United States received an instant outpouring of international support. As one French newspaper put it, 'We are all Americans.' When the administration of President George W. Bush moved to topple the Taliban regime that harboured al-Qaeda in Afghanistan, it received strong backing from its allies, and even from some enemies. The UN Security Council authorized the creation of the International Stabilization Force (ISAF) in December 2001 (subsequently, NATO assumed command of ISAF). By mid-2009, 42 nations had contributed troops to ISAF and the force stood at a troop strength of 64,500. Initial coalition victories against the Taliban seemed to hold out promise that Afghanistan could be stabilized and the power of the Taliban reduced. However, after US resources shifted to a new campaign in Iraq, beginning in the summer of 2003, the Taliban regrouped and began inflicting heavy casualties, especially in the area of southern Afghanistan. Between 2003 and 2009, a rapid increase in foreigners fighting alongside Taliban forces caused considerable concern. In light of the deteriorating situation on the ground in Afghanistan, in December 2009, the new US administration of President Barack Obama committed to a massive surge in American troops in an attempt to contain the Taliban and its allies.

The second stage of the 'war on terror', as it was called, began in 2002, when President Bush made a series of strident claims about the imminent threat posed by Iraqi President Saddam Hussein. US Secretary of State Colin Powell spoke forcefully before the United Nations, claiming that Iraq had breached the disarmament requirements imposed after the first Gulf War and was stockpiling both biological and chemical weapons. Arguing that the world's nations were either with the United States or against it, Bush accused Iraq of belonging to an 'axis of evil' that included Iran and North Korea. Iraq, according to the American

administration, not only possessed weapons of mass destruction and supported terrorist groups but was also poised to strike America and its allies at any moment.

Although Bush received heavy support from British Prime Minister Tony Blair, his policy toward Iraq alienated many nations that had backed the overthrow of the Taliban. Bush's strategy toward Iraq was widely viewed as part of a larger shift in American foreign policy. To neutralize perceived terrorist threats, the Bush administration adopted a doctrine of pre-emptive

Canadian Prime Minister Jean Chrétien looks up at the wreckage of what is left of the World Trade Center in New York, 29 September 2001. Twenty-four Canadians were among the 2,973 who died in the September 11 attacks. CP Archives (Tom Hanson).

action and embraced a form of unilateralism advocated by neo-conservative strategists, which, as UN Secretary-General Kofi Annan pointed out in September 2004, was an illegal act that violated the UN Charter. As had been the case during the Cold War, the American-led war on terror polarized international relations. When the United States invaded Iraq in March 2003, many

CANADA IN AFGHANISTAN

The Government of Canada committed troops to the Afghan mission in 2001, within a broad coalition of military and humanitarian forces. The stated mission of the Canadian effort—which is scheduled to conclude in 2011—is to 'help Afghans rebuild their country as a stable, democratic, and self-sufficient society'. Canada has focused on six priorities: security, the provision of basic services, humanitarian aid, border defence, the building of national institutions, and reconciliation among tribal factions. Approximately 2,800 members of the Canadian Forces were serving in the Joint Task Force Afghanistan (JTF-Afg) as of 2009, including a 1,000-member battle group based in Kandahar Province. Between 2001 and the end of October 2009, 133 members of the Canadian armed forces (including the first Canadian female combat soldier killed on the front lines), two aid workers, and one diplomat had been killed. A government report estimated the incremental cost of the mission at CAD$11.3 billion, including post-2011 disability and healthcare costs for veterans. Of this figure, military operations were projected at $9 billion and operations controlled by the Canadian International Development Agency (CIDA) at $1.7 billion.

As of 2009 Afghanistan was the single largest recipient of Canadian development aid. Public support for the Afghan mission has fluctuated, but in October 2009 surveys showed that 56 per cent of Canadians were opposed to the military mission. However, 49 per cent supported a civilian reconstruction role after the combat mission ends. This poll was taken shortly after the UN-backed Electoral Complaints Commission invalidated hundreds of thousands of ballots amid widespread claims of election fraud on the part of both incumbent President Hamid Karzai and his main rival, Abdullah Abdullah.

Progress on the priorities identified by the Canadian government remained difficult to assess. The government itself acknowledged that Kandahar Province is one of the most difficult environments in the world in which to operate. The area suffers from extreme poverty and, as a result, support for the Taliban remains high. Literacy rates (in this case measured in terms of the ability to read or write) are estimated at only 26 per cent of men and 5 per cent of women. The Kandahar Provincial Reconstruction Team, for which Canadian forces assumed responsibility in 2005, has focused on training local police forces, as well as providing assistance to infrastructure and healthcare projects including digging wells; building roads, bridges, and irrigation and sanitation facilities; clearing mines in order to return land to agricultural use; improving maternal healthcare; and eradicating polio. Government reports show considerable progress on some of these goals. The polio eradication campaign, for example, administered vaccinations to seven million children in 2007 and hopes to eliminate the disease entirely by 2011. However, the report on mine clearing stated that, in 2009, only 0.7 square kilometres of land was released for agricultural use.

Of greater concern has been the drastic increase in support of the Taliban in the region. Analysts now argue that a 'shadow Islamic Republic' headed by the group is already operating in Helmand, Kandahar, Zabol, Oruzgan, Paktia, and Paktika Provinces, with a new northern front opened in the summer of 2009. Across the border with Pakistan, Taliban forces—often aided by Pakistan's Directorate for Inter-Services Intelligence—have repeatedly engaged the Pakistani army and have gained firm control over the country's northwestern provinces.

of its allies, including Canada, refused to participate in the military campaign. Although Saddam Hussein's regime was quickly defeated, American forces failed to bring peace and stability to the country. As the conflict dragged on and casualties mounted, the long-term effects of the war on terror became more uncertain.[2]

By 2007, US forces were increasingly frustrated by Iraqi attacks. Casualty rates were rising every month, primarily from improvised explosive devices but also due to bolder attacks on American military outposts. General David Petraeus, newly appointed commanding general of the coalition forces in Iraq, called the spring of 2007 a 'horrific nightmare'. Petraeus thus undertook a comprehensive revision of American strategy in Iraq, accompanied by an increase in US troops of approximately 28,000, the majority of which were tasked with improving security in Baghdad. To that end Petraeus's advisors began negotiations with Sunni insurgents. Nearly 100,000 former opponents were given jobs with the American administration—at an estimated cost of US$30 million a month—in order to reign in the insurgency. Petraeus also began focusing on locally developed solutions rather than imposing American assumptions on the situation, often relying on former insurgents to provide new ideas as to how best to improve security.

In the end most analysts have rated the 'Petraeus Doctrine' as a military success: security on the ground improved, US casualties decreased, and the Obama administration was able to fulfill its promise to withdraw American forces from Iraqi cities at the end of June 2009. Nonetheless, some 130,000 American troops remain in Iraq, and the White House has acknowledged that many will have to stay beyond the formal military withdrawal targeted for August 2010. Critics have noted that the most intractable questions, including issues relating to the sharing of oil revenue; reconciliation among Sunni, Shia, and Kurdish peoples; and the role and influence of Iran in the region remain entirely unresolved. There are also lingering fears that another leader in the vein of Saddam Hussein may yet arise to impose order, in light of increasing factional violence directed against civilians since the American withdrawal from the cities. Thomas Ricks, a senior fellow at the Center for a New American Security, concluded that the whole situation 'is tainted by the original sin of invading a country preemptively on false premises. Our job now is to find the least bad answers. . . . he's [Obama] eventually going to have to settle into a long war with much smaller numbers of forces—35,000–50,000 troops—but probably for several more years of fighting.'

A NEW WORLD ORDER?

With the collapse of the Soviet Union, in December 1991, a number of analysts boldly predicted a new, unipolar world order. The Cold War was over; the West with its focus on free market capitalism and democracy had won. Two decades later, the situation seems far less clear. While the United States did move increasingly in the direction of unilateral action, especially after the events of 11 September 2001, the outcome has hardly been positive. By the end of George W. Bush's second term as president, the country's debt stood at US$10.5 trillion, at least $1.6 trillion of which was, according to a congressional committee report, a direct result of the unilateral American intervention in Iraq.[3] The Bush administration also rejected the Kyoto Protocol on carbon emissions standards, withdrew from the 1972 Antiballistic Missile (ABM) Treaty, and violated commitments to the 1970 Non-Proliferation Treaty (NPT).

Given the negative international view of American unilateralism, it was to be expected that the newly elected Democratic administration of Barack Obama would seek to reverse its predecessor's policies. Prior to his inauguration, the president-elect had committed to 'combine military power with strengthened diplomacy . . . [and] to build and forge stronger alliances around the world so that we are not carrying the burdens and these challenges by ourselves'. Secretary of State-elect Hillary Clinton echoed Obama when she noted that 'our security, our values, and our interests cannot be protected and advanced by force alone nor, indeed, by Americans [alone].' Whether this rhetoric will be matched by concrete policy changes remains to be seen, as the administration struggles with an economic recession, the continuing war in Iraq, and a renewed commitment to the Afghan War.

In attempting to identify those powers which might provide an effective counterweight to the United States, Russia must be considered. During the Boris Yeltsin regime (1991–9), Russia moved from one crisis to another as the transition to capitalism produced a disastrous economic situation. By the end of 1998, annual inflation had reached 70 per cent, the official unemployment rate approached 12 per cent, and over 44 million Russians lived below the poverty line. A survey of Russian citizens showed that almost 30 per cent expected to survive at only the most basic level; a further 48 per cent simply hoped to be no worse off than their neighbours. Meanwhile, Yeltsin clashed repeatedly with parliamentary factions which disagreed with his policies and with the draconian manner in which he controlled the country. When Yeltsin resigned on 31 December 1999 in favour of his hand-picked successor, Vladimir Putin, Russian power seemed to have been thoroughly broken.

However, high oil and gas prices in the first half of the 2000s, combined with what Putin referred to as 'managed democracy'—strengthening the powers of the central Russian state while reducing the powers of regional leaders[4]—ushered in a new era of economic growth and international influence. Powerful oligarchs who had enjoyed near limitless power in the Yeltsin era, including oil tycoons Boris Berezovsky and Mikhail Khodorkovsky, were pushed aside in favour of technocrats chosen by and loyal to Putin. Controls were placed on the independent media, and, during Putin's second term, new limits were placed on freedom of association, assembly, and expression. A 2008 Amnesty International report accused the Putin administration of using laws against extremism to target non-governmental organizations (NGOs) that refused to follow the Kremlin's dictates. Putin, however, argued that such limits were in keeping with Russian history and tradition. Democracy would be contained in such a way as to guarantee that there would be no return to the chaos of the Yeltsin era.

When, in 2008, constitutional safeguards prohibited him from seeking a third term (despite his tremendous popularity among the Russian people) Putin nominated his former presidential chief of staff and deputy prime minister, Dmitry Medvedev, to succeed him. Medvedev, in turn, promised to appoint Putin as Russia's prime minister. Together, the leaders have overseen Russia's re-emergence as a powerful regional actor, able to intervene without concern in the South Ossetia region of Georgia, even as Georgian President Mikheil Saakashvili was negotiating to bring his country into NATO. Medvedev spoke repeatedly of the importance of multilateralism as a cornerstone of Russian foreign policy, even as the Russians moved military units into South Ossetia, an irony that was hardly lost in the West.

As Russia was rebuilding its economic and political institutions, new powers were emerging to challenge the notion of a unipolar world. A 2006 briefing paper from the Bonn-based German Development Institute (DIE) argued that the rise of India and China had already produced a de facto multipolar configuration. As of 2005 China held over US$819 billion in currency reserves, the second largest total in the world; was the third largest trading nation in the world; and produced some 15 per cent of all US imports. In 2006 Chinese industry employed 83 million workers, with another 100 million able to move into the industrial sector should demand increase. One negative result of this massive industrial capacity has been an alarming increase in pollution: China is now one of the world's largest emitters of carbon dioxide. The DIE estimated that, by 2020, India would occupy China's current role in the global economy. Both countries have become increasingly important actors on the international stage due to their potential to impact the world economy and the environment.

GLOBALISM AND ITS DISCONTENTS

Two key and simultaneous forces evident in the last decades of the twentieth century seemed poised to shape global development in the twenty-first. One factor was the shift towards globalism in economic, cultural, and political organizations. The other was the ongoing fragmentation of nation-states into sub-national units as ethnic, religious, and political antagonisms resurfaced.

Definitions of globalism vary and few are value-neutral. In its most general sense, the term refers simply to the integration of economic, political, financial, technological, cultural, and social systems throughout the world. Most analysts agree that the pace of globalism increased markedly after 1980; however, there is extensive disagreement as to its overall impact. Some believe that globalism has increased opportunities for nations both to participate in and draw benefits from the global economy and the global trend towards democratization. Others view globalism as an entirely destructive process wherein smaller nations are reduced to being perpetual suppliers of cheap labour and raw material to the developed world.

It would be hard to argue that the gap between rich and poor nations has shown any sign of decreasing in the early twenty-first century. Forty-nine developing countries, home to some two billion people, have seen their share of global trade decline since 1980 and, as a result, per capita incomes in those nations have also dropped. In 2003 the Washington, DC-based Worldwatch Institute found that, despite a sevenfold increase in the global economy since 1950, the gross domestic product (GDP) gap between the 20 richest and 20 poorest nations had more than doubled. The United Nations Development Program (UNDP) noted in 2003 that just as globalization has systematically benefited some of the world's regions, it has bypassed others as well as many groups within countries. In the 1990s most of East and South Asia saw living standards improve dramatically. But large parts of Sub-Saharan Africa, parts of Eastern Europe and the Commonwealth of Independent States (CIS) and many countries in Latin America and the Middle East did not. In addition, epidemic disease, most dramatically HIV/AIDS, prey disproportionately on those left behind and push them back even further—trapping poor people in a vicious cycle of poverty and disease.

A similar phenomenon is evident within many nations. In Canada, studies of 2006 census data showed clearly that the gap between rich and poor has widened significantly. Incomes rose 16.4 per cent for the richest twenty per cent of the population between 1980 and 2005. In contrast, incomes for the poorest twenty per cent dropped by 20.6 per cent. Incomes in the middle range stagnated, despite the fact that the economy expanded over this 25-year period. More than one person in every ten in Canada was classified as living in a low-income household. Immigrant communities were highly likely to fall into the low-income category, with immigrant male workers earning only CAD$0.63 for every $1 earned by a Canadian-born male worker. Immigrant women earned only $0.56 cents for every $1 earned by Canadian-born women. Twenty-five years earlier the figure had been $0.85 to every $1 for both immigrant groups. Many analysts pointed to the more globalized economy as the cause of these increasing gaps. A larger global labour supply had served to depress wages and to eliminate many blue-collar jobs, as manufacturing moved offshore to low-labour–cost countries.

Nonetheless, World Bank data reveals that 24 countries, classified as 'developing' (including China, India, the Philippines, Malaysia, and Bangladesh) greatly increased their share of global trade and their per capita income after introducing economic reforms and free trade policies designed to integrate their countries into the global economy. This rise was, however, before the most recent global economic downturn, the full impact of which remains to be seen.

The fact is that confronting global poverty remains a key struggle in the twenty-first century. To this end, in September 2000, 189 UN countries adopted what was called the 'Millennium

Declaration'—a commitment to extend freedom, equality, solidarity, tolerance, respect for nature, and shared responsibility by 2015. Eight broad millennium development goals (MDGs) were identified: the eradication of extreme poverty and hunger; the achievement of universal primary education; the promotion of gender equality and the empowerment of women; the reduction of child mortality; the improvement of maternal health; the reduction of HIV/AIDS, malaria, and other diseases; the achievement of environmental sustainability; and the development of a global partnership for development. However, the 2009 progress report reveals just how intractable some of these problems are.

The MDG which shows the greatest progress is access to education, both primary and secondary. In Latin America and the Caribbean, for example, over half of the 29 countries within this group have reached the goal of universal access to primary education. Similarly, of 13 Middle Eastern/ North African nations only a slightly lower percentage has already met the target. However, when one looks at the goal of reducing child mortality, the situation appears bleak. The greatest progress has been made in Eastern Europe/ Central Asia and in South Asia; in both cases almost 40 per cent of countries are either on track to meet or have met the MDG. However, none of the 47 countries of Sub-Saharan Africa fall into this category: 45 per cent are off track and 53 per cent are seriously off track.[5] In the Middle East/North Africa, while approximately 50 per cent are on track, the remainder are either off track (40 per cent) or seriously off track (10 per cent). Likewise, on the issue of access to sanitation facilities (a sub-category of environmental sustainability, not one Sub-Saharan African country is on track to meet the MDG: 75 per cent are seriously off track, as are over 50 per cent of South Asian countries. On the broadest goal of all—eradicating extreme hunger and poverty—a great many countries have not even reported the data necessary to assess the MDG, but the trend is not promising among those that have. Only the region of Eastern Europe/Central Asia is showing substantial

progress, with 50 per cent on track and more than 10 per cent having already achieved the MDG. Even here, however, over 20 per cent are seriously off track. Over 50 per cent of South Asian countries reporting data are off track or seriously off track, as are 30 per cent of Latin American/ Caribbean countries.

One of the undeniable results of poverty and inequality has been an increase in ethnic, religious, and social tensions. In developed countries these pressures are usually contained, if barely so, by social welfare provisions. In developing states and states in the midst of rapid transitions, however, they can lead to fragmentation and even to the destruction of the nation-state itself. The dissolution of Yugoslavia, in the 1990s, stands as a cautionary example of what can happen when the pressures of the political transition from communism, traditional nationalisms, and economic disparity combine. Whereas Marshal Tito's Yugoslavia had contained socio-economic and religious tensions (by force where necessary), Slobodan Milošević sought to manipulate these tensions in pursuit of greater Serbian power within the federation. In the end, Yugoslavia dissolved into its constituent parts, but not before 191,000 people lost their lives in religious and ethnically based violence.

In Somalia, it was rapid Westernization—a last-ditch effort by the Somali dictator Mohamed Siad Barre to consolidate power over rebellious clans—that would end in the complete destruction of the state. In 1988 a civil war broke out between armed clans and the central government in Mogadishu. By 1991, Siad Barre, who had held power for 22 years, had been forced into exile and the central government dissolved in the face of numerous rival factions. In 1992 and 1993 a multinational force was sent, under UN auspices, to stabilize the situation sufficiently to deliver humanitarian aid. However, this intervention ended disastrously when 19 US troops were killed and another 80 were wounded in October 1993. In response, the United States withdrew its troops from Somalia and has since been extremely reluctant to intervene in subsequent African conflicts.

The Somali Civil War has continued, halted only briefly by efforts to negotiate power-sharing agreements and by an Ethiopian and an African Union military intervention. By 2009, though the northernmost area of Somalia had largely stabilized, the south remained deeply divided. Radical Islamist factions battled African Union troops and more secular regional warlords. Meanwhile, the area has become a primary training ground for Islamist terrorists, including members of al-Shabaab which is believed to be affiliated with al-Qaeda. Human rights groups estimate that, to date, the conflict has led to between 350,000 and 400,000 civilian deaths.

The failure of the Somali state has not only impacted the peoples of the immediate region. The lawless nature of the area has contributed to an extraordinary rise in piracy off the Somali coast, which has taken a costly toll on shipping through the Gulf of Aden and the Indian Ocean. The BBC estimated that, in 2008, shipping companies were forced to pay over US$80 million in ransom money to Somali pirates, who attempted at least 111 attacks, 42 of them successful. In early 2009 the number of attacks increased dramatically, leading to the deployment of more warships to the region.

ONE WORLD?

Sociologists have identified three phases of global interconnectedness. The first, from 1870 to 1914, was characterized by the rise of vast colonial economic networks, as well as the establishment of branch plants. The second, from 1950 to 1980, was propelled by the institutions created at the 1944 Bretton Woods Conference, including the International Bank for Reconstruction and Development (IBRD) and the International Monetary Fund (IMF), and established a general commitment among non-communist nations to free trade and open markets. But there can be little doubt that the third phase, beginning in about 1980, differs from the others in both qualitative and quantitative ways. In the realm of economics, Western hegemony in the IMF and World

Bank was challenged when the People's Republic of China assumed responsibility for the China seat (instead of Taiwan) in both organizations, after agreeing to follow a more market-oriented economic path.[6] In 1988 China held the ninth greatest voting power (2.58 per cent); by 2006 its share of votes had increased to 3.66 per cent, with a further increase projected between 2009 and 2011.

The 1980s also saw the IMF become more concerned that its funds were being misused by borrower nations. This suspicion led to a series of guidelines which not only increased the likelihood of repayment but also pushed countries along a similar economic path. Under the rubric of 'Structural Adjustment Programs' (SAPs) the IMF insisted that borrowers liberalize trade, increase privatization, devalue currencies, and reduce subsidies in order to qualify for further loans. Critics have argued that SAPs have destroyed local industry and oftentimes forced countries back into reliance on cash crops. Despite these claims, there is no denying that SAPs encouraged a shift to free trade throughout the developing world.

The use of SAP credit was particularly high among the states of the former Soviet bloc. As market economies re-emerged, use of IMF credit was commonplace, with Russia itself drawing heavily on SAP loans to complete its transition to a capitalist economy. Many of the Soviet bloc countries also sought admission into broader economic, political, and military alliances, in particular the European Union (EU) and NATO. In this way global interconnectedness has been further intensified. Since 1989 Latvia, Lithuania, Estonia, Poland, Hungary, the Czech Republic, Slovakia, Slovenia, Romania, and Bulgaria have joined the EU. As of 2009 Croatia and Macedonia are candidate countries. In 1999 the Czech Republic, Hungary, and Poland joined NATO. Since that time Bulgaria, Estonia, Latvia, Lithuania, Romania, Slovakia, Slovenia, Albania, and Croatia have also become member states.

Even before this EU expansion, new trade blocs were emerging, both to promote free trade and to increase regional economic strength. In 1984 the

Canada–US Free Trade Agreement was superseded by the North American Free Trade Agreement (NAFTA), which added Mexico to form a trilateral trading bloc. In 1991 the Treaty of Asunción created Mercosur, a free trade area among Argentina, Paraguay, Uruguay, and Brazil. Currently Bolivia, Chile, Colombia, Ecuador, and Peru have associate member status, and Venezuela's membership is pending. Most recently there have been efforts to transform the Mercosur Parliament into a more meaningful decision-making body. Meanwhile, the Association of Southeast Asian Nations (ASEAN) has become an increasingly influential regional actor.

The strength of these trading blocs pales in comparison, however, with the power of multinational corporations in the global economy. In 2005, 95 of the world's 150 largest economies were multinational corporations (MNCs), including Wal-Mart, Exxon Mobil, Mitsui, BP, Mitsubishi, Royal Dutch Shell, Allianz, Siemens, China National Petroleum, and Verizon. In a 1997 article, updated in the early 2000s, Robert Kaplan argued that multinational corporations were nothing less than the vanguard of a new Darwinian organization of politics. Because they are in the forefront of real globalization while the overwhelming majority of the world's inhabitants are still rooted in local terrain, corporations will be free for a few decades to leave behind the social and environmental wreckage they create—abruptly closing a factory here in order to open an unsafe facility with a cheaper work force there.

The connections created by MNCs, the IMF, and the World Bank have been intensified by technological developments which began in the late 1970s. E-mail was introduced in late 1971 and the World Wide Web in 1990 (in 1993 the web saw a 341,634 per cent increase in user traffic). Meanwhile, steady improvements in memory capacity made personal computers more efficient. In 1979 10,000 Tandy TRS-80 systems were sold in the first month after their release (Radio Shack had predicted sales of 3,000 per year). The system cost just less than US$600 and came with 4KB of memory. By 1982, the Commodore 64 offered 64KB of RAM. Two years later the Apple Macintosh was introduced with a 9-inch screen and 128KB of RAM, expandable—with some considerable effort—to 512KB; Windows 1.0 launched in November 1985.

By 2007, a combination of these early technologies had launched a communications revolution. Nearly 20 per cent of the world's population had access to the Internet, ranging from a high of 70 per cent in North America to a low of 5 per cent in Africa. A Pew Research Center survey conducted in 2007 showed that computer ownership had increased in 32 out of 34 countries surveyed between 2002 and 2007. Countries in the former Eastern bloc showed the most dramatic increases in computer ownership during this time, averaging between 10 and 28 per cent increases in ownership (Canada led the world with 77 per cent of the population owning a computer by 2007). Even in countries such as Côte d'Ivoire and Mali, where computer ownership remained very low, remarkable increases in computer use were recorded. In Côte d'Ivoire only 6 per cent reported owning a computer, but 41 per cent used one. Likewise in Mali, 6 per cent ownership contrasted with 38 per cent use.

Similarly, mobile phone ownership increased substantially in the early years of the twenty-first century. The Czech Republic and Kuwait led the way with 98 per cent of adults having a mobile phone in 2007. Between 2002 and 2007, mobile ownership soared around the developing world. In Nigeria ownership increased by more than half, to 67 per cent of the adult population. In Côte d'Ivoire the numbers increased by one-third, to 66 per cent of the adult population. And in India ownership increased from 12 per cent to 60 per cent of the population. In 2008, a massive campaign to extend mobile phone service into that country's rural areas meant that 347 million Indians had subscribed to mobile phone service by the end of the year.

The same survey also provides a number of useful insights into popular perceptions of twenty-first century trends. Respondents were asked whether or not they believed that most people are better off in a free market economy, even though some people are rich and some are poor. Respondents around the world overwhelmingly answered that they either mostly or completely agreed. In only 2 of 47 countries surveyed—Japan and Ethiopia—did a bare majority answer that they mostly or completely disagreed. Yet when asked whether they believed that their traditional way of life was either getting lost or remaining strong, respondents in the vast majority of countries answered in the affirmative. In only a small number of countries did 35 per cent or more answer that their traditional way of life remained strong: Sweden, Egypt, Jordan, the Palestinian Territories, Israel, Indonesia, and China. Sweden was the only country in which a majority indicated that their way of life did not need to be protected against foreign influence, though even Swedes agreed that the entry of people into their country should be restricted or controlled more so than at present. When asked whether their culture was superior to others, the only countries where a majority answered in the negative were Britain, France, Germany, and Sweden. And finally, when asked whether it was sometimes necessary to use military force to maintain world order, in only seven countries did a majority of those surveyed answer in the negative: Germany, Bulgaria, Slovakia, Egypt, Jordan, South Korea, and Ethiopia.

THE ENVIRONMENT

In the 1960s and 1970s environmental concerns became a central part of public discourse. Rachel Carson's seminal work, *Silent Spring,* first focused attention on the potentially harmful results of the use of DDT. The terrible impact on human health of such chemical defoliants as Agent Orange, widely used during the Vietnam War, was also a cause for great concern. Organizations such as Greenpeace were founded to focus the world's attention on the dangers of nuclear weapons and nuclear testing. Subsequently, many of these organizations broadened their focus to address other pressing environmental issues, in particular the damage done by industrial pollutants.

As the twenty-first century dawned, however, no one issue attracted greater attention than concerns over global climate change. Numerous scientific studies pointed to a pattern of climate change beginning during the Industrial Revolution and accelerating during the twentieth century. Critics countered that the global climate has always passed through cycles of heating and warming. But the alarming melting of polar ice caps at the turn of the century gave new weight to scientific warnings regarding the problem.

In 2007 the Intergovernmental Panel on Climate Change (IPCC), which was established in 1988 by the UN Environment Programme (UNEP) and the World Meteorological Organization (WMO), issued its fourth and most unequivocal report. The panel concluded that '[w]arming of the climate system is unequivocal, as is now evident from observations of increases in global average air and ocean temperatures, widespread melting of snow and ice and rising global average sea level.' As to the much-debated human origins of climate change the panel determined that '[t]here is very high confidence that the global average net effect of human activities since 1750 has been one of warming.'[7]

The IPCC report should have surprised no one. As early as the 1980s members of the scientific community had begun to issue warnings regarding climate change and its impact on the earth's ecosystem. Of particular concern were carbon dioxide emissions produced by the burning of fossil fuels, by large scale agribusiness, and by deforestation. However, public awareness remained minimal and government policy change virtually non-existent. In 1992 the United Nations hosted an 'Earth Summit' in Rio de Janeiro which produced Agenda 21, a series of protocols relating to development and the environment, sustainable forestry, biological diversity, and the Framework Convention on Climate Change by which the signatory nations (155 in total) agreed that carbon emissions should be kept to 1990 levels for 10 years. Compliance with the convention was, however, voluntary, and efforts to create a more binding means of restricting 'greenhouse gases' were soon underway.

In 1997 lengthy negotiations led to the Kyoto Protocol which, unlike the UN Convention on Climate Change, was binding on the signatory nations. The protocol, which has now been signed by 184 nations (the United States, the world's largest carbon emitter, withdrew in 2001), requires that the 37 industrialized nations plus the European Union reduce carbon emissions by an average of 5.2 per cent between 2008 and 2012. Reductions can be achieved by the still controversial practice of carbon credit trading, by developing clean energy projects domestically, or by partnering with other members to reduce emissions in the partner country. Efforts to achieve a binding agreement on a second phase of emissions reductions at a meeting in Copenhagen in December 2009 were largely unsuccessful. However, the active participation of the US in these discussions was viewed as a positive development.

To date progress on Kyoto targets has been mixed, with the greatest success in Europe and the greatest failure in Canada. Despite Spain, Italy, and Denmark failing to meet their targets, reductions in Sweden, Britain, Germany, Greece, and France have left Europe in a relatively good position. However, Canada, whose Conservative government rejected many of the initiatives of its predecessor with respect to Kyoto, may not only fail to reduce its overall emissions but may actually see an over 25 per cent increase.

Should the changes to the earth's climate continue, or even accelerate, the citizens of the

Raul Estrada Oyuela (centre), chairman of the Parties of the UN Framework Convention on Climate, and other meeting officials celebrate the adoption of the Kyoto Protocol, 11 December 1997. Kyodo/Associated Press.

twenty-first century will face a series of progressively difficult challenges. The IPCC report summarizes the effects with respect to water resources:

> Climate change is expected to exacerbate current stresses on water resources from population growth and economic and land-use change, including urbanisation. On a regional scale, mountain snow pack, glaciers and small ice caps play a crucial role in freshwater availability. Widespread mass losses from glaciers and reductions in snow cover over recent decades are projected to accelerate throughout the 21st century, reducing water availability, hydropower potential, and changing seasonality of flows in regions supplied by meltwater from major mountain ranges (e.g. Hindu-Kush, Himalaya, Andes), where more than one-sixth of the world population currently lives.

For a continent such as Africa, which has suffered from chronic famines and water shortages, the IPCC concludes that between 75 and 200 million people will be exposed to 'water stresses' which will severely compromise agricultural production in the range of 9 to 21 per cent. Food security will be compromised and malnutrition will rise. In the remainder of the world the risk of wildfires will increase, low-lying coastal areas will be inundated (in some regions by as early as 2050), and the toll from water-borne diseases will increase due to alternating cycles of flood and drought.

Despite an immensely negative outlook, scientists generally agree that new strategies can avert or at least mitigate the effects of climate change. Sustainable development policies in the industrialized world, combined with massive assistance to developing countries, could help to diminish the worst effects. However, carbon emissions in the developing world remain a major problem. Even with the policies currently in place (including the Kyoto Protocol), these emissions will continue to rise over the next several decades. As to the global economic cost of effective reduction strategies, a recent World Bank study put the cost at between US$75 and $100 billion per year for the period between 2010 and 2050.

Given the overlapping threats posed by environmental change, global poverty, disease, and military conflict, it is not hard to see why so little of the optimism that greeted the opening of the twentieth century remains in the twenty-first. It is clear, however, that these challenges will have to be confronted sooner rather than later in the century, especially if the predictions on climate change prove accurate.

SUMMARY

The twenty-first century opened with a mixture of fear and promise—fear generated by the Y2K panic and the collapse of nation-states; optimism engendered by the end of the tensions which had dominated the Cold War era. However, the events of 11 September 2001 focused global attention on the threat of terrorism. The resulting American intervention in Afghanistan and Iraq created a series of problems that dominated US policy-making for the remainder of the decade. The war in Afghanistan also became a major concern for Canadian policy-makers, who had committed troops and aid in support of their American ally.

Even as the United States became mired in the Iraq and Afghan wars, new powers emerged to challenge the post-Cold War American dominance over international affairs. As its economic and political situation stabilized, Russia moved to reclaim its traditional global power. Meanwhile, dramatic economic growth in China and India propelled both nations to influence on the world stage.

Other nations, in particular in Africa and Latin America, struggled just to maintain the status quo; many fell further behind, locked in a cycle of debt and dependency. An ambitious development program launched by the United Nations, under the rubric of 'Millennium Development Goals', produced few measurable successes in the most impoverished parts of the world. Still, economic globalization continued to integrate the world at a dramatic pace.

Finally, the early twenty-first century was dominated by concerns about the global environment and the devastating potential of climate change.

Scientists were able to show convincing evidence of a sustained transformation of the world's climate. The impact of this change, especially for the world's poorest countries, remained a topic of great debate as the decade drew to a close. Likewise, there was little consensus as to how best to deal with the challenges posed by the environment.

NOTES

1. Concerns over the Y2K bug largely obscured the issue that the new millennium actually began in the year 2001, not 2000.
2. As of September 2009 US forces had suffered 4,262 deaths, with 30,182 listed as wounded.
3. The Committee also noted that the incremental costs of the war (including healthcare for veterans and attendant economic impacts) could reach US$3.5 trillion by 2017.
4. A 2004 law abolished direct election of regional governors in favour of their appointment by the Kremlin.
5. The remaining 2 per cent is a result of insufficient data to obtain a measurement.
6. In December 2001, after agreeing to a lengthy series of tariff reductions, China officially joined the WTO.
7. 'Very high confidence' is defined by the IPCC as 90 per cent agreement (www.ipcc.ch/pdf/assessment-report/ar4/syr/ar4_syr.pdf).

QUESTIONS FOR CRITICAL THOUGHT

1. What lessons can be learned from the events following 11 September 2001?
2. What are the implications of the economic ascendance of India and China?
3. Discuss whether a democratic regime can succeed when it is forcibly imposed by outsiders.
4. Can the Millennium Development Goals be achieved, and in what ways can developed countries ensure that this happens?
5. How can organizations such as al-Qaeda be weakened or marginalized?
6. Has the end of the Cold War brought about the emergence of a unipolar world, or a multipolar one? Outline how each type influences global economic, political, and social systems.

WEBSITES FOR FURTHER REFERENCE

The CHOICES Program: Teaching with the News
www.choices.edu/resources/current.php

Intergovernmental Panel on Climate Change
www.ipcc.ch/

Library of Congress: Global Gateway
http://international.loc.gov/intldl/intldlhome.html

Resources on the events of 11 September 2001
www.nyu.edu/fas/projects/vcb/case_911/resources/web.htm

TIMELINE OF WORLD HISTORY 1900–2010

1900

- In August, a combined European force aided by Japan and the United States crushes the Boxer Rebellion in China, an uprising of Chinese nationalists in Beijing opposed to Western influence.

1902

- Threatened by Russian advances on Manchuria and the Korean Peninsula, Japan and Britain sign the Anglo–Japanese Treaty on 30 January.
- In May, the Boer (or South African) War, sparked in 1899 by the refusal of Dutch and Huguenot inhabitants of Southern Africa to grant equal rights to British immigrants, ends. The British victory is obtained through the use of almost half a million British and imperial troops. Over 7,000 Canadians take part in the war, which marks Canada's first military expedition abroad.

1903

- Lord Alverstone, Lord Chief Justice of England, supports the United States in its dispute with Canada over the boundary of the Alaska panhandle.
- In August, the Russian Socialist Democratic Party splits into two factions: the Bolsheviks, led by Vladimir Lenin, who oppose co-operation with moderate reformers and favour revolution by a small political elite prepared to shape the ideas of the working class; and the Mensheviks, who favour a looser party structure.

1904

- The Russo–Japanese War begins over territorial disputes in Manchuria and the Korean Peninsula. The war would end a year later with a series of humiliating defeats for the Russians. The peace settlement, signed in Portsmouth, New Hampshire, gives the Japanese ascendancy in the region.

1905

- The Russian Revolution of 1905 begins on 22 January, when tsarist troops in St Petersburg fire on a crowd of peaceful demonstrators protesting high taxes and Russian losses in the Russo–Japanese War. The uprising ends after Tsar Nicholas II makes a number of concessions, including the formation of an elected legislative body (the Duma).

1907

- On 31 August, Russia signs an agreement with Britain; together with France, the two countries form an alliance known as the Triple Entente, which would form the basis of the Allied powers in the First World War.

1908

- Austria–Hungary annexes the province of Bosnia–Herzegovina, drawing opposition from both Serbia and its ally Russia.
- Canada and Japan sign the Lemieux–Hayashi Gentleman's Agreement, setting a yearly limit on the number of Japanese immigrants to Canada; the cap would be lowered in 1923 and again in 1928.

1910

- On 22 August, Japan annexes Korea, which would remain a Japanese possession until the end of the Second World War.

1911

- On 10 October, a revolution breaks out in central China. Sun Yat-sen becomes the provisional president of the Republic of China after the ruling Qing Dynasty is overthrown.

1912

- The first of two Balkan wars results in Turkey's loss of Albania and Macedonia, leaving the area around Constantinople (Istanbul) as the only Ottoman territory in Europe. The Second Balkan War (1913) would result in the partition of Macedonia between Greece and Serbia.

1914

- The Panama Canal opens on 7 June under the administration of the United States, which began construction of the canal in 1904.
- On 28 June, Archduke Franz Ferdinand, heir to the Austro–Hungarian Empire, is assassinated by a Serbian nationalist in Sarajevo. A month later, Austria–Hungary declares war on Serbia, precipitating the First World War. Russia intervenes on behalf of its ally, Serbia; on 1 August, Germany, on the pretext of defending Austria–Hungary, declares war on Russia and (via neutral Belgium) France. On 4 August, King George V, on behalf of Britain and its dominions (including Canada), declares war on Germany. Japan enters the conflict on 15 August, declaring war on Germany. Turkey joins the Central Powers on 1 November.

1915

- The 1st Canadian Division sees its first action of the war in the second battle of Ypres, Belgium, fought in April and May. German troops use poison gas for the first time, and the battle ends in a stalemate.
- On 12 May, German submarines sink the British ocean liner *Lusitania*, killing 1,200 passengers. The loss of more than a hundred American lives in the attack draws calls for the United States to enter the war.

1916

- Between February and June, the French lose 350,000 troops while withstanding a prolonged German offensive on the fortified town of Verdun in northeastern France.
- Between July and November, more than a million British, French, and German soldiers are killed or wounded at the battle of the Somme river in northern France. On 1 July, the opening day of the battle, the 29th Division, with 800 soldiers of the Royal Newfoundland Regiment (RNR), takes part in a disastrous attack on the German position in the Beaumont Hamel valley. Over 700 members of the RNR are killed or wounded.
- An uprising against British rule in several cities in Ireland ends with the surrender of protesters; the Easter Rising would contribute to the establishment of the Irish Free State in 1921.

1917

- Wartime shortages of food and fuel lead to strikes and riots in St Petersburg and mark the start of the Russian Revolution. During the first phase (or February Revolution), Tsar Nicholas II abdicates and a provisional government is set up. During the second phase (or October Revolution), the Bolsheviks seize control of the government in a coup led by Lenin.
- On 6 April, the United States declares war on Germany and enters the First World War.
- On 9 April, Allied forces capture the German position of Vimy Ridge, near Arras, France. One of the key positions on the Western Front, it resisted earlier French and British assaults before being taken by Canadian troops.
- In July, British troops launch the third battle of Ypres near the village of Passchendaele, Belgium. In November, the village is captured after a two-week assault by the Canadian Corps, with Canadian losses of over 15,000 dead and wounded.
- In December, the counter-revolutionary 'White Russian' army begins armed opposition to the Bolshevik Red Army, as the Russian Civil War begins.

1918

- Soviet Russia signs the Treaty of Brest-Litovsk with Germany on 3 March, ending Russian participation in the First World War.
- In August, Canadian and Australian forces spearhead a successful four-day attack on the German

trenches around Amiens, earning a decisive victory for the Allies in the war's final phase.

- An armistice is signed on 11 November, marking the end of the First World War.

1919

- The Treaty of Versailles is signed in Paris on 29 June, officially ending the First World War. Germany is forced to cede Alsace–Lorraine to France and West Prussia to Poland, while agreeing to pay reparations and to accept restrictions on its armed forces. The treaty also establishes the League of Nations.

1920

- The League of Nations places the territory of Palestine under British administration, prompting a dramatic increase in Jewish immigration to the territory and increased calls for the land to be designated an independent Jewish state.

1921

- The Russian Civil War ends with the defeat of the White Russians, who lose despite receiving assistance from Britain, France, Japan, and the United States. The following year, the victorious Bolsheviks proclaim the Union of Soviet Socialist Republics (USSR).

1922

- Benito Mussolini, founder of the Italian Fascist Party, leads a march on Rome and, on 31 October, is appointed prime minister by King Victor Emmanuel III.

1923

- The Treaty of Lausanne ends the Turkish War of Independence, which began after the collapse of the Ottoman Empire at the end of the First World War. Turkey is proclaimed an independent republic with Mustafa Kemal Atatürk as its first president.

1925

- Britain, Germany, France, Belgium, Poland, and Czechoslovakia sign the Locarno Pact, a series of agreements guaranteeing the common borders of France, Germany, and Belgium and the demilitarization of the Rhineland, as specified by the Treaty of Versailles.

1926

- The Imperial Conference adopts the Balfour Report declaration, which states that Britain and its dominions are equal and autonomous communities within the British Empire. The declaration becomes the basis for the Statute of Westminster, which would be passed in 1931.
- Civil war begins in China, as Chiang Kai-shek, who succeeded Sun Yat-sen as leader of the nationalist Kuomintang Party in 1925, begins a purge of communists and launches a military campaign to unite China; he would become president in 1928.

1928

- On 17 July, the Kellogg–Briand Pact, renouncing war as an instrument of national policy, is signed in Paris by representatives of 15 nations.

1929

- The stock market crash of 29 October ('Black Tuesday') marks the start of the Great Depression, which would last throughout most of the 1930s.

1930

- In German legislative elections, in September, the Nazi Party becomes the second largest in Germany, its representation in the Reichstag increasing from 12 to 107.

1931

- On 18 September, the Japanese army begins its occupation of the Chinese province of Manchuria.
- In December, British Parliament passes the Statute of Westminster, giving autonomy to Canada and other dominions of the British Empire.

1932

- In March, a Manchurian independence movement, financed and controlled by the Japanese occupation army, establishes the sovereign state of Manchukuo, detached from China and under Japanese military protection.

1933

- Following his appointment as chancellor of Germany in January, Adolf Hitler overthrows the Weimar Republic and establishes the totalitarian Third Reich, proclaiming himself Führer.

1934

- The 'Long March' of Chinese communists, led by Mao Zedong, begins, as 100,000 people evacuate the Chinese communist headquarters in Jiangxi, destroyed by the nationalist Kuomintang forces, and trek over a distance of 9,600 kilometres to Yan'an in Shaanxi province.

1935

- Hitler formally rejects the disarmament provisions of the Treaty of Versailles, revealing on 9 March the existence of a German air force as well as plans to expand its size and strength and introducing, on 16 March, universal military conscription with the goal of creating a 36-division army. On 15 September, the Nazi Party passes the Nuremberg Laws, depriving German Jews of citizenship.
- On 3 October, Italy invades Ethiopia. The League of Nations, at the urging of British and French representatives (as well as Canadian representative Walter Riddell), condemns the offensive and imposes economic sanctions on Italy, straining the relationship between Italy and its erstwhile European allies.

1936

- Germany re-occupies the Rhineland.
- In July, a nationalist uprising, led by General Franco and supported by fascist Italy and Germany, against the Republican Popular Front government of Spain marks the start of the Spanish Civil War; it would last until 1939.

1937

- The second Sino–Japanese War begins, as Chinese Communist Party leader Mao Zedong

and Kuomintang leader Chiang Kai-shek join forces to oppose Japanese expansionism.

1938

- Germany invades Austria on 12 March, meeting no resistance from Austrian forces. On 10 April, a rigged plebiscite produces an overwhelming vote for *Anschluss*, the unification of Austria and Germany.
- On 29 September, Hitler meets with the leaders of Britain, France, and Italy in Munich; the parties conclude an agreement (the Munich Pact) that cedes the Sudetenland region of Czechoslovakia to Germany. The agreement represents a desperate move by Britain and France to quell German expansionism and avoid war.

1939

- On 23 August, Germany and the Soviet Union sign the Molotov–Ribbentrop non-aggression pact, ostensibly committing each to neutrality toward the other in the event of a European war but secretly setting the terms for the partition of Poland following a German attack on that country. On 1 September, Germany invades Poland, marking the start of the Second World War (1939–45). Warsaw surrenders on 27 September, and Germany and the Soviet Union partition the territory as agreed.
- On 3 September, Britain and France declare war on Germany. Canada declares war a week later.
- In Spain, Franco's nationalist forces capture Barcelona and Madrid, bringing the Spanish Civil War to an end. Franco establishes a fascist dictatorship that would last until his death in 1975.

1940

- In April, Germany occupies Denmark, Norway, the Netherlands, Belgium, and Luxembourg. In June, Allied troops retreat from the French town of Dunkirk, and Germany invades France, capturing Paris; French Prime Minister Philippe Pétain concludes an armistice with the Germans and establishes the French government at Vichy.

- In June, Italy declares war on Britain and France.
- From July until October, British and German air forces fight the Battle of Britain; the RAF's defence of the island against the numerically superior German air force leads Hitler to abandon a planned invasion of Britain.
- On 18 August, Canadian Prime Minister Mackenzie King and US President Franklin D. Roosevelt sign the Ogdensburg Agreement, establishing a Permanent Joint Board of Defence for 'defence of the northern half of the Western Hemisphere'.
- In September, Japan invades French Indochina.

1941

- Germany occupies the Balkans and invades the Soviet Union, coming to within 40 kilometres of Moscow and laying siege to Leningrad (St Petersburg).
- The United States and Britain sign the Lend–Lease Agreement, giving the US the use of British-owned military bases in exchange for military equipment.
- In April, Prime Minister King and President Roosevelt sign the Hyde Park Declaration, in which the United States agrees to increase its defence purchases of Canadian supplies, thereby easing the trade deficit between the two countries.
- In August, President Roosevelt and British Prime Minister Winston Churchill, meeting at sea off the coast of Newfoundland, sign the Atlantic Charter, which forms the ideological basis for the United Nations organization.
- Convinced of the inevitability of war with the United States after Washington imposed sanctions on the Japanese to protest their invasion of Indochina, Japan bombs American naval bases at Pearl Harbor, Hawaii, on 7 December and declares war on the US.

1942

- In February, the King government announces that it will relocate nearly 22,000 people of Japanese ancestry from the coastal areas of British Columbia to work camps and internment camps in the Interior; in the same month, President Roosevelt announces similar measures for the 120,000 Japanese Americans living on the US west coast.
- In June, the US navy repels a Japanese invasion fleet in the Battle of Midway, sinking four aircraft carriers and ending Japan's wartime expansion in the Pacific.
- In August, German troops reach Stalingrad and attempt to take the city but meet fierce resistance. Grim house-to-house fighting would occur until the surrender, in January 1943, of German troops after 300,000 casualties.
- In August, 5,000 Canadian and 1,000 British troops launch an amphibious raid on the French channel port of Dieppe; the raid ends disastrously with two-thirds of the Allied troops killed.

1943

- In July, Italian dictator Benito Mussolini is deposed in a coup and imprisoned; in September, having been rescued by German troops, he sets up a fascist republican government in northern Italy. The new government of Italy, under Pietro Badoglio, surrenders to the Allies.
- In August, President Roosevelt and Prime Minister Churchill meet in Quebec City to discuss the course of the war. The two leaders would meet again in Quebec in September 1944. Prime Minister King, while acting as host to the two leaders, does not take part in the strategy sessions.

1944

- On 6 June, 'D-Day', British, US, and Canadian forces land on beaches in Normandy in German-occupied northern France, establishing a bridgehead from which the Allies launch an offensive to drive the Germans out of France. In August, Paris is liberated.
- At a meeting at the Bretton Woods resort in New Hampshire, representatives of 44 allied nations establish the International Monetary Fund (IMF) and the International Bank for Reconstruction and Development (the World Bank) to help the post-war recovery of the

industrialized West by facilitating international trade and capital movements.

1945

- In February, Prime Minister Churchill and President Roosevelt meet with Soviet leader Joseph Stalin at Yalta to discuss the final stages of the war and the subsequent territorial division of Europe.
- In April, the United Nations is established by delegates of 50 states meeting in San Francisco, replacing the League of Nations; Canada signs the charter on 26 June. The UN General Assembly would meet for the first time on 10 January 1946, in London.
- On 8 May, Germany surrenders at Reims, France, ending the war in Europe.
- From 17 July until 2 August, US, British, and Soviet leaders meet in Potsdam, Germany, to establish the principles for the Allied occupation of Germany following the war. From this conference an ultimatum is sent to Japan demanding unconditional surrender.
- On 6 August, the US air force drops an atomic bomb on Hiroshima, Japan; three days later, a second bomb is dropped on Nagasaki. Japan surrenders, ending the Second World War.
- On 5 September, Igor Gouzenko, a cipher clerk working at the Soviet embassy in Ottawa, defects and presents Canadian authorities with documents that establish the existence of a spy ring in North America. Gouzenko's revelations would become public in February 1946, signalling for many the start of the Cold War.

1946

- In August, a referendum showing a majority of Greeks in favour of returning King George II— exiled during the German occupation of Greece 1941–5—to power sparks a civil war between communist opponents of the government and royalist supporters of the exiled king; the civil war would last until 1949.
- Civil war resumes in China following the surrender of Japan; it would last until 1949.

- Resistance to French control of Vietnam by Ho Chi Minh's communist-dominated nationalist movement, the Vietminh, leads to fighting between French and Vietnamese forces. Fighting would last until French defeat and withdrawal in 1954.

1947

- On 15 August, India is granted independence by Britain and is divided into the dominions of India (predominantly Hindu) and Pakistan (predominantly Muslim).
- The UN supports a British plan to partition Palestine—then under British administration— into separate Jewish and Arab states upon the expiry of the British mandate (1948).

1948

- On 25 February, communists seize control of Czechoslovakia, setting up a Stalinist government under Klement Gottwald.
- In South Africa, the Afrikaner National Party begins the policy of institutional racial segregation known as apartheid.
- The British mandate over Palestine ends, and on 14 May, the independent Jewish state of Israel is proclaimed. Israel is immediately attacked by the surrounding Arab states but withstands the assault; Israel would actually gain territory by the time a ceasefire is reached in 1949. During the course of the war, hundreds of thousands of Palestinian Arabs flee to neighbouring countries.
- In June, Russian forces blockade Berlin in an attempt to isolate it from the West and terminate the joint Allied military government of the city. In an effort to break the blockade, Britain and the United States airlift food and supplies to the city. The blockade would last until 1949, when the city would be formally divided into East and West Berlin.
- US Congress approves the European Recovery Program (the 'Marshall Plan') of US-sponsored financial aid designed to boost the economies of Western European countries after the war.

1949

- Japanese Canadians are permitted to return to the BC coast and given the right to vote.
- On 31 March, Newfoundland becomes Canada's tenth province.
- On 4 April, NATO is formed for the defence of North America and Europe against the perceived threat of Soviet aggression; the North Atlantic Treaty is signed by representatives of Canada, Britain, the United States, Belgium, Denmark, France, Iceland, Italy, Luxembourg, the Netherlands, Norway, and Portugal.
- On 18 April, the Republic of Ireland declares its independence from Britain and leaves the Commonwealth of Nations.
- On 21 May, the Federal Republic of Germany ('West Germany') is created from the zones occupied by Britain, the United States, and France.
- Civil war in China ends as the nationalist Kuomintang government of Chiang Kai-shek is overthrown by communist forces, and the People's Republic of China is declared on 1 October. Chiang Kai-shek and 500,000 nationalist troops withdraw to Taiwan, which becomes the headquarters of the Kuomintang.
- The Greek Civil War (1946–9) ends with the defeat of the communists and the re-establishment of the monarchy, under Paul.

1950

- On 24 June, Kim Il-Sung's Soviet-equipped North Korean military launches a surprise attack across the 38th parallel on the US-sponsored South. The UN votes to oppose the invasion, and UN troops—dominated by US forces—invade and advance to the border of North Korea with China. In November, China intervenes on the side of the North, setting the stage for a global conflict; however, peace negotiations would begin in 1951, and the Korean War would end in 1953.

1951

- The United States, Australia, and New Zealand sign the ANZUS Pact, a security treaty designed to protect the Pacific countries from armed attack.

1952

- The United States tests the first hydrogen bomb—more than a thousand times more powerful than the first atom bomb—at the Eniwetok Atoll in the Pacific Ocean in November; the Soviet Union would follow suit nine months later.
- The European Coal and Steel Community is established to regulate pricing, transport, and tariffs for the coal and steel industries of the member countries (originally France, West Germany, Italy, Belgium, the Netherlands, and Luxembourg); it is the first of the organizations that now make up the European Community.

1953

- The Korean War ends on 27 July; the previous boundary along the 38th parallel is restored.
- Soviet leader Joseph Stalin dies after 31 years as general secretary of the Communist Party (1922–53); he is succeeded by Nikita Khrushchev.

1954

- Shortly after the defeat of French troops at Dien Bien Phu, Vietnam, the Geneva Accords ending the eight-year war in Southeast Asia are signed in July. Vietnam is partitioned along the 17th parallel between communist North Vietnam (capital, Hanoi) and non-communist South Vietnam (capital, Saigon). The sovereignty of the royalist governments of Laos and Cambodia is formally recognized as well.
- The South-East Asia Treaty Organization (SEATO) is formed as a defence alliance, modelled on NATO, for countries of Southeast Asia and part of the Southwest Pacific. Orchestrated by Washington with the objective of defending Laos and Cambodia against communist aggression or insurgency and to protect South Vietnam against North Vietnam, the organization comprises the following members:

Australia, Britain, France, New Zealand, Pakistan, the Philippines, Thailand, and the United States.

1955

- West Germany is admitted as a member of NATO. In response, the communist states of Europe under Soviet influence sign the Eastern European Mutual Assistance Treaty (the 'Warsaw Pact'), a treaty of mutual defence and military aid, on 14 May.
- In July, Soviet and Western heads of state meet for the first time since the end of the Second World War, in Geneva. US President Dwight Eisenhower makes his 'open skies' proposal, which would allow the exchange of blueprints of US and Soviet military installations, along with aerial photo-reconnaissance on both sides. Soviet Premier Nikolai Bulganin proposes to prohibit the construction and use of nuclear weapons. The two sides discuss reunification of Germany. No agreements are reached.

1956

- In February, Nikita Khrushchev, speaking at a closed meeting of the Communist Party, launches a program of 'de-Stalinization' by denouncing the former Soviet leader and his repressive policies and calling for less arbitrary rules of political procedure. The speech implicitly endorses liberalization in the Soviet satellite states of Eastern Europe; it is followed two months later by the dissolution of the Communist Information Bureau (COMINFORM), created by Stalin at the start of the Cold War to promote the unity of European Communist parties and to ensure their subservience to the Soviet state.
- After Egyptian President Gamal Abdel Nasser nationalizes the Suez Canal on 26 July, Britain and France form a pact with Israel to regain control of the canal. On 29 October, Israeli troops attack Egypt and advance towards the canal. On 5 November, British and French paratroops arrive in Suez and Port Said, ostensibly to separate the two armies but in fact to

secure the canal. Strong opposition to the operation by US, Soviet, and Canadian officials, among others, forces the withdrawal of forces. Canadian Minister of External Affairs Lester B. Pearson lobbies for the creation of a UN emergency peacekeeping force, which is dispatched to the region.
- Khrushchev's denunciation of Stalin sparks anti-Soviet uprisings in Poland and Hungary in October. The violence in Poland ends when Polish leader Władysław Gomułka secures concessions from Moscow, including an easing of restrictions on civil liberties and of Soviet military authority in Poland; the violence in Hungary ends when Soviet troops enter Budapest and crush the liberal reform movement after Hungarian President Imre Nagy vows to withdraw from the Warsaw Pact. In 1956–7, Canada accepts 37,500 Hungarian refugees.

1957

- The Treaty of Rome is signed on 25 March by France, West Germany, Italy, Belgium, the Netherlands, and Luxembourg, setting the aims of the European Economic Community.
- On 12 September, Canada and the United States sign the North American Air Defence (NORAD) Agreement, designed to help integrate air reconnaissance and defence systems of the two countries.
- On 4 October, Sputnik is launched by the Soviet Union, becoming the first satellite to be placed in orbit.

1958

- Charles de Gaulle introduces a new French constitution that establishes a republican regime, the 'Fifth Republic'; he would become the new republic's first president the following year.
- Chinese leader Mao Zedong begins the 'Great Leap Forward', a policy designed to hasten industrialization and improve agricultural production by reorganizing the population into large rural collectives and by adopting labour-intensive industrial methods to lessen the need for expensive heavy machinery.

1959

- Fidel Castro, leader of a successful revolution against the right-wing dictatorship of President Fulgencio Batista, seizes power in Cuba and establishes a communist regime, of which he becomes prime minister.
- Chinese forces ruthlessly quell an armed insurrection by Tibetan rebels opposed to communist rule. Tibet's spiritual leader, the Dalai Lama, is forced into exile in India.

1960

- The Organization of the Petroleum Exporting Countries (OPEC) is founded to coordinate price and supply policies.
- A coalition of dissidents opposed to the government of South Vietnam forms the National Liberation Front. The group, contemptuously labelled 'Viet Cong' ('Vietnamese communist') by its opponents, declares its dedication to social reform, political liberalization, and neutrality for South Vietnam.

1961

- Communist authorities build a fortified and heavily guarded wall on the boundary between East and West Berlin, chiefly to curb the flow of East Germans to the West.
- On 17 April, 1,500 US-backed Cuban exiles land at the Bay of Pigs, Cuba, and make an unsuccessful attempt to invade the country and overthrow the Castro regime; within three days, the entire invasion force would be either killed or captured by Castro's forces.

1962

- In October, US reconnaissance planes overflying Cuba discover Soviet missile sites on the island. US President John F. Kennedy demands their removal and orders a naval blockade of Cuba to prevent the arrival of additional armaments. The threat of nuclear war looms for a week before Soviet Premier Khrushchev accedes to US demands in exchange for Washington's promise not to invade Cuba.

- Unable to work out an agreement on disputed territory along their mutual border, China, on 20 October, launches an attack on India. One month later, having achieved all of its territorial objectives, China imposes a unilateral ceasefire.

1963

- In May, representatives of 30 independent African states assemble in Addis Ababa, Ethiopia, to found the Organization of African Unity. Among the principal goals set out in the OAU Charter are to prevent territorial conflicts between rival African nations, to facilitate political unification of the continent, and to remain neutral in the Cold War.
- In August, Britain, the United States, and the Soviet Union sign the Test-Ban Treaty prohibiting nuclear tests both in the atmosphere and in the sea. Framed to prevent other nations from developing nuclear weapons as well as to protect the environment, the treaty would eventually be signed by more than 100 governments.
- US President Kennedy is assassinated on 22 November; he is succeeded by Lyndon B. Johnson.

1964

- On 4 August, North Vietnamese torpedo boats allegedly fire on two US destroyers in international waters in the Gulf of Tonkin. Although the Vietnamese vessels promptly retreat and neither American ship is damaged, the incident serves as a pretext for US President Johnson to step up American involvement in the war between North and South Vietnam.
- The Palestine Liberation Organization (PLO) is founded in Beirut, Lebanon, with the goal of uniting Palestinian Arab groups and achieving an independent state of Palestine.

1965

- In February, the United States launches a series of air strikes on North Vietnam in retaliation for a Viet Cong night raid on the barracks of a US airfield at Pleiku, which results in over 100 casualties. On 2 April, Canadian Prime

Minister Lester Pearson, during a convocation speech at Temple University in Philadelphia, criticizes the US's escalating military campaign in North Vietnam.

- An attempted communist coup against Indonesian President Achmed Sukarno is crushed by the military, under General Raden Suharto. Suharto's military proceeds to massacre between 200,000 and 700,000 Communist Party members and sympathizers. Over the next two years, Sukarno would steadily lose power to the military, eventually being ousted by Suharto in 1967.

1966

- A period of political upheaval begins in China, as Mao Zedong launches the Cultural Revolution, intended to bring about a return to revolutionary Maoist beliefs. The movement results in attacks on intellectuals, a large-scale purge in party posts, and considerable economic dislocation. The Cultural Revolution would last until 1968, when it would be brought to an end by Zhou Enlai.

1967

- In May, Egypt demands and obtains the removal of the UN peacekeeping force that has acted as a buffer between Egypt and Israel since the Suez Crisis, then closes the Straits of Tiran, an Israeli shipping route to the Red Sea. Egypt, Syria, Jordan, and Iraq sign mutual defence agreements and mass for an attack on Israel, which on 5 June launches a pre-emptive strike against Egypt and Syria. By the end of the Six Day War, Israeli forces would capture the entire Sinai peninsula from Egypt, the Golan Heights from Syria, and the West Bank of the Jordan River, including the Jordanian sector of the holy city of Jerusalem.

- On 24 July, during a state visit to Canada, French President Charles de Gaulle exclaims 'Vive le Québec libre!' to a crowd gathered at Montreal's city hall. The phrase would become a slogan of the separatist Parti Québécois, formed a year later.

1968

- On 30 January, Viet Cong guerrillas and North Vietnamese regulars launch the 'Tet Offensive', a surprise attack on 36 provincial capitals of South Vietnam. While the insurgents are repelled by a furious US–South Vietnamese counterattack, the incident discredits US claims of imminent victory. As opposition to the war grows in the United States, President Johnson announces in March that American bombings and ground forces will be scaled back. In May, the North Vietnamese government agrees to send a delegation to Paris to meet with US negotiators.

- In July, the United States, the Soviet Union, and Britain sign the Nuclear Non-Proliferation Treaty, which would come into force in March 1970 after being signed by 97 countries. According to the treaty, the nuclear powers (except for China and France, which refuse to sign) pledge never to furnish nuclear weapons or the technology to manufacture them to non-nuclear powers, while the non-nuclear countries promise never to produce or acquire them.

- In August, Soviet troops move into Czechoslovakia to crush a movement (the 'Prague Spring') to democratize and liberalize Czech political life.

1969

- Strained Sino–Soviet relations erupt in violence in March, as Chinese troops ambush a Soviet contingent near the disputed Damansky (or Chenpao) Island; 31 Soviet soldiers and an unknown number of Chinese die in the border clash. Subsequent skirmishes in the spring and summer accompanied by a renewal of Chinese territorial claims against the Soviet Union are followed by a gradual buildup of Soviet troops on the Chinese border over the next three years.

- Yasser Arafat becomes chairman of the PLO, a position he would hold until his death in 2004.

- In October, West German elections bring Willy Brandt to power as chancellor. As head of government he renews and intensifies his efforts to normalize West Germany's relations with its Eastern European neighbours ('*Ostpolitik*').

- In November, Soviet and US officials in Helsinki begin formal talks designed to limit nuclear weapons, under the title of Strategic Arms Limitation Talks (SALT).

1970

- The Canadian government, under Pierre Trudeau, extends diplomatic recognition to China.

1971

- Ugandan military leader Idi Amin seizes power from President Milton Obote and begins a rule characterized by the advancement of narrow tribal interests, the expulsion of non-Africans, and the murder of thousands of his political opponents.
- On 25 October, the People's Republic of China gains a seat at the UN, replacing the Republic of China (Taiwan), which it considers one of its provinces. The American refusal to veto the admission of communist China, together with US President Richard Nixon's visit to China in February 1972, signals a détente in Sino–American relations.
- Civil war breaks out in Pakistan after the separatist Awami League, a year after winning an overwhelming majority in East Pakistan, declares East Pakistan's independence from West Pakistan. In December, India intervenes on behalf of East Pakistan, which emerges the following year as the independent state of Bangladesh.

1972

- In May, President Richard Nixon visits Moscow; US and Soviet officials conclude an arms control agreement (SALT I).
- At the Summer Olympics in Munich, Germany, 11 members of the Israeli team are killed by Palestinian terrorists.

1973

- On 27 January, the United States and North Vietnam sign the Paris Peace Accords; the US agrees to remove all of its armed forces from South Vietnam within two months, and the two sides agree on an exchange of prisoners of war. The accord provides for a coalition government in the south that would conduct free elections there. Within two years of the US evacuation, all three of Indochina's pro-Western regimes would fall to communist-led insurgencies.
- In October, on the Jewish holy day of Yom Kippur, Egypt and Syria launch a surprise attack against Israel. Egyptian forces drive into the Sinai, while Syrian forces swarm the Golan Heights. After two weeks of fierce tank battles, Israel gains the upper hand, forcing the Syrians to within 30 kilometres of Damascus and encircling the Egyptian forces. Just as the US and the Soviet Union are set to deploy forces to the region in support of their respective clients, the UN Security Council passes a compromise resolution authorizing the deployment of 7,000 UN soldiers to supervise a ceasefire. In December, the Israeli and Arab representatives, with the support and participation of the superpowers, meet in Geneva for negotiations that would continue on and off for two years.
- In retaliation for American intervention in Israel, OPEC imposes a 5-month embargo on petroleum shipments to the United States and begins a series of dramatic increases in the price of crude oil.

1974

- In April, a leftist military coup in Portugal, led by army officers opposed to continuing colonial wars in Angola and Mozambique, ends a long period of right-wing dictatorship and leads to Portugal's rapid withdrawal from its African colonies and eventually to democratic reform.
- Ongoing tensions in Cyprus between Greek Cypriots (some favouring unification with Greece, or 'Enosis') and Turkish Cypriots come to a head when Turkish forces land on the northern part of the island following a coup by Greek officers of the Nationalist Guard and an Enosis extremist. Turkish troops partition

the island and proclaim the northern part the Turkish Federated State of Cyprus.

1975

- Friction between conservative Christian groups and left-wing Muslim groups escalates into all-out civil war in Lebanon, sparked on 13 April by the killing of 25 Palestinian Arabs by Maronite Christian militiamen in East Beirut.
- On 30 April, North Vietnamese forces capture the Southern capital of Saigon, ending the Vietnam War.
- Civil war ends in Cambodia as the Khmer Rouge, a communist guerrilla organization, seizes power. Under the dictatorship of Pol Pot, the Khmer Rouge would undertake a forced reconstruction of Cambodian society, involving massive deportation from the towns to the countryside and the execution of many thousands of Cambodians. More than two million would die before the regime is overthrown by the Vietnamese in 1979.

1976

- In January, Prime Minister Trudeau makes a controversial state visit to Cuba.
- North and South Vietnam are reunited under a communist regime.
- In September, Mao Zedong, chairman of the Chinese Communist Party from 1949 and China's most powerful politician, dies, paving the way for Deng Xiaoping's economic reforms.

1977

- Chinese statesman Deng Xiaoping, discredited during the Cultural Revolution, is reinstated and becomes the architect of ambitious plans for China's modernization, which involve major economic reforms, closer ties to the West, and a firm stance in relation to the Soviet Union.
- On 7 September, the United States, under President Jimmy Carter, signs a treaty with Panama that gives Panamanians legal jurisdiction over the Panama Canal as well as the sole right to operate and defend the canal by the end of the century.

1978

- In September, at the US presidential retreat at Camp David, Egyptian President Anwar Sadat and Israeli Prime Minister Menachem Begin sign an agreement calling for Israel to return the Sinai peninsula to Egypt in two stages (in 1980 and 1982) and for Egypt to recognize Israel's right to exist as a sovereign nation; the sensitive issue of Palestinian autonomy in the Gaza Strip and on the West Bank of the Jordan River is left for future negotiation. The two countries would sign a peace treaty in March 1979.
- President Carter announces that formal diplomatic relations between the United States and China will begin on 1 January 1979, and that the US defence treaty with Taiwan—a longtime partner in the war against communism—will expire the following year.

1979

- In January, Vietnamese troops capture the Cambodian (Kampuchean) capital of Phnom Penh, toppling the government of Pol Pot and establishing a pro-Vietnamese puppet regime. The ousted Khmer Rouge, under Pol Pot, wage guerrilla resistance to the Vietnamese-backed government.
- In February, after 16 years in exile, Shi'ite clerical leader Ayatollah Khomeini returns to Iran to lead an Islamic revolution, overthrowing the shah; he establishes an Islamic republic. In November, Iranian students seize the American embassy in Tehran, taking 69 hostages in an effort to force Washington to extradite the shah; though some of the hostages are released or escape, 53 would not be freed until January 1981.
- In June, the Strategic Arms Limitation Talks produce a second agreement, as US and Soviet officials sign the SALT II Treaty in Vienna; however, US Congress would fail to ratify the agreement.
- In December, Soviet troops enter Afghanistan and install a pro-Soviet government under Babrak Karmal.
- The left-wing Sandinista National Liberation Front, led by Daniel Ortega, overthrows the

dictatorship of Luis Somoza in Nicaragua. The Sandinistas would be opposed during most of their rule by the US-backed Contra guerrilla force.

1980

- In January, six Americans held hostage in the US embassy in Tehran, who escaped with the help of Canadian Ambassador Ken Taylor, return to the United States.
- In September, war breaks out between Iran and Iraq. Sparked ostensibly by a border dispute over the Shatt al-Arab River, the principal cause of the war is Iraqi President Saddam Hussein's concerns over the spread of Khomeini's Islamic Revolution, which could spark an uprising by Iraq's Shi'ite majority. The war would end inconclusively in 1988, after great loss of life on both sides.
- Solidarity is founded in Poland under Lech Wałęxa. The independent trade-union movement would develop into a mass campaign for political change and would inspire popular opposition to communist regimes in a number of Eastern European countries.

1982

- In April, Argentinian forces invade the Falkland Islands, which were administered by Britain, in support of their claim to sovereignty. In response, Britain sends a task force of ships and aircraft and forces the Argentinians to surrender six weeks after its arrival.
- On 17 April, Queen Elizabeth II signs the Constitution Act, marking the patriation of the Canadian Constitution so that the Canadian government can make legal changes to the constitution without having to go through Britain. The new constitution, containing a charter of rights and freedoms, is ratified by all provinces except Quebec.
- In June, Israel sends troops across the Lebanese border to overwhelm PLO strongholds in southern Lebanon, while American-built Israeli jet fighters knock out Soviet-built Syrian planes and surface-to-air missile sites in the Bekaa valley of northeastern Lebanon. By the end of the summer,

a US-sponsored agreement is worked out for the evacuation of Palestinian political leaders and military forces from Lebanon under the protection of a multinational peacekeeping force.

1983

- In Grenada, the seizure of power by the left-wing Revolutionary Military Council prompts an invasion, on 25 October, of 2,000 US and 300 Jamaican and Barbadian troops. The RMC forces are defeated.
- On 27 October, Prime Minister Trudeau begins his personal peace mission, on which he would visit several heads of state to lobby for the reduction of nuclear weapons.

1984

- China and Britain conclude an agreement on the political future of Hong Kong. Britain agrees to allow it to revert to Chinese sovereignty in 1997 in exchange for China's guarantee that the former crown colony will have the status of a special administrative region with a high degree of autonomy and the right to retain its capitalist economic system for at least 50 years after absorption.

1985

- On 11 March, Mikhail Gorbachev becomes general secretary of the Soviet Communist Party and begins a series of major political, economic, and cultural reforms that would include the eventual removal of the party's monopoly on power (*glasnost*) and movement towards a market economy (*perestroika*). He would play a significant role in ending the Cold War by negotiating a series of arms control agreements with the United States.
- In March, US President Ronald Reagan meets with Canadian Prime Minister Brian Mulroney in Quebec City. The 'Shamrock Summit' would lay the groundwork for the Canada–US Free Trade Agreement, signed in 1988.
- On 23 June, an Air India jet travelling from Montreal to London explodes and crashes into the Atlantic Ocean 240 kilometres off the

southwestern coast of Ireland, killing all 329 people aboard. A lengthy RCMP investigation would result, in 2000–1, in charges against three Sikh extremists.

1986

- The United States launches a punitive air strike against targets in Libya in retaliation for Libyan leader Muammer Qaddafi's alleged support for a number of international terrorist incidents, including the killing of a US soldier in Berlin earlier in the year.
- US Congressional hearings begin on the Iran–Contra Affair ('Irangate'); the hearings would reveal that the administration of Ronald Reagan secretly supplied weapons to Iran—then at war with Iraq—in order to secure the release of American hostages in Lebanon and that proceeds of the sales were used to supply arms to the anti-communist Contras in Nicaragua. Among those who would be implicated in the scandal are Lt Col. Oliver North, a military aide to the National Security Council, who supervised the illegal negotiations.

1987

- The *Intifada*, an uprising of Palestinians in the Israeli-occupied West Bank and Gaza Strip, begins as a spontaneous popular reaction to the failure of Israeli–Palestinian peace talks.
- On 1 July, the Single European Act comes into effect. The act, approved by the European Council in December 1985, calls for the removal of all barriers to the free movement of goods, services, capital, and labour among the 12 member states of the European Community by the start of January 1993.
- On 8 December, Reagan and Gorbachev meet in Washington to sign the INF Treaty, an agreement eliminating all intermediate-range nuclear forces (i.e. ground-based missiles with ranges of 500–5,500 kilometres) from Europe.

1988

- The Kremlin announces that all Soviet troops will be withdrawn from Afghanistan within 10 months, regardless of the fate of the Soviet-installed puppet regime in Kabul; the last retreating Soviet soldier would cross the frontier in February 1989.
- The war between Iran and Iraq war ends in August after 8 years of fighting.
- On 21 December, a Pan American airliner is destroyed by a bomb over Lockerbie, Scotland, killing all 259 people on board and 11 people on the ground. In February 2004, Libya would accept responsibility for the bombing.

1989

- On 1 January, the Canada–US Free Trade Agreement, signed by Mulroney and Reagan in 1988, comes into effect.
- In April, Tiananmen Square in Beijing, China, is occupied by hundreds of thousands of student-led demonstrators of the emerging pro-democracy movement. The demonstration ends when government troops open fire on unarmed protesters; it is estimated that over 2,000 are killed.
- In the fall, communist regimes are deposed in Hungary, Poland, East Germany, Czechoslovakia, Bulgaria, and Romania. On 10 November, the East German government opens its border, and the Berlin Wall, the most visible symbol of the 'Iron Curtain' between East and West for more than 27 years, is dismantled amid massive celebrations.
- F.W. de Klerk becomes president of South Africa and initiates a number of political reforms designed to promote racial reconciliation and the end of apartheid.
- Vietnam begins withdrawing troops from Cambodia. The complete withdrawal of Vietnamese troops, in September, coincides with an intensification of the civil war that has been ongoing in Cambodia since the Khmer Rouge regime was toppled in 1977.

1990

- In February, the South African government of F.W. de Klerk legalizes the African National Congress (ANC) and releases its deputy leader, Nelson Mandela, after 27 years in prison.

- In August, Iraq invades and annexes Kuwait on the pretext of redressing ancient territorial claims but in large part to gain control of the Kuwaiti oil industry. The UN condemns the invasion, imposing sanctions on Iraq and an ultimatum to withdraw its forces by 15 January 1991. Iraqi President Saddam Hussein redefines the impending confrontation as an Arab–Muslim 'Holy War' against the West and its ally in the region, Israel.
- On 3 October, East and West Germany are formally reunited.

1991

- In January, an international coalition of forces determined to compel Iraq to withdraw from Kuwait assembles in Saudi Arabia under the auspices of the UN but under the military leadership of the United States. On 15 January, the UN-imposed deadline for Iraqi withdrawal, the coalition forces attack. After a massive air attack followed by a ground assault, the Iraqis are quickly driven out, suffering heavy military and civilian casualties. Although the Gulf War ends in February, withdrawing Iraqi forces sabotage Kuwait's oil wells, starting hundreds of fires that would not be extinguished for several months.
- In June, a ceasefire ends the intermittent civil war in Cambodia; multiparty democracy and a free market economy are introduced in October.
- In July, Soviet leader Mikhail Gorbachev and US President George H.W. Bush sign the Strategic Arms Reduction Treaty (START I) that had been under consideration since 1982.
- In the summer, two of the six republics of Yugoslavia—Slovenia and Croatia—declare their independence amid sporadic clashes between the partisans of secession and the Yugoslav federal army. A ceasefire would restore peace to the two republics in early 1992.
- On 21 August, communist hardliners attempt a coup of the Soviet government of Mikhail Gorbachev. The attempt collapses as a result of the intervention of Boris Yeltsin, whose efforts win him the support of the public and the military, while Gorbachev would return to Moscow with

diminished authority. Following the secession of several constituent republics of the Soviet Union, 11 of these 15 new nations, on 21 December, form a confederation, the Commonwealth of Independent States. On 25 December, Mikhail Gorbachev resigns the presidency, and the Soviet Union is formally dissolved.
- In December, at a summit meeting in Maastricht, the heads of state of the 12 member states of the European Community agree to the Treaty on European Union, paving the way to full economic and monetary union within the EC.

1992

- In January, the European Community formally recognizes the independence of the former Yugoslav republics of Slovenia and Croatia. The neighbouring republics of Bosnia–Herzegovina and Macedonia subsequently declare independence, while Bosnian Serbs, unwilling to be governed by the republic's Muslim majority, declare the independence of their own ethnic enclave. Intense civil and ethnic conflict breaks out in these areas. The two remaining republics, Serbia and Montenegro, declare a new federal republic of Yugoslavia.
- The UN Security Council decides to intervene in Somalia, where the fall of the central government in 1991 and the declaration of an independent Somaliland Republic in the northern part of the country have sparked a massive tribal war causing starvation and disease among the Somali people. The US-led humanitarian force would succeed in opening up supply routes for relief operations, but sporadic clashes between UN troops and local militias and Somali civilians would continue until the end of the UN mandate in March 1995.

1993

- On 1 January, a single market within the European Community comes into effect, as called for in the 1987 Single European Act. On 1 November, the EC becomes part of the newly created European Union, which comprises the EC together with two intergovernmental organizations for dealing with foreign affairs and with immigration and justice.

- On 1 January, the two parts of the Czech and Slovak Federal Republic (as Czechoslovakia was renamed in 1990 following the collapse of Soviet power) separate, forming the countries Slovakia and the Czech Republic.
- On 3 January, Russian President Boris Yeltsin and US President George H.W. Bush sign the second Strategic Arms Reduction Treaty (START II).
- On 20 August, representatives of Israel and the PLO initial the Oslo Declaration of Principles, signed in Washington on 13 September by Israeli Prime Minister Yitzhak Rabin and PLO Chairman Yasser Arafat. The pact establishes a timetable for Israel's withdrawal from the Gaza Strip and the West Bank town of Jericho and for the transfer of control of the internal affairs of these regions to the new Palestinian Authority.
- In November, the Convention for a Democratic South Africa (CODESA) adopts an interim constitution abolishing the black homelands and establishing a democratically elected National Assembly; the first multiracial national elections with universal adult suffrage are scheduled for April 1994.
- The Canadian government disbands the Canadian Airborne Regiment after an investigation into the killing of a Somali teenager by members of the regiment serving in Somalia reveals a larger pattern of serious misconduct.

1994

- In January, the North American Free Trade Agreement, signed in October 1992 and ratified the following year, comes into effect; it is designed to eliminate barriers to trade between Canada, the United States, and Mexico.
- In April, Nelson Mandela is elected president in South Africa's first democratic elections, becoming the head of a multiracial, multiparty government; South Africa rejoins the Commonwealth, which it left in 1961.
- In April, the signing of the General Agreement on Tariffs and Trade Treaty (GATT) concludes the Uruguay Round of negotiations and paves the way for the gradual implementation of a multilateral agreement to cut global tariffs by an average of one-third.
- During the spring and summer, the military forces of the Rwandan Hutu massacre half a million members of the Tutsi minority. After the Tutsi-controlled Rwandan Patriotic Front gains the upper hand in the conflict, 2,000,000 desperate Hutu flee to refugee camps in Zaire and Tanzania.
- Canadian Prime Minister Jean Chrétien visits Beijing and Shanghai with a delegation of federal ministers and provincial and territorial leaders. During the visit, Chrétien and Chinese Premier Li Peng sign a nuclear co-operation agreement and a letter of intent for several other development projects. Chrétien would lead 'Team Canada' trade missions to China again in 1996, 1998, and 2001.
- On 9 December, Russian troops invade Chechnya to suppress a separatist rebellion in the province. A ceasefire would not be negotiated until the summer of 1996, and Chechen separatist activity would continue into the next century, supported by numerous acts of terrorism within Russia.

1995

- On 1 January, the World Trade Organization (WTO) formally replaces the 47-year-old GATT as the governing body of international trade rules.
- On 28 August, a Bosnian Serb mortar attack on a marketplace in Sarajevo kills 37 shoppers. The incident promps a massive NATO air assault against ethnic Serb positions throughout Bosnia–Herzegovina. After Bosnian Serbs agree to negotiate an end to the conflict, a ceasefire is declared, and the Dayton Agreement is signed on 21 November. The agreement preserves the sovereignty of Bosnia–Herzegovina but recognizes two separate self-governing entities within its borders: the Bosnian–Croat Federation and the Bosnian Serb Republic.
- On 3 November, Israeli Prime Minister Yitzhak Rabin is assassinated by an opponent of the peace process.

1996

- On 29 January France agrees to end all nuclear testing and subsequently signed and ratified the Comprehensive Nuclear-Test-Ban Treaty in 1998.
- A UN tribunal lays charges of war crimes against Bosnian Muslims and Croats on 22 March.
- The Taliban movement gains control of Kabul and sets up an Islamic state in Afghanistan on 27 September.

1997

- On 1 July, Britain's mandate over Hong Kong ends and the colony is turned over to China. In accordance with the agreement signed by Britain and China in 1984, Hong Kong becomes a special administrative region, with basic laws guaranteeing existing systems and lifestyles for 50 years.
- Following two-and-a-half years of ethnic violence in Zaire, President Mobuto Sese Seko is overthrown by forces supporting Laurent Kabila, who renames the country the Democratic Republic of the Congo.

1998

- Serbian forces enter the autonomous Serbian province of Kosovo to terrorize and expel its ethnic Albanian inhabitants, who make up 90 per cent of the province's population and some of whom have been calling for secession.

1999

- The euro, the single European currency, is introduced on 1 January.
- After talks between Serbian officials in Yugoslavia and Kosovar Albanian leaders fall apart, Yugoslav President Slobodan Milošević orders a new campaign of 'ethnic cleansing' in northern Kosovo: villages are burned and ethnic Albanians are forced to flee across the Albanian border. Between March and June, NATO mounts an air assault against military targets and civilian infrastructure throughout the Yugoslav republic of Serbia. On 10 June, Milošević's government agrees to withdraw all Yugoslav forces from Kosovo. During the crisis, Canada provides temporary shelter to more than 7,000 Kosovar refugees, many of whom would choose to resettle permanently in Canada.

2000

- Vicente Fox is elected president of Mexico on 2 July, ending three quarters of a century of political dominance by the Institutional Revolutionary Party (PRI).
- In September, 189 UN countries adopt the 'Millennium Declaration' to address global poverty, inequality, intolerance, and environmental challenges. Eight Millennium Development Goals (MDGs) are adopted to achieve these aims.
- On 5 October a popular uprising overthrows Yugoslav President Slobodan Milošević.
- A terrorist attack on the USS Cole on 12 October leaves 17 American sailors dead. Responsibility for the attack is subsequently laid on the Sudanese government and al-Qaeda operatives in Yemen.

2001

- Police and anti-globalization demonstrators clash at the Summit of the Americas, held in Quebec City on 20–2 April.
- On 28 June, former Yugoslav President Slobodan Milošević is turned over to the International Criminal Tribunal for the former Yugoslavia to face charges of genocide and war crime.
- 178 nations reach agreement on a modified version of the Kyoto Climate Protocol on 23 July. The United States does not sign the pact.
- On 11 September, two airliners hijacked by radical Islamists crash into the World Trade Center in New York; a third hijacked jet crashes into the Pentagon in Washington; a fourth, believed to be bound for Washington DC, crashes in a field in Pennsylvania. Nearly 3,000 people would die in the attacks.
- Blaming the 9/11 attacks on al-Qaeda, an Islamist organization established by Osama bin Laden, the United States leads an international force into Afghanistan on 7 October to topple

the Taliban regime that harboured al-Qaeda in that country.

- On 24 December, a ceasefire agreement is reached between the Tamil Tigers and the Sri Lankan government in an effort to bring almost two decades of civil war to an end. Tamil grievances, however, would ultimately lead to a return to fighting.

2002

- On 24 May, representatives from the United States and Russia sign the Strategic Offensive Reductions Treaty (SORT) which binds each country to limit its arsenal of deployed nuclear warheads.
- A terrorist attack, subsequently linked to al-Qaeda though carried out by Jemaah Islamiyah, kills 202 people, mainly foreign tourists in the resort area of Bali on 12 October.
- UN Security Council Resolution 1441 on 8 November calls on Iraq to comply with the provisions of previous disarmament resolutions, including re-admitting weapons inspectors, or else face 'serious consequences'.
- On 15 November, Hu Jintao replaces Jiang Zemin as general secretary of the Communist Party of China.

2003

- In his State of the Union address on 28 January, US President George W. Bush announces that he will attack Iraq with or without UN approval, a decision that UN Secretary-General Kofi Annan later labelled 'illegal'.
- The United States, aided by Great Britain and a loose coalition of allies, attacks Iraq on 19 March, arguing that Iraq was co-responsible in the 9/11 attacks and was concealing weapons of mass destruction. Both claims were later disproved decisively. On 1 May the US declares an end to major combat operations; the war, however, would continue past the end of the decade.
- NATO takes command of the International Security Assistance Force (ISAF) in Afghanistan on 11 August.

- The US-backed 'roadmap for peace in the Middle East' collapses in September and Israeli–Palestinian violence continues to escalate.
- On 13 December, Saddam Hussein is taken into custody by American troops.

2004

- On 11 March, in Madrid, a series of coordinated bombings leave 191 dead and almost 2,000 people injured. The terrorists were linked indirectly to al-Qaeda.
- NATO expands by seven countries to admit former Eastern bloc nations Estonia, Latvia, Lithuania, Romania, Bulgaria, Slovakia, and Slovenia, on 29 March.
- The European Union expands to include the Czech Republic, Estonia, Hungary, Latvia, Lithuania, Poland, Slovakia, and Slovenia, as well as Malta and Cyprus, on 1 May.
- With US casualties increasing in Iraq, power is transferred to an Interim Iraqi Government on 28 June. US military involvement continues.
- On 11 November, Yasser Arafat, head of the Palestinian Authority and of Fatah, the political wing of the PLO, dies in Paris.
- On 7 December, Hamid Karzai is inaugurated as the president of Afghanistan, despite widespread allegations of voter fraud.
- A massive tsunami decimates parts of the Indian Ocean basin on 26 December leading to a worldwide relief effort which stretches into 2005.

2005

- In the first Palestinian presidential election in almost a decade, Mahmoud Abbas is elected to head the Palestinian Authority on 9 January.
- On 30 January, elections are held in Iraq to form a new Transitional National Assembly.
- The Syrian military withdraws from Lebanon on 26 April, ending an occupation which had lasted for nearly three decades.
- Terrorist bombings in London, linked to al-Qaeda, paralyze transportation systems across the capital on 7 July and leave 52 people dead.
- On 28 July, the Irish Republican Army (IRA) officially renounces the use of violence and

commits itself to the political process in Northern Ireland, thereby dramatically accelerating the Northern Ireland Peace process. Splinter groups, such as the Real IRA, vow to fight on.

- The trial of Saddam Hussein for atrocities committed against his own people begins on 19 October. He would be found guilty and hanged in late 2006.

- Angela Merkel, leader of the centre-right Christian Democratic Union, becomes Germany's first female chancellor on 22 November.

2006

- On 25 January, Hamas defeats the more moderate Fatah to form the next government in Gaza. Despite the fact that the election was judged to be fair, several countries withdraw aid from Gaza.

- Despite efforts by the UN to prevent Iran from developing a nuclear program, on 11 April Iranian President Mahmoud Ahmadinejad announces that his country has successfully enriched uranium. North Korea contributes to global nuclear fears when, on 9 October, they test their own nuclear device.

- A series of train bombings in Mumbai on 11 July leave 209 people dead. The attacks are blamed on Islamist groups with ties to the Pakistani Inter-Services Intelligence (ISI). The attacks negatively impact Indian–Pakistani relations in the immediate aftermath; however, the two countries subsequently agree to address the threat of terrorism co-operatively.

- Israel launches a major military offensive into Lebanon which lasts from 12 July to 14 August.

- On 31 July, the ceasefire between the Tamil Tigers and the Sri Lankan government is broken.

2007

- Bulgaria and Romania join the EU on 1 January.

- The Intergovernmental Panel on Climate Change reviews and accepts the conclusions of its working group on human-created climate change on 1 February, after submitting the work to 650 scientists, governments, and organizations for review.

- The US military begins a massive surge in Iraq early in the year in the hopes of ending increasingly deadly attacks by insurgent militias.

- A power-sharing agreement is negotiated between Sinn Fein and the Democratic Unionist Party in Northern Ireland on 26 March.

- Pro-democracy forces in Burma are brutally attacked by the country's military government on 26 September. Despite global outrage, the government is able to suppress the democracy movement.

- On 2 September, the Bush administration agrees to provide aid to North Korea in exchange for an agreement to dismantle nuclear facilities in the country. Progress on nuclear disarmament has, however, been negligible since this time.

2008

- On 21 January, global markets plunge amidst fears of a worldwide economic depression.

- The former Yugoslav state of Kosovo declares its independence on 17 February; however, the potential for regional instability prevents several nations from recognizing the declaration as legitimate.

- On 19 February, Fidel Castro officially resigns as president and commander-in-chief of Cuba, handing power to his brother Raúl.

- After constitutional limits prevent Vladimir Putin from serving a third term as Russian president, Dmitry Medvedev, Putin's hand-picked candidate, is declared the winner of presidential elections on 3 March. In turn, Medvedev appoints Putin as prime minister on 8 May.

- The Treaty of Lisbon, which was designed to improve the functioning of the EU Parliament and to increase the scope of its powers, is rejected by Irish voters in a referendum on 12 June.

- Barack Obama accepts the nomination as the US Democratic presidential candidate on 28 August.

- Fears of a global economic depression intensify as the world's stock markets crash in October.

- On 4 November, Barack Obama is elected president of the United States, becoming the first African-American president.

2009

- Israeli troops enter Gaza on 3 January, after a week of air attacks against Hamas positions; fighting continues until 18 January leaving at least 1,200 Palestinians and 13 Israelis dead.
- On 17 February, the UN releases a report showing a 40 per cent increase in Afghan civilian casualties over the past year; 2,118 civilians died in 2008.
- North Korea defies international condemnation and tests its second nuclear device on 25 May.
- Centre-right parties gain ground in EU elections on 7 June.
- Iranian President Mahmoud Ahmadinejad wins re-election on 12 June despite widespread allegations of vote tampering, fraud, and intimidation. Ahmadinejad's victory begins a months-long campaign of anti-governmental protest.
- On 30 June, US forces hand control over Iraqi cities to Iraqi troops.

- Afghani incumbent Hamid Karzai claims victory after his country's 20 August presidential election; opponents file formal protests.
- The Japanese Liberal Democratic Party is defeated by the Democratic Party on 30 August ending a near stranglehold on political power dating back to the end of the Second World War.
- On 2 October, Irish voters ratify the Treaty of Lisbon paving the way for the treaty to become law on 1 December.
- Attacks by Pakistani militants (Tehrik-i-Taliban Pakistan) in Lahore, Islamabad, and Peshawar leave over 300 dead in late October; the Taliban, in turn, blames some of the attacks on Pakistani security forces attempting to discredit the TTP.
- On 18 December, at the end of the Copenhagen Climate Conference, the leaders of the United States, China, India, Brazil, and South Africa agree to a series of measures to address global climate change. However, the lack of a global agreement leads many analysts to brand the conference a failure.

GLOSSARY OF INTERNATIONAL ECONOMICS TERMINOLOGY

autarky   Total national economic self-sufficiency; that is, the ability to obtain all essential goods and services from domestic sources.

balance of payments   A summary statement of all economic transactions between private citizens or government agencies of one country and those of all other countries of the world during a particular year. The balance-of-payments statement includes not only exports and imports of merchandise (the *balance of trade*) but also such activities as foreign tourist expenditures, transportation costs, insurance premiums and indemnities, and investment income.

balance of trade   The difference in value between a nation's total merchandise imports and exports during a particular year. The balance of trade is only one part of the balance of total earnings and expenditures of a nation in its transactions with the rest of the world (the *balance of payments*).

barter   The exchange of specified quantities of products at a specified ratio without any monetary transactions taking place. Barter arrangements between countries are usually undertaken to circumvent obstacles to foreign exchange.

capital-intensive industry   An industry in which the cost of capital represents a relatively large percentage of the total production costs. (Compare *labour-intensive industry*, *land-intensive industry*, *technology-intensive industry*.)

central bank   A bank (such as the Bank of Canada, the Bank of England, the Federal Reserve Board in the United States, etc.) that holds the exclusive right to print and distribute the national currency of a country and coordinates a country's banking and monetary activities.

common market   A group of countries imposing few or no duties on trade with one another and a common tariff on trade with other countries.

comparative advantage   The particular ability of a country to produce a product or service relatively more cheaply than other products or services because of the *factors of production* (land, labour, capital, or technology) with which it is endowed. In international trade theory, the principle of comparative advantage explains why a particular country should concentrate on producing and exporting a product or service for which its cost advantage is greatest while importing from other countries those products or services for which it has a lesser cost advantage.

customs duty   See *tariff*.

debt service   The payment of interest and principal due on a debt.

deficit financing   The funding of government spending by borrowing.

deficit spending   Government spending, in excess of revenue, of funds raised by borrowing rather than by taxation.

depression   A long and severe recession in an economy or market, such as the financial slump that began in 1929 and lasted through much of the 1930s.

devaluation   A government-engineered reduction in the value of a national currency in relation to other national currencies or gold, usually undertaken to promote exports and reduce imports.

direct investment   The purchase by citizens of one country of the material assets or the stock of corporations located in another country that establishes ownership and control of the assets or the enterprise by the foreign investor.

duty   See *tariff*.

embargo   An official ban on trade or other commercial activity with a particular country.

exchange control   Government regulation of the purchase and sale of foreign currencies, usually undertaken to prevent the flight of capital abroad.

factor cost   The cost of an item of goods or a service in terms of the various productive factors that have played a part in its production or availability, exclusive of tax costs.

factor of production (or productive factor)   An economic resource that goes into the production of a good. The four major productive factors are land (including natural resources located on or under it), capital, labour, and technology.

foreign exchange   The purchase and sale of national currencies; often used to designate the total value of foreign currencies held by citizens of a particular country, as in 'Poland's shortage of foreign exchange'.

free trade   International trade left to its natural course without tariffs, quotas, or restrictions.

gold reserve   A quantity of gold held by a central bank to support the issue of currency.

gold standard   The system in which the value of a currency is defined in terms of gold, for which the currency may be exchanged.

gross domestic product (or GDP)   The total value of goods produced and services provided by a particular nation's economy during a particular year, excluding transactions with other countries.

gross national product (or GNP)   The total value of all goods produced and services provided by a particular nation's economy during a particular year.

human capital   The skills, knowledge, and experience possessed by a population, viewed in terms of their value or cost to a country.

import quota   A government-established restriction on the importation of items to a country. The quota may be specified in terms of either the monetary value or the physical amount of the imported item, and it may apply to all imports of a specific item or to all imports from a specific country.

labour-intensive industry   An industry in which the cost of labour represents a relatively large percentage of the total costs of production. (Compare *capital-intensive industry*, *land-intensive industry*, *technology-intensive industry*.)

land-intensive industry   An industry in which the cost of land represents a relatively large percentage of the total costs of production. (Compare *capital-intensive industry*, *labour-intensive industry*, *technology-intensive industry*.)

manufacturing industry   See *secondary industry*.

mixed economy   An economic system combining private and state enterprise.

most-favoured-nation principle   The requirement that all parties to a trade agreement must be granted any reduction in tariffs that is negotiated between or among any signatories of the agreement.

portfolio investment   The purchase by citizens of one country of the financial instruments or securities issued by a foreign government or corporation without the acquisition of ownership or control.

primary industry   An industry, such as mining, agriculture, or forestry, that is concerned with obtaining or providing natural raw materials for conversion into commodities and products for the consumer. (Compare *secondary industry*.)

protectionism   The practice of shielding a country's domestic industries from foreign competition by taxing imports.

quota   A limited quantity of a particular product that under official controls can be produced, exported, or imported. (See *import quota*.)

recession   A period of temporary economic decline during which trade and industrial activity are reduced, generally identified as the fall in gross domestic product in two successive quarters.

secondary industry (or manufacturing industry)   An industry that converts raw materials provided by primary industry into commodities or products for the consumer.

single market An association of countries trading with each other without restrictions or tariffs.

soft loan A loan, typically one to a developing country, made on terms very favourable to the borrower.

tariff (or customs duty) A tax on the importation of particular goods, levied by a national government and payable to it when the item crosses the nation's customs boundary. Originally a device to raise revenue, tariffs were subsequently employed to discourage imports that might undersell the products of domestic industries that the government wished to protect.

technology-intensive industry An industry in which the cost of technology represents a relatively large percentage of the total costs of production. (Compare *capital-intensive industry*, *labour-intensive industry*, *land-intensive industry*.)

terms of trade The ratio of an index of a country's export prices to an index of its import prices.

trade deficit The amount by which the cost of a country's imports exceeds the value of its exports.

BIBLIOGRAPHICAL ESSAY

Since this book is based entirely on secondary sources, the following bibliography makes no reference to available collections of primary sources (such as government records or the papers, diaries, and memoirs of policy-makers). Moreover, since the book is addressed principally to students and generalists rather than scholarly specialists, references to journal articles and foreign-language studies have been de-emphasized in favour of readily accessible general studies in English.

PROLOGUE: INTERNATIONAL RELATIONS AT THE BEGINNING OF THE TWENTIETH CENTURY

THE EUROPEANIZATION OF THE WORLD

Among the dozens of excellent general studies of European imperial expansion before the First World War, the following may be read with profit: Alan Hodgart, *The Economics of European Imperialism* (1977); A.P. Thornton, *Doctrines of Imperialism* (1965), which surveys the impact of imperialism from Roman times to the present; Tom Kemp, *Theories of Imperialism* (1969), which summarizes and evaluates the various contemporary and retrospective interpretations of the phenomenon; and George Lichtheim, *Imperialism* (1971), an elegant essay by a master analyst of twentieth-century political behaviour. Two comprehensive and perceptive treatments of British imperial policy are Ronald Robinson et al., *Africa and the Victorians* (1970), and Clive Dewey and A.G. Hopkins, eds, *The Imperial Impact: Studies in the Economic History of Africa and India* (1978), which stresses the long-term consequences of economic imperialism in the British Empire. The classic study of French imperialism, which de-emphasizes its economic motivation, is Henri Brunschwig, *French Colonialism, 1871–1914* (1966).

THE RISE OF JAPANESE POWER IN EAST ASIA

The three best studies of Japanese–American rivalry in the Pacific before the First World War are Edwin O. Reischauer, *The United States and Japan* (1965), which stresses the Japanese perspective; Charles E. Neu, *The Troubled Encounter: The United States and Japan* (1975), which pays attention to the evolution of American governmental policy toward Asia; and Akira Iriye, *Pacific Estrangement: Japanese and American Expansion, 1897–1911* (1972), a penetrating analysis. Two classic studies of the economic underpinnings of Japan's rise to great-power status are Lawrence Klein and Kazushi Ohkawa, eds, *Economic Growth: The Japanese Experience since the Meiji Era* (1968), and Henry Rosovsky, *Capital Formation in Japan, 1868–1940* (1961). Valuable monographs on Japanese imperial expansion in particular regions of East Asia include Hilary Conroy, *The Japanese Seizure of Korea, 1868–1910* (1960), which should be checked against C.I. Eugene Kim and Han-kyo Kim, *Korea and the Politics of Imperialism, 1876–1910* (1967). Andrew Molozenoff, *Russian Far Eastern Policy, 1881–1904* (1958), traces the background of Russo–Japanese conflict in East Asia, while Shumpei Okamoto, *The Japanese Oligarchy and Russo–Japanese War* (1970), probes the domestic context of Japanese decision-making leading to the war of 1904–5. The most authoritative treatment of anti-Japanese sentiment on the American west coast is Roger Daniels, *The Politics of*

Prejudice: The Anti-Japanese Movement in California and the Struggle for Japanese Exclusion (1962). For details on Canadian government policy concerning Japanese immigrants to and inhabitants of the West Coast see K. Adachi, *The Enemy That Never Was: A History of the Japanese Canadians* (1978). Another excellent Canadian study, which also covers attitudes towards the Chinese in British Columbia, is Patricia E. Roy, *The Oriental Question: Consolidating a White Man's Province, 1914–41* (2004).

THE EMERGENCE OF THE UNITED STATES/DEVELOPMENTS IN THE AMERICAS

A stimulating interpretive essay on the history of Latin America during the late nineteenth century is E. Bradford Burns, *The Poverty of Progress: Latin America in the Nineteenth Century* (1980), which emphasizes the conflict between the elites of the various Latin American states that were intent on pursuing industrial development on the European–American model and the peasant masses that resisted modernization. Two widely quoted surveys of US policy toward Latin America approach the subject from different perspectives and reach diametrically opposite conclusions: the classic study by Samuel Flagg Bemis, *The Latin American Policy of the United States* (1943), written by the dean of Latin American historians in the United States amid wartime anxiety about Axis intervention in the western hemisphere, stresses the benevolence and protectiveness of the United States toward its southern neighbours; Gordon Connell-Smith's *The United States and Latin America* (1974), an Englishman's caustic indictment of the US's economic subjugation of the republics in its hemisphere, reflects the influence of the Vietnam experience and Europe's resentment of American domination. Two less contentious accounts of the United States' replacement of the European states as the preeminent power in the Caribbean are Lester D. Langley, *Struggle*

for the American Mediterranean: United States–European Rivalry in the Gulf-Caribbean, 1776–1904 (1976), and Dana G. Munro, *Intervention and Dollar Diplomacy in the Caribbean, 1900–1921* (1964). Dexter Perkin's *History of the Monroe Doctrine* (1955) is still regarded by experts as the definitive work on that subject. A valuable collection of essays on American–European economic rivalry in Latin America is Marvin Bernstein, ed., *Foreign Investment in Latin America* (1966). A comprehensive treatment of British investments in the region during this period is J. Fred Rippy, *British Investments in Latin America, 1822–1949* (1949). For British commercial relations with Latin America before the First World War, see Desmond Platt, *Latin America and British Trade, 1806–1914* (1972).

For a discussion of the relationship between Canada, Britain, and the United States at the turn of the century, see J.L. Granatstein's essay *How Britain's Weakness Forced Canada into the Arms of the United States* (1989). Volume 1 of C.P. Stacey's *Canada and the Age of Conflict: A History of Canadian External Policies* (1984) is a classic account of Canadian foreign policy from Confederation through the 1920s, while Carl Berger, *The Sense of Power: Studies in the Ideas of Canadian Imperialism, 1867–1914* (1970), offers a pioneering account of English-Canadian nationalist ideology in the late nineteenth and early twentieth centuries. Other studies of Canadian identity at the turn of the century include H.V. Nelles, *The Art of Nation-Building: Pageantry and Spectacle in Quebec's Tercentenary* (2000), which examines the festivities surrounding the 300-year anniversary of Champlain's founding of Quebec City; Gerald Friesen, *Citizens and Nation: An Essay on History, Communications, and Canada* (2003), a social study of how storytelling has informed Canadian identity; and Ramsay Cook, *French-Canadian Nationalism: An Anthology* (1969). For an excellent study of turn-of-the-century economic relations between Canada and Latin America, see Christopher Armstrong and H.V. Nelles, *Southern*

Exposure: Canadian Promoters in Latin America and the Caribbean, 1896–1930 (1988). Canada's contribution to the Boer War is discussed by Carman Miller in *Painting the Map Red: Canada and the South African War, 1899–1902* (1993).

TECHNOLOGY AND THE GEOPOLITICAL WORLD VIEW

Two useful summaries of the principal theories of geopolitics (or political geography) are Hans W. Weigert et al., *Principles of Political Geography* (1960), and J.R.V. Prescott, *Boundaries and Frontiers* (1978). For brief treatments of the principal individual contributions to geopolitical theory, see Anthony J. Pearce's lucid introduction to Halford J. Mackinder, *Democratic Ideals and Reality* (1962); and Derwent Whittlesley, 'Haushofer: The Geopoliticians', and Margaret T. Sprout, 'Mahan: Evangelist of Sea power', both in E.M. Earle, ed., *Makers of Modern Strategy* (1970). For a brilliant analysis of the Mahan School and its role in the United States' rise to global power, see Richard D. Challener, *Admirals, Generals, and American Foreign Policy, 1898–1914* (1973). Two classic theoretical studies of international relations that emphasize geopolitical considerations are Raymond Aron, *Peace and War: A Theory of International Relations* (1966), and Hans J. Morgenthau, *Politics Among Nations: The Struggle for Power and Peace* (1973).

THE DEVELOPMENT OF AN INTERNATIONAL ECONOMY

The spread of industrialism and the foundation of a global network of trade and investment before the First World War is the subject of a number of useful general works. See, for example, William Woodruff, *The Emergence of an International Economy* (1970), a solid survey that pays attention to the non-Western aspects of the emerging world economic system. The same is true of A.J.H. Latham, *The International Economy and the Undeveloped World, 1865–1914* (1978), which rejects the notion that the international economy was a British and North American phenomenon and emphasizes the contribution of the southern hemisphere, especially Africa and Asia. More Eurocentric, but no less sweeping in their coverage of the subject, are W.W. Rostow, *The World Economy: History and Prospect* (1978), and William Ashworth, *A Short History of the International Economy since 1850* (1975). A lucidly written textbook, still worth reading for its theoretical as well as its historical treatment of international economics, is P.T. Ellsworth, *The International Economy* (1958). Valuable studies of particular aspects of the operation of the world economy before the First World War include J.H. Dunning, *Studies in International Investment* (1970); J.H. Adler, ed., *Capital Movements and International Development* (1967), the first three sections of which are historical in their orientation; A.K. Cairncross, *Home and Foreign Investment, 1870–1913* (1953), a classic study of British capital movements; W.M. Scammell, *The London Discount Market* (1968); and Herbert Feis, *Europe: The World's Banker, 1870–1914* (1965), a still useful summary. An excellent attempt to relate labour supply to economic development during this period is B. Thomas, *Migration and Economic Growth* (1973). On the role of technology in the growth and spread of industrialization, see B.R. Williams, ed., *Science and Technology in Economic Growth* (1973), and David Landes, *The Unbound Prometheus* (1969). For informative surveys of economic development in the major participants in the global economic system, see Charles Kindleberger, *Economic Growth in France and Britain, 1851–1950* (1964); S.B. Saul, *Studies in British Overseas Trade, 1870–1914* (1960); Maurice Levy-Leboyer, ed., *La Position internationale de la France* (1977); G. Stolper et al., *The German Economy, 1870 to the Present* (1965); L.E. Davis et al., *American Economic History: The Development of a National Economy* (1965); and G.C. Allen, *A Short Economic History of Modern Japan* (1972).

PART ONE: THE THIRTY YEARS' WAR (1914–1945)

CHAPTER 1: GERMANY'S BID FOR EUROPEAN DOMINANCE (1914–1918)

One of the best military histories of the First World War is B.H. Liddell Hart, *History of the First World War* (1970). An excellent summary of the important tactical and strategic aspects of the war may also be found in Theodore Ropp, *War in the Modern World* (1962). For the political context of the war, the splendid survey by David Stevenson, *The First World War and International Politics* (1988), is essential. The controversy over the war aims of imperial Germany sparked by Fritz Fischer's *Germany's Aims in the First World War* (1967) produced a variety of responses, many of which are summarized in John A. Moses, *The Politics of Illusion: The Fischer Controversy in German Historiography* (1975). See also David Calleo, *The German Problem Reconsidered: Germany and World Order, 1870 to the Present* (1978), which is dominated by the theme that Germany's ambitions constantly outstripped its resources. There have also been a number of incisive studies of the war aims of the other great powers. See, for example, V.H. Rothwell, *British War Aims and Peace Diplomacy, 1914–1918* (1971); Sir Llewellyn Woodward, *Great Britain and the War of 1914–1918* (1967); David F. Trask, *The United States in the Supreme War Council: American War Aims and Inter-Allied Strategy, 1917–18* (1961); David Stevenson, *French War Aims Against Germany, 1914–1918* (1982); Walter McDougall, *France's Rhineland Diplomacy, 1914–1924* (1978), which treats French efforts to detach this strategically and economically valuable region from Germany; Marc Trachtenberg, *Reparation and World Politics* (1980), which absolves France of the vindictive reparation policy traditionally imputed to it; and

Carl Parrini, *Heir to Empire: United States Economic Diplomacy, 1916–1923* (1969), which contains a useful analysis of the Paris Economic Conference and the European allies' plans to establish a post-war economic bloc excluding the United States and the Central Powers. America's shift from neutrality to intervention and the impact of that transformation on the international order has been the subject of a number of excellent studies. See Patrick Devlin, *Too Proud to Fight: Woodrow Wilson's Neutrality* (1975), which complements the earlier work by Ernest R. May, *The World War and American Isolation, 1914–1917* (1959); Ross Gregory, *The Origins of American Intervention in the First World War* (1971); Edward M. Coffmann, *The War to End All Wars* (1968), which focuses on the period of active American participation in the war effort; and N. Gordon Levin, *Woodrow Wilson and World Politics* (1968), which emphasizes the American president's attempt to promote a liberal capitalist alternative to traditional imperialism and Bolshevism, a theme also treated in Arno J. Mayer, *Wilson vs. Lenin: Political Origins of the New Diplomacy* (1959). Three studies by French scholars have traced the ambivalent relationship between France and the United States during the war: Yves-Henri Nouailhat, *La France et les Etats-Unis, août 1914–avril 1917* (1977); Andre Kaspi, *La France et le concours américain, février 1917–novembre 1918* (1975); and Denise Artaud, *La Question des dettes interalliés et la reconstruction de l'Europe* (1978), the definitive study of American war loans to the European allies and the resulting debt controversy. On Anglo–American relations during the war, see Parrini, op. cit., for a discussion of the two countries' economic rivalry and co-operation, and Basil Collier, *The Lion and the Eagle: British and Anglo–American Strategy, 1900–1950* (1972), for a treatment of their military relations. For accounts of Canada's role in the First World War see Pierre Berton, *Vimy* (1986); D.G. Dancocks, *Spearhead to Victory: Canada and the Great War* (1987); W.A.B. Douglas, *The Creation of the National Air Force* (1986); Desmond Morton, *A*

Peculiar Kind of Politics (1982); Desmond Morton and J.L. Granatstein, *Marching to Armageddon: Canada and the Great War 1914–18* (1989); and Shane B. Schreiber, *Shock Army of the British Empire: The Canadian Corps in the Last 100 Days of the Great War* (1997). Jonathan F. Vance, *Death So Noble: Memory, Meaning, and the First World War* (1999), offers an original view of Canada's war from a philosophical and cultural perspective. For the role of Canadian women during the war, see Linda Kealey, *Enlisting Women for the Cause: Women, Labour and the Left in Canada, 1890–1920* (1998). J.L. Granatstein and J.M Hitsman's *Broken Promises: A History of Conscription in Canada* (1977) offers an account of how the issue divided the country in both world wars. For more general accounts of Canadian foreign policy during this period see C.P. Stacey, op. cit., and Norman Hillmer and J.L. Granatstein, *From Empire to Umpire: Canada and the World to the 1990s* (1994). One of the best studies of the Russian withdrawal from World War I remains John W. Wheeler-Bennett, *Brest-Litovsk: The Forgotten Peace* (1971). The allied intervention in the Russian Civil War is covered by George Kennan, *The Decision to Intervene* (1958), by John Silverlight, *The Victors' Dilemma: Allied Intervention in the Russian Civil War* (1970), and by Betty Miller Unterberger, *The United States, Revolutionary Russia, and the Rise of Czechoslovakia* (1989).

CHAPTER 2: THE PEACE OF PARIS AND THE NEW INTERNATIONAL ORDER

There is a rich literature on particular aspects of the deliberations and decisions of the Paris Peace Conference and their impact on the world. A recent narrative account is Margaret MacMillan's *Paris 1919: Six Months that Changed the World* (2002). The most comprehensive study of the peace conference, though focusing primarily on American policy, is Arthur Walworth, *Wilson and His Peacemakers: American Diplomacy and the Paris Peace Conference, 1919* (1986). A much briefer study, but one with a much more multinational scope, is Alan Sharp's *The Versailles Settlement* (1991). Howard Elcock's *Portrait of a Decision: The Council of Four and the Treaty of Versailles* (1972) emphasizes the organizational context of decision-making and the clash of national interests. Michael G. Fry, *Illusions of Security: North Atlantic Diplomacy, 1918–22* (1972), Seth P. Tillman, *Anglo–American Relations at the Paris Peace Conference, 1919* (1961), Louis A.R. Yates, *The United States and French Security, 1917–1921* (1957), and Jon Paul Selsam, *The Attempts to Form an Anglo–French Alliance, 1919–1924* (1936), all treat the disintegration of the anti-German coalition and the advent of Anglo–American efforts to mitigate the alleged harshness of the peace treaty with Germany. Preliminary discussions of the related issues of inter-Allied debts and German reparations are exhaustively covered in Artaud, op. cit., and Trachtenberg, op. cit., respectively. The peacemakers' preoccupation with the ideological menace of Russian communism and their attempts to protect Europe from its westward advance is the dominant theme of Arno J. Mayer, *Politics and Diplomacy of Peacemaking: Containment and Counterrevolution at Versailles, 1918–1919* (1967). France's abortive effort to establish a client state in the Rhenish buffer zone is recounted in McDougall, op. cit. The collapse of the inter-Allied wartime economic partnership during the peace conference receives extensive treatment in Parrini, op. cit., Trachtenberg, op. cit., and Dan P. Silverman, *Reconstructing Europe After the Great War* (1982). Two excellent studies of the role of second-rank powers at the peace conference are René Albrecht-Carrie, *Italy at the Paris Peace Conference* (1966), originally published in 1938 but still useful, and Sally Marks's *Belgium at the Paris Peace Conference* (1981). George Parkin de Twenebroker's *Canada at the Paris Peace Conference* (1942) is a rather old but still useful study of Canada's role at the conference. For accounts and analysis of the Winnipeg General Strike, see J.M. Bumsted, *The Winnipeg General Strike of 1919: An Illustrated History* (1994), and Craig Heron, ed., *The Workers' Revolt in Canada, 1917–1925* (1997).

CHAPTER 3: THE 1920S: ERA OF ILLUSIONS

THE ILLUSION OF ECONOMIC RESTORATION

An ambitious attempt to make sense of the complex developments in international economic relations in the 1920s is Derek H. Aldcroft, *From Versailles to Wall Street: 1918–1929* (1977). America's rise to preeminence in the world economy at Britain's expense is treated in Parrini, op. cit., Joan Hoff-Wilson, *American Business and Foreign Policy, 1920–1933* (1971), Herbert Feis, *The Diplomacy of the Dollar: First Phase, 1919–1932* (1950), and Mira Wilkins, *The Maturing of Multinational Enterprise: American Business Interests Abroad from 1914 to 1970* (1974). Michael J. Hogan's *Informal Entente: The Private Structure of Cooperation in Anglo–American Economic Diplomacy, 1918–1928* (1977), emphasizes the co-operative spirit in which the two English-speaking powers strove to manage the economic recovery of the post-war world. Among the several studies that assess the attempts by the European belligerents to reconstruct their national financial and monetary systems, with or without American assistance, are Silverman, op. cit., Artaud, op. cit., Charles S. Maier, *Recasting Bourgeois Europe* (1975), Melvyn P. Leffler, *The Elusive Quest: America's Pursuit of European Stability and French Security, 1919–1933* (1979), and Stephen A. Schuker, *The End of French Predominance in Europe: The Financial Crisis of 1924 and the Adoption of the Dawes Plan* (1976). Jacques Bariéty, *Les relations franco–allemandes après la première guerre mondiale* (1977), is a brilliantly conceived and exhaustively researched assessment of the abortive attempts at Franco–German reconciliation through measures of economic co-operation similar to those successfully implemented a generation later. Trachtenberg's study of reparations, op. cit., should be supplemented by Herman J. Rupieper, *The Cuno Government and Reparations, 1921–1923* (1979), and David Felix, *Walther Rathenau and the Weimar Republic: The Politics of Reparations* (1971).

Benjamin M. Rowland, ed., *Balance of Power or Hegemony: The Interwar Monetary System* (1976), is a valuable collection of essays that may be read in conjunction with Stephen V.O. Clarke, *Central Bank Cooperation, 1924–1931* (1967). On Britain's post-war struggle to revive its industrial production, foreign trade, and international financial position, see B.W.E. Alford, *Depression and Recovery: British Economic Growth, 1918–1939* (1972), and Ian Drummond, *British Economic Policy and the Empire, 1919–1932* (1972).

THE CONFIRMATION OF US SUPREMACY IN LATIN AMERICA

United States military intervention and economic expansion in Latin America during and after the First World War has been recorded and evaluated in a number of important works. The best general studies of the subject include David Green, *The Containment of Latin America* (1971), C. Neal Ronning, *Intervention in Latin America* (1971), and Dana M. Munro, *The United States and the Caribbean Republics, 1921–1933* (1974). Joseph Tulchin's *Aftermath of War: World War I and United States Policy Toward Latin America* (1971) emphasizes the State Department's role in promoting American export interests in the region at the expense of European competitors. Kenneth J. Greib, *The Latin American Policy of Warren G. Harding* (1976), is a carefully researched study that also devotes considerable attention to America's expanding economic interests south of the border. Joseph Brandes, *Herbert Hoover and Economic Diplomacy: Department of Commerce Policy, 1921–1928* (1962), has much to say about the same subject. Alexander DeConde, *Herbert Hoover's Latin American Policy* (1951), remains a useful account of an important transitional period. Dick Steward, *Trade and Hemisphere* (1975), is a wide-ranging assessment of inter-American commercial relationships that emphasizes the United States' commanding position in hemispheric trade. Wilson, op. cit., and Mira Wilkins, *The Maturing of Multinational Enterprise: American Business Abroad From 1914–1970* (1974), though global in scope, accord extensive treatment to inter-American economic relationships.

THE ILLUSION OF CONTINENTAL SECURITY

The succession of attempts to promote continental stability and security in the 1920s inspired a number of early scholarly analyses that appeared while most of the European diplomatic archives remained inaccessible. Arnold Wolfers, *Britain and France Between the Wars: Conflicting Strategies of Peace* (1940), and W.M. Jordan, *Great Britain, France, and the German Problem* (1943), are two old classics that assess the Western allies' divergent efforts to preserve the post-war settlement. Yates, op. cit., and Selsam, op. cit., record the failure of successive French governments in the early 1920s to revive the defunct security pacts with the two 'Anglo-Saxon' powers, while Robert H. Ferrell, *Peace in Their Time: The Origins of the Kellogg-Briand Pact* (1952), demonstrates how the multilateral pledge to 'outlaw war' originated as a French ploy to secure the US's unilateral support against a resurgent Germany. The immediate consequences of the Great War and the European powers' clumsy attempts to cope with them in the early 1920s are admirably analyzed in Carole Fink, *The Genoa Conference: European Diplomacy, 1921–1922* (1984). The formation of the French alliance system in Eastern Europe and the internal contradictions that already plagued it in the early 1920s are carefully examined in Piotr Wandycz, *France and Her Eastern Allies, 1919–1925* (1962). Stresemann's reputation as a sincere advocate of treaty fulfillment is deflated in Hans Gatzke, *Stresemann and the Rearmament of Germany* (1954). The two most useful studies of Soviet foreign policy during this period are George Kennan, *Russia and the West Under Lenin and Stalin* (1960), and Adam Ulam, *Expansion and Coexistence: The History of Soviet Foreign Policy, 1917–1973* (1974). US relations with the transatlantic world during the 'era of isolationism' are shrewdly assessed in L. Ethan Ellis, *Republican Foreign Policy, 1921–1933* (1968); Jean-Baptiste Duroselle, *From Wilson to Roosevelt: The Foreign Policy of the United States, 1913–1935* (1963), and Selig Adler, *The Isolationist Impulse: Its Twentieth Century Reaction* (1951).

Many of these older studies were superseded by works that benefited from the opening of the European archives in the 1960s and 1970s. Two of the best general surveys of the period are Sally Marks, *The Illusion of Peace: Europe's International Relations, 1918–1933* (1976), and Arnold A. Offner, *The Origins of the Second World War: American Foreign Policy and World Politics, 1917–1941* (1975). A perceptive assessment of the shifting balance of power on the continent in the course of the 1920s may be found in William J. Newman, *The Balance of Power in the Interwar Years* (1969). Though heavily weighted toward economic matters, Bariéty's study of Franco–German relations in the 1920s, op. cit., also treats the security concerns and policies of the two antagonistic powers on the Rhine. Leffler, op. cit., updates and extends Yates's study of Franco–American relations up to 1933 but is based almost exclusively on American primary sources. Keith L. Nelson, *Victors Divided: America and the Allies in Germany, 1918–1923* (1975), is a carefully researched study of the tensions and policy disputes between the Allied occupation armies in the Rhineland. Judith Hughes, *To the Maginot Line* (1971), and Jacques Nere, *The Foreign Policy of France from 1914 to 1945* (1975), succinctly summarize the security dilemmas of the power whose primary responsibility it was to enforce the Versailles Treaty during this period. Two full-length studies of British foreign policy in the 1920s that were written after the opening of government records are Anne Orde, *Great Britain and International Security, 1920–1926* (1978), and Michael Howard, *The Continental Commitment: The Dilemma of British Defense Policy in the Era of the Two World Wars* (1972). On the operation of the League of Nations during its first decade in existence, see Ruth B. Henig, ed., *The League of Nations* (1973), and P. Raffo, *The League of Nations* (1974). Richard Veatch outlines Canada's post-war foreign policy and involvement in the League of Nations in *Canada and the League of Nations* (1975). The best study of the Locarno Conference and its aftermath is Jon Jacobson, *Locarno Diplomacy: Germany and the West, 1925–1929* (1972). For a brilliant reassessment of Soviet–American relations during the period of non-recognition, see Joan Hoff-Wilson, *Ideology and Economics: U.S. Relations with the Soviet Union, 1918–1933* (1974).

CHAPTER 4: THE 1930S: ILLUSIONS DISPELLED

THE COLLAPSE OF THE WORLD ECONOMIC ORDER

The definitive survey of the Great Depression and its global consequences, written by an economist with a flair for lucid historical narrative, is Charles Kindleberger's *The World in Depression, 1929–1939* (1973). The foreign economic policy of the Roosevelt administration in the 1930s is evaluated in Lloyd C. Gardner, *Economic Aspects of New Deal Diplomacy* (1964), and found to be motivated by a desire to preserve the open door for American trade. A useful monograph on one important institutional mechanism for the revival of American foreign trade in the Depression decade is Frederick C. Adams, *Economic Diplomacy: The Export–Import Bank and American Foreign Policy, 1934–1939* (1976). Wilkins, op. cit., remains the best general account of the expansion and contraction of American direct investment abroad. To the studies by Alford, op. cit., and Drummond, op. cit., of Britain's foreign economic policy in the inter-war years may be added H.W. Richardson, *Economic Recovery in Britain, 1932–1939* (1967). The two best studies of Nazi Germany's economic recovery and its relation to Hitler's war plans are B.H. Klein, *Germany's Economic Preparations for War* (1959), and Bernice A. Carroll, *Design for Total War: Arms and Economics in the Third Reich* (1968). Tom Kemp, *The French Economy, 1913–1939* (1972), chronicles the decline of French industrial productivity during the very time it was needed to fuel rearmament, while David Kaiser, *Economic Diplomacy and the Origins of the Second World War: Germany, Britain, France, and Eastern Europe, 1930–1939* (1980), demonstrates how the small nations of Eastern Europe became economically dependent on Germany even as they sought to preserve their political and military ties to France during the 1930s.

THE UNITED STATES AND LATIN AMERICA

US–Latin American relations during the period of Roosevelt's Good Neighbor Policy have been comprehensively treated in the following general works: Wilfred H. Callcott, *The Western Hemisphere: Its Influence on United States Foreign Policies to the End of World War II* (1968); Bryce Wood, *The Making of the Good Neighbor Policy* (1961), which de-emphasizes Hoover's contribution to the improvement of hemispheric relations and stresses Roosevelt's role; and Donald Dozier, *Are We Good Neighbors?* (1959). A number of works focus on the alleged threat of Axis intervention in the western hemisphere and the United States' efforts to mobilize its Latin American clients to combat it: Alton B. Frye, *Nazi Germany and the Western Hemisphere, 1933–1941* (1967) recounts the expansion of German economic activity and political intrigue in Latin America after Hitler's accession; Stanley E. Hilton, *Hitler's Secret War in South America, 1939–1945* (1981), is a well-documented account of German espionage in Brazil and of Brazilian–US efforts to counteract it. Hilton's *Brazil and the Great Powers, 1930–1939* (1975) and Frank D. McCann, Jr's *The Brazilian–American Alliance, 1937–1945* (1973) both show how Brazilian President Getúlio Vargas used his country's close relationship with the US to limit European influence and strengthen Brazil in its regional rivalry with Argentina. Alberto Conil Paz and Gustavo Ferrari, *Argentina's Foreign Policy, 1930–1962* (1962), is a well-documented account of Argentina's challenge to US interests and policies in Latin America. Three superb studies of the inter-American conferences and Washington's quest for a hemispheric security system are Samuel G. Inman, *Inter-American Conferences, 1926–1954* (1965); Tom J. Farer, ed., *The Future of the Inter-American System* (1979); and J. Lloyde Mecham, *The United States and Inter-American Security, 1889–1960* (1961). Bryce Wood, *The United States and the Latin American Wars, 1932–1942* (1966), documents American inaction and indifference in regard to the Chaco, Letitia, and Marañón conflicts in Latin America. In addition to those books on US–Latin American economic relations cited in the bibliography for Chapter 3, see Frederick C. Adams, *Economic Diplomacy: The Export–Import Bank and American Foreign Policy, 1934–1939* (1976), and Lloyd Gardner, *Economic Aspects of New Deal Diplomacy* (1964). Green, op. cit., offers the revisionist interpretation that Roosevelt's Good Neighbor Policy rhetoric masked a sustained effort to contain radical social reform and preserve American economic dominance in Latin America.

THE COLLAPSE OF THE EUROPEAN SECURITY SYSTEM

The enormous body of scholarly literature on the origins of the Second World War in Europe was greatly enriched by works based on the declassified records of the belligerent states. A.J.P. Taylor's controversial *Origins of the Second World War* (1961), written before all but the captured German documents were accessible, caused a sensation by emphasizing the continuity of German foreign policy throughout the inter-war period and depicting Hitler as a traditional German nationalist who implemented the policies of his republican predecessors by exploiting opportunities provided by the mistakes of weak-kneed British and French leaders. Two less tendentious and more recent studies of the subject are Joachim Remak, *The Origins of the Second World War* (1976), and Anthony Adamthwaite, *The Making of the Second World War* (1979). Gerhard Weinberg's magisterial two-volume work *The Foreign Policy of Hitler's Germany* (1970, 1979) is a solid narrative account based on primary sources from half a dozen countries, and it may be supplemented with Klaus Hildebrand, *The Foreign Policy of the Third Reich* (1973). Norman Rich, *Hitler's War Aims* (2 vols,

1973–4), focuses on the objectives of Nazi foreign policy and devotes less attention to the unfolding of events. Excellent studies of French foreign policy during the 1930s include Anthony T. Komjathy, *The Crises of France's East Central European Diplomacy, 1933–1938* (1977); Anthony Adamthwaite, *France and the Coming of the Second World War* (1977); Nicole Jordan, *The Popular Front and Central Europe: The Dilemma of French Impotence, 1918–1940* (1992), which, despite its subtitle, deals primarily with the 1930s; and Jean-Baptiste Duroselle, *La Decadence* (1980), a poignant account of French decline amid German renewal. Robert Young's *In Command of France* (1978) assesses the tactical and strategic thinking of the French general staff during the period of German rearmament and European crisis. Britain's shift from appeasement to rearmament is treated in William R. Rock, *British Appeasement in the 1930s* (1977); Keith Middlemas, *Diplomacy of Illusion: The British Government and Germany, 1937–1939* (1971); Maurice Cowling, *The Impact of Hitler: British Politics and British Policy, 1933–1940* (1975); Robert Paul Shay, *British Rearmament in the Thirties* (1977); and Michael Howard, op. cit. C.P. Stacey, one of Canada's greatest military and international historians, offers a classic account of Canadian foreign policy in the Mackenzie King era in volume 2 of *Canada and the Age of Conflict: A History of Canadian External Policy* (1984). King himself is the subject of a number of interesting studies, including C.P. Stacey, *A Very Double Life* (1976), and J.E. Esberey, *Knight of the Holy Spirit* (1980). For an even-handed treatment of Canadian policy towards Jewish immigrants in the 1930s and 1940s, see Abella Irving and Harold Troper, *None is Too Many: Canada and the Jews of Europe, 1933–1948* (1982).

The critical turning points in foreign policy between 1933 and 1939 have been analyzed in a number of monographs. The Ethiopian affair is treated exhaustively in Frank Hardie, *The Abyssinian Crisis* (1974), and George W. Baer, *Test Case: Italy, Ethiopia, and the League of Nations* (1976). For a Canadian perspective that focuses on League of Nations representative Walter Riddell's disregard for King's orders to keep Canada out of the conflict see Richard Veatch, op. cit. Hugh Thomas, *The Spanish Civil War* (1961), is an excellent general survey of the subject and may be read in conjunction with T. Harper, *German Economic Policy in Spain* (1967), and John F. Cloverdale, *Italian Intervention in the Spanish Civil War* (1975). For studies of Canadian participation see W.C. Beeching, *Canadian Volunteers: Spain, 1936–1939* (1990), and Mark Zuehlke, *The Gallant Cause: Canadians in the Spanish Civil War, 1936–1939* (1996). Important studies of Italian foreign policy include Elizabeth Wiskemann, *The Rome–Berlin Axis* (1966); Mario Toscano, *The Origins of the Pact of Steel* (1967); and Denis Mack Smith, *Mussolini's Roman Empire* (1976). The most comprehensive treatment of the German annexation of Austria is Gordon Brooke-Shepard, *Anschluss: The Rape of Austria* (1963). Of the numerous assessments of the Munich Crisis, the following may be recommended: Keith Robbins, *Munich* (1968); Roy Douglas, *In the Year of Munich* (1977); Keith Eubank, *Munich* (1963); and Robert M. Smelser, *The Sudeten Problem, 1933–1938* (1975), for a background to the crisis. The best study of the Polish problem at the end of the decade is Anna M. Cienciala, *Poland and the Western Powers, 1938–39* (1968). America's isolationism and its gradual turn toward involvement in the European crisis is covered in Arnold A. Offner, *American Appeasement: United States Foreign Policy and Germany, 1933–1938* (1969); Manfred Jonas, *Isolationism in America, 1935–1941* (1966); Robert A. Divine, *The Illusion of Neutrality* (1962); and Richard P. Traina, *American Diplomacy and the Spanish Civil War* (1968).

CHAPTER 5: GERMANY'S SECOND BID FOR EUROPEAN DOMINANCE (1939–1945)

The standard military history of the Second World War is B.H. Liddell Hart, *History of the Second World War* (1970). One of the best recent studies of the political, diplomatic, and economic context of the war is Gerhard Weinberg, *A World At Arms: A Global History of World War II* (1994). For exhaustive studies of individual campaigns, see General Andre Beaufre, *1940: The Fall of France* (1968); Telford Taylor, *The Breaking Wave* (1967); and Basil Calber, *The Battle of Britain* (1962), on the failure of Operation Sea-Lion; Paul Carill, *Hitler's War in Russia* (1964); and Trumbull Higgins, *Hitler and Russia: The Third Reich in a Two-Front War, 1937–1943* (1966), on Operation Barbarossa; Denis Whitaker, *Dieppe: Tragedy to Triumph* (1992), for a Canadian veteran's well-supported first-hand account of the Dieppe raid; Correlli Barnett, *The Desert Generals* (1960), on the North African campaign; Dominick Graham and Shelford Bidwell, *Tug of War: The Battle for Italy, 1943–1945* (1986); Daniel G. Dancocks, *The D-Day Dodgers: The Canadians in Italy, 1943–1945* (1992); L.R. Ellis, *Victory in the West: The Battle of Normandy* (1963); Terry Copp, *Fields of Fire: The Canadians in Normandy* (2003); and Stephen E. Ambrose, *D-Day June 6, 1944: The Climactic Battle of World War II* (2002), for a narrative account based on interviews with American, British, Canadian, French, and German veterans; Sir Charles Webster and Noble Frankland, *The Strategic Air Offensive Against Germany, 1939–1945* (4 vols., 1961); and Captain S.W. Roskill, *The War at Sea, 1939–1945* (3 vols, 1954–61). The critical role of Allied intelligence in the winning of the war is highlighted in F.W. Winterbotham, *The Ultra Secret* (1974). Two general surveys of the war that pay attention to the home front as well as the battlefront are worthy of mention: Gordon Wright, *The Ordeal of Total War, 1939–45* (1968), concentrates on the European theatre and is more analytical than narrative in its approach, while Peter Calvocoressi and Guy Wint, *Total War: Causes and Courses of the Second World War* (1979), is a comprehensive 900-page narrative treating every important aspect of the world struggle. A stimulating assessment of the European war before the intervention of the two superpowers may be found in John Lukacs, *The Last European War: September 1939–December 1941* (1976). One of the best studies of the economic dimensions of the war is Alan S. Milward, *War, Economy, and Society:*

1939–1945 (1977), a worthy successor to his *The German Economy at War* (1965). On the American role in the war and its relations with the European allies, see T.R. Fehrenbach, *FDR's Undeclared War, 1939–1941* (1967); Robert A. Divine, *Roosevelt and World War II* (1969); Philip Goodhart, *Fifty Ships That Saved the World: The Foundations of Anglo-American Alliance* (1965); Warren R. Kimball, *The Most Unsordid Act: Lend–Lease, 1939–1941* (1969); Theodore A. Wilson, *The First Summit: Roosevelt and Churchill at Placentia Bay, 1941* (1969); Robert Beitzell, *The Uneasy Alliance: America, Britain, and Russia, 1941–1943* (1972); and George C. Heering, Jr, *Aid to Russia, 1941–1946* (1973). Various aspects of Canada's role in the war are discussed in Donald H. Avery, *The Science of War: Canadian Scientists and Allied Military Technology during the Second World War* (1998); J.A. Boutilier, ed., *The RCN in Retrospect 1910–1968* (1982); J.L. Granatstein and Desmond Morton, *A Nation Forged in Fire: Canadians and the Second World War* (1989); Brereton Greenhous et al., *The Crucible of War, 1939–1945*, vol. 3: *The Official History of the Royal Canadian Air Force* (1994); Norman Hillmer et al., eds, *A Country of Limitations: Canada and the World in 1939* (1996); G.W.L. Nicholson, *The Canadians in Italy* (1956); and Mark Zuehlke, *Juno Beach: Canada's D-Day Victory: June 6, 1944* (2004). For a study of Canada's wartime policy see J.L. Granatstein, *Canada's War: The Politics of the Mackenzie King Government, 1939–1945* (1974), and C.P. Stacey, *Arms, Men, and Governments: The War Policies of Canada, 1939–1945* (1970). The diplomatic wrangling at the wartime conferences and the origins of Soviet–American disagreements on post-war policy are treated in Anne Armstrong, *Unconditional Surrender: The Impact of the Casablanca Policy Upon World War II* (1961); Diane Shaver Clemens, *Yalta* (1970); and Herbert Feis, *Between War and Peace: The Potsdam Conference* (1960), and his *Churchill, Roosevelt, Stalin* (1957). Among the various reliable surveys of the Holocaust are Lucy S. Dawidowicz, *The War Against the Jews* (1975); Michael R. Marrus, *The Holocaust in History* (1987); and Dan Stone, ed., *The Historiography of the Holocaust* (2004).

CHAPTER 6: THE CONFIRMATION OF JAPAN'S SUPREMACY IN EAST ASIA

PEACEFUL PENETRATION (1914–1930)

Readers unfamiliar with the history of Japan's foreign relations prior to the expansionist period of the 1930s may consult Ian Nish, *Japanese Foreign Policy, 1869–1942* (1977). The standard account of Japan's relations with the Western imperial powers in the Pacific in the decade after the First World War is Akira Iriye, *After Imperialism: The Search for Order in the Far East, 1921–1931* (1965). Japanese–American conflicts during the First World War and the Paris Peace Conference are judiciously assessed in James W. Morley, *The Japanese Thrust into Siberia, 1918* (1957), and Russell H. Fitfield, *Woodrow Wilson and the Far East: The Diplomacy of the Shantung Question* (1952). The background of the Washington Naval Conference is traced in Roger Dingman, *Power in the Pacific: The Origins of Naval Arms Limitation, 1914–1922* (1970). For the conference itself, see Sadao Asada, 'Japan's "Special Interests" and the Washington Conference, 1921–22', *American Historical Review* 67 (1961), and Thomas H. Buckley, *The United States and the Washington Naval Conference, 1921–1922* (1970).

For Anglo–American reactions to Japan's rise to great-power status in the Pacific, see Gerald E. Wheeler, *Prelude to Pearl Harbor: The United States Navy and the Far East, 1921–1931* (1963); Ian Nish, *Alliance in Decline: A Study of Anglo–Japanese Relations* (1972); and William Roger Louis, *British Strategy in the Far East, 1919–1939* (1971). The role of the British Pacific Dominions in the balance of power during the 1920s is evaluated in William S. Livingston and William Roger Louis, eds, *Australia, New Zealand, and the Pacific Islands since the First World War* (1979). A valuable collection of essays on Sino–Japanese relations during this period is Alvin D. Coox and Hilroy Conroy, eds, *China and Japan: Search for Balance since World War I* (1978). America's involvement in China has been analyzed in exhaustive detail in Roberta A.

Dayer, *Bankers and Diplomats in China, 1917–1925* (1980), which concentrates on Anglo–American rivalry; Barbara Tuchman, *Stilwell and the American Experience in China, 1911–1945* (1971); Warren I. Cohen, *America's Response to China: An Interpretive History of Sino–American Relations* (1971); and James L. Lawrence, *Organized Business and the Myth of the China Market* (1981), a monographic study of the American Asiatic Association and its lobbying efforts on behalf of American economic penetration of China. An authoritative study of the London Naval Conference is Raymond G. O'Connor, *Perilous Equilibrium: The United States and the London Naval Conference of 1930* (1962).

MILITARY EXPANSION (1931–1941)/ THE WAR IN ASIA (1941–1945)

Full-length studies of Japan's bid for supremacy in Manchuria and North China during the 1930s include James B. Crowley, *Japan's Quest for Autonomy: National Security and Foreign Policy, 1930–1938* (1966), and David J. Lu, *From the Marco Polo Bridge to Pearl Harbor: Japan's Entry into World War II* (1961). Four excellent analyses of Britain's ambivalent response to Japan's aggressive foreign policy in the 1930s appeared in the 1970s: Ann Trotter, *Britain and East Asia, 1933–1937* (1975); Stephen L. Endicott, *Diplomacy and Enterprise: British China Policy 1933–1937* (1975); Bradford A. Lee, *Britain and the Sino–Japanese War, 1937–1939* (1973); and Peter Lowe, *Great Britain and the Origins of the Pacific War* (1977). Among the many monographs on the Manchurian Crisis and its global ramifications, Sadaka Ogata, *Defiance in Manchuria: The Making of Japanese Foreign Policy, 1931–1932* (1964), and Takehiko Yoshihashi, *Conspiracy at Mukden: The Rise of the Japanese Military* (1963), emphasize the domestic determinants of the turn toward aggressiveness; Armin Rappaport, *Henry L. Stimson and Japan, 1931–1933* (1963), assesses the tepid American response; while Christopher Thorne, *The Limits of Foreign Policy: The West, the League, and the Far Eastern Crisis of 1931–1933* (1972), is a judicious account of the world community's paralysis in the face of Japanese action. On Japan's relations with the Axis powers in Europe, see James W. Morley, ed., *Deterrent Diplomacy: Japan, Germany and the USSR, 1935–1940* (1976); E.L. Presseisen, *Germany and Japan: A Study in Totalitarian Diplomacy* (1969); and J.M. Mestill, *The Hollow Alliance: Germany and Japan* (1966). The best studies of the diplomatic and naval decisions preceding the Pearl Harbor attack are Dorothy Borg and Shumpei Okomoto, eds, *Pearl Harbor as History: Japanese–American Relations, 1931–1941* (1973), a valuable collection of essays by Japanese and American scholars; and Paul Schroeder, *The Axis Alliance and Japanese–American Relations, 1941* (1958), a revisionist account of the Japanese–American negotiations that failed over the Pacific. The Pearl Harbor attack itself has generated a vast literature. Roberta Wohlstetter, *Pearl Harbor: Warning and Decision* (1962), remains a persuasive explanation of America's lack of preparedness, which the author attributes to an 'overload' of conflicting intelligence information rather than to deliberate blindness. Two notable presentations of this conspiracy theory are Charles C. Tansill, *Back Door to War: The Roosevelt Foreign Policy, 1933–1941* (1952), and Robert A. Theobald, *The Final Secret of Pearl Harbor: The Washington Contribution to the Japanese Attack* (1954). Two more recent tomes, John Toland, *Infamy: Pearl Harbor and its Aftermath* (1982), and Gordon Prang, *At Dawn We Slept* (1981), supply interesting details but fail to disprove Wohlstetter's convincing assessment. An authoritative account of the military and naval campaigns in the Pacific theatre is Basil Collier, *The War in the Far East* (1970). Three excellent studies of the diplomatic and political context of the war in the Pacific are Christopher Thorne, *Allies of a Kind: The United States, Britain, and the War Against Japan, 1941–1945* (1978); John Dower, *War Without Mercy: Race and Power in the Pacific War* (1986); and Akira Iriye, *Power and Culture: The Japanese–American War, 1941–1945* (1981). Several stimulating evaluations of Japan's war aims and its methods of achieving them appear in Joyce C. Lebra, *Japan's Greater East Asia Co-Prosperity Sphere in World War II* (1975), which supersedes F.C. Jones,

Japan's New Order in East Asia, 1937–1945 (1961). The evacuation of Japanese Americans from the Pacific Coast is treated in Roger Daniels, *Concentration Camps USA: Japanese-Americans and World War II* (1971), and Audrie Girdner and Annie Loftis, *The Great Betrayal: The Evacuation of the Japanese-Americans During World War II* (1969). Ann Sunahara, *The Politics of Racism: The Uprooting of Japanese Canadians during the Second World War* (1981), gives a trenchant analysis of Canada's policy towards Japanese Canadians during the war. Her book may be read in conjunction with B. Broadfoot, *Years of Sorrow, Years of Shame: The Story of Japanese Canadians in World War II* (1977). For two dissimilar accounts of the American decision to drop the atomic bombs on Japan, see Herbert Feis, *The Atomic Bomb and the End of World War II* (1966), and Martin J. Sherwin, *A World Destroyed* (1987).

PART TWO: THE COLD WAR BETWEEN THE SUPERPOWERS (1945–1985)

CHAPTER 7: THE FORMATION OF THE BIPOLAR WORLD IN THE TRUMAN–STALIN ERA (1945–1953)

The Cold War has generated dozens of polemical studies that strive to explain its origins by attributing primary or even exclusive responsibility to one or the other of the two superpowers. Most of these works concentrate on the period 1941–9, when the Soviet–American relationship was transformed from wartime partnership to global confrontation. But there are also a number of more comprehensive works that cover the entire history of the Cold War. Two of the most useful narrative accounts are Andre Fontaine, *History of the Cold War* (2 vols, 1968, 1969), and Colin Brown and Peter J. Mooney, *Cold War to Détente, 1945–1980* (1981). Walter LaFeber, *America, Russia, and the Cold War* (1976), is an even-handed analysis; and

Louis Halled, *The Cold War as History* (1967), is an elegant essay by a former State Department official. The Roots of the Cold War in Soviet–American disagreements concerning the political future of Europe are laid bare in Robert Beitzell, *The Uneasy Alliance: America, Britain, and Russia, 1941–1943* (1973); Lynn E. Davis, *The Cold War Begins: Soviet–American Conflict over Eastern Europe* (1974); Thomas Paterson, *Soviet–American Confrontation, Postwar Reconstruction, and the Origins of the Cold War* (1973); John Lewis Gaddis, *The United States and the Origins of the Cold War, 1941–47* (1972); Vojtech Mastny, *Russia's Road to the Cold War: Diplomacy, Warfare, and the Politics of Communism, 1941–45* (1979); Daniel Yergin, *Shattered Peace: The Origins of the Cold War and the National Security State* (1977); and Melvyn P. Leffler, *A Preponderance of Power: National Security, The Truman Administration, and the Cold War* (1992). Amy Knight, *How the Cold War Began: The Gouzenko Affair and the Hunt for Soviet Spies* (2005), examines the way the defection of the Russian cipher clerk in Ottawa gave Washington the evidence it needed to demonize the Soviet Union. Her work may be read together with Gouzenko's autobiography, *This Was My Choice* (1948). Studies that focus on the Cold War in Canada include Reg Whitaker and Steve Hewitt, *Canada and the Cold War* (2003), and Reg Whitaker and Gary Marcuse, *Cold War Canada: The Making of a National Insecurity State, 1945–1957* (1994).

For a stimulating assessment of Europe's position in the post-war bipolar system, see A.W. DePorte, *Europe Between the Superpowers* (1979). The role of Germany in the collapse of the Soviet–American wartime partnership has been treated in the following works: Warren F. Kimball, *Swords into Plowshares? The Morgenthau Plan for Defeated Nazi Germany, 1943–46* (1976); Stephen Ambrose, *Eiesenhower and Berlin, 1945* (1971); Bruce Kuklick, *American Policy and the Division of Germany* (1972); John H. Backer, *Priming the Germany Economy: American Occupation Policies, 1945–48* (1971); and Jean Smith, *The Defense of Berlin* (1963).

For specific studies of the Marshall Plan, the Truman Doctrine, the containment policy, and the

Soviet response, see the following: Joseph Jones, *The Fifteen Weeks* (1955), an insider's account of the decisions leading to the promulgation of the new policies; John Gimbel, *The Origins of the Marshall Plan* (1976); Michael J. Hogan, *The Marshall Plan: America, Britain, and the Reconstruction of Western Europe, 1947–1952* (1987); Robert A. Pollard, *Economic Security and the Origins of the Cold War* (1985); Richard Freeland, *The Truman Doctrine and the Origins of McCarthyism* (1971); Richard Barnet, *Intervention and Revolution* (1972); John O. Iatrides, *Revolt in Athens* (1972), which treats the 1944–5 phase of the Greek Civil War; Stephen G. Xydis, *Greece and the Great Powers, 1944–47* (1963); Bruce R. Kuniholm, *The Origins of the Cold War in the Near East: Great Power Conflict and Diplomacy in Iran, Turkey, and Greece* (1980); and Rouhollah K. Ramazani, *Iran's Foreign Policy, 1941–1973* (1975). The significance of America's atomic monopoly in superpower relations during the second half of the 1940s is treated in Gar Alperowitz, *Atomic Diplomacy* (1965); Sherwin, op. cit.; and Barton J. Bernstein, *The Atomic Bomb* (1975). On Soviet foreign policy toward Europe east and west after the war, see Martin McCauley, ed., *Communist Power in Europe, 1944–1949* (1977); Alvin Z. Rubenstein, *Soviet Foreign Policy since World War II* (1981); Peter J. Mooney, *The Soviet Superpower* (1982); Marshall D. Shulman, *Stalin's Foreign Policy Reappraised* (1963); Ulam, op cit.; and Thomas Wolfe, *Soviet Power and Europe, 1945–1970* (1970). On the origins and early years of the Atlantic alliance, see Lord Ismay, *NATO: The First Five Years, 1949–1954* (n.d.); Harlan Cleveland, *NATO: The Transatlantic Bargain* (1970); and Alfred Grosser, *The Western Alliance* (1980). Escott Reid, *Time of Fear and Hope: The Making of the North Atlantic Treaty 1947–1949* (1977), offers a first-hand account of Canada's role in shaping NATO, while J.T. Jackel, *No Boundaries Upstairs: Canada, the US and the Origins of North American Air Defence* (1987), examines Canada's role in NORAD. For a general study of Canadian foreign policy immediately after the Second World War see John Holmes, *The Shaping of Peace: Canada and the Search for World Order, 1943–1957* (1979).

CHAPTER 8: COEXISTENCE AND CONFRONTATION (1953–1962)

Useful general studies of American foreign policy in the Eisenhower years include Robert A. Divine, *Eisenhower and the Cold War* (1980); H. William Brands, Jr, *Cold Warriors: Eisenhower's Generation and American Foreign Policy* (1988); and Charles Alexander, *Holding the Line* (1975). For divergent evaluations of Eisenhower's controversial secretary of state and his diplomacy, see Michael Guhin, *John Foster Dulles: A Statesman and His Times* (1972), and Townsend Hoopes, *The Devil and John Foster Dulles* (1973); Hoopes is unsparingly critical of Dulles, while Guhin see his subject as more pragmatic and less rigidly ideological than he is customarily portrayed. On the post-Stalinist foreign policies of the Khrushchev era, see the titles on Soviet foreign policy cited above, as well as David J. Dallin, *Soviet Foreign Policy after Stalin* (1961), and Edward Crankshaw, *Khrushchev* (1966). For assessments of Russia's relations with the East European satellites during this transition period, see Robin A. Remington, *The Warsaw Pact* (1971); Michael Kaser, *Comecon: Integration Problems of the Planned Economies* (1967); H.G. Skilling, *Communism National and International: Eastern Europe after Stalin* (1964); Kurt London, ed., *Eastern Europe in Transition* (1966); and Alfred Zauberman, *Industrial Progress in Poland, Czechoslovakia, and East Germany, 1937–1962* (1964). The two most dramatic instances of Eastern European resistance to Soviet domination are treated in Stefan Brandt, *The East German Rising* (1957), and Paul E. Zinner, *Revolution in Hungary* (1964).

The challenge of organizing Western Europe's defence and managing the rearmament of West Germany in the 1950s is discussed in the following works: Daniel Lerner and Raymond Aron, *France Defeats EDC* (1957); Roger Morgan, *The United States and West Germany* (1974); Richard A. Neustadt, *Alliance Politics* (1970); Robert E. Osgood, *NATO: The Entangling Alliance* (1962); F. Roy Willis, *France, Germany, and the New Europe, 1945–1967* (1968); and Robert McGeehan, *The German Rearmament Question:*

American Diplomacy and European Defense after World War II (1971). Sean M. Maloney, War Without Battles: Canada's NATO Brigade in Germany, 1951–1993 (1997), offers a study of Canada's role in Germany.

The best study of the evolution of American defence strategy from 'massive retaliation' to 'flexible response' during the 1950s is Morton Halperin, Defense Strategies for the Seventies (1971), which, despite its title, presents an analytical review of changes in strategic doctrine since the Korean War. Edward A. Kolodziej, The Uncommon Defense and Congress, 1945–1963 (1966), is a massive study of congressional influences on the adoption of weapons systems and the evolution of strategic policy. For a comprehensive treatment of Warsaw Pact strategy, see Wolfe, op. cit. Attempts to impose limits on the arms race during the second half of the 1950s are covered in Robert A. Divine, Blowing on the Wind: The Nuclear Test Ban Debate, 1954–1960 (1978), and Lincoln Bloomfield et al., Khrushchev and the Arms Race: Soviet Interests in Arms Control and Disarmament, 1954–1964 (1966).

European decolonization and the Soviet Union's diplomatic offensive in the developing world have been the subject of a number of important studies. See, for example, John D. Hargreaves, The End of Colonial Rule in West Africa: Essays in Contemporary History (1979); Thomas J. Noer, Cold War and Black Liberation: The United States and White Rule in Africa, 1948–1968 (1985); Wynfred Joshua and Stephen P. Gilbert, Arms for the Third World: Soviet Military Aid Diplomacy (1969); Marshall I. Goldman, Soviet Foreign Aid (1967); Roger Kanet, ed., The Soviet Union and the Developing Nations (1974); and Edward Taborsky, Communist Penetration of the Third World (1963). On Moscow's relations with particular developing countries or regions during this period, see Helen Desfosses Cohn, Soviet Policy Toward Black Africa (1972); Robert H. Donaldson, Soviet Policy Toward India (1976); and Geoffrey Jukes, The Soviet Union in Asia (1973).

On the Anglo–French withdrawal from the Arab world see Ann Williams, Britain and France in the Middle East and North Africa, 1914–1967 (1969); Elizabeth Monroe, Britain's Moment in the Middle East, 1914–1956 (1963); and Howard M. Sachar, Europe Leaves the Middle East, 1936–1954 (1972). Among the best studies of the Suez Crisis are Hugh Thomas, The Suez Affair (1966), and Anthony Nutting, No End of a Lesson: The Story of Suez (1967), while Diane Kunz's The Economic Diplomacy of the Suez Crisis (1991) skilfully analyzes the Eisenhower administration's financial pressure on its European allies to abandon their aggressive plans for Egypt. Lester Pearson's role in diffusing the crisis is treated in James Eayrs and Robert Spencer, eds, 'Lester Pearson's Diplomacy', International Journal 29 (1), Winter 1973–4; John English, The Worldly Years: The Life of Lester Pearson 1949–1972 (1992); and Geoffrey Pearson, Seize the Day: Lester B. Pearson and Crisis Diplomacy (1993). For studies of France's war in Algeria, see Alistair Home, Savage War of Peace (1978), and John Talbott, The War Without a Name: The French in Algeria, 1954–1962 (1980). The transformation of Soviet policy toward the Arab–Israeli conflict in the Middle East is discussed in Arnold Krammer, The Forgotten Friendship: Israel and the Soviet Bloc, 1947–1953 (1974); Aaron S. Kleiman, Soviet Russia and the Middle East (1970); and Oles Smolansky, The Soviet Union and the Arab World Under Khrushchev (1974). The expanding role of the United States in this region is scrutinized in Kenneth Ray Bain, The March to Zion: United States Policy and the Founding of Israel (1979); W.R. Polk, The United States and the Arab World (1965); and Robert W. Stookey, America and the Arab States (1975). Nadav Safran, From War to War: The Arab–Israeli Confrontation, 1948–1967 (1969), is one of the most objective, comprehensive accounts of Arab–Israeli, inter-Arab, and superpower conflict in this region from the birth of Israel to the Six Day War.

The Berlin problem receives extensive treatment in Jack Schick, The Berlin Crises, 1958–62 (1974); Robert M. Slusser, The Berlin Crisis of 1961 (1973); and Honore M. Catudal, Jr, The Diplomacy of the Quadripartite Agreement on Berlin (1977). For studies of the Cuban Crisis and the advent of Soviet–American rivalry in Latin America, see Trumbull Higgins, *The Perfect Failure: Kennedy, Eisenhower, and the Bay of Pigs* (1987); D. Bruce Jackson, *Castro, The Kremlin, and Communism in Latin America* (1969); Richard E. Welch, *Response to Revolution: The United States and the Cuban Revolution, 1959–1961* (1985); Herbert S. Dinerstein, *The Making of a Missile Crisis: October 1962* (1976); Graham Allison, *Essence of Decision: Explaining the Cuban Missile Crisis* (1971); David Detzer, *The Brink* (1979); and Richard J. Walton, *Cold War and Counterrevolution: The Foreign Policy of John F. Kennedy* (1972). Canada's role in the crisis is analyzed in Commander Peter T. Haydon's *The 1962 Cuban Missile Crisis: Canadian Involvement Reconsidered* (1993), while James Eayrs, *In Defence of Canada,* vol. 4: *Growing Up Allied* (1980) offers an account of Canadian defence policy during this period. For a journalist's account of the difficult relationship between John Diefenbaker and John F. Kennedy, see Knowlton Nash, *Kennedy and Diefenbaker: Fear and Loathing across the Undefended Border* (1990).

CHAPTER 9: DÉTENTE AND MULTIPOLARITY (1962–1975)

Superpower attempts to reach agreement on arms control from the aftermath of the Cuban Missile Crisis to the conclusion of the *SALT* I Treaty are recounted in Christer Jonsson, *Soviet Bargaining Behavior: The Nuclear Test Ban Case* (1979); Thomas B. Larso *Disarmament and Soviet Policy, 1964–1968* (1969); Roman Kolkowicz et al., *The Soviet Union and Arms Control* (1973); John Newhouse, *Cold Dawn: The Story of SALT* (1973); Gerard C. Smith, *Doubletalk: The Story of the First Strategic Arms Limitation Talks* (1980); Mason Willrich and John Rhinelander, eds, *SALT: The Moscow Agreements and Beyond* (1974); Coral Bell, *The Diplomacy of Detente: The Kissinger Era* (1977); and Robert D. Schulzinger, *Henry Kissinger: Doctor of Diplomacy* (1989). The expansion of Soviet strategic and conventional power during the 1960s and the first half of the 1970s is treated in John Erickson, *Soviet Military Power* (1971); William R.

Kintner and Harriet F. Scott, eds, *The Nuclear Revolution in Soviet Military Affairs* (1968); Harriet F. Scott and William F. Scott, *The Armed Forces of the USSR* (1979); and C.G. Jacobsen, *Soviet Strategic Initiatives: Challenge and Response* (1979). On the Soviet naval buildup during the same period, see Michael McGwire and John Donnell, eds, *Soviet Naval Influence: Domestic and Foreign Dimensions* (1977), and Paul Nitze et al., *Securing the Seas: The Soviet Naval Challenge and Western Alliance Options* (1979). For studies of the American response to these developments, see William W. Kaufman, *The McNamara Strategy* (1964); Thomas B. Larson, *Soviet–American Rivalry* (1978); Richard J. Barnet, *The Giants: Russia and America* (1977); and Alexander L. George and Richard Smoke, *Deterrence in American Foreign Policy* (1975).

Canada's relationship with the United States during this period is treated in Greg Donaghy, *Tolerant Allies: Canada and the United States, 1963–1968* (2002); Robert Bothwell, *Canada and the United States: The Politics of Partnership* (1992); and John Herd Thompson and Stephen J. Randall, *Canada and the United States: Ambivalent Allies* (3rd edn, 2002). For an examination of foreign policy under Lester B. Pearson see Norman Hillmer, ed., *Pearson: The Unlikely Gladiator* (1999). The cancellation of the Avro Arrow has been the subject of a number of books aimed at substantiating or dispelling conspiracy theories around the project. Two of these are Creig Stewart, *Shutting Down the National Dream: A.V. Roe and the Tragedy of the Avro Arrow* (1996), and Palmiro Campagna, *Requiem for a Giant: A.V. Roe and the Avro Arrow* (2003). J.L. Granatstein, *Who Killed the Canadian Military?* (2004), treats this subject in the context of Canada's shrinking military since the Second World War.

The breakdown of the bipolar international system during the 1960s and the Gaullist challenge to American leadership of the Western alliance have been addressed in the following works: Edward Kolodziej, *French International Policy under De Gaulle and Pompidou* (1974); Michael Harrison, *Reluctant Ally: France and Atlantic Security* (1981); Wilfred L. Kohl, *French Nuclear Diplomacy* (1971); and Wolf Mendl, *Deterrence* and Persuasion: French Nuclear Armament in the Context of National Policy, 1945–1969 (1970). Britain's position between the US and an increasingly independent-minded continental Europe is discussed in Robert L. Pfaltzgraff, Jr, Britain Faces Europe (1969), and Andrew Pierre, Nuclear Politics: The British Experience with an Independent Strategic Force, 1939–1970 (1972). For the development of European economic integration and its implications for the East–West struggle, see Richard Mayne, The Recovery of Europe, 1945–1973 (1973); Ernst H. Van der Beugel, From Marshall Aid to Atlantic Partnership: European Integration as a Concern of American Foreign Policy (1966); Joseph Kraft, The Grand Design: From Common Market to Atlantic Partnership (1962); Miriam Camps, European Unification in the Sixties (1966); and A.E. Walsh and J. Paxton, Into Europe: The Structure and Development of the Common Market (1972).

The post-war international monetary system and its stresses and strains during the 1960s is covered in Robert Solomon, The International Monetary System, 1945–1976 (1977); Robert Triffin, The World Money Maze (1966); E.S. Mason and R.E. Asher, The World Bank since Bretton Woods (1973); B. Tew, International Monetary Cooperation, 1945–1970 (1970); and G. Bell, The Euro-Dollar Market and the International Financial System (1973).

The transformation of West Germany's foreign policy from the Adenauer to the Brandt era and the response of the Communist bloc is recounted in the following works: Karl Kaiser, German Foreign Policy in Transition (1968); Frederick H. Hartmann, Germany Between East and West: The Reunification Problem (1965); Zoltan M. Szaz, Germany's Eastern Frontiers: The Problem of the Oder–Niesse Line (1960); Gerhard Wettig, Community and Conflict in the Socialist Camp: The Soviet Union, East Germany, and the German Problem, 1965–1972 (1975); George B. Ginsburgs and Alvin Z. Rubenstein, eds, Soviet Foreign Policy Toward Western Europe (1978); Lawrence L. Whetten, Germany's Ostpolitik: Relations Between the Federal Republic and the Warsaw Pact Countries (1971); and William E. Griffith, The Ostpolitik of

the Federal Republic of Germany (1978). Studies of the Soviet Union's relationship with its East European satellites during the era of détente and polycentrism include Adam Bromke and Derry Novak, eds, The Communist States in the Era of Détente, 1971–1977 (1979); Henry W. Schaefer, COMECON and the Politics of Integration (1972); Joseph G. Whelan, World Communism, 1967–69: Soviet Efforts to Reestablish Control (1970); and Peter F. Sugar and Ivo J. Lederer, eds, Nationalism in Eastern Europe (1969). Useful studies in English of the causes and consequences of the Soviet intervention in Czechoslovakia include Pavel Tigrid, Why Dubček Fell (1971); Z.A.B. Zeman, Prague Spring (1969); and Jiri Valenta, Soviet Intervention in Czechoslovakia, 1968 (1979). The early years of Romania's bid for an independent foreign policy within the Communist bloc are covered in David Floyd, Rumania: Russia's Dissident Ally (1965).

The growing engagement of the two superpowers in the Middle East after the Suez Crisis is addressed in the following works: J.C. Hurewitz, Soviet–American Rivalry in the Middle East (1969); Steven L. Spiegel et al., eds, The Soviet–American Competition in the Middle East (1988); M. Confino and S. Shamir, eds, The USSR and the Middle East (1973); Dana Cass, Soviet Involvement in the Middle East: Policy Formulation, 1966–1973 (1978); Robert O. Freedman, Soviet Policy Toward the Middle East Since 1970 (1978); Edward F. Sheehan, The Arabs, Israelis, and Kissinger (1976); Abdalla M. Battah and Yehuda Lukacs, eds, The Arab–Israeli Conflict: Two Decades of Change (1988); and William B. Quant, Decade of Decision: American Policy Toward the Arab–Israeli Conflict, 1967–1976 (1977). On the internal struggle between Arabs and Israelis in the region, see Nadav Safran, Israel: The Embattled Ally (1978); Shaul Mishal, West Bank/East Bank: The Palestinians in Jordan, 1949–1967 (1978); and Dana A. Schmidt, Armageddon in the Middle East: Arab vs. Israeli through the October War (1974). An excellent study of Lebanon's precarious geopolitical position in the region is Kamal S. Salibi, Crossroads to Civil War: Lebanon, 1958–1976 (1976).

The position of Latin America in the inter-American system and the expansion of Soviet–American rivalry in the region is treated in the following works: Samuel Baily, *The United States and the Development of Latin America, 1945–1975* (1977); Nicola Miller, *Soviet Relations with Latin America, 1959–1987* (1989); Walter M. Davis, ed., *Latin America and the Cold War* (1978); Lester Langley, *The United States and the Caribbean in the Twentieth Century* (1985); and Herbert Goldhamer, *The Foreign Powers in Latin America* (1972).

CHAPTER 10: THE RISE OF CHINA AND THE COLD WAR IN ASIA

General studies of the birth of the People's Republic of China include John F. Melby, *The Mandate of Heaven* (1968), a lively account of the Chinese Civil War; Suzanne Pepper, *Civil War in China: The Political Struggle, 1945–1949* (1978), a comprehensive, exhaustively researched study; C.P. Fitzgerald, *The Birth of Communist China* (1966); Kenneth E. Shewmaker, *Americans and the Chinese Communists, 1927–1945* (1971); Tuchman, op. cit., which provides essential background on the Sino–American rift; John R. Beal, *Marshall in China* (1970), which claims that the Marshall mission in 1946 came close to mediating a settlement between the communists and the Nationalists; John K. Fairbank, *The United States and China* (1971), the standard study of Sino–American relations, which should be supplemented with Michael Schaller, *The United States and China in the Twentieth Century* (1990); and Rang Tsou, *America's Failure in China, 1941–1950* (1963), a reliable narrative account.

For the causes and consequences of the Korean War, see Glenn T. Page, *The Korean Decision* (1968); Robert R. Simmons, *The Strained Alliance* (1975); David Rees, *Korea: The Limited War* (1964); Bruce Cumings, *The Origins of the Korean War* (1981); and Allan Whiting, *China Crosses the Yalu* (1960). The Truman–MacArthur struggle is judiciously assessed in Trumbull Huggins, *Korea and the Fall of MacArthur* (1960), and John W. Spanier, *The Truman–MacArthur Controversy* (1959). Canada's role in the Korean War is considered in Denis Stairs, *The Diplomacy of Constraint: Canada, the*

Korean War, and the United States (1974). See also James Eayrs, *In Defence of Canada*, vol. 5: *Indochina: Roots of Complicity* (1983).

The re-engagement of American power in Asia is treated in Robert A. Hart, *The Eccentric Tradition: American Diplomacy in the Far East* (1976); Foster Rhea Dulles, *American Policy Toward Communist China, 1949–1969* (1972); Yonasuke Nagai and Akira Iriye, eds, *The Origins of the Cold War in Asia* (1977); Michael Schaller, *The American Occupation of Japan* (1985); F.S. Dunn, *Peacemaking and the Settlement with Japan* (1963); K. Kawai, *Japan's American Interlude* (1960); Reischauer, op. cit.; and Neu, op. cit. Valuable studies of Sino–Soviet relations before the rift include Robert C. North, *Moscow and the Chinese Communists* (1963); Robert R. Simmons, *The Strained Alliance: Peking, Pyongyang, Moscow, and the Politics of the Korean Civil War* (1975); and Cheng Chu-yuan, *Economic Relations Between Peking and Moscow, 1949–1963* (1964). Russia's relations with Japan after the Second World War are treated in Robert Searingen, *The Soviet Union and Postwar Japan: Escalating Challenge and Response* (1978); Young C. Kim, *Japanese–Soviet Relations* (1974); and Savitri Vishwanathan, *Normalization of Japanese–Soviet Relations, 1945–1970* (1973).

The Sino–Soviet split and its impact on the international communist movement has been the subject of a number of important studies. One of the most comprehensive treatments is Alfred D. Low, *The Sino–Soviet Dispute* (1978), but it is helpful to consult several earlier studies that appeared as the events of the dispute were unfolding: Donald S. Zagoria, *The Sino–Soviet Conflict, 1956–1961* (1962); David Floyd, *Mao Against Khrushchev* (1963); and William E. Griffith, *The Sino–Soviet Rift* (1964). The role of China's long-standing border grievances against the Soviet Union in the deterioration of relations between Moscow and Beijing is assessed in Tai Sung An, *The Sino–Soviet Territorial Dispute* (1973), and in George Ginsburgs and Carl F. Pinkele, *The Sino–Soviet Territorial Dispute, 1949–64* (1978). For lucid analyses of the impact of the Sino–Soviet split on Russia's relations with the East European satellites and the West European communist parties, see William E. Griffith, ed., *Communism in Europe: Continuity, Change, and the Sino–Soviet Dispute* (1966).

The most useful studies of the French phase of the Indochinese War include Ellen Hammer, *The Struggle for Indochina* (1966); F.E.M. Irving, *The First Indochina War: French and American Policy, 1945–1954* (1975); and Bernard Fall, *Hell Is a Very Small Place: The Siege of Dien Bien Phu* (1967). The involvement of foreign powers in the civil war in Laos is covered in Arthur J. Dommen, *Conflict in Laos: The Politics of Neutralization* (1971), and Charles A. Stevenson, *The End of Nowhere: American Policy Toward Laos since 1954* (1972). For the story of America's engagement and disengagement in Indochina, see Frances Fitzgerald, *Fire in the Lake* (1972); Peter Poole, *The United States and Indochina from FDR to Nixon* (1973); George C. Heering, *America's Longest War: The United States and Vietnam, 1950–1975* (1986); Stanley Karnow, *Vietnam: A History* (1983); and *The New York Times*, ed., *Pentagon Papers* (1971), a top-secret official history of the American involvement (including classified documents) that was leaked to the newspapers by a disillusioned contributor. For the decision-making process that led to the American escalation in Indochina, see David Halberstam, *The Best and the Brightest* (1972), and Doris Kearns, *Lyndon Johnson and the American Dream* (1976). For a critical analysis of Canada's role see Victor Levant, *Quiet Complicity: Canadian Involvement in the Vietnam War* (1986). There are also several accounts of the experiences of American draft dodgers and war resisters in Canada, including John Hagan, *Northern Passage: American Vietnam War Resisters in Canada* (2002), and Alan Haig-Brown, *Hell No, We Won't Go: Vietnam Draft Resisters in Canada* (1996).

The rapprochement between Washington and Beijing during the first half of the 1970s is discussed in Gene T. Hsiao, ed., *The Sino–American Detente and Its Policy Implications* (1974); Alan M. Jones, *U.S. Foreign Policy in a Changing World* (1973); Lloyd Gardner, ed., *The Great Nixon Turnaround* (1973); Harvey W. Nelsen, *Power and Insecurity: Beijing, Moscow, and Washington,* *1949–1988* (1989); and Donald F. Lach and Edmund S. Wehrle, *International Politics in East Asia Since World War II* (1975).

CHAPTER 11: THE RESURGENCE OF EAST–WEST TENSIONS (1975–1985)

Among the many studies covering this period of the Cold War, the following are worth consulting: W. Stevenson, *The Rise and Fall of Detente* (1985); Raymond L. Gartoff, *Detente and Confrontation* (1985); Joseph D. Douglass, Jr, *Soviet Military Strategy in Europe* (1980); Paul H. Nitze et al., *Securing the Seas: The Soviet Naval Challenge and Western Alliance Options* (1979); and Coit D. Blacker, *Reluctant Warriors: The United States, the Soviet Union, and Arms Control* (1987). The conflict over theatre nuclear weapons in Europe and its corrosive effect on the budding East–West rapprochement is ably treated in Hans-Henrich Holm and Nikolai Peterson, *The European Missiles Crisis* (1984). Vojtech Mastny summarizes the fading hopes for a European political settlement in his *Helsinki, Human Rights, and European Security* (1986). For a fascinating study of the attempts to forge a Paris–Bonn axis as the basis of a powerful European entity between the two superpowers, see Haig Simonian, *The Privileged Partnership: Franco–German Relations in the European Community, 1969–1984* (1985).

International economic relations from 1975 to 1985 are treated in the following works: Bela Belassa, *Change and Challenge in the World Economy* (1985); Theodore Geiger, *The Future of the International System: The United States and the World Political Economy* (1988); Mohammed E. Ahrari, *OPEC: The Failing Giant* (1986); and Omar F. Homouda et al., eds, *The Future of the International Monetary System* (1989). A provocative, sweeping assessment of the economic constraints on great-power diplomacy over the past four centuries is found in Paul Kennedy, *The Rise and Fall of the Great Powers* (1987).

The continuing tension in the Middle East and South Asia is treated in a number of important works. On the war in the Persian Gulf, see Ralph

King, *The Iran–Iraq War: The Political Implications* (1987), and Shahram Chubin, *Iran and Iraq at War* (1988). For analyses of the emergence of Islamic fundamentalism as a destabilizing influence on the politics of the region, see Dilip Hiro, *Holy Wars: The Rise of Islamic Fundamentalism* (1989), and Henry Munson, Jr, *Islam and Revolution in the Middle East* (1988). On the US debacle in Iran, see Barry Rubin, *Paved with Good Intentions: The American Experience in Iran* (1980). The Soviet intervention in Afghanistan is assessed in Rosanne Klass, ed., *Afghanistan: The Great Game Revisited* (1988), and Mark L. Urban, *War in Afghanistan* (1988). For a broader treatment of the entire sub-region of South Asia, see Stanley Wolpert, *Roots of Confrontation in South Asia: Afghanistan, Pakistan, India, and the Superpowers* (1982). On the Arab–Israeli conflict, and the Middle Eastern policies of the two superpowers in the aftermath of the Camp David agreement, see William B. Quandt, *Camp David: Peacemaking and Politics* (1986); Geoffrey Aronson, *Creating Facts: Israel, Palestinians, and the West Bank* (1987); Samuel F. Wells and Mark Bruzonsky, *Security in the Middle East: Regional Change and Great Power Strategies* (1987); William B. Quandt, ed., *The Middle East: Ten Years After Camp David* (1988); and Battah and Lukacs, op. cit. Lebanon's particular trauma in this period is ably recounted in David Gilmour, *Lebanon: The Fractured Country* (1983), and Thomas Friedman, *From Beirut to Jerusalem* (1989).

Pierre Trudeau, and his tenure as prime minister, has been the subject of a number of interesting studies. For a sympathetic assessment of Trudeau's efforts to remake Canadian foreign policy in the 1970s, see J.L. Granatstein and Robert Bothwell, *Pirouette: Pierre Trudeau and Canadian Foreign Policy* (1990). The importance of multilateralism to the Canadian foreign policy of this period is treated in Tom Keating, *Canada and World Order: The Multilateralist Tradition in Canadian Foreign Policy* (1993). An excellent biography of Trudeau is Richard Gwyn, *The Northern Magus* (1980). This may be read together with John English, Richard Gwyn, and P. Whitney Lackenbauer, eds, *The Hidden Pierre Elliott Trudeau: The Faith Behind the Politics* (2004), which offers the reflections and views of friends, family, and political colleagues of the popular Canadian leader.

CHAPTER 12: AFRICA: FROM INDEPENDENCE TO DEPENDENCY

On the extension of Soviet–American rivalry to the continent in Africa and the African response, see Olajide Aluko, *Africa and the Great Powers in the 1980s* (1987); Arthur Gavshon, *Crisis in Africa: Battleground of East and West* (1984); Peter Calvocoressi, *Independent Africa and the World* (1985); Tom J. Farer, *Clouds on the Horn of Africa: The Widening Storm* (1979); David Dickson, *United States Foreign Policy Towards Sub-Sahara Africa* (1985); David E. Albright, *The USSR and Sub-Sahara Africa in the 1980s* (1983); and Bala Mohammed, *Africa and Non-Alignment: A Study in the Foreign Relations of New Nations* (1982). For analyses of Africa's changing position in the international system, see Stephen Wright and Janice N. Brownfoot, *Africa and World Politics* (1987), and Ralph I. Onwuka and Timothy M. Shaw, *Africa and World Politics* (1989). For Canadian foreign policy towards South Africa, see Linda Freeman, *Ambiguous Champion: Canada and South Africa in the Trudeau and Mulroney Years* (1997), which challenges the notion that Canada was an international leader in the campaign against apartheid. See also David M. Black's essay 'How Exceptional? Assessing the Anti-Apartheid "Crusade"' in Kim R. Nossal and Nelson Michaud, eds, *Diplomatic Departures: The Conservative Era in Canadian Foreign Policy, 1984–93* (2001).

CHAPTER 13: THE FAR EAST: THE ROAD TO THE NEW CO-PROSPERITY SPHERE

The fundamental transformation of the geopolitical situation in East Asia following the collapse of the American position in Indochina in the middle of the 1970s has been treated in Ilpyong J. Kim, *The Strategic Triangle: China, The United States, and the Soviet Union* (1987); Steffan B. Linder, *The Pacific*

Century: Economic and Political Consequences of Asian-Pacific Dynamism (1986); W.W. Rostow, *The United States and the Regional Organization of Asia and the Pacific, 1965–1985* (1986); Bruce Dickson and Harry Harding, eds, *Economic Relations in the Asian–Pacific Region* (1987); Jon Woronoff, *Asia's 'Miracle Economies'* (1986); and Wolfgang Klenner, ed., *Trends of Economic Development in East Asia* (1989). On particular countries in the region, see the following: for China, Hsiang-tse Chiang, *The United States and China* (1988); Robert G. Sutter, *Chinese Foreign Policy: Developments After Mao* (1986); John Wong, *The Political Economy of China's Changing Relations with Southeast Asia* (1984); and Samuel S. Kim, *China and the World* (1989); for Japan, Herbert J. Ellison, *Japan and the Pacific Quadrille: The Major Powers in East Asia* (1987); Robert S. Ozaki and Walter Arnold, eds, *Japan's Foreign Relations: A Global Search for Economic Security* (1985); Karel G. von Wolferen, *The Enigma of Japanese Power* (1989); and Clyde V. Prestowitz, Jr, *Trading Places: How We Allowed Japan to Take the Lead* (1988). For a lucid study of an often-overlooked regional organization in Asia, see Michael Leifer, *ASEAN and the Security of South East Asia* (1988).

PART THREE: FROM COLD WAR TO NEW WORLD DISORDER (1985–2000)

CHAPTER 14: MOSCOW, WASHINGTON, AND THE END OF THE SOVIET EMPIRE

The most comprehensive treatment of the end of the Cold War and the breakup of the Soviet Union is Raymond L. Garthoff, *The Great Transition: American–Soviet Relations and the End of the Cold War* (1994). A perceptive assessment of the economic crisis of the former Soviet Union may be found in Marshall I. Goldman, *Lost Opportunity: Why Economic Reforms in Russia Have Not Worked*

(1994). Three astute assessments of the strategic implications of the disintegration of the Soviet Union are found in Roy Allison, *Military Forces in the Soviet Successor States* (1993), Renée de Nevers, *Russia's Strategic Renovation* (1994); and Roland Dannreuther, *Creating New States in Central Asia* (1994). For analyses of the end of the Cold War from an American perspective, see John Lewis Gaddis, *The United States and the End of the Cold War* (1992); Michael J. Hogan, ed., *The End of the Cold War: Its Meaning and Implications* (1992); and Michael Beschloss and Strobe Talbot, *At the Highest Level* (1993). From a more global perspective, Paul Kennedy's *Preparing for the Next Century* (1993) updates his sweeping analysis of the history of international relations in *The Rise and Fall of the Great Powers,* op. cit. For studies of Canadian post–Cold War foreign policy, see Andrew Cohen, *While Canada Slept: How We Lost our Place in the World* (2003); Claire Turenne Sjolander et al., eds, *Feminist Perspectives on Canadian Foreign Policy* (2003); and Lloyd Axworthy, *Liberals at the Border: We Stand on Guard for Whom* (2004).

CHAPTER 15: EUROPE: INTEGRATION AND DISINTEGRATION

On the relaunching of the movement toward European unity, see the concluding chapters in D.W. Urwin, *The Community of Europe: A History of European Integration since 1945* (1995), and William Wallace, *The Transformation of Western Europe* (1990). The best treatment of the development of the European monetary system is David Marsh, *The Bundesbank: The Bank That Rules Europe* (1994). For two shrewd assessments of the economic, political, and strategic context of German reunification, consult Timothy Gorton Ash, *In Europe's Name: Germany and the Divided Continent* (1993), and Konrad H. Jarausch, *The Rush to German Unity* (1994). The transformation of Europe's security environment in the early 1990s is treated in Edward Mortimer, *European Security After the Cold War* (1992), and Mathias Jopp,

The Strategic Implications of European Integration (1994). Gail Stokes, *The Walls Came Tumbling Down: The Collapse of Communism in Eastern Europe* (1993), traces the abrupt liberation of Moscow's satellite empire, while some of the unanticipated difficulties resulting from this transformation are summarized in Jan Zielonka, *Security in Central Europe* (1992). The origins of the seemingly endless crisis on the Balkan Peninsula are traced in Misha Glenny, *The Fall of Yugoslavia* (1992); John Zametica, *The Yugoslav Conflict* (1992); and David Fromkin, *Kosovo Crossing* (1999). For an analysis of the Mulroney government's attempt to take a more active role in international peacekeeping, see Nicholas Grammer, *From Peacekeeping to Peacemaking: Canada's Response to the Yugoslav Crisis* (2001), as well as Manon Tessier and Mic Fortmann, 'The Conservative Approach to International Peacekeeping', in Kim R. Nossal and Nelson Michaud, op. cit.

CHAPTER 16: ASIA AT THE CROSSROADS

The economic and strategic transformation of Asia has inspired a number of important studies from both a regional and a national perspective. For general studies of the economic development of the region and its subregions, see John P. Hardt and Young C. Kim, eds, *Economic Cooperation in the Asia–Pacific Region* (1990), Gavin Boyd, *Pacific Trade, Investment, and Politics* (1989); David Wurfel and Bruce Burton, eds, *The Political Economy of Foreign Policy in Southeast Asia* (1990); Jon Woronoff, *Asia's 'Miracle' Economies* (1991); and John Bresnan, *From Dominoes to Dynamos: The Transformation of Southeast Asia* (1997). On the strategic implications of the end of the Cold War in the Far East, see Raju G.C. Thomas, *South Asian Security in the 1990s* (1993); Amitav Acharya, *A New Regional Order in South-East Asia: ASEAN in the Post–Cold War Era* (1991); Stuart Harris and James Cotton, eds, *The End of the Cold War in Northeast Asia* (1991), and Kanti Bajpai, *South Asia after the Cold War: International Perspectives* (1993). China's headlong plunge into

the international economic order is addressed in Jude Howell, *China Opens Its Doors: The Politics of Economic Transition* (1993), and Robert Kleinberg, *China's 'Opening' to the Outside World: The Experiment with Foreign Capitalism* (1990).

On Japan's adjustment to new strategic and economic realities, see Philip Oppenheim, *Trade Wars: Japan versus the West* (1992); Gilbert Rozman, *Japan's Response to the Gorbachev Era* (1991); and Jeffrey E. Garten, *A Cold Peace: America, Japan, Germany, and the Struggle for Supremacy* (1992).

CHAPTER 17: AFRICA ON ITS OWN: ETHNIC CONFLICT, AUTOCRACY, AND UNDERDEVELOPMENT

The political and ethnic conflicts in Africa during the late twentieth century are reviewed in Basil Davidson, *The Black Man's Burden: Africa and the Curse of the Nation-State* (1992), and George B.N. Ayittey, *Africa in Chaos* (1998). The persistence of external involvement on the continent is treated in Keith Somerville, *Foreign Military Intervention in Africa* (1990). Two excellent studies of important subregions of the African continent are Samuel M. Makinda, *Security in the Horn of Africa* (1992), and Claire Spencer, *The Maghreb in the 1990s* (1993). Of the extensive recent literature on Africa's economic development and its financial relationship with the outside world, the following are particularly useful: Timothy Shaw, *Reformism and Revisionism in Africa's Political Economy in the 1990s* (1993); Trevor Parfitt, *The African Debt Crisis* (1989); Richard Sandbrook, *The Politics of Africa's Economic Recovery* (1993); and Christopher Clapham, *Africa and the International System: The Politics of State Survival* (1996).

For an account of the scandal involving the Canadian Airborne Regiment in Somalia, see David Bercuson, *Significant Incident: Canada's Army, the Airborne and the Murder in Somalia* (1996). Romeo Dallaire, *Shake Hands with the Devil: The Failure of Humanity in Rwanda* (2003), is a first-hand account of the Rwandan genocide by the Canadian leader of the UN peacekeeping mission to that country.

CHAPTER 18: THE MIDDLE EAST: THE ROCKY ROAD TO RECONCILIATION

The diplomatic background to the Gulf War of 1991 is explored in Laurence Freedman and Efraim Karsh, *The Gulf Conflict, 1990–91* (1993), while a more narrowly military account is provided in Jeffrey McCausland, *The Gulf Conflict: A Military Analysis* (1993). On the Arab–Israeli conflict since the Israeli invasion of Lebanon in 1982, see Ian S. Lustik, ed., *Arab–Israeli Relations in World Politics* (1994); Yossi Melman and Dan Raviv, *Behind the Uprising: Israelis, Jordanians, and Palestinians* (1989); Adam Garfinkle, *Israel and Jordan in the Shadow of War* (1992); and William B. Quandt, *Peace Process: American Diplomacy and the Arab–Israeli Conflict since 1967* (1993). Assessments of the role of foreign powers in the Middle East include A.F.K. Organsky, *The $36 Billion Bargain: Strategy and Politics in U.S. Assistance to Israel* (1990); David Schoenbaum, *The United States and the State of Israel* (1993); Efraim Karsh, *Soviet Policy Towards Syria Since 1970* (1991); and Oles M. Smolansky, *The USSR and Iraq: The Soviet Quest for Influence* (1991).

CHAPTER 19: LATIN AMERICA: DEMOCRACY, FREE MARKETS, AND REGIONAL STABILITY

For general analyses of the evolution of inter-American relations since the mid-1980s, see L. Erik Kjonnerod, ed., *Evolving U.S. Strategy for Latin America and the Caribbean* (1992); Michael C. Desch, *When the Third World Matters: Latin America and United States Grand Strategy* (1993); Robert A. Pastor, *Whirlpool: U.S. Foreign Policy toward Latin America and the Caribbean* (1992); Tom H. Carothers, *In the Name of Democracy: U.S. Policy Toward Latin America in the Reagan Years* (1991); and G. Pope Atkins, *Latin America in the International System* (1995). The US intervention in the Nicaraguan Civil War is detailed in Roy Gutman, *Banana Diplomacy: The Making of American Foreign Policy in Nicaragua* (1988), and William I. Robinson, *A Faustian Bargain: U.S. Intervention in the Nicaraguan Election and American Foreign Policy in the Post–Cold War Era* (1992). On the transition from dictatorship to representative government in many Latin American states during the 1980s, see Howard J. Wiarda, *The Democratic Revolution in Latin America* (1990). The resolution of the debt crisis in Latin America is discussed in Philip Brock et al., eds, *Latin American Debt and Readjustment* (1989); Miguel D. Ramirez, Antonio Jorge, and Jorge Salazar-Carrillo, eds., *The Latin American Debt* (1992); and *Mexico's Economic Crisis: Its Origins and Consequences* (1989). Volume 16 in the *Canada Among Nations* series, *Vanishing Borders* (2000), edited by Maureen Appel Molot and Fen Osler Hampson, looks at Canada's position in the western hemisphere, with a particular emphasis on how North American free trade has homogenized Canada, the United States, and Mexico.

CHAPTER 20: A UNIPOLAR WORLD OR A NEW MULTILATERALISM?

The new activism of the United Nations in peace-keeping missions is treated in Adam Roberts and Benedict Kingsburg, eds, *United Nations, Divided World: The U.N.'s Role in International Relations* (1993); Peter R. Baehr and Leon Gordenker, *The United Nations in the 1990s* (1992); and Mats R. Berdal, *Whither UN Peacekeeping?* (1993). On the arms control breakthroughs of the Gorbachev–Reagan era, see April Carter, *Success and Failure in Arms Control Negotiations* (1989); Steve Weber, *Cooperation and Discord in U.S.–Soviet Arms Control* (1991); and George L. Rueckert, *Global Double Zero: The INF Treaty From Its Origins to Implementation* (1993). The danger of nuclear proliferation in the post–Cold War era has inspired a number of important works, including Kathleen C. Bailey, *Doomsday Weapons in the Hands of Many* (1991); Harald Muller et al., *Nuclear Non-Proliferation and Global Order* (1994); and Trevor Taylor, *The Collapse of the Soviet Empire: Managing the Regional Fallout* (1992). On efforts to control the spread of conventional arms, see Anthony Sampson, *The Arms Bazaar in the Nineties: From Krupp to Saddam* (1991), and Schuyler Foerster et al., *Defining Stability: Conventional Arms Control in a Changing Europe* (1989). The best treatment of recent attempts to control chemical weapons is Brad Roberts, *Chemical Disarmament and International Security* (1992). For comprehensive analyses of the evolution of the international economic system after the end of the Cold War, see Joan E. Spero, *The Politics of International Economic Relations* (1992); Thomas D. Lairson and David Skidmore, *International Political Economy: The Struggle for Power and Wealth* (1993); and Jagdish Bhagwati, *The World Trading System at Risk* (1991). Among the most useful English-language sources for analyses of contemporary international developments are the following periodicals: *Foreign Affairs, Foreign Policy, World Politics, International Security, Survival, International History Review, Diplomatic History, Canadian Foreign Policy,* the occasional papers of the International Institute for Strategic Studies published under the rubric *Adelphi Papers,* and the indispensable annual publications of the latter organization, entitled *Strategic Survey* and *The Military Balance.*

CHAPTER 21: THE TWENTY-FIRST CENTURY

For an overview of the global situation at the end of the twentieth and beginning of the twenty-first centuries see Paul Kennedy, *Preparing for the Twenty-First Century* (1993); John Lukacs, *The End of the Twentieth Century and the End of the Modern Age* (1993); Felipe Fernandez-Armesto, *Millennium* (1995); and Thomas Homer-Dixon, *The Upside of Down: Catastrophe, Creativity, and the Renewal of Civilization* (2006). Francis Fukuyama analyzes the nation-state and global governance in the new century in *State-Building: Governance and World Order in the 21st Century* (2004). The new

balance of global economic power is examined in Andre Gunder Frank, *Reorient: Global Economics in the Asian Age* (1998). American global power is addressed in Noam Chomsky, *Hegemony or Survival: America's Quest for Global Dominance* (2003). For an in-depth review of the facts and circumstances surrounding the 11 September 2001 attacks, see *The 9/11 Commission Report* (2004), prepared by the National Commission on Terrorist Attacks Upon the United States, established by US Congress and President George W. Bush in 2002. The aftermath of the 9/11 attacks is analyzed in Jeremy Black, *War and the New Disorder in the 21st Century* (2004), and in Gwynne Dyer, *Future: Tense: The Coming World Order?* (2004). Volume 18 of *Canada Among Nations: A Fading Power* (2002), edited by Norman Hillmer and Maureen Appel Molot, looks at how Canada's relationship with the US has changed since the 11 September terrorist attacks. James Orbinski, *An Imperfect Offering: Humanitarian Action in the Twenty-first Century* (2008) examines the prospects for global peacekeeping operations in the twenty-first century. For Canadian perspectives on the globalization movement, see Naomi Klein, *No Logo: Taking Aim at the Brand Bullies* (2000); Mark Brawley, *The Politics of Globalization: Gaining Perspective, Assessing Consequences* (2002); Stephen Clarkson, *Uncle Sam and Us: Globalization, Neoconservatism, and the Canadian State* (2002); and Terry O'Reilly & Mike Tennant, *The Age of Persuasion: How Marketing Ate Our Culture* (2009). For a very different perspective see John Ralston Saul, *The Collapse of Globalism and the Reinvention of the World* (2005). On the environment and climate change see Jared Diamond, *Collapse: How Societies Choose to Fail or Succeed* (2005); Al Gore, *An Inconvenient Truth: The Planetary Emergency of Global Warming and What We Can Do About It* (2006); and Tim Flannery, *The Weather Makers: How We Are Changing the Climate and What It Means for Life on Earth* (2005).

INDEX